The Business Writer's Handbook

Fourth Edition

The Business Writer's Handbook

Fourth Edition

Charles T. Brusaw
NCR Corporation (retired)

Gerald J. Alred
University of Wisconsin—Milwaukee

Walter E. Oliu
U.S. Nuclear Regulatory Commission

St. Martin's Press

New York

For our wives and families

Senior editor: Catherine Pusateri
Development editor: Denise Quirk
Manager, publishing services: Emily Berleth
Production supervisor: Omega Publishing Services, Inc.
Cover design: Tom McKeveny

Library of Congress Catalog Card Number: 92-50042
Copyright © 1993 by St. Martin's Press, Inc.

Manufactured in the United States of America.
7654
fedc

For information, write:
St. Martin's Press, Inc.
175 Fifth Avenue
New York, NY 10010

ISBN: 0-312-05734-2 (Paper)
      0-312-08715-2 (Cloth)

Preface

The Business Writer's Handbook, Fourth Edition, is designed to be a comprehensive, thoroughly practical reference guide for students, as well as a desktop reference for people already working in industry or government. In the classroom, it can be used along with a standard textbook, although instructors wishing to avoid the constraints imposed by a textbook might easily use this handbook as the basic resource.

The *Handbook* offers coverage far beyond the scope of conventional English handbooks. In addition to a comprehensive treatment of grammar, usage, style, format, and writing procedures (planning, research, outlining, methods of development, and so forth), it provides information on all types of business communication—reports of various kinds (including oral presentations), proposals, instructions, job descriptions, letters, and memorandums. It also covers the use of word processors. It gives abundant examples, all drawn from business or industrial contexts to provide the greatest possible relevance for professionally oriented readers.

We believe that the unique four-way access system in *The Business Writer's Handbook* makes it more flexible and easier to use than other writing handbooks we have seen. The main body of the book is organized alphabetically, so that readers can usually go immediately to the topic at hand. The index provides an exhaustive list of the topics, indexed not only by the terms actually used in the entries but also by various other terms that readers might think of instead. The Topical Key to the Alphabetical Entries groups the entries into categories, helping readers pull together information on broad subjects covered by several different entries and facilitating correlation of the *Handbook* with standard textbooks or writing guides. Five Steps to Successful Writing offers a brief, step-by-step guide through the writing process, which is then summarized in list fashion, with page references to pertinent entries, by the Checklist of the Writing Process.

In preparing this fourth edition, we have carefully reexamined every entry, clarified or updated a great many, deleted a few that proved to have been seldom used, and added a substantial number of new ones. Among the entries added are those on **computer graphics, electronic mail, English as a second language, international correspondence, layout and design,** and **collaborative writing**. In addition to the new entries, major revisions have been made to the entries on **word processing, library research, documenting sources, graphs, illustrations, résumés, formal reports,** and a great many others. We have also added an instructor's manual to assist those who wish to use *The Business Writer's Handbook* as the primary text.

As in earlier editions, the entries themselves are complete without being exhaustive; that is, they focus on solutions to specific writing problems. Therefore, the general tone is prescriptive. For example, questions about the history of a term such as *data* and the controversy surrounding its use may be interesting, but they are secondary to the advice the user seeks. So, although debate over divided usage is acknowledged, a guideline is offered to get the writer on with the business of writing. This principle holds true for the grammatical entries as well; they do not attempt to settle the debate between traditional and linguistically oriented grammarians, although current linguistic thinking about grammatical problems is presented where it contributes to the explanation of a concept. The guidance offered in the entries will solve most of the problems users of this book will encounter. However, students should understand that some companies and government agencies have their own standards governing certain subjects dealt with in this book and their employees must conform to those standards.

The Business Writer's Handbook shares not only its format but a majority of the topics in the alphabetical entries with *Handbook of Technical Writing*, also published in a fourth edition by St. Martin's Press. Within the alphabetical entries common to both books, however, the examples given, as well as portions of the text, are often different—illustrating the same writing principles but in language that reflects a technical context in one handbook and a business context in the other. In a course combining both technical and business writing, either book might be used, the choice depending upon the emphasis the instructor thinks most appropriate.

We are deeply grateful to the many instructors, students, technical writers, and others who have helped us prepare *The Business Writer's Handbook.* For his contributions to the first edition, which continue to lend strength to the latest edition, we are indebted to Conrad R. Winterhalter, who reviewed the entire manuscript in several drafts and wrote the original entries on the **résumé, letter of application**, and **letter of acceptance**. Others whose suggestions for the first edition continue to be reflected here, and to whom we are happy to renew our thanks, are Clare Bedillion, James H. Chaffee, Merrily A. Enquist, Bertrand Heflin, Keith Palmer, Julie Whitmore, and Bobby Wooten.

For assistance with the second edition, we renew our thanks to Renu Juneja, Valparaiso University; George Love, Michigan Technological University; Judy McInish, Hornbake Library, University of Maryland; Wendy Osborne, Society of American Foresters; Marjorie Piechowski, Marquette University; C.J. Raeth, Miami University; Diana Reep, University of Akron; Charlene Schou, Idaho State University; Patricia Shoff, Williamsport Area Community College; Mabel Stonecipher, University of Kentucky; Jack Thompson, University of California at Davis; and Mary Thompson, Krannert Graduate School of Management, Purdue University.

For assistance with the third edition, we wish to recognize the contributions of William Van Pelt of the University of Wisconsin–Milwaukee, who wrote the entry on **word processing**; Eleanor Berry of the University of Wisconsin–Milwaukee, who contributed to the entry on **documenting sources**; Mary Mullins and Sandra Balzo of First Wisconsin National Bank who provided the sample newsletter article; and Ann Thomas, Rayleona Sanders, and Mimi Mejac—all of the Nuclear Regulatory Commission—for their helpful comments. We would also like to express our heartfelt appreciation to our academic reviewers for the third edition, who did a truly superb job: Kevin Harty, English Department, La Salle College, Philadelphia; Jane Parks-Clifford, Director of Composition, University of Missouri, St. Louis; Alan Glossner, Arts & Humanities Division, Monroe Community College, Rochester; and Thomas Willard, English Department, University of Arizona, Tucson.

For assistance with the fourth edition, we wish to thank Erik Thelen of the University of Wisconsin–Milwaukee, who served as a reviewer and also developed the entry on **international corre-

spondence, and Pat Goldstein of the University of Wisconsin–Milwaukee, who developed the **English as a second language** entry. For help with the entry on **computer graphics**, we wish to thank graphics designer Darlene Chang. We would also like to express our appreciation to our academic reviewers for the fourth edition: Erik A. Thelen, University of Wisconsin–Milwaukee; Patricia H. Graves, Georgia State University; Don Washington, Tulane University; and James B. Stull, San Jose State University.

We also express our appreciation to the following organizations for permission to use examples of their business writing: American Marketing Association, Allen Bradley Company, NCR Corporation, and Professional Secretaries International.

C.T.B.
G.J.A.
W.E.O.

Contents

Five Steps
to Successful Writing

Many business people have difficulty writing because they do not know how to begin. They sit down in front of a blank computer screen or with pen in hand and hope to fill the screen or the blank page without realizing that skill in writing, like the business skills in which they are proficient, requires a disciplined and systematic approach.

Successful writing on the job is not the product of inspiration, nor is it merely the spoken word transferred to paper. Rather, it is primarily the result of knowing how to structure ideas on paper. The best way to ensure that a writing task will be successful—whether it is a letter, a proposal, or a formal report—is to divide the writing process into the following five steps:

- Preparation
- Research
- Organization
- Writing the Draft
- Revision

At first, these five steps must be consciously—even self-consciously—followed. But so, at first, must the steps in operating a machine, designing a circuit, troubleshooting a motor, interviewing a candidate for a job, or chairing a meeting of a board of directors. With practice, the steps in each of these processes become nearly automatic. This is not to suggest that writing becomes easy; it does not because writing well requires that you exercise judgment during each step. But the easiest and most efficient way to do it is systematically.

As you master the five steps of the writing process, keep in mind that the steps are interrelated and overlap at points. For example, your reader's needs and your objective could affect decisions in each of the other steps. You may also find that you need to retrace steps.

As you organize the information you gathered, for example, you may discover a gap that will require further research.

Be aware also that the time required for each step varies with different writing tasks. For example, when writing a brief informal memo, you might follow the first three steps (preparation, research, and organization) by simply listing the points you want to cover in the order you want to cover them. In other words, the information gathering and organizing occurs mentally as you consider your purpose in writing the memo. For a formal report, on the other hand, these three steps require well-organized research, careful note taking, and detailed outlining. In short, the five steps expand, contract, and at times must be reviewed or even repeated to fit the complexity of the writing task.

Use the summary of the following five steps of the writing process to guide you. The Checklist of the Writing Process that follows this summary can also help you detect and solve problems by referring you to the specific entry that explains the cause of the problem and shows you how to solve it. In the following discussion, as elsewhere throughout this book, words and phrases printed in **boldface type** refer to specific alphabetical entries.

Step 1.   Preparation

Writing, like most business tasks, requires solid **preparation**. In fact, adequate preparation is as important as writing the draft. Preparation for writing consists of (1) establishing your objective, (2) identifying your reader, and (3) determining the scope of your coverage.

Establishing your **objective** is simply determining what you want your readers to know or be able to do when they have finished reading your report or paper. But you must be precise; it is all too common for a writer to state an objective in terms so broad that it is almost useless. An objective such as "To report on possible locations for a new manufacturing facility" is too general to be of real help. But "To compare the relative advantages of Chicago, Minneapolis, and Salt Lake City as possible locations for a new manufacturing facility so that top management can choose the best location" gives you an objective that can guide you throughout the writing process.

The next task is to identify your **reader**. Again, be precise. What are your reader's needs in relation to your subject? What does your reader already know about your subject? You need to know, for example, whether you must define basic terminology or whether such definitions will merely bore, or even insult, your reader. Is your reader actually several readers with different interests and levels of technical knowledge? For the objective stated in the previous paragraph, the reader was described as "top management." But *who* is included in this category? Will one of the people evaluating the report be the personnel manager? If so, that person is likely to have a special interest in such things as the availability of qualified personnel in each city, the presence of colleges where special training would be available for employees, housing conditions, and perhaps even recreational facilities. The purchasing manager will be concerned about available sources for the materials needed by the plant. The marketing manager will give priority to such things as the plant's closeness to its primary markets and the available transport facilities for distribution of the plant's products. The financial vice-president will want to know about land and building costs and the local tax structure. The president may be interested in *all* these things and even more; for example, he or she might be concerned about the convenience of personal travel between corporate headquarters and the new plant.

In addition to knowing the needs and interests of these readers, you should know as much as you can about their backgrounds. For example, have they visited all three cities? Have they already seen other studies of the three cities? Is this the first new plant, or have they chosen locations for new plants before? If you have many readers, one way to accommodate their needs is to combine all your readers into one composite reader and write for *that* reader. Another way is to aim parts of a document to different readers: an **executive summary** to a top manager and an **appendix** with detailed data to business specialists, and the body of the report to middle managers.

Determining your objective and identifying your readers will help you decide what to include and not to include in your writing. Then you will have established the **scope** of your writing project. If you do not clearly define the scope before beginning your research (the next step), you will spend needless extra hours on research because you will not be sure what kind of information you need, or even how much. For example, given the objective and reader established in the preceding two paragraphs, the scope of your report on plant locations would include such things as land and

building costs, available labor force, transportation facilities, proximity to sources of supply, and so forth; however, it probably would
not include the history of the cities being considered or the altitude
and geological features (unless these were directly related to your
particular business).

Step 2. Research

The purpose of most business writing is to explain something—
usually something that is complex. This kind of writing cannot be
done by someone who does not understand the subject he or she is
writing about. The only way to be sure that you can deal adequately
with a complex subject is to compile a complete set of notes during
your **research** and then to create a working outline from the notes.
Numerous sources of information are available to you: the library
(see **library research**), personal interviews (see **interviewing for
information** and **questionnaires**), your own knowledge (see **research**), and others. Consider them all when you begin your
research, and use those that fit your needs. Of course, the amount
of research you will need to do depends on your project; for a brief
memo or letter, your "research" may amount to nothing more than
jotting down the pertinent ideas before you begin to organize them.

Step 3. Organization

Without **organization**, the material gathered during your research
would be incomprehensible to your reader. Thus you must determine the best sequence in which your ideas should be presented—
that is, you must choose a **method of development**.

An appropriate method of development is the writer's tool for
keeping things under control and the reader's means of following
the writer's presentation. Your subject may readily lend itself to a
particular method of development. For example, if you were giving
instructions for starting an engine, you would naturally present the
steps of the process in the order of their occurrence. For this task,
the obvious method of development would be sequential. If you
were writing about the history of the computer, your account would
go from the beginning to the present. This is the chronological
method of development. If your subject, like those mentioned,
naturally lends itself to a certain method of development, use it—
don't attempt to impose another method on it. This book includes
all the methods of development that are likely to be used by business

people: chronological, sequential, spatial, increasing or decreasing order of importance, comparison, division and classification, analysis, general to specific, specific to general, and cause and effect. As the writer, you must choose the one that best suits your subject, your reader, and your objective. You are then ready to prepare your outline.

Outlining makes large or complex subjects easier for you to organize, by breaking them into manageable parts, and it ensures that your finished writing will move logically from idea to idea without omitting anything important. It also enables you to emphasize your key points by placing them in the positions of greatest importance. Finally, by forcing you to structure your thinking at an early stage, a good outline releases you to concentrate exclusively on writing when you begin the rough draft. Even if the task is only a letter or short memo, successful writing needs the logic and structure that a method of development and an outline provide, although for such simple projects, the method of development and outline may be in your head rather than on paper.

If you intend to include **illustrations** with your writing, a good time to think about them is when you have completed your outline— especially if the illustrations need to be prepared by someone else while you are writing and revising the draft. If your outline is reasonably detailed, you should be able to determine which ideas will benefit from graphic support.

Make sure at this point that you use **layout and design** and a **format** that are helpful to your reader and appropriate to your subject and objective.

Step 4. Writing the Draft

When you have established your objective, reader's needs, and scope and have completed your research and your outline, you will be well prepared to write your first draft. To do so, simply expand the notes from your outline into **paragraphs**, without worrying about **grammar**, refinements of language, or such mechanical aspects of writing as **spelling**. Refinements will come with revision.

Write the rough draft quickly, concentrating entirely on converting your outline to sentences and paragraphs. To facilitate this step, write as though you were explaining your subject to someone sitting across the desk from you. Don't worry about a good opening. Just start. There is no need in the rough draft to be concerned about an

introduction or **transition** unless they come quickly and easily—concentrate instead on *ideas*. Don't attempt to polish or revise. Writing and revising are different activities. Keep writing quickly so as to achieve **unity** and proportion.

Even with good preparation, writing the draft remains a chore for many writers. The entry on **writing the draft** describes tactics used by experienced writers to get started and keep moving. Discover which ones are the most helpful and appropriate for you.

However, the most effective way to start and keep going is to use a good outline as a map for your first draft. Above all, don't wait for inspiration—you need to treat writing a draft in business writing as you would any on-the-job task.

Step 5. Revision

Chances are that the clearer a piece of writing seems to the reader, the more effort the writer has put into **revision**. If you have followed the steps of the writing process to this point, you will have a very rough draft. Revision, the obvious final step, requires a different frame of mind than does writing the draft. Read and evaluate the draft from the reader's point of view. Be eager to find and correct faults, and be honest. Be hard on yourself for the reader's convenience; never be easy on yourself at the reader's expense.

Do not try to do all your revising at once. Read your rough draft several times, each time looking for and correcting a different set of problem or errors.

Check your draft for accuracy and completeness. Your draft should give readers exactly what they need, but it should not burden them with unnecessary information or sidetrack them into loosely related subjects.

If you have not yet written an **opening** or **introduction**, now is the time to do it. Your introduction should serve as a frame into which readers can fit the information that follows in the body of your draft; check your introduction to see that it does, in fact, provide readers with such assistance. Your opening should both announce the subject and give the reader essential background information about it.

Check your draft for unity, coherence, and transition. If it has unity, all of the sentences in each paragraph will contribute to the development of that paragraph's central idea (expressed in the topic sentence), and all of the paragraphs will contribute to the development of the main topic. If the draft has **coherence**, the sentences and the paragraphs will flow smoothly from one to the next, and the relationship of each sentence or paragraph to the one before it will be clear. Coherence can be achieved in many ways, but especially by the careful use of **transition** devices and by the maintenance of a consistent **point of view**. Also check your draft for the proper **emphasis** and **subordination** of your ideas. Now is also a good time to adjust the **pace**: if you find places where too many ideas are jammed together, space out the ideas and slow the pace; conversely, if you find a series of simple ideas expressed in short, choppy sentences, combine some of the sentences to quicken the pace.

Check your draft for **clarity**. Although much of your revising will already have improved the clarity, check now for any terms that must be defined or explained (see **defining terms**). In addition, check for **ambiguity**. Is your writing free of **affectation**? Is it free of **jargon** that your readers may not understand? Are there **abstract words** that could be replaced by concrete words? Check your entire draft for appropriate **word choice**.

Check your draft for **style**. By now you will have already done much to improve the style, but there is more you can do. Check for **conciseness**: can you eliminate useless words or phrases—what some writers call "deadwood"? It is almost always possible to do so, and your reader will benefit greatly. Get rid of **clichés** and other **trite language**. Is your writing active? Especially in business writing there is a great temptation to use the passive **voice** when the active voice would be far stronger and more concise. Replace negative writing with **positive writing**. Check, too, for **parallel structure**. Examine your **sentence construction**, and look for ways to create **sentence variety**.

Check your draft for **awkwardness** and for departures from the appropriate **tone**. Awkwardness and tone are hard to define because they are the result of a great many different things, most of which you will have already dealt with in your revision. Read your draft aloud, or have someone read it while you listen. You will recognize awkwardness because awkward writing sounds forced or clumsy—like something you would never say if you were *talking* to your reader because it would sound unnatural. You will recognize departures from the proper tone because they are words, phrases, or statements that are inappropriate to the relationship between you and your reader. For example, in a memo to a superior in your organization you would want to avoid phrases or statements that sound like lecturing. If your readers are serious about your subject (and it is best to assume that they are), don't try to be witty. Correcting the tone is frequently a matter of replacing a word with another that has more appropriate **connotations**. Consider the difference in tone between, "I'm puzzled by your *stubbornness* in opposing the plan," and "I'm puzzled by the *firmness* of your opposition to the plan." Finally, check slowly and carefully for problems of **grammar, punctuation**, and mechanics (**spelling, abbreviations, capital letters, acronyms and initialisms**, and the like).

The following Checklist of the Writing Process is designed to help you follow the five steps to successful writing. It can help you diagnose any writing problem you may have, and it refers you to the entry that explains the causes of the problem and shows you how to correct it.

Checklist of the Writing Process

This checklist arranges the key entries of the *Handbook* according to a recommended sequence of steps useful for any writing project. The exact titles of the entries are in **boldface type** for quick reference, followed by the page numbers. When you turn to the entries themselves, you will find boldface cross-references to other entries that may be helpful. (You may also wish to refer to the Topical Key to the Alphabetical Entries and to the index at the back of the book.)

5. Revision   597

Topical Key
to the Alphabetical Entries

This tabulation arranges the alphabetical entries into subject categories. Within each category the entries are listed mainly, but not strictly, in alphabetical order. Excluded from this tabulation are the numerous entries concerned with the usage of particular words or phrases (*imply/infer, already/all ready*, and the like). For a list of the key entries in a recommended sequence of steps for any writing project, see the Checklist of the Writing Process.

Types of Business Writing

Finding a Job

Planning and Research

Organization, Writing, and Revision

Paragraphs, Sentences, Clauses, and Phrases

Parts of Speech, Inflection, and Agreement

The Business Writer's Handbook

Fourth Edition

A

a/an

A and *an* are indefinite **articles**; "indefinite" implies that the **noun** designated by the article is not a specific person, place, or thing but is one of a group.

> EXAMPLE The insurance salesman sold *a* policy. (Not a specific policy, but an unnamed policy.)

Use *a* before words beginning with a consonant or consonant sound (including *y* or *w* sounds).

> EXAMPLES The year's activities are summarized in *a* one-page report. (Although the *o* in *one* is a vowel, the first *sound* is *w*, a consonant sound. Hence the article *a* precedes the word.)
> *A* manual has been written on that subject.
> It was *a* historic event for the company.
> The office manager felt that it was *a* unique situation.
> *A* sonar operator first detected the wreck.

Use *an* before words beginning with a vowel or vowel sound.

> EXAMPLES The report is *an* overview of the year's activities.
> He seems *an* unlikely candidate for the job.
> The interviewer arrived *an* hour early. (Although the *h* in *hour* is a consonant, the word begins on a vowel *sound*; hence it is preceded by *an*.)
> He bought *an* SLR camera.

Be careful not to use unnecessary indefinite articles in a sentence.

> CHANGE I will meet you in *a* half *an* hour.
> TO I will meet you in *a* half hour.
> OR I will meet you in half *an* hour.

a lot/alot

A lot is often incorrectly written as one word (*alot*). Write the **phrase** as two words: *a lot*. The phrase *a lot* is very informal, however, and should not normally be used in business writing.

> CHANGE They had *a lot* of objections.
> TO They had many objections.

abbreviations

Abbreviations may be shortened versions of words, or they may be formed by the first letters of words. (See also **acronyms and initialisms**.)

> EXAMPLES Mister/Mr.
> Avenue/Ave.
> September/Sept.
> dozen/doz
> National Retail Dry Goods Association/NRDGA
> cash on delivery/c.o.d.

Abbreviations, like **symbols**, can be important space savers in business writing, where it is often necessary to provide the maximum amount of information in a limited amount of space. Use abbreviations, however, only if you are certain that your **reader** will understand them as readily as he or she would the terms for which they stand. Remember also that a **memorandum** or **report** addressed to a specific person may be read by others and that you must consider those readers as well. Take into account your reader's level of knowledge of your subject when deciding whether to use abbreviations. Do not use them if they might become an inconvenience to the reader. A good rule of thumb: When in doubt, spell it out.

In general, use abbreviations only in charts, **tables**, **graphs**, footnotes, **bibliographies**, and other places where space is limited. Normally you should not make up your own abbreviations, for they will probably confuse your reader. Except for commonly used abbreviations (U.S.A., p.m.), a term to be abbreviated should be spelled out the first time it is used, with the abbreviation enclosed in **parentheses** following the term. Thereafter, the abbreviation may be used alone.

> EXAMPLE The annual report of the National Retail Dry Goods Association (NRDGA) will be issued next month. In it, the NRDGA will detail shortages in several widely used textiles.

Do not add an additional period at the end of a sentence that ends with an abbreviation.

> EXAMPLE The official name of the company is Data Base, Inc.

For abbreviations specific to your profession, use the style guide provided by your company or professional organization. (A listing of style guides appears at the end of **documenting sources**.)

FORMING ABBREVIATIONS

Measurements. When you abbreviate terms that refer to measurement, be sure your reader is familiar with the abbreviated form. The following list contains some common abbreviations used with units of measurement. Notice that except for *in.* (inch), *bar.* (barometer), and others that form words, abbreviations of measurements do not require periods.

amp, ampere

atm, atmosphere

bar., barometer

bbl, barrel

bhp, brake horsepower

Btu, British thermal unit

bu, bushel

cal, calorie

cm, centimeter

cos, cosine

ctn, cotangent

doz or dz, dozen

emf or EMF, electromotive force

F, Fahrenheit

fig., figure (illustration)

ft, foot (or feet)

gal., gallon

hp, horsepower

hr, hour

in., inch

kc, kilocycle

kg, kilogram

km, kilometer

lb, pound

min, minute

oz, ounce

ppm, parts per million

pt, pint

qt, quart

rad, radian

rev, revolution

sec, second or secant

tan., tangent

yd, yard

yr, year

Abbreviations of units of measure are identical in the singular and plural: one *cm* and three *cm* (not three *cms*).

Personal Names and Titles. Personal names should generally not be abbreviated.

> CHANGE Chas., Thos., Wm., Geo.
>   TO Charles, Thomas, William, George

An academic, civil, religious, or military title should be spelled out when it does not precede a name.

> EXAMPLE The doctor asked for the patient's chart.

When they precede names, some titles are customarily abbreviated. (See also **Ms./Miss/Mrs.**)

EXAMPLES Dr. Smith, Mr. Mills, Mrs. Katz

An abbreviation of a title may follow the name; however, be certain that it does not duplicate a title before the name.

CHANGE Dr. William Smith, Ph.D.
    TO Dr. William Smith
    OR William Smith, Ph.D.

When addressing **correspondence** and including names in other documents, you should normally spell out titles.

EXAMPLES The Honorable Mary J. Holt
    Professor Charles Matlin
    Captain Juan Ramirez
    Reverend James MacIntosh, D.D.

The following is a list of common abbreviations for personal and professional titles:

Atty.	Attorney
B.A.	Bachelor of Arts
B.S.	Bachelor of Science
B.S.E.E.	Bachelor of Science in Electrical Engineering
D.D.	Doctor of Divinity
D.D.S.	Doctor of Dental Science (or Surgery)
Dr.	Doctor (used with any doctor's degree)
Drs.	Plural of Dr.
Ed.D.	Doctor of Education
Hon.	Honorable
Jr.	Junior (used when a father with the same name is living)
LL.B.	Bachelor of Law
LL.D.	Doctor of Law
M.A.	Master of Arts
M.B.A.	Master of Business Administration
M.D.	Doctor of Medicine
Messrs.	Plural of Mr.
Mr.	Mister (spelled out only in the most formal contexts)
Mrs.	Married woman
Ms.	Woman of unspecified marital status
M.S.	Master of Science
Ph.D.	Doctor of Philosophy

Rev.   Reverend
Sr.   Senior (used when a son with the same name is living)

Names of Organizations. Many companies include in their names such terms as *Brothers, Incorporated, Corporation,* and *Company.* If these terms appear as abbreviations in the official company names, use them in their abbreviated forms: *Bros., Inc., Corp.,* and *Co.* If not abbreviated in the official names, such terms should be spelled out in most writing other than addresses, footnotes, **bibliographies**, and **lists**, where abbreviations may be used. A similar guideline applies for use of an **ampersand** (&); this symbol should be used only if it appears in an official company name. Titles of divisions within organizations, such as Department (Dept.) and Division (Div.) should be abbreviated only when space is limited.

Common Scholarly Abbreviations. The following is a partial list of abbreviations that are commonly used in reference books and for documenting sources in research papers and reports.

anon.	anonymous
assn.	association
bibliog.	**bibliography**, bibliographer, bibliographic, bibliographical
biog.	biography, biographer, biographical
bull.	bulletin
©	**copyright**
c., ca.	*circa,* "about" (used with approximate dates: c. 1756)
cf.	*confer,* "compare"
ch., chs.	chapter(s)
cit.	citation, cited
diss.	dissertation
ed., eds.	edited by, editor(s), edition(s)
e.g.	*exempli gratia,* "for example" (see **e.g./i.e.**)
enl.	enlarged (as in "rev. and enl. ed.")
esp.	especially
et al.	*et alii,* "and others"
etc.	*et cetera,* "and so forth" (see **etc.**)
f., ff.	and the following page(s) or line(s)
fig.	figure
fwd.	**foreword**, foreword by
GPO	Government Printing Office, Washington DC
i.e.	*id est,* "that is"

l., ll.	line, lines
MS, MSS	manuscript, manuscripts (see **MS/MSS**)
n., nn.	note, notes (used immediately after page number: 56n., 56n.3, 56nn.3–5)
NB	*Nota Bene,* "take notice, mark well" (always capitalized)
n.d.	no date (of publication)
n.p.	no place (of publication); no publisher
n. pag.	no pagination
p., pp.	page, pages
pref.	preface, preface by (see **Foreword/Preface**)
proc.	proceedings
pseud.	pseudonym
pub (publ.)	published by, publisher, publication
rept.	reported by, **report**
rev.	revised by, revision; review, reviewed by (spell out *review* where *rev.* might be ambiguous)
rpt.	reprinted by, reprint
sec., secs.	section, sections
soc.	society
supp.	supplement
trans.	translated by, translator, translation
UP	University Press (used in MLA style of **documenting sources**: Oxford UP)
viz.	*videlicet,* "namely"
vol., vols.	volume, volumes
vs., v.	versus, "against" (v. preferred in titles of legal cases)

Dates and Time. The following are common abbreviations.

A.D.	*anno Domini* (beginning of calendar time—A.D. 1790)	Jan.	January
		Feb.	February
B.C.	before Christ (before the beginning of calendar time— 647 B.C.)	Mar.	March
		Apr.	April
		Aug.	August
a.m.	*ante meridiem,* "before noon"	Sept.	September
p.m.	*post meridiem,* "after noon"	Dec.	December

Months should always be spelled out when only the month and year are given. The standard and alternative forms of abbreviations appear in current dictionaries, either in regular alphabetical order (by the letters of the abbreviation) or in a separate index. (See **dictionaries.**)

above

Avoid using *above* to refer to a preceding passage, **illustration,** or **table** in your writing. Its reference is often vague, and if the passage referred to is far from the current one, the use of *above* is distracting because your **reader** must go back to the earlier passage to understand your reference. The same is true of *aforesaid, aforementioned, above mentioned, the former,* and *the latter.* In addition to distracting the reader, these words also contribute to a heavy, wooden **style.** If you must refer to something previously mentioned, either repeat the **noun** or **pronoun** or construct your **paragraph** so that your reference is obvious (see also **former/latter** and **aforesaid**).

> CHANGE Please fill out and submit the above by March 1.
> TO Please fill out and submit the vacation schedule on the previous page by March 1.

absolute words

Absolute words (such as *round, unique, exact,* and *perfect*) are not logically subject to **comparison** (*rounder, roundest*); nevertheless, these words are sometimes used comparatively.

> CHANGE We modified our contract to *more exactly* reflect existing requirements.
> TO We modified our contract to *more closely* reflect existing requirements.

Absolute words should be used comparatively only with the greatest caution in business writing, where accuracy and precision are crucial.

absolutely

Absolutely means "definitely," "entirely," "completely," or "unquestionably." It is not an **intensifier** and should not be used to mean "very" or "much." When used as an intensifier, it can be deleted.

> CHANGE A new analysis is *absolutely* impossible.
> TO A new analysis is impossible.

abstracts

An *abstract* summarizes and highlights the major points of a longer piece of writing. Abstracts are written for many **formal reports**, **journal articles**, and most dissertations, as well as for many other long works. Their primary purpose is to enable readers to decide whether to read the work in full. (For a discussion of how summaries differ from abstracts, see **executive summaries**.)

Although abstracts are published with the longer works they condense, they are also often published independently in computer-retrievable periodical indexes. These periodicals, such as the *Accountant's Digest* and *Personnel & Training Abstracts*, are devoted exclusively to abstracting information in specific fields of study. They enable researchers to review a great deal of **literature** in a short time. (For a discussion of computer-retrievable indexes, see **library research**, and for a listing of typical periodicals that publish abstracts, see **reference books**.)

The abstracts for **reports** and articles are also frequently the source of terms (called *keywords*) used to **index** the original document by subject for computerized information-retrieval systems. Because they are the source of keywords, abstracts must accurately but concisely describe the original work so that researchers in the field will not miss valuable information. Accordingly, they should contain no information not discussed in the original. Abstracts do vary, however, in the amount of information they provide about the original work. Depending on their **scope**, abstracts are usually classified as either *descriptive* or *informative*.

DESCRIPTIVE ABSTRACTS

A descriptive abstract includes information about the purpose, scope, and methods used to arrive at the findings contained in the original document. It is almost an expanded **table of contents** in sentence form. A descriptive abstract need not be longer than several sentences if it adequately summarizes the information.

The following descriptive abstract comes from a 30-page report that describes how a select group of foreign countries provide engineering expertise to their control-room operators for round-the-clock shift work at nuclear power plants:

ABSTRACT

Purpose and This report describes the practices of selected foreign coun-
scope tries for providing engineering expertise on shift in nuclear

Methods used power plants. The report discusses the extent to which engineering expertise is made available and the alternative models of providing such expertise. The implications of foreign practices for U.S. consideration are discussed, with particular reference to the shift technical adviser position and to a proposed shift engineer position. The relevant information for this study came from the open literature, interviews with utility staff and officials, and governmental and nuclear utility reports.

INFORMATIVE ABSTRACTS

The informative abstract is an expanded version of the descriptive abstract. In addition to information about the purpose, scope, and methods of the original document, the informative abstract includes the results, **conclusions**, and recommendations, if any. The informative abstract retains the tone and essential scope of the original work while omitting its details.

The following informative abstract expands the scope of the sample descriptive abstract by including the report's findings, conclusions, and recommendation:

ABSTRACT

Purpose and scope This report describes the practices of selected foreign countries for providing engineering expertise on shift in nuclear power plants. The report discusses the extent to which engineering expertise is made available and the alternative models of providing such expertise. The implications of foreign practices for U.S. consideration are discussed, with particular reference to the shift technical adviser position and to a proposed

Methods used shift engineer position. The relevant information for this study came from the open literature, interviews with utility staff and officials, and governmental and nuclear utility reports.

Finding The countries studied used two approaches to provide engineering expertise on shift: (1) employing a graduate engineer in a line management operations position and (2) creating a specific engineering position to provide expertise to the operations staff. The comparison of these two models did not in-

General conclusions dicate that one system inherently functions more effectively than does the other for safe operations. However, the alternative modes are likely to affect crew relationships and performance; labor supply, recruitment, and retention; and system implementation. Of the two systems, the nonsupervisory

Recommen- dation engineering position seems more advantageous within the context of current recruitment and career-path practices.

Which of the two types should you write? The answer depends on the organization or publication for which you are writing. If it has a policy, comply with it. Otherwise, aim at the needs of the principal readers for your document. To satisfy the widest possible readership, including those who must index the original document based on the abstract, write informative abstracts. Descriptive abstracts, on the other hand, are indispensable for information surveys, conference proceedings, **progress reports** that combine information from more than one project, and other publications that compile a variety of information. For these types of publications, conclusions and recommendations either do not exist in the original or are too numerous to include in an abstract.

LENGTH OF ABSTRACTS

A long abstract defeats the purpose of an abstract. For this reason, abstracts are usually no longer than 200 to 250 words. Descriptive abstracts may be considerably shorter, of course.

SCOPE

Include in your abstract the following kinds of information, bearing in mind that your readers know nothing, except what your title announces, about your document:

- the subject of the study
- the scope of the study
- the purpose of the study
- the methods used
- the results obtained (informative abstract only)
- the recommendations made, if any (informative abstract only)

Do not include the following kinds of information:

- the background of the study
- a detailed discussion or explanation of the methods used
- administrative details about how the study was undertaken, who funded it, who worked on it, and the like
- figures, **tables**, charts, **maps**, and bibliographic references
- any information that does not appear in the original

Also, abstracts published independently of the main document will make no sense if they refer to tables or **illustrations** in the document;

therefore, the abstract must make no reference to such tables or illustrations.

WRITING STYLE

Write the abstract after completing the report, article, or other work. Otherwise, your abstract may not accurately reflect the original document. Use the major and minor heads of your outline to help distinguish primary from secondary ideas.

Begin with a topic sentence that announces at least the subject and scope of the original document. Then combine the other relevant material for conciseness and clarity, eliminating unnecessary words and ideas. Write in complete sentences, but instead of stringing a group of short sentences end to end, combine ideas by using **subordination** and **parallel structure**. The degree of conciseness possible for **abbreviations, acronyms**, and technical **jargon** will vary depending on your readers. As a rule, spell out all **acronyms and initialisms** and all but the most common abbreviations (C°, F°, mph). In your attempts to write concisely, do not slip into a **telegraphic style** in which you omit **articles** (*a, an, the*) and important transitional words (*however, therefore, but, in summary*). Finally, as you summarize, keep the **tone** and **emphasis** consistent with those of the original document. (For guidance about the placement of abstracts in **reports**, see **formal report**.)

abstract words/concrete words

The difference between abstract and concrete words is the difference between *durability* (abstract) and *stone* (concrete).

Abstract nouns and other words refer to general ideas, qualities, conditions, acts, or relationships. Abstract words refer to something that is intangible, something that cannot be discerned by the five senses.

> EXAMPLES   work, courage, crime, kindness, idealism, love, hate, fantasy, sportsmanship

Abstract words must frequently be qualified by other words.

> CHANGE   What the members of the Research and Development Department need is *freedom.*
>
> TO   What the members of the Research and Development Department need is *freedom to explore the problem further.*

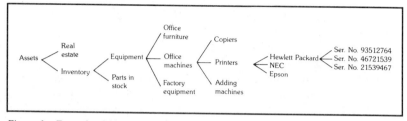

Figure 1   Example of Abstract to Concrete Words

Concrete nouns and other words refer to specific persons, objects, and acts that can be perceived by the senses.

> EXAMPLES   wrench, book, house, scissors, gold, water, glass
> *Skiing* (concrete) is a strenuous *sport* (abstract).

Concrete words are easier to understand, for they create images in the mind of your **reader**. Still, you cannot express ideas without using some abstract words. Actually, the two kinds of words are usually used best together, in support of each other. For example, the abstract idea of *transportation* is made clearer with the use of specific concrete words, such as *subways, jets,* or *automobiles.*

In fact, a word that is concrete in one context can be less concrete in another. The same word may even be abstract in one context and concrete in another. The choice between abstract and concrete terms always depends on the context. Just how concrete a particular context might require you to be is shown in Figure 1, which goes from the most abstract, on the left, to the most concrete, on the right.

The example represents seven levels of abstraction; which one would be appropriate depends on your purpose in writing and on the context in which you are using the word. For example, a company's **annual report** might logically use the most abstract term, *assets,* to refer to all the property and goods the firm owns; shareholders would probably not require a less abstract term. Interoffice **memorandums** between the company's accounting and legal departments would appropriately call the firm's holdings *real estate* and *inventory.* To the company's inventory control department, however, the word *inventory* is much too abstract to be useful, and a report on inventory might contain the more concrete terms *equipment* and *parts in stock.* But to the assistant inventory control manager in charge of equipment, that term is still too abstract; he or she would speak of several particular kinds of equipment: *office furniture, factory equipment,* and *office machines.* The breakdown of the types of office machines for which the inventory control assistant is responsible might include *copiers, adding machines,* and *printers.* But even this classification would not be concrete enough to enable the company's purchasing department to obtain service contracts for the normal maintenance of its printers. Because the department must deal with different printer manufacturers, *printers* would have to be listed by brand name: *Hewlett Packard, NEC,* and *Epson.* And the Epson technician who performs the maintenance must go one step further and identify each Epson printer by serial number. As the example in Figure 1 shows, then, a term that is sufficiently concrete in one context may be too abstract in another. (See also **word choice.**)

accept/except

Accept is a **verb** meaning "consent to," "agree to take," or "admit willingly."

EXAMPLE I *accept* the responsibility that goes with the appointment.

Except is normally a **preposition** meaning "other than" or "excluding."

EXAMPLE We agreed on everything *except* the schedule.

acceptance letters

When you have received an offer of a job that you want to accept, reply as soon as possible—certainly within a week. The **format** for such a letter is simple: Begin by accepting, with pleasure, the job you have been offered. Identify the job you are accepting, and state the salary so that there is no confusion on these two important points.

The second **paragraph** might go into detail about moving dates and reporting for work. The details will vary depending on what occurred during your job interview. Complete the letter with a statement that you are looking forward to working for your new employer. Figure 1 is an example of an acceptance letter. (See also **correspondence** and **refusal letters.**)

```
                                        2647 Patterson Road
                                        Beechwood, OH  45432
                                        March 6, 19--


        Mr. F. E. Cummins
        Personnel Manager
        Calcutex Industries, Inc.
        3275 Commercial Park Drive
        Bintonville, MI  49474

        Dear Mr. Cummins:

        I am pleased to accept your offer of a position as
        assistant personnel manager at a salary of $X,XXX per
        month.

        Since graduation is August 30, I plan to leave Dayton
        on Tuesday, September 2.  I should be able to locate
        suitable living accommodations within a few days and be
        ready to report for work on the following Monday,
        September 8.  Please let me know if this date is satis-
        factory to you.

        I look forward to a rewarding future with Calcutex.

                                Sincerely,

                                Craig Adderly
                                Craig Adderly
```

State the job and salary you are accepting. →

Specify the date on which you will report to work. →

State your pleasure at joining the firm. →

Figure 1   Acceptance Letter

accumulative/cumulative

Accumulative and *cumulative* are **synonyms** that mean "amassed" or "added up over a period of time." *Accumulative* is rarely used except with reference to accumulated property or wealth.

> EXAMPLES   Last month's expenses were acceptable, but the *cumulative* expenses since the project was begun are excessive.
> The corporation's *accumulative* holdings include nineteen real-estate properties.

acknowledgment letters

It is sometimes necessary (and always considerate), as well as good public relations, to let someone know that you have received something sent to you. An acknowledgment letter serves such a function. It should usually be a short, polite note that mentions when the item arrived and that expresses thanks. See the **correspondence** entry for details and general advice on letter writing; study the example (Figure 1) to get an idea of how to phrase an acknowledgment letter.

```
                        Energy Savings Systems
                          501 North Springfield
                           Phoenix, AZ 85302



        November 8, 19--

        Ms. Wanda Evans, Consultant
        936 East Avenue
        Phoenix, AZ 85301

        Dear Ms. Evans:

        I received your report today; it appears to be complete and
        well done.  Thank you for sending it so promptly.

        When I finish studying the report, I will send you our cost
        estimate for the installation of the Mark II Energy-Saving System.

        Sincerely,

        Robert A. Martinez

        Robert A. Martinez
        Administrative Assistant


        RAM/mo
```

Figure 1   Acknowledgment Letter

acronyms and initialisms

An acronym is an **abbreviation** that is formed by combining the first letter or letters of several words. Acronyms are pronounced as words and are written without periods.

> EXAMPLES   *r*adio *d*etecting *a*nd *r*anging/radar
> *C*ommon *B*usiness-*O*riented *L*anguage/COBOL
> *s*elf-*c*ontained *u*nderwater *b*reathing *a*pparatus/scuba

An *initialism* is an abbreviation that is formed by combining the initial letter of each word in a multiword term. Initialisms are pronounced as separate letters.

> EXAMPLES   *e*nd *o*f *m*onth/e.o.m.
> *c*ash *o*n *d*elivery/c.o.d.

In business, industry, and government, acronyms and initialisms are often used by people working together on particular projects or having the same specialties—as, for example, financial analysts or accountants. As long as such people are communicating with one another, the abbreviations are easily recognized and understood. If the same acronyms or initialisms were used in **correspondence** to someone outside the group, however, they might be incomprehensible to that **reader** and should be explained.

Acronyms and initialisms can be convenient—for the reader and the writer alike—if they are used appropriately. Business people, however, often overuse them, either as an **affectation** or in a misguided attempt to make their writing concise.

WHEN TO USE ACRONYMS AND INITIALISMS

The following are two sample guidelines to apply in deciding whether to use acronyms and initialisms:

1. If you must use a multiword term as much as once each **paragraph**, you should instead use its acronym or initialism. For example, a **phrase** such as "primary software overlay area" can become tiresome if repeated again and again in one piece of writing; it would be better, therefore, to use *PSOA*.
2. If something is better known by its acronym or initialism than by its formal term, you should use the abbreviated form. The initialism *a.m.*, for example, is much more common than the formal *ante meridiem*.

If these conditions do not exist, however, always spell out the full term.

HOW TO USE ACRONYMS AND INITIALISMS

The first time an acronym or initialism appears in a written work, write the complete term, followed by the abbreviated form in **parentheses**.

> EXAMPLE The Capital Appropriations Request (CAR) controls the spending of money.

Thereafter, you may use the acronym or initialism alone. In a long document, however, you will help your reader greatly by repeating the full term in parentheses after the abbreviation at regular intervals so that he or she does not have to search back to the first time the acronym or initialism was used to find its meaning.

> EXAMPLE Remember that the CAR (Capital Appropriations Request) controls the spending of money.

Write acronyms in **capital letters** without **periods**. The only exceptions are those acronyms that have become accepted as **common nouns**, which are written in lowercase letters.

> EXAMPLES NASA, HUD, laser, scuba

Initialisms may be written either uppercase or lowercase. Generally, do not use periods when they are uppercase, but use periods when they are lowercase. Two exceptions are geographic names and academic degrees.

> EXAMPLES COD/c.o.d., FOB/f.o.b., CIF/c.i.f., EOM/e.o.m.
> U.S.A., R.O.K.
> B.A., M.B.A.

Form the plural of an acronym or initialism by adding an *s*. Do not use an *apostrophe*.

> EXAMPLES MIRVs, CRTs

activate/actuate

Even linguists disagree on the distinction between these two words, although both mean "make active." *Actuate* is usually applied only to mechanical processes.

EXAMPLES The relay *actuates* the trip hammer. (mechanical process)
The electrolyte *activates* the battery. (chemical process)
The governor *activated* the National Guard. (legal process)

actually

Actually is an **adverb** meaning "really" or "in fact." Although it is often used for **emphasis** in speech, such use of the word should be avoided in writing. (See also **intensifiers**.)

CHANGE Did he *actually* finish the report on time?
TO Did he finish the report on time?

adapt/adept/adopt

Adapt is a **verb** meaning "adjust to a new situation." *Adept* is an **adjective** meaning "highly skilled." *Adopt* is a verb meaning "take or use as one's own."

EXAMPLE The company will *adopt* a policy of finding executives who are *adept* administrators and who can *adapt* to new situations.

ad hoc

Ad hoc is Latin for "for this" or "for this particular occasion." An ad hoc committee is one set up to consider a particular issue, as opposed to a permanent committee. This term has been fully assimilated into English and thus does not have to be italicized (or underlined). (See also **foreign words in English**.)

adjectives

An adjective makes the meaning of a **noun** or **pronoun** more specific by pointing out one of its qualities (descriptive adjective) or by imposing boundaries on it (limiting adjective).

EXAMPLES a *hot* iron (descriptive)
He is *cold*. (descriptive)
ten automobiles (limiting)
his desk (limiting)

Limiting adjectives include these common and important categories:

Articles (a, an, the)
Demonstrative adjectives (this, that, these, those)
Possessive adjectives (my, his, her, your, our, their)
Interrogative and relative adjectives (whose, which, what)
Numeral adjectives (two, first)
Indefinite adjectives (all, none, some, any)

The demonstrative adjectives are *this, these, that,* and *those.* They are adjectives that "point to" the thing they modify, specifying its position in space or time. *This* and *these* specify a closer position; *that* and *those* specify a more remote position.

EXAMPLES *This* proposal is the one we accepted.
That proposal would have been impracticable.
These problems remain to be solved.
Those problems are not insurmountable.

Because possessive adjectives (*my, your, our, his, her, its, their*) directly modify **nouns**, they function as adjectives, even though they are **pronoun** forms. Anything that modifies a noun functions as an adjective.

EXAMPLE The *proposal's* virtues outweighed *its* defects.

The possessives *mine, yours, hers, ours,* and *theirs* normally function as pronouns rather than as adjectives.

Like **relative pronouns**, the relative adjectives (*whose, which,* and *what*) are **pronoun** forms that link **dependent clauses** to main **clauses**. The difference is that relative pronouns perform this linking function while taking the place of **nouns**, and relative adjectives perform this linking function while *modifying* (describing) nouns. Examples of the uses of relative adjectives follow:

EXAMPLES The president commended the managers *whose* divisions were the most profitable. (*Whose* modifies "divisions.")
He also told us *which* divisions needed to show the greatest improvement. (*Which* modifies "divisions.")
Finally, he told us *what* steps we should take to improve our profits. (*What* modifies "steps.")

COMPARISON OF ADJECTIVES

Most adjectives add the **suffix** *-er* to show **comparison** with one other item and the suffix *-est* to show comparison with two or more other items. The three degrees of comparison are called the *positive, comparative,* and *superlative.*

EXAMPLES Interest rates at bank A are *high.* (positive form)
Interest rates at bank B are *higher.* (comparative form)
Interest rates at bank C are *highest.* (superlative form)

However, many two-syllable adjectives and most three-syllable adjectives are preceded by the words *more* or *most* to form the comparative or the superlative.

EXAMPLES The new facility is *more impressive* than the old one.
The new facility is the *most impressive* in the city.

A few adjectives have irregular forms of comparison (*much, more, most; little, less, least*).

Absolute words (round, unique) are not logically subject to comparison (rounder, roundest); nevertheless, these words are sometimes used comparatively.

CHANGE We recently modified our standard contract to make several clauses *more exact.*

TO We recently modified our standard contract to make several clauses *more accurate.*

PLACEMENT OF ADJECTIVES

When limiting and descriptive adjectives appear together, the limiting adjectives precede the descriptive adjectives, with the **articles** usually in the first position.

EXAMPLE *The ten gray cars* were parked in a row. (article, limiting adjective, descriptive adjective)

Within a sentence, adjectives may appear before the nouns they modify (the attributive position) or after the nouns they modify (the predicative position).

EXAMPLES The *small* jobs are given priority. (attributive position)
Priority is given to jobs that are *small.* (predicative position)

An adjective in an attributive position may shift to a predicative position in a larger, more complex construction.

EXAMPLES We passed a *big* budget. (attributive position)
We negotiated a contract *bigger by far than theirs.* (predicative position for adjective phrase)

When an adjective follows a **linking verb**, it is called a predicate adjective.

EXAMPLES The warehouse is *full*.
The lens is *convex*.
His department is *efficient*.

A predicate adjective is one kind of **subjective complement**. By completing the meaning of a linking verb, a predicate adjective describes or limits the subject of the **verb**.

EXAMPLES The job is *easy*.
The manager was very *demanding*.

An adjective that follows a transitive **verb** and modifies its direct **object** is one kind of **objective complement**. (See also **complements**.)

EXAMPLE We appointed Mr. Jones *chairman*.

USE OF ADJECTIVES

Because of the need for precise qualification in business writing, it is often necessary to use nouns as adjectives.

EXAMPLE The *test* conclusions led to a redesign of the system.

When adjectives modifying the same noun can be reversed and still make sense or when they can be separated by *and* or *or*, they should be separated by commas.

EXAMPLE The company is seeking a *young, energetic, creative* marketing team.

When an adjective modifies a phrase, no comma is required.

EXAMPLE He was wearing his *old cotton tennis hat* (*old* modifies the phrase *cotton tennis hat*).

Never separate a final adjective from its noun.

CHANGE He is a conscientious, honest, *reliable, worker*.
TO He is a conscientious, honest, *reliable worker*.

Business people frequently string together a series of nouns to form a unit modifier, thereby creating **jammed modifiers**. Be aware of this problem when using nouns as adjectives.

CHANGE The test control group meeting was held on Wednesday.
TO The meeting of the test control group was held on Wednesday.

As a rule of thumb, it is better to avoid general (*nice, fine, good*) and trite (a *fond* farewell) adjectives; in fact, it is good practice to question the need for most adjectives in your writing. Often, your writing will not only read as well without an adjective, but it may be even better without it. If an adjective is needed, try to find one that is as exact as possible for your meaning.

adjustment letters

An adjustment letter is written in response to a **complaint letter** and tells the customer what your firm intends to do about his or her complaint.

Although it is sent in response to a problem, an adjustment letter actually provides an excellent opportunity to build goodwill for the firm. An effective adjustment letter both repairs the damage that has been done and restores the customer's confidence in your firm.

You should settle claims quickly and courteously, trying always to satisfy the customer at a reasonable cost to your company. Grant adjustments graciously, for a settlement made grudgingly will do more harm than good. **Tone** is critical. No matter how unpleasant or unreasonable the complaint letter, your response must remain both respectful and positive. Avoid emphasizing the unfortunate situation at hand; put your **emphasis** instead on what you are doing to correct it. Not only must you be gracious, but also you must admit your error in such a way that the buyer will not lose confidence in your firm.

Before granting an adjustment to a claim for which your company is at fault, you must investigate what happened and decide what you can do to satisfy the customer. Be certain that you know your company's policy regarding adjustments before you attempt to write an adjustment letter. Also, be very careful about how you put certain words together; for example, "we have just received your letter of May 7 about our *defective product*" could be ruled in a court of law as an admission that the product is in fact defective. Treat every claim individually, and lean toward giving the customer the benefit of the doubt. The following guidelines might help you write adjustment letters.

1. Open with whatever you believe the **reader** will consider good news: *Grant the adjustment* for uncomplicated situations ("Enclosed is a replacement for the damaged part").

ELECTRONIC Parts Inc.
One South Park Avenue
Columbia, AL 36319

January 17, 19--

Mr. Paul E. Denlinger
Denlinger Television Services, Inc.
4873 Wenton Way
Birmingham, AL 35214

Dear Mr. Denlinger:

We have received your letter regarding your order for nine
TR-5771-3 tuners and have shipped the correct tuners by
United Parcel. You should receive them shortly after you
receive this letter. I have also instructed our Billing
Department to charge you our preferred-customer rate--
normally reserved for orders of more than $2000. Please
accept our apologies for not sending the proper tuners and
for incorrectly billing you.

Evidently, when your package arrived at our loading docks,
a dock worker failed to see your letter in the container.
We set the box aside with several boxes of parts destined
for our Rebuilt Parts Department; therefore, your note did
not come to the attention of our parts manager.

We appreciate your business and hope we have resolved your
problem to your satisfaction.

Sincerely,

Jonathan L. Pennington

Jonathan L. Pennington
Office Manager

JLP/jq

Figure 1 Adjustment Letter Granting the Claim

Reveal that you intend to grant the adjustment by admitting that the
customer was in the right ("Yes, you were incorrectly billed for
the oil delivery"). Then later explain the specific details of the
adjustment. This method is good for adjustments that require
detailed explanations.

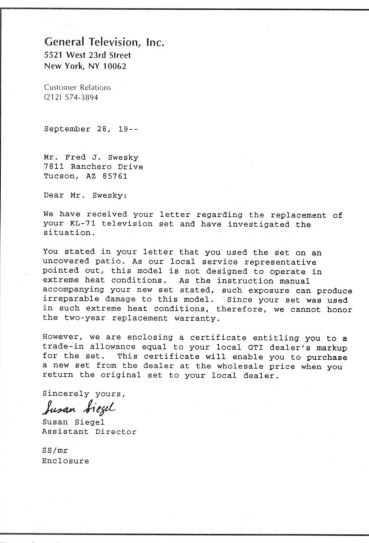

General Television, Inc.
5521 West 23rd Street
New York, NY 10062

Customer Relations
(212) 574-3894

September 28, 19--

Mr. Fred J. Swesky
7811 Ranchero Drive
Tucson, AZ 85761

Dear Mr. Swesky:

We have received your letter regarding the replacement of
your KL-71 television set and have investigated the
situation.

You stated in your letter that you used the set on an
uncovered patio. As our local service representative
pointed out, this model is not designed to operate in
extreme heat conditions. As the instruction manual
accompanying your new set stated, such exposure can produce
irreparable damage to this model. Since your set was used
in such extreme heat conditions, therefore, we cannot honor
the two-year replacement warranty.

However, we are enclosing a certificate entitling you to a
trade-in allowance equal to your local GTI dealer's markup
for the set. This certificate will enable you to purchase
a new set from the dealer at the wholesale price when you
return the original set to your local dealer.

Sincerely yours,

Susan Siegel

Susan Siegel
Assistant Director

SS/mr
Enclosure

Figure 2   Adjustment Letter Granting a Partial Adjustment

Apologize for the error ("Please accept our apologies for not acting
sooner to correct your account"). This method is effective when
the customer's inconvenience is as much an issue as money.
Use a combination of these techniques. Often, situations requiring an
adjustment are unique and do not fit a single pattern.

```
SWELCO Coffee Maker, Inc.
9025 North Main Street
Butte, MT 59702




August 26, 19--


Mr. Carlos Ortiz
638 McSwaney Drive
Butte, MT 59702

Dear Mr. Ortiz:

Enclosed is your SWELCO Coffee Maker, which you sent to us on
August 17.

In various parts of the country, tap water may contain a high
mineral content.  If you fill your SWELCO Coffee Maker with
water for breakfast coffee before going to bed, a mineral scale
will build up on the inner wall of the water tube--as explained
on page 2 of your SWELCO Instruction Booklet.

We have removed the mineral scale from the water tube of your
coffee maker and thoroughly cleaned the entire unit.  To ensure
the best service from your coffee maker in the future, clean
it once a month by operating it with four ounces of white vinegar
and eight cups of water.  To rinse out the vinegar taste, operate
the unit twice with clear water.

With proper care, your SWELCO Coffee Maker will serve you faithfully
and well for many years to come.

Sincerely,

Helen Upham

Helen Upham
Customer Services


HU/mo
Enclosure
```

Figure 3   Educational Adjustment Letter

2. Explain what caused the problem—if such an explanation will help restore your reader's confidence or goodwill.
3. Explain specifically how you intend to make the adjustment—if it is not obvious in your opening.
4. Express appreciation to the customer for calling your attention

to the situation, explaining that this helps your firm keep high the quality of its product or service.

5. Point out any steps you may be taking to prevent a recurrence of whatever went wrong, giving the customer as much credit as the facts allow.

6. Close pleasantly—looking forward, not back. Avoid recalling the problem in your closing ("Again, we apologize . . ."). A typical adjustment letter is shown in Figure 1 on page 23.

Sometimes you may decide to grant a partial adjustment, even though the claim is not really justified, as in Figure 2. (See also **refusal letters**.)

You may sometimes need to educate your reader about the use of your product or service. Customers sometimes submit claims that are not justified, even though they honestly believe them to be. The customer may actually be at fault—for not following maintenance instructions properly for example. Such a claim is granted only to build goodwill. When you write a letter of adjustment in such a situation, it is wise to give the explanation before granting the claim—otherwise, your reader may never get to the explanation. If your explanation establishes customer responsibility, be sure that it is by implication rather than by outright statement. Look at the example of such an educational adjustment letter shown in Figure 3.

adverbs

An adverb modifies the action or condition expressed by a **verb**.

> EXAMPLE   Three of the applicants passed the business aptitude tests *satisfactorily*. (The adverb tells *how* the applicants passed the test.)

An adverb may also modify an **adjective**, another adverb, or a **clause**.

> EXAMPLES   The graphics department used *extremely* bright colors. (modifying an adjective)
> The redesigned brake pad lasted *much* longer. (modifying another adverb)
> *Surprisingly*, the machine failed. (modifying a clause)

An adverb answers one of the following questions:

WHERE? (adverb of place)

> EXAMPLE   The office will be moved *downtown*.

WHEN? (adverb of time)

EXAMPLE Please give me the estimate *tomorrow*.

HOW? (adverb of manner)

EXAMPLE Open the container *gently*.

HOW MUCH? (adverb of degree)

EXAMPLE The *nearly* completed report was lost in the move.

TYPES OF ADVERBS

An adverb may be a common, a conjunctive, an interrogative, or a numeric **modifier**.

Typical **common adverbs** are *almost, seldom, down, also, now, ever,* and *always*.

EXAMPLE I *rarely* work on the weekend.

Typical **conjunctive adverbs** are *however, therefore, nonetheless, nevertheless, consequently, accordingly,* and *then*.

EXAMPLE I rarely work on the weekend; *however*, this weekend will be an exception.

Interrogative adverbs ask questions. Common interrogative adverbs include *where, when, why,* and *how*.

EXAMPLES *How* many hours did you work last week?
Where are we going when the new project is finished?
Why did it take so long to complete the job?

Typical **numeric adverbs** are *once* and *twice*.

EXAMPLE I have worked overtime *twice* this week.

COMPARISON OF ADVERBS

Adverbs are normally compared by adding *-er* or *-est* to them or by inserting *more* or *most* in front of them. One-syllable adverbs use the comparative ending *-er* and the superlative ending *-est*.

EXAMPLES This copier is *faster* than the old one.
This copier is the *fastest* of the three tested.

Most adverbs with two or more **syllables** end in *-ly*, and most adverbs ending in *-ly* are compared by inserting the comparative *more* or *less* or the superlative *most* or *least* in front of them.

EXAMPLES He moved *more quickly* than the other company's salesman.
Most surprisingly, the engine failed during the test phase.
He moved *less quickly* than the other company's salesman.
Least surprisingly, the engine failed during the test phase.

There are a few irregular adverbs that require a change in form to indicate **comparison**.

EXAMPLES The training program functions *well*.
Our training program functions *better* than most others in the industry.
Many consider our training program the *best* in the industry.

PLACEMENT OF ADVERBS

An adverb may appear almost anywhere in a sentence, but its position may affect the meaning of the sentence. Avoid placing an adverb between two verb forms where it can be read ambiguously as modifying either.

CHANGE The supplier wanted *belatedly* to thank the purchasing agent for the order.
TO The supplier *belatedly* wanted to thank the purchasing agent for the order.

The adverb is commonly placed in front of the verb it modifies.

EXAMPLE The accountant *meticulously* checked the figures.

An adverb may, however, follow the verb (or verb and its **object**) that it modifies.

EXAMPLES The gauge dipped *suddenly*.
They repaired the computer *quickly*.

The adverb may be placed between a **helping verb** and a main verb.

EXAMPLE He will *surely* call.

If an adverb modifies only the main verb, and not any accompanying helping verbs, place the adverb immediately before the main verb.

EXAMPLE The alternative proposal has been *effectively* presented.

An adverb **phrase** should not be inserted between the words of a compound verb.

CHANGE This suggestion has *time and time again* been rejected.
TO This suggestion has been rejected *time and time again*.

To place **emphasis** on an adverb, put it before the **subject** of the sentence.

EXAMPLES   *Clearly*, he was ready for the promotion when it came.
Unfortunately, fuel rationing has been unavoidable.

In writing, such adverbs as *nearly, only, almost, just,* and *hardly* are placed immediately before the words they limit. A speaker can place these words earlier and avoid **ambiguity** by stressing the word to be limited; in writing, however, only the appropriate placement of the adverb will ensure **clarity**.

CHANGE   The punch press with the auxiliary equipment *only* costs $47,000.
TO   The punch press with the auxiliary equipment costs *only* $47,000.

The first sentence is ambiguous because it might be understood to mean that *only* the punch press with auxiliary equipment costs $47,000. (See also **misplaced modifiers**.)

advice/advise

Advice is a **noun** that means "counsel" or "suggestion."

EXAMPLE   My *advice* is to sign the contract immediately.

Advise is a **verb** that means "give advice."

EXAMPLE   I *advise* you to sign the contract immediately.

affect/effect

Affect is a **verb** that means "influence."

EXAMPLE   The public utility commission's decisions *affect* all state utilities.

Effect can function either as a verb that means "bring about" or "cause" or as a **noun** that means "result." It is best, however, to avoid using *effect* as a verb. A less formal word, such as *made*, is usually preferable.

CHANGE   The new manager *effected* several changes that had a good *effect* on morale.
TO   The new manager *made* several changes that had a good *effect* on morale.

affectation

Affectation is the use of language that is more technical, formal, or showy than is necessary to communicate information to the **reader**. A writer who is unnecessarily ornate, pompous, or pretentious is usually attempting to impress the reader by showing off a repertoire of fancy or flashy words and phrases. Using unnecessarily formal words (such as *herewith*) and outdated phrases (such as *please find enclosed*) is another cause of affectation.

> EXAMPLES *pursuant to* (instead of *about* or *regarding*)
> *in view of the foregoing* (instead of *therefore*)
> *in view of the fact that* (instead of *because*)
> *it is interesting to note that* (omit)
> *it may be said that* (omit)

Affected writing forces the reader to work harder to understand the writer's meaning. Affected writing typically contains abstract, highly technical, pseudotechnical, pseudolegal, or foreign words and is often liberally sprinkled with **vogue words. Jargon** can become affectation if it is misused. **Euphemisms** can contribute to affected writing, especially when their purpose is to conceal facts.

The easiest kind of affectation to be lured into is the use of **long variants**: words created by adding **prefixes** and **suffixes** to simpler words (*analyzation* for analysis, *telephonic communication* for telephone call). The practice of **elegant variation**—attempting to avoid repeating the same word in the same **paragraph** by substituting pretentious **synonyms**—is also a form of affectation. Another contributor to affectation is **gobbledygook**, which is wordy, roundabout writing that has many pseudolegal and pseudoscientific terms sprinkled throughout.

Attempts to make the trivial seem important can cause affectation. This attempt is apparent in the first version of the following example, taken from a specification soliciting bids from local merchants for the operation of a television repair shop in an Air Force Post Exchange.

> CHANGE In addition to performing interior housekeeping services, the concessionaire shall perform custodial maintenance on the exterior of the facility and grounds. Where a concessionaire shares a facility with one or more other concessionaires, exterior custodial maintenance responsibilities will be assigned by Post Exchange management on a fair and equi-

table basis. In those instances where the concessionaire's activity is located in a Post Exchange complex wherein predominant tenancy is by Post Exchange-operated activities, then Post Exchange management shall be responsible for exterior custodial maintenance except for those described in 1, 2, 3, and 4 below. The necessary equipment and labor to perform exterior custodial maintenance, when such a responsibility has been assigned to the concessionaire, shall be furnished by the concessionaire. Exterior custodial maintenance shall include the following tasks:

1. Clean entrance door and exterior of storefront windows daily.
2. Sweep and clean the entrance and customer walks daily.
3. Empty and clean waste and smoking receptacles daily.
4. Check exterior lighting and report failures to the contracting officer's representative daily.

TO The merchant will, with his or her own equipment, perform the following duties daily:

1. Maintain a clean and neat appearance inside the store.
2. Clean the entrance door and the outsides of the store windows.
3. Sweep the entrance and the sidewalk.
4. Empty and clean wastebaskets and ashtrays.
5. Check the exterior lighting, and report failures to the representative of the contracting officer.

The merchant will also maintain the grounds surrounding the store. Where two or more merchants share the same building, Post Exchange management will assign responsibility for the grounds. Where the merchant's store is in a building that is occupied predominantly by Post Exchange operations, Post Exchange management will be responsible for the grounds.

Affectation is a widespread problem in business writing because many people apparently feel that affectation lends a degree of formality, and hence authority, to their writing. Nothing could be further from the truth. Affectation puts up a smoke screen that the reader must penetrate to get to the writer's meaning. It can alienate the customer or client, making him or her feel that the writer is difficult to communicate with. (See also **conciseness/wordiness, clichés**, and **nominalizations**.)

affinity

Affinity refers to the attraction of two persons or things to each other.

> EXAMPLE The *affinity* between the two executives can be explained by the similarity of their business philosophies.

Affinity should never be used to mean "ability" or "aptitude."

> CHANGE She has an *affinity* for economics.
> TO She has an *aptitude* for economics.
> OR She has a *talent* for economics.

aforesaid

Aforesaid means "stated previously," but it is legal **jargon** and should be avoided in writing. (See also **above**.)

> CHANGE The *aforesaid* problems can be solved in six months.
> TO The three problems explained in the preceding paragraphs can be solved in six months.

agree to/agree with

When you *agree to* something, you are "giving consent."

> EXAMPLE I *agree to* the terms of the contract.

When you *agree with* something, you are "in accord" with it.

> EXAMPLE I *agree with* the recommendations of the advisory board.

agreement

Agreement, grammatically, means the correspondence in form between different elements of a sentence to indicate **person**, **number**, **gender**, and **case**. A **pronoun** must agree with its antecedent, and a **verb** must agree with its **subject**.

A subject and its verb must agree in number and in person.

> EXAMPLES *I am* going to approve his promotion. (The first person singular subject, *I*, requires the first person singular verb, *am*.)
> The *subsidiaries were* incorporated into the company as divisions. (The third person plural subject, *subsidiaries*, requires the third person plural form of the verb, *were*.)

A pronoun and its antecedent must agree in person, number, and gender.

EXAMPLES   The *employees* report that *they* become less efficient as the humidity rises. (The third person plural subject, *employees*, requires the third person plural pronoun, *they*.)

Mr. Joiner said that *he* would serve as a negotiator. (The third person singular, masculine subject, *Mr. Joiner*, requires the third person singular, masculine form of the pronoun, *he*.)

(See also **agreement of pronouns and antecedents** and **agreement of subjects and verbs**.)

agreement of pronouns and antecedents

Every **pronoun** must have an antecedent, or a **noun** to which it refers. In the following example, the pronoun *it* has no noun to which it could logically refer. The solution is to use a noun instead of the pronoun or to provide a noun to which it could logically refer.

CHANGE   Economists must constantly struggle to keep up with the professional literature because *it* is a dynamic science.

TO   Economists must constantly struggle to keep up with the professional literature because *economics* is a dynamic science.

OR   Economists must continue to study *economics* because *it* is a dynamic science.

Using the **relative pronoun** *which* to refer to an idea instead of a specific noun can be confusing.

CHANGE   He acted independently on the advice of his consultant, *which* the others thought unjust. (Was it the fact that he acted independently or was it the advice that the others thought unjust?)

TO   The others thought it unjust for him to act independently.

OR   The others thought it unjust for him to act on the advice of his consultant.

Using the pronouns *it, they, these, those, that*, and *this* can also lead to vague or uncertain references.

CHANGE   Studs and thick treads make snow tires effective. *They* are implanted with an air gun. (Which are implanted with an air gun: studs or thick treads?)

TO   Studs and thick treads make snow tires effective. *The studs* are implanted with an air gun.

CHANGE   The inadequate quality-control procedure has resulted in an equipment failure. *This* is our most serious problem at present. (Which is our most serious problem at present: the procedure or the failure?)

TO   The inadequate quality-control procedure has resulted in an equipment failure. Quality control is our most serious problem at present.

OR   The inadequate quality-control procedure has resulted in an equipment failure. The equipment failure is our most serious problem at present.

GENDER

A pronoun must agree in **gender** with its antecedent.

EXAMPLE   Mr. Swivet in the Accounting Department acknowledges *his* share of the responsibility for the misunderstanding, just as Ms. Barkley in the Research Division must acknowledge *hers*.

Traditionally, a masculine, singular pronoun has been used to agree with such indefinite antecedents as *anyone* and *person*.

EXAMPLE   *Each* may stay or go as *he* chooses.

It is now recognized that there is an implied sexual bias in such usage. When alternatives are available, use them. One solution is to use the plural. Another is to use both feminine and masculine pronouns, although this combination is clumsy when used too often.

CHANGE   Every *employee* must sign *his* time card.
TO   All *employees* must sign *their* time cards.
OR   Every *employee* must sign *his* or *her* time card.

Do not, however, attempt to avoid expressing gender by resorting to a plural pronoun when the antecedent is singular.

CHANGE   An *accountant* can expect to advance on *their* merit.
TO   *Accountants* can expect to advance on *their* merit.
OR   An *accountant* can expect to advance on *his or her* merit.

NUMBER

A pronoun must agree with its antecedent in **number**. Many problems of agreement are caused by expressions that are not clear in number.

CHANGE   Although the typical *engine* runs well in moderate temperatures, *they* often stall in extreme cold.

TO   Although the typical *engine* runs well in moderate temperatures, *it* often stalls in extreme cold.

Use singular pronouns with the antecedents *everybody* and *everyone* unless to do so would be illogical because the meaning is obviously plural. (See also **everybody/everyone**.)

EXAMPLES   *Everyone* pulled *his* share of the load.
Everyone laughed at my sales slogan, and I really couldn't blame *them.*

The demonstrative adjectives sometimes cause problems with agreement of number. *This* and *that* are used with singular **nouns**, and *these* and *those* are used with plural nouns. Demonstrative adjectives often cause problems when they modify the nouns *kind, type,* and *sort.* Demonstrative adjectives used with these nouns should agree with them in **number**.

EXAMPLES   this kind / these kinds
that type / those types
this sort / these sorts

Confusion often develops when the **preposition** *of* is added ("this kind *of,*" "these kinds *of*") and the **object** of the preposition is not made to conform in number to the demonstrative adjective and its noun.

CHANGE   *This kind* of hydraulic *cranes* is best.
TO   *This kind* of hydraulic *crane* is best.
CHANGE   *These kinds* of hydraulic *crane* are best.
TO   *These kinds* of hydraulic *cranes* are best.

The error can be avoided by remembering to make the demonstrative adjective, the noun, and the object of the preposition—all three—agree in number. This **agreement** makes the sentence not only correct but also more precise.

Using demonstrative adjectives with words like *kind, type,* and *sort* can easily lead to vagueness. It is better to be more specific.

CHANGE   *These kinds* of hydraulic cranes are best.
TO   *Computer-controlled* hydraulic cranes are best.

A compound antecedent joined by *or* or *nor* is singular if both elements are singular, and plural if both elements are plural.

EXAMPLES Neither the *engineer* nor the *draftsman* could do *his* job until *he* understood the new concept.

Neither the *executives* nor the *directors* were pleased at the performance of *their* company.

When one of the antecedents connected by *or* or *nor* is singular and the other plural, the pronoun agrees with the nearer antecedent.

EXAMPLES Either the *supervisor* or the *operators* will have *their* licenses suspended.

Either the *operators* or the *supervisor* will have *his* license suspended.

A compound antecedent with its elements joined by *and* requires a plural pronoun.

EXAMPLE Martha and Joan took *their* layout drawings with *them.*

If both elements refer to the same person, however, use the singular pronoun.

EXAMPLE The respected *economist and author* departed from *her* prepared speech.

Collective nouns may be singular or plural, depending on meaning.

EXAMPLES The *committee* arrived at the recommended solutions only after *it* had deliberated for days.

The *committee* quit for the day and went to *their* respective homes.

agreement of subjects and verbs

A **verb** must agree with its **subject**. Do not let intervening **phrases** and **clauses** mislead you.

CHANGE The *program,* despite the new instructional materials, still *take* several days to install.

TO The *program,* despite the new instructional materials, still *takes* several days to install. (The verb *takes* must agree in **number** with the subject, *program,* rather than *materials.*)

CHANGE The use of these new accounting procedures, although they offer unquestionable benefits, often result in more errors.

TO The *use* of these new accounting procedures, although they offer unquestionable benefits, often *results* in more errors. (The verb *results* must agree with the subject of the sentence, *use*, rather than with the subject of the preceding clause, *they*.)

Be careful to avoid making the verb agree with the **noun** immediately in front of it if that noun is not its subject. This problem is especially likely to occur when a plural noun falls between a singular subject and its verb.

EXAMPLES Only *one* of the emergency lights *was* functioning when the accident occurred. (The subject of the verb is *one*, not *lights*.)
Each of the switches *controls* a separate circuit. (The subject of the verb is *each*, not *switches*.)
Each of the managers *supervises* a very large region. (The subject of the verb is *each*, not *managers*.)

Be careful not to let modifying phrases obscure a simple subject.

EXAMPLE The *advice* of two engineers, one lawyer, and three executives *was* obtained prior to making a commitment. (The subject of the verb is *advice*, not *executives*.)

Sentences with inverted word order can cause problems with agreement between subject and verb.

EXAMPLE From this work *have come* several important *improvements*. (The subject of the verb is *improvements*, not *work*.)

Such words as *type, part, series,* and *portion* take singular verbs even when they precede a phrase containing a plural noun.

EXAMPLES A *series* of meetings *was* held about the best way to market the new product.
A large *portion* of most industrial annual reports *is* devoted to promoting the corporate image.

Subjects expressing measurement, weight, mass, or total often take singular verbs even when the subject word is plural in form. Such subjects are treated as a unit.

EXAMPLES *Four years is* the normal duration of the training program.
Twenty dollars is the wholesale price of each unit.

Indefinite pronouns such as *some, none, all, more,* and *most* may be singular or plural depending upon whether they are used with a mass noun (*oil* in the following examples) or with a count noun (*drivers* in the following examples). Mass nouns are singular and count nouns are plural.

EXAMPLES   *None* of the oil *is* to be used.
None of the truck drivers *are* to go.
Most of the oil *has* been used.
Most of the drivers *know* why they are here.
Some of the oil *has* leaked.
Some of the drivers *have* gone.

One and *each* are normally singular.

EXAMPLES   *One* of the brake drums *is* still scored.
Each of the original founders *is* scheduled to speak at the dedication ceremony.

A verb following the **relative pronouns** *who* and *that* agrees in number with the noun to which the **pronoun** refers (its antecedent).

EXAMPLES   Steel is one of those *industries* that *are* hardest hit by high energy costs. (*That* refers to *industries*.)
This is one of those engineering *problems* that *require* careful analysis. (*That* refers to *problems*.)
She is one of those *employees* who *are* rarely absent. (*Who* refers to *employees*.)

The word *number* sometimes causes confusion. When used to mean a specific number, it is singular.

EXAMPLE   *The number* of committee members *was* six.

When used to mean an approximate number, it is plural.

EXAMPLE   *A number* of people *were* waiting for the announcement.

Relative pronouns (*who, which, that*) may take either singular or plural verbs, depending upon whether the antecedent is singular or plural. (See also **who/whom**.)

EXAMPLES   He is a bookkeeper *who takes* work home at night.
He is one of those bookkeepers *who take* work home at night.

Some **abstract nouns** are singular in meaning though plural in form: *mathematics, news, physics,* and *economics*.

EXAMPLES   *News* of the merger *is* on page four of the *Chronicle*.
Textiles is an industry in need of import quotas.

Some words are always plural, such as *trousers* and *scissors*.

EXAMPLE   His *trousers were* torn by the machine.
BUT   A *pair* of trousers *is* on order.

Collective subjects take singular verbs when the group is thought of as a unit, plural verbs when the individuals are thought of separately. (See also **collective nouns.**)

A singular subject that is followed by a phrase or clause containing a plural noun still requires a singular verb.

> CHANGE One in twenty transistors we receive from our suppliers are faulty.
> TO *One* in twenty transistors we receive from our suppliers *is* faulty. (The subject is *one*, not *transistors*.)

The number of a **subjective complement** does not affect the number of the verb—the verb must always agree with the subject.

> EXAMPLE The *topic* of his report *was* rivers. (The subject of the sentence is *topic*, not *rivers*.)

A book with a plural title requires a single verb.

> EXAMPLE *Monetary Theories is* a useful source.

COMPOUND SUBJECTS

A compound subject is one that is composed of two or more elements joined by a **conjunction** such as *and, or, nor, either . . . or,* or *neither . . . nor.* Usually, when the elements are connected by *and,* the subject is plural and requires a plural verb.

> EXAMPLE *Chemistry and accounting are* both prerequisites for this position.

One exception occurs when the elements connected by *and* form a unit or refer to the same thing. In this case, the subject is regarded as singular and takes a singular verb.

> EXAMPLES *Bacon and eggs is* a high-cholesterol meal.
> The *red, white, and blue flutters* from the top of the Capitol.
> Our greatest *business opportunity and technical breakthrough is* the Model MX Calculator.

A compound subject with a singular and a plural element joined by *or* or *nor* requires that the verb agree with the element nearest to it.

> EXAMPLES Neither the office manager nor the *secretaries were* there.
> Neither the secretaries nor the officer *manager was* there.
> Either they or *I am* going to write the report.
> Either I or *they are* going to write the report.

If *each* or *every* modifies the elements of a compound subject, use the singular verb.

> EXAMPLES *Each* manager and supervisor *has* a production goal to meet.
> *Every* manager and supervisor *has* a production goal to meet.

all around/all-around/all-round

All-round and *all-around* both mean "comprehensive" or "versatile."

> EXAMPLE The company started an *all-round* training program.

Do not confuse these words with the two-word **phrase** *all around*, as in "The fence was installed *all around* the building."

all right/all-right/alright

All right means "all correct," as in "The answers were all right." In formal writing it should not be used to mean "good" or "acceptable." It is always written as two words, with no **hyphen**; *all-right* and *alright* both are incorrect.

> CHANGE The decision that the committee reached was *all right*.
> TO The decision that the committee reached was acceptable.

all together/altogether

All together means "all acting together," or "all in one place."

> EXAMPLE The parties involved in the merger were *all together* at the attorney's office.

Altogether means "entirely" or "completely."

> EXAMPLE The trip was *altogether* unnecessary.

allude/elude/refer

Allude means to make an indirect reference to something not specifically mentioned.

> EXAMPLE The report simply *alluded* to the problem rather than stating it clearly.

Elude means to escape notice or detection.

EXAMPLES The discrepancy in the account *eluded* the auditor.
The leak *eluded* the inspectors.

Refer is used to indicate a direct reference to something.

EXAMPLE He *referred* to the chart three times during his speech.

allusion

The use of allusion (implied or indirect reference) promotes economical writing because it is a shorthand way of referring to a body of material in a few words, or of helping to explain a new and unfamiliar process in terms of one that is familiar. Be sure, however, that your **reader** is familiar with the material to which you allude. In the following **paragraph**, the writer sums up the argument he has been developing with an allusion to the Bible. The biblical story is well known, and the allusion, with its implicit reference to "right standing up to might," concisely emphasizes the writer's point.

EXAMPLE As it presently exists, the review process involves the consumer's attorney sitting alone, usually without adequate technical assistance, faced by two or three government attorneys, two or three attorneys from the XYZ Corporation, and large teams of experts who support the government and corporation's attorneys. The entire proceeding is reminiscent of David versus Goliath.

Allusions should be used with restraint. If overdone, they can lead to **affectation**. (See also **analogy** and **international correspondence**.)

allusion / illusion

An *allusion* is an indirect reference to something not specifically mentioned.

EXAMPLE The report made an *allusion* to the company's declining sales.

An *illusion* is a mistaken perception or a false image.

EXAMPLE The general manager is under the *illusion* that all is going well in the manufacturing department.

almost/most

Do not use *most* as a colloquial substitute for *almost* in your writing.

> CHANGE New shipments arrive *most* every day.
>   TO New shipments arrive *almost* every day.

If you can substitute *almost* for *most* in a sentence, *almost* is the word you need.

already/all ready

Already is an **adverb** expressing time.

> EXAMPLE We had *already* shipped the parts when the stop order arrived.

All ready is a two-word **phrase** meaning "completely prepared."

> EXAMPLE He was *all ready* to start work on the project when it was suddenly canceled.

also

Also is an **adverb** that means "additionally."

> EXAMPLE He brought the reports and letters. He *also* brought the section supervisor's recommendations.

It should not be used as a **connective** in the sense of "and."

> CHANGE He brought the reports, letters, *also* the section supervisor's recommendations.
>   TO He brought the reports, letters, *and* the section supervisor's recommendations.

Avoid opening sentences with *also*. It is a weak transitional word that suggests an afterthought rather than planned writing.

> CHANGE *Also* he brought statistical data to support his proposal.
>   TO *In addition*, he brought statistical data to support his proposal.
>   OR He *also* brought statistical data to support his proposal.

ambiguity

A word or passage is ambiguous when it is susceptible to two or more interpretations, yet provides the **reader** with no certain basis for choosing among the alternatives.

EXAMPLE   Mathematics is more valuable to an accountant than a calculator. (Does this mean that an accountant is more in need of
mathematics than a calculator is? Or does it mean that mathematics is more valuable to an accountant than a calculator is?)

Ambiguity can take many forms: ambiguous **pronoun reference**,
misplaced modifiers, **dangling modifiers**, ambiguous coordination,
ambiguous juxtaposition, incomplete **comparison**, incomplete
idiom, ambiguous **word choice**, and so on.

CHANGE   Inadequate quality-control procedures have resulted in more
equipment failures. *This is* our most serious problem at
present. (ambiguous pronoun reference; does *this* refer to
"quality-control procedures" or "equipment failures"?)

TO   Inadequate quality-control procedures have resulted in more
equipment failures. These failures are our most serious
problem at present.

OR   Inadequate quality-control procedures have resulted in more
equipment failures. Quality control is our most serious
problem at present.

CHANGE   Ms. Jones values rigid quality-control standards more than
Mr. Rosenblum. (incomplete comparison)

TO   Ms. Jones values rigid quality-control standards more than
Mr. Rosenblum *does*.

CHANGE   His hobby was cooking. He was especially fond of cocker
spaniels. (missing modifier)

TO   His hobby was cooking. He was *also* especially fond of cocker
spaniels.

CHANGE   She *almost* wrote a million dollars in insurance policies last
month. (misplaced modifier)

TO   She wrote *almost* a million dollars in insurance policies last
month.

Ambiguity is also often caused by thoughtless word choice.

CHANGE   The general manager has denied reports that the plant's recent fuel allocation cut will be *restored*. (inappropriate word
choice)

TO   The general manager has denied reports that the plant's recent fuel allocation cut will be *rescinded*.

amount/number

Amount is used with things thought of in bulk (mass nouns).

EXAMPLES   The *amount* of electricity available for industrial use is limited.
The *amount* of oxygen was insufficient for combustion.

Number is used with things that can be counted as individual items (count nouns).

> EXAMPLES   A large *number* of stockholders attended the meeting.
> The *number* of employees who are qualified for early retirement has increased in recent years.

Avoid using *amount* when referring to countable items.

> CHANGE   The *amount* of people in the room gradually increased.
> TO   The *number* of people in the room gradually increased.
> CHANGE   Because the *amount* of thefts has increased, the doors will be locked in the evening.
> TO   Because the *number* of thefts has increased, the doors will be locked in the evening.
> CHANGE   I was surprised at the *amount* of errors in the report.
> TO   I was surprised at the *number* of errors in the report.

ampersands

The ampersand (&) is a symbol sometimes used to represent the word *and*, especially in the names of organizations.

> EXAMPLES   Chicago & Northwestern Railway
> Watkins & Watkins, Inc.

The ampersand is appropriate for footnotes, **bibliographies**, **lists**, and references if the ampersand appears in the name being listed. When writing the name of an organization in sentences or in an address, however, spell out the word *and* unless the ampersand appears in the official name of the company. (See also **abbreviations**.)

An ampersand must always be set off by normal word spacing but should never be preceded by a **comma**.

> CHANGE   Carlton, Dillon, & Manchester, Inc.
> TO   Carlton, Dillon & Manchester, Inc.

analogy

Analogy is a **comparison** between two objects or concepts to show ways in which they are similar. In effect, analogies say, "A is to B as C is to D."

> EXAMPLE   Pollution is to the environment as cancer is to the body.

The resemblance between the concepts represented in an analogy must be close enough to illuminate the relationship the writer wants to establish. Analogies may be brief or extended, depending on the writer's purpose. Analogy often helps writers explain unfamiliar things by comparing them to things with which the reader is familiar.

Analogy can be a particularly useful tool to the business person writing for an intelligent and educated but nontechnical audience, such as top management, because of its effectiveness in **defining terms** and explaining processes. Like all figurative language, analogy can provide a shortcut means of communication if it is used with care and restraint.

The following example explains a computer search technique for finding information in a data file by comparing it to the method used by most people to find a word in a **dictionary**.

> The search technique used in this kind of file processing is similar to the search technique used to look up a word in a dictionary. To locate a specific word, you scan the key words located at the top of each dictionary page (these key words identify the first and last words on the page) until you find the key words that confine your word to a specific page. Assume that all the key words that reference the last word on each page of a dictionary were placed in a file, along with their corresponding page numbers, and that all the words in the dictionary were placed in another file. To locate any word, you would simply scan the first file until you found a key word greater in alphabetical sequence than the desired word and go to the place in the second file indicated by the key word to find the desired word. This search technique is called indexed sequential processing.
>
> —*The NCR File Management Manual* (Dayton: NCR Corporation).

and/or

And/or means that either both circumstances are possible or only one of two circumstances is possible; however, it is clumsy and awkward because it makes the **reader** stop to puzzle over your distinction. Also, writers more often than not use the term inexactly. As Wilson Follett said, "English speakers and writers have managed to express this simple relationship without *and/or* for over six centuries." Avoid it.

CHANGE Use A and/or B.

TO Use A or B or both.

annual reports

The corporate annual report is a legally required document that is, in effect, a "state of the company" message. It is written primarily for stockholders, although many other audiences must be kept in mind when the report is prepared (bankers, financial press, labor unions, employees, and the like). An annual report usually covers the high points of the previous year's operations and finances and attempts to forecast the coming year's operations. It may also explain the company's present directions and highlight its present strengths. If weaknesses have developed or failures have occurred, the annual report may analyze them and explain the efforts being made to overcome them.

A wide variety of annual reports are published every year. Some are lavish in presentation and paint the company and its operations in glowing terms; others are spartan financial recitations that merely meet the legal requirements for annual financial reporting. Most annual reports are combinations of legally required financial reporting and narrative articles presenting the company with its best foot forward.

Although they vary greatly, annual reports typically have five major divisions: (1) financial highlights, (2) a statement to the stockholders or letter from the president, (3) a narrative section containing articles on the company's operations, (4) a financial statement, and (5) a listing of the company's board of directors and officers.

Financial Highlights. The financial highlights section is a quick review of the company's sales and earnings that usually precedes the president's message to the stockholders, sometimes even appearing on the inside of the front cover. The most-read part of the annual report, this section often compares sales and earnings for three years, and it often includes the percentage of change from year to year.

Statement to Stockholders. This section of the annual report is a direct statement to stockholders from the company's president or chairman of the board of directors. This statement (which is sometimes presented in the form of a letter) is second in readership only to the financial highlights. It is the place to set the stage for the rest of the report. It should avoid repeating financial facts already cited in the financial highlights; instead, it can be used to (1) interpret the entire year's performance, (2) touch upon plans and future directions, and (3) give the company's explanations for any failures.

The statement to stockholders may be an in-depth review of the company's operations during the past year, or it may be a brief summary of the entire report. A brief summary of the annual report is sometimes followed by an article in "interview" (question and answer) **format** that reviews the past year's operations as though an actual interview were taking place between the writer and the president of the company. Avoid stereotyped language, **clichés**, and technical terms when you write this statement. Use simple sentences and short **paragraphs**, and use a straightforward and informal **style**.

Narrative Feature Articles. This section of the annual report is normally used to present company operations and new products or developments in a positive light. Select the **topic** for these articles very carefully, making certain that they are timely and meaningful and that they contribute to the primary objective of the annual report. The following list includes topics that are often dealt with in annual reports:

Major profit factors in last year's performance
Sales trends
The company's performance compared with that of its competition
International operations
World problems that affect the company
The dependability of the company's overseas markets
Research and development efforts
Significant organizational changes
The company's labor relations outlook
Productivity
Acquisitions and their significance
Prospects for increasing stock dividends
Outlook for next year (for the company as a whole or by divisions)
Significant new products or services
Current market performance of existing products or services
Service and support operations
Social responsibilities—on environmental protection, energy conservation, safety, hiring minorities and the handicapped, and so on. (Be certain to document the company's efforts in this area because overstated claims by a few companies in the past have generated suspicion of all such claims.)

Most **readers** merely scan an annual report, but they do stop to look at **photographs** and **illustrations** and to read their captions. Therefore, use photographs and illustrations liberally in this section of the annual report, and make your captions informative and well written.

Financial Statement. The financial statement should not be forbidding in appearance; it should be uncluttered, inviting, and consistent with the other sections of the annual report. The financial statement may appear at the beginning, middle, or end of the annual report; however, it most often appears at the end. It is frequently prepared as a separate booklet, printed on colored paper, and then stitched into the report.

Minimum normal contents of the financial statement include (1) balance sheet, (2) statement of income, (3) changes in financial position, (4) the auditor's statement, and (5) footnotes. Most annual reports also include a fairly comprehensive **comparison** of financial results of the past ten to fifteen years.

Footnotes in the financial section should be written in simple, direct language rather than in accounting terms. The auditor's statement should be limited to no more than one-third of a page.

Board of Directors and Company Officers. The final part of the annual report lists the company's board of directors, along with their corporate affiliations. Many annual reports also include a portrait photograph of each director, and the company's officers are listed by name and title (sometimes with photographs). These generally include the chairman of the board of directors, president, vice-presidents, secretary, treasurer, and legal counsel. To avoid hard feelings about some being shown in photographs and others not, establish a logical cutoff point. For example, if there are too many officers to include photographs of them all, show only the executive committee. Do not, however, underestimate the importance of these photographs; all your reading audiences are interested in seeing what your company's top executives look like.

PREPARING THE REPORT

Assuming you are to prepare the annual report, the first thing you must do is interview the president of the company or the chairman of the board of directors to determine the general directions the report is to take. Next, you must interview the various vice-presidents, or division heads, to learn the highlights of each division's operations during the year. Determine from these executives the proper **emphasis** to place on their divisions' performances—but stay within the general direction established by the president or chairman of the board.

The primary objective of the annual report often depends on which of several audiences (shareholders, bankers, business and financial analysts, the financial press, employees, labor unions, the communities in which your company operates) you are most concerned about. Since you cannot satisfy all these groups with one report, you must establish priorities among them. Having done that, you can compose a list of "must" topics, then a list of secondary topics (such as diversification, expansion of markets, and product development). You can also select the main topics for brief coverage in the statement to stockholders, decide whether to show sales and earnings by division, determine the amount of space to allot to various divisions and subsidiaries, determine the contents of charts and graphs, decide whether to include photographs of the executives of branches, divisions, and subsidiaries, decide whether to include a frank discussion of company problems and solutions, and decide how lavish or spartan the report should be in appearance and costs.

Tone is a critical factor in writing and designing an annual report. Companies are as different as people; some are conservative, and some are aggressively youthful. The annual report should convey the image your company has established or wants to establish. A static, formal page layout with traditional typography will suggest a conservative, dignified company, for example; and bold graphics, a dynamic design, and unusual typography will suggest an aggressive company. Don't mix the two, however; photographs of executives in dark business suits would not be compatible with bold graphics.

Be selective in your choice of photographs and illustrations, choosing only those that will make the maximum contribution to the report's theme. Remember that most readers merely scan an annual report, looking carefully only at photographs and captions. So both photographs and their captions are critical to the success of your annual report. A photograph of a machine can be dull. But put an operator in it, and the caption can tell what the operator is doing, and why it is meaningful.

Study your company's annual reports of the past several years for content, style, and format. Within reason, try to emulate these. Then review the writing process outlined in the Checklist of the Writing Process at the beginning of this book, and use all the steps listed there to the best of your ability—your company's annual report could well be the most important writing you will ever be asked to do.

The following information is normally printed on the inside front and back covers of the annual report: (1) notice of the annual meeting, (2) corporate address, (3) names of transfer agents, (4) registrar, and (5) stock exchange. Some annual reports use the inside front cover for the announcement of the annual meeting alone.

Use of Charts and Graphs. **Graphs** and charts enable readers to grasp statistical material quickly and easily—provided the charts and graphs are not so complex that they defeat that purpose. Some companies scatter graphs throughout the annual report at strategic locations near the financial highlights, in the statement to stockholders, throughout the feature articles, and so forth. Others group them in the financial statement.

The subjects that most easily lend themselves to graphs and charts—usually shown in a five-year comparison arrangement—are assets, capital expenditures, dividends, earnings (by product groups or by divisions), industry growth, inventories, liabilities, net worth, prices (trend of), reserves, sales (by product groups or by divisions), and source and disposition of funds (taxes, wages, working capital).

ante-/anti-

Ante- means "before" or "in front of."

EXAMPLES   *ante*room, *ante*date, *ante*diluvian (before the flood)

Anti- means "against" or "opposed to."

EXAMPLES   *anti*body, *anti*clerical, *anti*social

Anti- is hyphenated when joined to proper nouns or to words beginning with the letter *i*.

EXAMPLES   *anti*-American, *anti*-intellectual

When in doubt, consult your **dictionary**. (See also **prefixes**.)

antonyms

An antonym is a word that is nearly the opposite, in meaning, of another word.

EXAMPLES   good/bad, well/ill, fresh/stale

Many pairs of words that look as if they are antonyms are not. Be careful not to use these words incorrectly.

EXAMPLES famous/infamous, flammable/inflammable, limit/delimit

When in doubt about the pronunciation, correct use, or exact meaning of a word, use your **dictionary**.

apostrophes

The apostrophe (') is used to show possession, to mark the omission of letters, and sometimes to indicate the plural of arabic numbers, letters, and **acronyms**. Do not confuse the apostrophe used to show the plural with the apostrophe used to show possession.

EXAMPLES The entry required five 7's in the appropriate columns. (The apostrophe is used here to indicate the plural, not possession.)
The letter's purpose was clearly evident in its opening paragraph. (The apostrophe here is used to show possession, not the plural.)

TO SHOW POSSESSION

An apostrophe is used with an *s* to form the possessive **case** of some **nouns**.

EXAMPLE A recent scientific analysis of New York City's atmosphere concluded that a New Yorker on the street took into his or her lungs the equivalent in toxic materials of 38 cigarettes a day.

With coordinate nouns, the last noun takes the possessive form to show joint possession.

EXAMPLE Michelson and Morley's famous experiment on the velocity of light was made in 1887.

To show individual possession with coordinate nouns, each noun should take the possessive form.

EXAMPLE Tom's and Mary's desks are at opposite ends of the office.

Singular nouns ending in *s* may form the possessive either by an apostrophe alone or by 's. Whichever way you do it, however, be consistent.

EXAMPLES   a waitress' uniform, an actress' career
a waitress's uniform, an actress's career

Singular nouns of one syllable form the possessive by adding *'s*.

EXAMPLE   The boss's desk was cluttered.

Use only an apostrophe with plural nouns ending in *s*.

EXAMPLES   a managers' meeting, the technicians' handbook, the waitresses' lounge

When adding an *'s* would result in a noun ending in multiple consecutive *s* sounds, add only an apostrophe.

EXAMPLES   the Joneses' test result

The apostrophe is not used with possessive **pronouns**.

EXAMPLES   yours, its, his, ours, whose, theirs

It's is a **contraction** of *it is; its* is the possessive form of the **pronoun**. Be careful not to confuse the two words. (See **its/it's**.)

EXAMPLE   *It's* important that the sales force meet *its* quota.

In names of places and institutions, the apostrophe is usually omitted.

EXAMPLES   Harpers Ferry, Writers Book Club

TO SHOW OMISSION

An apostrophe is used to mark the omission of letters in a word or date.

EXAMPLES   can't, I'm, I'll
the class of '61

TO FORM PLURALS

An apostrophe and an *s* may be added to show the plural of a word as a word. (The word itself is underlined, or italicized, to call attention to its use.)

EXAMPLE   There were five *and's* in his first sentence.

If the term is in all **capital letters** or ends with a capital letter, however, the apostrophe is not required to form the plural. (See also **acronyms and initialisms**.)

EXAMPLES   The university awarded seven *Ph.D.s* in engineering last year.
He had included 43 *ADDs* in his computer program.

Do not use an apostrophe to indicate the plural of numbers and letters unless confusion would result without one.

EXAMPLES   5s, 30s, two 100s, seven i's

appendix / appendixes / appendices

An appendix contains material at the end of a **formal report** or book that supplements or clarifies. (The plural form of the word may be either **appendixes** or **appendices**.)

Although not a mandatory part of a **report**, an appendix can be useful for explanations that are too long for notes but that could be helpful to the reader seeking further assistance or a clarification of points made in the report. Information placed in an appendix is too detailed or voluminous to appear in text without impeding the orderly presentation of ideas. This information typically includes passages from documents and laws that reinforce or illustrate the text, long lists of charts and **tables**, letters and other supporting documents, calculations (in full), computer printouts of raw data, and case histories. An appendix, however, should not be used for miscellaneous bits and pieces of information you were unable to work into the text.

Generally, each appendix contains only one type of information. The contents of each appendix should be identifiable without the reader having to refer to the body of the report. An introductory paragraph describing the contents of the appendix, therefore, is necessary for some appendixes, especially those containing computer printouts of data, long tables, or similar information.

When the report contains more than one appendix, arrange them in the order in which they are referred to in the text. Thus, a reference in the text to Appendix A should precede the first text reference to Appendix B.

Each appendix begins on a new page. (For guidance on where to locate appendixes in reports, see **formal reports**.) Identify each with a **title** and a **head**:

Appendix A
Sample Questionnaire

Appendixes are ordinarily labeled Appendix A, Appendix B, and so on. If your report has only one appendix, label it Appendix, followed by the title. To call it Appendix A implies that an Appendix B will follow.

The titles and beginning page numbers of the appendixes are listed in the **table of contents** of the report in which they appear.

application letters

The letter of application is essentially a **sales letter**. You are marketing your skills, abilities, and knowledge. Remember that you may be competing with many other applicants. The immediate **objective** of an application letter is to get the attention of the person who screens and hires job applicants. Your ultimate goal is to obtain a job interview (see **interviewing for a job**).

The successful application letter does three things: catches the **reader's** favorable attention, convinces the reader that you are qualified for consideration, and requests an interview. It should be concisely written.

A letter of application should provide the following information:

1. Identify an employment area or state a specific job title.
2. Point out your source of information about the job.
3. Summarize your qualifications for the job, specifically education, work experience, and activities showing leadership skills.
4. Refer the reader to your **résumé**.
5. Ask for an interview, stating where you can be reached and when you will be available for an interview.

If you are applying for a specific job, include information pertinent to the position—details not included on the more general résumé.

Personnel directors review many letters each week. To save them time, you should state your job objective directly at the beginning of the letter.

> EXAMPLE I am seeking a position in an accounting department where I can use my financial training to solve business problems.

If you have been referred to a prospective employer by one if its employees, a placement counselor, a professor, or someone else, however, you might say so before stating your job objective.

> EXAMPLE During the recent NOMAD convention in Washington, D.C., a member of your sales staff, Mr. Dale Jarrett, informed me of a possible opening for a manager in your Dealer Sales Division. I believe that my extensive background in the of-

6819 Locustview Drive
Topeka, Kansas 66614
June 14, 19--

Loudons, Inc.
4619 Drove Lane
Kansas City, Kansas 63511

Dear Personnel Manager:

The Kansas Dispatch recently reported that
Loudons is building a new data processing
center just north of Kansas City. I would
like to apply for a position as an entry-
level programmer at the center.

I am a recent graduate of Fairview Community
College in Topeka, with an Associate Degree
in Computer Science. In addition to taking a
broad range of courses, I have served as a
computer consultant at the college's computer
center, where I helped train novice computer
users. Since I understand Loudons produces
both in-house and customer documentation, my
technical writing skills (as described in the
enclosed resume) may be particularly useful.

I will be happy to meet with you at your convenience and provide any additional information you may need. You can reach me either at
my home address or at (913) 233-1552.

Sincerely,

David B. Edwards

David B. Edwards

Enclosure: Resume

Figure 1 Sample Application Letter

273 East Sixth Street
Bloomington, IN 47401
May 29, 19--

Ms. Laura Goldman
Personnel Manager
Acton, Inc.
80 Roseville Road
St. Louis, MO 63130

Dear Ms. Goldman:

I am seeking a responsible position as a financial research assistant in which I may use my
training to solve financial problems. I would
be interested in exploring the possibility of
obtaining such a position within your firm.

I expect to receive a Bachelor of Business
Administration degree in finance from Indiana
University in June. Since September 19--
I have been participating, through the university,
in the Professional Training Program at Computer
Systems International, in Indianapolis. In the
program I was assigned, on a rotating basis, to
several staff sections in apprentice positions.
Most recently I have been a financial trainee in
the Accounting Department and have gained a
great deal of experience. Details of the academic courses I have taken are contained in the
enclosed resume.

I look forward to meeting you soon in an interview. I can be contacted at my office (812-
866-7000, ext. 312) or at home (812-256-6320).

Sincerely yours,

Carol Ann Walker

Carol Ann Walker

Enclosure: Resume

Figure 2   Sample Application Letter

522 Beethoven Drive
Roanoke, Virginia 24017
November 15, 19--

Ms. Cecilia Smathers
Vice President, Dealer Sales
Hamilton Office Machines, Inc.
6194 Main Street
Hampton, Virginia 23661

Dear Ms. Smathers:

During the recent NOMAD convention in Washington,
a member of your sales staff, Mr. Dale Jarrett,
informed me of a possible opening for a Manager
in your Dealer Sales Division. I believe that
my extensive background in the office machine
industry qualifies me for the position.

I was with the Technology, Inc., Dealer Division
from its formation in 19-- to its phase-out
last year. During this period, I was involved
in all areas of dealer sales, both within Technology, Inc., and through personal contact with
a number of independent dealers. Between 19--
and 19-- I served as Assistant to the Dealer
Sales Manager as a Special Representative.
My education and work experience are detailed
in the enclosed resume.

I would like to discuss my qualifications in
an interview at your convenience. Please write
to me or telephone me at 703-449-6743 any weekday.

Sincerely,

Gregory Mindukakis

Gregory Mindukakis

Enclosure: Resume

Figure 3 Sample Application Letter

fice machine industry makes me highly qualified for the position.

In succeeding **paragraphs** expand upon the qualifications you mentioned in your **opening**. Add any appropriate details, highlighting the experience listed on your résumé that is especially pertinent to the job you are seeking. Close your letter with a request for an interview.

Type your letter, proofread it carefully for errors, and *keep a copy* for future reference. (See also **proofreading**.)

Three sample letters of application are presented here. The first one is written by a recent college graduate, the second by a college student about to graduate, and the third by a writer with many years of work experience.

Figure 1 is in response to a local newspaper article about a company's plan to build a new plant. The writer is not applying for a specific job opening but describes the position he is looking for. In Figure 2 the writer does not specify where she learned of the opening because she does not know whether a position is actually available. Figure 3 opens with an indication of where the writer learned of the job vacancy. (See also **job search** and **reference letters**.)

appositives

An appositive is a **noun** or noun **phrase** that follows and amplifies another noun or noun phrase. It has the same grammatical function as the noun it complements.

> EXAMPLES Dennis Gabor, *a British scientist*, experimented with coherent light in the 1940s.
> The British scientist *Dennis Gabor* experimented with coherent light in the 1940s.
> George Thomas, *head of the Economic and Planning Branch of PRC*, summarized the president's speech in a confidential memo to the advertising staff.

For detailed information on the use of **commas** with appositives, see **restrictive and nonrestrictive elements**.

When in doubt about the **case** of an appositive, you can check it by substituting the appositive for the noun it modifies.

> EXAMPLE My boss gave the two of us, Jim and *me*, the day off. (You wouldn't say, "My boss gave *I* the day off.")

articles

As a **part of speech**, articles are considered to be **adjectives** because they modify the items they designate by either limiting them or making them more precise. There are two kinds of articles, indefinite and definite.

Indefinite: *a* and *an* (denotes an unspecified item)

> EXAMPLE *A* program was run on our new computer. (Not a specific program, but an unspecified program. Therefore, the article is indefinite.)

Definite: *the* (denotes a particular item)

> EXAMPLE *The* program was run on the computer. (Not just any program, but *the* specific program. Therefore, the article is definite.)

The choice between *a* and *an* depends on the sound rather than the letter following the article. Use *a* before words beginning with a consonant sound (*a* person, *a* happy person, *a* historical event). Use *an* before words beginning with a vowel sound (*an* uncle, *an* hour). With **abbreviations**, use *a* before initial letters having a consonant sound: *a* TWA flight. Use *an* before initial letters having a vowel sound: *an* SLN report (note that the first sound is "ess").

Do not omit all articles from your writing. This is, unfortunately, an easy habit to develop. To include the articles costs nothing; to eliminate them makes the reading more difficult. (See also **telegraphic style**.)

> CHANGE Pass card through punch area for any debris.
> TO Pass *a* card through *the* punch area *to clear away* any debris.
> CHANGE There has been decline in domestic output of crude oil.
> TO There has been *a* decline in *the* domestic output of crude oil.

On the other hand, don't overdo it. An article can be superfluous.

> EXAMPLES I'll meet you in *a* half *an* hour. (Choose one and eliminate the other.)
> Fill with *a* half *a* pint of fluid. (Choose one and eliminate the other.)

Do not capitalize articles when they appear in titles except as the first word of the title. (See also **capital letters**.)

> EXAMPLE *Time* magazine reviewed *The Old World's New Order.*

as (see also **like/as**)

Since *as* can mean so many things (*since, because, for, that, at that time, when, while*, and the like) and can be at least four **parts of speech (conjunction, preposition, adverb, pronoun)**, it is often overused and misused, especially in speech. In writing, *as* is often weak or even ambiguous. Notice that the following sentence has two possible meanings:

>EXAMPLE *As* we were together, he revealed his plans.
>MEANS *Because* we were together, he revealed his plans.
>OR *While* we were together, he revealed his plans.

The word *as* can also contribute to **awkwardness** by appearing too many times in a sentence.

>CHANGE *As* we realized *as* soon *as* we began the project, the problem needed a solution.
>TO We realized the moment we began the project that the problem needed a solution.

(See also **because**.)

as much as/more than

These two **phrases** are sometimes incorrectly run together, especially when intervening phrases delay the completion of the phrase.

>CHANGE The engineers had *as much*, if not *more*, influence in planning the program *than* the accountants.
>TO The engineers had *as much* influence in planning the program *as* the accountants, if not *more*.
>OR The engineers had *as much* influence *as* the accountants, if not *more*, in planning the program.

as regards/with regard to/in regard to/regarding

With regards to and *in regards to* are incorrect **idioms** for *with regard to* and *in regard to*. *As regards* and *regarding* both are acceptable variants.

>CHANGE *With regards to* the building contract, this question is pertinent.
>TO *With regard to* the building contract, this question is pertinent.
>OR *In regard to* the building contract, this question is pertinent.
>OR *As regards* the building contract, this question is pertinent.
>OR *Regarding* the building contract, this question is pertinent.

as such

The **phrase** *as such* is seldom useful and should be omitted.

> CHANGE The accounting department, *as such*, worked overtime to meet the deadline.
> TO The accounting department worked overtime to meet the deadline.
> CHANGE This procedure is poor. *As such*, it should be eliminated.
> TO This procedure is poor and should be eliminated.

as to whether

The **phrase** *as to whether* (*as to when* or *as to where*) is clumsy and redundant. Either omit it altogether or use only *whether*.

> CHANGE *As to whether* we will commit our firm to a long-term contract, we have decided to do so.
> TO We have decided to commit our firm to a long-term contract.

Be wary of all phrases starting with *as to*; they are often redundant, vague, or indirect.

> CHANGE *As to* his policy, I am in full agreement.
> TO I am in full agreement with his policy.

as well as

Do not use *as well as* together with *both*. The two expressions have similar meanings; use one or the other.

> CHANGE *Both* General Motors, *as well as* Ford, are developing electric cars.
> TO *Both* General Motors *and* Ford are developing electric cars.
> OR General Motors, *as well as* Ford, is developing an electric car.

attribute/contribute

Attribute (with the accent on the second syllable) is a **verb** that means "point to a cause or source."

> EXAMPLE He *attributes* the plant's improved safety record to the new training program.

Attribute (with the first syllable accented) is a **noun** meaning a quality or characteristic belonging to someone or something.

EXAMPLE His mathematical skill is his most valuable *attribute*.

Contribute means "give."

EXAMPLE His mathematical skills will *contribute* much to the project.

audience (see reader)

augment/supplement

Augment means to increase or magnify in size, degree, or effect.

EXAMPLE Many employees *augment* their incomes by working overtime.

Supplement means to add something to make up for a deficiency.

EXAMPLE The physician told him to *supplement* his diet with vitamins.

average/mean/median

The *average*, or arithmetical *mean*, is determined by dividing a sum of two or more quantities by the number of quantities. For example, if one report is 10 pages, another is 30 pages, and a third is 20 pages, their *average* (or *mean*) length is 20 pages. It is incorrect, therefore, to say that "*each* averages 20 pages" because *each* report is a specific length.

CHANGE Each report *averages* 20 pages.
TO The three reports *average* 20 pages.

A *median* is the middle number in a sequence of numbers.

EXAMPLE The *median* of the series, 1, 3, 4, 7, 8, is 4.

awhile/a while

Awhile is an **adverb** meaning "for a short time." It is not preceded by *for* because the meaning of *for* is inherent in the meaning of *awhile*. *A while* is a **noun** phrase that means "a period of time."

CHANGE Wait for *awhile* before investing more heavily.
TO Wait for *a while* before investing more heavily.
OR Wait *awhile* before investing more heavily.

awkwardness

Any writing that strikes the **reader** as awkward—that is, as forced or unnatural—impedes the reader's understanding. Awkwardness has many causes, including overloaded sentences, overlapping **subordination**, grammatical errors, ambiguous statements, overuse of **expletives** or of the passive **voice**, faulty **logic**, unintentional **repetition**, **garbled sentences**, and **jammed modifiers**.

To avoid awkwardness, make your writing as direct and concise as possible. The following three guidelines will help you smooth out most awkward passages: (1) In general, you should keep your sentences uncomplicated. (2) Use the active voice unless you have a particular reason to use the passive voice. (3) Tighten up your writing by eliminating excess words.

B

bad/badly

Bad is the **adjective** form that follows such **linking verbs** as *feel* and *look*.

> EXAMPLES With the flu, you will feel *bad* for three days.
> We don't want our department to look *bad* at the meeting.

Badly is an **adverb**.

> EXAMPLE The test model performed *badly* during the trial run.

To say "I feel badly" would mean, literally, that your sense of touch was impaired. (See also **good/well**.)

balance/remainder

One meaning of *balance* is "a state of equilibrium"; another meaning is "the amount remaining in a bank account after balancing deposits and withdrawals." *Remainder*, in all applications, is "what is left over." *Remainder* is the more accurate word, therefore, to mean "that which is left over."

> EXAMPLES The personnel department must attempt to maintain a *balance* between looking after the company's best interests and being sensitive to the needs of individuals.
> The *balance* in the corporate account after the payroll has been met is a matter for concern.
> Round the fraction off to its nearest whole number and drop the *remainder*.

When using these words figuratively (outside of banking and mathematical contexts), use *remainder* to mean "what is left over."

> CHANGE Four of the cars in the auto show were from General Motors, and the *balance* were from Ford and Chrysler.
> TO Four of the cars in the auto show were from General Motors, and the *remainder* were from Ford and Chrysler.

be sure and/be sure to

The **phrase** *be sure and* is colloquial and unidiomatic when used for *be sure to*. (See also **idioms**.)

> CHANGE   When you get to the branch office, *be sure and* phone me.
> TO   When you get to the branch office, *be sure to* phone me.

because

To express cause, *because* is the strongest and most specific connective (others are *for, since, as, inasmuch as, insofar as*). *Because* is unequivocal in stating causal relationship.

> EXAMPLE   We didn't complete the project *because* the raw materials became too costly. (The use of *because* emphasizes the cause-and-effect relationship.)

For can express causal relationships, but it is weaker than *because*, and it allows the **clause** that follows to be a separate **independent clause**.

> EXAMPLE   We didn't complete the project, *for* raw materials became too costly. (The use of *for* expresses but does not emphasize the cause-and-effect relationship.)

As a connective to express cause, *since* is also a weak substitute for *because*.

> EXAMPLE   *Since* the computer is broken, paychecks will be delayed.

However, *since* is an appropriate connective when the **emphasis** is on circumstances, conditions, or time rather than on cause and effect.

> EXAMPLES   *Since* I was in town anyway, I stopped at the branch office.
> *Since* 1984, the company has earned a profit every year.

As is the least definite connective to indicate cause; its use for this purpose is better avoided.

> CHANGE   I left the office early, *as* I had finished my work.
> TO   I left the office early *because* I had finished my work.
> OR   *Since* I had finished my work, I left the office early.

Inasmuch as implies concession; that is, it suggests that a statement is true "in view of the circumstances."

EXAMPLE You may as well complete the project, *inasmuch as* you have already begun it.

(See also **reason is because**.)

being as/being that

These **phrases** are nonstandard English and should not be used in writing. Use *because* or *since*.

beside/besides

Besides, meaning "in addition to" or "other than," should be carefully distinguished from *beside*, meaning "next to" or "apart from."

EXAMPLE *Besides* the two of us from the Marketing Department, three people from Production were standing *beside* the president when he presented the award.

between/among

Between is normally used to relate two items or persons.

EXAMPLES The roll pin is located *between* the grommet and the knob. Preferred stock offers a buyer a middle ground *between* bonds and common stock.

Among is used to relate more than two.

EXAMPLE The subcontracting was distributed *among* the three firms.

between you and me

People sometimes use the incorrect expression *between you and I*. Because the **pronouns** are **objects** of the **preposition** *between*, the objective form of the **personal pronoun** (*me*) must be used. (See also **case [grammar]**.)

CHANGE *Between you and I*, John should be taken off the job.
TO *Between you and me*, John should be taken off the job.

bi/semi

When used with periods of time, *bi* means "two" or "every two." Bimonthly means "once in two months"; biweekly means "once in two weeks."

When used with periods of time, *semi* means "half of" or "occurring twice within a period of time." Semimonthly means "twice a month"; semiweekly means "twice a week."

Both *bi* and *semi* are normally joined with the following element without space or **hyphen**.

biannual/biennial

By conventional usage, *biannual* means "twice during the year," and *biennial* means "every other year." (See also **bi/semi**.)

bibliography

A bibliography is a list of the books, articles, and other source materials consulted in the preparation of a paper, **report**, or article. It provides a convenient alphabetical listing of these sources in a standardized form for **readers** interested in getting further information on the topic or in assessing the scope of the **research**. A bibliography is normally placed at the end of a document. (See **formal reports** for guidance on the placement of a bibliography in a report.)

Those works consulted for background information, in addition to those actually cited in the text, should be included in a bibliography. A bibliography is often appropriate as a supplement to **lists** of "Works Cited" or "Reference" sections, since they include only works actually referred to in the text. If a list of "References" or "Works Cited" is used, the bibliography should follow the same format. (See **documenting sources** for detailed format guidelines.)

The entries in a bibliography are listed alphabetically by the author's last name. If the author is unknown, the entry is alphabetized by the first word in the title (following *a, an,* or *the*). Entries may also be arranged into subject categories and then by alphabetical order within these categories.

An annotated bibliography is one that includes complete bibliographic information about a work (author, title, publisher) followed by a brief description or evaluation of the work. (See also **literature reviews**.) The following annotation concisely evaluates a book:

> Freiberger, Paul, and Michael Swaine. *Fire in the Valley: The Making of the Personal Computer.* Berkeley, CA: Osborne/McGraw, 1984. This history of the development of the personal computer industry focuses on California's Silicon

Valley in the seventies. The book is based on personal interviews with the technological innovators–turned-entrepre-
neurs who led the transformation of garage electronics
shops into multimillion dollar corporations and made the
computer a machine for the people.

The format of this sample entry follows the guidelines in the
Modern Language Association's *MLA Handbook for Writers of Research
Papers*, 3rd ed. For explanations and further samples of this and
other formats, see **documenting sources**.

blend words

A blend word is formed by combining part of one word with part
of another.

> EXAMPLES   motor + hotel = motel
> breakfast + lunch = brunch
> smoke + fog = smog
> electric + execute = electrocute

Although blend words (sometimes called "portmanteau words")
may occasionally be created by a specialist to meet a specific need—
such as *stagflation* (a stagnant economy coupled with inflation)—resist creating blend words in your writing unless an obvious need
arises. If you must create a blend word, be sure to define it clearly
for your **reader**. Otherwise, creating blend words is at best merely
"cute" and could be confusing. (See also **new words**.)

both . . . and

Statements using the *both . . . and* construction should always be balanced both grammatically and logically.

> EXAMPLE   A successful photograph must be *both* clearly focused *and* ade-
> quately lighted.

Notice that *both* and *and* are followed logically by ideas of equal
weight and grammatically by identical constructions.

> CHANGE   For success in management, it is necessary both *to develop* writ-
> ing skills and *mastering* speaking.
> TO   For success in management, it is necessary both *to develop* writ-
> ing skills and *to master* speaking.

Be careful to avoid the common error of substituting *as well as* for *and* in this construction.

> CHANGE For success in management, it is necessary *both* to develop writing skills *as well as* to master speaking.
>
> TO For success in management, it is necessary *both* to develop writing skills *and* to master speaking.

(See also **parallel structure** and **correlative conjunctions**.)

brackets

The primary use of brackets is to enclose a word or words inserted by an editor or writer into a **quotation** from another source.

> EXAMPLE He stated, "Wheat prices will continue to rise [no doubt because of the Russian wheat purchase] until next year."

Brackets are also used to set off a parenthetical item within **parentheses**.

> EXAMPLE We should be sure to give Emanuel Foose (and his brother Emilio [1812–1882] as well) credit for his role in founding the institute.

Brackets are also used in academic writing to insert the Latin word *sic*, which indicates that the writer has quoted material exactly as it appears in the original, even though it contains an obvious error.

> EXAMPLE Dr. Smith pointed out that "the earth does not revolve around the son [*sic*] at a constant rate."

bunch

Bunch refers to like things that grow or are fastened together. Do not use the word *bunch* to refer to people.

> CHANGE A *bunch* of trainees toured the site.
> TO A *group* of trainees toured the site.

business writing style

At one time, business writing style was as formal as the starched collars every businessman wore. The following example was typical:

> My Dear Sir:
> Yours of the 12th received and in reply beg to state that herewith are forwarded the reports under consideration. Please be advised of general concurrence in desire to expedite matters. . . .

This style is extremely formal and impersonal by today's standards. Business writing today (especially business **correspondence**) is generally much more personal and conversational, as the following revision of the previous example illustrates.

> Dear Mr. Watson:
> I have received your letter of the 12th, and I am enclosing the reports for your company to study. Certainly, we agree with you that time is important to the project. . . .

Even though business writing style is less formal today than in the past, it must adhere to the conventions of standard English by using conventional **spelling** and standard grammatical forms.

Business writing may legitimately vary all the way from the chatty style of a letter to a close business associate to the very formal style found in contracts. In **memorandums** and letters, however, a position between the two extremes is generally appropriate. Writing that is too formal can be irritating to the **reader**, and an obvious attempt to be casual and informal may strike the reader as insincere. In business writing, as in all writing, knowing your reader is critical.

> CHANGE Dear Jane,
> I'm crazy about your proposal! . . .
> TO Dear Jane:
> Your proposal arrived today, and it seems fine. . . .

Your use of **personal pronouns** is important in letters and memorandums. For example, do not use *one* (or *the writer*) to refer to yourself; it is perfectly natural and appropriate to refer to yourself as *I* and to the reader as *you*. In a **report**, however, you may not be writing to a single reader and should not normally refer to collective readers as *you*. Be careful also when you use the **pronoun** *we* in a business letter that is written on company stationery, since it commits your company to what you have written. When a statement is your opinion, use *I*; when it is company policy, use *we*. (See also **point of view**.)

The best writers strive to write in a style that is so clear that their message cannot be misunderstood. **Clarity** should be the ultimate

PLR Air Conditioning Center 27 West Elm Street • Plaines City, IA 50705

March 6, 19--

Ms. Harriet L. Bussman, President
Bussman Engineering, Inc.
2731 Janus Street
Plaines City, IA 50505

Dear Ms. Bussman:

Thank you very much for allowing us to present our recommendation for a PLR Air Conditioning System. We would like
also to express our appreciation to Mr. Lindsay and Mrs.
Smoot for the time and courtesy they extended to us as we
collected the data necessary for this proposal.

After thoroughly analyzing your company's management and
engineering requirements, we believe that this proposed PLR
system will provide the maximum return on your investment
dollar. In addition, the PLR system protects you against
obsolescence in the near future--if your business continues
to experience the normal growth you have experienced the
last few years--because the equipment PLR proposes to install is a modular design to which you may add additional
units as the need arises. The system we have designed for
you provides flexibility, allowing for any special conditions your company may wish to incorporate.

We believe that you will find this system practical, efficient, and economical for your company, both now and in the
future. It is our sincere hope that the information in the
enclosed proposal will make your decision to install a PLR
Air Conditioning System much easier.

Sincerely yours,

James P. Callahan

James P. Callahan
Sales Manager

JPC/mo
Enclosure

Figure 1   Business Writing Style

goal of your business writing style. A clear style is achieved primarily
through proper and conscientious use of the different steps of the
writing process—**preparation**, **research**, **organization**, **writing the
draft**, and **revision**. (See also the Checklist of the Writing Process.)

One way to achieve a clear style, especially during revision, is to eliminate overuse of the passive **voice**, which is prevalent in most poor business writing. The passive voice not only saps the life of your writing; it can sometimes be ambiguous, uninformative, or overly impersonal.

CHANGE It was discovered that salary totals were incorrect. (Who discovered it?)

TO The Accounting Department discovered that the salary totals were incorrect.

You can also achieve clarity with **conciseness**. Proceed cautiously here, however, because business writing should not be **telegraphic**, with an endless series of short, choppy sentences.

Furthermore, don't be so concise that you are blunt. If you respond to a written request that you cannot understand with "Your request was unclear" or "I don't understand your question," you will probably offend your reader. Instead of attacking the writer's ability to phrase a request, consider that what you are really doing is asking for more information. Say so: "I will need more information before I can answer your request. Specifically, can you give me the title and the date of the report you are looking for?" The second version is a little longer than the first, but it is both more polite and more helpful. (See also **you viewpoint**.)

Finally, clarity is achieved through the wise use of **punctuation**. The businessperson who says "I don't worry about every **comma**; I get my message across" does not realize that a misplaced comma (or other mark of punctuation) can often cause misunderstanding and confusion.

In Figure 1 notice that the **tone** is dignified, yet neither too formal nor too informal. Extensive use of the active voice keeps the **pace** of the letter moving well. Use of personal pronouns and a positive point of view keeps the writing interesting. (See also **formal writing style**, **informal writing style**, and **English, varieties of**.)

C

can/may

In writing, *can* refers to capability, and *may* refers to possibility or permission.

    EXAMPLES I *can* have the project finished by January 1. (capability)
                I *may* be in Boston on Thursday. (possibility)
                I *can* be in Boston on Thursday. (capability)
                May I have an extra week to finish the project? (permission)

cannot/can not

Cannot is one word.

    CHANGE We *can not* meet the deadline specified in the contract.
        TO We *cannot* meet the deadline specified in the contract.

cannot help but

Avoid the **phrase** *cannot help but* in writing. (See also **double negatives**.)

    CHANGE We *cannot help but* cut our staff.
        TO We cannot avoid cutting our staff.

canvas/canvass

Canvas is a **noun** meaning "heavy, coarse, closely woven cotton or hemp fabric." *Canvass* is a **verb** meaning "to solicit votes or opinions."

    EXAMPLES The maintenance crew spread the *canvas* over the equipment.
                The executive committee decided to *canvass* the employees.

capital/capitol

Capital may refer either to financial assets or to the city that hosts the government of a state or a nation. *Capitol* refers to the building in which the state or national legislature meets. *Capitol* is often written with a small *c* when it refers to a state building, but it is always capitalized when it refers to the home of the United States Congress in Washington, D.C.

capital letters

The use of capital letters (or uppercase letters) is determined by custom and tradition. Capital letters are used to call attention to certain words, such as **proper nouns** and the first word of a sentence. Care must be exercised in using capital letters because they can affect the meaning of words (march/March, china/China, turkey/Turkey). Thus, capital letters can help eliminate **ambiguity**.

PROPER NOUNS

Proper nouns name a specific person, place, thing, concept, or quality and therefore are capitalized.

> EXAMPLES Physics 101, General Electric, John Doe

COMMON NOUNS

Common nouns name a general class or category of persons, places, things, concepts, or qualities rather than specific ones and therefore are not capitalized.

> EXAMPLES a physics class, a company, a person

FIRST WORDS

The first letter of the first word in a sentence is always capitalized.

> EXAMPLE Of all the plans you mentioned, the first one seems the best.

The first word after a **colon** may be capitalized if the statement following is a complete sentence or if it introduces a formal resolution or question.

> EXAMPLE Today's meeting will deal with only one issue: What is the firm's role in environmental protection?

If a subordinate element follows the colon, however, or if the thought is closely related, use a lowercase letter following the colon.

> EXAMPLE We had to keep working for one reason: our deadline was upon us.

The first word of a complete sentence in **quotation marks** is capitalized.

EXAMPLE He said, "When I arrive, we will begin."

Complete sentences contained as numbered items within a sentence may also be capitalized.

EXAMPLE He recommended two ways to increase sales: (1) Next year we should spend more on television advertising, and (2) Our quality control should be improved immediately.

The first word in the salutation and complimentary close of a letter is capitalized. (See also **correspondence**.)

EXAMPLES Dear Mr. Smith:
Sincerely yours,
Best regards,

SPECIFIC PEOPLE AND GROUPS

Capitalize all personal names.

EXAMPLES Walter Bunch, Mary Fortunato, Bill Krebs

Capitalize names of ethnic groups and nationalities.

EXAMPLES American Indian, Italian, Jew, Chicano
Thus Italian immigrants contributed much to the industrialization of the United States.

Do not capitalize names of social and economic groups.

EXAMPLES middle class, working class, ghetto dwellers

SPECIFIC PLACES

Capitalize the names of all political divisions.

EXAMPLES Chicago, Cook County, Illinois, Ontario, Iran, Ward Six

Capitalize the names of geographical divisions.

EXAMPLES Europe, Asia, North America, the Middle East, the Orient

Do not capitalize geographic features unless they are part of a proper name.

EXAMPLE The mountains in some areas, such as the Great Smoky Mountains, make television transmission difficult.

The words *north, south, east,* and *west* are capitalized when they refer to sections of the country. They are not capitalized when they refer to directions.

> EXAMPLES I may travel south when I relocate to Delaware.
> We may build a new plant in the South next year.
> State Street runs east and west.

Capitalize the names of stars, constellations, and planets.

> EXAMPLES Saturn, Andromeda, Jupiter, Milky Way

Do not capitalize *earth, sun,* and *moon,* however, except when they are used with the names of other planets.

> EXAMPLES Although the sun rises in the east and sets in the west, the moon may appear in any part of the evening sky when darkness settles over the earth.
> Mars, Pluto, and Earth were discussed at the symposium.

SPECIFIC INSTITUTIONS, EVENTS, AND CONCEPTS

Capitalize the names of institutions, organizations, and associations.

> EXAMPLE The American Management Association and the Department of Housing and Urban Development are cooperating in the project.

An organization usually capitalizes the names of its internal divisions and departments.

> EXAMPLES Faculty, Board of Directors, Accounting Department

Types of organizations are not capitalized unless they are part of an official name.

> EXAMPLES Our group decided to form a writers' association; we called it the American Association of Writers.
> I attended Post High School. What high school did you attend?

Capitalize historical events.

> EXAMPLE Dr. Jellison discussed the Boston Tea Party at the last class.

Capitalize words that designate specific periods of time.

EXAMPLES Labor Day, the Renaissance, the Enlightenment, January, Monday, the Great Depression, Lent

Do not, however, capitalize seasons of the year.

EXAMPLES spring, autumn, winter, summer

Capitalize scientific names of classes, families, and orders, but do not capitalize species or English derivatives of scientific names.

EXAMPLES Mammalia, Carnivora/mammal, carnivorous

TITLES OF BOOKS, ARTICLES, PLAYS, FILMS, REPORTS, AND MEMOS (SUBJECT LINE)

Capitalize the initial letters of the first and last words of a title of a book, article, play, or film, as well as all major words in the title. Do not capitalize **articles** (*a, an, the*), **conjunctions** (*and, but, if*), or short **prepositions** (*at, in, on, of*) unless they begin the title. Capitalize prepositions that contain more than four letters (*between, because, until, after*).

EXAMPLES The author worked three years writing the book *The Many Lives of an Organization.*
The article "Year After Year" describes the life of a turn-of-the-century industrialist.
The report entitled "Alternative Sites for Plant Relocation" was submitted in February.
The memo "Analysis of Division Accounting Procedures," dated November 13, explains the problem.

PERSONAL, PROFESSIONAL, AND JOB TITLES

Titles preceding proper names are capitalized.

EXAMPLES Miss March, Professor Galbraith

Appositives following proper names are not normally capitalized. (The word *President* is usually capitalized when it refers to the chief executive of a national government.)

EXAMPLE Frank Jones, senator from New Mexico (but Senator Jones)

The only exception is an epithet, which actually renames the person.

EXAMPLES Alexander the Great, Solomon the Wise

Job titles used with personal names are capitalized.

> EXAMPLE John Reems, Division Manager, will meet with us on Wednes-
> day.

Job titles used without personal names are not capitalized.

> EXAMPLE The division manager will meet with us on Wednesday.

Use capital letters to designate family relationships only when they
occur before a name or substitute for a name.

> EXAMPLES One of my favorite people is Uncle Fred.
> Jim and Mother went along.
> Jim and my mother went along.

ABBREVIATIONS

Capitalize **abbreviations** if the words they stand for would be capitalized.

> EXAMPLES UCLA (University of California at Los Angeles)
> p. (page)
> Ph.D. (Doctor of Philosophy)

LETTERS

Certain single letters are always capitalized. Capitalize the **pronoun**
I and the **interjection** *O* (but do not capitalize *oh* unless it is the first
word in a sentence).

> EXAMPLES When I say writing, O believe me, I mean rewriting.
> When I say writing, oh believe me, I mean rewriting.

Capitalize letters that serve as names or indicate shapes.

> EXAMPLES X-ray, vitamin B, T-square, U-turn, I-beam

MISCELLANEOUS CAPITALIZATIONS

The word *Bible* is capitalized when it refers to the Jewish or Christian
Scriptures; otherwise, it is not capitalized.

> EXAMPLE He quoted a verse from the Bible, then read from Blackstone,
> the lawyer's bible.

All references to deities (Allah, God, Jehovah, Yahweh) are capitalized.

EXAMPLE God is the One who sustains us.

A complete sentence enclosed in **dashes**, **brackets**, or **parentheses** is not capitalized when it appears as part of another sentence.

EXAMPLES We must make an extra effort in safety this year (last year's sales were down 10 percent).
Extra effort in sales should be made next year. (Last year's sales were down 10 percent.)

Certain units, such as rooms in buildings and parts and chapters of books, when specifically identified by number, are normally capitalized.

EXAMPLES Chapter 5, Ch. 5, Room 72, Rm. 72

Minor divisions within such units are not capitalized unless they begin a sentence.

EXAMPLES page 11, verse 14, seat 12

When in doubt about whether or not to capitalize, check a **dictionary** or a secretarial manual, such as the current edition of *The Gregg Reference Manual* by William A. Sabin (McGraw).

case (grammar)

Grammatically, *case* indicates the functional relationship of a **noun** or a **pronoun** to the other words in a sentence. Nouns change form only in the possessive case; pronouns may show change for the subjective, the objective, or the possessive case. The case of a noun or pronoun is always determined by its function in its **phrase, clause,** or sentence. If it is the **subject** of its phrase, clause, or sentence, it is in the subjective case; if it is an **object** within its phrase, clause, or sentence, it is in the objective case; if it reflects possession or ownership and modifies a noun, it is in the possessive case. The subjective case indicates the person or thing acting (*He* sued the vendor); the objective case indicates the thing acted upon (The vendor sued *him*); and the possessive case indicates the person or thing owning or possessing something (It was *his* company).

The different forms of a noun or pronoun indicate whether it is functioning as a subject (subjective case), as a **complement** (usually objective case), or as a **modifier** (possessive case).

Subjective Case	Objective Case	Possessive Case
I	me	my, mine
we	us	our, ours
he	him	his, his
she	her	her, hers
they	them	their, theirs
you	you	your, yours
who	whom	whose
it	it	its

SUBJECTIVE CASE

A pronoun is in the subjective case (also called the nominative case) when it represents the person or thing acting.

> EXAMPLE　*I* wrote a letter to that company before I graduated.

A **linking verb** links a pronoun to its antecedent to show that they identify the same thing. Because they represent the same thing, the pronoun is in the subjective case even when it follows the **verb**, which makes it a **subjective complement**.

> EXAMPLES　*He* is the president of the company. (subject)
> The president of the company is *he*. (subjective complement)

Whether a pronoun is a subject or a subjective complement, it is in the subjective case.

The subjective case is used after the words *than* and *as* because of the understood (although unstated) portion of the clauses in which these words appear.

> EXAMPLES　George is as good a designer as *I* [am].
> Our subsidiary can do the job better than *we* [can].

OBJECTIVE CASE

A pronoun is in the objective case when it indicates the person or thing receiving the action expressed by the verb. (The objective case is also called the accusative case.)

> EXAMPLE　They informed *me* by letter that they had received my résumé.

A pronoun is in the objective case when it is the object of a verb, **gerund**, or **preposition** and when it is the subject of an **infinitive**. Pronouns that follow prepositions must be in the objective case.

EXAMPLES   Between you and *me*, his facts are questionable.
Many of *us* attended the conference.

Pronouns that follow action verbs (which excludes all forms of the verb *be*) must be in the objective case. Don't be confused by an additional name.

EXAMPLES   The company promoted *me* in June.
The company promoted John and *me* in June.

Pronouns that follow gerunds must be in the objective case.

EXAMPLE   Phoning *him* was the best thing I could have done.

Subjects of infinitives must be in the objective case.

EXAMPLE   We asked *them* to return the deposit.

For determining the case of an object, English does not differentiate between direct objects and indirect objects; both require the objective form of the pronoun. (See also **complements**.)

EXAMPLES   The interviewer seemed to like *me*. (direct object)
They wrote *me* a letter. (indirect object)

POSSESSIVE CASE
A noun or a pronoun is in the possessive case when it represents a person or thing owning or possessing something.

EXAMPLE   John's intelligence was evident in *his* work.

Nouns.   Although exceptions are relatively common, it is a good rule of thumb to use the *'s* form of the possessive case with nouns referring to persons and living things, and to use an *of* phrase for the possessive case of nouns referring to inanimate objects.

EXAMPLES   The *chairman's* address was well received.
The leaves *of the tree* look healthy.

If this rule leads to awkwardness or wordiness, however, be flexible.

EXAMPLES   The *company's* branches are doing well.
The *plane's* landing gear failed.

Only the possessive form of a noun or pronoun should precede a **gerund**.

> EXAMPLES   John's working has not affected his grades.
> His working has not affected his grades.

The established **idiom** calls for the possessive case in many stock phrases.

> EXAMPLES   A day's journey, a day's work, a moment's notice, at his wit's end, the law's delay

In a few cases, the idiom even calls for a double possessive employing both the *of* and *'s* forms.

> EXAMPLE   That friend *of* George's was at the meeting yesterday.

Plural words ending in *s* need only add an **apostrophe** to form the possessive case.

> EXAMPLE   the *laborers'* union

With a multiword term, add *'s* to the last word only.

> EXAMPLES   The *Chairman of the Board's* statement was brief.
> The fact that his *father-in-law's* business address was the Pentagon gave rise to some suspicion.

To show individual possession with coordinate nouns, make both nouns possessive.

> EXAMPLE   The *Senate's and House's* chambers were packed.

To show joint possession with coordinate nouns, make only the last possessive.

> EXAMPLE   The *Senate and House's* joint declaration was read to the press.

Pronouns. The use of possessive pronouns does not normally cause problems except with gerunds and **indefinite pronouns**. Several indefinite pronouns (*all, any, each, few, most, none,* and *some*) require *of* phrases to form the possessive case.

> EXAMPLE   Both dies were stored in the warehouse, but rust had ruined the surface *of each.*

Others, however, use the apostrophe.

> EXAMPLE   *Anyone's* contribution is welcome.

Only the possessive form of a pronoun should be used with a gerund.

EXAMPLES The boss objected to *my* arriving late every morning.
My working has not affected my grades.

Pronouns in compound constructions should be in the same case.

EXAMPLES This is just between *them* and *us*.
Both *they* and *we* must agree to the arrangement.

APPOSITIVES

An appositive is a noun or noun phrase that follows and amplifies another noun or noun phrase. Because it has the same grammatical function as the noun it complements, an appositive should be in the same case as the noun with which it is in apposition.

EXAMPLES Two accountants, Merle Fosnight and *I*, were appointed to represent the department. (subjective case)
The accountants selected two members to represent the department—Merle Fosnight and *me*. (objective case)
We all came—Jim and Carol and *I*. (subjective case)
He gave us both, Rod and *me*, a week to make up our minds. (objective case)

TIPS ON DETERMINING THE CASE OF PRONOUNS

One test to determine the proper case of a pronoun is to try it with some transitive **verb** such as *resembled* or *hit*. If the pronoun would logically precede the verb, use the subjective case; if it would logically follow the verb, use the objective case.

EXAMPLES *She* (he, they) resembled her father. (subjective case)
Angela resembled *him* (her, them). (objective case)

In the following type of sentence, try omitting the noun to determine the case of the pronoun.

EXAMPLES (*We/Us*) pilots fly our own airplanes.
We [pilots] fly our own airplanes. (This correct usage sounds right.)
Us [pilots] fly our own airplanes. (This incorrect usage is obviously wrong.)

To determine the case of a pronoun that follows *as* or *than*, try mentally adding the words that are normally omitted.

EXAMPLES The other bookkeeper is not paid as well *as she* [is paid]. (You would not write, "*Her* is paid.")

His partner was better informed that *he* [was informed]. (You would not write, "*Him* was informed.")

If compound pronouns cause problems, try using them singly to determine the proper case.

EXAMPLES (*We/Us*) and the Johnsons are going to the Grand Canyon.

We are going to the Grand Canyon. (You would not write, "*Us* are going to the Grand Canyon.")

WHO/WHOM

Who and *whom* cause much trouble in determining case. *Who* is the subjective case form, whereas *whom* is the objective case form. When in doubt about which form to use, try substituting a personal pronoun to see which one fits. If *he* or *they* fits, use *who*.

EXAMPLES *Who* is the congressman from the 45th district?

He is the congressman from the 45th district.

If *him* or *them* fits, use *whom*.

EXAMPLES It depended on *them*.

It depended on *whom*?

It was they on *whom* it depended.

It is becoming common to use *who* for the objective case when it begins a clause or sentence, although some readers still object to such an "ungrammatical" construction, especially in formal contexts.

EXAMPLE *Who* should I call to report a fire?

The best advice is to know your **reader**. (See also **who/whom**.)

case (usage)

The word *case* is often merely filler. Be critical of the word, and eliminate it if it contributes nothing.

CHANGE An exception was made in the *case* of those closely connected with the project.

TO An exception was made for those closely connected with the project.

cause-and-effect method of development

When your purpose is to explain why something happened or why you think something will happen, the cause-and-effect **method of development** is a useful writing strategy.

The goal of the cause-and-effect method of development is to make as plausible as possible the relationship between a situation and either its cause or its effect. The conclusions you draw about the relationships should be based on the evidence you have gathered. Because not all evidence will be of equal value to you, keep some guidelines in mind for evaluating evidence.

EVALUATING EVIDENCE

The facts and arguments you gather should be pertinent to your **topic**. Be careful not to draw a conclusion that your evidence does not lead to or support. You may have researched some statistics, for example, which show that an increasing number of Americans are licensed to fly small airplanes. But you cannot use this information as evidence that there is a slowdown in interstate highway construction in the United States—the evidence does not lead to that conclusion. Statistics on the increase in small-plane licensing may be relevant to other conclusions, however. You could argue that the upswing has occurred because small planes save travel time, provide easy access to remote areas, and, once they are purchased, are economical to operate.

Your evidence should be adequate. Incomplete evidence can lead to false conclusions.

> EXAMPLE   Driver training classes do not help prevent auto accidents. Two people I know who completed driver training classes were involved in accidents.

Although the evidence cited to support the conclusion may be accurate, there is not enough of it. A thorough investigation of the usefulness of driver training classes in keeping down the accident rate would require many more than two examples. And it would require a comparison of the driving records of those who had completed driver training with drivers who had not.

Your evidence should be representative. If you conduct a survey to obtain your evidence, be sure that you do not solicit responses only from individuals or groups whose views are identical to yours; that is, be sure you obtain a representative sampling.

Your evidence should also be plausible. Two events that occur close to each other in time or place may or may not be causally related. Thunder and black clouds do not always signal rain, but they do so often enough that if we are outdoors and the sky darkens and we hear thunder, we seek shelter unless we're prepared to get wet. If you walk under a ladder and shortly afterward sprain your ankle on a curb, however, you cannot conclude that walking under a ladder brings bad luck—unless you are superstitious. Merely to say that *X* caused *Y* (or will cause *Y*) is inadequate. You must demonstrate the relationship with pertinent facts and arguments.

LINKING CAUSES TO EFFECTS

To show a true relationship between a cause and an effect, you must demonstrate that the existence of the one *requires* the existence of the other. It is often difficult to establish beyond any doubt that one event was *the* cause of another event. More often, a result will have more than one cause. As you research your subject, your task is to determine which cause or causes are the most plausible.

When several probable causes are equally valid, report your findings accordingly, as in the following **paragraph** on the use of an energy-saving device called a furnace-vent damper. The damper is a metal plate fitted inside the flue or vent pipe of natural-gas or fuel-oil furnaces. When the furnace is on, the damper opens to allow the gases to escape up the flue. When the furnace shuts off, the damper closes, thus preventing warm air from escaping up the flue stack. The dampers are potentially dangerous, however. If the dampers fail to open at the proper time, they could allow poisonous furnace gases to back into the house and asphyxiate anyone in a matter of minutes. Tests run on several dampers showed a number of probable causes for their malfunctioning.

> EXAMPLE   One damper was sold without proper installation instructions, and another was wired incorrectly. Two of the units had slow-opening dampers (15 seconds) that prevented the [furnace] burner from firing. And one damper jammed when exposed to a simulated fuel temperature of more than 700 degrees.
> —Don DeBat, "Save Energy but Save Your Life, Too," *Family Safety* Fall 1978: 27.

The investigator located all the causes of damper malfunctions and reported on them. Without such a thorough account, recommendations to prevent similar malfunctions would be based on incomplete evidence.

MEMORANDUM

To: James K. Arburg, Safety Officer
From: Lawrence T. Baker, Foreman of Section A-40 *LTB*
Date: November 30, 19--

Subject: Personal-Injury Accident in Section A-40
           October 10, 19--

On October 10, 19--, at 10:15 p.m., Jim Hollander, operating
punch press #16, accidentally brushed the knee switch of his
punch press with his right knee as he swung a metal sheet over
the punching surface. The switch activated the punching unit,
which severed Hollander's left thumb between the first and second
joints as his hand passed through the punch station. While an
ambulance was being summoned, Margaret Wilson, R.N., administered
first aid at the plant dispensary. There were no witnesses to
the accident.
     The ambulance arrived from Mercy Hospital at 10:45 p.m., and
Hollander was admitted to the emergency room at the hospital at
11:00 p.m. He was treated and kept overnight for observation,
then released the next morning.
     Hollander returned to work one week later, on October 17.
He has been given temporary duties in the tool room until his
injury heals.

Conclusions About the Cause of the Accident

The Maxwell punch press on which Hollander was working has two
switches, a hand switch and a knee switch, and both must be
pressed to activate the punch mechanism. The hand switch must be
pressed first, and then the knee switch, to trip the punch
mechanism. The purpose of the knee switch is to leave the
operator's hands free to hold the panel being punched. The hand
switch, in contrast, is a safety feature. Because the knee
switch cannot activate the press until the hand switch has been
pressed, the operator cannot trip the punching mechanism by
touching the knee switch accidentally.
     Inspection of the punch press that Hollander was operating
at the time of the accident made it clear that Hollander had
taped the hand switch of his machine in the ON position,
effectively eliminating its safety function. He could then pick
up a panel, swing it onto the machine's punching surface, press
the knee switch, stack the newly punched panel, and grab the next
unpunched panel, all in one continuous motion--eliminating the
need to let go of the panel, after placing it on the punching
surface, in order to press the hand switch.

Preventive Training

To prevent a recurrence of this accident, I have conducted a
brief safety session with all punch press operators, at which I
described Hollander's experience and cautioned them against
tampering with the safety features of their machines.

mo

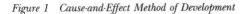

Figure 1   Cause-and-Effect Method of Development

By substituting *problem* for "cause" and *solution* for "effect," you
can use the same approach to develop a **report** dealing with a solution to a problem.

The report shown in Figure 1 is developed from effect to cause.

center around

Substitute *on* or *in* for *around* in this redundant and illogical expression.

> CHANGE The experiments *center around* the new discovery.
>   TO The experiments *center on* the new discovery.

Usually the idea intended by *center around* is best expressed by *revolve around*.

> EXAMPLE The Senate hearings on no-fault insurance *revolve around* present insurance rates.

chair/chairperson/chairman/chairwoman

The terms *chair, chairperson, chairman*, and *chairwoman* all are used to refer to a presiding officer. The titles *chair* and *chairperson*, however, avoid any sexual bias that might be implied by the other titles.

> EXAMPLES Mary Roberts preceded John Stevens as *chairperson* (or *chair*) of the executive committee.
>   Mary Roberts was *chairwoman* of the executive committee before John Stevens became *chairman*.

character

Character, used in the sense of "nature" or "quality," is often an unnecessary and inexact filler that should be omitted from your writing. Choose instead a word that conveys your meaning more specifically.

> CHANGE The modifications changed the whole *character* of the engine.
>   TO The modifications changed the performance of the engine.

chronological method of development

The chronological method of development arranges the events under discussion in sequential order, beginning with the first event and continuing chronologically to the last event. **Trip reports**, work schedules, some **minutes of meetings**, and certain **trouble reports** are among the types of writing in which information is organized chronologically.

```
To:      Joanna Sanchez
From:    Larry Brown      𝓛𝓑
Date:    November 5, 19--

Subject: Reducing Shoplifting

Over the past year my staff and I have taken a number of measures
to try to reduce the amount of shoplifting in the downtown store.
As you know, we've spent much time, effort, and money on the
problem, which we hope will be alleviated during the Christmas
shopping season.  Let me recap the specific steps we have taken.


Task Force

We formed a task force of salespeople, buyers, managers, and ex-
ecutive staff to recommend ways of curtailing shoplifting and
methods of implementing our recommendations.  We met four times
during January and twice in March to reach our final recommenda-
tions.  During the meetings. . . .


Mark IV Surveillance System

In April we installed a Mark IV System, which uses closed-circuit
TV cameras at each exit.  The cameras are linked with our secu-
rity office and are capable of taping signals from all exits si-
multaneously.  The task force felt the Mark IV System might be
useful in detecting a pattern of specific individuals entering
and leaving the store.  This system, which was operational on
April 20, has been very helpful in. . . .


Employee Training

During May and June we held workshops for employees on detecting
shoplifters.  We used the consulting firm of Security, Inc.,
which provided not only lectures and tips on spotting shoplifters
but also demonstrations of common techniques used to divert store
personnel.  All those who attended the workshops thought they
were quite helpful. . . .


Other Steps Taken

Since the task force determined that certain items were particu-
larly vulnerable to shoplifters, we decided to restructure some
of the display areas.  Our purpose was to make these areas less
isolated from the view of clerks and other store personnel and
thus less vulnerable.  The remodeling, most of which was rela-
tively minor, was completed over the summer months.

     For the fall and holiday sales, we have hired extra uni-
formed security guards.  These guards, also from Security, Inc.,
should deter first-time shoplifters, although we know that. . . .

     We believe the steps we have taken will substantially reduce
theft.  Of course, after we've reviewed the figures at the end of
the year, the task force intends to meet again in January to re-
view the success of the methods we have employed.  If you need
more details, please let me know.


bb
```

Figure 1   Chronological Method of Development

In the **report** shown in Figure 1, the writer describes one department store's efforts to reduce shoplifting. After providing an **opening** to orient the **reader,** the writer presents the steps taken in chronological order.

cite/site/sight

Cite means "acknowledge" or "quote an authority"; *site* is the place or plot of land where something is located; *sight* is the ability to see.

EXAMPLES The speaker *cited* several famous economists to support his prediction about the stock market.

The *site* for the new factory is three miles from the middle of town.

After the accident, his vision was blurred, and he feared that he might lose his *sight*.

clarity

No element is more essential to writing than clarity. You should strive to make all of your writing direct, orderly, and precise. Many factors contribute to clarity just as many other elements can defeat it. Logical development, unity, coherence, emphasis, subordination, pace, transition, an established point of view, conciseness, and word choice contribute to clarity. **Ambiguity**, **awkwardness**, vagueness, poor use of **idiom**, **clichés**, and inappropriate level of usage detract from clarity.

It is surely evident that a logical **method of development** and a good outline are essential to clarity. Without a logical method of development and an outline, you may communicate only isolated thoughts to your **reader**, and your **objective** cannot be achieved by a jumble of isolated thoughts. You must use a method of development that puts your thoughts together in a logical, meaningful sequence. Only then will your writing achieve the **unity** and **coherence** so vital to clarity.

Proper **emphasis** and **subordination** are mandatory if you wish to achieve clarity. If you do not use these two complementary techniques wisely, your **clauses** and sentences all may appear to be of equal importance. Your reader will be forced to guess which are most important, which are least important, and which fall between the two extremes. At the very least, this will puzzle and annoy your reader; at worst, it will render your writing incoherent.

The **pace** at which you present your ideas is important to clarity because if the pace is not carefully adjusted to both the **topic** and the reader, your writing will appear cluttered and unclear.

Point of view establishes through whose eyes, or from what vantage point, the reader views the subject. A consistent point of view is essential to clarity; if you switch from the first person to the third person in midsentence, you are certain to confuse your reader.

Clear **transition** contributes to clarity by providing the smooth flow that enables the reader to connect your thoughts with one another without conscious effort. This enables the reader to concentrate solely on absorbing your ideas.

That **conciseness** is a requirement of clearly written communication should be evident to anyone who has ever attempted to decipher an insurance policy or legal contract. Although words are our chief means of communication, too many of them can impede communication just as effectively as too many cars on a highway can impede traffic. For the sake of clarity, prune excess verbiage from your writing.

The selection of precise words over **vague words** is **word choice**. Thoughtful choice of the right word advances clarity by defeating ambiguity and awkwardness.

Another important contributor to clarity is a careful and methodical approach to your writing project, including proper application of all the steps of the writing process—**preparation**, **research**, **organization**, **writing the draft**, and **revision**.

clauses

A clause is a syntactical construction, or group of words, that contains a **subject** and a **predicate** and functions as part of a sentence. A clause that could stand alone as a **simple sentence** is an **independent clause**.

> EXAMPLE *The scaffolding fell* when the rope broke.

A clause that could not stand alone if the rest of the sentence were deleted is a **dependent clause**.

> EXAMPLE I was at the St. Louis branch *when the decision was made.*

Every subject–predicate word group in a sentence is a clause. Unlike a **phrase**, a clause can make a complete statement because it contains a finite **verb** (as opposed to **verbals**) as well as a subject. Every sentence must contain at least one independent clause, with the obvious exception of minor sentences—**sentence fragments** that are acceptable because the missing part is clearly understood, such as "At last." or "So much for that."

A clause may function as a **noun**, an **adjective**, or an **adverb** in a larger sentence, or it may be modified by one or more other clauses that are subordinate to it.

EXAMPLE   While I was in college, I studied differential equations.

While I was in college is an **adverb clause** modifying the verb of the independent clause *I studied differential equations.*

A clause may be connected with the rest of its sentence by a **coordinating conjunction**, a **subordinating conjunction**, a **relative pronoun**, or a **conjunctive adverb**.

EXAMPLES   It was 500 miles to the facility, *so* we made arrangements to fly. (coordinating conjunction)
She left the office *after* she finished the report. (subordinating conjunction)
It was the traffic manager *who* approved the new truck route. (relative pronoun)
It was dark when we arrived; *nevertheless,* we began the tour of the factory. (conjunctive adverb)

INDEPENDENT CLAUSES

Unlike a dependent clause, which is part of a larger construction, an independent clause is complete in itself; it could stand alone as a separate sentence if taken out of its larger sentence.

EXAMPLE   *We abandoned the project* because the cost was excessive.

DEPENDENT CLAUSES

A dependent, or subordinate, clause is a group of words that has a subject and a verb but must nonetheless depend on a main clause to complete its meaning. Within the sentence as a whole, a dependent clause can function as a noun, an adjective, or an adverb.

A **noun clause** is a subordinate clause that functions as a noun. It can be a subject, an **object**, or a **complement**.

EXAMPLES   *Why the report took three months to prepare* is a mystery to me. (subject)
Mr. Yen told me *that you are a key-punch operator.* (direct object)
That is not *what I meant.* (subjective complement)

Noun clauses are frequently introduced by interrogative and **relative pronouns** and adverbs (*which, who, what, when, where,* and *why*).

The **conjunction** *that* (not the relative pronoun) is also commonly used.

A noun clause can fit any sentence position that can be occupied by a noun.

EXAMPLES *That we had succeeded* pleased us. (subject)

The treasurer admitted *that he had made a mistake.* (direct object of verb)

Upon retirement, she's going back to *where she came from.* (object of preposition)

Help out by doing *what you can.* (direct object of gerund)

Give *whoever comes* a ticket. (indirect object)

The main thing we should remember, *that we are in business to make a profit,* is the thing we seem to be forgetting. (appositive)

He made himself *what he wanted to be.* (objective complement)

Noun clauses appear often in definitions and explanations as **subjective complements**.

EXAMPLE A common theory is *that competition keeps prices low.*

An adjective clause is a subordinate **clause** that functions as an adjective by modifying a noun or pronoun in another clause.

EXAMPLE The designer *we commissioned last year* (modifying "designer") has delivered the drawings *which we have approved* (modifying "drawings").

Adjective clauses are often introduced by **relative pronouns** (*who, that,* and *which*).

EXAMPLE Our culture is beginning to produce a breed of people *who are very mobile.*

Adjective clauses are also sometimes introduced by relative adverbs (*when, where,* and *why*).

EXAMPLE The fourth quarter is the period *when cost control will be crucial.*

Adjective clauses may be **restrictive** or nonrestrictive. If the clause is essential to limiting the meaning of the noun, it is restrictive and not set off by **commas**.

EXAMPLE The statistics *that accompany this report* were compiled from a series of questionnaires.

If the clause is not intended to limit the meaning of the noun but merely provides further information about it, the clause is nonrestrictive and set off by commas.

> EXAMPLE New statistics, *which we will submit soon*, suggest a different conclusion.

If adjective clauses are not placed carefully, they may appear to modify the wrong noun or pronoun.

> CHANGE The factory in the suburbs *that we bought* has increased in value. (This sentence implies that we bought the suburbs rather than the factory.)
> TO The factory *that we bought* in the suburbs has increased in value.
> OR The suburban factory *that we bought* has increased in value.

(See also **that/which/who**.)

An adverb clause is a subordinate clause used to modify a verb, adjective, or adverb in the main clause.

> EXAMPLE The property is located *where the railroad track crosses the road.*

Like adverbs, adverb clauses normally express such ideas as those of time, place, condition, cause, manner, or **comparison**.

> EXAMPLES It stopped *after we installed the new bearings.* (time)
> It stopped *where the previous model stopped.* (place)
> *If we install the new bearings again*, it will stop again. (condition)
> It stopped *because we installed the bearings.* (cause)
> It stopped *as though it had run into a wall.* (manner)
> The new bearings perform no better *than the old bearings did.* (comparison)

Adverb clauses are often introduced by **subordinating conjunctions** (*because, when, where, since, though*, and the like). If the adverb clause follows the main clause, a **comma** should not normally separate the two clauses.

> EXAMPLE We are being especially cautious about expansion *because interest rates are rising.*

If the adverb clause precedes the main clause, the adverb clause should be set off by a comma.

> EXAMPLE *Because interest rates are rising*, we are being especially cautious about expansion.

Placement of an adverb clause can change the **emphasis** of a sentence. Do not allow this to happen inadvertently.

EXAMPLES   Ruins and artifacts are mere objects of curiosity *unless they are used to reconstruct the daily activities of prehistoric peoples.*
Unless they are used to reconstruct the daily activities of prehistoric peoples, ruins and artifacts are mere objects of curiosity.
Ruins and artifacts, *unless they are used to reconstruct the daily activities of prehistoric peoples,* are mere objects of curiosity.

An adverb clause cannot act as the **subject** of a sentence.

CHANGE   *Because medical expenses have increased* is the reason health insurance rates have gone up.

TO   Health insurance rates have gone up *because medical expenses have increased.*

OR   *Because medical expenses have increased,* health insurance rates have gone up.

cliches

A cliché is an expression that has been used for so long that it is no longer fresh (although some clichés were, at one time, fresh **figures of speech**). Because they have been used continually over a long period of time, clichés come to mind easily. In addition to being stale, clichés are usually wordy and often vague. Each of the following clichés is followed by better, more direct, words or expressions:

EXAMPLES   quick as a flash   quickly, in five minutes
straight from the shoulder   frank
last but not least   last, finally
as plain as day   clear, obvious
abreast of the times   up to date, current
the modern business world   business today

Clichés are often used in an attempt to make writing elegant or impressive. (See also **affectation**.) Because they are wordy and vague, however, they slow communication and can even irritate your **reader**. So, although clichés come to mind easily while you are **writing the draft**, they normally should be eliminated during the **revision** phase of the writing process.

On rare occasions, certain clichés, because they are so much a part of the language, may provide (much like **jargon**) a time-saving and efficient means of relating an idea. For example, "guardedly optimistic" or "if I can help further, please let me know" may, in appropriate contexts, best express your idea—provided you are certain that the expression is meaningful and acceptable to your reader. Be on guard, however, because clichés can too easily become the pattern of your **word choice**. The best advice is to avoid clichés if *any* other choice of words will work. Consider the following **paragraphs**, first with clichés and then rewritten without them:

> CHANGE Our new computer system will have a positive impact on the company *as a whole*. It will keep us *abreast of the times* and make our competition *green with envy*. The committee deserves a *pat on the back* for its *herculean efforts* in convincing management that it was *the thing to do*. I'm sure that their *untiring efforts* will *not go unrewarded*.

> TO Our new computer system will have a positive impact throughout the company. It will keep our operations up-to-date and make our competition envious. The committee deserves credit for their efforts in convincing management of the need for the computer. I'm sure that the value of their efforts will be recognized.

clipped forms of words

When the beginning or end of a word is cut off to create a shorter word, the result is called a *clipped form*.

> EXAMPLES dorm, lab, demo, phone, memo

In the insurance business, for example, policies that pay dividends are called *participating* policies, and policies that do not pay dividends are called *nonparticipating* policies. In the insurance industry, they are known respectively as *par* and *nonpar* policies. As a rule, it is better to avoid clipped forms; however, where these are part of a special vocabulary, such as *par* and *nonpar* in the insurance industry, they are acceptable.

Apostrophes are not normally used with clipped forms of words (not *'phone*, but *phone*). Since they are not strictly **abbreviations**, clipped forms are not followed by **periods** (not *lab.*, but *lab*).

Do not use clipped forms of **spelling** (*thru*, *nite*, and the like).

coherence

Writing is coherent when the relationships among ideas are made clear to the reader. Coherent writing moves logically and consistently from point to point. Each idea should relate clearly to others, with one idea flowing smoothly to the next. Many elements contribute to smooth and coherent writing; however, the major components are (1) a logical sequence of ideas and (2) clear **transitions** between ideas.

A logical sequence of presentation is the most important single requirement in achieving coherence, and the key to achieving the most logical sequence of presentation is the use of a good **outline**. The outline forces you to establish a beginning (**introduction**), a middle (body), and an end (**conclusion**), and this alone contributes greatly to coherence. The outline also enables you to lay out the most direct route to your **objective**—without digressing into interesting but only loosely related side issues, a habit that inevitably defeats coherence. Drawing up an outline permits you to experiment with different sequences and choose the best one.

Thoughtful transition is also essential to coherence, for without it your writing cannot achieve the smooth flow from sentence to sentence and from **paragraph** to paragraph that is required for coherence. Notice the difference between the following two paragraphs; the first has no transition and the second has transition added.

CHANGE The moon has always been an object of interest to human beings. Until the 1960s, getting there was only a dream. Some thought that we were not meant to go to the moon. In 1969 Neil Armstrong stepped onto the lunar surface. Moon landings became routine to the general public.

TO The moon has always been an object of interest to human beings, *but* until the 1960s, getting there was only a dream. *In fact*, some thought that we were not meant to go to the moon. *However*, in 1969 Neil Armstrong stepped onto the lunar surface. *After that* moon landings became routine to the general public.

The transitional words and expressions of the second paragraph fit the ideas snugly together, making that paragraph read more smoothly than the first. Attention to transition in longer works is essential if your reader is to move smoothly from point to point in your writing.

Providing your readers with sentence variety also contributes greatly to making your writing coherent: provide variety in **sentence construction** (not beginning every sentence with an **article** and a **noun**, for example), in **sentence types** (using **complex sentences**, for example, in addition to **simple sentences** and **compound sentences**), and in sentence length (if you write only long sentences, you'll put your readers to sleep; if you write only short sentences, you'll have a jack-hammer effect on them).

Check your draft carefully for coherence during **revision**; if your writing is not coherent, you are not really communicating with your **reader**.

collaborative writing

Collaborative writing occurs when two or more writers work to-gether to produce a single document for which they share respon-sibility and decision-making authority. The collaborating writers make approximately equal contributions, and communication among them is among equals, never superior to subordinate.

Collaborative writing teams are formed when (1) the size of a project or the time constraints imposed on it requires collaboration, (2) the project needs multiple areas of expertise, or (3) the project requires the melding of divergent views to form a single perspective that is acceptable to the whole collaborating team or another group.

Although the collaborative writing team is composed of peers, its members recognize and take advantage of the expertise of each member. Team members must respect the professional capabilities of one another and be compatible enough to work together in harmony, although some conflict is a natural part of any group project.

The team must designate one person as its leader, although that person does not have decision-making authority, just the extra re-sponsibility of coordinating the activities of the team members and organizing the project. Team leadership can be by mutual agree-ment of the team members, or it can be on a rotating basis if the team produces multiple documents. Being team leader bestows no par-ticular advantages; the team leader just does administrative work in addition to his or her normal writing duties.

TASKS OF THE COLLABORATIVE WRITING TEAM

The collaborative writing team normally has four tasks: planning the document, researching and writing the draft, reviewing the drafts of other team members, and revising the drafts on the basis of the reviewers' comments.

Planning. The team, collectively, should identify the audience, purpose, and scope of the project, as well as its goals and the most

effective organization for the whole document. The team analyzes the overall project, conceptualizes the document to be produced, creates a broad outline of the document, divides the document into segments, and assigns different segments to individual team members (often on the basis of expertise).

The team then plans, as a group, to the lowest level that is practical. Beyond a certain level, of course, the group does not have sufficient command of details to plan realistically and must leave any further planning to the individual team member who has the assigned responsibility for researching a specific section of the document.

In the planning stage, the team should produce a projected schedule and set any writing style standards that team members will be expected to meet. The agreed-on schedule should include the due dates for drafts, for reviews of the drafts by other team members, and for revisions. It is important that these deadlines be met, even if the drafts are not quite as polished as the individual author would like, because a missed deadline by one team member holds up the work of the entire team. All members should be familiar with the schedule and make every effort to meet it.

The team should not insist that the agreed-on broad outline be followed slavishly by individual team members. Once into the assignment, an individual writer may—and often will—find that the broad outline for a specific segment was based on insufficient knowledge and presents a plan that, in fact, is not possible or not desirable. The individual team member must be allowed the freedom to alter the broad outline on the basis of what is possible, more appropriate, or clearly more desirable.

Research and Writing. Planning is followed by research and writing, a period of intense independent activity by the individual members of the team. Each member researches his or her assigned segment of the document, fleshes out the broad outline with greater detail, and produces a draft from the detailed outline. The writers revise their drafts until they are as good as the individual writers can make them. Then, by the deadline established for drafts, the individual writers submit copies of their drafts to all other members of the team for review.

Reviewing. During the review stage, team members assume the role of the reading audience and try to clear up in advance any problems that might arise for the reader. Each team member reviews the

work of the other team members carefully and critically, but diplomatically. Team members review for things both large and small: They evaluate the organization of each segment, as well as each sentence and paragraph. They offer any advice or help that will enable the individual writer to improve his or her segment of the document.

The review stage may lead to renewed planning. If, for example, review makes it obvious that the original planning for a section was inadequate or incorrect, or if new information becomes available, the team must rethink the plan for that segment of the document on the basis of the newer understanding and knowledge.

Revising. The individual writers evaluate the reviews of all other team members and accept or reject their suggestions. Writers must be careful not to let ego get in the way of good judgment. They must evaluate each suggestion objectively—on the basis of its merit—rather than emotionally. The ability to accept criticism and use it to produce a better end product is one of the critical differences between an effective collaborator and an ineffective one.

Conflict. Members of a team never have exactly the same perspective on any subject, and differing perspectives can easily lead to conflict. A team that can tolerate some disharmony yet work through conflicting opinions to reach consensus produces better results. Although mutual respect among team members is necessary, too much deference can inhibit challenges—and that actually reduces the team's creativity. Writers must be willing to challenge one another—tactfully and diplomatically, however.

It is critically important to the quality of the document being produced that all viewpoints be considered. Under such circumstances, conflicts will occur, ranging from relatively mild differences over minor points to major conflicts over the basic approach. Regardless of the severity of the conflict, it must be worked through to a conclusion or a compromise that all team members can accept, even though all might not entirely agree.

THE ADVANTAGES OF COLLABORATIVE WRITING

The work a collaborative writing team produces can be considerably better than the work any one of its members could have produced alone. This is true, at least in part, because team members lead each other to consider ideas different from those they would have explored individually.

Getting immediate feedback—even if it is sometimes contested and debated—is one of the great advantages of the peer writing team. Team members easily detect problems with organization, clarity, logic, and substance, and they point these things out during reviews.

Another advantage is that team members play devil's advocate for one another, taking contrary points of view to try to make certain that all important points are covered and that all potential problems have been exposed and resolved.

As a team member, you become more aware of, and involved in, the planning of a document than you would working alone, because of the team discussions that take place during the planning stage. The same is true of reviewing and revising.

collection letters

With the expansion of credit in recent decades, all companies now need to send collection letters. These letters serve a two-fold purpose of (1) collecting the overdue bill and (2) preserving the customer relationship.

Most companies send a series of collection letters in which the letters become increasingly demanding and urgent, though the number and frequency of letters sent varies from one company to another. Although many firms rely on form letters, a short, personal note will usually motivate a customer to pay a bill faster than will a form letter. Collection letters should be polite; you can demonstrate insistence with the letters' frequency as well as with their **tone**. The intervals between letters should be long enough for the customer to respond, however. Generally, you should be more patient with a steady, long-time customer than with a new or unknown customer.

The collection process may vary from one business to another. A furrier, for example, might give customers a longer time to pay than would a discount hardware store. Competition is also a factor: If your major competitors give customers eight months before starting legal action, you should not take action after only two months.

A series of collection letters usually proceeds in three stages, each of which may include several letters. All letters, even form messages, must be courteous and should show a genuine interest in the customer as well as concern for whatever problems are preventing prompt payment.

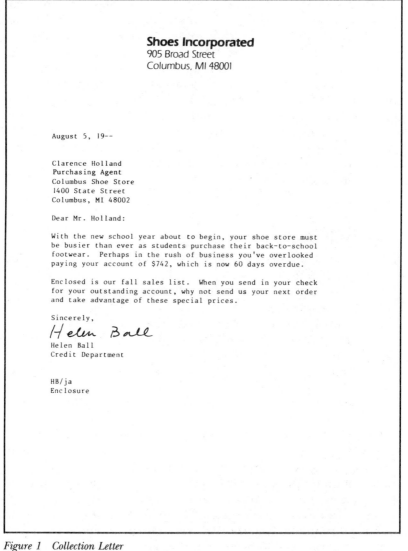

Figure 1 *Collection Letter*

The first stage of collection letters consists of reminders stamped on the invoice, form letters, or brief personal notes. These early reminders should maintain a friendly tone that emphasizes the customer's good credit record until now. You should remind him or her

---

Shoes Incorporated
905 Broad Street
Columbus, MI 48001

November 5, 19--

Clarence Holland
Purchasing Agent
Columbus Shoe Store
1400 State Street
Columbus, MI 48002

Dear Mr. Holland:

We are concerned that we have not heard from you about your
overdue account of $742, even though we have written 3 times
in the past 90 days. Since you have always been one of our
best customers, we have to wonder whether some special circumstances
have caused the delay; if so, please feel free to discuss the
matter with us.

By sending us a check today, you can preserve your excellent
credit record. Because you have always paid you account promptly
in the past, we are sure that you will want to settle this balance
now. If your balance is more than you can pay right now, we
will be happy to work out satisfactory payment arrangements.

Please use the enclosed envelope to send in your check, or call
(800) 526-1945, toll-free, to discuss your account.

Sincerely,

Helen Ball

Helen Ball
Credit Department

HB/ja
Enclosure

Figure 2   Collection Letter

of the debt and indicate that you are sure that payment has merely
been overlooked. You may even solicit additional business by including promotion for new sales items, as is done in Figure 1.

Shoes Incorporated
905 Broad Street
Columbus, MI 48001

December 5, 19--

Clarence Holland
Purchasing Agent
Columbus Shoe Store
1400 State Street
Columbus, MI 48002

Dear Mr. Holland:

Your account in the amount of $742 is now 120 days overdue.
You have already received a generous extension of time, and in
fairness to our other customers, we cannot permit a longer delay
in payment.

Because you have not responded to any of our letters, we will
be forced to turn your account over to our attorney for collection
if we do not receive payment immediately. Such action, of course,
will damage your previously fine credit rating.

Why not avoid this unpleasant situation by sending your check
in the enclosed return envelope within 10 days or by calling
(800) 526-1945 to discuss payment.

Sincerely,

Helen Ball

Helen Ball
Credit Department

HB/ja
Enclosure

Figure 3   Collection Letter

In the second stage the collection letters are more than just
reminders. You now assume that some circumstances are preventing
payment. Ask directly for payment, and inquire about possible
problems, perhaps inviting the customer to discuss the matter with

you. If you have a standard optional payment plan, you might suggest it to him. Mention the importance of good credit, appealing to
his pride and self-esteem as well as to his sense of fair play. Remind
him that he has always received good value from you. Make it easy
to respond by enclosing a return envelope or by offering a toll-free
telephone number. In this stage your tone should be firmer and
more direct than in the early stage, but never rude, sarcastic, or
threatening. Notice that Figure 2 is more direct than the first letter,
but no less polite.

The third stage of collection letters reflects a sense of urgency, for
the customer has not responded to your previous letters. Although
your tone should remain courteous, make your demand for payment explicit. Point out how reasonable you have been, and urge the
customer to pay at once to avoid legal action. Again, make it easy
to respond by providing a return envelope and a toll-free telephone
number, as is done in Figure 3.

collective nouns

Collective nouns name a group or collection of persons, places,
things, concepts, actions, or qualities.

> EXAMPLE army, committee, crowd, team, public, class, jury, humanity

When a collective noun refers to a group as a whole, it takes a singular verb and pronoun.

> EXAMPLE The staff *was* divided on the issue and could not reach *its* deci-
> sion until May 15.

When a collective noun refers to individuals within a group, it takes
a plural verb and pronoun.

> EXAMPLE The staff returned to *their* offices after the conference.

A better way to emphasize the individuals on the staff would be to
use the phrase *members of the staff*.

> EXAMPLE The members of the staff returned to *their* offices after the
> conference.

Organizational titles, such as *company* and *department*, can be either
singular or plural.

EXAMPLES LRM Company has grown 200 percent in the last three years; *it* will move to a new facility in January.

LRM Company will submit an environmental report in November. *They* will present it at the next County Commission meeting.

Where any **pronoun reference** confusion could occur, substitute an appropriate noun.

EXAMPLE LRM Company submitted several environmental impact statements. LRM *scientists* [rather than *they*] are meeting with government officials to revise these statements.

Some collective nouns regularly take singular verbs (*crowd*); others do not (*people*).

EXAMPLES *The crowd was* growing impatient.
Many *people were* able to watch the first space shuttle land safely.

Some collective nouns have regular plural forms (*team, teams*); others do not (*sheep*). (For additional information about the **case**, **number**, and function of collective nouns, see **nouns**.)

colloquialism (see **English, varieties of**)

colons

The colon is a mark of anticipation and introduction that alerts the **reader** to the close connection between the first statement and the one that follows it.

A colon may be used to connect a list or series to the **clause**, word, or **phrase** with which it is in apposition.

EXAMPLE We carry two brands of watches: Timex and Bulova.

Do not, however, place a colon between a **verb** and its **objects**.

CHANGE The three fluids for cleaning pipettes are: water, alcohol, and acetone.
TO The three fluids for cleaning pipettes are water, alcohol, and acetone.

One common exception is made when a verb is followed by a stacked list.

EXAMPLE The corporations that manufacture computers include:
NCR   CDC   DEC
Compaq   IBM   Apple
Unisys

Do not use a colon between a **preposition** and its object.

CHANGE I would like to be transferred to: Tucson, Boston, or Miami.
TO I would like to be transferred to Tucson, Boston, or Miami.

A colon may be used to link one statement to another that develops, explains, amplifies, or illustrates the first. A colon may be used in this way to link two **independent clauses**.

EXAMPLE Any large organization is confronted with two separate, though related, information problems: it must maintain an effective internal communication system, and it must see that an effective overall communication system is maintained.

A colon may be used to link an **appositive** phrase to its related statement if greater **emphasis** is needed.

EXAMPLE There is only one thing that will satisfy Mr. Sturgess: our finished report.

Colons are used to link numbers signifying different identifying **nouns**.

EXAMPLES Matthew 14:1 (chapter 14, verse 1)
9:30 a.m. (9 hours, 30 minutes)

In proportions, the colon indicates the ratio of one amount to another.

EXAMPLE The cement is mixed with the water and sand at 7:5:14. (In this case, the colon replaces *to*.)

Colons are often used in mathematical ratios.

EXAMPLE $7:3 = 14:x$

In **bibliography** and footnote entries, colons may link the place of publication with the publisher and perform other specialized functions.

EXAMPLE Aaron, John. *Business Letters*. Boston: Bane, 1970.

A colon follows the salutation in business letters:

EXAMPLES   Dear Ms. Jeffers:
Dear Manager:
Dear George:

The initial **capital letter** of a **quotation** is retained following a colon if the quoted material originally began with a capital letter.

EXAMPLE   The senator issued the following statement: "We are not concerned about the present. We are worried about the future."

A colon always goes outside **quotation marks**.

EXAMPLE   This was the real meaning of his "suggestion": the division must show a profit by the end of the year.

When quoting material that ends in a colon, drop the colon and replace it with **ellipses**.

CHANGE   "Any large corporation is confronted with two separate, though related, information problems:"

TO   "Any large corporation is confronted with two separate, though related, information problems . . ."

The first word after a colon may be capitalized if (1) the statement following is a complete **sentence** or (2) it introduces a formal resolution or question.

EXAMPLE   The members attending this year's conference passed a single resolution: Voting will be open to associate members next year.

If a subordinate element follows the colon, however, use a lowercase letter following the colon.

EXAMPLE   There is only one way to stay within our present budget: to reduce expenditures for research and development.

comma splice

Do not attempt to join two **independent clauses** with only a **comma**; this is called a *comma splice*.

EXAMPLE   It was five hundred miles to the facility, we made arrangements to fly.

Such a comma splice could be corrected in several ways.

1. Substitute a **semicolon**, or a semicolon and a **conjunctive adverb**.

> CHANGE It was five hundred miles to the facility, we made arrangements to fly.
>
> TO It was five hundred miles to the facility; we made arrangements to fly.
>
> OR It was five hundred miles to the facility; *therefore*, we made arrangements to fly.

2. Add a **coordinating conjunction** following the comma.

> EXAMPLE It was five hundred miles to the facility, *so* we made arrangements to fly.

3. Create two sentences. (Be aware, however, that putting a **period** between two closely related and brief statements may result in two weak sentences.)

> EXAMPLE It was five hundred miles to the facility. We made arrangements to fly.

4. Subordinate one **clause** to the other.

> EXAMPLE *Because* it was five hundred miles to the facility, we made arrangements to fly.

When a conjunctive adverb connects two independent clauses, the conjunctive adverb *must* be preceded by a semicolon and followed by a comma.

> CHANGE It was five hundred miles to the facility, therefore, we made arrangements to fly.
>
> TO It was five hundred miles to the facility; therefore, we made arrangements to fly.

commas

Like all **punctuation**, the comma helps **readers** understand the writer's meaning and prevents **ambiguity**. Notice how the comma helps make the meaning clear in the following examples:

> CHANGE To be successful managers with MBAs must continue to learn. (At first reading, the sentence, seems to be about "successful managers with MBAs.")
>
> TO To be successful, managers with MBAs must continue to learn. (The comma makes clear where the main part of the sentence begins.)

CHANGE   When you see an airport fly directly over it at an altitude of
1,500 feet. (At first glance, the sentence seems to have the
airport flying.)

TO   When you see an airport, fly directly over it at an altitude of
1,500 feet. (The comma makes clear where the main part of
the sentence begins.)

As these examples illustrate, effective use of the comma depends on
your understanding of **sentence construction**.

To help you find the advice you need, the following entry is divided into the following uses of the comma:

Linking Independent Clauses
Enclosing Elements
Introducing Elements
  Clauses and Phrases
  Words and Quotations
Separating Items in a Series
Clarifying and Contrasting
Showing Omissions
Using with Other Punctuation
Using with Numbers and Names
Avoiding Unnecessary Commas

LINKING INDEPENDENT CLAUSES

Use a comma between **independent clauses** that are linked by a
coordinating conjunction (*and, but, or, nor*, and sometimes *so, yet,* and
for). The comma precedes the **conjunction**.

EXAMPLE   Human beings have always prided themselves on their unique
capacity to create and manipulate symbols, but today computers are manipulating symbols.

Although many writers omit the comma when the **clauses** are short
and closely related, the comma can never be wrong.

EXAMPLES   The cable snapped and the power failed.
The cable snapped, and the power failed.

ENCLOSING ELEMENTS

Commas are used to enclose nonrestrictive clauses and parenthetical elements. (For other means of punctuating parenthetical elements, see **dashes** and **parentheses**.)

EXAMPLES   Our new Detroit factory, *which began operations last month,* should add 25 percent to total output. (nonrestrictive clause)

We can, *of course,* expect their lawyer to call us. (parenthetical element).

(See also **restrictive and nonrestrictive elements.**)

Yes and *no* are set off by commas in such uses as the following:

EXAMPLES   I agree with you, *yes.*

No, I do not think we can finish as soon as we would like.

A **direct address** should be enclosed in commas.

EXAMPLE   You will note, *Mark,* that the surface of the brake shoe complies with the specifications.

Phrases in apposition (which identify another expression) are enclosed in commas.

EXAMPLE   Our company, *The Blaylok Precision Company,* did well this year.

Commas enclose nonrestrictive **participial phrases.**

EXAMPLE   The lathe operator, *working quickly and efficiently,* finished early.

Interrupting transitional words or phrases are usually set off with commas.

EXAMPLE   We must wait for the written authorization to arrive, *however,* before we can begin work on the project.

Commas are omitted when the word or phrase does not interrupt the continuity of thought.

EXAMPLE   I *therefore* suggest that we begin construction.

INTRODUCING ELEMENTS

Clauses and Phrases. It is generally a good rule of thumb to put a comma after an introductory clause or phrase. Identifying where the introductory element ends helps indicate where the main part of the sentence begins.

EXAMPLE   *Since many rare fossils seem never to occur free from their matrix,* it is wise to scan every slab with a hand lens.

In all cases, use a comma following a long introductory dependent clause.

EXAMPLES When they artificially stimulated the electrochemical action of the brain, scientists learned more about the brain.
While the angry crowd outside the embassy waited, the ambassador drank cocktails.

When long modifying phrases precede the main clause, they should always be followed by a comma.

EXAMPLE *During the first series of field-performance tests last year at our Colorado proving ground,* the new motor failed to meet our expectations.

When an introductory phrase is short and closely related to the main clause, the comma may be omitted.

EXAMPLE *In five minutes* the meeting will begin.

A comma should always follow an introductory absolute phrase.

EXAMPLE *The tests completed,* we organized the data for the final report.

Words and Quotations. Certain types of introductory words are followed by a comma. One such is a **noun** used in direct address.

EXAMPLE *Bill,* enclosed is the statement you asked me to audit.

An introductory **interjection** (such as *oh, well, why, indeed, yes,* and *no*) is followed by a comma.

EXAMPLES *Yes,* I will make sure your request is approved.
Indeed, I will be glad to send you further information.

A transitional word or phrase like *moreover* or *furthermore* is usually followed by a comma.

EXAMPLE *Moreover,* our balance of payments will be better because of this policy.

Introductory **adverbs** and adverb phrases are set off with a comma when they serve the dual function of modifying the idea that follows and connecting it to the idea in the previous sentence. (See also **transition**.)

EXAMPLE We can expect a better balance of payments in the coming year. *In addition,* we should look for a better world market as a result. *However,* we should expect some shortages due to the overall economic climate.

When adverbs closely modify the **verb** or the entire sentence, however, they should not be followed by a comma.

EXAMPLE *Perhaps* we can still solve the environmental problem. *Certainly* we should try.

Use a comma to separate a direct quotation from its introduction.

EXAMPLE Morton and Lucia White said, "Men live in cities but dream of the countryside."

Do not use a comma, however, when giving an indirect quotation.

EXAMPLE Morton and Lucia White said that men dream of the countryside, even though they live in cities.

SEPARATING ITEMS IN A SERIES

Although the comma before the last word in a series is sometimes omitted, it is generally clearer to include it. The confusion that can result from omitting the comma is illustrated in the following example.

CHANGE Random House, Irwin, Doubleday and Dell are publishing companies. (Is "Doubleday and Dell" one company or two?)

TO Random House, Irwin, Doubleday, and Dell are publishing companies.

The presence of a comma removes the ambiguity.

Phrases and clauses in coordinate series, like words, are punctuated with commas.

EXAMPLE It is well known that plants absorb noxious gases, act as receptors of dirt particles, and cleanse the air of other impurities.

When **adjectives** modifying the same noun can be reversed and make sense, or when they can be separated by *and* or *or*, they should be separated by commas.

EXAMPLE The company is seeking a *young, energetic, creative* marketing team.

When an adjective modifies a phrase, no comma is required.

EXAMPLE He was wearing his *old cotton tennis hat*. (*old* modifies the phrase *cotton tennis hat*.)

Never separate a final adjective from its noun.

CHANGE He is a conscientious, honest, reliable, worker.

TO He is a conscientious, honest, reliable worker.

CLARIFYING AND CONTRASTING

If you find you need a comma to separate the consecutive use of the same word to prevent misreading, rewrite the sentence.

CHANGE The assets we had, had surprised us.
TO We were surprised at the assets we had.

Use a comma to separate two contrasting thoughts or ideas.

EXAMPLES The project was finished on time, but not within the budget.
The plans call for 100-pound beams, not 1,000-pound beams.
The project was finished on time, wasn't it?
It was Bill, not Matt, who decided to change the terms.
I generally agreed with him, but not completely.

Use a comma following an independent clause that is only loosely related to the **dependent clause** that follows it.

EXAMPLE The plan should be finished by July, even though I lost time because of illness.

SHOWING OMISSIONS

A comma sometimes replaces a verb in certain elliptical constructions.

EXAMPLE Some were punctual; *others, late.* (replaces *were*)

However, it is better to avoid such constructions in on-the-job writing.

USING WITH OTHER PUNCTUATION

Conjunctive adverbs (*however, nevertheless, consequently, for example, on the other hand*) joining independent clauses are preceded by a **semicolon** and followed by a comma. Such adverbs function as both **modifiers** and connectives.

EXAMPLES Your idea is good; *however,* your format is poor.
He has held the project together; *moreover,* he has helped everyone's morale.

Use a semicolon to separate phrases or clauses in a series when one or more of the phrases or clauses contain commas.

EXAMPLE Among those present were John Howard, president of the Howard Paper Company; Thomas Martin, president of Copco Corp.; and Larry Stanley, president of Stanley Papers.

A comma always goes inside **quotation marks**.

EXAMPLE Although he called his presentation "adequate," the audience thought it was superb.

When an introductory phrase or clause ends with a parenthesis, the comma separating the introductory phrase or clause from the rest of the sentence always appears outside the parenthesis.

CHANGE Although we left late (at 7:30 p.m.,) we arrived in time for the keynote address.

TO Although we left late (at 7:30 p.m.), we arrived in time for the keynote address.

Except with **abbreviations**, a comma should not be used with a **period, question mark, exclamation mark**, or **dash**.

CHANGE "I have finished the project.," he said.

TO "I have finished the project," he said. (omit the period)

CHANGE "Have you finished the project?," I asked.

TO "Have you finished the project?" I asked. (omit the comma)

USING WITH NUMBERS AND NAMES

Commas are conventionally used to separate distinct items. Use commas between the elements of an address written on the same line.

EXAMPLE Walter James, 4119 Mill Road, Dayton, Ohio 45401

A date can be written with or without a comma following the year if the date is in the month–day–year format.

EXAMPLES October 26, 19--, was the date the project began.
October 26, 19-- was the date the project began.

If the date is in the day–month–year format, do not set off the date with commas.

EXAMPLE The date was 26 October 19-- when the project began.

Use commas to separate the elements of arabic **numbers**.

EXAMPLE 1,528,200

A comma may be substituted for the **colon** in a personal letter. Do not use a comma in a business letter, however, even if you use the person's first name.

EXAMPLES Dear John, (personal letter)
Dear John: (business letter)

Use commas to separate the elements of geographical names.

EXAMPLE   Toronto, Ontario, Canada

Use a comma to separate names that are reversed or that are followed by an **abbreviation**.

EXAMPLE   Smith, Alvin
Jane Rogers, Ph.D.
LMB, Inc.

Use commas to separate certain elements of footnote and **bibliography** entries.

EXAMPLES   Bibliography—Young, Gerald, ed. *Handbook of Management Information Systems.* Westport, CT: MIS, 1992.
Footnote—[1]Young, Gerald, ed. *Handbook of Management Information Systems* (Westport, CT: MIS, 1992) 30.

AVOIDING UNNECESSARY COMMAS

A number of common writing errors involve placing commas where they do not belong. These errors often occur because writers assume that a pause in a sentence should be indicated by a comma. It is true that commas usually signal pauses, but it is not true that pauses *necessarily* call for commas.

Be careful not to place a comma between a **subject** and verb or between a verb and its **object**.

CHANGE   The cold conditions at the test site in the Arctic, made accurate readings difficult.

TO   The cold conditions at the test site in the Arctic made accurate readings difficult.

CHANGE   He has often said, that one company's failure is another's opportunity.

TO   He has often said that one company's failure is another's opportunity.

Do not use a comma between the elements of a compound subject or a compound **predicate** consisting of only two elements.

CHANGE   The director of the engineering department, and the supervisor of the quality-control section both were opposed to the new schedules.

TO   The director of the engineering department and the supervisor of the quality-control section both were opposed to the new schedules.

CHANGE The director of the engineering department listed five major objections, and asked that the new schedule be reconsidered.

TO The director of the engineering department listed five major objections and asked that the new schedule be reconsidered.

An especially common error is the placing of a comma after a coordinating conjunction such as *and* or *but* (especially *but*).

CHANGE The chairman formally adjourned the meeting, but, the members of the committee continued to argue.

TO The chairman formally adjourned the meeting, but the members of the committee continued to argue.

CHANGE I argued against the proposal. And, I gave good reasons for my position.

TO I argued against the proposal. And I gave good reasons for my position.

Do not place a comma before the first or after the last item of a series.

CHANGE We are considering a number of new products, such as, calculators, scanners, and cameras.

TO We are considering a number of new products, such as calculators, scanners, and cameras.

CHANGE It was a fast, simple, inexpensive, process.

TO It was a fast, simple, inexpensive process.

Do not unnecessarily separate a prepositional phrase from the rest of the sentence with a comma.

CHANGE He met me, in the conference room, down the hall.

TO He met me in the conference room down the hall.

CHANGE We discussed the final report, on the new project.

TO We discussed the final report on the new project.

committee

Committee is a **collective noun** that takes a singular **verb**.

EXAMPLE The *committee is* to meet at 3:30 p.m.

If you wish to emphasize the individuals on the committee, use *the members of the committee* with the plural verb form.

EXAMPLE The *members of the committee were* all in agreement.

common nouns

A common noun names general classes or categories of persons, places, things, concepts, actions, or qualities. Common nouns can be abstract (*justice*), concrete (*jail*), or **collective** (*jury*).

Common Nouns	Proper Nouns
boy	Toby Wilson
city	Chicago
company	General Electric
day	Tuesday
document	Declaration of Independence

Common nouns are not capitalized unless they begin a sentence. (For information about the **case**, **number**, and function of common nouns, see **nouns**.)

comparative degree

Most **adjectives** and **adverbs** can be compared. Their common forms of **comparison** are as follows:

EXAMPLES The new copier is *fast*. (positive)
The new copier is *faster* than the old one. (comparative)
The new copier is the *fastest* I have ever used. (superlative)

Most one-syllable words use the comparative ending *-er* and the superlative ending *-est*.

EXAMPLES Ours was the *faster* of the two cars tested.
Ours was the *fastest* car on the track.

Most words with more than one syllable form the comparative degree by using the word *more* and the superlative degree by using the word *most*.

EXAMPLES She is *more* talented than the rest of the writers on the staff.
She is the *most* talented writer on the staff.

Some words may use either means of expressing degree.

EXAMPLES He was the *most* able technician at the meeting.
He was the *ablest* technician at the meeting.

A few words have irregular forms of comparison.

    EXAMPLES much, more, most
                  good, better, best

Writers often use the comparative degree when comparing two persons or things and the superlative degree when comparing three or more.

    EXAMPLES This is the *newer* of the two policies.
                  This is the *newest* of the three policies.

The superlative form is sometimes also used in expressions that do not really express comparison (*best* wishes, *deepest* sympathy, *highest* praise, and *most* sincerely).

compare/contrast

When you *compare* things, you point out similarities or both similarities and differences. When you *contrast* things, you point out only the differences. In either case, you compare or contrast only things that are part of a common category.

    EXAMPLES He *compared* all the features of the two brands before buying.
                  Their styles of selling *contrasted* sharply.

When *compare* is used to establish a general similarity, it is followed by *to*.

    EXAMPLE *Compared to* the computer, the abacus is a primitive device.

When *compare* is used to indicate a close examination of similarities or differences, it is followed by *with* in formal **usage**.

    EXAMPLE We *compared* the features of the new capacitor very carefully *with* those of the old one.

Contrast is normally followed by *with*.

    EXAMPLE The new policy *contrasts* sharply *with* the earlier one in requiring that sealed bids be submitted.

When the **noun** form of *contrast* is used, one speaks of the *contrast between* two things or of one thing being *in contrast to* the other.

    EXAMPLES There is a sharp *contrast between* the old and new policies.
                 The new policy is *in* sharp *contrast to* the earlier one.

comparison

When making a comparison, make certain that both or all the elements being compared are clearly evident to your **reader**.

> CHANGE The third-generation computer is *better*.
> TO The third-generation computer is *better than the second-generation computer.*

The things being compared must be of the same kind.

> CHANGE *Imitation alligator hide* is almost as tough as a *real alligator*.
> TO *Imitation alligator hide* is almost as tough as *real alligator hide*.

Be sure to point out the parallels or differences between the things being compared. Don't assume your reader will know what you mean.

> CHANGE Washington is farther from Boston *than Philadelphia*.
> TO Washington is farther from Boston *than it is from* Philadelphia.
> OR Washington is farther from Boston *than Philadelphia is*.

A double comparison in the same sentence requires that the first be completed before the second is stated.

> CHANGE The discovery of electricity was *one of the great if not the greatest* scientific discoveries in history.
> TO The discovery of electricity was *one of the great* scientific discoveries in history, *if not the greatest*.

Do not attempt to compare things that are not comparable.

> CHANGE Farmers say that storage space is reduced by 40 percent compared with baled hay. (*Storage space* is not comparable to *baled hay*.)
> TO Farmers say that baled hay requires 40 percent less storage space than loose hay requires.

comparison method of development

As a **method of development**, comparison points out similarities and differences between the elements of your subject. The comparison method of development can be especially effective because it can explain a difficult or unfamiliar subject by relating it to a simpler or more familiar one.

You must first determine the basis for the **comparison**. For example, if you were responsible for the purchase of chain saws for a logging company, you would have a number of factors to take into account in order to establish your bases of comparison. Because loggers use the equipment daily, you would have to select durable saws with the appropriate size engines, chain thicknesses, and bar lengths for the type of wood most frequently cut. Since chain saws produce noise and vibration, you would want to compare the quality and cost of the various silencers on the market. You would not include in your comparison such irrelevant factors as color or place of manufacture. Taking into account all of the important elements, however, you would establish a number of bases for choosing from among the available chain saws—engine size, chain thickness, bar length, and noise mufflers.

Once you have determined the basis (or bases) for comparison, you must decide how to present it. In the whole-by-whole method, all the relevant characteristics of one item are discussed before those of the next item are considered. In the part-by-part method, the relevant features of each item are compared one by one. The following discussion of typical woodworking glues, organized according to the whole-by-whole method, describes each type of glue and its characteristics before going on to the next type.

> *White glue* is the most useful all-purpose adhesive for light construction, but it cannot be used on projects that will be exposed to moisture, high temperature, or great stress. Wood that is being joined with white glue must remain in a clamp until the glue dries, which will take about 30 minutes.
>
> *Aliphatic resin glue* has a stronger and more moisture-resistant bond than white glue. It must be used at temperatures above 50°F. The wood should be clamped for about 30 minutes....
>
> *Plastic resin glue* is the strongest of the common wood adhesives. It is highly moisture resistant—though not completely waterproof. Sold in powdered form, this glue must be mixed with water and used at temperatures above 70°F. It is slow setting and the joint should be clamped for four to six hours....
>
> *Contact cement* is a very strong adhesive that bonds so quickly it must be used with great care. It is ideal for mounting sheets of plastic laminate on wood. It is also useful for attaching strips of veneer to the edges of plywood. Since this adhesive bonds immediately when two pieces are pressed together, clamping is not necessary, but the parts to be joined must be very carefully aligned before being placed together. Most

brands are quite flammable and the fumes can be harmful if inhaled. To meet current safety standards, this type of glue must be used in a well-ventilated area, away from flames or heat.

—*Space and Storage* (Alexandria, VA: Time-Life, 1977) 61.

As is often the case when the whole-by-whole method is used, the purpose of this comparison is to weigh the advantages and disadvantages of each glue for certain kinds of woodworking. The comparison could be expanded, of course, by the addition of other types of glue. If, on the other hand, your purpose were to consider, one at a time, the various characteristics of all the glues, the information might be arranged according to the part-by-part method, as in the following example:

Woodworking adhesives are rated primarily according to their bonding strength, moisture resistance, and setting times.

Bonding strengths are categorized as very strong, moderately strong, or adequate for use with little stress. Contact cement and plastic resin glue bond very strongly, while aliphatic resin glue bonds moderately strongly. White glue provides a bond least resistant to stress.

The moisture resistance of woodworking glues is rated as high, moderate, and low. Plastic resin glues are highly moisture resistant. Aliphatic resin glues are moderately moisture resistant; white glue is least moisture resistant.

Setting times for these glues vary from an immediate bond to a four-to-six-hour bond. Contact cement bonds immediately and requires no clamping. Because the bond is immediate, surfaces being joined must be carefully aligned before being placed together. White glue and aliphatic resin glue set in thirty minutes; both require clamping to secure the bond. Plastic resin, the strongest wood glue, sets in four to six hours and also requires clamping.

The part-by-part method could accommodate further comparison. Comparisons might be made according to temperature ranges, special warnings, common uses, and so on.

complaint letters

Businesses sometimes err when providing goods and services to customers, and so customers write complaint letters (or claim letters) asking that such situations be corrected. The **tone** of such a letter

BAKER MEMORIAL HOSPITAL | *Television Services*
501 Main Street
Springfield, OH 45321
(513) 683-8100

September 23, 19--

General Television, Inc.
5521 West 23rd Street
New York, NY 10062

Attention: Customer Relations Manager

On July 9th I ordered nine TV tuners for your model MX-15 color receiver.
The tuner part number is TR-5771-3.

On August 2nd I received from your Newark, New Jersey, parts warehouse
seven tuners, labeled TR-413-7. I immediately returned these tuners
with a note indicating the mistake that had been made. However, not
only have I failed to receive the tuners I ordered, but I have also
been billed repeatedly.

Please either send me the tuners I ordered or cancel my order. I
have enclosed a copy of my original order and the most recent bill.

Sincerely,

Paul Denlinger
Manager

PD:sj
Enclosure

Figure 1   Complaint Letter

is important; the most effective complaint letters do not sound angry.
Do not use a complaint letter to vent your anger; remember that the
reader of your letter probably had nothing to do with whatever went
wrong, and berating that person is not likely to achieve anything

positive. In most cases, you need only state your claim, support it with all the pertinent facts, and then ask for the desired adjustment. Most companies are very willing to correct whatever went wrong.

The **opening** of your complaint letter should include all identifying data concerning the transaction: item, date of purchase, place of purchase if pertinent, cost, invoice number, and so on.

The body of your letter should explain logically and clearly what happened. You should present any facts that prove the validity of your claim. Be sure of your facts, and present them concisely and objectively, carefully avoiding any overtones of accusation or threat. You may, however, wish to state any inconvenience or loss created by the problem, such as a broken machine stopping an entire assembly line.

Your **conclusion** should be friendly, and it should request action. State what you would like your reader to do to solve your problem.

Large organizations often have special departments to handle complaints. If you address your letter to one of these departments— for example, to Customer Relations or Consumer Affairs—it should reach someone who can respond to your claim. In smaller organizations you might write to a vice-president in charge of sales or service. For a very small business, write directly to the owner.

The example shown in Figure 1 is a typical complaint letter. (See also **adjustment letters** and **refusal letters**.)

complement/compliment

Complement means "anything that completes a whole." It is used as either a **noun** or a **verb**.

> EXAMPLES   A *complement* of four employees would bring our staff up to its normal strength. (noun)
> The two programs *complement* one another perfectly. (verb)

Compliment means "praise." It too is used as either a noun or a verb.

> EXAMPLES   The manager *complimented* the staff on its efficient job. (verb)
> The manager's *compliment* boosted staff morale. (noun)

complements

A complement is a word, **phrase**, or **clause** used in the **predicate** of a sentence to complete the meaning of the sentence.

EXAMPLES   Pilots fly *airplanes*. (word)
     To live is *to risk death*. (phrase)
     John knew *that he would be late*. (clause)

Four kinds of complements are generally recognized: direct object (which completes the sense of a transitive **verb**), indirect object (which completes the meaning of a transitive verb and the verb's direct object), **objective complement** (which completes the meaning of a verb's object), and **subjective complement** (which completes the meaning of the subject).

A direct object is a **noun** or noun equivalent that receives the action of a transitive verb; it answers the question *what* or *whom* after the verb.

EXAMPLES   John built *a business*. (noun)
     I like *to work*. (verbal)
     I like *it*. (pronoun)
     I like *what I saw*. (noun clause)

An indirect object is a noun or noun equivalent that occurs with a direct object after certain kinds of transitive verbs such as *give, wish, cause*, and *tell*. It answers the question *to whom* or *for whom* (or *to what* or *for what*).

EXAMPLES   Give *John* a wrench. (*wrench* is the direct object)
     We should buy *the Milwaukee office* a color copier. (*color copier* is the direct object)

An objective complement completes the meaning of a sentence by revealing something about the object of its transitive verb. An objective complement may be either a noun or an **adjective**.

EXAMPLES   They call him *a genius*. (noun)
     We painted the building *white*. (adjective)

A subjective complement, which follows a **linking verb** rather than a transitive verb, describes the **subject**. A subjective complement may be either a noun or an adjective.

EXAMPLES   His sister is *an accountant*. (noun)
     His brother is *ill*. (adjective)

complex sentences

The complex sentence provides a means of subordinating one thought to another (or, put another way, of emphasizing one thought

over another) because it contains one **independent clause** and at
least one **dependent clause** that expresses a subordinate idea.

> EXAMPLE   We lost some of our efficiency (independent clause) when we
> moved (dependent clause).

Normally, the independent clause carries a main point, and the dependent clause carries a related subordinate point. A dependent
clause may occur before, after, or within the independent clause.
The dependent clause can serve within the sentence as its **subject**,
as an **object**, or as a **modifier**.

> EXAMPLES   *What he proposed* is irrelevant. (subject)
> We know *where it is supposed to be.* (object)
> The computer, *which can make more calculations in one hour than
> thousands of scientists could make in a lifetime*, is perhaps one
> of the greatest challenges people have ever had to face.
> (modifier)

Complex sentences offer more variety than **simple sentences**. And
frequently the meaning of a **compound sentence** can be made more
precise by subordinating one of the two independent clauses to the
other to create a complex sentence (thereby establishing the relationship of the two parts more clearly). (See also **subordination**.)

> EXAMPLES   We moved *and* we lost some of our efficiency. (compound sen-
> tence with **coordinating conjunction**)
> *When* we moved, we lost some of our efficiency. (complex sen-
> tence with **subordinating conjunction**)

Learn to handle the complex sentence well; it can be a useful tool
with which to express your thoughts clearly and exactly. However, be
on guard against placing the main idea of a complex sentence in a
dependent clause; this is one of the most common errors made with
the complex sentence. For example, do not write the first sentence
below if what you mean is expressed by the second sentence.

> EXAMPLES   Production was not as great as we expected, although we met
> our quota. (The main idea expressed here is that production
> fell short of expectations.)
> Although production was not as great as we expected, we met
> our quota. (The main idea expressed here is that the pro-
> duction quota was met.)

compound sentences

A compound sentence combines two or more related **independent clauses** that are of equal importance.

> EXAMPLE Drilling a well is the only sure way to determine the presence of oil, *but* it is a very costly endeavor.

The independent clauses of a compound sentence may be joined by a **comma** and a **coordinating conjunction**, by a **semicolon**, or by a **conjunctive adverb** preceded by a semicolon and followed by a comma.

> EXAMPLES People deplore violence, *but* they have an insatiable appetite for it on television and in films. (coordinating conjunction)
> There is little similarity between the chemical composition of sea water and river water; the various elements are present in entirely different proportions. (semicolon)
> People deplore violence; *however*, they have an insatiable appetite for it on television and in films. (conjunctive adverb)

A compound sentence is balanced when its clauses are of similar length and construction.

> EXAMPLES The plan was sound, and the staff was eager to begin.
> Fingerprints were used for personal identification in 200 B.C., but they were not used for criminal identification until about A.D. 1880.

compound-complex sentences

A compound-complex sentence consists of two or more **independent clauses** and at least one **dependent clause**.

> EXAMPLE At the same time *that the new system improves employee morale*, it provides incentives for better productivity; it uses a variation of "flex-time" working hours, *which the union has been advocating;* and *since the system involves employees in the decision-making process*, it helps them appreciate the dilemmas faced by management.

Here, the three parallel independent clauses are joined in a series linked by **semicolons** and the **coordinating conjunction** *and*; each independent clause contains a dependent clause (in **italics**). The first two dependent clauses are adjective clauses modifying *time* and *"flex-time" working hours*, and the third is an **adverb clause** that modifies its independent clause as a whole.

The compound-complex sentence offers a vehicle for a more elaborate grouping of ideas than other sentence types permit. It is not really recommended for inexperienced writers because it is difficult to handle skillfully and often leads them into sentences that become so complicated that they lose all **logic** and **coherence**. The result can be a garbled sentence. The more technically complex the subject, the more difficult the compound-complex sentence is to control effectively.

compound words

A compound word is made from two or more words that are either hyphenated or written as one word. (If you are not certain whether a compound word should be hyphenated, check a **dictionary**).

EXAMPLES nevertheless, mother-in-law, courthouse, run-of-the-mill, low-level, high-energy

Be careful to distinguish between compound words and words that frequently appear together but do not constitute compound words, such as *high school* and *post office*. Also be careful to distinguish between compound words and word pairs that mean different things, such as *greenhouse* and *green house*.

Plurals of compound words are usually formed by adding an *s* to the last letter.

EXAMPLES bedrooms, masterminds, overcoats, cupfuls

When the first word of the compound is more important to its meaning than the last, however, the first word takes the *s* (when in doubt, check your dictionary).

EXAMPLES editors-in-chief, fathers-in-law

Possessives are formed by adding '*s* to the end of the compound word.

EXAMPLES the *vice-president's* speech, his *brother-in-law's* car, the *pipeline's* diameter, the *antibody's* action

comprise/compose

Comprise means "include," "contain," or "consist of." The whole *comprises* the parts.

> EXAMPLE   The review panel *comprises* seven members.

Compose means "create" or "make up the whole." The parts *compose* the whole.

> EXAMPLE   The seven members *compose* the review panel.
> OR   The review panel *is composed of* seven members.

Do not use *comprise* in place of *compose*.

> CHANGE   The sales force *is comprised of* 12 representatives.
> TO   The sales force *comprises* 12 representatives.
> OR   The sales force *is composed of* 12 representatives.

computer graphics

Computer graphics is among the fastest developing areas of applications software for personal computers. Both new software and novel combinations of existing software are continually being developed. Accordingly, rather than attempting a definitive classification of this field, this entry provides a concise, basic introduction to the most common types of graphics software and their capabilities. The discussion focuses on graphics produced primarily for use in documents rather than for use in oral or multimedia presentations.

Graphics software for personal computers can be divided into two broad categories: *business graphics* and *free-form graphics*.

BUSINESS GRAPHICS

Business graphics programs, also called *charting* programs, produce preformatted charts, **graphs**, and **tables** based on numerical data taken either from a computer spreadsheet program, as in Figure 1, or from text and data entered from the computer keyboard. Figure 2 shows a range of typical bar and pie charts created by business graphics software.

FREE-FORM GRAPHICS

In free-form graphics, images are not automatically preformatted to become charts, graphs, and tables that display numerical data. In-

Capacity of Oil Storage Facilities (in millions of barrels)			
Storage Facility	Planned Volume	Completed Volume	Permanent Capacity Planned
Bayou Choctaw	48.3	48.2	46
Bryan Mound	74.5	78.2	66
Sulphur Mines	27.4	27.3	26
Weeks Island	73.1	73.1	73
West Hackberry	51.1	50.6	49
Total	274.4	272	260

Figure 1   Spreadsheet Table to Graph Image

stead, you control the image by manipulating a variety of strokes, lines, shapes, and symbols, much as an artist wields pencil, brush, charcoal, templates, and other tools to create images on paper and canvas. Many such programs also contain "clip art" libraries of ready-to-use electronic images of various symbols, shapes, and pictures, a sample of which is shown in Figure 3.

Figure 2   Typical Computer-generated Bar and Pie Charts

Figure 3   Sample Computer Clip Art

Free-form programs are further subdivided into *paint* and *draw programs,* categories defined by the software technology each uses. *Paint programs* allow you to create freehand images on screen, usually with a mouse. You can control images created with paint programs down to the individual dot, "bit," or picture element (known as a pixel) on the screen. Because of this capability, these programs are often referred to as *pixel* or *bit mapped*. Pixels are similar to the dots that make up the images on a television screen. Figure 4 shows a paint-program image. Note how the pixels create a "fuzzy" image.

Figure 4   Image Created from a Paint Program

Draw programs allow you the freedom to create images on screen but differ from paint programs in that you manipulate predefined shapes, called *graphics primitives* (boxes, triangles, arcs, lines, and so on), rather than pixels; that is, you create images by manipulating existing "building block" configurations, like those shown in Figure 5.

Figure 5   Graphics Primitives

Figure 6   Image Created from a Draw Program

The images are manipulated and saved to memory by the coordinates, or vectors, of the beginning and end points of the lines that form them. For this reason, these programs are sometimes called *vector-* or *object-oriented.* These images can be combined to form graphs, line drawings, and flow and organizational charts. Figure 6 shows an image rendered with draw-program software. Note the crispness of this image compared with the same subject created with a paint program in Figure 4.

SPECIALIZED GRAPHICS PROGRAMS

Other computer graphics programs are available for creating **maps**, statistical analyses, animation, and computer-aided design (CAD) images used in engineering and manufacturing. They offer specialized applications for the graphics, engineering, architectural, or scientific professional that are beyond the scope of this text.

GRAPHICS STANDARDS

As you create computer graphics, apply the principles specific to each type presented throughout this book, recognizing that software packages often have inflexible settings for some features, like the sequence in which segments appear on a pie chart, or the size and kind of typeface used for words and numbers on the graphic. After creating your graphics, follow the guidelines listed in **illustrations** for integrating them into your document.

concept/conception

A *concept* is a thought or an idea. A *conception* is the sum of a person's ideas, or concepts, on a subject.

> EXAMPLES   This final *conception* of the whole process evolved from many smaller *concepts*.
> From the *concept* of combustion evolved the *conception* of the internal combustion engine.

conciseness/wordiness

Effective writers make all words, sentences, and **paragraphs** count by eliminating unnecessary words and phrases. Wordiness results from needless **repetition** of the same idea in different words.

> CHANGE   Modern students *of today* are more technologically sophisticated than their parents. (The phrase *of today* repeats the thought already expressed by the adjective *modern*.)
> TO   Modern students are more technologically sophisticated than their parents.
> CHANGE   The walls were sky-blue *in color*. (The phrase *in color* is redundant.)
> TO   The walls were sky-blue.

Careful writers remove every word, **phrase**, **clause**, or sentence they can without sacrificing **clarity**. In doing so, they are striving to be as concise as **clarity** permits—but note that conciseness is not a synonym for brevity. In fact, when brevity is overdone it can become **telegraphic style**. Brevity may or may not be desirable in a given passage, depending on the writer's **objective**, but conciseness is always desirable. The writer must distinguish between language that is used for effect and mere wordiness that stems from lack of care or judgment, such as the use of **nominalizations**. The following **anecdote** was related by Benjamin Franklin to Thomas Jefferson as members of the Continental Congress undertook to trim excess words and phrases from the Declaration of Independence:

> The wise old Pennsylvanian told Jefferson, in an aside, about a hatter who was opening a shop and wanted a signboard for it. What the new proprietor had in mind was a message reading, "John Thompson, Hatter, makes and sells hats for ready money," but one of his friends suggested that the word "hat-

ter" was superfluous. Another told him that no buyer would care who made the hats, so the word "makes" was omitted. Someone else advised him to leave out "ready money," since nobody expected to buy on credit, and yet another man said that since Thompson did not propose to give the hats away the word "sells" should go. When the sign was finally erected, Franklin smiled, all that remained was the name "John Thompson" and the picture of a hat.

—Richard M. Ketchum, *The Winter Soldiers* (New York: Doubleday, 1973) 19.

A concise sentence is not guaranteed to be effective, but a wordy sentence always loses some of its readability and **coherence** because of the extra load it must carry. Wordiness is to be expected in a first draft, but it should never survive **revision**. "I would have written a shorter letter if I'd had more time" is a truism.

CAUSES OF WORDINESS

Modifiers that repeat an idea already implicit or present in the word being modified contribute to wordiness by being redundant.

EXAMPLES   *active* consideration   *present* status
           final outcome   *true* facts
           personal opinion   *past* history
           completely finished   isolated *by himself*
           round circles   *tall* skyscrapers
           basic essentials   descended *down*
           hot boiling water   circle *around*
           advance planning   square *in shape*
           small *in size*   worthy *of merit*
           balance *of equilibrium*   the reason *is because*
           realization of a dream *come true*   cooperate *together*
           visible *to the eye*

Another cause of wordiness is the "it . . . that . . ." construction. Not only is this construction wordy, but often it forces you to use the passive **voice** (a major cause of wordiness in its own right).

CHANGE   *It* is agreed *that* our sales quota will increase next year.
    TO   We agree that our sales quota will increase next year.

The **gobbledygook** addict is fond of such words and phrases as *factor, case, basis, elements, field, phenomenon, in terms of, in the nature of, with reference to.* Key words that seem to invite redundancy are *situation, angle, line, factor, aspect, element, consideration, considering.* Although all these words have legitimate uses, business people seem to have a particular weakness for their overuse and inexact use, under the mistaken impression that they add formality to writing.

Coordinating synonyms that merely repeat one another contribute to wordiness.

EXAMPLES   *any and all*   *each and every*
           finally and for good   *basic and fundamental*
           first and foremost

Wordiness can be caused by unnecessary or redundant phrases and clauses.

EXAMPLE   Our domestic retail outlets, *which are located in this country,* are more profitable than our South American retail outlets.

Excess qualification also contributes to wordiness, as the following examples demonstrate:

EXAMPLES   utterly rejected—rejected
           perfectly clear—clear
           completely compatible—compatible
           completely accurate—accurate
           radically new—new

The use of **expletives, relative pronouns**, and relative adjectives, although they have legitimate purposes, often results in wordiness.

CHANGE   *There are* (expletive) many supervisors in the area *who* (relative pronoun) are planning to attend the workshop *which* (relative adjective) is scheduled for Friday.
TO   Many supervisors in the area plan to attend the workshop scheduled for Friday.

Circumlocution (a long, indirect way of expressing things) is a leading cause of wordiness.

CHANGE   We urge you to submit any suggestions you may have on the subject, and you may be certain that your suggestions will be given our most careful attention.
TO   Please give us your suggestions. We will consider them carefully.

Conciseness can be overdone. If you respond to a written request that you cannot understand with "Your request was unclear" or "I don't understand," you will probably offend your reader. Instead of attacking the writer's ability to phrase a request, consider that what you are really doing is asking for more information. Say so.

> EXAMPLE   I will need more information before I can answer your request. Specifically, can you give me the title and the date of the report you are looking for?

This version is a little longer than the others, but it is both more polite and more helpful.

Although conciseness and clarity *usually* reinforce each other, there are times when clarity legitimately demands more words. See the example of "rendering" in **descriptions** as an example. (See also **telegraphic style**.)

HOW TO ACHIEVE CONCISENESS

Conciseness can be achieved by effective use of **subordination**. This is, in fact, the best means of tightening wordy writing.

> CHANGE   The law clerk's report was carefully illustrated, and it covered five pages.
> TO   The law clerk's five-page report was carefully illustrated.

Conciseness can be achieved by using simple words and phrases.

> CHANGE   It is the policy of the company to provide the proper equipment to enable each employee to conduct the telephonic communication necessary to discharge his responsibilities; such should not be utilized for personal communications.
> TO   Your telephone is provided for company business; do not use it for personal calls.

Conciseness can be achieved by eliminating undesirable **repetition**.

> CHANGE   This tuning, which is offered to all our customers at no further cost to them whatsoever, is available with each piano purchased from this company.
> TO   Free piano tuning is offered with each purchase.

Conciseness can be achieved by making sentences positive. (See also **positive writing**.)

> CHANGE   If the error does not involve data transmission, the special function is not used.
> TO   The special function is used only when the error involves data transmission.

Conciseness can sometimes be achieved by changing a sentence from the passive to the active voice or from the indicative to the imperative **mood**. The following example does both:

CHANGE   Card codes are normally used when it is known that the cards are to be processed by a computer, and control punches are normally used when it is known that the cards are designed to be processed at a tab installation.

TO   Use card codes when you process the cards on a computer, and use control punches when you process them at a tab installation.

Eliminate wordy introductory phrases or pretentious words and phrases of any kind.

EXAMPLES   In view of the foregoing   As you may recall
It appears that   As you know
In the case of   Needless to say
It may be said that   In view of the fact that
It is interesting to note that

CHANGE   *In connection with* your recent accident, we must *discontinue* your insurance *due to the fact that* this is your third claim within the past year. *Inasmuch* as you were insured with us *at the time of the accident, we are prepared* to honor your claim *along the lines* of your policy.

TO   Concerning your recent accident, we are canceling your insurance because you have filed three claims in the past year. Since you were insured with us at the time of the accident, however, we will honor your claim.

CHANGE   in order to, so as to, so as to be able to, with a view to
TO   to

CHANGE   due to the fact that, for the reason that, owing to the fact that, the reason for
TO   because

CHANGE   by means of, by using, utilizing, through the use of
TO   by or with

CHANGE   at this time, at this point in time, at present, at the present
TO   now

CHANGE   at that time, at that point, at that point in time, as of that date, during that period
TO   then

Overuse of **intensifiers** (such as *very, more, most, best, quite*) contributes to wordiness; conciseness can be achieved by eliminating them. The same is true of excessive use of **adjectives** and **adverbs**. (See also **nominalizations** and **pace**.)

concluding

Concluding a piece of writing not only ties together all the main ideas but can do so emphatically by making a final significant point. This final point may be to recommend a course of action, to make a prediction, to offer a final judgment, to speculate on the implications of your ideas, or merely to summarize your main points.

The way you conclude depends on both the purpose of your writing and the needs of your **reader**. For example, a committee **report** about possible locations for a new manufacturing plant could end with a recommendation. A report on a company's annual sales figures might conclude with a judgment about why sales are up or down. A letter about consumer trends could end by speculating on the implications of these trends. A document that is particularly lengthy will often end with a summary of its main points. Study the following examples:

Recommen-
dation

These results indicate that you need to alter your testing procedure to eliminate the impurities we found in specimens A through E.

Prediction

Although my original estimate on equipment ($20,000) has been exceeded by $2,300, my original labor estimate ($60,000) has been reduced by $3,500; therefore, I will easily stay within the limits of my original bid. In addition, I see no difficulty in having the arena finished for the December 23 Christmas program.

Judgment

Although our estimate calls for a substantially higher budget than in the three previous years, we believe that it is justified by our planned expansion.

Summary

As this letter has indicated, we would attract more recent graduates by (1) increasing our advertising in local student newspapers, (2) resuming our co-op program, (3) sending a representative to career day programs at local colleges, (4) inviting local college instructors to teach in-house courses here at the plant, and (5) encouraging our employees to attend evening classes at local colleges.

The concluding statement may merely present ideas for consideration, but it may also call for action or deliberately provoke thought.

Ideas for
consideration

The new prices become effective the first of the year. Price adjustments are routine for the company, but some of your customers will not consider them so. Please consider the needs of both your customers and the company as you implement these new prices.

Call for action   Send us a check for $250 now if you wish to keep your account active. If you have not responded to our previous letters because of some special hardship, I will be glad personally to work out a solution with you.

Thought-provoking statement   Can we continue to accept the losses incurred by careless workmanship? Must we accept it as inevitable? Or should we consider steps to control it firmly now?

Because this statement appears in a position of great **emphasis**, be careful to avoid closing with a cliché. Some such expressions do say what you want to say so precisely that they are considered acceptable closings, however.

EXAMPLES   It has been a pleasure to be of assistance.
May we thank you again for your cooperation.
If I can provide further information, please let me know.

Be especially careful not to introduce a new **topic** when you conclude. A concluding thought should always relate to and reinforce the ideas presented in your writing. (See also **conclusions**.)

conclusions

The conclusion section of a **report** or article pulls together the results or findings and interprets them in the light of the purpose of the study and of the methods by which it was conducted. Consequently, the conclusion is the focal point of the work, the goal toward which the study was aiming. The evidence for these findings makes up the discussions in the body of the report or article; the conclusions must grow out of the information discussed there. Moreover, the conclusions must be consistent with what the **introduction** stated that the report would examine (its purpose) and how it would do so (its method). If the introduction stated that the report had as its **objective** to learn the economic costs of relocating a plant from one city to another, then the conclusion should not discuss the social or aesthetic impacts the new plant could have on the new location. Of course, if "costs" are defined in the introduction to include social and aesthetic concerns, then these also must be accounted for in the report and discussed in the conclusions.

The sample conclusion shown in Figure 1 comes from a report about how community growth and real estate values in four specific

CONCLUSIONS

Brief statement of purpose

This study was undertaken to test the hypotheses that nuclear power plants have an adverse effect on (1) community growth and (2) residential property values. Implicit in the second hypothesis is that prices paid for residential properties reflect perceptions of house and lot quality, community services and attributes, and environmental characteristics. If people in general perceive nuclear plants as a possible threat to health and safety, they will tend to avoid living close to them. Such actions should be reflected in the real estate market for residential properties, and everything else being equal, the closer to the plant, the lower the price for housing.

Findings based on methods specified in introduction

The following conclusions are apparent from an analysis of time series data on total assessed real property values from 1960 to 1976 and from a regression analysis of 540 single-family house sales in 1975, 1976, and 1977 in the vicinity of four nuclear power generating plants in the Northeast.

1. Assuming that the real (deflated) increase in total assessed property values is a good indicator of growth, the presence of the nuclear plants has had no adverse effects on the growth rates of communities in close proximity to such plants.

2. Because (a) growth rates were inversely related to distance from the plant and (b) annual growth rates for the years following plant construction were higher than for the years before plant construction, with the increase in the growth rate for the host communities being higher than the increase for the region as a whole, the presence of the nuclear plant may actually stimulate growth. The likely explanation for this is the lower tax rates in the host municipalities, which are made possible by the large tax assessments levied on the plants.

3. The presence of the nuclear power plants, at least in 1975, 1976, and 1977, exerted no influence on the price of single-family housing within 20 miles of these plants. Therefore, our hypothesis that residential property values are directly related to distance from the nuclear power plants must be rejected and the null hypothesis accepted.

4. For most people in these study areas, the proximity of a nuclear power plant does not appear as a factor in residential location choice. The fears for health and safety expressed by some individuals and groups in society are not reflected in the housing decisions of residents in communities near the nuclear plants studied.

Restatement of scope and its implications

These conclusions apply only to the four areas studied. Since the plants were preselected and do not represent a random sample of all nuclear plants, the findings cannot be used to predict influences on growth and property values at other plant sites. Moreover, society's perceptions and values change over time, and what may have been true in the mid-1970s may not hold true in the future.

Figure 1   Sample Conclusion

areas were affected by nearby nuclear power plants. Note that the authors briefly restate the purpose of the study: to test two hypotheses. They then clarify some implicit assumptions in their original purpose before indicating that the findings are based on the methods specified in the introduction to the report (that is, the analysis of time series data and a regression analysis). After listing the findings, they go on to qualify these carefully, noting that the results are valid for the scope of this study but that they may not apply to areas at other plant sites. Notice that a conclusion is often more than a simple summary.

Not all reports or articles require a separate conclusions section. Periodic **progress reports** for a long-term project, for example, may simply indicate what was done during the last month or quarter. The final report for such a project, however, would require a conclusions section in which the findings and their implications were discussed. Nor do many other types of writing require a fully developed conclusion. For examples of less formal conclusions, see **concluding**.

Finally, because the conclusions are frequently read independently of the rest of the work, they should be written accordingly. The conclusions should restate the purpose of the document and specify the methodology (as was done in the power plant sample), and should define **symbols** and **abbreviations** as though they were being used for the first time. (For guidance about the location of the conclusions section in a report, see **formal reports**.)

conjunctions

A conjunction connects words, **phrases**, or **clauses**. A conjunction can also indicate the relationship between the two elements it connects (*and* joins together, *or* selects and separates).

Occasionally, a conjunction may begin a sentence and even a paragraph, as in the following example:

> EXAMPLE Unemployment resulting from social, locational, technological, and specific market factors unrelated to overall weakness in the economy is called structural unemployment.
>
> *But* when unemployment increases by the hundreds of thousands or millions over the course of a single year, you can be sure the change is not due to structural factors but to a business slump—and insufficient aggregate demand.
> —Leonard Silk, *Economics in Plain English* (New York: Simon, 1978) 86.

TYPES OF CONJUNCTIONS

A **coordinating conjunction** is a word that joins two sentence elements that have identical functions. The coordinating conjunctions are *and, but, or, for, nor, yet,* and *so.*

EXAMPLES   Betty *and* John work at the Los Angeles office. (joining two
proper nouns)

To hear *and* to obey are two different things. (joining two
phrases)

He would like to include the test results, *but* that would make
the report too long. (joining two clauses).

Correlative conjunctions are coordinating conjunctions that are
used in pairs. The correlative conjunctions are *either ... or, neither
... nor, not only ... but also, both ... and,* and *whether ... or.*

EXAMPLE   Bill will arrive *either* on Wednesday *or* on Thursday.

A **subordinating conjunction** connects sentence elements of different weights, normally **independent clauses** and **dependent clauses**.
The most frequently used are *so, although, after, because, if, where, than,
since, as, unless, before, that, though, when,* and *whereas.*

EXAMPLE   I left the office *after* I had finished writing the report.

A **conjunctive adverb** is an **adverb** that has the force of a conjunction because it is used to join two independent clauses. The most
common conjunctive adverbs are *however, moreover, therefore, further,
then, consequently, besides, accordingly, also, thus.*

EXAMPLE   The engine performed well in the laboratory; *however*, it failed
under road conditions.

PUNCTUATING CONJUNCTIONS

Two independent clauses separated by a coordinating conjunction
should have a **comma** immediately preceding the coordinating conjunction if the clauses are relatively long.

EXAMPLE   The Alpha project was her third assignment, *and* it was the one
that made her reputation as a project leader.

If two independent clauses that are joined by a coordinating conjunction have commas within them, a **semicolon** may precede the
conjunction.

EXAMPLE   Even though the schedule is tight, we must meet our deadline;
and all the staff, including programmers, will have to work
overtime this week.

Two independent clauses that are joined by a conjunctive adverb
require a **semicolon** before and a **comma** after the conjunctive

adverb because the conjunctive adverb is introducing the independent clause that follows it and is indicating its relationship with the
independent clause preceding it. The conjunctive adverb connects
ideas but does not grammatically connect the clause stating the
ideas; the semicolon must do that. The conjunctive adverb both
connects and modifies. As a **modifier**, it is part of one of the two
clauses that it connects. The use of the semicolon makes it a part of
the clause it modifies.

> EXAMPLE   The building was not finished on the scheduled date; *never-*
> *theless*, Rogers moved in and began to conduct the business
> of the department from the unfinished offices.

CONJUNCTIONS IN TITLES

Conjunctions in the titles of books, articles, plays, movies, and so on
should not be capitalized unless they are the first or last word in the
title. (See also **capital letters**.)

> EXAMPLE   The book *Technical and Professional Writing* was edited by
> Herman Estrin.

conjunctive adverbs

A conjunctive adverb is an **adverb** because it modifies the **clause** that
it introduces; it operates as a **conjunction** because it joins two
independent clauses. The most common conjunctive adverbs are
however, nevertheless, moreover, therefore, further, then, consequently, besides,
accordingly, also, and *thus.*

> EXAMPLE   The engine performed well in the laboratory; *however*, it failed
> under road conditions.

The two independent clauses that are joined by a conjunctive adverb
require a **semicolon** before and a **comma** after the conjunctive
adverb. The conjunctive adverb both connects and modifies. As a
modifier, it is part of one of the two clauses that it connects, and the
use of the semicolon makes it a part of the clause that it modifies.
(See also **transition**.)

> EXAMPLE   The new project is almost completed and is already over cost
> estimates; *however*, we must emphasize the importance of
> adequate drainage.

connected with/in connection with

Connected with and *in connection with* are wordy **phrases** that can usually be replaced by *in* or *with*.

> CHANGE He is *connected with* the First National Bank.
>   TO He is *with* the First National Bank.
>   OR He is employed by the First National Bank.

> CHANGE The fringe benefits *in connection with* (or *connected with*) the job are quite good.
>   TO The fringe benefits with the job are quite good.

connotation/denotation

The terms *connotation* and *denotation* refer to two different ways of interpreting a word's meaning. The *denotation* of a word is its literal and objective meaning. Defined this way, *communism* is a socioeconomic system that aims at a classless society, and a *bureaucrat* is an unelected public official who administers government policy. Of course both words bring to mind a host of secondary or implied meanings that arise from our emotional reactions to them. Many Americans react negatively to the word *communism*, associating it with a totalitarian form of government that is antireligious and, until recent dramatic changes in the former Soviet Union, committed to world conquest. Likewise, the word *bureaucrat* frequently conjures up visions of someone who insists on rigid adherence to arbitrary rules and regulations. These secondary meanings are a word's connotations.

In your writing you must be sure to consider the connotations of your words. You know what you mean to say, but you must be careful to say it in words that will not be misinterpreted by your **reader**. For example, you might not want to refer to an item as *cheap*, meaning inexpensive, for the word *cheap* also implies shoddy workmanship or poor materials. The **usage** notes in a reputable dictionary can help you make these distinctions. Business writing in particular requires an objective and impartial presentation of information, and so you should always be as careful as possible to use words without misleading or unwanted connotations.

On the other hand, a word may have several equally valid denotative meanings. Context will make the meaning clear, as in the following varied uses of the word *check*:

EXAMPLES The bank verified the *check*.

The driver was instructed to *check* the oil before every trip.

The chess champion was in *check* three times, but he eventually won the match.

The hockey player executed a bruising *check*.

(See also **defining terms**.)

consensus of opinion

Since *consensus* normally means "harmony of opinion," the **phrase** *consensus of opinion* is redundant. The word *consensus* can be used only of a group, never one or two people.

CHANGE The *consensus of opinion* of the members was that the committee should change its name.

TO The *consensus* of the members was that the committee should change its name.

continual/continuous

Continual means "happening over and over" or "frequently repeated."

EXAMPLE Writing well requires *continual* practice.

Continuous means "occurring without interruption" or "unbroken."

EXAMPLE The *continuous* roar of the machines was deafening.

contractions

A contraction is a shortened **spelling** of a word or **phrase** with an **apostrophe** substituting for the missing letters.

EXAMPLES		
	cannot	can't
	will not	won't
	have not	haven't
	it is	it's

Contractions are often used in speech but should be used discriminatingly in **reports**, formal letters, and most business writing. (See also **style**.)

coordinating conjunctions

A coordinating conjunction is a word that joins two sentence elements that have identical functions. The coordinating conjunctions include *and, but, or, for, nor, yet,* and *so.*

> EXAMPLE The first impact of the cutback was on the purchasing department, *but* it is now making itself felt in our department as well.

Coordinating conjunctions can join words, **phrases**, or **clauses** of equal rank.

> EXAMPLES Only crabs *and* sponges managed to escape the red tide. (words)
>
> Our twin objectives are to increase sales *and* to lower production costs. (phrases)
>
> The average city dweller in the United States now has 0.17 parts per million of lead in his blood, *and* the amount is increasing yearly. (clauses)

Under normal circumstances, use coordinating conjunctions only to connect **parallel structures**.

copyright

Copyright is the right of exclusive ownership by an author of the benefits resulting from the creation of his or her work. This right gives authors, or others to whom they transfer ownership of copyright, control over the reproduction and dissemination of their works. Once copyrighted, a work cannot be indiscriminately reproduced unless the copyright owner is compensated by royalties or other arrangements.

This right is protected for the life of the author plus 50 years by a federal law that became effective on January 1, 1978. This law protects any work from the moment of its creation, regardless of whether it is ever published and whether it contains a notice of copyright. At the end of the copyright period, the work becomes "public domain" and may be published or reproduced by anyone without permission or compensation to the copyright owner's estate.

The copyright law provides a "fair use" provision that allows teachers, librarians, reviewers, and others to reproduce copyrighted materials for educational and illustrative purposes without compensation to the copyright owners. The law refers to such purposes as "criticism, comment, news reporting, teaching (including multiple copies for classroom use), scholarship, or research." Although the law does not exactly define "fair use," it sets out four criteria for determining whether a given use is fair: (1) the purpose and nature of the use, (2) the amount of material used in relation to the copyrighted work as a whole, (3) the nature of the copyrighted work, and (4) the effect of the use on the potential market for or value of the copyrighted work. Publications that explain the copyright law in detail are available from the Copyright Office, Library of Congress, Washington, DC 20559.

If you use copyrighted materials in your written work, be aware of the following guidelines:

1. A small amount of material from a copyrighted source may be used in your written work without permission or payment as long as the use is reasonable and not harmful to the rights of the copyright owner.

2. A work created after January 1, 1978, receives copyright protection whether or not it bears a notice of copyright, although all published materials should contain such a notice, usually on the back of the title page. (For an example of a copyright notice, turn to the back of the title page of this book.)

3. All publications of U.S. government agencies are in the public domain—that is, they are *not* copyrighted.

4. One way to determine whether a work from which you wish to quote is in the public domain is to write to the Copyright Office at the address cited in this entry. There is a search fee for this service.

(See also **plagiarism**.)

correlative conjunctions

Correlative conjunctions are **coordinating conjunctions** that are used in pairs. The correlative conjunctions are *either . . . or, neither . . . nor, not only . . . but also, both . . . and,* and *whether . . . or.*

> EXAMPLES   The shipment will arrive *either* on Wednesday *or* on Thursday.
> The shipment contains the parts *not only* for the seven machines scheduled for delivery this month *but also* for those scheduled for delivery next month.

To add not only symmetry but also logic to your writing, follow correlative conjunctions with parallel sentence elements (such as *on Wednesday* and *on Thursday* in the previous example).

A problem can develop with correlative conjunctions joining a singular **noun** to a plural noun. The problem is with the **verb**. If you use this construction, make the verb agree with the nearest noun.

> EXAMPLE Neither the treasurer nor his *associates deny* his guilt. ("Neither the treasurer nor his associates denies his guilt" would be grammatically incorrect.)

A common solution is to change the construction of the sentence.

> EXAMPLE His guilt is denied by neither the treasurer nor his associates.

(See also **parallel structure**.)

correspondence

The process of writing letters involves many of the same steps that go into most other on-the-job tasks. The following list summarizes these steps:

1. Establish your **objective**, and determine your **reader's** attitude and needs.
2. Prepare an **outline**, even if it is only a list of points to be covered in the order you wish to cover them.
3. Write the first draft (see also **writing the draft**).
4. Allow a "cooling" period (time for weaknesses to become obvious).
5. Revise the draft (see also **revision**).
6. Use **proofreading** techniques.

These guidelines will help you write a clear, well-organized letter. (See also **memorandums**.) You might also find it valuable to look at the "Five Steps to Successful Writing" at the front of this book. Keep in mind, however, that one very important element in business letters is the impression they leave on the reader. To convey the right impression—of yourself as well as of your company or organization—you must take particular care with both the **tone** and the **style** of your writing.

TONE

Letters are generally written directly to another person who is identified by name. You may or may not know the person, but never forget that you are writing to another human being. For this reason, letters are always more personal than are **reports** or other forms of business writing. Successful writers find that it helps to imagine their reader sitting across the desk from them as they write; they then write to the reader as if they were talking to him or her in person. This technique helps them keep their language natural. Of course, they adhere to all the guidelines of good writing, including grammar and punctuation. As a letter writer addressing yourself directly to your reader, you are in a good position to take into account your reader's needs. If you ask yourself, "How might I feel if I were the recipient of such a letter?" you can gain some insight into the likely needs and feelings of your reader—and then tailor your message to fit those needs and feelings. Furthermore, you have a chance to build goodwill for your business or organization. Many companies spend millions of dollars to create a favorable public image. A letter to a customer that sounds impersonal and unfriendly can quickly tarnish that image, but a thoughtful letter that communicates sincerity can greatly enhance it.

Suppose, for example, you are a department-store manager who receives a request for a refund from a customer who forgot to enclose the receipt with the request. In a letter to that customer, you might write the following:

> EXAMPLE   The sales receipt must be enclosed with the merchandise before we can process a refund.

But if you consider how you might keep the goodwill of the customer, you might word the request this way:

> EXAMPLE   Please enclose the sales receipt with the merchandise so that we can send you your refund promptly.

However, you can go one step further as a business-letter writer. You can put the reader's needs and interests at the center of the letter by writing from the reader's perspective. Often, although not always, doing so means using the words *you* and *your* rather than *we, our, I,* and *mine.* That is why the technique has been referred to as the **you viewpoint.** Consider the following revision, which is written with the "you" viewpoint:

EXAMPLE So that you can receive your refund promptly, please enclose the sales receipt with the merchandise.

In this example, the reader's benefit and interest is stressed: to get a refund as quickly as possible. By emphasizing the reader's needs, the writer will be more likely to accomplish his or her objective: to get the reader to act.

Obviously, both goodwill and the "you" viewpoint can be overdone. Used thoughtlessly, both techniques can produce a fawning, insincere tone—what might be called "plastic goodwill," as in the following:

CHANGE You're the sort of forward-thinking person whose outstanding good judgment is obvious from your selection of the Model K-50 word processor.

TO Congratulations on selecting the Model K-50 word processor. We believe the K-50 is one of the finest on the market.

Language that is full of false praise will seem insincere and thus be counterproductive.

DIRECT AND INDIRECT PATTERN: GOOD NEWS AND BAD NEWS LETTERS

It is generally more effective to present good news directly and bad news indirectly, because readers form their impressions and attitudes very early in letters. In fact, some readers do not finish reading a letter when bad news is presented first. Other readers may finish a letter that presents bad news at the outset, but they tend to read what follows with a predetermined opinion. They may be very skeptical about an explanation, or they may reject a reasonable alternative presented by the writer. Furthermore, even if you must refuse a person's request or say no to someone, you still may wish to work with him or her in the future, and an abruptly phrased rejection early in the letter may prevent you from reestablishing an amicable relationship in the future.

Consider the thoughtlessness of the rejection in Figure 1. Although the letter is direct and uses the pronouns *you* and *your*, the writer has apparently not considered how the reader will feel as she reads the letter. There is no expression of regret that Mrs. Mauer is being rejected for the position nor any appreciation of her efforts in applying for the job. The letter is, in short, rude. The pattern of this letter is (1) bad news, (2) explanation, and (3) close.

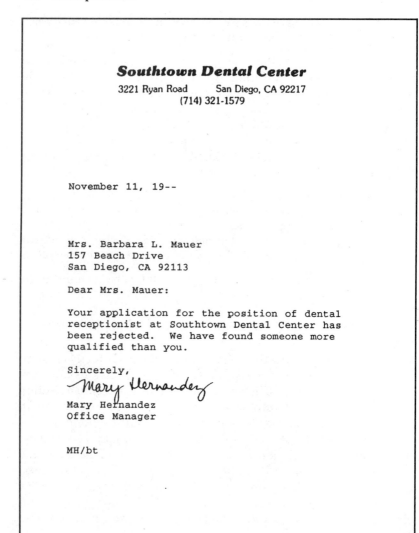

Southtown Dental Center

3221 Ryan Road   San Diego, CA 92217
(714) 321-1579

November 11, 19--

Mrs. Barbara L. Mauer
157 Beach Drive
San Diego, CA 92113

Dear Mrs. Mauer:

Your application for the position of dental
receptionist at Southtown Dental Center has
been rejected. We have found someone more
qualified than you.

Sincerely,

Mary Hernandez

Mary Hernandez
Office Manager

MH/bt

Figure 1   Poor "Bad News" Letter

A better general pattern for "bad news" letters is as follows:

1. Buffer
2. Bad news
3. Goodwill

The "buffer" may be either neutral information or an explanation that makes the bad news *understandable*. Bad news is never pleasant; however, information that either puts the bad news in perspective or makes the bad news seem reasonable maintains goodwill between the writer and the reader. Consider, for example, a revision of the rejection letter, as shown in Figure 2.

Figure 2 carries the same disappointing news as the first one does, but the writer is careful to thank the reader for her time and effort, to explain why she was not accepted for the job, and to offer her encouragement in finding a position in another office. Presenting good news is, of course, easier. Present good news early—at the outset, if at all possible. The pattern for "good news" letters should be as follows:

1. Good news
2. Explanation or facts
3. Goodwill

By presenting the good news first, you will increase the likelihood that the reader will pay careful attention to details, and you will achieve goodwill from the start. Figure 3 is a good example of a "good news" letter.

The following tips will help you achieve a tone that builds goodwill with the reader:

1. *Be respectful, not demanding.*

> CHANGE Submit your answer in one week.
> TO I would appreciate your answer within one week.

2. *Be modest, not arrogant.*

> CHANGE My report is thorough, and I'm sure that you won't be able to continue without it.
> TO I have tried to be as thorough as possible in my report, and I hope you find it useful.

Southtown Dental Center

3221 Ryan Road   San Diego, CA 92217
(714) 321-1579

November 11, 19--

Mrs. Barbara L. Mauer
157 Beach Drive
San Diego, CA 92113

Dear Mrs. Mauer:

Buffer

Thank you for your time and effort in applying for the position of dental receptionist
at Southtown Dental Center.

Bad News

Since we need someone who can assume the
duties here with a minimum of training, we
have selected an applicant with over ten
years of experience.

Goodwill

I am sure that with your excellent college
record you will find a position in another
office.

Sincerely,

Mary Hernandez

Mary Hernandez
Office Manager

MH/bt

Figure 2   Courteous and Effective "Bad News" Letter

Southtown Dental Center

3221 Ryan Road   San Diego, CA 92217
(714) 321-1579

November 11, 19--

Mrs. Barbara L. Mauer
157 Beach Drive
San Diego, CA 92113

Dear Mrs. Mauer:

Good News   Please accept our offer for the position of dental receptionist at Southtown Dental Center.

Explanation   If the terms we discussed in the interview are acceptable to you, please come in at 9:30 a.m. on November 15. At that time we will ask you to complete our personnel form, in addition to. . . .

Goodwill   Everyone here at Southtown is looking forward to working with you. We all were very favorably impressed with you during your interview.

Sincerely,

Mary Hernandez

Mary Hernandez
Office Manager

MH/bt

Figure 3   Effective "Good News" Letter

3. *Be polite, not sarcastic.*

> CHANGE I just received the shipment we ordered six months ago. I'm sending it back—we can't use it now. Thanks!
>
> TO I am returning the shipment we ordered on March 12, 19--. Unfortunately, it arrived too late for us to be able to use it.

4. *Be positive and tactful, not negative and condescending.*

> CHANGE Your complaint about our prices is way off target. Our prices are definitely not any higher than those of our competitors.
>
> TO Thank you for your suggestion concerning our prices. We believe, however, that our prices are competitive with, and in some cases are below, those of our competitors.

WRITING STYLE

Letter-writing style may legitimately vary from informal, in a letter to a close business associate, to formal, or restrained, in a letter to someone you do not know. (Even if you are writing a business letter to a close associate, you should always follow the rules of standard grammar, spelling, and punctuation.)

> INFORMAL It worked! The new process is better than we had dreamed.
>
> RESTRAINED You will be pleased to know that the new process is more effective than we had expected.

You will probably find yourself relying on the restrained style more frequently than on the informal one, since an obvious attempt to sound casual, like overdone goodwill, may strike the reader as insincere. Do not adopt such a formal style, however, that your letters read like legal contracts. Using legalistic-sounding words in an effort to impress your reader will make your writing seem stuffy and pompous—and may well irritate your reader.

> CHANGE In response to your query, I wish to state that we no longer have an original copy of the brochure requested. Be advised that a photographic copy is enclosed herewith. Address further correspondence to this office for assistance as required.
>
> TO Because we are currently out of original copies of our brochure, I am sending you a photocopy of it. If I can help further, please let me know.

The excessively formal writing style in the original version is full of largely out-of-date business language; expressions like *query, I wish to state, be advised that,* and *herewith* are both old-fashioned and pretentious. Good business letters today have a more personal, down-to-earth style, as the revision illustrates.

The revised version not only is less stuffy but also slightly more concise. Being concise in writing is important, but don't be so concise that you become blunt (or lapse into **telegraphic style**). If you respond to a written request that you cannot understand with "Your request was unclear" or "I don't understand," you will probably offend your reader. Instead of attacking the writer's ability to phrase a request, consider that what you are really doing is asking for more information. Say so.

> EXAMPLE I will need more information before I can answer your request. Specifically, can you give me the title and the date of the report you are looking for?

This version is a bit longer, but it is both more polite and more helpful.

ACCURACY

Since a letter is a written record, it must be accurate. Facts, figures, dates, and explanations that are incorrect or misleading may cost time, money, and goodwill. Remember that when you sign a letter, you are responsible for its contents. Always allow yourself time to review a letter before mailing it. When time permits, ask someone who is familiar with its contents to review an important letter. Listen with an open mind to the criticism of others about what you have said, and make any changes you believe necessary.

A second kind of accuracy to check for is the mechanics of writing—**punctuation**, **grammar**, and **spelling**. Regardless of who types the letter, if you sign it, you are responsible for its contents and form.

APPEARANCE

The appearance of a business letter may be crucial in influencing a recipient who has never seen you. The rules for preparing a neat, attractive letter are not difficult to master, and they are important—particularly if you type your own letters. Type on unruled white bond paper of standard size, and use envelopes of the same quality. Center the letter on the page vertically and horizontally—a "picture frame" of white space should surround the contents. When you use your company's letterhead stationery, consider the bottom of the letterhead as the top edge of the paper.

PARTS OF A BUSINESS LETTER

If your employer recommends or requires a particular **format** and typing style, use it. You may also wish to consult a secretarial guide, such as *The Gregg Reference Manual* by William A. Sabin (McGraw). Otherwise, follow the guidelines provided here, and review the illustrations for placement with full- and modified-block style (pp. 163–164).

Heading. The writer's full address (street, city, state, and ZIP code) and the date are given in the heading. Because the writer's name appears at the end of the letter, it need not be included in the heading. Words like *street, avenue, first,* or *west* should be spelled out rather than abbreviated. You may either spell out the name of the state in full or use the U.S. Postal Service abbreviations. The date usually goes directly beneath the last line of the address. Do not abbreviate the name of the month.

> EXAMPLE   1638 Parkhill Drive East
> Great Falls, MT 59407
> April 8, 19—

Align the heading on the page at the center line. If you are using company letterhead that gives the address, type in only the date, two spaces below the last line of printed copy.

The Inside Address. The recipient's full name and address are given in the inside address. You can begin the inside address two spaces below the date if the letter is long, or four spaces below if the letter is quite short. The inside address should be aligned with the left margin—and the left margin should be at least one inch wide. Include the reader's full name and title (if you know them) and his or her full address, including ZIP code.

> EXAMPLE   Ms. Gail Silver
> Production Manager
> Quicksilver Printing Company
> 14 President Street
> Sarasota, FL 33546

The Salutation. Place the salutation, or greeting, two spaces below the inside address, also aligned with the left margin. In most business letters, the salutation contains the recipient's title (*Mr., Ms., Dr.,* and so on) and last name, followed by a **colon**. If you are on a first-name basis with the recipient, include his or her title and full name on the inside address, but use only the first name in the salutation. Notice that the titles *Mr., Ms., Mrs.,* and *Dr.* may be abbreviated but that other titles, such as *Captain* or *Professor,* should always be spelled out.

EXAMPLES   Dear Ms. Silver:
Dear Dr. Lee:
Dear Captain Ortiz:
Dear Professor Murphy:
Dear George:

Address women without a professional title as *Ms.,* whether they are married or unmarried. If a woman has expressed a preference for *Miss* or *Mrs.,* however, honor her preference. If you do not know whether the recipient is a man or a woman, you may use a title appropriate to the context of the letter. The following are examples of the kinds of titles you may find suitable:

EXAMPLES   Dear Customer: (Letter from a department store)
Dear Homeowner: (Letter from an insurance agent soliciting business)
Dear Parts Manager: (Letter to an auto-parts dealer)

In the past, correspondence to large companies or organizations was customarily addressed to "Gentlemen." Today, however, writers who do not know the name or title of the recipient often address the letter to an appropriate department or identify the subject in a "subject line" and use no salutation.

EXAMPLE   National Business Systems
501 West National Avenue
Minneapolis, MN 55407

Attention: Customer Relations Department

I am returning three calculators that failed to operate. . . .

EXAMPLE   National Business Systems
501 West National Avenue
Minneapolis, MN 55407

Subject: Defective Parts for SL-100 Calculators

I am returning three calculators that failed to operate. . . .

When a person's first name could be either feminine or masculine, one solution is to use both the first and the last name in the salutation.

EXAMPLE   Dear Pat Smith:

Avoid using "To Whom It May Concern" because it is impersonal and dated.

The Body. The body of the letter should begin two spaces below the salutation (or directly below the heading if there is no salutation). Single-space within paragraphs, and double-space between paragraphs. If a letter is very short and you want to suggest a fuller appearance, you may instead double-space throughout and indicate paragraphs by indenting the first line of each paragraph five spaces from the left. The right margin should be approximately as wide as the left margin. (In very short letters, you may increase both margins to about an inch and a half.)

Two very important elements in the body are the **opening** and closing. One effective way to arrange your letter is to open with a short **paragraph**, followed by one or more longer paragraphs for the message and another short paragraph for concluding. This is called a diamond arrangement, and it can help focus your letter whether you are using the direct or indirect pattern. Never underestimate the importance of the opening and closing; in fact, their positions of **emphasis** make them particularly significant.

In your opening you should identify your subject so as to focus its relevance for the reader. Remember that your reader may not immediately recognize or see the importance of your topic—indeed, he or she may be preoccupied with some other business. Therefore, it is important to focus his or her attention on the subject at hand. Be particularly careful to get directly to the point; leave out any less important details.

EXAMPLE   Yesterday, I received your letter and the defective tuner, number AJ #50172, that you described. I sent the tuner to our laboratory for tests.

Carol Moore, our lead technician, reports that preliminary tests indicate. . . .

Your closing should let the reader know what he or she should do next or establish goodwill—or often both.

EXAMPLE   Thanks again for the report, and let me know if you want me to send you a printout of the tests.

Because a closing is in a position of emphasis, be especially careful to avoid **clichés**. Of course, some very commonly used closings are so precise that they are hard to replace.

EXAMPLES Thank you for your advice.

If you have further questions, please let me know.

The Complimentary Closing. Type the complimentary closing two spaces below the body. Use a standard expression like *Yours truly, Sincerely,* or *Sincerely yours.* (If the recipient is a friend as well as a business associate, you can use a less formal closing, such as *Best wishes* or *Best regards.*) Capitalize only the initial letter of the first word, and follow the expression with a **comma.** Type your full name four spaces below, aligned with the closing at the left. On the next line you may type in your business title, if it is appropriate to do so. Write your signature in the space between the complimentary closing and your typed name. If you are writing to someone with whom you are on a first-name basis, it is acceptable to sign only your given name; otherwise, sign your full name.

EXAMPLE Sincerely,

Thomas R. Castle

Thomas R. Castle
Treasurer

Sometimes the complimentary closing is followed by the name of the firm. Then comes the actual signature, between the name of the firm and the typed name.

EXAMPLE Sincerely yours,
VIKING SUPPLY COMPANY, INC.

Laura A. Newland

Laura A. Newland
Controller

A Second Page. If a letter requires a second page, always carry at least two lines of the body text over to that page; do not use a continuation page to type only the letter's closing. The second page should be typed on plain paper of quality equivalent to that of the letterhead stationery. It should have a heading with the recipient's name, the page number, and the date. The heading may go in the upper left-hand corner or across the page, as Figure 4 shows.

```
    Ms. M. C. Marks
    Page 2
    March 12, 19--
```

```
    Ms. M. C. Marks              2              March 12, 19--
```

Figure 4   Headings for the Second Page of a Letter

Additional Information. Business letters sometimes require the typist's initials, an enclosure notation, or a notation that a copy of the letter is being sent to one or more people. Place any such information at the left margin, two spaces below the last line of the complimentary closing in a long letter, four spaces below in a short letter.

The *typist's initials* should follow the letter writer's initials, and the two sets of initials should be separated by either a colon or a slash. The writer's initials should be in capital letters, and the typist's initials should be in lowercase letters. (When the writer is also the typist, no initials are needed.)

EXAMPLES JTM:mgm
MHR/jbr

Enclosure notations indicate that the writer is sending material along with the letter (an invoice, an article, and so on). They may take several forms, as illustrated below.

EXAMPLES Enclosure: Preliminary report invoice
Enclosures (2)
Enc. (or Encs.)

Enclosure notations are included in long, formal letters or in any letters where the enclosed items would not be obvious to the reader. Remember, though, that an enclosure notation cannot stand alone. You must mention the enclosed material in the body of the letter.

Letterhead	**EVANS & ASSOCIATES** 520 Niagara Street Lexington, KY 40502 (502) 787-1175 TELEX 5-72118
Date	May 15, 19--
Inside address	Mr. George W. Nagel Director of Operations Boston Transit Authority 57 West City Avenue Boston, MA 02110
Salutation	Dear Mr. Nagel:
Body	Enclosed is our final report evaluating the safety measures for the Boston Intercity Transit System. We believe the report covers the issues you raised and that it is self-explanatory. However, if you have any further questions, we would be happy to meet with you at your convenience. We would also like to express our appreciation to Mr. L. K. Sullivan of your committee for his generous help during our trips to Boston.
Complimentary close	Sincerely,
Signature	*Carolyn Brown*
Typed name	Carolyn Brown, Ph.D.
Title	Director of Research
Additional information	CB/la Enclosure: Final Safety Report cc: ITS Safety Committee Members

Figure 5   Business Letter (Full Block) with Standard Elements

Copy notations tell the reader that a copy of the letter is being sent to one or more named individuals. You should add a copy notation for both carbon copies and photocopies.

EXAMPLE cc: Ms. Marlene Brier

A letter may contain all three items of additional information.

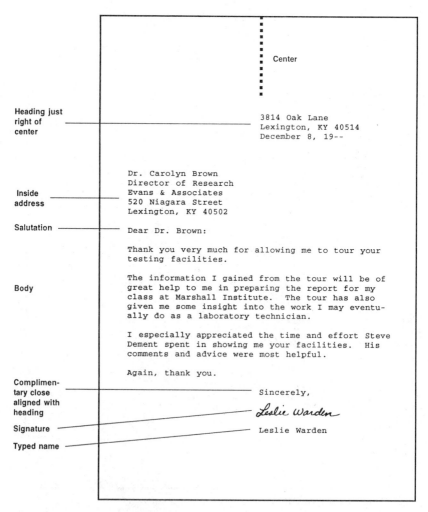

Center

Heading just right of center ————— 3814 Oak Lane
Lexington, KY 40514
December 8, 19--

Inside address ————— Dr. Carolyn Brown
Director of Research
Evans & Associates
520 Niagara Street
Lexington, KY 40502

Salutation ————— Dear Dr. Brown:

Thank you very much for allowing me to tour your testing facilities.

Body ————— The information I gained from the tour will be of great help to me in preparing the report for my class at Marshall Institute. The tour has also given me some insight into the work I may eventually do as a laboratory technician.

I especially appreciated the time and effort Steve Dement spent in showing me your facilities. His comments and advice were most helpful.

Again, thank you.

Complimentary close aligned with heading ————— Sincerely,

Leslie Warden

Signature ————— Leslie Warden

Typed name —————

Figure 6   Modified Block Style

EXAMPLE Sincerely yours,

Jane T. Rogers

Jane T. Rogers

JTR/pst
Enclosure: Preliminary report invoice
cc: Ms. Marlene Brier

Figure 5 shows a typical business letter using most of the standard elements.

LETTER FORMATS

The two most common formats of business letters are the full block style (shown in Figure 5) and the modified block style. The full block style, though easier to type because every line begins at the left margin, is suitable only with business letterhead stationery. In the modified block style, the return address, the date, and the complimentary closing all begin at the center of the page, and the other elements are aligned at the left margin. All other letter styles are variations of these two styles. Again, if your employer recommends or requires a particular style, follow it carefully. Otherwise, choose a style and follow it consistently. Figure 6 is an example of the modified block style.

THE ENVELOPE

The most widely used format for typing envelopes is the block form. Figure 7 shows the block form used with a number 10 business envelope. Figure 8 illustrates the proper technique for folding 8-1/2-by-11-inch stationery into a standard (10) envelope:

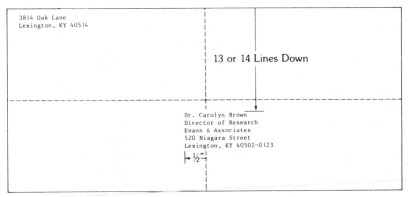

Figure 7   Address on Standard Business Envelope

Figure 8 Folding Business Stationery into a Number 10 Envelope

For information on specific types of correspondence, see **form letters, acceptance letters, acknowledgment letters, adjustment letters, application letters, collection letters, complaint letters, credit letters, inquiry letters, order letters, reference letters, refusal letters, resignation letter or memorandum, sales letters,** and **memorandums.**

credible/creditable

Something is *credible* if it is believable.

> EXAMPLE The statistics in this report are *credible*.

Something is *creditable* if it is worthy of praise or credit.

> EXAMPLE The chief engineer did a *creditable* job.

credit letters

A letter discussing credit must be worded carefully. Because credit is linked so closely to a person's integrity and financial reputation, the credit applicant will be particularly sensitive to any **tone** or **word choice** that seems to cast doubt on his or her character or finances. When you must refuse credit, be particularly sensitive to the danger of offending the credit applicant. Brief form letters that bluntly deny credit without giving reasons or suggesting alternatives can be particularly upsetting. Whatever the credit situation, you should always emphasize that your company remains anxious to serve the applicant. A bad credit risk might still be a good cash customer— and perhaps a good credit risk in the future.

When requesting information from a credit bureau or another company or when supplying credit information, ask specific questions and give specific answers.

CHANGE Please tell us if Joseph Rauch was a faithful employee.
    TO Please give us the dates of employment for Joseph Rauch.
CHANGE Mr. Rauch worked for us many years.
    TO Mr. Rauch was employed with us from September 4, 1964, to January 18, 1979.

If you must report unfavorable credit information in response to an inquiry about a customer, choose your words carefully and stick to the facts.

EXAMPLE We have had difficulty collecting for Mr. Johnson's May and June orders, and we are now on a cash basis.

If you are writing a letter inviting someone to apply for credit, take advantage of the opportunity to explain any special products or services. Emphasize the benefits of your credit plan, and suggest immediate action.

EXAMPLE Stop in this week and fill out a credit application. Take advantage of a special 10 percent discount on your first $100 in purchases.

Your first letter to an applicant might be merely an acknowledgment of his or her request for credit. This letter should be prompt and courteous but noncommittal. Be careful not to imply that credit will be approved before the references are checked. This **acknowledgment letter** offers an excellent opportunity to point out the benefits of doing business with your firm.

EXAMPLE I am enclosing a brochure explaining our unique home decorator department.

Granting credit is easy. Emphasize how happy you are to be establishing an account for the customer. Include a clear explanation of the terms of the credit plan, and point out the benefits of the plan. Again take the opportunity to stimulate enthusiasm for your company. Make the customer welcome, and invite immediate use of your new credit relationship. The example shown in Figure 1 is typical.

Refusing credit is always an unpleasant task, and demands particular tact. Be prompt and courteous, as in all **correspondence**. Open pleasantly, thanking the customer for interest in your company. Next, indicate that you have carefully considered the matter, and explain the reasons for your refusal. Suggest alternatives if there are any.

Highland Appliances, Inc.
9000 South Main Street
Pittsburgh, PA 15230
February 19, 19--

Janet Lisle
5014 Long Island Avenue
Pittsburgh, PA 15220

Dear Ms. Lisle:

Because of your excellent credit rating, we are happy to
open an account for you immediately at Highland Appliances,
Inc. As the enclosed credit agreement specifies, you will
receive an itemized statement on the fifteenth of each
month. A discount of 2 percent is available for payment
within ten days.

You can now take advantage of our special fall sale on
brand-name household appliances. Use our shop-at-home number
(555-1233) to place your order today.

Sincerely,

Brenda E. Long

Brenda E. Long
Finance Department

BEL/ja
Enclosure

Figure 1   Credit Letter

There are several common reasons for refusing credit. Most often these include generally unfavorable business conditions or the weak financial standing or poor credit record of the applicant. If the reason for refusal is a poor business climate, emphasize that you are therefore not extending credit to anyone (if this is the case). Figures 2 and 3 are two examples of such credit letters.

If the applicant's poor credit record is the cause for refusal, be brief but tactful. Remain neutral in tone, and do not criticize or of-

---

Titus Packaging, Inc.
40 North East Street
Baywood City, CA 95524
February 9, 19--

Debra Kohls
10 South Perry Street
Baywood City, CA 95524

Dear Ms. Kohls:

We appreciate your interest in establishing an open account at Titus Packaging, Inc. In the two years since you began operations in Baywood City, your firm has earned an excellent reputation in the business community. As you know, however, interest rates have been rising sharply this past year, and sales are generally down. The economic climate is so poor that we have decided not to establish any new open accounts during this calendar year.

We plan to review this policy and all pending applications after the first of the year. In the meantime, we would be pleased to continue our present cash relationship, with a 2 percent discount for payment within ten days. Just call our Sales Department (712-4034) to place an order, and your shipment will be on its way immediately.

Sincerely,

Gerald M. Bellows

Gerald M. Bellows
Manager, Finance Department

CMB/mo

Figure 2   Credit Letter

White Line Chemicals
405 Fairview Avenue
Decatur, Illinois 62525

March 12, 19--

Frank Forester, President
Forester Chemical Company
205 North Main Street
Decatur, Illinois 62525

Dear Mr. Forester:

Thank you for your order for White Line Chemicals. We are happy to
have you as a customer and look forward to establishing a good business
relationship.

Most business experts, as you know, suggest that a company maintain
an assets-to-liabilities ratio of 2 to 1. Since you are just getting
started in business, your ratio is still below that figure. We certainly
expect that as your business grows, Mr. Forester, you will be able
to reach the 2-to-1 ratio quickly and that we can then set up an open
account for you.

Although we cannot now give you the credit terms you requested, we
are happy to serve you in the meantime on a cash basis, with a special
3 percent discount for payment within ten days. Call us toll-free
at (800) 964-2996 if you wish your order shipped immediately.

Sincerely,

Dale M. Everet

Dale M. Everet
Manager, Credit Department

DME/bb

Figure 3   Credit Letter

fer condescending advice. It is usually not necessary to say too much
about the customer's poor payment record—he or she knows it.
Close the letter with an upbeat message designed to show that you
do still value the customer on a cash basis, as is done in Figure 4.

Packard's Pharmacy
One Smith Drive
Jackson, Mississippi 39205

June 16, 19--

Mildred Freeman
16 Alabaster Road
Jackson, Mississippi 39205

Dear Ms. Freeman:

Thank you for your recent request for a charge account at Packard's
Pharmacy.

We have carefully checked the credit references you supplied and
believe that it would be best to continue serving you on a cash basis.

We do hope, of course, that we can continue to offer you savings on
all your drugstore needs. Enclosed is the list of sale items for April.

We hope to see you in our store soon.

Sincerely,

Carl E. Reynolds

Carl E. Reynolds
Manager

CER/ja
Enclosure

Figure 4   Credit Letter

The credit letter, though often difficult to write, does present an opportunity to demonstrate your firm's willingness to be friendly and understanding. (See also **correspondence** and **collection letters**.)

criterion/criteria/criterions

Criterion means "an established standard for judging or testing." *Criteria* and *criterions* both are acceptable plural forms of *criterion*, but *criteria* is generally preferred.

> EXAMPLE In evaluating this job, we must use three *criteria*. The most important *criterion* is quality of workmanship.

critique

A *critique* is a written or oral evaluation of something. It is a **noun**. Avoid using *critique* as a **verb** meaning "criticize."

> CHANGE Please *critique* his job description.
> TO Please prepare a *critique* of his job description.

D

dangling modifiers

Verbal phrases (**gerund**, **participle**, **infinitive**) that do not clearly and logically refer to the proper **noun** or **pronoun** are called *dangling modifiers*. Dangling modifiers usually appear at the beginning of a sentence as an introductory phrase.

> CHANGE While eating lunch in the cafeteria, the computer malfunc-
> tioned. (The problem, of course, is that the sentence ne-
> glects to mention *who* was eating lunch in the cafeteria.)
>
> TO While *the operator* was eating lunch in the cafeteria, the com-
> puter malfunctioned.

Dangling modifiers can, however, appear at the end of the sentence as well. Probably the clearest example of this type of dangling modifier is the sentence "The mouse was caught *using the trap*." For a more business-oriented example, consider the following sentence:

> CHANGE The problem was eventually solved, working with them. (*Who*
> was working with them? An action is stated, but no one is
> identified who could perform the stated action.)
>
> TO Working with them, *we* solved the problem.
>
> OR *We* solved the problem by working with them.

Edmund Weiss, in *The Writing System for Engineers and Scientists*, offers this example: "The car was designed by our new safety engineer with an impact-absorbing rear end."

Dangling modifiers are often caused by overuse of the passive **voice**. In an active-voice clause, the doer of the action appears in front of the verb; since the doer of the action is normally the intended subject of the introductory phrase, the phrase does not dangle. If the clause is in the passive voice, however, the doer of the action appears after the verb or is not identified, thereby causing the phrase to dangle.

> CHANGE To evaluate the feasibility of the project, the centralized plan
> will be compared with the present system of dispersing facil-
> ity sites. (The main clause is in the passive voice, and the
> doer of the action expressed by the verb *compared* is not iden-
> tified; therefore, the introductory phrase "To evaluate the

feasibility of the project" has nothing that it can logically modify because there is no one in the main clause who could possibly evaluate anything.)

TO   To evaluate the feasibility of the project, *the committee* will compare the centralized plan with the present system of dispersing facility sites.

DANGLING GERUND PHRASES

A dangling gerund phrase can be corrected by adding a noun or a pronoun for it to modify.

CHANGE   After finishing the research, the job was easy.

TO   After finishing the research, *we* found the job to be easy.

Another way to correct a dangling gerund phrase is to make the **phrase** into a **clause**.

CHANGE   After finishing the research, the job was easy.

TO   After we finished the research, the job was easy.

OR   The job was easy after we finished the research.

DANGLING PARTICIPIAL PHRASES

A dangling **participial phrase** can be corrected by providing a subject that stands near the phrase.

CHANGE   Keeping busy, the afternoon passed swiftly.

TO   Keeping busy, *I* felt that the afternoon passed swiftly.

A dangling participial phrase may also be corrected by making the phrase into a clause.

CHANGE   Keeping busy, the afternoon passed swiftly.

TO   Because I kept busy, the afternoon passed swiftly.

CHANGE   Entering the gate, the administration building is visible.

TO   As you enter the gate, the administration building is visible.

CHANGE   Being a poor speller, a word processor with a large dictionary is important to me.

TO   Because I am a poor speller, a word processor with a large dictionary is important to me.

DANGLING INFINITIVE PHRASES

Correct a dangling **infinitive phrase** by supplying the missing noun or pronoun that provides the subject of the infinitive phrase.

CHANGE   To improve typing skills, practice is needed.

TO   To improve typing skills, *you* must practice.

CHANGE   To evaluate the feasibility of the project, the centralized plan will be compared with the present system of dispersing facility sites.

TO   To evaluate the feasibility of the project, the *committee* will compare the centralized plan with the present system of dispersing facility sites.

DANGLING SUBORDINATE CLAUSES

Occasionally a **subject** and **verb** are omitted from a **dependent clause**, forming what is known as an *elliptical clause*. If the omitted subject of the elliptical clause is not the same as the subject of the main clause, the construction will dangle. Simply adding the subject and verb to the elliptical clause solves the problem.

CHANGE   When ten years old, his father started the company.

TO   When *Bill* was ten years old, his father started the company.

OR   Bill was ten years old when his father started the company.

(See also **misplaced modifiers** and **verbals**.)

dashes

The dash is a versatile, yet limited, mark of **punctuation**. It is versatile because it can perform all the duties of punctuation (to link, to separate, and to enclose). It is limited because it is an especially emphatic mark that is easily overused. Use the dash cautiously, therefore, to indicate more informality or **emphasis** (a dash gives an impression of abruptness) than would be achieved by the conventional punctuation marks. In some situations, a dash is required; in others, a dash is a forceful substitute for other marks.

A dash can emphasize a sharp turn in thought.

EXAMPLE   The project will end on January 15—unless the company provides additional funds.

A dash can indicate an emphatic pause.

EXAMPLES   Consider the potential danger of a household item that contains mercury—a very toxic substance.

The job will be done—after we are under contract.

Sometimes, to emphasize contrast, a dash is also used with *but*.

> EXAMPLE   We may have produced work more quickly—but the result was not as good.

A dash can be used before a final summarizing statement or before **repetition** that has the effect of an afterthought.

> EXAMPLE   It was hot near the ovens—steaming hot.

Such a thought may also complete the meaning.

> EXAMPLE   We try to speak as we write—or so we believe.

A dash can be used to set off an explanatory or **appositive** series.

> EXAMPLE   Three of the applicants—John Evans, Mary Fontana, and Thomas Lopez—seem well qualified for the job.

Dashes set off parenthetical elements more sharply and emphatically than do **commas**. Unlike dashes, **parentheses** tend to reduce the importance of what they enclose. Compare the following sentences:

> EXAMPLES   Only one person—the president—can authorize such activity.
> Only one person, the president, can authorize such activity.
> Only one person (the president) can authorize such activity.

Use dashes for **clarity** when commas appear within a parenthetical element; this avoids the confusion of too many commas.

> EXAMPLE   Retinal images are patterns in the eye—made up of light and dark shapes, in addition to areas of color—but we do not see patterns; we see objects.

The first word after a dash is never capitalized unless it is a proper noun. In typing, use two consecutive **hyphens** (--) to indicate a dash, with no spaces before or after the hyphens.

data/datum

The debate over whether *data* should be treated as a plural or a collective singular noun continues. In much business writing, **data** is considered a collective singular. In formal and scholarly writing, however, *data* is generally used as a plural, with *datum* as the singular form.

EXAMPLES   The *data are* voluminous in support of a link between smoking
and lung cancer. (formal)
The *data is* now ready to be evaluated. (less formal)

Base your decision on whether your **reader** should consider the data
as a single collection or as a group of individual facts. Whatever you
decide, be sure that your **pronouns** and **verbs** agree in **number** with
the selected **usage**.

EXAMPLES   The *data are* voluminous. *They indicate* a link between smoking
and lung cancer.
The *data is* now ready for evaluation. *It is* in the mail.

dates

In business and industry, dates have traditionally been indicated by
the month, day, and year, with a **comma** separating the figures.

EXAMPLE   October 26, 19--

The day-month-year system used by the military does not require
commas.

EXAMPLE   26 October 19--

A date can be written with or without a comma following the year
if the date is in the month-day-year format.

EXAMPLES   October 26, 19--, was the date the project began.
October 26, 19-- was the date the project began.

If the date is in the day-month-year format, do not set off the date
with commas.

EXAMPLE   The project began on 26 October 19--.

The strictly numerical form for dates (10/26/87) should be used
sparingly, and never on business letters or formal documents, since
it is less immediately clear. When this form is used, the order in
American usage is always month/day/year. For example, 5/7/87 is
May 7, 1987.

CENTURIES

Confusion often occurs because the spelled-out names of centuries
do not correspond to the numbers of the years. (See also **numbers**.)

EXAMPLES   The twentieth century is the 1900s (1900–1999).
The nineteenth century is the 1800s (1800–1899).
The fifth century is the 400s (400–499).

When the century is written as a noun, do not use a hyphen.

EXAMPLE   The sixteenth century produced great literature.

When the century is written as an adjective, however, use a hyphen.

EXAMPLE   Twentieth-century business must rely on clear business communications.

decided/decisive

When something is *decided*, it is "clear-cut," "without doubt," "unmistakable." When something is *decisive*, it is "conclusive" or "has the power to settle a dispute."

EXAMPLE   The executive committee's *decisive* action gave our firm a *decided* advantage over the competition.

decreasing-order-of-importance method of development

Decreasing order of importance is a **method of development** in which the writer's major points are arranged in descending order of importance. It begins with the most important fact or point, then goes to the next most important, and so on, ending with the least important. It is an especially appropriate method of development for a **report** addressed to a busy decision maker, who may be able to reach a decision after considering only the most important points, or for a report addressed to various **readers**, some of whom may be interested only in the major points and others in all of the points.

The advantages of this method of development are that (1) it gets the reader's attention immediately by presenting the most important point first, (2) it makes a strong initial impression, and (3) it ensures that the hurried reader will not miss the most important point.

The example shown in Figure 1 uses decreasing order of importance.

INTEROFFICE MEMORANDUM

To: Mary Vincenti, Chief, Personnel Department
From: Frank W. Russo, Chief, Claims Department *FWR*
Date: November 13, 19--
Subject: Selection of Chief of the Claims Processing Section

I feel there are three possible candidates for the position of Chief of
the Claims Processing Section.

The most qualified candidate for Chief of the Claims Processing Section
is Mildred Bryand, who is at present Acting Chief of the Claims Processing Section. In her twelve years in the Claims Department, Ms. Bryand
has gained wide experience in all facets of the department's operations.
She has maintained a consistently high production record and has demonstrated the skills and knowledge that are required for the supervisory
duties she is now handling in an acting capacity. A number of additional qualifications also make her the best candidate: her valuable
contributions to and cooperation during the automation of the
department's claims records; her performance on several occasions as
acting chief in other sections of the Claims Department; the continual
rating of "outstanding" she has received in all categories of her job-
performance appraisals.

Michael Bastik, Claims Coordinator, our second choice, also has strong
potential for the position. An able administrator, he has been with the
company for seven years. For the past year he has been enrolled in
several management training courses at the university. He is ranked
second, however, because he lacks supervisory experience and because his
most recent work has been with the department's maintenance and supply
components. He would be the best person to fill many of Mildred
Bryand's responsibilities if she should be made full-time Chief of the
Claims Processing Section.

Jane Fine, our third-ranking candidate, has shown herself a skilled
administrator in her three years with the Claims Consideration Section.
Despite her obvious potential, my main objection to her is that compared
with the other top candidates, she lacks the breadth of experience in
claims processing that would be required of someone responsible for
managing the Claims Processing Section. Jane Fine also lacks on-the-job
supervisory experience.

Please let me have your recommendations on filling this position at your
earliest convenience

mo

Figure 1 Decreasing Order of Importance

de facto/de jure

De facto means that something "exists" or is "a fact" and therefore
is accepted for practical purposes. *De jure* means that something
"legally" exists.

EXAMPLE The law states that no signs should be erected along Highway
127. Store owners have disregarded this law, and many signs
exist along Highway 127. The presence of the signs along
Highway 127 is *de facto* but not *de jure*—their presence is "a
fact," but it is not "lawful."

defective / deficient

If something is *defective*, it is faulty.

EXAMPLE The wiring was *defective*.

If something is *deficient*, it lacks a necessary ingredient.

EXAMPLE The compound was found to be *deficient* in calcium.

defining terms

One of the most basic rules of good writing is to be sure that your
readers understand and follow what they are reading. You must always keep in mind their familiarity with the topic and be careful to
define any terms that they may not understand.

Terms can be defined either formally or informally, depending on
your purpose and on your readers. (For techniques on expanding
a definition to explain the meaning of a term, see **definition method
of development**.)

A *formal definition* is a form of classification. A term is defined by
placing it in a category and then identifying what features distinguish it from other members of the same category. Several examples
of formal definitions are given in the table on page 181. An *informal
definition* explains a term by giving a familiar word or **phrase** as a
synonym.

EXAMPLES An *invoice* is a bill.
Many states have set up wildlife *habitats* (or living spaces).
Plants have a *symbiotic*, or mutually beneficial, relationship
with certain kinds of bacteria.

Definitions should normally be stated positively; focus on what the
term is rather than on what it is not. For example, "In a legal transaction, real property is not personal property," although a true
statement, does not tell the reader exactly what real property *is*. The
definition could just as easily be stated positively: "Real property is

Term	Category	Distinguishing Features
A spoon is	an eating utensil	that consists of a small shallow bowl on the end of a handle.
An auction is	a public sale	in which property passes to the highest bidder through successively increased offers.
An annual is	a plant	that completes its life cycle, from seed to natural death, in one growing season.
A contract is	a binding agreement	between two or more persons or parties.
A lease is	a contract	that conveys real estate for a term of years at a specified rent.

legal terminology for the right or interest a person has in land and the permanent structures on that land." (For a discussion of when negative definitions are appropriate, see **definition method of development.**)

When writing a definition, keep in mind the following pitfalls that may result in confusing, inaccurate, or incomplete definitions:

Avoid circular definitions, which merely restate the term to be defined and therefore fail to clarify it.

CIRCULAR *Spontaneous combustion* is fire that begins spontaneously.

REVISED *Spontaneous combustion* is the self-ignition of a flammable material through a chemical reaction like oxidation and temperature buildup.

Avoid "is when" and "is where" definitions. Such definitions fail to include the category and are too indirect: They say when or where rather than what.

"IS WHEN" A *contract* is when two or more people agree to something.

REVISED A *contract* is a binding agreement between two or more people.

"IS WHERE" A *day-care center* is where working parents can leave their preschool children during the day.

REVISED A *day-care center* is a facility at which working parents can leave their preschool children during the day.

Avoid definitions that include terms that may be unfamiliar to your readers. Even informal writing will occasionally require terms used in a special sense that your readers may not understand; such terms should always be defined.

> EXAMPLE In these specifications the term *safety can* refers to an approved container of not more than five-gallon capacity having a spring-closing spout cover designed to relieve internal pressure when the can is exposed to fire.

definite/definitive

Definite and *definitive* both apply to what is "precisely defined," but *definitive* more often refers to what is complete and authoritative.

> EXAMPLE When the committee took a *definite* stand, the president made it the *definitive* company policy.

definition method of development

To define something is basically to identify precisely its fundamental qualities. In business writing, as in all writing, clear and accurate definitions are critical. Sometimes simple, dictionarylike definitions suffice (see **defining terms**), but at other times definitions need to be expanded with additional details, examples, comparisons, or other explanatory devices.

When more than a **phrase** or a sentence or two is needed to explain an idea, use an *extended definition,* which explores a number of qualities of the item being defined. How an extended definition is developed depends on your reader's needs and on the complexity of the subject. A **reader** familiar with a **topic** or an area might be able to handle a long, fairly technical definition, whereas one less familiar with a topic would require simpler language and more basic information.

Probably the easiest way to give an extended definition is with specific examples. Listing examples gives your reader easy-to-picture details that help him or her to see and thus to understand the term being defined.

> EXAMPLE Form, which is the shape of landscape features, can best be represented by both small-scale features, such as *trees and shrubs,* and by large-scale elements, such as *mountains and mountain ranges.*

Another useful way to define a difficult concept, especially when you are writing for nonspecialists, is to use an **analogy** to link the unfamiliar concept with a simpler or more familiar one. An analogy is a resemblance in certain aspects between things otherwise unalike, and it can help the reader understand an unfamiliar term by showing its similarities with a more familiar one. Notice in the following description of *management by objective* how the writer develops an analogy to make his point.

EXAMPLE   Management by objective has been quite popular, but it is important to remember that the selection of objectives is the key to successfully adopting this principle. Think, for example, of a golfer who wishes to improve by hitting the ball farther. The golfer sets a goal of hitting every drive as far as possible. Every decision the golfer makes is governed by that goal—hitting the ball as far as possible. The golfer would then be managing his or her game by objective. However, the golfer is shortsighted because golf is as much a game of accuracy as it is of hitting balls for distance. Some of the decisions the golfer makes, therefore, might well be counterproductive to achieving the larger goal of obtaining the lowest score possible. Therefore, when a company decides to use a management by objective strategy, it must be certain that the objective is appropriate for achieving the desired result.

Some terms are best defined by an explanation of their causes, as the following explanation of the term *stagflation* demonstrates:

EXAMPLE   Traditional economic theory said that a decline in business activity and employment caused a decrease in the rate of inflation. In recent history, however, economists have learned that inflation can continue while business and employment decline. These combined factors produce an economy that is sluggish and a general attitude that inflation will continue. This condition has been called *stagflation*.

Sometimes a formal definition of a concept can be made simpler by breaking the concept into its component parts. In the following example, the formal definition of *fire* is given in the first paragraph, and the component parts are given in the second:

EXAMPLE   Fire is the visible heat energy released from the rapid oxidation of a fuel. A substance is "on fire" when the release of heat energy from the oxidation process reaches visible light levels.

> The classic fire triangle illustrates the elements necessary to create fire: *oxygen, heat,* and *burnable material* or *fuel.* Air provides sufficient oxygen for combustion; the intensity of the heat needed to start a fire depends on the characteristics of the burnable material or fuel. A burnable substance is one that will sustain combustion after an initial application of heat to start it.

Under certain circumstances, the meaning of a term can be clarified and made easier to remember by an exploration of its origin. Scientific and medical terms, because of their sometimes unfamiliar Greek and Latin roots, benefit especially from an explanation of this type. Tracing the derivation of a word can also be useful when you want to explain why a word has favorable or unfavorable associations—particularly if your goal is to influence your reader's attitude toward an idea or an activity.

EXAMPLE   Efforts to influence legislation generally fall under the head of *lobbying,* a term that once referred to people who prowl the lobbies of houses of government, buttonholing lawmakers and trying to get them to take certain positions. Lobbying today is all of this, and much more, too. It is a respected—and necessary—activity. It tells the legislator which way the winds of public opinion are blowing, and it helps inform him of the implications of certain bills, debates, and resolutions he must contend with.
—Bill Vogt, *How to Build a Better Outdoors* (New York: McKay, 1978) 93.

Sometimes it is useful to point out what something is *not* in order to clarify what it is. A negative definition is effective only when the reader is familiar with the item with which the defined item is contrasted. If you say *x* is not *y*, your readers must understand the meaning of *y* for the explanation to make sense. In a crane operators' manual, for instance, a negative definition is used to show that for safety reasons, a hydraulic crane cannot be operated in the same manner as a lattice boom crane.

EXAMPLE   A hydraulic crane is *not* like a lattice boom crane in one very important way. In most cases, the safe lifting capacity of a lattice boom crane is based on the *weight needed to tip the machine.* Therefore, operators of friction machines sometimes depend on signs that the machine might tip to warn them of impending danger.
This practice is very dangerous with a hydraulic crane. . . .
—*Operator's Manual* (Model W-180), Harnishfeger Corporation.

demonstrative adjectives

The demonstrative adjectives are *this, these, that,* and *those.* They are **adjectives** that "point to" the thing they modify, specifying its position in space or time. *This* and *these* specify a closer position; *that* and *those* specify a more remote position.

EXAMPLES   *This* proposal is the one we accepted.
That proposal would have been impracticable.
These problems remain to be solved.
These problems are not insurmountable.

Notice that *this* and *that* are used with singular **nouns** and that *these* and *those* are used with plural nouns. Demonstrative adjectives often cause problems when they modify the nouns *kind, type,* and *sort.* Demonstrative adjectives used with these nouns should agree with them in **number**.

EXAMPLES   this kind/these kinds
that type/those types
this sort/these sorts

Confusion often develops when the **preposition** *of* is added ("this kind *of,*" "these kinds *of*") and the **object** of the preposition is not made to conform in number to the demonstrative adjective and its noun.

CHANGE   *This kind* of hydraulic *cranes* is best.
TO   *This kind* of hydraulic *crane* is best.

CHANGE   *These kinds* of hydraulic *crane* are best.
TO   *These kinds* of hydraulic *cranes* are best.

The error can be avoided by remembering to make the demonstrative adjective, the noun, and the object of the preposition—all three—agree in number. This **agreement** makes the sentence not only correct but also more precise.

Using demonstrative adjectives with words like *kind, type,* and *sort* can easily lead to vagueness. It is better to be more specific.

CHANGE   It was *kind of* a bad year for the firm.
TO   The firm's profits were down 10 percent from last year.

Do not use the pronoun *this* and *that* to make broad or ambiguous references to a whole sentence or to an abstract thought. (See also **pronoun reference**.) For recommendations on the placement and usage of demonstrative adjectives, see **adjectives**.

demonstrative pronouns

Demonstrative pronouns are actually the same words as **demonstrative adjectives**, but they differ in **usage** (a demonstrative adjective modifies a **noun**, a demonstrative pronoun substitutes for a noun). The antecedent of a demonstrative pronoun must either be the last noun of the preceding sentence—not the idea of the sentence—or be clearly identified within the same sentence, as in the following examples:

> EXAMPLES　*This* is the *specification* as we wrote it.
> *These* are the *statistics* we needed to begin the project.
> *That* was a *proposal* for drilling a water well.
> *Those* were *salesmen.*

Notice that as with demonstrative adjectives, *this* and *that* are used for singular nouns and *these* and *those* for plural nouns. Do not use the pronoun *this* and *that* to make broad or ambiguous references to a whole sentence or to an abstract thought. (See also **pronoun reference**.) One way to avoid the problem is to insert the noun immediately after the pronoun.

> CHANGE　The inadequate quality-control procedure has resulted in an equipment failure. *This* is our most serious problem at present.
> TO　The inadequate quality-control procedure has resulted in an equipment failure. *This failure* is our most serious problem at present.

dependent clauses

A dependent (or subordinate) clause is a group of words that has a **subject** and a **predicate** but nonetheless depends on a main **clause** to complete its meaning. A dependent clause can function in a sentence as a **noun**, an **adjective**, or an **adverb**.

As nouns, dependent clauses may function in the sentence as subjects, **objects**, or **complements**.

> EXAMPLES　*That human beings can learn to control their glands and internal organs by direct or indirect means* is an established fact. (subject)
> I learned *that drugs ordered by brand name can cost several times as much as drugs ordered by generic name.* (direct object)
> The trouble is *that we cannot finish the project by May.* (subjective complement)

As adjectives, dependent clauses can modify nouns or **pronouns**. Dependent clauses are often introduced by **relative pronouns** and relative adjectives (*who, which, that*).

 EXAMPLE The man *who called earlier* is here. (modifying *man*)

As adverbs, dependent clauses may express relationships of time, cause, result, or degree.

 EXAMPLES You are making an investment *when you buy a house.* (time)
    A title search was necessary *because the bank would not issue a loan without one.* (cause)
    The cost of financing a home will be higher *if discount points are charged.* (result)
    Monthly mortgage payments should not be much more *than a person earns in one week.* (degree)

Dependent clauses are useful in making the relationship between thoughts more precise and succinct than if the ideas were presented in a series of **simple sentences** or **compound sentences**.

 CHANGE The sewage plant is located between Millville and Darrtown. Both villages use it. (two thoughts of approximately equal importance)
   TO The sewage plant, *which is located between Millville and Darrtown,* is used by both villages. (one thought subordinated to the other)

 CHANGE Title insurance is a policy issued by a title insurance company, *and* it protects against any title defects, such as outside claimants. (two thoughts of approximately equal importance)
   TO Title insurance, *which* protects against any title defects, such as outside claimants, is a policy issued by a title insurance company. (one thought subordinated to the other)

Subordinate clauses are especially effective, therefore, for expressing thoughts that describe or explain another statement. Too much **subordination**, or a string of dependent clauses, however, may be worse than none at all.

 CHANGE Since interest rates on conventional loans tend to follow general conditions in the money market, *if* money is plentiful for lending and the demand for loans is low, interest rates will be forced down, *whereas* if money is scarce and the demand for loans is high, interest rates will be forced up.

TO   Interest rates on conventional loans tend to follow general conditions in the money market: if money is plentiful for lending and the demand for loans is low, interest rates will be forced down; if money is scarce and the demand for loans is high, interest rates will be forced up.

CHANGE   He had selected teachers *who* taught classes *that* had a slant *that* was specifically directed toward students *who* intended to go into business.

TO   He had selected teachers *who* taught classes *that* were specifically directed to business students.

description

Effective description uses words to transfer a mental image from the writer's mind to the reader's. The key to effective description is the accurate presentation of details. To select appropriate details, determine what use your **reader** will make of the description. Will it be used to identify an object? Will it be used to repair or assemble the device you are describing?

Descriptions can be brief and simple, or they can be highly complex. Simple descriptions usually require only a simple listing of key features. A purchase order is a typical example of simple descriptive writing (see accompanying example). Purchase-order descriptions should be clear and specific. An inaccurate or omitted detail may result in the delivery of the wrong item. Even an order for something as ordinary as trash compactor bags needed, in addition to the part number, five specific descriptive details.

PURCHASE ORDER

Part No.	Description	Quantity
GL/020	Trash compactor bags, 31″ × 50″ tubular, non-transparent, 5-mil thickness, including 100 tie wraps per carton	5 cartons @ 100 per carton

Complex descriptions, of course, require even more details than do simple descriptions. The details you select should accurately and vividly convey what you are describing. If it is useful for your reader to visualize an object, for instance, include details—like color and shape—that appeal to the sense of sight. The following description of a corporate headquarters uses details, partly based on shapes, to convey an image to the reader. The writer assumes that the reader knows such terms as *colonial design* and *champaign elm*.

Sets scene | Their corporate headquarters, which reminded me of a rural college campus, is located just north of the city in a 90-acre wooded area. It consists of five 3-story buildings of colonial design. The buildings are spaced about 50 feet apart and are
Integrates scene with U-shaped image | built in a *U* shape, with the main building at the bottom of the *U*. The driveway that runs in front of the buildings is lined with overarching champaign elms. Employee and visitor parking lots are nearly hidden behind each building.

An aspect of description sometimes called *rendering* is the act of show-ing or demonstrating, as opposed to telling, primarily through the use of images and details. Rendering makes writing more vivid and interesting by giving the reader more details and a sense of immedi-acy. This technique is especially useful to business people because it can help clarify and make more concrete the complex, abstract, and sometimes subtle subjects with which they must deal. It also uses **analogy** to explain unfamiliar concepts in terms of familiar con-cepts. For example, the plastic device that holds the letters and sym-bols for some typewriters and word-processing printers is a wheel-shaped piece of plastic, with each letter and symbol positioned at the circumference of the wheel and attached to the hub at the center of the wheel by thin plastic strips. Using **analogy**, the strips can be thought of as petals radiating from the center of a flower. Because the strips are uniform in length and width, similar to the petals of a daisy, the print elements are commonly referred to, in an extension of the flower analogy, as daisy wheel print elements.

The following sentence, typical of much business writing, con-tains a number of complex notions unfamiliar to the nonexpert:

EXAMPLE Computers can scan and read punched cards.

The complex thought contained in this sentence can be rendered clearly by the skillful use of images and details from everyday life (the familiar) used as a bridge to the unfamiliar.

Familiar (print/page) | When information appears in print, as on this page, people like you and me are able to read and understand it. However, if information is to be processed by a machine, like a com-puter, then other ways must be found to put these same letters

Unfamiliar (machine) and words into the machine. Computers, of course, do not have eyes like humans—but they do have electrical sensing equipment that in certain ways does almost the same thing.

Familiar (doors at market)

For example, most of us have walked into supermarkets through doors that open by themselves. These doors are controlled by electrical sensing equipment known as photoelectric cells, which act like eyes. Each door is controlled by two

Unfamiliar (photoelectric cell) photoelectric cells that shine a beam of light to each other. As you walk through the door, the light beam is broken causing the photoelectric cells or "eyes" to sense that someone is beginning to enter. The electric eye reacts in a split second by sending a burst of electrical energy to the door's mechanical hinge, and this automatically swings the door open.

Transitional ideas (beam of light/hole in card)

The photoelectric sensing idea can also be used to detect the presence of a hole in a card or piece of paper.

New concept (machine "reading" text)

Thus, if holes are punched in paper to represent certain letters of the alphabet or words, it is possible for the machine to electronically sense or read this information.

—Joseph Becker, *The First Book of Information Science* (Washington, DC: U.S. Atomic Energy Commission, 1973) 20.

Illustrations can be powerful aids in descriptive writing, especially when they show details too cumbersome to explain in writing.

despite/in spite of

Despite and *in spite of* (both meaning "notwithstanding") should not be blended into *despite of*.

CHANGE *Despite of* our best efforts, the plan failed.

TO *In spite of* (or *despite*) our best efforts, the plan failed.

Although there is no literal difference between *despite* and *in spite of*, *despite* suggests an effort to avoid blame.

EXAMPLES *Despite* our best efforts, the plan failed. (We are not to blame for the failure.)

In spite of our best efforts, the plan failed. (We did everything possible, but failure overcame us.)

diacritical marks

Diacritical marks are **symbols** added to letters to indicate their specific sounds. They include the phonetic symbols used by **dictionar-**

ies as well as the marks used with foreign words. Some dictionaries place a reference list of common marks and sounds at the bottom of each page. The accompanying list presents common diacritical marks with their equivalent sound values. (See also **foreign words in English**.)

Name	Symbol	Example	Meaning
macron	¯	cāke	a "long" sound that signifies the standard pronunciation of the letter
breve	˘	bracket	a "short" sound, in contrast to the standard pronunciation of the letter
dieresis	¨	coöperate	indicates that the second of two consecutive vowels is to be pronounced separately
acute accent	´	cliché	indicates a primary vocal stress on the indicated letter
grave accent	`	crèche	indicates a deep sound articulated toward the back of the mouth
circumflex	^	crêpe	indicates a very soft sound
tilde	~	cañon	a Spanish diacritical mark identifying the palatal nasal "ny" sound
cedilla	ç	garçon	a mark placed beneath the letter *c* in French, Portuguese, and Spanish to indicate an *s* sound

diagnosis / prognosis

Because they sound somewhat alike, these words are often confused with each other. *Diagnosis* means "an analysis of the nature of something" or "the conclusions reached by such analysis."

> EXAMPLE The chairman of the board *diagnosed* the problem as the allocation of too few dollars for research.

Prognosis means "a forecast or prediction."

> EXAMPLE He offered his *prognosis* that the problem would be solved next year.

dictation

If you write many short letters or **memorandums**, dictation may save you numerous hours each week. (See also **correspondence**.)

You should be aware, however, that dictation has certain limitations. First, although some people can compose sentences easily while speaking into a microphone or telephone, others find dictating a chore and can compose faster on paper. Only experience will tell whether dictation is for you. Second, certain kinds of material do not lend themselves to dictation. **Reports**, for example, or any material with mathematical equations, **tables**, **graphs**, or scientific terminology pose special problems for the person dictating as well as for the person transcribing. In general, dictation proves less effective with materials that have a complicated **format**. Finally, dictation sometimes causes a choppy and unconversational **style**, and so you may need to allow time to edit and polish your draft after you receive the transcription from the typist.

If you determine that dictation will save you time and effort, you may find the following tips helpful:

1. Once you learn how to use your firm's dictating equipment, you might want to make a few practice runs in order to become familiar with switches and buttons or the response time of a centralized dictating service.

2. Outline before you dictate. The length and complexity of the letter will determine how detailed your outline should be. However, even if you jot down only several key words in the order you wish to present your ideas, don't skip the outline—it will help prevent you from "freezing" when the machine is running.

3. Begin your dictation with any special **instructions** for the person transcribing: "This is a rough draft—please double-space" or "Prepare four copies."

4. Speak in a normal voice and enunciate clearly. Avoid vocal pauses ("uh," "er," "hm"); simply stop speaking or turn off the machine when you cannot think of what to say next.

5. Spell out words that sound like other words (*ensure, insure*); personal or company names when used for the first time (spell out the name MacGillis as "capital *M*, small *a*, *c*, capital *G*, small *i*, *l*, *l*, *i*, *s*"); **abbreviations**, and unusual terms.

6. Slow down for **numbers**, addresses, and difficult phrases ("*send six showroom* display cases").

7. Dictate as much **punctuation** as your transcriber needs; however, *always* specify "paragraph," "quote," "unquote," "open parenthesis," "close parenthesis," and "underline."
8. Give a good secretary or transcriber the latitude to make corrections in punctuation, grammar, or **usage**. You, however, are responsible for the content and **tone**.
9. Proofread the transcribed dictation carefully, and make any necessary revisions—especially in important correspondence. Never skip this important stage, no matter how much you trust the person transcribing the dictation. (See also **proofreading**.)
10. Set a time each day for dictation, preferably early enough to allow time to review the correspondence before mailing it.

diction

The term *diction* is often misunderstood because it means both "the choice of words used in writing and speech" *and* "the degree of distinctness of enunciation of speech." In discussions of writing, *diction* applies to choice of words. (See also **word choice**.)

dictionaries

A dictionary lists, in alphabetical order, a selection of the words in a language. It defines them, gives their **spelling** and pronunciation, and indicates their function as a **part of speech**. In addition, it provides information about a word's origin and historical development. Often it provides a list of **synonyms** for a word and, where pertinent, an **illustration** to help clarify the meaning of the word.

The explanation of a word's meaning makes up the bulk of a dictionary entry. A dictionary gives primarily denotative rather than connotative meanings. It also labels the field of knowledge to which a specific meaning applies (grid, *electricity*; merger, *law*). Some specialized dictionaries list such technical terms exclusively. (See **library research** for examples.) The order in which a word's meanings are given varies. Some dictionaries give the most widely accepted current meaning first; others list the meaning in historical order, with the oldest meaning first and the current meaning last. If a word has two or more fundamental meanings, they are listed in separate paragraphs, with secondary meanings numbered consecutively within each paragraph. A dictionary's preface normally indicates whether current or historical meanings are listed in an entry.

A dictionary entry also includes a word's spelling. It lists any variant spellings (align/aline, catalog/catalogue) and indicates which is most commonly used. Entries show if and where a word ought to be hyphenated—information especially helpful for **compound words**—and how the word can be abbreviated.

A word's pronunciation, indicated by phonetic symbols, is also given. The **symbols** are explained in a key in the front pages of the dictionary, and an abbreviated symbol key is often found at the bottom of each page as well. (See also **diacritical marks**.)

Information about the origin and history of a word (its etymology) is also given, usually in **brackets** at the end of the entry. This information can help clarify a word's current meaning.

Entries also include information about a word's part of speech and its inflected forms (how it forms plurals or how it changes form to express comparative and superlative degree). Many entries include a list of synonyms in a separate paragraph following the main paragraph. Some dictionaries label words according to **usage** levels to indicate whether a word is considered standard English, nonstandard English, slang, and so on. Many dictionaries supplement a word's definition by providing illustrations in the form of **maps**, **photographs**, **tables**, **graphs**, and the like.

TYPES OF DICTIONARIES

Desk dictionaries are often abridged versions of larger dictionaries. There is no single "best" dictionary, but there are several guidelines for selecting a good desk dictionary. Choose a recent edition. The older the dictionary, the less likely it is to have the up-to-date information you need. Select a dictionary with upward of 125,000 entries. Pocket dictionaries are convenient for checking spelling, but for detailed information the larger range of a desk dictionary is necessary. The following are considered good desk dictionaries:

1. *The Random House College Dictionary*. Rev. ed. New York: Random.
2. *The American Heritage Dictionary of the English Language*. Boston: Houghton.
3. *Funk and Wagnalls Standard College Dictionary*. New, updated ed. New York: Funk.

4. *Webster's New World Dictionary of the American Language.* Cleveland: World.
5. *Webster's Ninth New Collegiate Dictionary.* Springfield, MA: Merriam.

Unabridged dictionaries provide complete and authoritative linguistic information, but they are impractical for desk use because of their size and expense.

1. *Webster's Third New International Dictionary of the English Language, Unabridged* (Springfield, MA: Merriam, 1981) contains over 450,000 entries. Since word meanings are listed in historical order, the current meaning is given last. This dictionary does not list personal and geographical names, nor does it include usage information. *Webster's Third* is updated with periodic supplements that define thousands of new terms that have entered the language since 1981.
2. *The Random House Dictionary of the English Language,* 2nd ed. (New York: Random, 1987) contains nearly 300,000 entries, many illustrations, a 31-page color atlas, a manual of style, a chart of the chemical elements, and quick translating dictionaries of French, German, Spanish, and Italian. It gives a word's widely used current meaning first, and includes personal and geographic names.

The following unabridged dictionary attempts to be exhaustive:

The Oxford English Dictionary, 2nd ed. (Oxford, England: Clarendon, 1991) is the standard historical dictionary of the English language, with definitions of over 500,000 terms. It follows the chronological development of the terms defined, beginning about the year 1000, providing numerous examples of usage and sources. The 20-volume second edition integrates the original dictionary, published in 1928, with the four supplemental volumes published between 1972 and 1986, into one alphabetical sequence.

(See also **reference books.**)

differ from/differ with

Differ from is used to suggest that two things are not alike.

EXAMPLE The vice-president's background *differs from* the general manager's background.

Differ with is used to indicate disagreement between persons.

> EXAMPLE Our attorney *differed with* theirs over the selection of the last jury member.

different from/different than

In formal writing, the **preposition** *from* is used with *different*.

> EXAMPLE The fourth-generation computer is *different from* the third-generation computer.

Different than is acceptable when it is followed by a **clause**.

> EXAMPLE The job cost was *different than* we had estimated it.

direct address

Direct address refers to a sentence or **phrase** in which the person being spoken or written to is explicity named.

> EXAMPLE *John*, call me as soon as you arrive at the airport.
> Call me, *John*, as soon as you arrive at the airport.

Notice that the person's name in a direct address is set off by **commas**.

discreet/discrete

Discreet means "having or showing prudent or careful behavior."

> EXAMPLE Since the matter was personal, he asked Bob to be *discreet* about it at the office.

Discrete means something is "separate, distinct, or individual."

> EXAMPLE The publications department was a *discrete* unit of the marketing division.

disinterested/uninterested

Disinterested means "impartial, objective, unbiased."

> EXAMPLE Like good judges, scientists should be passionately interested in the problems they tackle but completely *disinterested* when they seek to solve these problems.

Uninterested means simply "not interested."

EXAMPLE Despite Jane's enthusiasm, her manager remained *uninterested* in the project.

division-and-classification method of development

One effective way to develop a complex subject is to divide it into logical parts and then go on to explain each part separately. This technique is especially well suited to subjects that can be readily broken down into units, and it can be used as the **method of development** in much business writing. You might use this approach to describe a physical object, like a machine; to examine an idea, like the terms of a new labor-management contract; to explain a process, like the stages of an illness; or to give **instructions**, like the steps necessary to prepare a rusty metal surface for painting.

To explain the different types of printing processes currently in use, for example, you could divide the field into its major components, and where a fuller explanation is required, subdivide those (Figure 1). The emphasis in division is on breaking down a complex whole into a number of like units, because it is easier to consider smaller units and to examine the relationship of each to the other.

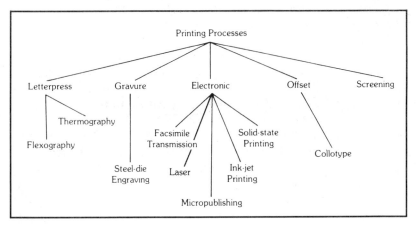

Figure 1   Printing Processes

The process by which a subject is divided is similar to the process by which a subject is classified. Division involves the separation of a whole into its component parts; classification is the grouping of a number of units (people, objects, ideas, and so on) into related categories. Consider the following list:

Triangle file	Steel tape ruler
Needle-nose pliers	Vise
Pipe wrench	Keyhole saw
Mallet	Tin snips
C clamps	Rasp
Hacksaw	Plane
Glass cutter	Ball-peen hammer
Steel square	Spring clamp
Claw hammer	Utility knife
Crescent wrench	Folding extension ruler
Slip-joint pliers	Crosscut saw
Tack hammer	Utility scissors

To group the items in the list, you would first determine what they have in common. The most obvious characteristic they share is that they all belong in a carpenter's tool chest. With that observation as a starting point, you can begin to group the tools into related categories. Pipe wrenches belong with slip-joint pliers because both tools grip objects. The rasp and the plane belong with the triangular file because all three tools smooth rough surfaces. By applying this kind of thinking to all the items in the list, you can group each tool according to function (Figure 2).

To divide or classify a subject, you must first divide the subject into its largest number of equal units. The basis for division depends, of course, on your subject and your purpose. For explaining the functions of tools, the classifications in Figure 2 (smoothing, hammering, measuring, gripping, and cutting) are excellent. For recommending which tools a new homeowner should buy first, however, the classifications are not helpful—they *all* contain tools that a new homeowner might want to purchase right away. To give homeowners advice on purchasing tools, you should clarify the types of repairs they are most likely to have to do. That classification can serve as a guide to tool purchase.

Once you have established the basis for the division or classification, apply it consistently, putting each item in only one category. For example, it might seem logical to classify needle-nose pliers both as "tools that cut" and as "tools that grip" because most needle-nose pliers have a small section for cutting wires. However, the *primary*

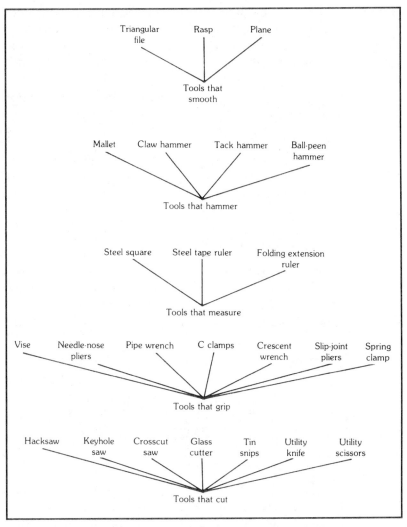

Figure 2   Division and Classification of Tools

function of needle-nose pliers is to grip. So listing them only under "tools that grip" would be more consistent with the basis used for listing the other tools.

The **memorandum** shown in Figure 3 uses the division and classification method of development. The writer, a company president, wishes to explain his goals for the company. He first divides the subject into the topics he considers the most important—productivity, marketing and sales, research and development, and human resources—and then classifies the plans, goals, and recent developments under each of those divisions. The following is an abridged version of the resulting memo:

To: All Employees
From: Barry E. Silvers BES

Date: April 22, 19--

One year ago today our company became a part of Altair Industries. It is appropriate, therefore, for us not only to look back at what we have accomplished but also to reassess now our goals for the next five years. I would like to share with you my thoughts and plans about the areas I believe are important to all of us in the years ahead.

<u>Productivity</u>

I am sure that you are all aware of the effort throughout our country to improve productivity. Over the past year we have made heavy capital investments to improve our position. Productivity, however, depends not only on the acquisition of more efficient equipment but also on the commitment of each employee to seek creative ways of using resources most efficiently. Certainly, I share your concern. . . .

<u>Marketing and Sales</u>

You may be aware that our CHRIS sales program has helped us to improve our sales by slightly over 15 percent. Although that result is gratifying, it is not large enough to offset the weak position in which we found ourselves two years ago. Therefore, I am setting a goal of a 25 percent increase in sales for this next year. To help make this goal possible, I am announcing today the expansion of our Marketing Division. . . .

<u>Research and Development</u>

Any company in our business must aggressively develop new and better products. Consequently, we have expanded our research facilities, which will certainly make us more competitive. But innovative ideas do not come from only R and D divisions; they also come from the creative thinking and participation of all employees. One way we have begun to tap the resources of our employees is through our new computerized suggestion network. I urge all of you to become familiar. . . .

<u>Human Resources</u>

As my comments about research and development suggest, our company's most valuable resources are its employees. Every progressive company makes a point of offering its employees strong training and room to grow professionally. In the years ahead I would like to see our efforts doubled in on-the-job training and intercompany placement. To achieve this goal I have asked Barbara Johnson to head a new department, Human Resources and Employee Development, which will coordinate a companywide effort....

I hope you share the excitement I feel as we implement these plans. Indeed, you must actively participate if they are to have a chance for success.

ja

Figure 3   Division-and-Classification Method of Development

documentation

In the academic world, *documentation* means giving formal credit to sources used or quoted in a research paper or **report**—that is, in a **bibliography** or a footnote. In the business and industrial world, documentation may refer also to information that is recorded, or "documented," on paper. The technical manuals provided to customers by manufacturers are examples of such documentation. Even **flowcharts** and engineering drawings are considered documentation.

documenting sources

By documenting sources, writers identify where they obtained the facts, ideas, **quotations**, and **paraphrases** they used in preparing a report, **journal article**, book, or other document. The information can come from books, manuals, correspondence, interviews, software documentation, reference works, and many other kinds of sources. Full and accurate documentation allows readers to locate and consult the information given and to find further information on the subject. It also gives proper credit to others so that the writer avoids **plagiarism**. The sources of all facts and ideas that are not common knowledge to the intended audience should be documented. The documentation must be complete, accurate, and consistent in format.

This entry describes and provides examples of the three principal methods of documenting sources: (1) *parenthetical documentation*—putting brief citations in parentheses in the text and providing full information in a list of "Works Cited"; (2) *reference documentation*—referring to sources with numbers in parentheses or by superscripts in the text and providing full information in a "References" section where the entries are listed numerically in the order of their first citation in the text; and (3) *notational documentation*—using superscript numbers in the text to refer to notes either at the bottom of the page (footnotes) or at the end of the paper, article, or chapter (endnotes).

Many professional organizations and journals publish style manuals that describe their own formats for documenting sources. A list of such style manuals appears at the end of this entry. If you are writing for publication in a professional field, consult the manual for the particular field or the style sheet for the journal to which you are submitting your article, and follow it exactly. Otherwise, follow one of the formats described in this entry. Whatever format you choose, be sure to follow it consistently—in every detail of order, **punctuation**, and capitalization.

Use the following contents guide to this entry to locate information quickly. Samples of each format appear at the end of each discussion. Parenthetical samples begin on page 206; reference samples begin on page 209; notational samples begin on page 213.

PARENTHETICAL DOCUMENTATION

The parenthetical method that follows is recommended by the Modern Language Association of America (MLA) in the *MLA Handbook for Writers of Research Papers*, 3rd ed. This method gives an abbreviated reference to a source parenthetically in the text and lists full information about the source in a separate section called "Works Cited" at the end of the report or article.

When documenting sources in text, include only the author and page number in parentheses. If the author's name is mentioned in the text, include only the page number of the source. The parenthetical citation should include no more information than is necessary to enable the reader to relate it to the corresponding entry in the list of "Works Cited." When referring to an entire work rather than to a particular page in a work, mention the author's name in the text, and omit the parenthetical citation.

The following passages contain sample parenthetical citations.

Examples

Steve Wozniak's first computer was the so-called Cream Soda Computer, which he and a friend built in 1971, staying up all night and drinking cream soda (Freiberger and Swaine 205).

According to Freiberger and Swaine, the development of the BASIC programming language by two Dartmouth professors in 1964 gave ordinary people the means of using the computing power put in their hands by microprocessor technology and its commercial exploitation (140).

When placing parenthetical citations in text, insert them between the closing quotation mark or the last word of the sentence (or clause) and the period or other punctuation. Use the spacing shown above. If the parenthetical citation follows an extended quotation or paraphrase, however, place it outside the last sentence of the quotation or paraphrase, followed by two spaces between the period and the first parenthesis. Within the citation itself, allow one space (no punctuation) between the name of the author and the page number. Don't use the word *page* or its abbreviation.

If you are citing a page or pages of a multivolume work, give the volume number, followed by a colon, space, and page number: (Jones 2: 53). If the entire volume is being cited, identify the author and volume as follows: (Smith, vol. 3).

If your list of "Works Cited" includes more than one work by the same author, include the title of the work (or a shortened version if the title is long) in the parenthetical citation, unless you mention it in the text. If, for example, your list of "Works Cited" included more than one work by Alvin von Auw, a proper parenthetical citation for his book *Heritage and Destiny: Reflections on the Bell System in Transition* would appear as in the following sample:

In the late seventies, a conflict arose between the Bell System's engineers and its "marketeers" over whether R & D should determine what the sales force had to market or marketing research should determine what the technologists would develop (von Auw, Heritage and Destiny 172-73).

Use only one space between the title and the page number.

The works cited in the sample passages given would be listed alphabetically, as follows, in a "Works Cited" section:

Freiberger, Paul, and Michael Swaine. Fire in the Valley: The Making of the
    Personal Computer. Berkeley: Osborne/McGraw, 1984.
von Auw, Alvin. Heritage and Destiny: Reflections on the Bell System in
    Transition. New York: Praeger, 1983.

The following section explains the content and format of entries in a list of "Works Cited." The format style described is that recommended in the *MLA Handbook for Writers of Research Papers*, 3rd ed.

CITATION FORMAT FOR WORKS CITED

The list of "Works Cited" should begin on the first new page following the end of the text. Each new entry should begin at the left margin, with the second and subsequent lines within an entry indented five spaces. Double-space within and between entries.

AUTHOR

Entries appear in alphabetical order by the author's last name (by the last name of the first author if the work has more than one author). Works by the same author should be alphabetized by the first major word of the title (following *a, an,* or *the*). If the author is a corporation, the entry should be alphabetized by the name of the corporation; if the author is a government agency, entries are alphabetized by the government, followed by the agency (for example, "United States. Dept. of Health and Human Services."). Some require more than one agency name (for example, "United States. Dept. of Labor. Bureau of Labor Statistics."). If no author is given, the entry should begin with the title and be alphabetized by the first significant word in the title. (Articles in reference works, like encyclopedias, are sometimes signed with initials; you will find a list of the contributors' initials and full names elsewhere in the work, probably near the introductory material or the index.)

After the first listing for an author, put three hyphens and a period in place of the name for the subsequent entries with the same author. An editor's name is followed by the abbreviation "ed."

McNeill, William H. The Pursuit of Power. Chicago: U of Chicago P, 1982.

———. The Rise of the West. Chicago: U of Chicago P, 1963.

TITLE

The second element is the title of the work. Capitalize the first word and each significant word thereafter. Underline the title of a book or pamphlet. Place quotation marks around the title of an article in a periodical, an essay in a collection, and a paper in a proceedings. Each title should be followed by a period.

PERIODICALS

For an article in a periodical (journal, magazine, or newspaper), the volume number (for a magazine or newspaper, simply the date), and the page numbers should immediately follow the title of the periodical. See the sample entries for proper punctuation.

SERIES OR MULTIVOLUME WORKS

For works in a series and multivolume works, the name of the series and the series number of the work in question, or the number of volumes, should follow the title. If the edition used is not the first, the edition should be specified.

PUBLISHING INFORMATION

The final elements of the entry for a book, pamphlet, or conference proceedings are the place of publication, publisher, and date of publication. Use a shortened form of the publisher's name (for example, *St. Martin's* for *St. Martin's Press, Inc., Random* for *Random House, Oxford UP* for *Oxford University Press*). If any of these cannot be found in the work, use the abbreviations n.p. (no publication place), n.p. (no publisher), and n.d. (no date), respectively. For familiar reference works, list only the edition and year of publication.

SAMPLE ENTRIES (MLA STYLE)

Book with One Author

von Auw, Alvin. Heritage and Destiny: Reflections on the Bell System in
    Transition. New York: Praeger, 1983.

Book with Two or More Authors

Freiberger, Paul, and Michael Swaine. Fire in the Valley: The Making of the
    Personal Computer. Berkeley: Osborne/McGraw, 1984.

Book with a Corporate Author

NEC Home Electronics. PC-8201A User's Guide. Tokyo: NEC, 1983.

Translated Book

Cardos, Fernando Henrique, and Enzo Faletto. Dependency and Development in
    Latin America. Trans. Marjory Mattingly Urquidi. Berkeley: U of California
    P, 1979.

Book Edition, If Not the First

Galbraith, John Kenneth. The Affluent Society. 3rd ed. Boston: Houghton, 1976.

Multivolume Book

Faber, Mike, and Dudley Seers, eds. The Crisis in Planning. 2 vols. London:
    Chatto, 1972.

Book in a Series

Kendrick, John W., and Beatrice N. Vaccar. New Developments in Productivity
    Measurement and Analysis. Studies in Income and Wealth 44. Chicago: U
    of Chicago P, 1980.

Work in an Edited Collection

Mundell, Robert A. "International Monetary Reform: The Optimal Mix in Big
    Countries." Macroeconomics, Prices, and Quantities: Essays in Memory
    of Arthur M. Okun. Ed. James Tobin. Washington, DC: Brookings, 1983.
    285–95.

Report

United States. Dept. of Labor. Bureau of Labor Statistics. Publications of the
    Bureau of Labor Statistics July-December 1980. Report 641. Washington,
    DC: US Dept. of Labor, 1981.

Proceedings

De Schutter, J., and G. Bemer, eds. Fundamental Aspects of Appropriate
    Technology. Proc. of the International Workshop on Appropriate Technol-
    ogy. 4–7 Sept. 1980. Delft, Neth.: Delft UP, 1980.

Paper in a Proceedings
Carr, Marilyn. "Appropriate Technology: Theory, Policy and Practice."
   Fundamental Aspects of Appropriate Technology. Proc. of the International
   Workshop on Appropriate Technology. 4–7 Sept. 1980. Ed. J. de Schutter
   and G. Bemer. Delft, Neth.: Delft UP, 1980. 145–53.

Paper Presented at a Conference
Van Pelt, William. "Microcomputers and the Business Writing Classroom."
   Midwest Regional Conference, Association for Business Communication.
   Milwaukee, 18 Apr. 1985.

Journal Article
Stevens, William P., Kathleen C. Stevens, and William Raabe, Jr. "Communication in Accounting: Readability of F.A.S.B. Statements." Review of Business and Economic Research 19(1983): 110–18.

Magazine Article
Wantuck, Mary-Margaret. "Bottom Line 101." Nation's Business Oct. 1985:
   24–32.

Anonymous Article (in Weekly Periodical)
"Western Union Ties PCs and Data Service." Infoworld 20 Jan. 1986: 48.

Newspaper Article (On Discontinuous Pages)
Chira, Susan. "Minebea: Takeover Quandary." New York Times 19 Oct. 1985,
   national ed.: 21 +.

Encyclopedia Entry
Tannenbaum, Morris. "Automation." Encyclopaedia Britannica: Macropaedia.
   15th ed. 1982.

Thesis or Dissertation
Kyj, Myroslaw J. "The Meaning and Uses of Customer Service in Industrial
   Products Markets." Diss. Temple U. 1985.

Letter from One Official to Another
Brown, Charles L. Letter to retired members of Bell System Presidents' Conference. 8 Jan. 1982.

Letter Personally Received
Harris, Robert S. Letter to the author. 3 Dec. 1985.

Personal Interview
Denlinger, Virgil, Assistant Chief of Police, Alexandria, VA. Personal interview.
   15 Mar. 1980.

Computer Software
FormBase. Vers. 1.1. Computer software. Ventura Software, 1991. IBM MS-DOS
3.1 or higher, 640K RAM.

REFERENCE DOCUMENTATION

The reference system of documenting sources lists the numbered documentation references at the end of the work. The references on the list are identified by numbers in the text that correspond to their numbers in the list. The reference list cites only those works referred to in the text.

The styles for references vary. The format style described here is recommended by the American National Standards Institute (ANSI) in *American National Standard for Bibliographic References*, Z39.29-1977.

The citations in a reference list are arranged in numerical sequence (1, 2, 3), according to the order in which they are first mentioned in the text. The most common method for directing readers from your text to specific references is to place the reference number in parentheses after the work cited. Thus in the text, the number one in parentheses (1) after a reference to a book, article, or other work refers the reader to the first citation in the reference list. The number five in parentheses (5) refers the reader to the fifth citation in the reference list. A second number in the parentheses, separated from the first by a colon (3:27), refers to the page number of the source from which the information was taken. There are several other common methods for directing readers from your text to specific references. You can place the word *Reference*, or the abbreviation *Ref.*, within parentheses with the numbers: (Reference 1) or (Ref. 1). Or you can write the reference number as a superscript: text[1]. Sometimes you may cite your sources within a sentence in the text; then you should spell out the word *Reference*: "The data in Reference 3 include. . . ." For subsequent references in the text, simply repeat the reference number of the first citation.

CITATION FORMAT FOR REFERENCES

In the numbered reference list, the number begins at the left margin, followed by a period. Then leave two spaces and begin the entry, indenting the second and subsequent lines to be even with the first. Single-space within entries, and double-space between them.

The recommended order for information groupings within an entry and punctuation within and between these groups are shown in the samples beginning on page 210. In general, put a period between groups and at the end of the entry, a semicolon between elements within a group, and a comma between subelements or closely related elements.

AUTHOR

Authors' names should be given with the last name first. If a work has two authors, both names should be given, with the last name first, separated by a semicolon. If a work has more than two authors, the first author should be cited, last name first, followed by "and others" in square brackets. For an edited work (if you are listing the whole work, not just an article in it) begin the entry with the editor, giving the names as described for the authors, followed by a comma and the abbreviation "ed."

TITLE

Only the first word and any proper nouns should be capitalized in a book or article title. The title of an article, followed by a period, should precede the title of the journal or book in which it appears. In journal or magazine titles, abbreviations may be used, and all significant words (or abbreviations for them) should be capitalized.

In an entry for an article or paper in an edited collection, the authorship group and title group for the article are followed by the editors and title group for the collection.

PUBLISHING INFORMATION

For a book, the publishing information consists of the place of publication followed by a colon, the publisher followed by a semicolon, and the year of publication followed by a period. For a journal or magazine, the date (in year–month–day order) may either precede or follow the volume number, issue number, and pages, separated from them by a semicolon. The volume number is followed by the issue number in parentheses, a colon after the closing parenthesis, and then the pages of the article. (The ANSI style for magazine articles is the same as for journal articles.)

SAMPLE REFERENCES (ANSI STYLE)

The following examples will acquaint you with the ANSI style. If you need to list a source for which no example is given, follow the pattern from the examples that are most like it. If you are uncertain whether to include a piece of information about the source, include it. (Note that the ANSI standard does not cover personal communications, interviews, speeches, and the like for which no print, manuscript, or electronic record exists.)

Book, One Author

1. von Auw, Alvin. Heritage and destiny: reflections on the Bell System in transition. New York: Praeger, 1983.

Book, Two Authors

2. Freiberger, Paul; Swaine, Michael. Fire in the valley: the making of the personal computer. Berkeley: Osborne/McGraw-Hill; 1984.

Book, Corporate Author

3. NEC Home Electronics. PC-8201A user's guide. Tokyo: NEC, 1983.

Work in an Edited Collection

4. Mundell, Robert A. International monetary reform: the optimal mix in big countries. In: Tobin, James, ed. Macroeconomics, prices, and quantities: essays in memory of Arthur M. Okun. Washington, DC: Brookings Institution, 1983: 285–295.

Book Edition, If Not the First

5. Galbraith, John Kenneth. The affluent society. 3rd ed. Boston: Houghton Mifflin; 1976.

Multivolume Work

6. Faber, Mike; Seers, Dudley, eds. The crisis in planning. London: Chatto and Windus; 1972. 2 v.

Book in a Series

7. Kendrick, John W.; Vaccara, Beatrice N. New developments in productivity measurement and analysis. Chicago: Univ. of Chicago; 1980. (Studies in income and wealth; v. 44.)

Report

8. Gould, John D. Composing letters with computer-based text editors. IBM Computer Science Research Report. 1980; IBM Report RC 8446 (#36750).

Thesis or Dissertation

9. McQuarrie, Edward Francis. Commitment to home computing: a joint result of action and evaluation. Cincinnati: Univ. of Cincinnati; 1985. 154 p. Dissertation.

Paper in a Conference Proceedings

10. Carr, Marilyn. Appropriate technology: theory, policy, and practice.
    de Schutter, J.; Bemer, G. eds. Fundamental aspects of appropriate technology. Proceedings of the international workshop on appropriate technology; 1980 September 4–7; Delft, Neth. Delft: Delft University Press; 1980: 145–153.

Unpublished Paper

11. Van Pelt, William. Microcomputers and the business writing classroom. 1985. Unpublished draft supplied to author by William Van Pelt.

Journal Article

12. Bryan, Lowell L. A blueprint for financial reconstruction. Harvard Business Review. 1991; 69: 73–86.

Computer Software

13. PowerEdit. vers. 1.0. (Computer software). Dallas, TX: Artificial Linguistics, 1991. IBM MS-DOS 3.0 or higher, 470 RAM.

NOTATIONAL DOCUMENTATION

Notes in publications have two uses: (1) to provide background information or explanations that would interrupt the flow of thought in the text and (2) to provide documentation references. (For guidance on footnotes used with tables, see **tables**.)

EXPLANATORY FOOTNOTES

Explanatory or content notes are useful when the basis for an assumption should be made explicit but spelling it out in the text might make readers lose the flow of an argument. Because explanatory or content notes can be distracting, however, they should be kept to a minimum. If you cannot work the explanatory or background material into your text, it may not belong there. Lengthy explanations should be placed in an appendix. (See **appendix/ appendixes/appendices**.)

DOCUMENTATION NOTES

Notes that document sources can appear as either endnotes or footnotes. Endnotes are placed in a separate section at the end of a report, article, chapter, or book; footnotes (including explanatory notes) are placed at the bottom of a text page. Endnotes are easy to type, but readers may find them inconvenient to find and difficult to correlate with the text. Footnotes are tricky to type unless you have a word-processing program that automatically allocates the right amount of space at the bottom of each page. They are, however, convenient for readers.

Use superscript numbers in the text to refer readers to notes, and number them consecutively from the beginning of the report, article, or chapter to the end. Place each superscript number at the end of a sentence, **clause**, or **phrase**, at a natural pause point like this,[1] right after the **period**, **comma**, or other punctuation mark (except a **dash**, which the number should precede[2]—as here).

FOOTNOTE FORMAT

To type footnotes, leave two line spaces beneath the text on a page, and indent the first line of each footnote five spaces. Begin each note with the appropriate superscript number, and skip one space between the number and the text of the footnote. If the footnote runs longer than one line, the second and subsequent lines should begin at the left margin. Single-space within each footnote, and double-space between footnotes.

Example

Assume that this is the last line of text on a page.

[1] Begin the first footnote at this position. When it runs longer than one line, begin the second and all following lines at the left margin.

[2] The second footnote follows the same spacing as the first. Single-space within footnotes, and double-space between them.

ENDNOTE FORMAT

Endnotes should begin on a separate page entitled "Works Cited" or "References" after the end of the text. The individual notes should be typed as for footnotes. Double-space within and between endnotes.

DOCUMENTATION NOTE STYLE

The following guidelines for documentation note style are based on those provided in the Modern Language Association's *MLA Handbook for Writers of Research Papers*, 3rd ed.

Documentation notes give the author's full name, title, and publication information for the source, including the page or pages from which material was taken. This information is given in full in the first note for the source, and the second and subsequent notes give abbreviated author and title information.

In a footnote or endnote, the information is given in a somewhat different order and uses somewhat different punctuation than in a bibliography or a list of "References" or "Works Cited." The author's name is given in normal order (Jane F. Smith) rather than last name first; the elements of the entry are separated by commas rather than periods; and the publication information for a book is enclosed in parentheses. The first reference to a book appears as follows:

[1] Alvin von Auw, Heritage and Destiny: Reflections on the Bell System in Transition (New York: Praeger, 1983) 140.

There is no punctuation mark between the title and the opening parenthesis or between the closing parenthesis and the page number, and the page number is not preceded by the word *page* or its abbreviation. Compare this sample note with how the same book would be listed in a bibliography or list of "Works Cited":

von Auw, Alvin. Heritage and Destiny: Reflections on the Bell System in Transition. New York: Praeger, 1983.

SAMPLE ENTRIES (MLA STYLE)

The following sample notes for first references are based on the format style of the *MLA Handbook*:

Book with a Corporate Author

[2] Borland International, Turbo Pascal Version 2.0 Reference Manual (Scotts Valley, CA: Borland, 1984) 157.

Work in an Edited Collection

[3] Robert A. Mundell, "International Monetary Reform: The Optimal Mix in Big Countries," Macroeconomics, Prices, and Quantities: Essays in Memory of Arthur M. Okun. ed. James Tobin (Washington, DC: Brookings, 1983) 289.

Report

[4] United States, Dept. of Labor, Bureau of Labor Statistics, Publications of the Bureau of Labor Statistics July-December 1980, Report No. 641 (Washington, DC: U.S. Dept. of Labor, 1981) 73.

Paper Presented at a Conference

[5] William Van Pelt, "Microcomputers and the Business Writing Classroom," Midwest Regional Conference, Association for Business Communication, Milwaukee, 18 Apr. 1985.

Journal Article

[6] Lowell L. Bryan, "A Blueprint for Financial Reconstruction," Harvard Business Review 69 (1991): 73.

Magazine Article

[7] Mary-Margaret Wantuck, "Bottom Line 101," Nation's Business Oct. 1985: 25.

Thesis or Dissertation

[8] Myroslaw J. Kyj, "The Meaning and Uses of Customer Service in Industrial Products Markets," diss., Temple UP, 1985, 96.

For periodicals, the date, enclosed in parentheses (if the periodical is a journal) is followed by a colon.

SECOND AND SUBSEQUENT REFERENCES

Notes for second and subsequent references to works should contain only enough information to allow the reader to relate it to the note for the first reference. Generally, the author's name and page number will suffice:

[9] Mundell 290.

Even if the second reference immediately follows the first, put the author's last name and the page number as shown. (The abbreviations *ibid.* and *op. cit.*, which you may encounter in older books and articles, are no longer recommended as ways to refer to previous citations.)

If two or more works by the same author are cited, include a shortened version of the title in the second and subsequent notes. Insert a comma between the author's name and the title, with no punctuation between the title and the page number.

BIBLIOGRAPHY FORMAT (MLA STYLE)

The following list shows how each of the works cited in the sample notes would appear in a bibliography:

Book with a Corporate Author

Borland International. <u>Turbo Pascal Version 2.0 Reference Manual.</u> Scotts Valley,
CA: Borland, 1984.

Work in an Edited Collection

Mundell, Robert A. "International Monetary Reform: The Optimal Mix in Big
Countries." <u>Macroeconomics, Prices, and Quantities: Essays in Memory</u>
<u>of Arthur M. Okun.</u> Ed. James Tobin. Washington, DC: Brookings, 1983.
285–95.

Report

United States. Dept. of Labor. Bureau of Labor Statistics. <u>Publications of the</u>
<u>Bureau of Labor Statistics July-December 1980.</u> Report No. 641. Washing-
ton, DC: U.S. Dept. of Labor, 1981.

Paper Presented at a Conference

Van Pelt, William. "Microcomputers and the Business Writing Classroom."
Midwest Regional Conference, Association for Business Communication.
Milwaukee, 18 Apr. 1985.

Journal Article

Bryan, Lowell L. "A Blueprint for Financial Reconstruction." <u>Harvard Business</u>
<u>Review</u> 69 (1991): 73–86.

Magazine Article

Wantuck, Mary-Margaret. "Bottom Line 101." <u>Nation's Business</u> Oct. 1985:
24–32.

Thesis or Dissertation

Kyj, Myroslaw J. "The Meaning and Uses of Customer Service in Industrial
Products Markets." Diss. Temple UP, 1985.

STYLE MANUALS

Many professional societies, publishing companies, and other organizations publish manuals that prescribe bibliographic reference
formats for their publications or publications in their fields. For an
annotated bibliography of style manuals issued by commercial publishers, government agencies, and university presses for fields ranging from agriculture to zoology, see John Bruce Howell, *Style Manuals of the English-speaking World* (Phoenix: Oryx, 1983).

The following is a list of style manuals for various fields:

Biology

Council of Biology Editors. *CBE style manual: a guide for authors, editors, and publishers in the biological sciences.* 5th ed. Bethesda: Council of Biology Editors, 1983.

Business

Moyer, Ruth (and others). *The research and report handbook for managers and executives in business, industry, and government.* New York: Wiley, 1981.

Chemistry

American Chemical Society. *ACS style guide: a manual for authors and editors.* Washington, DC: American Chemical Soc., 1986.

Geology

U. S. Geological Survey. *Suggestions to authors of the reports of the United States Geological Survey.* 7th ed. Washington, DC: U.S. GPO, 1991.

Mathematics

American Mathematical Society. *A manual for authors of mathematical papers.* Providence, RI: American Mathematical Soc., 1990.

Medicine

International Steering Committee of Medical Editors. *Uniform requirements for manuscripts submitted to biomedical journals.* Annals of Internal Medicine. 90 (Jan. 1978): 95–99.

Physics

American Institute of Physics, Publications Board. *AIP style manual.* 4th ed. New York: American Institute of Physics, 1990.

Psychology

American Psychological Association. *Publication manual of the American Psychological Association.* 3rd ed. Washington, DC: American Psychological Assn., 1983.

General

American national standard for bibliographic references. New York: American National Standards Institute, 1977. ANSI Z39.29—1977.

The Chicago manual of style. 13th ed. Chicago: U of Chicago P, 1982.

Gibaldi, Joseph, and Walter S. Achtert. *MLA handbook for writers of research papers.* 3rd ed. New York: Modern Language Assn. of America, 1988.

National Information Standards Organization. *Scientific and technical reports: organization, preparation, and production.* New York: National Information Standards Org., 1987. ANSI Z39.18—1987.

Skillin, M. E., and Gay, R. M. *Words into type.* 3rd ed. Englewood Cliffs, NJ: Prentice, 1974.

Turabian, K. L. *A manual for writers of term papers, theses, and dissertations.* 4th ed. Chicago: U of Chicago P, 1973.

United States Government Printing Office style manual. Washington, DC: U.S. GPO, 1984.

double negatives

A double negative is the use of an additional negative word to reinforce an expression that is already negative. It is an attempt to emphasize the negative, but the result is only awkward. Double negatives should never be used in writing.

> CHANGE   I *haven't* got *none.*
> TO   I have *none.*

Barely, hardly, and *scarcely* cause problems because writers sometimes do not recognize that these words are already negative.

> CHANGE   I *don't hardly* ever have time to read these days.
> TO   I *hardly* ever have time to read these days.

Not unfriendly, not without, and similar constructions are not double negatives because in such constructions two negatives are meant to suggest the gray area of meaning between negative and positive. Be careful, however, how you use these constructions; they are often confusing to the reader and should be used only if they serve a purpose.

> EXAMPLES   He is *not unfriendly.* (meaning that he is neither hostile nor friendly)
> It is *not without* regret that I offer my resignation. (implying mixed feelings rather than only regret)

The **correlative conjunctions** *neither* and *nor* may appear together in a clause without creating a double negative, so long as the writer does not attempt to use the word *not* in the same clause.

> CHANGE   It was *not,* as a matter of fact, *neither* his duty *nor* his desire to fire the man.
> TO   It was *neither,* as a matter of fact, his duty *nor* his desire to fire the man.
> OR   It was *not,* as a matter of fact, *either* his duty *or* his desire to fire the man.

Negative forms are full of traps that often entice inexperienced writers into errors of **logic,** as illustrated in the following example:

EXAMPLE There is *nothing* in the book that has *not* already been published in some form, but some of it is, I believe, very little known.

In this sentence, "some of it," logically, can refer only to "*nothing* in the book that has *not* already been published." The sentence can be corrected in one of two ways. The pronoun *it* can be replaced by a specific noun.

EXAMPLE There is nothing in the book that has not already been published in some form, but some of the *information* is, I believe, very little known.

Or the idea can be stated positively. (See also **positive writing**.)

EXAMPLE Everything in the book has been published in some form, but some of it is, I believe, very little known.

due to/because of

Due to (meaning "caused by") is acceptable following a **linking verb**.

EXAMPLES His short temper was *due to* work strain.
His short temper, which was *due to* work strain, made him inefficient.

Due to is not acceptable, however, when it is used with a nonlinking verb to replace *because of*.

CHANGE He went home *due to* illness.
TO He went home *because of* illness.

E

each

When *each* is used as a **subject**, it takes a singular **verb** or **pronoun**.

EXAMPLES *Each* of the reports *is* to be submitted ten weeks after *it* is assigned.

Each worked as fast as *his* ability would permit.

When *each* occurs after a plural subject with which it is in apposition, it takes a plural verb or pronoun. (See also **agreement**.)

EXAMPLE The reports *each have* white embossed titles on *their* covers.

each and every

Although the phrase *each and every* is commonly used in speech in an attempt to emphasize a point, the phrase is redundant and should be eliminated from your writing. Replace it with *each* or *every*.

CHANGE *Each and every* part was accounted for.
TO *Each* part was accounted for.
OR *Every* part was accounted for.

economic/economical

Economic refers to the production, development, and management of material wealth. *Economical* simply means "not wasteful or extravagant."

EXAMPLES The strike at General Motors had an *economic* impact on the country.

Since gasoline will be in short supply, drivers should be as *economical* as possible with its use.

e.g./i.e.

The **abbreviation** *e.g.* stands for the Latin *exempli gratia*, meaning "for example." Since a perfectly good English expression exists for the same use (*for example*), there is no need to use a Latin expression or abbreviation except in notes and illustrations where you need to save space. In addition, many people confuse *e.g.* with *i.e.*, which means "that is." The abbreviation *e.g.* does not save enough space to justify possible misunderstanding. Avoid *e.g.* in your writing.

> CHANGE Some terms of the contract (*e.g.*, duration and job classification) were settled in the first two bargaining sessions.
>
> TO Some terms of the contract (*for example*, duration and job classification) were settled in the first two bargaining sessions.
>
> OR Some terms of the contract, *such as* duration and job classification, were settled in the first two bargaining sessions.

The abbreviation *i.e.* stands for the Latin *id est*, meaning "that is." Since *that is* is a perfectly good English expression, there is no need to use a Latin expression or its abbreviation. In addition, many people confuse *i.e.* with *e.g.*, never being certain which means what. This abbreviation does not save enough space to justify having one person misunderstand its meaning; avoid *i.e.* in your writing.

> CHANGE We were a fairly heterogeneous group; *i.e.*, there were managers, foremen, and vice-presidents at the meeting.
>
> TO We were a fairly heterogeneous group; *that is*, there were managers, foremen, and vice-presidents at the meeting.

If you must use *i.e.* or *e.g.*, punctuate them as follows. If *i.e.* or *e.g.* connects two **independent clauses**, a **semicolon** should precede it and a **comma** should follow it, as in the preceding example. If *i.e.* or *e.g.* connects a **noun** with **appositives**, a comma should precede and follow it.

> EXAMPLES We were a fairly heterogeneous group, *i.e.*, managers, foremen, and vice-presidents.
>
> We were a fairly heterogeneous group; *i.e.*, we were managers, foremen, and vice-presidents.

electronic mail

Electronic mail (E-mail) refers to the transmission of messages from one person to another through a computer network. The messages are sent to and stored in a computer file called an electronic "mail box" until they are retrieved by the recipient. The recipient can display the message on the computer screen, print the message as a permanent record, forward the message to others, or send a reply to the original sender. E-mail is especially useful for employees within a large organization who must send **memorandums, reports, correspondence**, meeting notices, and even **questionnaires** to co-workers throughout the organization.

This method of communication offers a variety of advantages. The message—whether sent across the hall or across the continent—reaches its audience within minutes at a cost well below overnight mail service. Because the information is transmitted in machine-readable form, the text can be printed, revised and sent back, or incorporated directly into another computer file without being retyped.

WRITING STYLE

Although E-mail messages are like conventional job-related writing in most respects, they tend to be less formal, more conversational—somewhere between a telephone conversation and a memorandum—because of the immediacy of the transmission and the fact that it usually occurs directly between two people. Construct your messages accordingly. Avoid long, complicated sentences that are dense with unnecessary technical **jargon** that can confuse the reader and convey the wrong message. Keep in mind, too, that although you want to keep sentences brief and words short, you should not use a **telegraphic style** that leaves important information unsaid or only partly said. Think carefully about the **reader**, the accuracy of your information, and the level of detail necessary to communicate your message clearly and concisely to that reader.

REVIEW AND PRIVACY IMPLICATIONS

E-mail communications require that the writer consider the inadvisability of sending unreviewed or unedited text and the privacy implications of what's being transmitted.

The likelihood is high that E-mail messages written at the computer terminal will be sent directly to the recipient by the sender. This practice, although technically efficient, has pitfalls. Avoid the temptation to "dash off" a first draft and send it as is. Unless carefully reviewed, the information sent could contain errors of fact and of **grammar**, be ambiguous, contain unintended implications, or inadvertently omit crucial details.

Consider privacy, too. Because E-mail messages are recorded on computer tape for retrieval and storage, they could be read or printed by someone other than the intended recipient. This may happen not only during transmission but subsequent to it. Consider all your messages in the light of these possibilities.

elegant variation

The attempt to avoid repeating a **noun** in a **paragraph** by substituting other words (often pretentious **synonyms**) is called *elegant variation*. Avoid this practice—repeat a word if it says what you mean, or use a suitable **pronoun**. (See also **affectation** and **long variants**.)

> CHANGE The *use* of modules in the assembly process has increased production. *Modular utilization* has also cut costs.
>
>   TO The *use* of modules in the assembly process has increased production. The *use* of modules has also cut costs.
>
>   OR The use of modules in the assembly process has increased production and also cut costs.

(See also **thesaurus**.)

ellipses

When you omit words in quoted material, use a series of three spaced periods—called *ellipsis* dots—to indicate the omission. However, such an omission should not detract from or alter the essential meaning of the sentence.

> EXAMPLES Technical material distributed for promotional use is sometimes charged for, particularly in high-volume distribution to schools, although prices for these publications are not uniformly based on the cost of developing them. (without omission)
>
> Technical material distributed for promotional use is sometimes charged for . . . although prices for these publications are not uniformly based on the cost of developing them. (with omission)

When the omitted portion comes at the beginning of the sentence, begin the **quotation** with a lowercase letter.

> EXAMPLES "When the programmer has determined a system of runs, he must create a system flowchart to provide a picture of the data flow through the system." (without omission)
>
> The letter states that the programmer "must create a system flowchart to provide a picture of the data flow through the system." (with omission)

When the omission comes at the end of a sentence and you continue the quotation following the omission, use four periods to indicate both the final period to end the sentence and the omission.

EXAMPLE In all publications departments except ours, publications funds—once they are initially allocated by higher management—are controlled by publications personnel. Our company is the only one to have nonpublications people control funding within a budgeted period. In addition, all publications departments control printing funds as well. (without omission)

In all publications departments except ours, publications funds—once they are initially allocated by higher management—are controlled by publications personnel. . . . In addition, all publications departments control printing funds as well. (with omission)

Use a full line of periods across the page to indicate the omission of one or more **paragraphs**.

EXAMPLE A computer system operates with two types of programs: the software programs supplied by the manufacturer and the programs created by the user. The manufacturer's software consists of a number of programs that enable the system to perform complicated manipulations of data from the relatively simple instructions specified in the user's program.

Programmers must take a systematic approach to solving any data-processing problem. They must first clearly define the problem, and then they must define a system of runs that will solve the problem. For example, a given problem may require a validation and sort run to handle account numbers or employee numbers, a computation and update run to manipulate the data for the output reports, and a print run to produce the output reports.

When a system of runs has been determined, the programmer must create a system flowchart to provide a picture of the data flow through the system. (without omission)

A computer system operates with two types of programs: the software programs supplied by the manufacturer and the programs created by the user. The manufacturer's software consists of a number of programs that enable the system to perform complicated manipulations of data from the relatively simple instructions specified in the user's program.

. . . .

> When a system of runs has been determined, the program-
> mer must create a system flowchart to provide a picture of the
> data flow through the system. (with omission)

Do not use ellipsis dots for any purpose other than to indicate omission. Advertising copywriters, particularly those not skilled at
achieving the effect they strive for with words, often use ellipsis dots
to substitute for all marks of **punctuation**—and sometimes even use
them where no punctuation is needed. This practice achieves no
positive effect, and it is a poor one to emulate.

eminent/imminent

Someone or something that is *eminent,* is outstanding or distinguished.

> EXAMPLE   She is an *eminent* scientist.

If something is *imminent*, it is about to happen.

> EXAMPLE   He paced nervously, knowing that the committee's decision
> was *imminent.*

emphasis

Emphasis is the principle by which ideas in writing are stressed
according to their importance. The first step in achieving emphasis
is to write simply and concisely. If a sentence expresses the writer's
meaning simply and directly, it has the proper emphasis. But there
are also mechanical means of achieving emphasis: by position with-
in a sentence, **paragraph**, or **report**; by the use of **repetition**; by selection of sentence type; by varying the length of sentences; by the use
of climactic order within a sentence; by **punctuation** (use of the
dash); by the use of **intensifiers**; by the use of mechanical devices,
such as **italics** and **capital letters**; and by direct statement (using such
terms as *most important* and *foremost*).

Emphasis can be achieved by position because the first and last
words of a sentence stand out in the reader's mind.

> CHANGE   Because they reflect geological history, moon craters are im-
> portant to understanding the earth's history.
> TO   Moon craters are important to understanding the earth's his-
> tory because they reflect geological history.
> OR   Because moon craters reflect geological history, they are im-
> portant to understanding the earth's history.

Notice that the revised versions of the sentence emphasize moon craters simply because the term is in the front part of the sentence. Similarly, the first and last sentences in a paragraph and the first and last paragraphs in a report or paper tend to be the most emphatic to the reader.

EXAMPLE   Energy does far more than simply make our daily lives more comfortable and convenient. Suppose you wanted to stop—and reverse—the economic progress of this nation. What would be the surest and quickest way to do it? Find a way to cut off the nation's oil resources! Industrial plants would shut down, public utilities would stand idle, all forms of transportation would halt. The country would be paralyzed, and our economy would plummet into the abyss of national economic ruin. *Our economy, in short, is energy-based.*
—*The Baker World* (Los Angeles: Baker Oil Tools, 1964) 2.

Another way to achieve emphasis is to follow a very long sentence, or a series of long sentences, with a very short one.

EXAMPLE   We have already reviewed the problem the bookkeeping department has experienced during the past year. We could continue to examine the causes of our problems and point an accusing finger at all the culprits beyond our control, but in the end it all leads to one simple conclusion. *We must cut costs.*

Emphasis can be achieved by the repetition of key words and phrases.

EXAMPLE   Similarly, atoms *come and go* in a molecule, but the molecule *remains*; molecules *come and go* in a cell, but the cell *remains*; cells *come and go* in a body, but the body *remains*; persons *come and go* in an organization, but the organization *remains.*
—Kenneth Boulding, *Beyond Economics* (Ann Arbor: U of Michigan P, 1968) 131.

Different emphasis can be achieved by the selection of a **compound sentence**, **complex sentence**, or **simple sentence**.

EXAMPLES   The report turned in by the police detective was carefully illustrated, and it covered five pages of single-spaced copy. (This compound sentence carries no special emphasis because it contains two coordinate independent clauses.)
The police detective's report, which was carefully illustrated, covered five pages of single-spaced copy. (This complex sentence emphasizes the size of the report.)

> The carefully illustrated report turned in by the police detective covered five pages of single-spaced copy. (This simple sentence emphasizes that the report was carefully illustrated.)

Emphasis can be achieved by a climactic order of ideas or facts within a sentence.

> EXAMPLE Over subsequent weeks the industrial relations department worked diligently, management showed tact and patience, and the employees finally accepted the new policy.

Emphasis can be achieved by setting an item apart with a **dash**.

> EXAMPLE Here is where all the trouble begins—in the American confidence that technology is ultimately the medicine for all ills.

Emphasis can be achieved by the use of intensifiers (*most, very, really*), but this technique is so easily abused that it should be used only with caution.

> EXAMPLE The final proposal is *much* more persuasive than the first.

Emphasis can be achieved by such mechanical devices as italics (underlining) and capital letters. But this technique is also easily abused and should be used with caution.

> EXAMPLE When we add the commonplace situations that allow these systems to function for hundreds of researchers *simultaneously* and on all five continents, the power of this new information medium is even more remarkable.

However, do not use all capital letters to try to show emphasis. Doing so can cause confusion because capital letters are used for so many other reasons.

The word *do* (or *does*) may be used for emphasis, but this is also easily overdone, so proceed with caution. Compare the following examples:

> EXAMPLES You believe weekly staff meetings are essential, don't you? (unemphatic)
> You *do* believe weekly staff meetings are essential, don't you? (emphatic)

Direct address may also be used for emphasis in **correspondence**.

> EXAMPLE John, I believe we should rethink our plans.

(See also **subordination**.)

English, varieties of

There are two broad varieties of written English: standard and non-standard. These varieties are determined through **usage** by those who write in the English language. Standard English (also called American edited English) is used to carry on the daily business of the nation. It is the language of business, industry, government, education, and the professions. Standard English is characterized by exacting standards of **punctuation** and capitalization, by accurate **spelling**, by exact **diction**, by an expressive vocabulary, and by knowledgeable usage choices. Nonstandard English, on the other hand, is the language of those not familiar with the standards of written English. This form of English rarely appears in printed material except when it is used for special effect by fiction writers. Nonstandard English is characterized by inexact or inconsistent punctuation, capitalization, spelling, diction, and usage choices. Both standard and nonstandard English find their way into everyday speech and writing in the forms of the following subcategories.

COLLOQUIAL

Colloquial English is spoken standard English or writing that attempts to re-create the flavor of this kind of speech by using words and expressions common to casual conversation. Colloquial English is appropriate to some kinds of writing (personal letters, notes, and the like) but not to most business writing.

VERNACULAR

Vernacular English is the spoken form of the language, as opposed to its written form. It is the form used by the majority of those who speak the language. To write "in the vernacular" is to imitate this kind of language. Ordinarily, such writing is confined to fiction. Vernacular can also refer to the manner of expression common to a trade or profession (one might speak of "the legal vernacular"), although **jargon** more clearly expresses this meaning.

DIALECT

Dialectal English is a social or regional variety of the language that is comprehensible to people to that social group or region but that may be incomprehensible to outsiders. Dialect, which is usually nonstandard English, involves distinct **word choices**, grammatical forms, and pronunciations. Business writing, because it aims at a broad audience, should be free of dialect.

LOCALISM

A localism is a word or phrase that is unique to a geographical region. For example, the words *poke, sack,* and *bag* all denote "a paper container," each term being peculiar to a different region of the United States. Such words should normally be avoided in writing because knowledge of their meanings is too narrowly restricted.

SLANG

Slang refers to a manner of expressing common ideas in new, often humorous or exaggerated, ways. Slang often finds new use for familiar words ("He *crashed* early last night"—meaning that he went to bed early) or coins words ("He's a *kook*"—meaning that he is offbeat, unconventional). Slang expressions usually come and go very quickly. The fact that a fair number of words in the present standard English vocabulary were once considered slang indicates that when a slang word fills a legitimate need it is accepted into the language. *Skyscraper, bus,* and *date* (as in "to go on a date"), for example, were once considered slang expressions. Although slang may have a valid place in some writing, particularly in fiction, be careful not to let it creep into business writing.

BARBARISM

A barbarism is any obvious misuse of standard words, grammatical forms, or expressions. Examples include *ain't, irregardless, done got, drownded.*

English as a second language (ESL)

Learning to write well in a second language takes a great deal of effort and practice. The best and easiest way to improve your written command of English is to read widely beyond reports and professional articles: Read magazine and newspaper articles, novels, biographies, short stories, or any other writing that interests you.

This entry is a guide to some of the more common problems nonnative speakers experience when writing English. Use the cross-references to other entries and the references at the end of this entry for further study. For specific help when you are writing a memo or report, ask a native speaker.

Persistent problem areas for nonnative speakers include the following:

- count and noncount **nouns**
- **articles**
- **gerunds** and **infinitives**
- adjective **clauses**
- present perfect **verb** tense

COUNT AND NONCOUNT NOUNS

Count nouns refer to things that can be separated into countable units: *tables, pencils, projects, specialists.* Noncount nouns identify things that comprise a mass that cannot be counted: *electricity, water, oil, air, wood* (noncount nouns also describe abstract qualities such as *love, loyalty, pride,* and *harmony*).

The distinction between whether something can or cannot be counted is important for nonnative speakers to master because it determines the form of the noun to use (singular or plural), the kind of article that precedes it (*a, an, the,* or no article), and the kind of limiting adjective it requires (*fewer* or *less, much* or *many,* and so on). This distinction can be confusing with such words as *electricity* or *oil.* Although we can count Watt hours of electricity or barrels of oil, counting becomes inappropriate when we use the words *electricity* and *oil* in a general sense, as in "*Oil* is a limited resource." For a more complete list of typical count and noncount nouns, refer to the discussion of nouns in one of the texts cited at the end of this entry.

ARTICLES

This discussion of articles applies only to common nouns (not to proper nouns, such as the names of people) because count and noncount nouns are always common nouns.

The general rule is that every count noun must be preceded by an article (*a, an,* or *the*), a **demonstrative adjective** (*this, that, these*), a possessive **adjective** (*my, her, their,* and so on), or some expression of quantity (such as *one, two, several, many, a few, a lot of, some,* and *no*). The article, adjective, or expression of quantity appears either directly in front of the noun or in front of the whole noun phrase.

EXAMPLE Mary read *a* book last week. (The article *a* appears directly in front of the noun *book*.)

EXAMPLE Mary read *a* long, boring book last week. (The article *a* precedes the noun phrase *long, boring book*.)

EXAMPLE *Those* books Mary read were long and boring. The demonstrative adjective *those* appears directly in front of the noun *books*.)

EXAMPLE *Their* book was long and boring. (The possessive adjective *their* appears directly in front of the noun *book*.)

EXAMPLE *Some* books Mary read were long and boring. (The indefinite adjective *some* appears directly in front of the noun *books*.)

The articles *a* and *an* are used with nouns that refer to any one thing out of the whole class of those items.

EXAMPLE Bill has *a* pen. (Bill could have *any* pen.)

The article *the* is used with nouns that refer to a specific item that both the reader and writer can identify.

EXAMPLE Bill has *the* pen. (Bill has *a specific* pen and both the reader and the writer know which specific one it is.)

The only exception to this rule occurs when the writer is making a generalization. When making generalizations with count nouns, writers can either use *a* or *an* with a singular count noun, or they can use no article with a plural count noun. Consider the following generalization using an article.

EXAMPLE *An* egg is a good source of protein. (*any egg, all eggs, eggs in general*)

However, the following generalization uses a plural noun with no article.

EXAMPLE Eggs are good sources of protein. (*any egg, all eggs, eggs in general*)

When making generalizations with noncount nouns, do not use an article in front of the noncount noun, as shown in the following example.

EXAMPLE Sugar is bad for your teeth.

For a fuller explanation of this difficult problem, consult one of the texts listed at the end of this entry.

GERUNDS AND INFINITIVES

Nonnative writers are often puzzled by which form of a **verbal** (a verb used as a noun) to use when it functions as the direct **object** of a verb. No consistent rule exists for distinguishing between the use of an infinitive or a gerund after a verb when it is used as an object. Sometimes a verb takes an infinitive as its object, sometimes it takes a gerund, and sometimes it takes either an infinitive or a gerund. At times, even the base form of the verb is used.

Using a Gerund as a Complement

EXAMPLES　He enjoys *working.*
　　　　　　She denied *saying* that.
　　　　　　Did Alice finish *reading* the report?

Using an Infinitive as a Complement

EXAMPLES　He wants *to attend* the meeting in Los Angeles.
　　　　　　The company expects *to sign* the contract soon.
　　　　　　He promised *to fulfill* his part of the contract.

Using a Gerund or an Infinitive as a Complement

EXAMPLES　It began *raining* soon after we arrived. (gerund)
　　　　　　It began *to rain* soon after we arrived. (infinitive)

Using the Basic Verb Form as a Complement

EXAMPLES　Let Maria *finish* the project by herself.
　　　　　　The president had the technician *reassigned* to another project.

To make these distinctions accurately, you must rely on what you hear native speakers use or on what you read to determine the proper choices. Many ESL texts contain chapters on infinitive and gerund use that list verbs with their appropriate complements.

ADJECTIVE CLAUSES

Because of the variety of ways adjective clauses are constructed in different languages, they can be particularly troublesome for nonnative speakers. You need to remember a few guidelines when using adjective clauses in order to form them correctly.

First, place an adjective clause directly after the noun it modifies.

INCORRECT　The tall man is a vice-president of the company *who is standing across the room.*

CORRECT　The tall man *who is standing across the room* is a vice-president of the company.

The adjective clause *who is standing across the room* modifies *man,* not *company,* and thus comes directly after *man.*

Second, do not omit the relative pronoun when it is in the subject position of its clause. If, however, the relative pronoun is in the object position in its clause, it may be omitted. Notice the difference in these two sentences.

> EXAMPLE   The man *who sits at that desk* is my boss. (The relative pronoun *who* is in the subject position.)

> EXAMPLE   The man *whom we met* at the meeting is on the board of directors. (The relative pronoun *whom* is in the object position.)

> OR   The man we met at the meeting is on the board of directors. (The relative pronoun is omitted.)

Finally, make sure to avoid using a relative pronoun with another pronoun in an adjective clause.

> INCORRECT   The man *who he* sits at that desk is my boss.
> CORRECT   The man *who* sits at that desk is my boss.
> INCORRECT   The man *whom* we met *him* at the meeting is on the board of directors.
> CORRECT   The man *whom* we met at the meeting is on the board of directors.

PRESENT PERFECT VERB TENSE

Because it is so closely related to the past tense, the present perfect tense in English remains one of the most problematic of all tenses for nonnative speakers. A few guidelines, however, will help you remember the correct use of this tense. As a general rule, use the present perfect tense when referring to events completed in the past, but at nonspecified times. When a specific time is mentioned, use the simple past. Notice the difference in the two sentences following.

> EXAMPLE   I *wrote* the letter yesterday. (simple past tense *wrote.* The time when the action took place is mentioned.)

> EXAMPLE   I *have written* the letter. (present perfect tense *have written.* No specific time is mentioned; it could have been yesterday, last week, or ten years ago.)

Also use the present perfect tense to describe actions that were repeated several or many times in the unspecified past.

EXAMPLE She *has written* that report three times.

EXAMPLE The president and his chief technical advisor *have met* many times over the past few months.

Finally, use the present perfect with a *since* or *for* phrase when describing actions that began in the past and continue up to the present.

EXAMPLE This company *has been* in business *for* ten years.

EXAMPLE This company *has been* in business *since* 1983.

ADDITIONAL WRITING PROBLEMS

Other writing problems for nonnative speakers include subject-verb **agreement** and connectives between sentences and paragraphs (see **transition**). **Preposition** combinations as they appear in **idioms** or two-word verb structures also create problems for nonnative speakers. For additional help with these and other structural problems, consult one of the following texts. Please keep in mind, however, that the best source for learning correct usage of English structures for ESL writers comes from general reading, not from textbooks.

Azar, Betty Schrampfer. *Basic English Grammar.* Englewood Cliffs, NJ: Prentice, 1984.

———. *Fundamentals of English Grammar.* Englewood Cliffs, NJ: Prentice, 1985.

———. *Understanding and Using English Grammar.* 2nd ed. Englewood Cliffs, NJ: Prentice Regents, 1989.

The Azar books constitute a series of grammar texts that begin with fundamental structures and progress to more complex structures. The first book contains fundamental structures; the second contains intermediate structures; and the third contains the most complex structures.

Raimes, Ann. *How English Works: A Grammar Handbook with Readings.* New York: St. Martin's, 1990.

This book offers grammatical instruction and exercises for intermediate and advanced ESL students. It is unique in that it includes published readings with each grammar chapter and more complete readings at the end of the text.

Alexander, L. G. *Longman English Grammar.* London: Longman, 1988.

This book is a good, accurate, and concise reference for intermediate and advanced ESL learners. It has no exercises, but it covers a range of structures a writer should be familiar with.

equal/unique/perfect

Logically, *equal* (meaning "having the same quantity or value as another"), *unique* (meaning "one of a kind"), and *perfect* (meaning "a state of highest excellence") are **absolute words** and therefore should not be compared. However, colloquial usage of *more* and *most* as **modifiers** of *equal, unique,* and *perfect* is so common that an absolute prohibition against such use is impossible.

> EXAMPLE Yours is a *more unique* (or *perfect*) coin than mine.

Some writers try to overcome the problem by using *more nearly equal (unique, perfect)*. When **clarity** and preciseness are critical, the use of **comparative degrees** with *equal, unique,* and *perfect* can be misleading. The best rule of thumb is to avoid using the comparative degrees with absolute terms.

> CHANGE Ours is a more *equal* percentage split than theirs.
> TO Our percentage split is 51–49; theirs is 54–46.

-ese

The **suffix** *-ese* is used to designate types of **jargon** or certain languages or literary **styles** (official*ese*, journal*ese*, Chin*ese*, Pentagon*ese*).

etc.

Etc. is an **abbreviation** for the Latin *et cetera*, meaning "and others" or "and so forth"; therefore, *etc.* should not be used with *and*.

> CHANGE He brought pencils, pads, erasers, a calculator, *and etc.*
> TO He brought pencils, pads, erasers, a calculator, *etc.*

Do not use *etc.* at the end of a list or series introduced by the **phrases** *such as* or *for example* because these phrases already indicate that there are other things of the same category that are not named.

> CHANGE He brought camping items, *such as* backpacks, sleeping bags, tents, *etc.*, even though he didn't need them.
> TO He brought backpacks, sleeping bags, tents, *etc.*, even though he didn't need them.
> OR He brought camping items, *such as* backpacks, sleeping bags, and tents, even though he didn't need them.

In careful writing, *etc.* should be used only when there is logical progression (1, 2, 3, etc.) and when at least two items are named. It is often better to avoid *etc.* altogether, however, because there may be confusion as to the identity of the "class" of items listed.

EXAMPLE He brought backpacks, sleeping bags, tents, and other camping items.

euphemism

A euphemism is a word that is an inoffensive substitute for one that could be distasteful, offensive, or too blunt.

EXAMPLES *remains* for *corpse*
passed away for *died*
marketing representative for *salesman*
previously owned or *preowned* for *used*

Used judiciously, a euphemism might help you avoid embarrassing or offending someone. Overused, however, euphemisms can hide the facts of a situation (such as *incident* for *accident*) or be a form of *affectation*. (See also **word choice**.)

everybody / everyone

Both *everybody* and *everyone* are usually considered singular and so take singular **verbs** and **pronouns**.

EXAMPLES *Everybody is* happy with the new contract.
Everyone here *eats* at 11:30 a.m.
Everybody at the meeting made *his* proposals separately.
Everyone went *his* separate way after the meeting.

One exception is when the meaning is obviously plural.

EXAMPLE *Everyone* laughed at my sales slogan, and I really couldn't blame *them.*

Another exception is when the use of singular verbs and pronouns would be offensive by implying sexual bias; in such a situation, it is better to use plural verbs and pronouns or to use the expression "his or her."

CHANGE *Everyone* went *his* separate way after the meeting.
TO *They* all went *their* separate ways after the meeting.
OR Everyone went *his or her* separate way after the meeting.

Although normally written as one word, *everyone* is written as two words when each individual in a group should be emphasized.

EXAMPLES   *Everyone* here comes and goes as he pleases.
Every one of the team members contributed to this discovery.

(See also **indefinite pronouns**.)

ex post facto

The expression *ex post facto*, which is Latin for "after the fact," refers to something that operates retroactively. The term is normally used to refer to laws and is best avoided in other contexts.

CHANGE   The contract will be in effect *ex post facto* of the negotiations.
TO   The contract will be in effect after the negotiations.

exclamation marks

The purpose of the exclamation mark (!) is to indicate the expression of strong feeling. It can signal surprise, fear, indignation, or excitement. It cannot make an argument more convincing, lend force to a weak statement, or call attention to an intended irony—no matter how many are stacked like fence posts at the end of a sentence.

USES

The most common use of an exclamation mark is after a word (**interjection**), **phrase**, **clause**, or sentence to indicate surprise. Interjections are words that express strong emotion.

EXAMPLES   Ouch! Wow! Oh! Stop! Hurry!

An exclamation mark can also be used after a whole sentence, or even an element of a sentence.

EXAMPLES   The subject of this meeting—please note it well!—is our budget deficit.
How exciting is Stravinsky's *Rite of Spring!*

An exclamation mark is sometimes used after a title that is an exclamatory word, phrase or sentence.

EXAMPLES   "Our Marketing Strategy Must Change!" is an article by Richard Moody.
The Cancer with No Cure! is a book by Wilbur Moody.

When used with **quotation marks,** the exclamation mark goes outside, unless what is quoted is an exclamation.

> EXAMPLE The boss yelled, "Get in here!" Then Ben, according to Ray, "jumped like a kangaroo"!

executive summaries

The purpose of an executive summary is to consolidate the principal points of a **report** in one place. It must cover the information in the report in enough detail to reflect accurately its contents but concisely enough to permit an executive to digest the significance of the report without having to read it in full. They are called *executive summaries* because the intended audience is the busy executive who may have to make funding, personnel, or policy decisions based on findings or recommendations reported for a project.

The executive summary is a comprehensive restatement of the document's purpose, **scope,** methods, results, **conclusions,** findings, and recommendations. The executive summary condenses the entire work or explains how the results were obtained or why the recommendations were made. It simply states the results and recommendations, providing only enough information for a reader to decide whether to read the entire work.

Because they are comprehensive, executive summaries tend to be proportional in length to the larger work they summarize. The typical summary is 10 percent of the length of the report.

The sample executive summary in Figure 1 is from a market analyst's report for the executive staff of a corporation. The executive summary is usually organized according to the sequence of chapters or sections of the report it summarizes. It should be written so that it can be read independently of the report. It must not refer by number to figures, **tables,** or references contained elsewhere in the report. Executive summaries do occasionally contain a figure, table, or footnote, a practice appropriate as long as that information is integral to the summary. Because executive summaries are frequently read in place of the full report, all uncommon **symbols, abbreviations,** and **acronyms** must be spelled out. (For guidance on the location of executive summaries in reports, see **formal reports** and **abstracts.**)

Executive summaries differ from **abstracts** and **introductions.** An abstract is intended to be a snapshot of a longer work, most useful

EXECUTIVE SUMMARY

Background
and
purpose

Many recent business reports and academic papers have suggested that
businesses like ours must alter our marketing approaches to benefit
society as well as business. They advocate that our marketing decisions
should consider not only the profitability of new products but also
the value of those products to society. As in most companies, Blyco
Corporation has seldom given much consideration to the societal value
of new products. In practice, our overriding concern has always been
profitability and the competitive position of our firm in the marketplace.

Findings

This report says that this attitude will change, but slowly and only
with strong pressures from both consumers and lawmakers, and concludes
that the change will occur because our nation will eventually have
to make more efficient use of our resources. Today we may still be
able to ask only "Will it sell?" Tomorrow we will be forced to ask
also "Do we need it?"

Producers of frivolous products will disappear because their
markets will evaporate. Producers of marginally useful goods will
face shrinking markets. The firms that survive will do so only by
making major shifts in both direction and emphasis.

Scope

For business to make this change, however, government must put
profit in the area of social responsibility. Only by so doing can
government assure the maximum response from the business community.
If government does not take this necessary step, it will have to resort
to laws and regulations to force business to make the needed adjustments.

Blyco can take a lead in meeting this challenge by working with
government to ensure that we become partners rather than adversaries.
We can take the following specific steps to establish this relationship:

Recommendations

- Include on our board of directors a representative of a responsible
  consumer group and a person with legislative experience.
- Employ a person to act as a legislative liaison with congressional
  committees concerned with consumer issues.
- Implement a policy of considering the social impact of new
  products as we make marketing decisions.
- Publicize our willingness to cooperate with the government
  and responsible consumer groups in this area.

Taking these steps will not mean that we must abandon our traditional
concern for profitability; rather it will help us gain new respect
from consumers and will place us in a better position as legislative
bodies scrutinize the marketing practices of large corporations in
the years to come.

Figure 1   Executive Summary

for readers deciding whether to read the entire work based on its subject matter and purpose. An executive summary, by contrast, may be the only section of a longer work read by many readers, so it must cover the information in more detail. Although abstracts also summarize and highlight the major points of a report or article, they do so in a highly condensed form, seldom running longer than 200 or 250 words. Abstracts may also vary in the type of information they provide. *Descriptive* abstracts, for example, include information about the purpose, scope, and methodology of the longer work, whereas *informative* abstracts expand on the scope of descriptive abstracts to include any results, conclusions, and recommendations arrived at in the works being abstracted.

Introductions differ from abstracts and executive summaries in that they provide readers with essential background information needed to understand better the detailed information in the longer work. They announce the purpose, scope of coverage, and methodology used. They also decribe how the longer work is organized, but as with descriptive abstracts, introductions exclude findings, conclusions, and recommendations. As part of essential background information, introductions may also highlight the relationship of the work to a specific project or program and discuss any special circumstances leading to the study, especially when a **foreword** or **preface** is not included.

ADDITIONAL GUIDELINES ON WRITING AN EXECUTIVE SUMMARY

1. Write the executive summary after completing the report.
2. Avoid using technical terminology if your readers will include people not familiar with the topic.
3. Make the summary concise but not brusque. Be especially careful not to omit transitional words and **phrases** (such as *however, moreover, therefore, for example,* and *in summary*).
4. Finally, introduce no information not discussed in the report.

explaining a process (see process explanation)

expletives

An expletive is a word that fills the position of another word, phrase, or **clause**. *It* and *there* are the usual expletives.

EXAMPLE *It* is certain that he will go.

In this example, the expletive *it* occupies the position of subject in place of the real subject, *that he will go*. Although expletives are sometimes necessary to avoid **awkwardness**, they are commonly overused and most sentences can be better stated without them.

CHANGE *There are* several reasons that I did it.
TO I did it for several reasons.

CHANGE *There were* many orders lost for unexplained reasons.
TO Many orders were lost for unexplained reasons.
OR We lost many orders for unexplained reasons.

In addition to its usage as a grammatical term, the word *expletive* means an exclamation or oath, especially one that is profane.

explicit/implicit

An explicit statement is one expressed directly, with precision and clarity. An implicit meaning may be found within a statement, even though it is not directly expressed.

EXAMPLES His directions to the new plant were *explicit*, and we found it with no trouble.
Although he did not mention the nation's financial condition, the danger of an economic recession was *implicit* in the President's speech.

exposition

Exposition, or expository writing, informs the **reader** by presenting facts and ideas in direct and concise language that is usually not adorned with colorful or figurative words and **phrases**. Expository writing attempts to explain to the reader what its subject is, how it works, and how it relates to something else. Exposition is aimed at the reader's understanding, rather than at his or her imagination or emotions; it is a sharing of the writer's knowledge with the reader. The most important function of exposition is to give accurate and complete information to the reader and analyze it.

Figure 1 explains the use of software in a computer system by defining it, explaining how it works, and showing how it functions with the hardware equipment:

A major component of an electronic data processing system is the software—the programs supplied by the manufacturer to direct the computer's internal operation. The software supplied with the NCR Century 50 System is an extensive package that includes the operating system, utility routines, applied programs, and the NEAT/3 Compiler. These programs have been designed to perform specific functions but, at the same time, to interact with one another to increase processing efficiency and to avoid duplication.

To conserve valuable memory space, a large portion of the software package remains on disc; only the most frequently used portion resides in internal memory all of the time. The disc-resident software is organized into small modules that are called into memory as needed to perform specific functions.

The memory-resident portion of the operating system maintains strict control of processing. It consists of routines, subroutines, lists, and tables that are used to perform common program functions, such as processing input and output operations, calling other software routines from disc as needed, and processing errors.

The disc-resident portion of the operating system contains routines that are used less frequently in system operation, such as the peripheral-related software routines that are used for correcting errors encountered on the various units, and the log and display routines that record unusual operating conditions in the system log. The disc-resident portion of the operating system also contains Monitor, the software program that supervises the loading of utility routines and the user's programs.

—*NCR Century Elementary Systems Manual*

Figure 1   Expository Writing

Because it is the most effective **form of discourse** for explaining difficult subjects, exposition is widely used in business writing. To write exposition, you must have a thorough knowledge of your subject. As with all writing, how much of that knowledge you pass on to your reader should depend on the reader's needs and your **objective**.

F

fact

Expressions containing the word *fact* ("due to the *fact* that," "except for the *fact* that," "as a matter of *fact*," or "because of the *fact* that") are often wordy substitutes for more accurate terms.

> CHANGE *Due to the fact that* the sales force has a high turnover rate, sales have declined.
>
> TO *Because* the sales force has a high turnover rate, sales have declined.

The word *fact* is, of course, valid when facts are what is meant.

> EXAMPLE Our research has brought out numerous *facts* to support your proposal.

Do not use the word *fact*, however, to refer to matters of judgment or opinion.

> CHANGE *It is a fact that* sales are poor in the Midwest because of insufficient market research.
>
> TO In my opinion, sales are poor in the Midwest because of insufficient market research.
>
> OR Our analysis of the statistics indicates that sales are poor in the Midwest because of insufficient market research.
>
> OR We infer from our statistics that sales are poor in the Midwest because of insufficient market research.

(See also **logic**.)

feasibility reports

When the managers of an organization plan to undertake a new project—a move, the development of a new product, an expansion, or the purchase of new equipment—they try to determine the project's chances for success. A feasibility report is the study conducted to help them make this determination. This **report** presents evidence about the practicality of the proposed project: How much will it cost? Is sufficient manpower available? Are any legal or other special requirements necessary? Based on the evidence, the writer of the feasibility report recommends whether or not the project should be carried out. Management officials then consider the recommendation.

The most efficient way to begin work on a feasibility report is to state clearly and concisely the purpose of the study.

EXAMPLES The purpose of this study is to determine what type and how many new vans should be purchased to expand our present delivery fleet.

This study will determine which of three possible sites should be selected for our new warehouse.

A clearly worded statement of purpose acts as an effective guide for gathering and organizing information for the study. It both states the objective and defines the **scope** of the study. In a feasibility study, the scope includes the alternatives for accomplishing the purpose and the criteria by which each alternative will be examined.

A firm needing to upgrade its word-processing software, for example, might conduct a feasibility study to determine which software would best suit its requirements. The firm's requirements would establish the criteria by which each alternative is evaluated. The following example shows how the preliminary topic outline for such a study might be organized:

I. Purpose: To determine which word-processing software would best serve our office needs.

II. Alternatives: List of software and their features from various vendors.

III. Criteria:
   A. Current task requirements
      1. Memos and letters—100 per month
      2. Brief interoffice reports—8–10 per month
      3. One or two 30- to 50-page reports per month
      4. Numerous financial tables: need to link data between spreadsheet programs and text tables
      5. Occasional need to create and edit business graphics— bar and pie charts
   B. Compatibility with present hardware
      1. Need to upgrade hard-disk memory?
      2. Need to upgrade printers and purchase font cartridges?
   C. Costs
      1. Purchase of new software or upgrade of present software?
      2. Installation and transfer of existing working files
      3. Training of professional and secretarial staffs

In writing a feasibility report, you must first identify the alternatives and then evaluate each against your established criteria. After completing these analyses, summarize them in a **conclusion**. This summary of relative strengths and weaknesses usually points to one alternative as the best, or most feasible. Make your recommendation on the basis of this conclusion.

The structure of a feasibility report depends on its scope. Some studies are brief and informal; others are detailed and formal. Although the order of elements may vary, every feasibility report should contain the following sections: (1) an introduction, (2) a body, (3) a conclusion, and (4) a recommendation.

INTRODUCTION

The introduction should state the purpose of the report, describe the problems that led to it, and include any pertinent background information. You may discuss the scope or extent of the report. You might also discuss procedures or methods used in analyses of alternatives: Were any special techniques used to gather or analyze information? Was information obtained by interviews, an examination of financial records, computer analyses, or other means? Any limitations on the study should be noted here: Does a deadline have to be met? Were there any restrictions on how data could be obtained?

BODY

The body of the report should present a detailed evaluation of all alternatives under consideration. Evaluate each alternative according to your established criteria. Ordinarily, each evaluation would comprise a separate section of the report.

CONCLUSION

The conclusion should summarize the evaluation of each alternative, usually in the order in which they are discussed in the body of the report. In your conclusion you may also want to interpret the detailed evaluations.

RECOMMENDATION

This section must state the alternative that best meets the criteria.

SAMPLE FEASIBILITY REPORT

The sample feasibility report shown in Figure 1 opens with an **introduction** that states the purpose of the report, the problem that prompted the study, the alternatives that were examined, and the criteria used. The body presents a detailed discussion of each alternative, particularly in terms of the criteria stated in the introduction. The conclusion draws together and summarizes the details in the body of the study. The recommendation section suggests the course of action that the company should take.

INTRODUCTION

The purpose of this report is to determine which of two proposed computer processors would best enable the Jonesville Engineering and Manufacturing Branch to increase its data-processing capacity and thus to meet its expanding production requirements.

Problem

In October 19-- the Information Systems and Support Group at Jonesville put the MISSION System into operation. Since then the volume of processing transactions has increased fivefold (from 1,000 to 5,000 updates per day). This increase has severely impaired system response time from less than 10 seconds in 1988 to 120 seconds on average at present. Degraded performance is also apparent in the backlog of batch-processing transactions. During a recent check 70 real-time and approximately 2,000 secondary transactions were backlogged. In addition, the ARC 98 Processor that runs MISSION is nine years old and frequently breaks down. Downtime caused by these repairs must be made up in overtime. In a recent 10-day period in January, processor downtime averaged 25 percent during working hours (7:30 a.m. to 6:00 p.m.). In February the system was down often enough that the entire plant production schedule was endangered.

Finally, because the ARC 98 cannot keep up with the current workload, the following new systems, all essential to increased plant efficiency and productivity, cannot be implemented: shipping and billing, labor collection, master scheduling, and capacity planning.

Scope

Two alternative solutions to provide increased processing capacity have been investigated: (1) purchase of a new ARC 98 Processor to supplement the first, and (2) purchase of a

---

Figure 1   Feasibility Report

Landmark I Processor to replace the current ARC 98. The two alternatives will be evaluated primarily according to cost and, to a lesser extent, according to expanded capacity for future operations.

PURCHASING A SECOND ARC 98 PROCESSOR

This alternative would require additional annual maintenance costs, salary for an additional computer operator, increased energy costs, and a one-time construction cost for a new facility to house the processor.

Annual maintenance costs	$ 45,000
Annual salary for computer operator	28,000
Annual increased energy costs	7,500
Annual operating costs	$ 80,500
Facility cost (one-time)	$ 50,000
Total first-year cost	$130,500

These costs for the installation and operation of another ARC 98 Processor are expected to produce the following anticipated savings in hardware reliability and system readiness.

Hardware Reliability
A second ARC 98 would reduce current downtime periods from four to two per week. Downtime recovery averages 30 minutes and affects 40 users. Assuming that 50 percent of users require the system at a given time, we determined that the following reliability savings would result:

2 downtimes × 0.5 hours × 40 users × 50% × $12.00/ hour overtime × 52 weeks = $12,480 (annual savings)

System Readiness
Currently, an average of one day of batch processing per week cannot be completed. This gap prevents online system readiness when users report to work and affects all users at least one hour per week. Improved productivity would yield these savings:

40 users × 1 hour/week × $9.00/hour average wage rate × 52 weeks = $18,720 (annual savings)

Figure 1   Feasibility Report (continued)

Summary of Savings

Hardware reliability	$12,480
System readiness	18,720
Total annual savings	$31,200

Costs and Savings for ARC 98 Processor

Costs

Annual	$ 80,500
One-time	50,000
First-year total	$130,500
	− 50,000
Annual total	$ 80,500

Savings

Hardware reliability	$ 12,480
System readiness	18,720
Total annual savings	$ 31,200

Annual Costs Less Savings

Annual costs	$ 80,500
Annual savings	− 31,200
Net additional annual operating cost	$ 49,300

ARC 98 Capacity
By adding a second ARC 98 processor, current capacity will be doubled. Each processor could process 2,500 transactions per day while cutting response time from 120 seconds to 60 seconds. However, if new systems essential to increased plant productivity are added to the MISSION System, efficiency could be degraded to its present level in the next three to five years. This estimate is based on the assumption that the new systems will add between 250 and 500 transactions per day immediately. These figures could increase tenfold in the next several years if current rates of expansion continue.

Figure 1   Feasibility Report

PURCHASING A LANDMARK I PROCESSOR

This alternative will require additional annual maintenance costs, increased energy costs, and a one-time facility adaption cost.

Annual maintenance costs	$ 75,000
Annual energy costs	9,000
Annual operating costs	$ 84,000
Cost of adapting existing facility	$ 24,500
Total first-year cost	$108,500

These costs for installation of the Landmark I Processor are expected to produce the following anticipated savings in hardware reliability, system readiness, and staffing for the Information Systems and Services Department.

Hardware Reliability
Annual savings will be the same as those for the ARC 98 Processor: $12,480.

System Readiness
Annual savings will be the same as those for the ARC 98 Processor: $18,720.

Wages for the Information Systems and Services Department
New system efficiencies would permit the following wage reductions in the department:

One computer operator (wages and fringe benefits)	$28,000
One-shift overtime premium (at $100/week × 52 weeks)	10,400
Total annual wage savings	$38,400

Summary of Savings

Hardware reliability	$12,480
System readiness	18,720
Wages	38,400
Total annual savings	$69,600

Figure 1   Feasibility Report (continued)

Cost and Savings for Landmark I Processor

<u>Costs</u>

Annual	$ 84,000
One-time	24,500
First-year total	$108,500
	– 24,500
Annual total	$ 84,000

<u>Savings</u>

Hardware reliability	$ 12,480
System readiness	18,720
Wages	38,400
Total annual savings	$ 69,600

<u>Annual Costs Less Savings</u>

Annual costs	$ 84,000
Annual savings	– 69,600
Net additional annual operating cost	$ 14,400

Landmark I Capacity

The Landmark I processor can process 5,000 transactions per day with an average response time of 10 seconds per transaction. Should the volume of future transactions double, the Landmark I could process 10,000 transactions per day without exceeding 20 seconds per transaction on average. This increase in capacity over the present system would permit implementation of plans to add four new systems to MISSION.

CONCLUSION

A comparison of costs for both systems indicates that the Landmark I would cost $60,400 less in first-year costs.

<u>ARC 98 Costs</u>

Net additional annual operating	$49,300
One-time facility	50,000
First-year total	$99,300

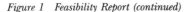

Figure 1 Feasibility Report (continued)

Landmark I Costs	
Net additional operating	$14,400
One-time facility	24,500
First-year total	$38,900

Installation of a second ARC 98 Processor will permit the present information-processing systems to operate relatively smoothly and efficiently. It will not, however, provide the expanded processing capacity that the Landmark I Processor would for implementing new subsystems essential to improved production and record keeping.

RECOMMENDATION

The Landmark I Processor should be purchased because of the initial and long-term savings and because its expanded capacity will allow the addition of essential systems.

Figure 1   Feasibility Report (continued)

female

Female is usually restricted to scientific, legal, or medical contexts (a *female* patient or suspect). Keep in mind that this term sounds cold and impersonal. The terms *girl, woman,* and *lady* are acceptable substitutes in other contexts; however, be aware that these substitute words have connotations involving age, dignity, and social position. (See also **male**.)

few/a few

In certain contexts, *few* carries more negative overtones than the phrase *a few* does.

EXAMPLES They have *a few* scruples. (positive)
They have *few* scruples. (negative)
There are *a few* good things about your report. (positive)
There are *few* good things about your report. (negative)

fewer/less

Fewer refers to items that can be counted (count nouns).

EXAMPLES A good diet can mean *fewer* colds.
Fewer members took the offer than we expected.

Less refers to mass quantities or amounts (mass nouns).

EXAMPLES *Less* vitamin C in your diet may mean more, not *fewer*, colds.
The crop yield decreased this year because we had *less* rain than necessary for an optimum yield.

figuratively/literally

These two words are often confused. *Literally* means "really" and should not be used in place of *figuratively*, which means "metaphorically." Do not say that someone "literally turned green with envy" unless that person actually changed color.

EXAMPLES In the winner's circle the jockey was, *figuratively* speaking, ten feet tall.
When he said, "Let's run it up the flagpole," he did not mean it *literally*.

Avoid the use of *literally* to reinforce the importance of something.

CHANGE She was *literally* the best of the group.
TO She was the best of the group.

figures of speech

A figure of speech is an imaginative **comparison**, either stated or implied, between two things that are basically unlike but have at least one thing in common. If a device is cone shaped with an opening at the top, for example, you might say that it looks like a volcano.

Business people may find themselves using figures of speech to clarify the unfamiliar by relating a new and difficult concept to one with which the **reader** is familiar. In this respect, figures of speech help establish a common ground of understanding between the specialist and the nonspecialist. Business people may also use figures of speech to help translate the abstract into the concrete; in the process of doing so, figures of speech also make writing more colorful and graphic.

Although figures of speech are not used extensively in business writing, a particularly apt figure of speech may be just the right tool when you must explain or describe a complex concept. A figure of speech must be appropriate, however, to achieve the desired effect.

CHANGE Without the fuel of tax incentives, our economic engine would operate less efficiently. (It would not operate at all without fuel.)

TO Without the fuel of tax incentives, our economic engine would sputter and die. (This is not only apt, but it also states a rather dry fact in a colorful manner—always a desirable objective.)

A figure of speech must also be consistent to be effective.

CHANGE We must get our research program back *on the track*, and we are counting on you to *carry the ball*. (inconsistent)

TO We must get our research program back on the track, and we are counting on you to do it. (inconsistency removed)

A figure of speech should not, however, attract more attention to itself than to the point the writer is making.

EXAMPLE The whine of the engine sounded like ten thousand cats having their tails pulled by ten thousand mischievous children.

Trite figures of speech, which are called **clichés**, defeat the purpose of a figure of speech—to be fresh, original, and vivid. A surprise that comes "like a bolt out of the blue" is not much of a surprise. It is better to use no figure of speech than to use a trite one.

TYPES OF FIGURES OF SPEECH

Analogy is a comparison between two objects or concepts that shows ways in which they are similar. It is very useful in business writing, especially when you are writing to an educated but nontechnical audience. In effect, analogies say "A is to B as C is to D." The resemblance between these concepts is partial but close enough to provide a striking way of illuminating the relationship the writer wishes to establish.

EXAMPLE Pollution (A) is to the environment (B) as cancer (C) is to the body (D).

Antithesis is a statement in which two contrasting ideas are set off against each other in a balanced syntactical structure.

EXAMPLES Man proposes, but God disposes.
Art is long, but life is short.

Hyperbole is gross exaggeration used to achieve an effect or **emphasis**.

EXAMPLE He *murdered* me on the tennis court.

Litotes are understatements, for emphasis or effect, achieved by denying the opposite of the point you are making.

> EXAMPLES Einstein was no dummy.
> Seventy dollars is not a small price for a book.

Metaphor is a figure of speech that points out similarities between two things by treating them as though they were the same thing. Metaphor states that the thing being described *is* the thing to which it is being compared.

> EXAMPLE He is the sales department's *utility infielder*.

Metonymy is a figure of speech that uses one aspect of a thing to represent it, such as *the red, white, and blue* for the American flag, *the blue* for the sky, and *wheels* for an automobile. This device is common in everyday speech because it gives our expressions a colorful twist.

> EXAMPLE *The hard hat* area of the labor force was especially hurt by the current economic recession.

Simile is a direct comparison of two essentially unlike things, linking them with the word *like* or *as*.

> EXAMPLE His feelings about his business rival are so bitter that in recent conversations with his staff he has returned to the subject compulsively, *like a man scratching an itch*.

Personification is a figure of speech that attributes human characteristics to nonhuman things or abstract ideas. One characteristically speaks of the *birth* of a planet and the *stubbornness* of an engine that will not start.

> EXAMPLE Early tribes of human beings attributed scientific discoveries to gods. To them, fire was not a *child of man's brain* but a gift from Prometheus.

fine

When used in expressions such as "I feel *fine*" or "a *fine* surf," fine is colloquial. The colloquial use of *fine*, like that of *nice*, is too vague for business writing. In writing, the word *fine* should retain the sense of "refined," "delicate," or "pure."

> EXAMPLES A *fine* film of oil covered the surface of the water.
> There was a *fine* distinction between the two possible meanings of the disputed passage.
> *Fine* crystal is currently made in Austria.

first/firstly

Firstly—like *secondly, thirdly . . . lastly*—is an unnecessary attempt to add the *-ly* form to an **adverb**. *First* is an adverb in its own right, and sounds much less stiff than *firstly*.

> CHANGE　*Firstly*, we should ask for an estimate.
> TO　*First*, we should ask for an estimate.

flammable/inflammable/nonflammable

Both *flammable* and *inflammable* mean "capable of being set on fire." Since the *-in* **prefix** usually causes the word following to take its opposite meaning (*incapable, incompetent*), *flammable* is preferable to *inflammable* because it avoids possible misunderstanding.

> EXAMPLE　The cargo of gasoline is *flammable*.

Nonflammable is the opposite, meaning "not capable of being set on fire."

> EXAMPLE　The asbestos suit was *nonflammable*.

flowcharts

A flowchart is a diagram of a process that involves stages, with the sequence of stages shown from beginning to end. The flowchart presents an overview of the process that allows the **reader** to grasp the essential steps of the process quickly and easily. The process being illustrated could range from the steps involved in assembling a bicycle to the stages by which bauxite ore is refined into aluminum ingots for fabrication.

Flowcharts can take several forms to represent the steps in a process. They can consist of labeled blocks (Figure 1), pictorial representations (Figure 2), or standardized symbols (Figure 3); the items in any flowchart are always connected according to the sequence in

Figure 1　Example of a Block Flowchart

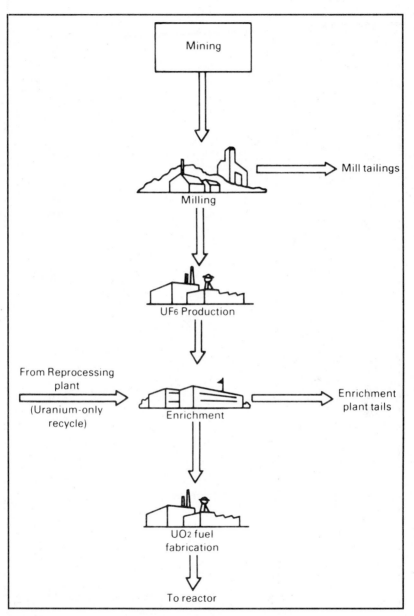

Figure 2   Pictorial Flowchart of Light-Water Reactor Uranium Fuel Cycle

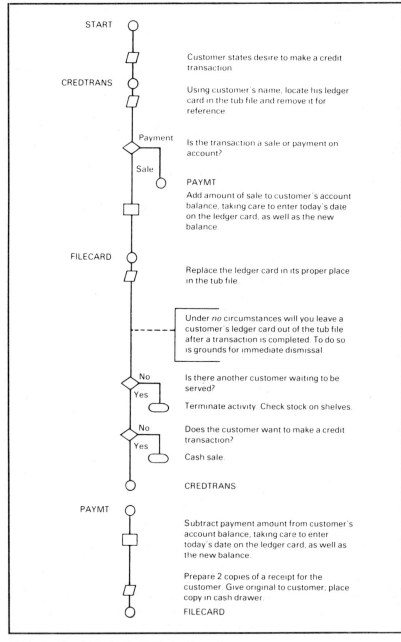

START — Customer states desire to make a credit transaction

CREDTRANS — Using customer's name, locate his ledger card in the tub file and remove it for reference

Payment — Is the transaction a sale or payment on account?

Sale

PAYMT — Add amount of sale to customer's account balance, taking care to enter today's date on the ledger card, as well as the new balance.

FILECARD — Replace the ledger card in its proper place in the tub file.

Under *no* circumstances will you leave a customer's ledger card out of the tub file after a transaction is completed. To do so is grounds for immediate dismissal.

No — Is there another customer waiting to be served?

Yes — Terminate activity. Check stock on shelves.

No — Does the customer want to make a credit transaction?

Yes — Cash sale.

CREDTRANS

PAYMT — Subtract payment amount from customer's account balance, taking care to enter today's date on the ledger card, as well as the new balance.

Prepare 2 copies of a receipt for the customer. Give original to customer; place copy in cash drawer.

FILECARD

Figure 3   Flowchart of a Credit Transaction

which the steps occur. The normal direction of flow in a chart is left to right or top to bottom. When the flow is otherwise, be sure to indicate it with arrows.

Flowcharts that document computer programs and other information-processing procedures use standardized **symbols**. The standards are set forth in *Information Processing—Documentation Symbols and Conventions for Data, Program and System Flowcharts, Program Network Charts and System Resources Charts,* published by the International Organization for Standardization, publication ISO 5807–1985 (E). When creating a flowchart, follow the general guidelines for creating and integrating illustrations with text in the **illustration** entry, in addition to the following guidelines specific to flowcharts:

1. Label each step in the process, or identify it with a conventional symbol. Steps can also be represented pictorially or by labeled blocks.
2. With flowcharts made up of labeled blocks and standardized symbols, use arrows to show the direction of flow only if the flow is opposite to the normal direction. With pictorial representation, use arrows to show the direction of all flow.
3. Include a key if the flowchart contains symbols your readers may not understand.

forceful/forcible

Although *forceful* and *forcible* both are **adjectives** meaning "characterized by or full of force," *forceful* is usually limited to persuasive ability and *forcible* to physical force.

EXAMPLES   The thief made a *forcible* entry into my apartment.
John made a *forceful* presentation at the committee meeting.

foreign words in English

The English language has a long history of borrowing words from other languages. Most of these borrowings occurred so long ago that we seldom recognize the borrowed terms (also called *loan words*) as being of foreign origin. To check the origin of a word, consult the etymology portion of its **dictionary** entry.

EXAMPLES   whiskey (Gaelic), animal (Latin), church (Greek)

GUIDELINES FOR USE OF FOREIGN WORDS IN ENGLISH
Foreign expressions should be used only if they serve a real need. The overuse of foreign words in an attempt to impress your **reader** or to be elegant is **affectation**. Your goal of effective communication can be accomplished only if your reader understands what you write; choose foreign expressions, therefore, only when they make an idea clearer.

Words not fully assimilated into the English language are set in **italics** if printed (underlined in typed manuscript).

> EXAMPLES   *sine qua non, coup de grâce, in res, in camera*

Words and abbreviations that have been fully assimilated need not be italicized. When in doubt, consult a current dictionary.

> EXAMPLES   cliché, etiquette, vis-à-vis, de facto, résumé, etc., i.e., e.g.

As foreign words become current in English, their plural forms give way to English plurals.

> EXAMPLES   *formulae* becomes *formulas*
> *agenda* becomes *agendas*

In addition, accent marks tend to be dropped from words (especially from French words) the longer they are used in English. But because not all foreign words shed their accent marks with the passage of time, consult a dictionary whenever you are in doubt. Foreign **diacritcal marks** are often written in pen because most American typewriters do not have them. (See also **e.g./i.e.** and **etc.**)

foreword/forward

Although the pronunciation is the same, the spellings and meanings of these two words are quite different. The word *foreword* is a **noun** meaning "introductory statement at the beginning of a book or other work."

> EXAMPLE   The department chairperson was asked to write a *foreword* for the professor's book.

The word *forward* is an **adjective** or **adverb** meaning "at or toward the front."

> EXAMPLES   Move the lever to the *forward* position on the panel. (adjective)
> Turn the dial until the needle begins to move *forward*. (adverb)

foreword/preface

The terms *foreword* and *preface* are occasionally used interchangeably but are usually differentiated. A foreword is an optional introductory statement about a book or **formal report** written by someone other than the author. The writer of the foreword is usually an authority in the field, whose name and affiliation and the date the statement was written appear at the end of the foreword. The foreword may discuss the purpose of the study, but it generally provides background information about the study's significance or places the study in the context of other works written in the field. If the work was done under contract to a sponsoring organization, the manager of the project at the sponsoring organization may indicate how the work pertains to specific programs or goals of that organization. The foreword always precedes the preface when a work has both.

The preface, an optional introductory statement to a book or formal report, is usually written by the author, but is not signed. The preface may announce the purpose, background, and scope of the work. Typically, it highlights the relationship of the work to a given project or program and discusses any special circumstances leading to the study. A preface may also specify the audience for whom the work is intended. It may contain acknowledgments of help received during the course of the project or in the preparation of the publication. Works that acknowledge help received but that do not have a preface typically include a section entitled "Acknowledgments." Such a section appears on a separate page following the table of contents and preceding the introduction. Finally, a preface may cite permission obtained for the use of copyrighted works.

If you do not have a foreword or preface, place the type of information they typically contain, if it is essential, in the introduction. (For guidance about the location of a foreword and preface in a report, see **formal report**.) For an example of a preface, see the preface of this text at the beginning of the book.

form letters

A form letter is a type of correspondence in which the identical message is sent to more than one person; only the name and address of each recipient differ from letter to letter. The text and the recipients' names and addresses are stored in a computer, merged on command, and printed on single sheets of stationery. The **reader's** impression is that the letter has been written directly and exclusively to him or her. (See **word processing**.)

Millions of form letters are mailed each year; used wisely, they can save a firm thousands of dollars because they reduce the time for **dictation**, transcription, handling, and filing. They can improve a firm's sales and customer relations by giving customers information about new products and services and by providing customers with faster service for routine or recurring situations.

WHEN TO USE FORM LETTERS

Form letters are ideal for simultaneously reaching hundreds or thousands of customers, clients, or employees with announcements and other information. In fact, **sales letters** are usually mass-produced as form letters. Form letters are also useful for situations that occur often, such as responses to inquiries, standard orders, acknowledgments of orders, credit matters, and early-stage **collection letters**. (See **acknowledgment letters**, **credit letters**, **inquiry letters and responses**, and **order letters**.) Of course, if a particular situation calls for a more personal response (such as an **adjustment letter** in response to a complaint), a form letter can be damaging. Most people resent casual or impersonal treatment when they believe they deserve individual attention.

For routine circumstances, however, an undisguised form letter results in a more positive response than do form letters that masquerade as personal messages but fail because of discrepancies in type, faculty alignment, or inappropriate wording. Furthermore, few customers object to form letters for recurring circumstances, since they know that using a form letter saves the writer money.

WRITING FORM LETTERS

Because form letters save so much time in the long run, it is worth spending extra time in the beginning to write an effective letter. By using the principles of **correspondence** and the **you viewpoint**, you can produce a form letter tailored to your potential readers and **objective**. Even though a reader may know he or she is reading a form letter, you should *give each the feeling that the letter fits his or her situation.* Avoid the mistake of broadcasting that the message is a form.

CHANGE To all our customers:
　　　Whether you live in Maine or California, we have provided the
　　　following toll-free number to help. . . .
　TO If you have a problem with your word processor and cannot
　　　find the answer in the *User's Guide*, someone will help you
　　　at the following toll-free number:

Since not all form letters need to be disguised, they often use a
"headline lead" to replace the standard salutation, as shown in Figure 1. By talking directly to the reader, you can make form letters
seem less stiff and impersonal. Some form letters can be personalized by adding a typed or handwritten postscript. However, if you
suspect that the reader would resent a form letter, even if it is personalized, either write an individual letter or perhaps use a "guide
letter."

A guide letter is individually typed and composed of several
optional sentences or paragraphs that can be combined to produce
a single letter. In effect, writing a guide letter is like selecting a meal
in a cafeteria line: you compose the letter by selecting and then
arranging previously written parts rather than writing sentences
from scratch.

Guide letters are ideal in recurring circumstances that require
more personal or varied responses than form letters provide. They
are useful, for example, when you wish either to tailor parts of the
letter for particular readers or to construct sets of letters from standardized parts, as in **application letters**, **reference letters**, **refusal
letters**, and some **memorandums**. Since guide letters are formed
from various prewritten parts, they require careful preparation. In
most cases, an office must create a guide-letter manual containing
paragraphs that are labeled with some sort of code—often combinations of letters and numbers (A-1, A-2, B-1, B-2, and so on). Then the

```
       Here's your copy of

       the User's Guide


       for your X-WRITER system.  This publication

       is designed to acquaint you with the hardware

       and WORDWRITE software. . . .
```

Figure 1

writer can dictate the parts and the order in which they should appear for a particular letter ("A-2, B-3, C-2, D-4"). Obviously, word processors, with their storage and retrieval capabilities, are ideal for managing and producing guide letters.

Those who work in offices that produce high volumes of letters benefit most from form and guide letters; however, anyone can adopt these concepts for his or her own correspondence. By keeping copies of each letter you write and by refining the language on each new occasion, you can create your own bank of form and guide letters that will save you time and effort. By carefully crafting a letter the first time you write it, you can use it later, in whole or in part, as a model for future letters.

formal reports

Formal reports are the written accounts of major projects. Projects that are likely to produce formal reports include research into new developments in a field, explorations of the advisability of launching a new product or an expanded service, or an end-of-year review of developments within an organization. The scope and complexity of the project will determine how long and how complex the report should be. Most formal reports—certainly those that are long and complex—require a carefully planned structure that offers the **readers** an easy-to-recognize guide to the material in the reports. Such aids as a **table of contents**, an **executive summary**, and an **abstract** make the information in the report more accessible. Making a formal topic outline that lists the major facts and ideas in the report and indicates their relationship to one another should help you write a well-organized report.

Most formal reports are divided into three major parts—front matter, body, and back matter—each of which contains a number of elements. Just how many elements are needed for a particular report depends on the subject, the length of the report, and the kinds of material covered. In fact, the number and arrangement of the elements in a formal report may vary.

ORDER OF ELEMENTS IN A FORMAL REPORT

Many companies and governmental and other institutions have a preferred style for formal reports and furnish guidelines that staff members must follow. If your employer has prepared a set of style guidelines, follow it; if not, use the format recommended in this entry. The following list includes most of the elements a formal report might contain.

Front Matter

Title page
Abstract
Table of contents
List of figures
List of tables
Foreword
Preface
List of abbreviations and symbols

Body

Executive summary
Introduction
Text (including headings)
Conclusions
Recommendations
References

Back Matter

Bibliography
Appendixes
Glossary
Index

FRONT MATTER

The front matter, which includes all the elements that precede the body of the report, serves several purposes: it gives the reader a general idea of the author's purpose in writing the report; it indicates whether the report contains the kind of information the reader is looking for; and it lists where in the report the reader can find specific chapters, **headings**, illustrations, and **tables**. Not all formal reports require every element of front matter. A title page and table of contents are usually mandatory, but whether an abstract, a preface, and lists of figures, tables, **abbreviations**, and **symbols** are included will depend on the **scope** of the report and its intended audience. The front matter pages are numbered with lowercase roman numerals. Throughout the report, page numbers should be centered near the bottom of each page.

Title Page. The formats of title pages for formal reports vary, but the page should include the following information:

1. The full **title** of the report. The title should indicate the topic and announce the scope and **objective** of the report. Titles often provide the only basis on which readers can decide whether to read a report. Titles that are too vague or too long not only hinder readers but also can prevent efficient filing and information retrieval by librarians and other information specialists. Follow these guidelines when creating the title:
   - Do not use "Report on ...," "Technical Report on ...," or "XYZ Corporation Report on ...," in the title, since the fact that the information appears in a report will be self-evident to your reader.
   - Do not use abbreviations in the title. Use **acronyms** only when the report is intended for an audience familiar enough with the topic that the acronym will not confuse them.
   - Do not include the period covered by a report in the title; include that information in a subtitle:

   EFFECTS OF PROPOSED HIGHWAY
   CONSTRUCTION ON PROPERTY VALUES
   Annual Report, 19--

2. The name of the writer, principal investigator, or compiler. Frequently, contributors simply list their names and almost never list their academic degrees. Sometimes they identify themselves by their job title in the organization (Jane R. Doe, Cost Analyst; Jack T. Doe, Head, Research and Development). Sometimes contributors identify themselves by their tasks in contributing to the report (Jane R. Doe, Compiler; Jack T. Doe, Principal Investigator).

3. The date or dates of the report. For one-time reports, list the date when the report is to be distributed. For periodic reports, which may be issued monthly or quarterly, list in a subtitle the time period that the present report covers. Elsewhere on the title page, list the date when the report is to be distributed.

4. The name of the organization for which the writer works.

5. The name of the organization to which the report is being submitted, if the work is being done for a customer or client.

These categories are standard on most title pages, but some organizations may require additional information.

The title page, although unnumbered, is considered page i (small Roman numeral 1). The back of the title page, which is blank and unnumbered, is considered page ii, and the abstract then falls on page iii so that it appears on a right-hand (i.e., odd-numbered) page. For reports with printing on both sides of each sheet of paper, right-hand pages are always odd-numbered and left-hand pages are always even-numbered. (Note the pagination in this book.) New sections and chapters of reports typically begin on a new right-hand page. Reports with printing on only one side of each sheet can be numbered consecutively regardless of where new sections begin.

Abstract. An abstract, which normally follows the title page and is page iii, is a condensed version of a longer piece of writing that summarizes and highlights the major points, enabling the prospective reader to decide whether to read the entire report. Usually 200 to 250 words or less, abstracts must make sense independently of the works they summarize. (For a complete discussion of abstract writing supported with samples, see **abstracts**.)

Table of Contents. A table of contents lists all the major **headings** or sections of the report in their order of appearance, along with their page numbers. It lists all front matter and back matter except the title page and the table of contents itself. The table of contents begins on a new page, numbered page iv, because it follows the title page (page i) and the abstract (page iii). By convention, the table of contents and its page number are not listed in the table of contents page.

Along with the abstract, a table of contents permits the reader to assess the value of a report. It also aids a reader who may want to look at only certain sections of the report. For this reason, the wording of chapter and section titles in the table of contents should be identical to those in the text. (For a sample contents page, see **table of contents**.) The table of contents need not list all headings in the report. Generally no more than three levels are listed. However, when any heading of a given level is listed, all headings of that level must also be listed in the contents.

Sometimes the table of contents is followed by lists of the figures and tables contained in the report. These lists should always be presented separately, and a page number should be given for each item.

List of Figures. Figures include all **illustrations—drawings, photographs, maps,** charts, and **graphs**—contained in the report. When a report contains more than five figures, they should be listed, along with their page numbers, in a separate section immediately following the table of contents. The section should be entitled "List of Figures" and should begin on a new page. Figure numbers, titles, and page numbers should be identical to those in the text. In most reports figures are numbered consecutively with arabic numbers.

List of Tables. When a report contains more than five tables, they should be listed, along with their titles and page numbers, in a separate section entitled "List of Tables," immediately following the list of figures (if there is one). Tables are numbered consecutively with arabic numbers throughout most reports.

Foreword. A foreword is an optional introductory statement written by someone other than the author. The foreword may discuss the purpose of the report but generally provides background information about its significance or places it in the context of other works written in the field.

The foreword always precedes the preface when the report contains both. (See also **foreword/preface.**)

Preface. The preface is an optional introductory statement, usually written by the author, that announces the purpose, background, and scope of the report. Sometimes the preface specifies the audience for whom the report is intended; it may also highlight the relationship of the report to a given project or program. A preface may contain acknowledgments of help received during the course of the project or in the preparation of the report. Finally, it may cite permission obtained for the use of copyrighted works. If the report does not require a preface, place this type of information, if it is essential, in the introduction.

The preface follows the table of contents (and the lists of figures or tables if they are included) and it begins on a separate page entitled "Preface." (See also **foreword/preface.**)

List of Abbreviations and Symbols. When the abbreviations and symbols used in the report are numerous and there is a chance that the reader will not be able to interpret them, the front matter should include a list of all symbols and abbreviations (including **acronyms**) and what they stand for in the report. Such a list, which follows the preface, is particularly helpful for reports on specialized subjects whose audience will include nonspecialists. Such a list, appropriately titled, begins on a new page.

BODY (TEXT)

The body is that portion of the report in which the author introduces the subject, describes in detail the methods and procedures used in the study, demonstrates how results were obtained, and draws conclusions on which any recommendations are based.

The first page of the body is numbered 1. This and all subsequent pages in the report are usually numbered in arabic numbers, unlike the front matter, which is numbered in lowercase roman numerals.

Executive Summary. The body of the report begins with an executive summary that provides a more complete overview of a report than either a descriptive or an informative abstract does. The summary states the purpose and nature of the investigation and gives major findings, conclusions, and—if any are to be made—recommendations. It also provides an account of the procedures used to conduct the study. Although more complete than an abstract, the summary should not contain a detailed description of the work on which the findings, conclusions, and recommendations were based. The size of an executive summary is proportional to the size of the report; a rule of thumb is that the length of the executive summary should be approximately 10 percent of the length of the report.

Some summaries are written to follow the organization of the report. Others highlight the findings, conclusions, and recommendations by summarizing them first before going on to discuss procedures or methodology.

A summary enables people who may not have time to read a lengthy report to scan its primary points and then decide whether they need to read the entire report. Because they are often intended for busy executives, summaries are sometimes called executive summaries. Addressed primarily to this audience, summaries often appear as the first section of the body of a report. Like abstracts, summaries should not contain tables, illustrations, or bibliographic citations. The summary is considered part of the body of the report. (For a more detailed discussion of summaries and a sample summary, see **executive summaries**.)

Introduction. The purpose of an introduction is to give the readers any general information they must have in order to understand the detailed information in the rest of the report. An introduction sets the stage for the report, providing a frame of reference for the details contained in the body of the report. In writing the introduction, you need to state the subject, the purpose, the scope, and the way you plan to develop the topic. You may also describe how the report will be organized. (For a detailed discussion of introductions, with samples, see **introductions**.)

Text. Generally the longest section of the report, the text (or body) presents the details of how the topic was investigated, how the problem was solved, how the best choice from among alternatives was selected, or whatever else the report covers. This information is often clarified and further developed by the use of illustrations and tables and may be supported by references to other studies.

Most formal reports have no single best organization. How the text is organized will depend on the topic and on how you have investigated it (survey, analysis, feasibility study, laboratory experiment, or whatever). The text is ordinarily divided into several major sections, comparable to the chapters in a book. These sections are then subdivided to reflect the logical divisions in your main sections. (For a discussion of the writing process, see "The Five Steps of Successful Writing" at the beginning of this book.)

Conclusions. The conclusion section pulls together the results of your study in one place. Here you tell the reader what you have learned and its implications. You show how the results follow from the study objectives and method. You should also point out any unexpected results. (For a fuller discussion of this section of a report, see **conclusions**.)

Recommendations. Recommendations, which are sometimes combined with the conclusions section, state what course of action should be taken based on the results of the study. Of the three possible locations for a new warehouse, which is the best? Which make of delivery van should be purchased to replace the existing fleet? Which contractor has submitted the best proposal for remodeling the company cafeteria? Which type of microcomputer equipment should the office buy? Should the equipment be leased rather than purchased? The recommendations section says, in effect, "I think we should purchase this, or do that, or hire them."

The emphasis is on the verb *should.* Recommendations advise the reader on the best course of action based on the researcher's findings. Generally someone up the organizational ladder, or a customer or client, makes the final decision about whether to accept the recommendations.

References. If in your report, you refer to material in or quote directly from a published work or other research source, you must provide a list of references in a separate section called references. If your employer has a preferred reference style, follow it; otherwise, use the guidelines provided in **documenting sources**.

For a relatively short report, the references should go at the end of the report. For a report with a number of sections or chapters, the reference section should fall at the end of each major section or chapter. In either case, every reference section should be labeled as such and should start on a new page. If a particular reference appears in more than one section or chapter, it should be repeated in full in each appropriate reference section.

BACK MATTER

The back matter of a formal report contains supplemental information, such as where to find additional information about the topic (**bibliography**) and how the information in the report can be easily located (**index**), clarified (**glossary**), and explained in more detail (appendix).

Bibliography. A **bibliography** is a list, usually in alphabetical order, of all sources that were consulted in researching the report but that are not cited in the text. A bibliography may not be necessary, however, when the reference listing contains a complete list of sources. When a report has both, the bibliography follows the reference section. This section is often entitled "Works Cited," especially when the sources include nonprint information like computer codes, microfiche, or video material.

Like the other elements in the front and back matter, the bibliography starts on a new page and is labeled by name. (For detailed information about creating a bibliography, see **bibliography**.)

Appendixes. An appendix contains information that clarifies or supplements the text. This type of information is placed at the back of the report because it is too detailed or voluminous to appear in the text without impeding the orderly presentation of ideas. Material typically placed in an appendix includes long charts and supplementary graphs or tables, copies of **questionnaires** and other material used in gathering information, texts of interviews, pertinent correspondence, and explanations too long for explanatory footnotes but helpful to the reader who is seeking further assistance or clarification.

A report may have one or more appendixes; generally, each appendix contains one type of material. For example, a report with two appendixes may have a questionnaire in one and a detailed computer printout tabulating the questionnaire's results in the other.

Place the first appendix on a new page directly after the bibliography. Additional appendixes also begin on a new page. Identify each with a title and a heading. Appendixes are ordinarily labeled Appendix A, Appendix B, and so on. If your report has only one appendix, simply label it Appendix, followed by its title. To call it Appendix A would imply that an Appendix B will follow. (For a detailed discussion of appendixes, see **appendix/appendixes/appendices**.)

Glossary. A glossary is a list of selected terms on a particular subject that are defined and explained. Include a glossary only if your report contains many words and expressions that will be unfamiliar to your intended readers. Arrange the terms alphabetically, with each entry beginning on a new line. The definitions then follow each term, dictionary style. The glossary, labeled as such, appears directly after the appendix and begins on a new page.

Even though the report may contain a glossary, you should also define all unfamiliar terms or terms having a special meaning in your study when they are first mentioned in the text. (See **defining terms**.)

Index. An index is an alphabetical list of all the major topics discussed in the report. It cites the pages where each topic can be found and thus allows readers to find information on topics quickly and easily. The index is always the final section of the report. The index to this volume can be found at the back of the book.

An index is an optional finding device in a report because a detailed table of contents usually gives readers adequate information about topics covered. Indexes are most useful for reference works like handbooks and manuals. (For guidance on creating an index, see **indexing**.)

format

Format has at least two distinct, but related, meanings. It can refer (1) to the sequence in which information is presented in a publication, and (2) to the physical arrangement of information on the page and to the general physical appearance of the finished publication. The first meaning applies to the standard arrangement or layout of information in many of the following types of job-related writing:

- **formal reports**
- **memorandums**
- **questionnaires**
- **proposals**
- **correspondence**
- **trip reports**
- **résumés**

These types of writing are characterized by conventions that govern where each section will be placed. In **formal reports**, for example, the **table of contents** precedes the preface but follows the title page and **abstract**. Likewise, although variations exist, letters typically are written according to the following standard pattern:

- letterhead
- date
- inside address
- salutation
- body
- complimentary close
- signature
- typed name and title
- additional information (initials, enclosure, and "carbon copy" notation)

These conventions also pertain to the use of **heads, illustrations**, and **indentation**. (For detailed information about numbered and unnumbered heading systems in reports and manuals, see **heads**.)

In recent years, a body of information has been published that expands the concept of format to encompass all typographic and graphic principles used to depict information in a document. (See **layout and design**.)

former/latter

Former and *latter* should be used to refer to only two items in a sentence or **paragraph**.

EXAMPLE The president and his trusted aide emerged from the conference, the *former* looking nervous and the *latter* looking downright glum.

Because these terms make the **reader** look back to previous material to identify the reference, they impede reading and are best avoided.

CHANGE We spent a great deal of time on the Jones account and very little on the Evans account, the *former* being highly profitable and the *latter* only marginally so.

TO We spent a great deal of time on the Jones account, which was highly profitable, and very little time on the Evans account, which produced only marginal profits.

forms design

Forms provide a time-saving and uniform way to record data. It is easier and quicker to supply information by filling out a form than by writing a **memorandum**, letter, or **report**. Also, it is far easier to read, tabulate, and evaluate information on a form than in more individual kinds of writing. Figures 1 and 2 are two examples of forms.

PREPARING A FORM

To be effective, a form should make it easy for one person to supply information and for another person to retrieve and interpret the information. Ideally, a form should be self-explanatory, even to a person who is seeing it for the first time. If you are preparing a form, plan carefully. Determine what kind of information you will be seeking, and arrange the questions in a logical order.

Writing Instructions and Captions. Instructions should go at the beginning of the form and are often preceded by a **head** designed to attract the attention of the **reader**:

Instructions for Completing This Form

1. Complete the applicable blue shaded portions on the front of pages 1, 2, and 3.
2. Mail page 1 to the Securi-Med Insurance Company at the address shown above.
3. Give page 2 to your doctor.
4. If services are rendered in a hospital, give page 3 to the hospital.
5. Use the back of page 1 to itemize bills that are to go toward your major medical deduction.

Annual Reappointment Form   July 1, 19___ to June 30, 19___

CHILDREN'S MEDICAL CENTER

1735 Chapel Street

Toledo, Ohio 43692

NAME:

List appointments or offices held, teaching positions, independent
studies in medical or dental societies or other medical organizations,
and any other professional recognitions you would like to have included
in your file:

_____

_____

_____

_____

_____

_____

_____

_____

Do you wish a change in your privileges? If so, specify:_____

_____

Have there been any changes in your board specialties? Yes☐ No☐

        If yes: Date_____

                 Specialty Board_____

Signature_____

Date_____

                          Return to: Chairman
                                      Credentials & Nominating Comm.

Figure 1   Example of a Form

CHILDREN'S MEDICAL CENTER

PHYSICIAN:	DEPARTMENT:
OFFICE ADDRESS:	SECTION:
OFFICE PHONE:	OHIO LICENSE NO:
STAFF STATUS:	BIRTHDATE:

****

1978–79		1979–80		1980–81		1981–82	
Satisfactory Health Status		Satisfactory Health Status		Satisfactory Health Status		Satisfactory Health Status	
Satisfactory Meeting Attendance		Satisfactory Meeting Attendance		Satisfactory Meeting Attendance		Satisfactory Meeting Attendance	
Satisfactory Medical Record Completion		Satisfactory Medical Record Completion		Satisfactory Medical Record Completion		Satisfactory Medical Record Completion	
No Disciplinary Action		No Disciplinary Action		No Disciplinary Action		No Disciplinary Action	
COMMITTEE APPOINTMENTS		COMMITTEE APPOINTMENTS		COMMITTEE APPOINTMENTS		COMMITTEE APPOINTMENTS	
APPROVED	DATE	APPROVED	DATE	APPROVED	DATE	APPROVED	DATE
Chairman, Credentials Comm.		Chairman, Credentials Comm.		Chairman, Credentials Comm.		Chairman, Credentials Comm.	
Chief of Staff		Chief of Staff		Chief of Staff		Chief of Staff	
Secretary, Board of Trustees		Secretary, Board of Trustees		Secretary, Board of Trustees		Secretary, Board of Trustees	

Figure 2　Example of a Form

Instructions for distributing the various copies of multiple-copy forms are normally placed at the bottom of the form and are repeated on every copy of the form.

Requests for information on the form are normally worded as captions. Keep captions brief and to the point; avoid unnecessary **repetition** by combining related information under an explanatory heading.

CHANGE What make of car do you drive? _____

          What year was it manufactured? _____

          What model is it? _____

          What is the body style? _____

TO Vehicle Information

          Make _____ Year _____

          Model _____ Body Style _____

Planning for Responses. Forms should ask questions that can be answered simply and briefly. The best responses are check marks, circles, or underlining; next best are numbers, single words, or brief **phrases**. Sentence responses are the least effective, since they take the most time to write and to read.

Make captions as specific as possible. For example, if a requested date is other than the date on which the form is being filled out, make the caption read, "Effective date," "Date issued," or whatever it may be, rather than simply "Date." As in all business writing, put yourself in your reader's place and imagine what sort of requests would be clear.

Sequencing Data. Try to arrange requests for information in an order that will be most helpful to the person filling out the form. At the top of the form, include preliminary information, such as the name of your organization, the title of your form, and any file number or reference number. In the main portion of the form, include the entries you need in order to obtain the necessary data. At the end of the form, include space for a signature and a date.

The arrangement of the entries depends on several factors. First, the subject matter of the entries will frequently determine the most logical order. A form requesting reimbursement for travel expenses, for instance, would logically begin with the first day of the week (or month) and end with the last day of the appropriate period. Second, if the response to one item is based on the response to another item, be sure that the items appear in the correct order. Third, group requests for related information together whenever possible. Finally, entries should, in general, be arranged on the form from left to right and from top to bottom, since that is the way we are accustomed to reading.

DESIGNING A FORM

When you prepare the final version of a form, pay particular attention to design details—especially to the placement of entry lines and the amount of space allowed for responses.

Entry Lines. The form can be laid out so that the person filling it out supplies information on a writing line, in a writing block, or in square boxes. The *writing line* is simply a rule with a caption.

(Name)	(Telephone)
(Street Address)	
(City)	(State) (Zip Code)

The *writing block* is essentially the same, except that each entry is enclosed in a ruled block, making it impossible for the person filling out the form to associate a caption with the wrong line.

Name		Telephone
Street Address		
City	State	Zip Code

On some forms, the captions are set horizontally.

Destination	Source	Supplier	Method of Shipment

On other forms, they are set vertically.

Destination	
Source	
Supplier	
Method of Shipment	

When it is possible to anticipate all likely responses, you can make the form easy to fill out by writing the question on the form, supplying a labeled box for each possible answer, and asking people to put an X in the appropriate box. Such a plan also makes it easy to retrieve the data. Be sure that your questions are both simple and specific.

EXAMPLE Would you buy another Whapo?   ☐ Yes   ☐ No

Spacing. Be sure to provide enough space to enable the person filling out the form to enter the data. Insufficient writing space makes it difficult for people to respond—and thus causes responses that are hard to read. Reading responses that are too tightly spaced or that snake around the side of the form can cause headaches and errors.

Forms may be filled out either in longhand or on a typewriter. Always allow sufficient space to accommodate both. If you think that some people will fill out the form in longhand, provide adequate space for relatively large handwriting. It is especially important to plan for typewritten responses if you intend to have your form typeset. If you do not inform the typesetter that the printed form must be easy to answer on a typewriter, those who do may have difficulty aligning the form vertically in their machines. The reason is simple: On a typewriter, there are 6 lines to the inch, but on typesetting equipment there are 6.0386 lines to the inch—there's a hairline less space between typeset lines than between typewritten lines—and any typewriter will be off the writing line by the time it nears the bottom of a page-long form. Be sure to remind the typesetter to set *exactly* 6 lines to the inch. If the form contains more than one response per line, align the column entries vertically if possible, so that the person filling it out can set tabs on the typewriter.

forms of discourse

There are four forms of discourse: exposition, description, persuasion, and narration. **Exposition** is the straightforward presentation of facts and ideas with the **objective** of informing the **reader**; **description** is an attempt to re-create an object or situation with words so that the reader can visualize it mentally; **persuasion** attempts to convince the reader that the writer's point of view is the correct or desirable one; and **narration** is the presentation of a series of events in chronological order. These types of writing rarely exist in pure form; rather, they usually appear in combination.

formula/formulae/formulas

The plural form of *formula* is either *formulae* (a Latin derivative) or *formulas*. *Formulas* is more common, however, since it is the more natural English plural. (See also **foreign words in English**.)

> EXAMPLE   You may present the underlying theory in your introduction, but save proofs or *formulas* for the body of your report.

fortuitous/fortunate

When an event is *fortuitous*, it happens by chance or accident and without plan. Such an event may be lucky, unlucky, or neutral.

> EXAMPLE   My encounter with the general manager in Denver was entirely *fortuitous*; I had no idea he was there.

When an event is *fortunate*, it happens by good fortune or happens favorably.

> EXAMPLE   Our chance meeting had a *fortunate* outcome.

functional shift

Many words shift easily from one **part of speech** to another, depending on how they are used. When they do, the process is called a *functional shift*, or a shift in function.

> EXAMPLES   It takes ten minutes to *walk* from the sales office to the accounting department. (verb)
> The long *walk* from the sales office to the accounting department reduces efficiency. (noun)

Let us *run* the new data through the computer. (verb)
May I see the last computer *run*? (noun)

I talk to the Chicago office on the *telephone* every day. (noun)
Sometimes I have to call from a *telephone* booth. (adjective)
He will *telephone* the home office from London. (verb)

After we discuss the project, we will begin work. (conjunction)
After lengthy discussions, we began work. (preposition)
The partners worked well together forever *after*. (adverb)

Do not arbitrarily shift the function of a word in an attempt to shorten a **phrase** or expression. Such attempts at achieving **conciseness** can result in the worst kind of **jargon**, as in the following examples:

EXAMPLES In medical jargon, an *attending physician* becomes an "attending." (a shift from an adjective to a noun)
In computer jargon, *to pass a signal through a computer logic gate* becomes "to gate." (a shift from a noun to a verb)
In nuclear energy jargon, a *reactor containment building* becomes a "containment." (a shift from an adjective to a noun)

Avoid these shortcut versions; they are unnecessary. Linguistically acceptable ways for saying the same things already exist. If you are unsure about how to use similar words and expressions, consult a **dictionary** for both the word's meaning and its part of speech. Identifying the word's part of speech will allow you to determine quickly whether or not you are using it properly. (See also **new words**.)

G

garbled sentences

A garbled sentence is one that is so tangled with structural and grammatical problems that it cannot be repaired by simply replacing words or rewriting **phrases**. The following nearly unreadable sentence appeared in an actual **memorandum**:

> EXAMPLE My job objectives are accomplished by my having a diversified background which enables me to operate effectively and efficiently, consisting of a degree in mechanical engineering, along with twelve years of experience, including three years in Staff Engineering-Packaging sets a foundation for a strong background in areas of analyzing problems and assessing economical and reasonable solutions.

A garbled sentence often results from an attempt to squeeze too many ideas into one sentence. Do not try to patch such a sentence; rather, analyze the ideas it contains, list them in a logical sequence, and then construct one or more entirely new sentences. An analysis of the previous example yields the following five ideas:

> EXAMPLES My job requires that I analyze problems and find economical and workable solutions to them.
> My diversified background helps me accomplish my job.
> I have a mechanical engineering degree.
> I have twelve years of job experience.
> Three of these years have been in Staff Engineering-Packaging.

Using these ideas, the writer might have described his job as follows:

> EXAMPLE My job requires that I analyze problems and find economical and workable solutions to them. Both my training and my experience help me achieve this goal. Specifically, I have a mechanical engineering degree and twelve years of job experience, three of which have been in the Staff Engineering-Packaging Department.

Notice that the revised job description contains three sentences with logical development and clear **transitions**. Such analysis and rewrit-

ing is useful for any sentence or **paragraph** that you cannot repair with minor editing. (See also **clarity** and **complex sentences**.)

gender

In grammar, gender is a term for the way words are formed to designate sex. The English language provides for recognition of three genders: masculine, feminine, and neuter (to designate those objects that have no definable sex characteristics). The gender of most words can be identified only by the choice of the appropriate **pronoun** (*he, she, it*). Only these pronouns and a select few **nouns** (*waiter/waitress*) reflect gender.

Gender is important to writers because they must be sure that nouns and pronouns within a grammatical construction agree in gender. A pronoun, for example, must agree with its noun antecedent in gender. We must refer to a woman as *she* or *her*, not as *it*; to a man as *he* or *him*, not as *it*; to a barn as *it*, not *he* or *she*.

An antecedent that includes both sexes, such as *everyone* and *student*, has traditionally taken a masculine pronoun. Since this **usage** might be offensive by implying sexual bias, however, it is better to use plural nouns and pronouns.

> CHANGE Every *employee* should be aware of *his* insurance benefits.
>   TO All *employees* should be aware of *their* insurance benefits.

It is best (though not always possible) to avoid the awkward "his or her," "he or she" type of construction. (See also **he/she**.)

general-to-specific method of development

In a general-to-specific **method of development**, you begin with a general statement and then provide facts or examples to develop and support that statement. For example, if you begin a **report** with the general statement "Companies that diversify are more successful than those that do not," the remainder of the report would offer examples and statistics that prove to your **reader** that companies that diversify are, in fact, more successful than companies that do not.

A **memorandum** or report organized in a general-to-specific sequence discusses only one point—the point made in the opening general statement. All other information in the memo or report supports the general statement, as in Figure 1.

<table>
<tr><td>General
statement</td><td>

Locating Additional Circuit Suppliers

Based on information presented at the Supply Committee meeting on April 14, we recommend that the company locate additional suppliers of integrated circuits. Several related events make such an action necessary.

Our current supplier, ABC Electronics, is reducing its output. Specifically, we can expect a reduction of between 800 and 1,000 units per month for the remainder of this fiscal year. The number of units should stabilize at 15,000 units per month thereafter.

</td></tr>
</table>

General
statement

Specific
supporting
information

Locating Additional Circuit Suppliers

Based on information presented at the Supply Committee meeting on April 14, we recommend that the company locate additional suppliers of integrated circuits. Several related events make such an action necessary.

Our current supplier, ABC Electronics, is reducing its output. Specifically, we can expect a reduction of between 800 and 1,000 units per month for the remainder of this fiscal year. The number of units should stabilize at 15,000 units per month thereafter.

Domestic demand for our calculators continues to grow. Demand during the current fiscal year is up 25,000 units over the last fiscal year. Sales Department projections for the next five years show that demand should peak next year at 50,000 units and then remain at that figure for at least the following four years.

Finally, our overseas expansion into England and West Germany will require additional shipments of 5,000 units per quarter to each country for the remainder of this fiscal year. Sales Department projections put calculator sales for each country at double this rate, or 20,000 units in a fiscal year, for the next five years.

Figure 1   General-to-Specific Method of Development

gerunds

A gerund is a **verbal** ending in *-ing* that is used as a **noun**.

EXAMPLE   *Typing* is a useful skill.

A gerund may be used as a **subject**, a direct **object**, an object of a **preposition**, a **subjective complement**, or an **appositive**.

EXAMPLES   *Estimating* is an important managerial skill. (subject)
I find *estimating* difficult. (direct object)
We were unprepared for their *coming*. (object of a preposition)
Seeing is *believing*. (subjective complement)
My primary departmental function, *programming*, occupies about two-thirds of my time on the job. (appositive)

Only the possessive form of a noun or **pronoun** should precede a gerund.

EXAMPLES   *John's* working has not affected his grades.
His working has not affected his grades.

Do not confuse a gerund with a present **participle**, which has the same form but functions as an **adjective**.

EXAMPLES   The job involves a great deal of *writing*. (gerund, used as a noun)
You must improve your *writing* skills. (particle, used as an adjective)

glossary

A glossary is a selected list of terms defined and explained for a particular field of knowledge. An alphabetical glossary, such as is often found at the end of a textbook or a **formal report**, can be helpful for quick reference.

If you are writing a report that will go to people who are not familiar with many of your technical terms, you may want to include a glossary. Inclusion of a glossary does not relieve you of the responsibility of defining in the text any terms you are certain your reader will not know, however. If you do, keep the entries concise and be sure they are so clear that any reader can understand the definitions. (See also **defining terms**.)

EXAMPLES   *Bearish:* Characterized by falling stock market prices.
Bullish: Characterized by rising stock market prices.
Certificate of Deposit: A certificate from a bank stating that the named person has a specified sum on deposit.
Debenture: A certificate or voucher acknowledging a debt.

gobbledygook

Gobbledygook is writing that suffers from an overdose of traits guaranteed to make it stuffy, pretentious, and wordy. These traits include the overuse of big and mostly **abstract words, affectation**, inappropriate **jargon, long variants**, stale expressions, **euphemisms, jammed modifiers, vogue words**, and deadwood. Gobbledygook is writing that attempts to sound official (officialese), legal (legalese), or scientific; it tries to make a "natural elevation of the geosphere's outer crust" out of a molehill. Consider the following statement from an auto repair release form:

CHANGE I hereby authorize the above repair work to be done along with the necessary material and hereby grant you and/or your employees permission to operate the car or truck herein described on streets, highways, or elsewhere for the purpose of testing and/or inspection. An express mechanic's lien is hereby acknowledged on above car or truck to secure the amount of repairs thereto.

TO You have my permission to do the repair work listed on this work order and to use the necessary material. You may drive my vehicle to test its performance. I understand that you will keep my vehicle until I have paid for all repairs.

Translated into straightforward English, the statement gains in clarity what it loses in pomposity without losing its legal meaning. Today, many organizations are working to eliminate gobbledygook.

Gobbledygook (also called "bombast" and "pedantic writing") is packed with unusual words when more common ones would be clearer; it is heavy with foreign words when their English equivalents would be more appropriate; and it generally stresses trivial matters in the hope that the **reader** will be impressed with the writer's mental agility. George Orwell parodies such writing in the essay "Politics and the English Language," from which the following excerpt is taken:

EXAMPLE Objective consideration of contemporary phenomena compels the conclusion that success or failure in competitive activities exhibits no tendency to be commensurate with innate capacity, but that a considerable element of the unpredictable must invariably be taken into account.

The following revision of Orwell's passage demonstrates the clarity of direct writing.

EXAMPLE Success or failure today depends as much on chance as on your capabilities.

(See also **affectation**, **conciseness/wordiness**, and **word choice**.)

good/well

The confusion about the use of *good* and *well* can be cleared up by remembering that *good* is an **adjective** and *well* is an **adverb**.

EXAMPLES John presented a *good* plan.
The plan was presented *well*.

However, *well* can also be used as an adjective to describe someone's health.

EXAMPLES   She is not a *well* woman.
Jane is looking *well*.

(See also **bad/badly**.)

grammar

Grammar is the systematic description of the way words work together to form a coherent language; in this sense, it is an explanation of the structure of a language. However, grammar is popularly taken to mean the set of "rules" that governs how a language ought to be spoken and written; in this sense, it refers to the **usage** conventions of a language.

These two meanings of grammar—how the language functions and how it ought to function—are easily confused. To clarify the distinction, consider the expression *ain't*. Unless used purposely for its colloquial flavor, *ain't* is unacceptable to careful speakers and writers because a convention of usage prohibits its use. Yet taken strictly as a **part of speech**, the term functions perfectly well as a **verb**; whether it appears in a declarative sentence ("I ain't going.") or an interrogative sentence ("Ain't I going?"), it conforms to the normal pattern for all verbs in the English language. Although we may not approve of its use in a sentence, we cannot argue that it is ungrammatical.

To achieve **clarity**, writers need to know both grammar (as a description of the way words work together) and the conventions of usage. Knowing the conventions of usage helps writers select the appropriate over the inappropriate word or expression. A knowledge of grammar helps them diagnose and correct problems arising from how words and **phrases** function in relation to one another. For example, knowing that certain words and phrases function to modify other words and phrases gives the writer a basis for correcting those **modifiers** that are not doing their job. Understanding **dangling modifiers** helps the writer avoid or correct a construction that obscures the intended meaning. In short, an understanding of grammar and its special terminology is valuable for writers chiefly because it enables them to recognize problems and thus communicate clearly and precisely.

graphs

A graph presents numerical data in visual form. This method has several advantages over presenting data in **tables** or within the text. Trends, movements, distributions, and cycles are more readily apparent in graphs than they are in tables. By providing a means for ready comparisons, a graph often shows a significance in the data not otherwise immediately apparent. Be aware, however, that although graphs present statistics in a more interesting and comprehensible form than tables do, they are less accurate. For this reason, they are often accompanied by tables giving the exact data. The main types of graphs are line graphs, bar graphs, pie graphs, and picture graphs. When creating graphs, follow the general guidelines for identifying graphs and integrating them with text in the **illustration** entry, in addition to following the guidelines throughout this entry specific to the types of graphs described.

LINE GRAPHS

The line graph shows the relationship between two sets of numbers by means of points plotted in relation to two axes drawn at right angles. The points, once plotted, are connected to one another to form a continuous line. In this way, what was merely a set of dots having abstract mathematical significance becomes graphic, and the relationship between the two sets of figures can easily be seen.

The line graph's vertical axis usually represents amounts, and its horizontal axis usually represents increments of time, as shown in Figure 1.

Line graphs with more than one line are common because they allow for comparisons between two sets of statistics for the same period of time. In creating such graphs, be certain to identify each line with a label or a legend, as the example in Figure 2 shows. The difference between the two lines can be emphasized by shading the space between them.

Tips on Preparing Line Graphs

1. Indicate the zero point of the graph (the point where the two axes meet). If the range of data shown makes it inconvenient to begin at zero, insert a break in the scale, as in Figure 3.

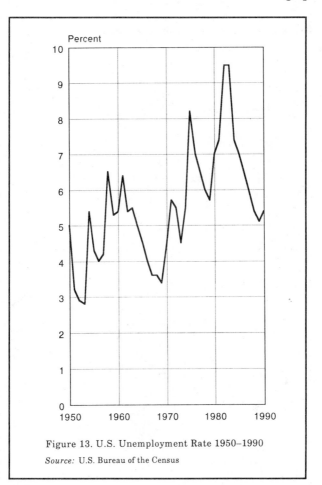

Figure 13. U.S. Unemployment Rate 1950–1990

Source: U.S. Bureau of the Census

Figure 1   Single-Line Graph

2. Graduate the vertical axis in equal portions from the least amount at the bottom to the greatest amount at the top. Ordinarily, the caption for this scale is placed at the upper left.
3. Graduate the horizontal axis in equal units from left to right. If a caption is necessary, center it directly beneath the scale.
4. Graduate the vertical and horizontal scales so that they give an accurate visual impression of the data, since the angle at which

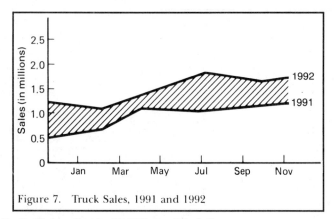

Figure 7.   Truck Sales, 1991 and 1992

Figure 2   Double-Line Graph with Difference "Shaded"

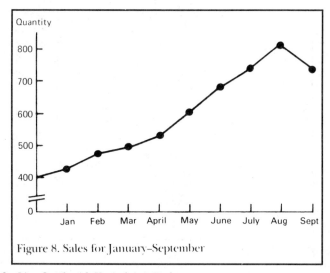

Figure 8. Sales for January–September

Figure 3   Line Graph with Vertical Axis Broken

the curved line rises and falls is determined by the scales of the
two axes. The curve can be kept free of distortion if the scales
maintain a constant ratio with each other. See Figures 4 and 5.
5. Hold grid lines to a minimum so that curved lines stand out.
Since precise values are usually shown in a table of data accom-

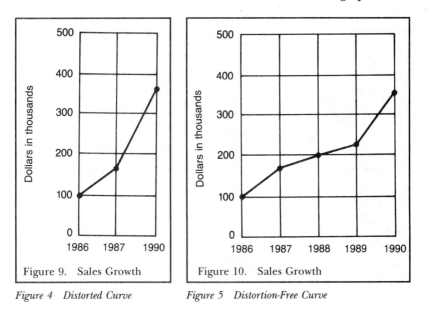

Figure 9. Sales Growth

Figure 10. Sales Growth

Figure 4   Distorted Curve

Figure 5   Distortion-Free Curve

panying a graph, detailed grid lines are unnecessary. Note the increasing clarity of the three graphs in Figures 6, 7, and 8.
  6. Include a key (which lists and explains **symbols**) when necessary, as in Figure 7. At times a label will do just as well, as in Figure 8.

BAR GRAPHS

Bar graphs consist of horizontal or vertical bars of equal width but scaled in length to represent some quantity. They are commonly used to show (1) quantities of the same item at different times, (2) quantities of different items for the same time period, or (3) quantities of the different parts of an item that make up the whole.

Figure 9 is an example of a bar graph showing varying quantities of the same item (population) at the same time (1980). Here each bar, which represents a different quantity of the same item, includes specific population data. The graph also provides additional information for each city in the form of land area and population density.

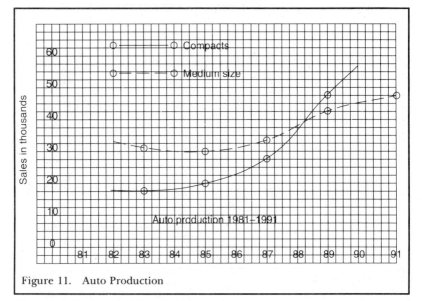

Figure 11.   Auto Production

Figure 6   Difficult-to-Read Line Graph

Figure 12.   Auto Production

Figure 7   A More Legible Version of Figure 6

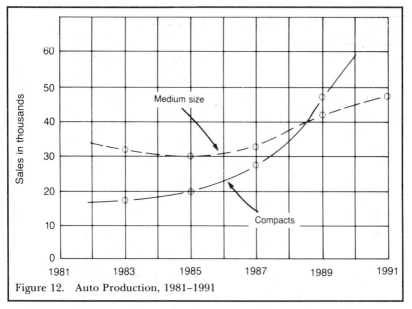

Figure 12.   Auto Production, 1981–1991

Figure 8   Clear Version of Figure 6

Some bar graphs show the quantities of different items for the same period of time. See Figure 10. (A bar graph with vertical bars is also called a column graph.)

Bar graphs can also show the different portions of an item that make up the whole. Here the bar is equivalent to 100 percent. It is then divided according to the appropriate proportions of the item sampled. This type of graph can be constructed vertically or horizontally and can indicate more than one whole when comparisons are necessary. See Figures 11 and 12.

If the bar is not labeled, each portion must be marked clearly by shading or crosshatching. Include a key that identifies the subdivisions.

PIE GRAPHS

A pie graph presents data as wedge-shaped sections of a circle. The circle must equal 100 percent, or the whole, of some quantity (a tax dollar, a bus fare, the hours of a working day), with the wedges representing the various ways in which the whole is divided. In Fig-

Supercity*	1980 Population	Land Area (Square Miles)	Population Density (People per Square Mile)
New York City/ Northeastern New Jersey/ Southern Connecticut	17,606,680	3,656	4,616
Los Angeles/Long Beach/ San Bernardino/Riverside	10,184,611	2,187	4,657
Chicago/Northwest Indiana/ Aurora/Elgin/Joliet	7,212,778	1,675	4,306
Philadelphia/ Wilmington/Trenton	4,779,796	1,270	3,764
San Francisco/San Jose	4,434,650	1,122	3,952
Detroit	3,809,327	1,044	3,649
Boston/Brockton/Lowell/ Lawrence/Haverhill	3,225,386	1,064	2,975
Miami/Fort Lauderdale/ Hollywood/West Palm Beach	3,103,729	816	3,804
Washington, D.C.	2,763,105	807	3,424
Houston/ Texas City/Lamarque	2,521,856	1,169	2,157
Cleveland/Akron/ Lorain/Elyria	2,493,475	989	2,521
Dallas/Fort Worth	2,451,390	1,280	1,915
St. Louis	1,848,590	597	3,096
Pittsburgh	1,810,038	713	2,539
Seattle/ Everett/Tacoma	1,793,612	672	2,669
Minneapolis/St. Paul	1,787,564	980	1,824
Baltimore	1,755,477	523	3,357
San Diego	1,704,352	611	2,789
Atlanta	1,613,357	905	1,783
Phoenix	1,409,279	641	2,199
Tampa/St. Petersburg	1,354,249	527	2,570
Denver	1,352,070	439	3,080
Cincinnati/Hamilton	1,228,438	465	2,642
Milwaukee	1,207,008	496	2,433
Newport News/Hampton/ Norfolk/Portsmouth	1,099,360	614	1,790
Kansas City	1,097,793	589	1,864
New Orleans	1,078,299	230	4,688
Portland	1,026,144	349	2,940
Buffalo	1,002,285	266	3,768

*Cities in bold type lost population in the 1980s.

Figure 14. Urban areas of 1 million or more population, with land area and population density. Source: *Scientific American*.

Figure 9   Bar Graph of Varying Quantities of the Same Item at the Same Time

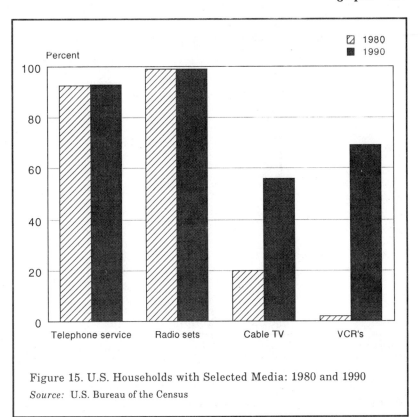

Figure 15. U.S. Households with Selected Media: 1980 and 1990

Source: U.S. Bureau of the Census

Figure 10   Bar Graph of Quantities of Different Items (Shown for Two Separate Years)

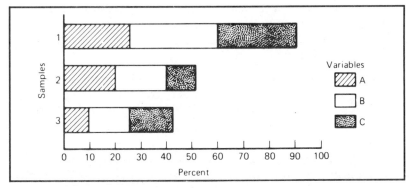

Figure 11   Bar Graph Showing Variables in Three Samples

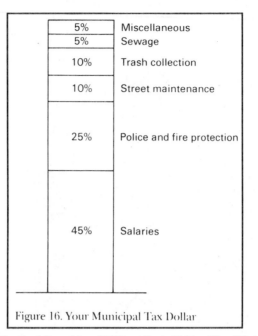

5%	Miscellaneous
5%	Sewage
10%	Trash collection
10%	Street maintenance
25%	Police and fire protection
45%	Salaries

Figure 16. Your Municipal Tax Dollar

Figure 12   Bar Graph of Quantities of Different Parts Making Up a Whole

ure 13, for example, the circle stands for a city tax dollar, and it is divided into units equivalent to the percentage of the tax dollar spent on various city services.

Pie graphs provide a quicker way of presenting the same information that can be shown on a table; in fact, a table often accompanies a pie graph with a more detailed breakdown of the same information.

Tips on Preparing Pie Graphs

1. The complete 360° circle is equivalent to 100 percent; therefore, each percentage point is equivalent to 3.6°.
2. To make the relative percentages clear, begin at the 12 o'clock position and sequence the wedges clockwise, from largest to smallest.
3. If you shade the wedges, do so clockwise and from light to dark.
4. Keep all labels horizontal, and most important, give the percentage value of each wedge.

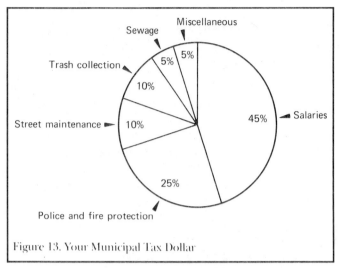

Figure 13. Your Municipal Tax Dollar

Figure 13   Pie Graph

5. Finally, check to see that all wedges, as well as the percentage values given for them, add up to 100 percent.

Although pie graphs have strong visual impact, they also have drawbacks. If more than five or six items are presented, the graph looks cluttered. Also, since they usually present percentages of something, they must often be accompanied by a table listing precise statistics. Further, unless percentages are shown on the individual sections, the reader cannot compare the values of the sections as accurately as is possible with a bar graph. (The terms that identify each segment of the graph are referred to as *callouts*.)

PICTURE GRAPHS

Picture graphs are modified bar graphs that use picture symbols of the item presented. Each symbol corresponds to a specified quantity of the item. See Figure 14. Note that precise figures are included, since the graph can present only approximate figures.

Tips on Preparing Picture Graphs

1. Make the symbol self-explanatory.
2. Have each symbol represent a single unit.

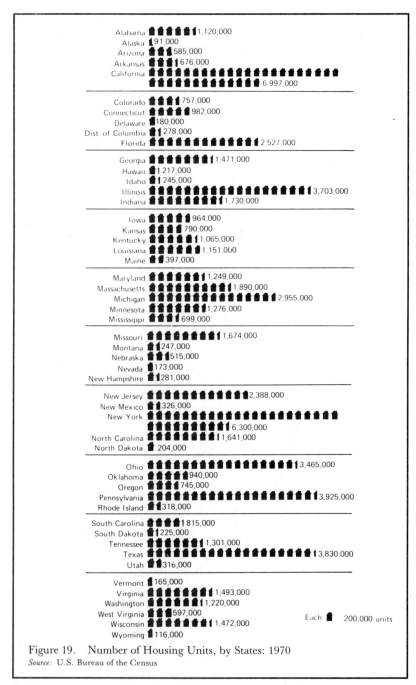

Figure 19.   Number of Housing Units, by States: 1970
Source: U.S. Bureau of the Census

Figure 14   Picture Graph

296

3. Show larger quantities by increasing the number of symbols rather than by creating a larger symbol. (It is difficult to judge relative sizes accurately.)

4. Consult a good graphics manual for details about preparing graphs. See **reference books** for a list of useful manuals.

H

half

Half a, half an, and *a half* all are correct idiomatic uses of the word *half.*

> EXAMPLES Your call to London will be completed in *half a* minute.
> Call the client in *half an* hour.
> The sales meeting lasted *a half* hour.

A half a (or *a half an*) is colloquial, however, and should be avoided in writing.

> CHANGE I will finish the sales report in *a half an* hour.
> TO I will finish the sale report in *half an* hour.

he/she

Since there is no singular **personal pronoun** in English that refers to both sexes, the word *he* was traditionally used when the sex of the antecedent is unknown.

> EXAMPLE Whoever is appointed [either a man or woman] will find *his* task difficult.

Because the use of a masculine **pronoun** when both sexes are being referred to is now recognized as offensive, it is better to rewrite the sentence in the plural (or avoid use of a pronoun altogether) than to offend.

> EXAMPLES *Employees* should take advantage of *their* insurance benefits.
> *Whoever* is appointed will find *the* task difficult.

You could also use the **phrases** *he or she* and *his or her.*

> EXAMPLE *Whoever* is appointed will find *his or her* task difficult.

Unfortunately, *he or she* and *his or her* are clumsy when used repeatedly and *s/he* is awkward; the best advice is to reword the sentence to use a plural **pronoun.** Be sure also to change to its plural form the **noun** to which the pronoun refers. (See also **plurals, gender,** and **Ms./Miss/Mrs.**)

CHANGE The financial analyst cannot do *his or her* job until *he or she* understands the concept.

TO The financial analysts cannot do *their* jobs until *they* understand the concept.

heads

Heads (also called headings) are **titles** or subtitles within the body of a long piece of writing that serve as guideposts for the **reader**. They divide the material into manageable segments, call attention to the main topics, and signal changes of topic. If a **report**, **proposal**, or other document you are writing is long or complicated, you may need several levels of heads to indicate major divisions, subdivisions, and even smaller units of those. In extremely technical material as many as five levels of heads may be appropriate, but as a general rule it is rarely necessary (and usually confusing) to use more than three.

The best advice on the effective use of heads is to be sure to prepare a good topic outline before writing your draft and then to use as heads the major topics of your outline (without roman numerals and capital letters). In a short document, you probably will use only the major divisions of your topic outline as heads, but in a longer document, you may use both the major and minor divisions. Be careful, however, not to use too many heads; four or five on a page would certainly be too many under most circumstances.

If your document requires only one level of head, you may use any form (all **capital letters**, initial capital letters only, and so on). For example, capitalizing the first letter of all the main words (as in a title) and then underlining them is very common.

The example shown in Figure 1, greatly shortened, is intended only to illustrate the use of the heads—in this case, three levels (beyond the title of the entire report). See page 300.

As you can infer from this example, the heads you use grow naturally from the divisions and subdivisions prepared in **outlining**. If more of this example were given, the heads would look like this:

CHICAGO
Location
Transportation
Rail Transportation
Sea Transportation

Interim Report of the Committee to Investigate New Factory Locations

The committee initially considered thirty possible locations for the proposed new factory. Of these, twenty were eliminated almost immediately for one reason or another (unfavorable tax structure, remoteness from rail service, inadequate labor supply, etc.). Of the remaining ten locations, the committee selected for intensive study the three that seemed most promising: Chicago, Minneapolis, and Salt Lake City. These three cities we have now visited, and our observations on each of them follow.

CHICAGO

Of the three cities, Chicago presently seems to the committee to offer the greatest advantages, although we wish to examine these more carefully before making a final recommendation.

Location

Though not at the geographical center of the United States, Chicago is centrally located in an area that contains more than three-quarters of the U.S. population. It is within easy reach of our corporate headquarters in New York. And it is close to several of our most important suppliers of components and raw materials—those, for example, in Columbus, Detroit, and St. Louis.

Transportation

Rail Transportation. Chicago is served by the following major railroads. . . .

Sea Transportation. Except during the winter months when the Great Lakes are frozen, Chicago is an international seaport. . . .

Air Transportation. Chicago has two major airports (O'Hare and Midway) and is contemplating building a third. Both domestic and international air cargo service are available. . . .

Transportation by Truck. Virtually all of the major U.S. carriers have terminals in Chicago. . . .

Figure 1   The Use of Heads

Air Transportation
Truck Transportation
Labor Supply
Engineering Personnel
Manufacturing Personnel
Outside and Consulting Services
Tax Structure
Living Conditions
Housing
Education
Recreation
Climate
MINNEAPOLIS
Location
Transportation

There is no one correct format for heads. Sometimes a company settles on a standard format, which everyone within the company is then expected to follow. Or a customer for whom a report or proposal is being prepared may specify a particular format. In the absence of such guidelines, the system used in the example should serve you well. Note the following format characteristics: (1) The first-level head is in all capital letters, typed flush to the left margin on a line by itself and separated by a line space from the material it introduces. (2) The second-level head is in capital and lowercase letters, also typed flush to the left margin on a line by itself and also separated by a line space from the material it introduces. (3) The third-level head is in capital and lowercase letters, but it is "run in" right on the same line with the first sentence of the material it introduces. Therefore, it is followed by a period to set it apart from what follows, and it is underlined or italicized so that it will stand out clearly on the page.

The following are some important points to keep in mind about heads:

1. They should signal a shift to a new topic (or, if they are lower-level heads, a new "subtopic" within the larger topic).
2. Within the larger unit they subdivide, all heads at any one level should be consistent in their relationship to the topic of the larger unit. For instance, notice in the extended list of heads in our sample that the first-level heads ("CHICAGO" and "MINNEAP-

OLIS") both bear the same relationship to the larger topic of the report (possible factory locations). When the discussion narrows to Chicago, all of the second-level heads within that unit bear the same relationship to the first-level head ("CHICAGO"): they refer to Chicago's location, its transportation, its labor supply, its tax structure, and its living conditions. And the third-level heads conform to the same principle within their units.

3. The fact that one unit at a particular level is subdivided by lower-level heads does not mean that *every* unit at that particular level must also include lower-level heads. In the example, notice that under the first-level head "CHICAGO," some of the second-level units (for instance, "Transportation") are further subdivided by third-level heads and some (for instance, "Location") are not.

4. All heads at any one level within the same next-larger unit should be parallel with one another in structure (see **parallel structure**). For instance, note in the example that all of the heads are **nouns** or noun **phrases**.

5. Too many heads, or too many levels of heads, can be as bad as too few. A highway map that showed only New York and San Francisco would not be very helpful, even to the traveler driving from New York to San Francisco. But a map that tried to show every street and every building in every town along the way would not be much better. Keep in mind the needs of your reader.

6. If your document needs a **table of contents**, create it from your heads and subheads. Be sure that the wording in your table of contents is the same as the wording in your text.

7. The head does not substitute for the discussion; the text should read as if the head were not there. In particular, don't use a **pronoun** in the text to refer to a noun in the head.

(See also **layout and design**.)

healthful/healthy

If something is *healthful*, it promotes good health. If something is *healthy*, it has good health. Carrots are *healthful*; people can be *healthy*.

> EXAMPLES Yogurt is *healthful*.
>
> We provide *healthful* lunches in the cafeteria because we want our employees to be *healthy*.

helping verbs

A helping verb (also called an auxiliary verb) is a **verb** that is added to a main verb to help it indicate **mood**, **tense**, and **voice**. In doing so, it also forms a verb **phrase**.

> EXAMPLES   I *am* going.
> I *will* go.
> I *should have* gone.
> I *should have been* gone.
> The order *was* given.

All helping verbs (*be, have, do, shall, will, may, can, must, ought*) can function alone as main verbs, but they usually function as helping verbs in verb phrases. Notice that the principal helping verbs are the various forms of the main verbs *be, have,* and *do.*

herein/herewith

The words *herein* and *herewith* are a type of **gobbledygook** that should be avoided.

> CHANGE   I have *herewith* enclosed a copy of the contract.
> TO   I have enclosed a copy of the contract.

hyperbole

Hyperbole is exaggeration to achieve an effect or **emphasis**. It is a device used to emphasize or intensify a point by going beyond the literal facts. It distorts to heighten effect.

> EXAMPLES   They *murdered* us at the negotiating session.
> The hail was like *boulders.*

Used cautiously, hyperbole can magnify an idea without distorting it; therefore, it plays a large role in advertising.

> EXAMPLE   A box of Clenso detergent can clean a *mountain of clothes.*

Everyday speech abounds in hyperbole.

> EXAMPLES   I'm *starved.* (meaning "hungry")
> I'm *dead.* (meaning "tired")

Because business writing needs to be as accurate and precise as possible, always avoid hyperbole. (See also **figures of speech**.)

hyphens

Although the hyphen functions primarily as a **spelling** device, it also functions to link and to separate words; in addition, it occasionally replaces the **preposition** *to* (0–100 for 0 *to* 100). The most common use of the hyphen, however, is to join **compound words**.

EXAMPLES   able-bodied, self-contained, carry-all, brother-in-law

A hyphen is used to form compound **numbers** from twenty-one to ninety-nine and fractions when they are written out.

EXAMPLES   twenty-one, one forty-second

When in doubt about whether or where to hyphenate a word, check your **dictionary**.

HYPHENS USED WITH MODIFIERS

Two-word and three-word unit **modifiers** that express a single thought are hyphenated when they precede a **noun** (an *out-of-date* car, a *clear-cut* decision). If each of the words can modify the noun without the aid of the other modifying word or words, however, do not use a hyphen (a *new digital* computer—no hyphen). Also, if the first word is an **adverb** ending in *-ly*, do not use a hyphen (a *hardly* used computer, a *badly* needed micrometer).

The presence or absence of a hyphen can alter the meaning of a sentence.

EXAMPLE   We need a biological waste management system.
COULD
MEAN   We need a biological-waste management system.
OR   We need a biological waste-management system.

A modifying **phrase** is not hyphenated when it follows the noun it modifies.

EXAMPLE   Our office equipment is *out of date*.

A hyphen is always used as part of a letter or number modifier.

EXAMPLES   5-cent, 9-inch, A-frame, H-bomb

In a series of unit modifiers that all have the same term following the hyphen, the term following the hyphen need not be repeated throughout the series; for greater smoothness and brevity, use the term only at the end of the series.

CHANGE   The third-floor, fourth-floor, fifth-floor rooms have recently
         been painted.
     TO The third-, fourth-, and fifth-floor rooms have recently been
         painted.

HYPHENS USED WITH PREFIXES AND SUFFIXES

A hyphen is used with a **prefix** when the root word is a **proper noun**.

EXAMPLES   pre-Sputnik, anti-Stalinist, post-Newtonian

A hyphen may optionally be used when the prefix ends and the root
word begins with the same vowel. When the repeated vowel is *i*, a
hyphen is almost always used.

EXAMPLES   re-elect, re-enter, anti-inflationary

A hyphen is used when *ex-* means "former."

EXAMPLES   ex-partners, ex-wife

A hyphen may be used to emphasize a prefix.

EXAMPLE   He was *anti-everything*.

The **suffix** *-elect* is hyphenated.

EXAMPLES   president-elect, commissioner-elect

OTHER USES OF THE HYPHEN

To avoid confusion, some words and modifiers should always be hyphenated. *Re-cover* does not mean the same thing as *recover*, for example; the same is true of *re-sent* and *resent*, *re-form* and *reform*, *re-sign* and
resign.

Hyphens should be used between letters showing how a word is
spelled.

EXAMPLE   In his letter he misspelled *believed* b-e-l-e-i-v-e-d.

Hyphens identify prefixes, suffixes, or written syllables.

EXAMPLE   *Re-*, *ism*, and *ex-* are word parts that cause spelling problems.

A hyphen can stand for *to* or *through* between letters and numbers.

EXAMPLES   pp. 44-46
           the Detroit-Toledo Expressway
           A-L and M-Z

Finally, hyphens are used to divide words at the end of a line. Avoid dividing words whenever possible, but, if you must, use the following guidelines for hyphenation:

Divide

- Between syllables (but leave at least three letters on each line)
  EXAMPLE let-ter
- Between the compounding parts of compound words
  EXAMPLE time-table
- After a single-letter syllable in the middle of the root word
  EXAMPLE sepa-rate
- After a prefix
  EXAMPLE pre-view
- Before a suffix
  EXAMPLE cap-tion
- Between two consecutive vowels with separate sounds
  EXAMPLE gladi-ator

Do Not Divide

- A word that is pronounced as one syllable
  EXAMPLE shipped
- A contraction
  EXAMPLE you're
- An **abbreviation** or **acronym**
  EXAMPLE AOPA
- A proper **noun**
  EXAMPLE Jim Wilson

If a word is spelled with a hyphen, divide it only at the hyphen break, unless dividing a word there would confuse the reader because the hyphen is essential to the word's meaning.

> EXAMPLE The accidents had all occurred during the post-
> blast period.

(See also **syllabication** and **jammed modifiers**.)

I

idea

The word *idea* means the "mental representation of an object of thought."

> EXAMPLE He didn't accept my idea about how to reorganize the branch.

Use *impression* or *intention* when they convey more precisely what you mean to say.

> CHANGE We started out with the *idea* of returning early.
> TO We started out with the *intention* of returning early.

> CHANGE She left me with the *idea* that he was in favor of the proposal.
> TO She left me with the *impression* that he was in favor of the proposal.

idioms

Idioms are groups of words that have a special meaning apart from their literal meaning. Someone who "runs for office" in the United States, for example, need not be a track star. The same person would "stand for office" in England. In both nations, the individual is seeking public office; only the idioms of the two countries differ. This difference indicates why idioms give foreign writers and speakers trouble (see also **English as a second language**).

> EXAMPLES The judge *threw the book* at the convicted arsonist.
> The company's legal advisers debated whether to *stand fast* or to *press forward* with the lawsuit.

The foreigner must memorize such expressions; they cannot logically be understood. The native writer has little trouble understanding idioms and need not attempt to avoid them in writing, provided the **reader** is equally at home with them. Idioms are often helpful shortcuts, in fact, that can make writing more vigorous and natural.

If there is any chance that your writing might be translated into another language or read in other English-speaking countries, eliminate obvious idiomatic expressions that might puzzle readers. For example, the owner's manual for a Volvo automobile was obviously translated into English with British drivers in mind. Where the

American expression would be "filling up," there are references to "topping up" various fluids; where Americans would expect "windshield wipers," they find "windscreen wipers"; and the rearview mirror has an "antidazzle knob" instead of an "antiglare adjustment" for night driving. Such idiomatic expressions can be an annoying hindrance to clear understanding.

Idioms are the reason that certain **prepositions** follow certain **verbs, nouns**, and **adjectives**. Since there is no sure system to explain such **usages**, the best advice is to check in a **dictionary**. The following are some common pairings that give writers trouble:

absolve from (responsibility)
absolve of (crimes)
accede to
accord/accordance with
according to
accountable for (actions)
accountable to (a person)
accused by (a person)
accused of (a deed)
acquaint with

adapt for (a purpose)
adapt to (a situation)
adapt from (change)
adept in
adhere to
adverse to
affinity between, with
agree on (terms)
agree to (a plan)
agree with (a person)

angry with (a person)
angry at, about (a thing)
approve of
apply for (a position)
apply to (contact)
argue for, against (a policy)
argue with (a person)

arrive in (a city, country)
arrive at (a specific location, conclusion)
based on, upon

blame for (an action)
blame on (a person)
compare with (things of the same kind to determine similarities and differences)
compare to (things that are similar but not the same kind)
comply with
concur in (consensus)
concur with (a person)
conform to
consist of
convenient for (a purpose)
convenient to (a place)
correspond to, with (a thing)
correspond with (a person)

deal with
depend on
deprive of
devoid of
differ about, over (an issue)
differ from (a thing)
differ with (a person)

differ on (amounts, terms)
different from
disagree on (an issue, plan)
disagree with (a person)
disappointed in
disapprove of
disdain for
divide between, among
divide into (parts)
engage in
exclude from
expect from (things)
expect of (people)
expert in

identical with, to
imply that
impose on
improve on
inconsistent with
independent of

infer from
inferior to
inseparable from
mediate between, among
necessary for (an action)

occupied with (actions)
opposite of (qualities)
opposite to (positions)
part from (a person)
part with (a thing)
proceed with (a project)
proceed to (begin)
proficient in

profit by (things)
profit from (actions)
prohibit from
qualify as (a person)
qualify by (experience, actions)
qualify for (a position, award)

rely on
responsibility for, of
reward for (an action)
reward with (a gift)
similar to
surrounded by (people)
surrounded with (things)
talk to (a group)
talk with (a person)
wait at (a place)
wait for (a person, event)

(See also **English as a second language** and **international correspondence.**)

illegal/illicit

If something is *illegal*, it is prohibited by law. If something is *illicit*, it is prohibited by law *or custom*. *Illicit* behavior may or may not be *illegal*, but it does violate custom or moral codes and therefore usually has a clandestine or immoral **connotation**.

> EXAMPLES Their *illicit* behavior caused a scandal, and the district attorney charged that *illegal* acts were committed.
> Explicit sexual material may be *illicit* without being *illegal*.

illustrations

The objective of using an illustration is to help your **reader** absorb the facts and ideas you are presenting. When used well, an illustration can convey an idea that words alone could never really make clear. Notice how the illustration in Figure 1 demonstrates how an accounting system can be computerized much more clearly and easily than could be done with words alone.

Illustrations should never be used as ornaments, however; they should always be functional working parts of your writing. Be careful not to overillustrate; use an illustration only when you are sure that it makes a direct contribution to your reader's understanding of your subject. When creating illustrations, always consider your objective and your reader. You would use different illustrations of an X-ray machine, for example, for a high school science class than you would for a group of X-ray technicians. Many of the attributes of good writing—simplicity, **clarity**, **conciseness**, directness—are equally important in creating and using illustrations.

The most common types of illustrations are **photographs**, **graphs**, **tables**, **drawings**, **flowcharts**, **organizational charts**, and **maps**. Your material will normally suggest one of these types when an illustration is needed.

CREATING ILLUSTRATIONS AND INTEGRATING THEM WITH TEXT

Each type of illustration has its unique strengths and weaknesses. The guidelines presented here apply to most visual material you use to supplement or clarify the information in your text. (The term *illustrations* in this entry refers to both graphics and tables.) The following tips will help you create and present your illustrations to good effect.

1. Be sure to make clear in the text why the illustration is included. The amount of discussion that each illustration requires will vary with its importance to the text. An illustration showing an important feature or system may be the central focus of an entire discussion. The complexity of the illustration will also affect the discussion, as will the background your readers bring to the information. Nonexperts require lengthier explanations than experts do, as a rule.

2. Keep the illustration as brief and simple as possible by including only information necessary to the discussion in the text.

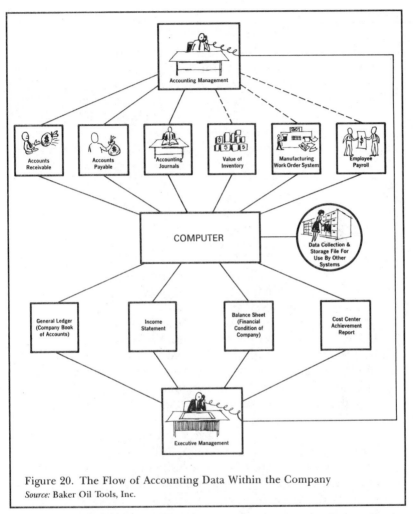

Figure 20. The Flow of Accounting Data Within the Company
Source: Baker Oil Tools, Inc.

Figure 1   Drawing Illustrating a Process

3. Try to present only one type of information in each illustration.
4. Keep terminology consistent. Do not refer to something as a "proportion" in the text and as a "percentage" in the illustration.
5. Specify the proportions used or include a scale of relative distances, when appropriate.
6. Position the lettering of any explanatory text on the illustration horizontally for ease of reading, if possible.

7. Give each illustration a concise title that clearly describes its contents.

8. Assign a figure or table number, particularly if your document contains five or more illustrations. The figure or table number precedes the title: *Figure 1 Widget Production for Fiscal 19___.* Note that graphics illustrations (photographs, drawings, maps, etc.) are generically referred to as "figures," while tables are referred to simply as "tables."

9. Refer to the illustration in your text by its figure or table number.

10. If the illustration is central to the discussion, illuminating or strongly reinforcing it, place it as close as possible to the text that discusses it. However, no illustration should precede its first text mention. Its appearance without an introduction in the text will confuse readers. But, if the illustration is lengthy, detailed, and peripheral to the discussion, place it in an appendix or elsewhere at the back of the text. However, even material in an appendix should be referred to in the text. Otherwise, the illustration is superfluous and need not be included. (See **appendix/appendixes/appendices**.)

11. Allow adequate white space on the page around and within the illustration. (See **layout and design**.)

12. In documents with more than five illustrations, list them by title, together with figure and page numbers, or table and page numbers, following the report's **table of contents**. The figures so listed should be titled "List of Figures." The tables so listed should be titled "List of Tables."

13. If you wish to use an illustration from a copyrighted publication, first obtain a written release to do so from the **copyright** holder. Acknowledge such borrowings in a source or credit line below the caption for a figure and below any footnotes at the bottom of a **table**. Illustrated materials in publications of the federal government are not copyrighted. You need not obtain written permission to reproduce them, although you should acknowledge their source in a credit line. (Such a source line appears in Figure 1.)

imply/infer

These words are not interchangeable. If you *imply* something, you hint or suggest it. If you *infer* something, you reach a conclusion on the basis of evidence.

EXAMPLES His memo *implied* that the project would be delayed.
The general manager *inferred* from the memo that the project would be delayed.

in/into

In means "inside of"; *into* implies movement from the outside to the inside.

EXAMPLE He went back *into* the building to get the new sales brochure, which he had left *in* his office.

in order to

The **phrase** *in order to* is sometimes essential to the meaning of a sentence.

EXAMPLE If the vertical scale of a graph line would not normally show the zero point, use a horizontal break in the graph *in order to* include the zero point.

The phrase *in order to* also helps control the **pace** of a sentence, even though it is not essential to the meaning of the sentence.

EXAMPLE The committee must know the estimated costs *in order to* evaluate the feasibility of the project.

Most often, however, the phrase *in order to* is just a meaningless filler phrase that is dropped into a sentence without thought.

CHANGE *In order to* meet the deadline, we must work overtime.
TO To meet the deadline, we must work overtime.

Search for these thoughtless uses of the phrase *in order to* in your writing and eliminate them.

in terms of

When used to indicate a shift from one kind of language or terminology to another, the **phrase** *in terms of* can be useful.

EXAMPLE *In terms of* gross sales, the year has been relatively successful; however, *in terms of* net income, it has been discouraging.

When simply dropped into a sentence because it comes easily to mind, however, the phrase *in terms of* is meaningless **affectation**.

CHANGE She was thinking *in terms of* subcontracting much of the work.
TO She was thinking *about* subcontracting much of the work.
OR She was thinking *of* subcontracting much of the work.

inasmuch as/insofar as

Inasmuch as, meaning "because," is a weak **connective** for stating causal relationships.

CHANGE *Inasmuch as* the heavy spring rains delayed construction, the office building will not be completed on schedule.
TO *Because* the heavy spring rains delayed construction, the office building will not be completed on schedule.

Insofar as, meaning "to the extent that," should be reserved for that explicit **usage** rather than being used to mean *since*.

EXAMPLE *Insofar as* this report analyzes the reasons for the decline in sales, it can help us improve our sales performance next year.

CHANGE *Insofar as* you are here, we will review the material.
TO *Since* you are here, we will review the material.

increasing-order-of-importance method of development

When you want the most important of several ideas to be freshest in your **reader's** mind at the end of your writing, organize your information by increasing order of importance. This sequence begins with the least important point or fact, then moves to the next least important, and builds finally to the most important point at the end. Increasing order of importance is often used when the writer is leading up to an unpleasant or unexpected conclusion.

Writing organized by increasing order of importance has the disadvantage of beginning weakly, with the least important information, which can cause your reader to become impatient before reaching your main point. But when you build a case in which the ideas lead, point by point, to an important **conclusion**, increasing order of importance is an effective method of **organization**. **Reports** on production or personnel goals are often arranged by this method, as are **oral presentations**.

In Figure 1, the writer begins with the least productive source of applicants and builds up to the most productive source.

MEMORANDUM

To: William D. Vane, Vice President for Operations
From: Harry Matthews. Personnel Department ⅄ℳ
Date: December 3, 19--
Subject: Recruiting Qualified Electronics Technicians

To keep our company staffed with qualified electronics technicians, we will have to redirect our recruiting program.

Least important source

In the past dozen years, we have relied heavily on the recruit-ment of skilled veterans. An end to the military buildup, as well as attractive reenlistment bonuses for skilled technicians now in uniform, has all but eliminated veterans as a source of trained employees. Our attempts to reach this group through ads in service newspapers and daily newspaper ads has not been successful recently. I think that the want ads should continue, although each passing month brings fewer and fewer veterans as job applicants.

Our in-house apprentice program has not provided the needed personnel either. High-school enrollments in the area are con-tinually dropping. Each year, fewer high-school graduates, our one source of trainees for the apprentice program, enter the shop. Even vigorous Career Day recruiting has yielded disap-pointing results. The number of students interested in the apprentice program has declined proportionately as school enroll-ment goes down.

Most important source

The local and regional technical schools produce the greatest number of qualified electronics technicians. These graduates tend to be highly motivated, in part because many have obtained their education at their own expense. The training and experi-ence they have received in the tech program, moreover, are first-rate. Competition for these graduates is keen, but I recommend that we increase our recruiting efforts and hire a larger share of this group than we have been doing.

I would like to meet with you soon to discuss the detail of a more dynamic recruiting program in the technical schools. I am certain that with the right recruitment campaign we can find the skilled personnel essential to our expanding role in electronics products and service.

mo

Figure 1   Increasing-Order-of-Importance Method of Development

incredible/incredulous

Something that is unbelievable or nearly unbelievable is *incredible*.

> EXAMPLE   The stock market rally was *incredible* in view of the recent price of gold on the world market.

Incredulous means that a person is skeptical or unbelieving about some thing or some event.

> EXAMPLE   He was *incredulous* at the report of the market's rally.

indefinite adjectives

Indefinite adjectives are so called because they do not designate anything specific about the **nouns** they modify.

> EXAMPLES   *some* circuit boards, *any* branches, *all* aircraft engines

Notice that the **articles** *a* and *an* are included among the indefinite adjectives. (See also **a, an**.)

> EXAMPLE   The meeting will not start for *an* hour.

For recommendations on the placement and **usage** of adjectives, see **adjectives**.

indefinite pronouns

Indefinite pronouns do not specify a particular person or thing; they specify any one of a class or group of persons or things. *Any, another, anyone, anything, both, each, either, everybody, few, many, most, much, neither, none, several, some* and *such* are indefinite pronouns. Most indefinite **pronouns** require singular **verbs**.

> EXAMPLES   If *either* of the vice-presidents *is* late, we will delay the meeting.
> *Neither* of them *was* available for comment.
> *Each* of the writers *has* a unique style.
> *Everyone* in our department *has* completed the form.

Some indefinite pronouns require plural verbs.

> EXAMPLES   *Many are* called, but *few are* chosen.
> *Several* of them *are* aware of the problem.

A few indefinite pronouns may take either plural or singular verbs, depending on whether the **nouns** they stand for are plural or singular.

EXAMPLES   *Most* of the employees *are* pleased, but *some are* not.
Most of the oil *is* imported, but *some is* domestic.

indentation

Type that is indented is set in from the margin. The most common use of indentation is at the beginning of a **paragraph**, where the first line is usually indented five spaces in a typed manuscript and one inch in a longhand manuscript.

EXAMPLE   It is hard to say when the stock market boom of the nineteen-twenties began. There were sound reasons why, during these years, the prices of common stocks should rise. Corporate earnings were good and growing. The prospect seemed benign. In the early twenties stock prices were low and yields favorable.

In the last six months of 1924, the prices of securities began to rise, and the increase was continued and extended through 1925. Thus at the end of May, 1924, the *New York Times* average of the prices of twenty-five industrial stocks was 106; by the end of the year it was 134.
—John Kenneth Galbraith, *The Great Crash* (Boston: Houghton, 1961) 12.

Another use of indentation is in **outlining**, in which each subordinate entry is indented under its major entry.

EXAMPLE   II. Types of Outlines
A. The Sentence Outline
1. A sentence outline provides order and establishes the relationship of topics to one another to a greater degree than a topic outline.

Finally, a block **quotation** may be indented within a manuscript instead of being enclosed in **quotation marks**; it must, in this case, be single-spaced. Set off the indented material from the text by indenting five spaces from the left margin and five spaces from the right margin and by double-spacing above and below the passage.

EXAMPLE   *The Operator's Manual* states:

This is a very dangerous thing to do with a hydraulic crane. Hydraulic crane ratings are based on the strength of the material of the boom (and other components). . . .

A hydraulic crane is not like a lattice boom friction crane in one very important way. In most cases, the safe lifting capacity of the lattice boom crane is based on the weight needed to tip the machine. Therefore, operators of friction machines sometimes depend on signs that the machine might tip to warn them of impending danger.

This warning was given because many operators were accustomed to. . . .

independent clauses

An independent clause is a group of words containing a **subject** and a **predicate** that expresses a complete statement and that could stand alone as a separate sentence.

> EXAMPLE   *Production was not as great as we had expected*, although we met our quota.

In the example the independent **clause** is italicized and could clearly stand alone as a complete sentence. The second, unitalicized clause is a **dependent clause**; although it contains a subject and predicate, it does not express a complete thought and could not stand alone as a sentence.

indexing

An index is an alphabetical list of all the major topics discussed in a written work. It cites the pages where each topic can be found and thus allows **readers** to find information on particular topics quickly and easily. The index falls at the very end of the work.

The key to compiling a useful index is selectivity. Instead of listing every possible reference to a topic, select references to passages where the topic is discussed fully or where a significant point is made about it. For actual index entries choose those words or **phrases** that best represent a topic. For example, the key terms in a reference to the development of legislation about environmental impact statements would probably be *legislation* and *environmental impact statement*, not *development*. Key terms are those that a reader would most likely look for in an index. In selecting terms for index entries, use chapter or section titles only if they include such key words. For index entries on **tables** and **illustrations**, use the key words in their titles.

COMPILING AN INDEX

Do not attempt to compile an index until the final manuscript is completed, because terminology and page numbers will not be accurate before then. The best way to compile your list of topics is with 3 × 5-inch index cards. Read through your written work from the beginning; each time a key term appears in a significant context, enter the term and its page number on a separate index card.

An index entry can consist solely of a main entry and its page number.

EXAMPLE Aquatic monitoring programs, 42

An index entry can also include a main entry, subentries, and even sub-subentries, as in Figure 1. A subentry indicates pages where a specific subcategory or subdivision of a main topic can be found. When compiling index entries on cards, enter a subentry on its own separate card, but include the main entry as well. Also put a sub-entry on a separate index card, but include the entry and subentry to which it is related. You must include all this information so that you will be able to tell where each card belongs when you arrange the cards in alphabetical order. (See Figure 2.)

When you have completed this process for the entire work, arrange the cards alphabetically and type the index, two columns

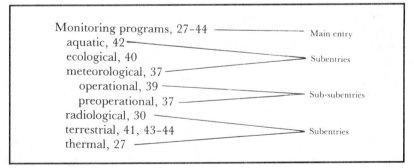

Figure 1   Index Entry with Main Entry, Subentries, and Sub-subentries

Figure 2 Sample Index Cards

to a page, from the cards. Be sure to arrange subentries and sub-subentries alphabetically beneath the proper main entry.

WORDING INDEX ENTRIES

The first word of an index entry should be the principal word because the reader will look for topics alphabetically by their main words. Selecting the right word to list first is of course easier for some topics than for others. For instance, *Tips on repairing electrical wire* would not be a suitable index entry because a reader looking for information on electrical wire would not look under the word *tips*. Whether you select *electrical wire; wire, electrical;* or *repairing electrical wire* depends on the purpose and **scope** of your report. Ordinarily, an entry with two key words, like *electrical wire*, should be indexed under each word. (When entering words on index cards you make out one card for *electrical wire* and another for *wire, electrical*.) An index entry should be written as a **noun** or a noun **phrase** rather than as an **adjective** alone.

CHANGE Electrical
grounding, 21
insulation, 20
repairing, 22
size, 21
wire, 20–22
TO Electrical wire, 20–22
grounding, 21
insulation, 20
repairing, 22
size, 21

CROSS-REFERENCING

Cross-references in an index guide the reader to other pertinent topics in the text. A reader looking up *business writing*, for example, might find a cross-reference to *memorandum*. Cross-references do not include page numbers; they merely direct the reader to another index entry, which of course does include pages. There are two kinds of cross-references: *see* references and *see also* references.

See references are most commonly used with topics that can be identified by several different terms. Listing the topic page numbers by only one of the terms, the indexer then lists the other terms throughout the index as *see* references.

EXAMPLE Economic costs. *See* Benefit-cost analyses

See references also direct readers to index entries where a topic is listed as a subentry.

EXAMPLE L-shaped fittings. *See* Elbows, L-shaped fittings

See also references indicate other entries that include additional information on a topic.

EXAMPLE Ecological programs, 40–49
See also Monitoring programs

STYLING THE INDEX

Capitalize the first word of a main entry and all other terms normally capitalized in the text. Do not capitalize the first words in subentries and sub-subentries unless they appear that way in the text. Italicize (underline) the cross-reference terms *see* and *see also*.

Place each subentry in the index on a separate line, indented from its main entry. Indent sub-subentries from the preceding subentry. These indentations allow readers to scan a column quickly for pertinent subentries or sub-subentries.

Separate entries from page numbers with **commas**. Type the index in a double-column format, as is done in the index to this book.

indiscreet/indiscrete

Indiscreet means "lacking in prudence or sound judgment."

> EXAMPLE His public discussion of the proposed merger was *indiscreet*.

Indiscrete means "not divided or divisible into parts."

> EXAMPLE The separate units, once combined, become *indiscrete*.

(See also **discreet/discrete**.)

individual

Avoid using *individual* as a **noun** if *person* is more appropriate.

> CHANGE Several *individuals* on the panel did not vote.
> TO Several *persons* on the panel did not vote.
> OR Several *people* on the panel did not vote.

> CHANGE She is an *individual* who says what she thinks.
> TO She is a *person* who says what she thinks.
> OR She says what she thinks.

Individual is most appropriate when used as an **adjective** to distinguish a single person from a group.

> EXAMPLE The *individual* employee's obligations to the firm are detailed in the booklet that describes company policies.

(See also **persons/people**.)

infinitive phrases

An infinitive phrase consists of an **infinitive** (usually with *to*) and any **modifiers** or **complements**.

> EXAMPLE The product must be able *to resist repeated hammer blows*.

Do not confuse a **prepositional phrase** beginning with *to* with an infinitive phrase. In the infinitive phrase, the *to* is followed by a **verb**; in the prepositional phrase, *to* is followed by a **noun** or **pronoun**.

> EXAMPLES   We went *to the building site.* (prepositional phrase)
> Our firm tries *to provide a comprehensive training program.* (infinitive phrase)

An infinitive phrase may function as a noun, an **adjective**, or an **adverb**.

> EXAMPLES   His goal is *to become sales manager.* (noun)
> The need *to increase sales* should be obvious. (adjective)
> We must work *to increase sales.* (adverb)

An infinitive phrase that functions as a noun may serve within the sentence as **subject**, **object**, **subjective complement**, or **appositive**.

> EXAMPLES   *To form her own company* was her lifelong ambition. (subject)
> They want *to know when we can begin the project.* (direct object)
> His objective is *to live well.* (subjective complement)
> His ambition, *to form his own company,* is soon to be realized. (appositive)

The implied subject of an introductory infinitive phrase should be the same as the subject of the sentence. If it is not, the **phrase** is a **dangling modifier**. In the following example, the implied subject of the infinitive is *you,* or *one,* not *practice.*

> CHANGE   *To learn shorthand,* practice is needed.
> TO   *To learn shorthand,* you must practice.
> OR   *To learn shorthand,* one must practice.

infinitives

An infinitive is the uninflected form of a **verb** (*go, run, fall, talk, dress, shout*) without the restrictions imposed by **person** and **number**. Along with the **gerund** and **participle**, it is one of the nonfinite verb forms. The infinitive is generally preceded by the word *to,* which, although not an inherent part of the infinitive, is considered to be the sign of an infinitive.

> EXAMPLES   It is time *to go* to work.
> We met in the conference room *to talk* about the new project.

An infinitive is a **verbal** and may function as a **noun**, an **adjective**, or an **adverb**.

> EXAMPLES *To expand* is not the only objective. (noun)
> These are the instructions *to follow*. (adjective)
> The company struggled *to survive*. (adverb)

The infinitive may reflect two **tenses**: the present and (with a **helping verb**) the present perfect.

> EXAMPLES to go (present tense)
> to have gone (present perfect tense)

The most common mistake made with infinitives is to use the present perfect tense when the simple present tense is sufficient.

> CHANGE I should not have tried *to have gone* so early.
> TO I should not have tried *to go* so early.

Infinitives formed with the root form of **transitive verbs** can express both active and (with a helping verb) passive **voice**.

> EXAMPLES to hit (present tense, active voice)
> to have hit (present perfect tense, active voice)
> to be hit (present tense, passive voice)
> to have been hit (present perfect tense, passive voice)

SPLITTING INFINITIVES

A split infinitive is one in which an adverb is placed between the sign of the infinitive, *to*, and the infinitive itself. Because they make up a grammatical unit, the infinitive and its sign are better left intact than separated by an intervening adverb.

> CHANGE *To* quickly *improve* our profit margin, we must reduce our overhead costs.
> TO *To improve* our profit margin quickly, we must reduce our overhead costs.

However, it may occasionally be better to split an infinitive than to allow a sentence to become awkward, ambiguous, or incoherent.

> CHANGE She agreed immediately to deliver the toxic materials. (Could be interpreted to mean that she agreed immediately.)
> TO She agreed to immediately deliver the toxic materials. (No longer ambiguous.)

ingenious/ingenuous

Ingenious means "marked by cleverness and originality," and *ingenuous* means "straightforward" or "characterized by innocence and simplicity."

EXAMPLES   Wilson's *ingenious* plan, which streamlined production in Department L, was the beginning of his rise within the company.
I believe that the *ingenuous* co-op students bring some freshness into the company.

inquiry letters and responses

An *inquiry letter* may be as simple as requesting a free brochure or as complex as asking a financial consultant to define the specific requirements for floating a multimillion-dollar bond issue.

There are two broad categories of inquiry letters. One kind provides a benefit (or potential benefit) to the reader: you may ask, for instance, for information about a product that a company has recently advertised. Be clear, concise, and accurate in stating your inquiry. The second kind of inquiry letter primarily benefits the writer; an example is a request to a public utility for information on the energy-related project you are developing. This kind of letter requires the use of persuasion and special consideration of your **reader's** needs.

WRITING AN INQUIRY LETTER

Your **objective** in writing the letter will probably be to obtain, within a reasonable period of time, answers to specific questions. You will be more likely to receive a prompt, helpful reply if you make it easy for the reader to respond, by following these guidelines:

1. Keep your questions concise but specific and clear.
2. Phrase your questions so that the reader will know immediately what type of information you are seeking, why you are seeking it, and how you will use it.
3. If possible, present your questions in a numbered list.
4. Keep the number of questions to a minimum, to save the reader's time.

5. Offer some inducement for the reader to respond, such as promising to share the results of your research.
6. Promise to keep responses confidential, especially if you are asking the recipient to complete a **questionnaire**.

At the end of the letter, thank the reader for taking the time and trouble to respond, and do not forget to include the address to which the material is to be sent. Your chances of getting a reply will improve if you enclose a stamped, self-addressed return envelope, especially if you are writing to someone who is self-employed. Figure 1 is a typical inquiry letter.

RESPONSE TO AN INQUIRY LETTER

When you receive an inquiry letter, first read it quickly to determine whether you are the right person in your organization to answer it—that is, whether you are the one who has both the information and authority to respond. If you are in a position to answer, do so as promptly as you can, and be sure to answer every question the writer has asked. How long your responses should be and how much technical language you should use depend, of course, on the nature of the question and on what information the writer has provided about himself or herself. Even if the writer has asked a question to which the answer is obvious or a question that seems foolish, answer it as completely as you can, and do so courteously. You may point out that the reader has omitted or misunderstood a particular piece of information or has in some other way introduced an error, but be tactful in your correction so that he or she will not feel foolish or ignorant. And at the end of the letter, offer to provide further assistance, if necessary.

Sometimes a letter of inquiry sent to a large company arrives at the desk of a staff member who realizes that he or she is not the employee best able to answer the letter. If you have received a letter that you feel you cannot answer, find out who can. Then forward the letter to that person. This person should state in the first paragraph of his or her letter that although the letter was addressed to you, it is being answered by someone else in the firm because he or she has the information needed to respond to the inquiry. Figure 2 indicates to the inquirer that her letter has been forwarded, and Figure 3 shows a typical response to an inquiry. (See also **correspondence**.)

P.O. Box 113
University of Dayton
Dayton, OH 45409
March 11, 19—

Ms. Jane Metcalf
Engineering Services
Miami Valley Power Company
P.O. Box 1444
Miamitown. OH 45733

Dear Ms. Metcalf:

I am an architectural student at the University
of Dayton and I need your help.

Could you please send me some information on
heating systems for a computer-controlled,
energy-efficient, middle-priced house that our
systems design class at the University of Dayton
is designing. The house, which contains 2,000
square feet of living space (17,600 cubic feet),
meets all the requirements stipulated in your
brochure "Insulating for Efficiency."

We need the following information:

1. The proper size heat pump to use in this
   climate for such a home;

2. The wattage of the supplemental electrical
   furnace that would be required for this
   climate; and

3. The estimated power consumption, and current rates, of these units for one year.

We will be happy to send you a copy of our
preliminary design report. Thank you very
much.

Sincerely yours,

Kathryn J. Parsons

Kathryn J. Parsons

Figure 1   Inquiry Letter

■■■■■■■■■■■■ **MIAMI VALLEY POWER COMPANY** ■■■■■■■■■■■
P.O. BOX 1444
MIAMITOWN, OH 45733

(513) 264-4800

March 15, 19--

Ms. Kathryn J. Parsons
P.O. Box 113
University of Dayton
Dayton, OH 45409

Dear Ms. Parsons:

Thank you for inquiring about the heating
system we would recommend for use in homes
designed according to the specifications outlined in our brochure "Insulating for Efficiency."

Since I cannot answer your specific questions, I have forwarded your letter to Mr.
Michael Stott, Engineering Assistant in our
development group. He should be able to answer the questions you have raised.

Sincerely,

Jane E. Metcalf

Jane E. Metcalf
Director of Public Information

JEM/mk
cc: Michael Stott

Figure 2   Letter Indicating That Inquiry Has Been Forwarded

MIAMI VALLEY POWER COMPANY
P.O. BOX 1444
MIAMITOWN, OH 45733

(513) 264-4800

March 24, 19--

Ms. Kathryn Parsons
P.O. Box 113
University of Dayton
Dayton, OH 45409

Dear Ms. Parsons:

Jane Metcalf has forwarded your letter of
March 11 about the house that your systems
design class is designing. I can estimate the
insulation requirements of a typical home of
17,600 cubic feet, as follows:

1. We would generally recommend, for such a
   home, a heat pump capable of delivering
   40,000 BTUs. Our model AL-42 (17 kilowatts)
   meets this requirement.

2. With the efficiency of the AL-42, you would
   not need a supplemental electrical furnace.

3. Depending on usage, the AL-42 unit averages
   between 1,000 and 1,500 kilowatt hours from
   December through March. To determine the
   current rate for such usage, check with the
   Dayton Power and Light Company.

I can give you an answer that would apply
specifically to your house only with information about its particular design (such as
number of stories, windows, and entrances).
If you would send me more details, I would be
happy to provide more precise figures--your
project sounds interesting.

Sincerely,

Michael Stott

Michael Stott
Engineering Assistant

MS/mo

Figure 3   Response to an Inquiry

inside/inside of

In the **phrase** *inside of,* the word *of* is redundant and should be omitted.

> CHANGE The switch is just *inside of* the door.
> TO The switch is just *inside* the door.

Using *inside of* to mean "in less time than" is colloquial but should be avoided in writing.

> CHANGE They were finished *inside of* an hour.
> TO They were finished *in less than* an hour.

insoluble/unsolvable

Although *insoluble* and *unsolvable* are sometimes used interchangeably to mean "incapable of being solved," careful writers distinguish between them. *Insoluble* means "incapable of being dissolved." *Unsolvable* means "incapable of being solved."

> EXAMPLES The plastic is *insoluble* in most household solvents.
> Until yesterday, the production problem seemed *unsolvable.*

instructions

When you explain how to perform a specific task—however simple or complex it may be—you are giving instructions. Written instructions that are based on clear thinking and careful planning should enable a **reader** to carry out the task successfully.

To write instructions that are accurate and easily understandable, you first must thoroughly understand the task you are describing. Otherwise, your instructions could prove confusing or even dangerous. If you are unfamiliar with the task you are describing, you should watch someone who is familiar with the task go through each step. As you watch, ask questions about any step that is not clear to you. Such direct observation should help you to write instructions that are exact, complete, and easy to follow.

Keep in mind your reader's level of knowledge and experience. Is he at all skilled in the kind of task for which you are writing instructions? If you know that your reader has a good background in the topic, you might feel free to use fairly specialized words. If, on the other hand, he has little or no knowledge of the subject, you would more appropriately use simple, everyday language—and avoid specialized terms as much as possible.

If the task requires any special tools or materials, say so at the beginning of the instructions. List all essential equipment at the beginning, in a section labeled "Tools Required" or "Materials Required."

The clearest, simplest instructions are written as commands, in the imperative **mood**.

> CHANGE The operator should raise the access lid. (indicative)
> TO Raise the access lid. (imperative)

Phrase instructions concisely but not as if they were telegrams. You can make sentences shorter by leaving out **articles** (*a, an, the*), some **pronouns** (*you, this, these*), and some **verbs**, but sometimes such sentences sound very **telegraphic** and are difficult to understand. The first version of the following instruction for cleaning a computer punch card assembly, for example, is confusing and difficult to understand.

> CHANGE Pass card through punch area for debris.
> TO Pass *a* card through *the* punch area *to clear away* any debris.

The meaning of the **phrase** *for debris* needed to be made clearer. The revised instruction is easily and quickly understood.

One good way to make instructions easy to follow is to divide them into short, simple steps. Be sure to order the steps in the proper sequence. Steps can be organized in one of two ways: with numbers or with words. You can label each step with a sequential number.

> EXAMPLE 1. Fill in the blanks for each section of the form. . . .
> 2. Sign and date the form in the appropriate place. . . .
> 3. Mail the form to. . . .

Or you can use words that indicate time or sequence.

> EXAMPLE *First*, determine what the customer's problem is with the computer. *Next*, observe the system in operation. *At that time*, question the operator until you are sure that the problem has been explained completely.

Plan ahead for your reader. If the instructions in step 2 will affect a process in step 9, say so in step 2. Otherwise, your reader may reach step 9 before discovering that an important piece of information—that should have been given in advance—is missing.

Sometimes your instructions have to make clear that two operations must be performed at the same time. Either state this fact in an **introduction** to the specific instructions or include both operations in the appropriate step.

> CHANGE 4. Hold the CONTROL key down.
> 5. Press the BELL key before releasing the CONTROL key.
> TO 4. While holding the CONTROL key down, press the BELL key.

In any operation certain steps must be performed with more preciseness than others. Alert your reader to those steps that require especially precise timing or measurement. Also warn of potentially hazardous steps or materials. If the instructions call for materials that are flammable or that give off noxious fumes, let the reader know before he or she reaches the step for which the material is needed.

If your instructions involve a great many steps, break them into stages, each with a separate **head** so that each stage begins again with step 1. Using heads as dividers is especially important if your reader is likely to be performing the operation as he or she reads the instructions.

Clear and well-planned **illustrations** can make even complex instructions easily understandable. Illustrations often simplify instructions by reducing the number of words necessary to explain a process or procedure. Appropriate pictures and diagrams will enable your reader to identify parts and the relationships between parts more easily than will long explanations. They will also free you, the writer, to focus on the steps making up the instructions rather than on the descriptions of parts. Not all instructions require illustrations, of course. Whether or not illustrations will be useful depends on your reader's needs as well as on the nature of the project. Instructions for inexperienced readers need to be more heavily illustrated than do those for experienced readers.

To test the accuracy and **clarity** of your instructions, ask someone who is not familiar with the operation to follow your written directions. A novice will quickly spot missing steps or point out passages that should be worded more clearly.

The instructions in Figure 1 guide the reader through the steps of "streaking" a saucer-sized disk of material (called *agar*) used to grow bacteria colonies. The object is to thin out the original speci-

INSTRUCTIONS

Distribute the inoculum over the surface of
the agar in the following manner:

(1) Beginning at one edge of the saucer, thin
     the inoculum by streaking back and forth
     over the same area several times, sweeping
     across the agar surface until approximately
     one quarter of the surface has been covered.

(2) Sterilize the loop in an open flame.

(3) Streak at right angles to the originally
     inoculated area, carrying the inoculum out
     from the streaked areas onto the sterile
     surface with only the first stroke of the
     wire. Cover half of the remaining sterile
     agar surface.

(4) Sterilize the loop.

(5) Repeat as described in step (3), covering
     the remaining sterile agar surface.

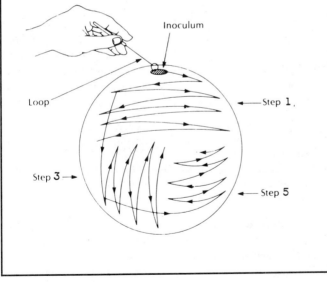

Figure 1   Illustrated Instructions

men (the inoculum) so that the bacteria will grow in small, isolated colonies. The streaking process makes certain that part of the saucer is inoculated heavily, whereas its remaining portions are inoculated progressively more lightly. The streaking is done by hand with a thin wire, looped at one end for holding a small sample of the inoculum. (See also **process explanation**.)

insure/ensure/assure

Insure, ensure, and *assure* all mean "make secure or certain." *Assure* refers to persons, and it alone has the **connotation** of setting a person's mind at rest. *Ensure* and *insure* also mean "make secure from harm." Only *insure* is widely used in the sense of guaranteeing the value of life or property against risk.

> EXAMPLES I *assure* you that the equipment will be available.
> We need all the data to *ensure* the success of the project.
> We should *insure* the contents of the building.

intensifiers

Intensifiers are **adverbs** that emphasize degree, such as *very, quite, rather, such,* and *too*. Although they serve a legitimate and necessary function, they can also seduce the unwary writer who is not on guard against overusing them. Too many intensifiers weaken your writing. When revising your draft, either eliminate intensifiers that do not make a definite contribution, or replace them with specific details.

> CHANGE It was *quite* a happy salesman who received the *very* good news that he had been offered a promotion with a *rather* substantial increase in salary.
> TO It was a happy salesman who received the good news that he had been offered a promotion with a 10 percent increase in salary.

The difference is not that the first example is wrong and the second one right but that the intensifiers in the first example add nothing to the sentence and are therefore superfluous.

Some words (such as *unique, perfect, impossible, final, permanent, infinite,* and *complete*) do not logically permit intensification because they do not permit degrees of comparison. Although **usage** often ignores this logical restriction, the writer should be aware that to ignore it is, strictly speaking, to defy the basic meanings of these words. (For more detailed information, see **comparative degree**.)

> CHANGE It is *quite* impossible to implement that sales program.
> TO It is impossible to implement that sales program.

interface

An *interface* is the "surface providing a common boundary between two bodies or areas." The bodies or areas may be physical (the *interface* of piston and cylinder) or conceptual (the *interface* of mathematics and statistics). Do not use *interface* as a substitute for the **verbs** *cooperate, interact,* or even *work.*

> CHANGE The art department will *interface* with the public relations staff on this project.
> TO The art department will *work* with the public relations staff on this project.

interjections

An interjection is a word or **phrase** of exclamation that is used independently to express emotion or surprise or to summon attention. *Hey! Ouch!* and *Wow!* are strong interjections. *Oh, well,* and *indeed* are mild ones. An interjection functions much as do *yes* or *no,* in that it has no grammatical connection with the rest of the sentence in which it appears. When an interjection expresses a sudden or strong emotion, punctuate it with an **exclamation mark**.

> EXAMPLE His only reaction was a resounding *Wow!*

Because they get their main expressive force from sound, interjections are more common in speech than in writing. They are rarely appropriate to business writing.

internal proposals

The purpose of an internal proposal is to suggest a change or an improvement within an organization. For example, one might be written to propose initiating a new management reporting system, expanding the cafeteria service, or changing the policy on parking privileges. An internal proposal, usually in a memo format, is prepared by a person or a department and is sent to a higher-ranking person who has the authority to accept or reject the proposal.

In the **opening** of a **proposal**, you must establish that a problem exists that needs a solution. If the person to judge the proposal is not convinced that there is a problem, your proposal will have no chance of success. Notice how the following opening to a proposal states its problem directly:

> Date: December 5, 19—
> To: Harriet Sullivan
> From: Christine Thomas *CT*
> Subject: Advantages of Expanding HVS Computing Facilities
>
> As we discussed earlier, because our computing facilities currently operate at maximum capacity, we are turning new customers away in growing numbers and will soon have to deny present customers computer time for emergencies or overload backups. By purchasing a new VT-8000 minicomputer and expanding our staff, we could respond to new service requests, provide better service to valued customers, and attract new customers who would not have previously considered using our service.

The body of a proposal should offer a practical solution to the problem. In building a case for a solution, be as specific as possible. When it is appropriate, include (1) a breakdown of costs; (2) information about equipment, material, and personnel requirements; and (3) a schedule for completing the task. Such information can help your **reader** to think about the proposal and thus may stimulate him or her to act. The following is an example:

> Last month we turned away 21 new service requests. At least 6 of these requests were equal to the largest accounts we currently serve. Furthermore, since our aging mainframe computer cannot handle the latest software available from ABC Systems, we can neither offer improved, faster services to our most profitable accounts (such as First International Savings and Loan) nor attract the new customers who are eager to take advantage of the most recent advances in computer technology.
>
> The VT-8000 is a very fast, reasonably priced minicomputer with massive peripheral memory capacity in the form of removable disk packs. This machine would triple our current processing capacity and enable us to use the full range of new

VRX software now available. The following details show how purchasing the VT-8000 system would triple our number of customers and pay for itself within two years.

Cost of New Equipment

VT-8000 minicomputer	$ 12,500
Two 3033 disks and disk drives	1,800
One VT80 computer terminal	980
New VRX software	1,050
Total cost of equipment	$ 16,330

Increases in Annual Operating Budget

Salaries: Computer operator	$ 19,000
Data entry technician	12,000
Total increase in annual operating budget	$ 31,000

Total Costs

First year	$ 47,330
Second year	26,200
Two-year total cost	$ 73,530

Increased Income Generated by Expansion

First-year estimate (45 new customers)	$ 37,010
Second-year estimate (50 new customers) plus the 45 of the first year	$ 64,400
Total	$101,410

Since the purchase of the VT-8000 system is a one-time investment a profit of $27,880 will be generated by the end of the second year. The estimates are based on the $751 average annual value of accounts over the past two years.

Because this system is reliable, easy to install, and easy to operate, we could have it running in three weeks with little disturbance of our normal office routine. More importantly, buying the VT-8000 will provide a cost-effective solution to the current problem of overburdened computing resources and will clear the way for meeting the demands of a growing base of customers. Although the VT-8000 printer is somewhat noisier than the VT-3400 printer, soundproofing the computer room is something that we had planned to do anyway.

The **conclusion** should be brief but must tie everything together. It is a good idea to restate recommendations here. Be careful, of course, to conclude in a spirit of cooperation, offering to set up a meeting, supply further facts and figures, or provide any other assistance that might solve the problem, as is done in the following example:

> On the basis of these details, I recommend that we expand HVS services by purchasing the VT-8000 system. An enclosed brochure describes the system in more detail. I will be happy to provide additional information about the system at your request.

A proposal to commit large sums of money is a common internal proposal. Although such internal proposals have various names, *capital appropriations proposal* is a common and descriptive name for them.

The introduction to such a proposal should provide any background information your reader might need in order to make the decision in question. The introduction should also briefly describe any feasibility study you may have conducted, the conclusions the study led you to reach, and the decision you made on the basis of those conclusions.

The body of the proposal should identify all the equipment or property you are asking to acquire and should state the economic justification for the expenditure involved. If you need to purchase equipment, be sure to list *all* of it so that later you don't have to prepare another proposal to purchase the rest of it. Include an economic justification of either the calculated return on investment or the internal rate of return. Your proposal should include all of the following items that are applicable to your particular request:

1. A brief description of the item to be purchased.
2. The alternative choices you considered before deciding on the one you are recommending.
3. The specific products or projects to be supported by the item.
4. The volume of usage that the item would receive over a specified period of time, such as the next two years.
5. If the company already has some of the item, an explanation of why you require an additional purchase.
6. The life expectancy of the item and of the product or project it is to support.

7. Any future products or projects that the item could be used to support.

8. Whether a leasing arrangement is available and more economical than purchasing the item.

9. The impact on the company if the item is not acquired.

10. The latest feasible date of acquisition, including the impact that a ninety-day delay would have.

11. The calculated return on investment, or the internal rate of return.

With your capital appropriations request, you should also submit a cover **memorandum**. The memo, which should be no more than one page long, should give a brief description of the item and the reason it is needed. Figure 1 is such a capital appropriations proposal.

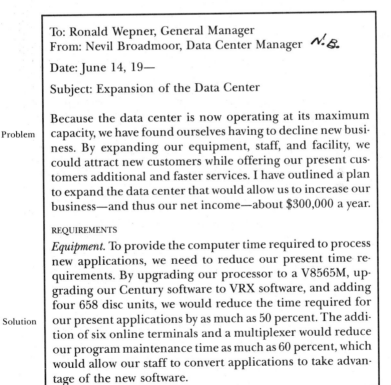

To: Ronald Wepner, General Manager
From: Nevil Broadmoor, Data Center Manager *N. B.*

Date: June 14, 19—

Subject: Expansion of the Data Center

Problem

Because the data center is now operating at its maximum capacity, we have found ourselves having to decline new business. By expanding our equipment, staff, and facility, we could attract new customers while offering our present customers additional and faster services. I have outlined a plan to expand the data center that would allow us to increase our business—and thus our net income—about $300,000 a year.

REQUIREMENTS

Equipment. To provide the computer time required to process new applications, we need to reduce our present time requirements. By upgrading our processor to a V8565M, upgrading our Century software to VRX software, and adding four 658 disc units, we would reduce the time required for

Solution

our present applications by as much as 50 percent. The addition of six online terminals and a multiplexer would reduce our program maintenance time as much as 60 percent, which would allow our staff to convert applications to take advantage of the new software.

Figure 1   Internal Proposal

Staff. To convert present applications to VRX software and to develop and support new applications, we need to increase our programming staff by three people (one senior programmer and two junior programmers).

Facility. To house the additional staff, we need to expand our office area and to purchase additional office furniture for the six online terminals we would place in the programmers' offices. The V8565M requires less space than the present processor, however, so we could rearrange the computer room to provide space for the multiplexer and additional disc units.

BENEFITS

On the basis of the business available in this area, we could expect to increase our net income by $300,000 a year. We would be able to attract new customers—as well as new business from our present customers—by offering additional and faster services. The increase in our operating budget would actually be small because of the reduction in time requirements provided by the new equipment.

COSTS

Equipment. The purchase of new equipment—reduced by the trade-in allowance on our old processor—would be $383,000.

Cost breakdown

Processor	$250,000
Integrated Disc Controller	20,000
Disc Units (four @ $20,000 each)	80,000
Integrated Multiplexer	10,000
Online Terminals (six @ $3,000 each)	18,000
VRX Software	5,000

Budget. The annual increase in our operating budget would be $86,800.

Salaries	$75,000
Benefits	6,800
Office Supplies	1,000
Utilities	1,000
Equipment Maintenance	3,000

Figure 1   Internal Proposal (continued)

Facility. The cost of expanding our facility would be $33,000.

Office Area	$20,000
Computer Room	10,000
Furniture	3,000

SCHEDULE

To achieve the expected net income increase, we would need to meet the following schedule in the expansion.

July 1–Order the required equipment.
September 1–Begin recruiting efforts.
September 15–Start expanding the office area.
October 1–Order the required office furniture.
November 1–Start soliciting new business.
November 5–Finish expanding office area.
November 5–Fill programming positions.
November 10–Start new applications design.
November 10–Start conversion effort.
December 1–Install new equipment.
December 15–Implement the first new customer application.

Conclusion

I feel that this expansion plan would enable us to meet the requirements of the businesses in this area. I have looked at the alternative equipment and believe that the V8565M offers better performance than the other hardware available in this price range. The design of the V8565M would allow us to grow with a minimum of effort as the business in this area grows. I would like to meet with you Friday to discuss this plan and will be happy to explain any details or to gather any additional information that you may desire. Please let me know if we can get together then to discuss this proposed expansion of the data center.

Figure 1   Internal Proposal (continued)

international correspondence

Organizations of all sizes are becoming increasingly aware of the advantages and challenges of participating in the global marketplace. Many businesses now rely on overseas markets and suppliers, employ workers and managers from different countries, and maintain plants and offices abroad. Such companies need to communicate effectively with readers from diverse cultural and linguistic backgrounds. These readers may be outside the organization, as in the case of foreign suppliers and distributors, but they may also be inside the organization, as in the case of foreign branch offices that hire employees locally.

Just as American **business writing style** has changed over time, ideas about appropriate business writing style vary from culture to culture. Writers must be alert to the special needs and expectations of readers from different cultural and linguistic backgrounds. Although business writing should always be courteous and efficient, experienced writers understand that the forms of courtesy and ideas about efficiency vary from country to country.

STYLE AND USAGE IN INTERNATIONAL CORRESPONDENCE

Because English is not your reader's native language, it is especially important to write clear, complete sentences. (See **English as a second language**.) Unusual syntax, **jammed modifiers**, and rambling sentences will hinder a nonnative user of English. Long sentences that contain more information than the reader can comfortably absorb should be divided into two or more sentences (see **sentence construction** and **sentence faults**).

Take special care to avoid American **idioms**, **affectation**, unusual **figures of speech**, **allusions**, and localism, any of which could easily confuse your reader. Humor, particularly sarcasm, and **euphemisms** should also be avoided because they are easily misunderstood outside their cultural context.

Elegant variation, especially the use of **long variants** or pretentious synonyms, will also impede the reader's understanding. Ask yourself whether the words you choose might be found in the abbreviated English-language dictionary that your reader would likely have close at hand.

Proofread your letters carefully; a misspelled word will be particularly troublesome for someone reading in a second language (especially if that reader turns to a dictionary for help and cannot find the word because it is misspelled). Finally, read your writing aloud to identify overly long sentences and to eliminate any possible **ambiguity**.

While it is important to choose your words carefully and to write clear, complete sentences, you should also avoid using an overly simplified "storybook" style. A reader who has studied English as a second language might be insulted by a condescending tone and childish language. Above all, avoid writing in short, choppy sentences. This **telegraphic style** makes even readers who are fluent in English work harder to mentally "fill in" the missing articles, pronouns, conjunctions, and transitional expressions; a reader who is not fluent in English is quite likely to misunderstand messages written in this style.

TRANSLATION

Because English is increasingly being taught and used as an international business language, most international correspondence will not require translation. If you do employ a translator, however, be sure that the translator understands the **objective** of the document you are preparing. It is also prudent to let your reader know (in the letter itself or in a postscript) that a translator helped write the document. For first-time contacts, consider sending a translation along with the English version of the letter.

DATES, TIME, AND MEASUREMENT

Different countries use a variety of formats to represent dates, time, and other kinds of measurement. To represent **dates**, Europeans typically write the day before the month and year. In England, for example, 1/11/92 means 1 November 1992; in the United States, it means January 11, 1992. The strictly numerical form for dates, therefore, should never be used in international correspondence. Writing out the name of the month makes the entire date immediately clear to any reader, whichever format you use. Time poses similar problems: particularly in this age of instantaneous communication and high-speed transportation, you may need to specify time zones or to refer to international standards, such as Greenwich Mean Time, to ensure clarity.

Your use of other international standards, such as the metric system, will also help your reader. For up-to-date information about accepted conventions for numbers and symbols in chemical, electrical, data processing, radiation, pharmaceutical, and other fields, consult guides and manuals specific to the subject matter.

CULTURE, TRADITION, AND BUSINESS WRITING STYLE

The style of business writing is an important variable in international correspondence. In American business writing, traditional salutations like *Dear* and cordial closings like *Yours truly* have, through custom and long use, acquired meanings quite distinct from their dictionary definitions. Understanding the unspoken meanings of these forms and using them "naturally" is a significant mark of being a part of American business culture. Be aware that such customary expressions and formal amenities vary from culture to culture; when you read foreign correspondence, be alert to these differences.

Japanese business writers, for example, often use traditional openings that reflect on the season, compliment the reader's success, and offer hopes for the reader's continued prosperity. These traditional openings may strike some American readers as being overly elaborate or "literary." Where Americans value directness and employ a forthright **tone** in their **correspondence**, Japanese readers might find the writing blunt and tactless. Remember that our ideas about business writing have evolved in a particular educational, social, economic, and cultural context. Be sensitive to the expectations of readers who judge effective and appropriate communication from the vantage of a different cultural tradition.

Decision-making styles also vary from culture to culture and from country to country. Consequently, the correspondence, reports, and memorandums that support decision-making processes will vary as well. Indeed, readers from different business writing backgrounds may interpret the objective of a particular letter or memo in dramatically different ways. The different decision-making strategies, and the stylistic preferences they inspire, reflect larger cultural differences. Whereas an American business writer might consider one brief letter sufficient to communicate a need or transmit a request, for example, a writer in another cultural setting may expect an exchange of three or four longer letters in order to pave the way for action.

For an overview of recent research in international communication, see Mohan R. Limaye and David A. Victor, "Cross-Cultural Business Communication Research: State of the Art and Hypothesis for the 1990's" *Journal of Business Communication* 28.3 (Summer 1991): 277–99.

interviewing for information

The **scope** of coverage that you have established for your writing project may require more information (or more current information) than is available in written form (in the library, in corporate specifications, in trade journals, and so on). When you reach this point, consider a personal interview with an expert in your subject.

A discussion of interviewing can be divided into three parts: (1) determining the proper person to interview, (2) preparing for the interview, and (3) conducting the interview.

DETERMINING THE PROPER PERSON TO INTERVIEW

Many times your subject, or your **objective** in writing about the subject, logically points to the proper person to interview. If you were writing about the use of a freeway onramp metering device on Highway 103, for example, you would want to interview the Director of the Traffic Engineering Department; if you were writing about the design of the device, you would want to interview the manufacturer's design engineer. You may interview a professor who specializes in your subject, in addition to getting leads from him or her as to others you might interview. Other sources available to help you determine the appropriate person to interview are (1) the city directory in the library, (2) professional societies, (3) the yellow pages in the local telephone directory, or (4) a local firm that is involved with all or some aspects of your subject.

PREPARING FOR THE INTERVIEW

After determining the name of the person you want to interview, you must request the interview. You can do this either by telephone or by letter, although a letter may be too slow to allow you to meet your deadline.

Learn as much as possible about the person you are going to interview and about the company or agency for which he works. When you make contact with your interviewee, whether by letter or by telephone, explain (1) who you are, (2) why you are contacting him, (3) why you chose him for the interview, (4) the subject of the interview, (5) that you would like to arrange an interview at his convenience, and (6) that you will allow him to review your draft.

Prepare a list of specific questions to ask your interviewee. The natural temptation for the untrained writer is to ask general questions rather than specific ones. "What are you doing about air pollution?" for example, may be too general to elicit specific and useful information. "Residents in the east end of town complain about the black smoke that pours from your east-end plant; are you doing anything to relieve the problem?" is a more specific question. Analyze your questions to be certain that they are specific and to the point.

CONDUCTING THE INTERVIEW

When you arrive for the interview, be prepared to guide the discussion. The following list of points should help you to do so:

1. Be pleasant, but purposeful. You are there to get information, so don't be timid about asking leading questions on the subject.
2. Use the list of questions you have prepared.
3. Let your interviewee do the talking. Don't try to impress him with your own knowledge of the subject on which he is presumably an expert.
4. Be objective. Don't offer your opinions on the subject. You are there to get information, not to debate.
5. Some answers prompt additional questions; ask them. If you do not ask these questions as they arise, you may find later that you have forgotten to ask them at all.
6. When the interviewee gets off the subject, be ready with a specific and direct question to guide him back onto the track.
7. Take only memory-jogging notes that will help you recall the conversation later. Do not ask your interviewee to slow down so you can take detailed notes. To do so would not only be an undue imposition on the interviewee's time but might also disturb or destroy his or her train of thought.
8. The use of a tape recorder is often unwise, since it often puts people on edge and requires tedious transcription after the interview. On the other hand, a tape recorder does allow you to listen more intently instead of taking notes. If you do use one, do not let it lure you into relaxing so that you neglect to ask crucial questions.

Immediately after leaving the interview, use your memory-jogging notes to help you mentally review the interview and record your detailed notes. Do not postpone this step. No matter how good your memory is, you will forget some important points if you do not do this at once.

interviewing for a job

A job interview may last for thirty minutes, or it may take several hours; it may be conducted by one person or by several, either at one time or in a series of interviews. Since it is impossible to know exactly what to expect, it is important to be as well prepared as possible.

BEFORE THE INTERVIEW

Learn as much as you can about your potential employer before the interview. What kind of business is it? Is the company locally owned? Is it a nonprofit organization? If the job is public employment, at what level of government is it? Does the business provide a service, and, if so, what kind? How large is the firm? Is the owner self-employed? Is it a subsidiary of a larger operation? Is it expanding? Where will you fit in? This kind of information can be obtained from current employees, from company publications, or from back issues of the local newspaper's business section (available at the public library). You should try to learn about the company's size, sales volume, products and new products, credit rating, and subsidiary companies from its **annual reports**, and from other business reference sources such as *Moody's Industrials, Dun and Bradstreet, Standard and Poor's*, and *Thomas' Register*. Such preparation will help you to speak knowledgeably about the firm or industry as well as to ask intelligent questions of the interviewer.

It is a good idea to try to anticipate the questions an interviewer might ask and to prepare your answers in advance. The following is a list of some typical questions posed in job interviews:

What are your short-term and long-term occupational goals?
What are your major strengths and weaknesses?
Do you work better alone or with others?
Why do you want to work for this company?
How do you spend your free time?

DURING THE INTERVIEW

Promptness is very important. Be sure to arrive for an interview at the appointed time. It is usually a good idea, in fact, to arrive ahead of time, since you may be asked to fill out an application before meeting the interviewer. Take along your **résumé**, even if the company already has a copy. For one thing, the interviewer may want another copy; for another, the résumé contains most of the information required on an application.

Remember that the interview will actually begin before you are seated. What you wear and how you act will be closely observed. The way you dress matters: It is usually best to dress conservatively and to be well groomed.

Remain standing until you are offered a seat. Then sit up straight—good posture suggests self-assurance—and look at the interviewer, trying to appear relaxed and confident. It is natural to be nervous during an interview, but be careful to remain alert. Listen carefully and make an effort to remember especially important information. (See **listening**.) Do not attempt to take extensive notes during an interview, although it is acceptable to jot down a few facts and figures.

When answering questions, don't ramble or stray from the subject. Take a minute to think before you answer difficult questions; not only will the time help you collect your thoughts, but it will also make you appear careful in your answer. Say only what you must in order to answer each question and then stop; however, avoid giving just yes and no answers, which usually don't permit the interviewer to learn enough about you. Some interviewers allow a silence to fall just to see how you will react. The burden of conducting the interview is the interviewer's, not yours—and he or she may interpret it as a sign of insecurity if you rush in to fill a void in the conversation. But if such a silence would make you uncomfortable, be ready to ask an intelligent question about the company.

Highlight your qualifications for the job, but admit obvious limitations as well. Remember also that the job, the company, and the location must be right for you. Ask about such factors as opportunity for advancement, fringe benefits (but don't create the impression that your primary interest is security), educational opportunity and assistance, and community recreational and cultural activities (if the job would require you to relocate).

If the interviewer overlooks important points, bring them up. But if possible, let the interviewer mention salary first. If you are forced to bring up the subject, ask it as a straightforward question. Knowing the prevailing salaries in your field will make you better prepared to discuss salary. It is usually unwise to bargain, especially if you are a recent graduate. Many companies have inflexible starting salaries for beginners.

Interviewers look for self-confidence and an understanding, on the part of the candidate, of the field in which he or she is applying. Less is expected of a beginner, but even a newcomer must show some knowledge of the field. One way to impress your interviewer is to ask questions about the company that are related to your line of work. Interviewers respond favorably to people who can communicate easily and present themselves well. Jobs today require interactions of all kinds: person-to-person, department-to-department, division-to-division.

At the conclusion of the interview, thank your interviewer for his or her time. Indicate that you are interested in the job (if true), and try tactfully to get an idea of when you can expect to hear from the company.

AFTER THE INTERVIEW

When you leave, jot down pertinent information you learned during the interview. (This information will be especially helpful in comparing job offers.) A day or two later, send the interviewer a brief note of thanks, saying that you find the job attractive (if true) and feel you can fill it well. Figure 1 is typical.

(See also **job search, résumés, application letters, listening,** and **acceptance letters.**)

introductions

The purpose of an introduction is to give your readers enough general information about your topic to enable them to understand the detailed information in the body of the paper or report. The introduction should explain the context out of which the work grew and establish the reasons that it was written. If you don't need to set the stage in this way, turn to the entry on **openings** for a variety of interesting ways to begin without writing an introduction. If you are writing a **newsletter article,** an **annual report,** a **proposal,** a **memorandum,** or something similar, you will probably find one of the various types of openings more appropriate than an introduction. If you are preparing a **formal report,** a **journal article,** a conference paper, or some similar writing project, however, you will need to present your readers with some general information before getting into the body of your report.

                                    2647 Sitwell Road
                                    Charlotte, NC 28210
                                    March 17, 19--

Mr. F. E. Vallone
Personnel Manager
Calcutex Industries, Inc.
3275 Commercial Park Drive
Raleigh, NC 27609

Dear Mr. Vallone:

Thank you for the informative and pleasant interview we had last
Wednesday. Please extend my thanks to Mr. Wilson of the Servocontrol
Group as well. I came away from our meeting most favorably impressed
with Calcutex Industries.

I find the position to be an attractive one and feel confident that
my qualifications would enable me to perform the duties to everyone's
advantage.

I look forward to hearing from you soon.

                                    Sincerely yours,

                                    Philip Ming.
                                    Philip Ming

Figure 1   Follow-up Letter to a Job Interview

STATING THE SUBJECT

In stating the subject, it may be helpful to the reader if you include a small amount of information on the history or theory of the subject. In addition to stating the subject, you may need to define it if it is one with which some of your readers may be unfamiliar. (See **definition method of development**.)

STATING THE PURPOSE

The statement of purpose in your introduction should function for your article or paper much as a **topic sentence** functions in a **paragraph**. It should make your readers aware of your goal as they read your supporting statements and examples. It should also tell them why you are writing about the subject: whether your material provides a new perspective or clarifies an existing perspective.

STATING THE SCOPE

Stating the **scope** of your article or report tells your reader how much or how little detail to expect. Does your article or report present a broad survey of your **topic**, or does it concentrate on one facet of the topic? Keep the statement of scope brief and simple, however; lack of restraint could lead you to write an **abstract** of your article or paper instead of a simple statement of scope in your introduction.

STATING THE DEVELOPMENT OF THE SUBJECT

In a larger work, it may be helpful to your reader if you state how you plan to develop the subject. Is the work an analysis of the component parts of some whole? Is the material presented in chronological sequence? Or does it involve an inductive or deductive approach? Providing such information makes it easier for your readers to anticipate how the subject will be presented (see **methods of development**), and it gives them a basis for evaluating how you arrived at your **conclusions** or recommendations. The following is an example:

> The steady increase in incoming orders over the past eighteen months represents a significant increase in the corporation's percentage of the market for office furniture, and the market survey conducted by a consulting firm indicates that the increase is permanent. Therefore, at its September meeting, the

corporation's board of directors approved the construction of
Subject   a new manufacturing plant to increase our manufacturing capacity to accommodate the present increase in demand and
the anticipated increase indicated by the market survey.

A committee was appointed by the president of the corporation to investigate various potential sites for the new manufacturing plant. The committee was to investigate all potential
building sites and select several of the best alternative sites for
manufacturing office furniture. These selections were to be
made on the basis of such considerations as the availability of
Purpose   transportation, the local tax structure, the availability of labor,
and   and the local living conditions. The purpose of this report is
scope   to submit the results of that investigation. The report offers first
a brief background, or summary, of the committee's complete
investigation; then it presents, in complete detail, the results
of the studies conducted on the three most promising building
sites for the new manufacturing plant.

The committee initially considered thirty possible locations
for the proposed new factory. Of these, twenty were eliminated
Background   almost immediately for one reason or another (unfavorable
tax structure, inadequate labor supply, and the like). Of the remaining ten locations, the committee selected for intensive
study the three that seemed the most promising: Chicago,
Minneapolis, and Salt Lake City. The committee then visited
these three cities, and its observations on each of them are
contained in the body of this report.

The report presents the significant details of each city in the
Development   following sequence: (1) the location of the city, (2) the availability of air, highway, and rail transportation, (3) the availability of labor, (4) the local tax structure, and (5) the local living conditions (housing, education, recreation, and climate).

CHICAGO

Body of   Of the three cities, Chicago presently seems to the committee
report   to offer the greatest advantages. . . .

TIPS ON WRITING INTRODUCTIONS

Not every document needs an introduction. When your readers are
already familiar with the major elements of your topic, you can save
them time and hold their interest better by getting on to the details.
If you do not need a full-scale introduction, turn to the entry on
openings for a variety of interesting ways to begin without an introduction.

Make your **point of view** toward the subject obvious to the readers. Do not assume that readers knowledgeable about your topic will instinctively know your point of view toward it. Be brief, if that will suffice, but be explicit.

Finally, consider writing the introduction last. Many writers find it helpful to write the introduction last because they feel that only then do they have a full enough perspective on the writing to introduce it adequately.

investigative reports

When a person investigates, or checks into, a particular topic, he or she might write up the results in an investigative report. For example, the report could summarize the findings of an opinion survey, of a product evaluation, or of a marketing study. It could review the published work on a particular topic or compare the different procedures used to perform the same operation. An investigative report gives a precise analysis of its topic and then offers the writer's conclusions and recommendations.

Open such a **report** with a statement of its purpose. In the body of the report, first define the **scope** of your investigation. If the report is on a survey of opinions, for example, you might need to indicate the number of people and the geographical areas surveyed as well as the income categories, the occupations, the age groups, and possibly even the racial groups of those surveyed. Include any information that is pertinent in defining the extent of the investigation. Then report your findings and, if necessary, discuss their significance. End your report with your conclusions and, if appropriate, any recommendations.

Notice that the sample investigative report (Figure 1, on p. 354) opens by stating its purpose and ends with its recommendations.

irregardless/regardless

Irregardless is nonstandard English because it expresses a double negative. The word *regardless* is already negative, meaning, "unmindful." Always use *regardless* or *irrespective*.

CHANGE *Irregardless* of the price, I will buy 100 shares of the stock.
TO *Regardless* of the price, I will buy 100 shares of the stock.

MEMORANDUM

To: Noreen Rinaldo, Training Manager
From: Charles Lapinski, Senior Instructor CL
Date: February 14, 19--

Subject: Addison Corporation's Basic English Program

Purpose

As you requested, I have investigated Addison's program to determine whether we might also adopt such a program. The purpose of the Addison Basic English course is to teach foreign mechanics who do not speak or read English to understand repair manuals written in a special 800-word vocabulary called "Basic English," and thus eliminate the need for Addison to translate its manuals into a number of different languages. The Basic English Program does not attempt to teach the mechanics to be fluent in English but, rather, to recognize the 800 basic words that appear in the repair manuals.

The course does not train mechanics. Students must know, in their own language, what a word like <u>torque</u> means; the course simply teaches them the English term for it. As prerequisites for the course, students must have a basic knowledge of their trade, must be able to identify a part in an illustrated parts book, must have served as a mechanic on Addison products for at least one year, and must be able to read and write in their own language.

Scope

Students are given the specially prepared instruction manual, an illustrated book of parts and their English names, and a pocket reference containing all 800 words of the Basic English vocabulary plus the English names of parts (students can write the corresponding word in their language beside the English words and then use the pocket reference as a bilingual dictionary). The course consists of thirty two-hour lessons, each lesson introducing approximately 27 words. No effort is made to teach pronunciation; the course teaches only recognition of the 800 words, which include 450 nouns, 70 verbs, 180 adjectives and adverbs, and 100 articles, prepositions, conjunctions, and pronouns.

The 800-word vocabulary enables the writers of the manuals to provide mechanics with any information that might be required, because the area of communication is strictly limited to maintenance, inspection, troubleshooting, safety, and the operation of Addison equipment. All nonessential words (such as <u>apple</u>, <u>father</u>, <u>mountain</u>, and so on) have been eliminated, as have most synonyms (for example <u>under</u> appears, but <u>beneath</u> does not).

<u>Conclusions</u>

I see three possible ways in which we might be able to use some or all of the elements of the Basic English Program: (1) in the preparation of all our student manuals, (2) in the preparation of student manuals for the international students in our service school, or (3) as Addison uses the program.

I think it would be unnecessary to use the Basic English methods in the preparation of student manuals for <u>all</u> our students. Most of our students are English-speaking people to whom an unrestricted vocabulary presents no problem.

Recommen-dations

In conjunction with the preparation of student manuals for international students, the program might have more appeal. Students would take the Basic English course either before coming to this country to attend school or after arriving but before beginning their technical training.

As for our initiating a Basic English Program similar to Addison's, we could create our own version of the Basic English vocabulary and write our service manuals in it. Since our product lines are much broader than Addison's, however, we would need to create illustrated parts books for each of the different product lines.

Figure 1   Investigative Report

it

The **pronoun** *it* has a number of uses. First, it can refer to a preceding **noun** that names an object or idea or to a baby or animal whose sex is unknown or unimportant to the point. *It* should have a clear antecedent.

> EXAMPLES Darwinism made an impact on nineteenth-century American thought. *It* even influenced economics.
> The Moodys' baby is generally healthy, but *it* has a cold at the moment.

It can also serve as an **expletive**.

> EXAMPLES *It* is necessary to sand the hull before you paint it.
> *It* is a truth universally acknowledged that there is no such thing as a free lunch.

Be on guard against overusing expletives, however.

> CHANGE *It* is seldom that we go.
> TO We seldom go.

(See also **its/it's** and **pronoun reference**.)

italics

Italics (indicated on the typewriter by underlining) is a style of type used to denote **emphasis** and to distinguish foreign expressions, book titles, and certain other elements. *This sentence is printed in italics.* You may need to italicize words that require special emphasis in a sentence.

> EXAMPLE Contrary to projections, sales have *not* improved since we started the new procedure.

Do not overuse italics for emphasis, however.

> CHANGE This will hurt *you* more than *me*.
> TO This will hurt you more than me!

TITLES

Italicize the titles of books, periodicals, newspapers, movies, and paintings.

EXAMPLES The book *Statistical Methods* was published in 1991.
The *Cincinnati Enquirer* is one of our oldest newspapers.
Journal of Marketing is published monthly for those engaged in marketing.

Abbreviations of such titles are italicized if their spelled-out forms would be italicized.

EXAMPLE The *Journal of QA Technology* is an informative publication.

Titles of chapters or articles within publications and titles of reports are placed in **quotation marks**, not italicized.

EXAMPLE The article, "Does Advertising Lower Consumer Prices?" was published in the *Journal of Marketing*.

Titles of holy books and legislative documents are not italicized.

EXAMPLE The Bible and the Magna Carta changed the history of Western civilization.

Titles of long poems and musical works are italicized, but titles of short poems and musical works and songs are enclosed in quotation marks.

EXAMPLES Milton's *Paradise Lost* (long poem)
Handel's *Messiah* (long musical work)
T.S. Eliot's "The Love Song of J. Alfred Prufrock" (short poem)
Leonard Cohen's "Suzanne" (song)

PROPER NAMES

The names of ships, trains, and aircraft (but not the companies that own them) are italicized.

EXAMPLE They sailed to Africa on the Onassis *Clipper* but flew back on the TWA *New Yorker*.

The exceptions are craft known by model or serial designations. These are not italicized.

EXAMPLES DC-7, Boeing 747

WORDS, LETTERS, AND FIGURES

Words, letters, and figures discussed as such are italicized.

EXAMPLES The word *inflammable* is often misinterpreted.
I should replace the *s* and the *6* keys on my dad's old typewriter.

FOREIGN WORDS

Foreign words that have not been assimilated into the English language are italicized.

EXAMPLES   *sine qua non, coup de grâce, in res, in camera*

Foreign words that have been fully assimilated into the language, however, need not be italicized.

EXAMPLES   cliché, etiquette, vis-à-vis, de facto, siesta

When in doubt about whether or not to italicize a foreign word, consult a current **dictionary**. (See also **foreign words in English**.)

SUBHEADS

Subheads in a report are sometimes italicized—or underlined in traditional typescript. (See also **heads**.)

EXAMPLE   There was no publications department as such, and the writing groups were duplicated at each plant or location. Wellington, for example, had such a large number of publications groups that their publication efforts can only be described as disorganized. Their duplication of effort must have been enormous.
Training Writers
We are certainly leading the way in developing first-line managers (or writing supervisors) who are not only technically competent but can also train the writers under their direction and be responsible for writing quality as well.

its/it's

Be careful never to confuse these two words: *Its* is a possessive **pronoun**, whereas *it's* is a **contraction** of *it is*.

EXAMPLE   *It's* important that the factory meet *its* quota.

Although nouns normally form the possessive by the addition of an **apostrophe** and an *s*, the contraction of *it is* (*it's*) has already used that device; therefore, the possessive form of the pronoun *it* is formed by adding only the *s*.

J

jammed modifiers

Some writing is unclear or difficult to read because it contains jammed modifiers, or strings of **modifiers** preceding **nouns**.

> CHANGE Your *staffing level authorization reassessment* plan should result in a major improvement.

In this sentence the noun *plan* is preceded by four modifiers; this string of modifiers slows the **reader** down and makes the sentence awkward and clumsy. Jammed modifiers often result from an overuse of **jargon** or **vogue words**. Occasionally, they occur when writers mistakenly attempt to be concise by eliminating short **prepositions** or connectives—exactly the words that help to make sentences clear. See how breaking up the jammed modifiers makes the previous example easier to read.

> CHANGE TO Your plan for the reassessment of staffing-level authorizations should result in a major improvement.
> OR Your plan to reassess authorizations for staffing levels should result in a major improvement.

(See also **conciseness**, **gobbledygook**, and **telegraphic style**.)

jargon

Jargon is a highly specialized technical slang that is unique to an occupational group. If all your **readers** are members of a particular occupational group, jargon may provide a time-saving and efficient means of communicating with them. For example, a declining stock market is called a "bear" market. In normal English, it is a falling market; in the jargon of the stock brokers, it is a bear market. If you have any doubt that your entire reading audience is a part of this group, however, avoid using jargon.

When jargon becomes so specialized that it applies only to one company or a subgroup of an occupation, it is referred to as *shop talk*. Obviously, shop talk is appropriate only for those familiar with its special vocabulary and should be reserved for speech or informal **memorandums**.

When jargon becomes enmeshed in a tangle of **abstract words**, many of them pseudoscientific or pseudolegal, it becomes an **affectation** known as **gobbledygook**. Jargon, used to this extreme, is "language more technical than the ideas it serves to express."*

Jargon and shop talk are similar in many ways to *lingo* and *cant*, which are terms used to describe language that is intended to exclude outsiders from a select circle of the initiated.

job descriptions

Most large companies and many small ones specify, in a formal job description, the duties of and requirements for many of the jobs in the firm. Job descriptions fill several important functions: They provide information on which equitable salary scales can be based; they help management determine whether all responsibilities within a company are adequately covered; and they let both prospective and current employees know exactly what is expected of them. Together, all of the job descriptions in a firm present a picture of the organization's structure.

Sometimes plant or office supervisors are given the task of writing the job descriptions of the employees assigned to them. In many organizations, though, an employee may draft his or her own job description, which the immediate superior then checks and approves.

A FORMAT FOR WRITING JOB DESCRIPTIONS

Although job description formats vary from organization to organization, they commonly contain the following sections:

Accountability.   This section identifies, by title, the person or persons to whom the employee reports.

Scope of responsibilities.   This section provides an overview of the primary and secondary functions of the job and states, if applicable, who reports to the employee.

Specific duties.   This section gives a detailed account of the specific duties of the job, as concisely as possible.

Personal requirements.   This section lists the education, training, experience, and licensing required or desired for the job.

---

*Susanne K. Langer, *Mind: An Essay on Human Feeling* (Baltimore: Johns Hopkins U P, 1967) 36.

TIPS FOR WRITING JOB DESCRIPTIONS

If you have been asked to prepare a job description for your position, the following guidelines should help:

1. Before attempting to write your job description, make a list of all the different tasks you do for a week or a month. Otherwise, you will almost certainly leave out some of your duties.
2. Focus on content. Remember that you are describing your job, not yourself.
3. List your duties in decreasing order of importance. Knowing how your various duties rank in importance makes it easier to set valid job qualifications.
4. Begin each statement of a duty with a **verb**, and be specific. Write "Answer and route incoming telephone calls" rather than "Handle telephone calls."
5. Review existing job descriptions that have been successful.

The job description in Figure 1, which is a typical one, never mentions the person holding the job described; it focuses, instead, on the job and on the qualifications *any* person must possess to fill the position.

For additional and detailed information on the use and creation of job descriptions, see Joseph J. Famularo, *Handbook of Human Resources Administration* (McGraw, 1985).

Publications Manager

ACCOUNTABILITY

Reports directly to the Vice President, Advertising and Public Relations.

SCOPE OF RESPONSIBILITIES

The Publications Manager is expected to plan, coordinate, and supervise the design and development of sales brochures, advertisements, and customer manuals required to support the sale, installation, and maintenance of company products and services. The manager is responsible for the administration of the Publications Department. The supervisor of customer publications and the supervisor of internal publications report to the Publications Manager.

Figure 1 Job Description

SPECIFIC DUTIES

Directs an organization presently composed of 20 people, including supervisors, writers, artists, and typists.

Screens, selects, and hires qualified applicants for the department.

Prepares a formal orientation program to familiarize trainees with the production of printed materials.

Evaluates the performance of and determines salary adjustments for all personnel in the department.

Plans documentation for the support of new and existing products.

Determines the need for subcontracted publications and acts as a purchasing agent when they are needed.

Offers editorial advice to supervisors.

Develops and manages an annual budget for the Publications Department.

Recommends new and appropriate uses for the department within the company.

Keeps up with new techniques in printing processes, typesetting, computerized text editing, art, and graphics and uses them to the company's advantage.

PERSONAL REQUIREMENTS

B.A. (or equivalent background and experience) desired.

Minimum of three years professional writing experience and a general knowledge of graphics and production techniques.

Minimum of two years management experience and a knowledge of the general principles of management.

Must be conversant with the needs of support people, technical people, and customers.

Figure 1   Job Description (continued)

job search

To begin an effective search for a job, you must know essentially three things: (1) yourself (your specific skills, your goals, and so forth), (2) the job you are searching for (geographical area, likely industries, likely companies, and so on), and (3) where to get all the information you need to conduct an effective job search.

YOURSELF

Do some homework on yourself—some real soul searching. Decide exactly what your goals are. What would you like to do in the immediate future? When you have answered that, think about the kind of work you would like to be doing two years from now. Then think seriously about what you would like to be doing five years from now. When you have pinned down these answers, you have established your goals.

You must also know exactly what your strongest skills are, for they are your most salable products. You must know your appropriate level of entry into a job requiring those skills (entry level for the inexperienced, intermediate level for the moderately experienced, and senior level for the very experienced). Then you must know where you would be most likely to find a need for those skills (geographical location, professional vocation, which industries, which companies).

Determine how you are different, or better qualified, for a job than the other people who are likely to apply for it. Are you expert in your field? Are you especially painstaking with details? Are you particularly good with people? Are you persistent and determined in solving problems? Do you have any particular skills or talents, such as writing, public speaking, or analytical ability? If you know what makes you stand out and can communicate it during an interview, you greatly increase your chances.

THE JOB

Start with the geographical area that would most favor your job search or in which you prefer to live. Then narrow the geographical area by determining the field in which you prefer to work. Then narrow the field by identifying those specializations within that field that interest you most. Finally, pinpoint those companies within your selected specializations that need your skills and for which you feel you could work comfortably. Be sure to include small and even very small companies, since collectively, they create far more jobs than do large companies.

Thoroughly **research** each company. Visit the library to find information about the company in sources such as **annual reports**, the *Standard and Poor's Directory*, and *Thomas' Register of American Manufacturers* (see also **library research**). Ask family, friends, and even casual acquaintances about the companies. One of the key things to learn is who in the company has the authority to hire you. For a recent graduate, this may be the personnel manager; for a highly experienced professional, it is more likely to be the manager of the department doing the hiring. Your goal should be to get a face-to-face meeting with that person.

SOURCES OF INFORMATION

The information you need to help you land a job can come from a number of sources: classified ads, **inquiry letters**, trade and professional journals, school placement services, employment agencies, friends already employed within your area of interest, and others.

Classified Ads. Many employers advertise in the classified sections of newspapers. For the widest selection, look in the Sunday editions of local and big city newspapers. Although reading want ads can be tedious, an item-by-item check is necessary if you are to make a thorough search. The job you are looking for might be listed in the classified ads under various titles. For example, an accountant seeking a job might find the specialty listed under "General Accountant," "Cost Analyst," or "Budget Analyst." So play it safe—read *all* the ads.

Occasionally, newspapers print special employment supplements that provide valuable information on many facets of the job market. Watch for these. As you read the ads, note such factors as salary ranges, job locations, and job duties and responsibilities.

Watch out for fake ads. These are ads for jobs that don't exist, run by placement firms to fatten their "résumé bank" for future clout with employers. They usually tell you nothing more than a job title and a salary (usually inflated).

Blind ads (no company name, just a box number) rarely prove worthwhile. Legitimate advertisers have nothing to hide.

Do not place a "job wanted" ad yourself, because potential employers don't read them—but placement services do (generally the less reputable ones).

Inquiry Letters. If you are interested in a particular company, write and ask whether it has an opening for someone with your skills and qualifications. This is essentially an **application letter**, except that you are not responding to an advertisement for a job. Normally you should send the letter either to the director of personnel or to the specific department head; for a small company, however, you can write to the president.

Trade and Professional Journals. Many occupations have associations that publish periodicals containing listings of current job opportunities. If you are seeking a job in forestry, for example, you could check the job listings in the *Journal of Forestry,* published by the Society of American Foresters. To learn about the trade or professional associations for your occupation, consult the following reference books:

Encyclopedia of Associations
Encyclopedia of Business Information Sources
National Directory of Employment Services

For a listing of journal ads, see *900,000 Plus Jobs Annually: Published Sources of Employment Listings,* by Norman S. Fiengold and Glenda Ann Winkler, Garrett Park Press, Garrett Park, MD 20896. This document lists more than 900 journals that carry want ads.

School Placement Services. Check with the career counselors in your school's job-placement office (you can sometimes use the job-placement services of other schools as well). Government, business, and industry recruiters often visit job-placement offices to interview prospective employees; the recruiters also keep college placement offices aware of their company's current employment needs.

While you are in the placement office, ask to see a current issue of the *College Placement Annual.* This publication lists the occupational requirements and addresses of over a thousand industry, business, and government employers.

Another document you can examine in most college placement offices is the *Directory of Career Planning and Placement Offices,* published by the College Placement Council, Inc., Box 2263, Bethlehem, PA 18001.

State Employment Agencies. Most states have free employment agencies that function specifically to match applicants and jobs. If your state has one, register with the local employment office. It may have just the job you want; if not, it will keep your résumé on file and call you if such a job comes along.

Private Employment Agencies. Private employment agencies are profit-making organizations that are in business to help people find jobs—for a fee. Reputable private employment agencies give you job leads and help you organize your campaign for the job you want. They may also provide useful information on the companies doing the hiring. Choose a private employment agency carefully. Some are well established and quite reputable, but others have questionable reputations. Check with your local Better Business Bureau as well as with friends and acquaintances before signing an agreement with a private employment agency.

Who will pay the fee if you are offered a job through a private agency? Sometimes the employer will pay the agency's fee; if not, you must pay either a set fee or a percentage of your first month's

salary. In general, if the employer pays the fee, the job is a prized position that is hard to fill, and the fact that the employer is paying the
fee is a good indication that the employment agency is reputable.
Before signing a contract, be sure you understand who is paying the
fee and, if *you* are, how much you are agreeing to pay. As with any
written agreement, read the fine print carefully.

Do not give a private employment agency "exclusive handling."
If you do, and you find *yourself* a job independent of the agency, you
may still have to pay it a fee.

Other Sources. When searching for a job, consult with people whose
judgment you respect. Use all available resources. Recruit family
members and friends to help and alert as many people as possible
to your search. Talk especially with people who are already working
in your chosen field.

Local, state, and federal government agencies offer many employment opportunities. Local government agencies are listed in
the white pages of your telephone directory under the name of your
city, county, or state. For information about jobs with the federal
government, contact the U.S. Office of Personnel Management or
the Federal Job Information Center; both have branches in most major cities. The offices are listed in the white pages of the telephone
directory under "U.S. Government."

If you are a veteran, local and campus Veteran's Administration
offices can provide material on special placement programs for veterans. Such agencies will supply you with the necessary information
about the particular requirements or entrance tests for your occupation.

The following registers might also be helpful:

Federal Career Opportunities, for government jobs, published biweekly
by Federal Research Service, Inc., 370 Maple Avenue West, Box 1059,
Vienna, VA 22180. This document lists over 3,200 available federal
jobs in the United States and overseas.

International Employment Hotline, for overseas jobs, published monthly
by International Employment Hotline, P.O. Box 6170, McLean, VA
22106.

The NELS Monthly Bulletin, for jobs in criminal justice, published by
the National Employment Listing Service, Criminal Justice Center,
Sam Houston State University, Huntsville, TX 77341.

Executive search firms are also available for those who consider themselves to be executives—such firms are not, of course, for recent college graduates. For the executive job searcher, the following documents might be useful:

Executive Employment Guide, published by the American Management Association, 135 W. 50th St., New York, NY 10020.

Recruiting and Research Report, published by Kenneth Cole, Box 895, Naperville, IL 60566.

Directory of Executive Recruiters, published by Consultant News, Templeton Rd., Fitzwilliam, NH 03447.

The Association of Executive Recruiting Consultants, 151 Railroad Avenue, Greenwich, CT 06830, also publishes a list of 60 top executive recruiters.

Keep a loose-leaf notebook with *dated* job ads, copies of letters of applications and résumés, notes sent in regard to interviews, and the names of important contacts. This notebook can act as a future resource and as a tickler file. (See also **résumé**, **interviewing for a job**, and **acceptance letter**.)

journal articles

A journal article is an article written on a specific subject for a professional periodical. These periodicals are often the official publications of professional societies. The *Journal of Business Communication,* for example, is an official voice of the Association for Business Communication. Other professional publications include *Journal of Accounting, Journal of Marketing,* and *Business Education Forum.* There are hundreds of periodicals, of course, ranging from scholarly journals that publish articles on advanced research in highly specialized areas to industrial and business periodicals that publish material of more general interest.

From time to time in your career, you may wish to write a journal article about something you know that would be of interest to others in your field. Such an article makes your work more widely known, provides favorable publicity for your employer, gives you a sense of satisfaction, and may even improve your chances for professional advancement.

PLANNING THE ARTICLE

When thinking about writing such an article, ask yourself the following questions:

- Is your work or your knowledge of the subject original? If not, what is there about your approach that justifies publication?
- Will the significance of the article justify the time and effort needed to write it?
- What parts of your work, project, or study are most appropriate to include in the article?

To help you answer these questions, learn about the periodical or periodicals to which you will send the article, and consult your colleagues for advice. Once you have decided on several journals, consider the following factors about each:

- the size and professional interests of its readership
- the professional reputation of the journal
- the appropriateness of your article to the journal's goals, as stated on the "masthead" page
- the frequency with which its articles are cited in other journals

After you have settled on the right journal, read back issues to find out such information as the amount and kind of details that the articles include, their length, and the typical writing **style**.

If your subject involves a particular project, you should begin work on it, ideally, when the project is in progress. Doing so will permit you to devote short periods during the project to writing various sections of the article, thereby writing the draft in manageable increments. This practice makes the writing integral to the project and may even reveal any weaknesses in the design or details of the project, such as the need for more data.

As you plan your article, decide whether to invite one or more coauthors to join you. Coauthors can add strength and substance to the paper but can add complications as well. To minimize potential problems, one of you should take the responsibility of being the primary author. That person creates the **outline**, makes assignments, sets up a schedule, and keeps the various parts in perspective. The primary author must also take responsibility for ensuring that the finished paper reads as smoothly as if it had been written by one person. Review the entry **revision** before revising for such consistency. (See also **collaborative writing**.)

GATHERING THE DATA

As you gather information, take notes from all the sources available to you, such as the following:

- published material on the subject
- your own experience
- notebooks recorded during your research
- survey results
- progress reports
- test data
- performance records
- patent disclosures

You should begin your **research** with a careful review of the literature to establish what has been published about your topic. A review of the relevant information in your field can be insurance against writing an article that in essence has already been published. (Some articles, in fact, begin with a **literature review**.) As you compile this information, record your references in full; that is, include all the information you would need to document the source (see **documenting sources**).

Be aware that published material may contain a number of flaws, such as incomplete and inaccurate citations; irrelevant citations; references to hard-to-find books, articles, and other material; and two slightly different versions of the same article published in separate journals. (See **library research** for advice about finding published sources.)

ORGANIZING THE DRAFT

Some journals (particularly in the sciences) use a prescribed organization for the major sections, such as the following:

- Introduction
- Materials and methods
- Results
- Discussion
- Literature cited

If the major organization is not prescribed, choose and arrange the various sections of the draft in a way that shows your results to best advantage.

In any case, the best guarantee of a logically organized article is a good outline. In addition to shaping your information in a logical order, outlining helps you organize your thinking. Moving topics about in an outline to produce the best organizational arrangement is easier and faster than moving whole paragraphs and pages of text in a manuscript. If you have coauthors, it is *essential* that the writing team work from a common, well-developed outline; otherwise, coordinating the various writers' work will be impossible, and the parts produced by each will not fit together logically as a whole.

As you prepare the outline, use the following questions to guide your thinking:

- What is the primary thesis?
- What are the key ideas?
- What details need to be included, considering your readers and your purpose?
- What data should be presented in illustrations or tables?

Once you have written your outline, however, consider it to be flexible; you may well change and improve your organization as you write the rough draft.

PREPARING SECTIONS OF THE ARTICLE

Introduction. The purpose of an introduction is to give your **readers** enough general information about your topic for them to be able to understand the detailed information in the body of the article. The introduction should include the following:

- the purpose of the article
- a definition of the problem examined
- the scope of the article
- the rationale for your approach to the problem or project and the reasons you rejected alternative approaches
- previous work in the field, including other approaches described in previously published articles

Emphasize what is new and different about your approach, especially if you are not dealing with a new concept. Show the overall significance of your project or approach by explaining how it fills a need, solves a current problem, or offers a useful application. For detailed guidance on writing introductions, see **introductions**.

Conclusion. The conclusion section pulls together your results and findings and interprets them based on the purpose of the study and the methods used to conduct it. Thus, the conclusion is the focal point of the article, the goal toward which the study was aimed. Your conclusions must grow out of the evidence for the findings in the body of the article. They must also be consistent with the scope of information presented in the introduction. For detailed guidance on writing conclusions, see **conclusions**.

Abstract. After the article is written, you will need to write an abstract. Be sure to follow any instructions provided by the journal on writing abstracts, and review previously published abstracts in that journal. Prepare your abstract carefully, since it will be the basis on which many other researchers will decide whether to read the work in full. Abstracts are often published independently in abstract journals (see **reference books**) and are used as a source of terms (called *keywords*) used to index, by subject, the original article for computerized information-retrieval systems. Abstract journals and computer searches allow researchers to review a great deal of literature in a short time. (For details on writing abstracts, see **abstracts**.)

Illustrations and Tables. Use illustrations and tables wherever they are appropriate, but design each for a specific purpose:

- to describe a function
- to show an external appearance
- to show internal construction (with cutaway or exploded-view drawings, for example)
- to display statistical data
- to indicate trends

Consider working your rough illustrations into your outline so that you decide on your illustrations as you write your manuscript. Used effectively and appropriately, illustrative material can clarify information in ways that text alone cannot. (For details, see **illustrations** and **tables**.)

Heads. The use of **heads** throughout your manuscript is important because they break the manuscript into manageable portions. They allow journal readers to understand the development of your topic and pinpoint sections of particular interest to them. The main headings in your outline will often become the headings in your final manuscript.

References. This section of the article lists the sources used or quoted in the article. The specific format for listing these sources varies from field to field. Usually the journal to which the article is submitted will specify the form the editors require for citing sources. (For a detailed discussion of using and citing sources, see **documenting sources** and **quotations**.)

PREPARING THE MANUSCRIPT

Some journals make available, or at least recommend, a "style sheet" with detailed guidelines on the style and **format** of the article. Such style sheets often include specific instructions about how the manuscript should be typed, the style for **abbreviations, symbols**, and units (like the International System of Units), how to handle mathematical equations, how many copies to submit, and the like. The following guidelines are typical:

- Double-space the manuscript, using at least one-inch margins all around, and number each page.
- Make sure that the captions for figures and tables are specific, accurate, and self-explanatory. Use labels (known as *callouts*) with those illustrations that need them.
- Provide clean, even, line work and accurately worded axes and labels for your drawings if the journal will not be redrawing them.
- Place mathematical equations, either typed or legibly printed in black ink, on separate lines in the text, and number them consecutively.
- If you include **photographs**, use glossy-finish black and white prints. Both the photograph and the contrast should be of good quality. Identify each photograph on the back; don't write on the face of it, and don't write on the back of it with a heavy hand. If necessary, indicate which edge of the photograph is the top.

OBTAINING PUBLICATION CLEARANCE

After the manuscript has been prepared, submit a copy to your employer for review before sending it to the journal. This review will make sure that no proprietary information or other kinds of trade secrets have been inadvertently revealed and that classified or other restricted information has not been disclosed. Likewise, secure ahead of time permission to print information for which someone else holds the **copyright**. At times, your employer may require that the published article contain a statement indicating approval or clearance for publication.

THE REFEREE PROCESS

Many journals use reviewers called *referees*—experts in the field— to evaluate manuscripts before they are accepted for publication. Their appraisals not only help maintain the quality of the journal but also help prospective authors by finding weaknesses and errors that can be corrected before publication.

The editor of the journal acts as an arbiter between the author and referees. Because they are anonymous (as the author is to them), they can be as critical as necessary without concern that the author knows their identities. The editor may send the referees' comments back verbatim or may only summarize them. These comments must be evaluated carefully and objectively. If you find misunderstanding or bias, bring it to the editor's attention. The editor then will make the final decision on the adequacy of the author's response or revision.

After such a review, you may be asked to revise your article before the journal will accept it for publication. Do not let this request discourage you, as the revision will probably be beneficial.

judicial/judicious

Judicial is a term that pertains only to law.

EXAMPLE The *judicial* branch is one of the three branches of the United States government.

Judicious refers to careful or wise judgment.

EXAMPLE The reorganization was accomplished smoothly by *judicious* management.

K

kind of/sort of

Kind of and *sort of* should be used in writing only to refer to a class or type of things.

> EXAMPLE We use a different *kind of* sales slip for cash transactions.

Do not use *kind of* or *sort of* to mean "rather," "somewhat," or "somehow."

> CHANGE It was *kind of* a bad year for the firm.
> TO It was a bad year for the firm.

know-how

An informal term for "special competence or knowledge," *know-how* should be avoided in **formal writing**.

> CHANGE He has a reputation for marketing *know-how*.
> TO He has a reputation for marketing *skill*.

(See also **English, varieties of.**)

L

lay/lie

Lay is a transitive verb (a **verb** that has a direct **object** to complete its meaning) and means "place" or "put." Its present **tense** form is *lay*.

> EXAMPLE We *lay* the foundation of the building one section at a time.

The past tense form of *lay* is *laid*.

> EXAMPLE We *laid* the first section of the foundation on the 27th of June.

The perfect tense form of *lay* is also *laid*.

> EXAMPLE Since June we *have laid* all but two sections of the foundation.

Lay is frequently confused with *lie*, which is an intransitive verb (a verb that does not require an object to complete its meaning) meaning "recline" or "remain." Its present tense form is *lie*.

> EXAMPLE Injured employees should *lie* down and remain still until the doctor arrives.

The past tense form of *lie* is *lay*. (This form causes the confusion between *lie* and *lay*.)

> EXAMPLE The injured employee *lay* still for approximately five minutes.

The perfect tense form of *lie* is *lain*.

> EXAMPLE The injured employee *had lain* still for approximately five minutes when the doctor arrived.

layout and design

Good visual design is crucial to the success of a document, whether it is a **résumé**, **formal report**, **newsletter**, or **proposal**. A well-designed document should make even complex information look accessible and give **readers** a favorable impression of the writer and the organization. To accomplish those goals, a good design should

- be visually simple and uncluttered
- highlight structure, hierarchy, and order
- help readers find information they need
- help reinforce an organization's image

Good design achieves visual simplicity by establishing compatible or harmonious relationships, such as using the same family of type in a document or the same highlighting device for similar items. Useful design reduces the complexity of prose, for example, by creating "chunks" of information that can be quickly noticed and absorbed. Effective design also reveals hierarchy by signaling the difference between topics and subtopics, between primary and secondary information, and between general points and examples. Visual cues make information easy to find the first and subsequent times it is sought. They also make information accessible to different readers within an audience by allowing them to locate the information they need. Finally, the design of a document should project the appropriate image of an organization. Good design can build both goodwill for the writer and the organization and respect for a company's products or services. (Some organizations, of course, have established design and **format** guidelines that you will need to follow.)

Writers can achieve effective layout and design through their selection of type for the text, their choice of devices that highlight information, and their arrangement of text and visual components on a page.

USING TYPOGRAPHY

Typography refers to the style and arrangement of type on a printed page. The letters comprising a typeface have a number of distinctive characteristics, some of which are shown in Figure 1. A complete set of all the words, numbers, and symbols available in one typeface (or style) is called a *font*.

Selecting a Typeface. Well over 10,000 different typefaces are available, each with a distinctive appearance and often having many variations within the same "family." For most on-the-job writing, select a typeface primarily for its legibility, which is the speed with which readers can recognize each letter and word. Avoid typefaces that may distract readers with contrasts in thickness or with odd features, as is often the case with script, or cursive, typefaces. In addi-

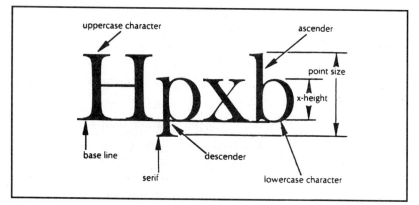

Figure 1   Primary Components of Letter Characters

tion, avoid typefaces that fade when printed or copied. Choose popular typefaces with which readers are familiar, such as the following typefaces:

- Baskerville
- Bodoni
- Caslon
- Century
- Futura

- Garamond
- Gill Sans
- Helvetica
- Times Roman
- Univers

As you are considering typefaces, keep in mind that you should not use more than two families of typeface in a document, *even though you may have access to many more.* If you wish to create a dramatic contrast between headlines and text, as in a newsletter, use a typefce that is distinctively different from the text. You may also wish to use a noticeably different typeface *inside* a graphic element. In any case, experiment with different typefaces before making final decisions, and keep in mind that not all fonts have the same assortment of symbols and other characters. Consult a book of type fonts and styles, beginning with those listed at the end of this entry.

One of the most basic distinctions of typefaces is between *serif* and *sans serif* type. Serifs, shown in Figure 1, are the small projections at the end of each stroke in a letter. Serif type styles have these lines; sans (French for "without") serif styles do not. Although sans serif type has a modern look, serif type is easier to read, especially in the smaller sizes. Sans serif, however, does work well for headings. If you do choose sans serif typefaces for text, pick one with large "counters," the fully or partially enclosed white spaces in letters like *c* and *b*.

Do not use a type that is too small for text because it will cause eye strain and make the text look crammed and uninviting. Six-point type is the smallest that can be read without a magnifying glass (see Figure 2). Type that is too large (1) may use more space than necessary, (2) can make reading difficult and inefficient, and (3) can make readers perceive words in parts rather than wholes.

Ideal point sizes for text range from 8 to 12 points (see Figure 2); 10-point type is most commonly used.

6 pt.	Type size can determine legibility.
8 pt.	Type size can determine legibility.
10 pt.	Type size can determine legibility.
12 pt.	Type size can determine legibility.
14 pt.	Type size can determine legibility.

Figure 2   Samples of 6- to 14-Point Type

Look at samples of text in various type sizes and typefaces—and trust your reaction to them. Remember, too, that the longer the lines, the larger the type size should be; hence shorter lines can accommodate smaller type.

The distance from which a document will be read should help determine type size. For example, a set of **instructions** on a table with the user standing requires a larger typeface. Consider the audience's age too. Visually impaired readers and some older adults may need large type sizes.

Adjusting Line Length and Leading. Designers sometimes use the following rule of thumb for determining optimal line length in typeset copy: Double the point size of the typeface for line length in picas. (There are six picas to an inch.) Thus, if the type size is 12 points, the line length should be 24 picas (or 4 inches). Other designers suggest that a maximum of 10 to 12 words on a line is acceptable for many typefaces, depending on the amount of white space on the page, as well as other elements discussed later in this entry.

Leading refers to the space between lines. Leading should be proportional to line length and point size—about 20 percent of the

Type Size (in points)	Line Length (in picas)	Line Length (in inches)	Leading (in points)
6	12	2	1(0–1)
8	16	2⅔	1½ (0–2)
9	18	3	2(0–3)
10	20	3⅓	2(0–3)
11	22	3⅔	2(1–3)
12	24	4	3(2–4)

Figure 3 Optimal Type Sizes, Line Lengths, and Leading

point size. The table in Figure 3 shows standard type sizes with recommended proportional line lengths and leading. Ranges are given (in parentheses) because some typefaces can affect the leading you should use. You may also use extra leading between paragraphs as well as indention for **paragraphs** to achieve maximum readability.

Choosing Justified or Ragged Right Margins. Ragged right margins are generally *easier* to read than justified right margins because the uneven contour of the right margin provides the eyes with more landmarks to identify. Ragged right may also be preferable if justification or proportional spacing in your **word processing** software inserts irregular-sized spaces between words, producing unwanted "rivers" of white space or unevenness in blocks of text.

Because ragged right margins look slightly informal, justified text is appropriate for publications aimed at a broad readership that expects a more formal, polished appearance. Further, justification is often useful with multiple-column formats because the spaces between the columns (called *alleys*) need the definition that justification provides. Regardless of your choice, do not justify short lines; doing so will leave huge gaps between words.

USING HIGHLIGHTING DEVICES

Writers use a number of means to emphasize important words, passages, and sections within documents:

- typographical devices
- headings and captions

- headers and footers
- rules and boxes
- icons and pictograms
- color and screening

When used thoughtfully, such highlighting and finding devices give a document a visible sense of **logic** and **organization**. For example, they can set off steps or **illustrations** from surrounding explanations.

Keep in mind also that typographical devices and special graphic effects should be used in moderation. Just because a feature is possible does not mean that you should use it. In fact, too many design devices clutter a page and interfere with comprehension. Check for clutter by simply counting the *number* of visual elements in a text and their frequency.

Remember that consistency is important. When you choose a highlighting technique to designate a particular feature, always use the same technique for that feature throughout your document.

Typographical Emphasis. One easily available method of typographical emphasis is the use of uppercase or **capital letters**. BUT ALL UPPERCASE LETTERS ARE DIFFICULT TO READ AT LONG STRETCHES BECAUSE THEIR UNIFORMITY OF SIZE AND SHAPE DEPRIVES READERS OF IMPORTANT VISUAL CLUES AND THUS SLOWS READING. Letters in lowercase have ascenders and descenders (see Figure 1) that make the letters distinctive and easy to identify; therefore, a mixture of uppercase and lowercase is most readable. You should use all uppercase letters only in short spans—three or four words, as in headings.

As with all uppercase letters, use **italics** sparingly. *Continuous italic type reduces legibility and thus slows readers because they must expend extra effort.* Of course, italics may be useful where you wish to slow readers, as in cautions and warnings. **Boldface**, used to cross-reference entries in this handbook, may be the best cuing device because it is visually different yet retains the customary shape of the letters and numbers.

Headings and Captions. Headings are signposts that give the reader a sense of what is covered in a section of a document. Headings (or **heads**) also reveal the organization of the document and indicate hierarchy within it. Many readers scan a document's headings before reading any text. Headings should therefore help readers decide which sections they need to read. Using too few headings forces readers to work to find their way; conversely, using too many headings can confuse readers and make a document look like an outline. Captions are key words (or *glosses*) that highlight or describe illustrations or blocks of text. Captions often appear in the left or right margins of textbooks to summarize passages. Keep in mind that they can be easily overused and do not emphasize hierarchy.

Numerous heading formats are possible, and organizations often set standards to ensure a consistent look for headings in their documents. Headings may appear in many typeface variations (boldface being most common) and often use sans serif styles. Although others are possible, the most common positions for headings and subheadings are centered, flush left, indented, or by themselves in a wide left margin. Major section or chapter headings normally appear at the top of a new page. Never leave a heading on the final line of a page. Instead, carry the heading over to the start of the next page. Insert one additional line of space or extra leading above a heading to emphasize that it marks a logical division.

Headers and Footers. A *header* contains the identifying information carried at the top of each page; a *footer* contains a similar information at the bottom of each page. Pages may have one or the other or both. Although practices vary, **headers and footers** carry such information as the topic or subtopic of a section, identifying numbers, a document date, page numbers, document name, and section title. Although headers and footers are important reference devices, too much information in them can create visual clutter.

Rules, Icons, and Color. *Rules* are vertical or horizontal lines used to divide one area of the page from another, such as setting off headers and footers from the rest of the page. Rules can also be combined to box off elements on the page. Do not overuse rules; too many rules and boxed elements can create a cluttered look.

An *icon* is a pictorial representation of an idea; it can be used to identify specific actions, objects, or sections of a document. The most widely used icons include the symbols used to designate men's and women's restrooms, wheelchair accessibility, and parking for the handicapped.

In documents, icons are useful to identify sections and to warn readers of danger, especially impaired readers. To be effective, icons must be simple and intuitively recognizable—or at least easy to define. Icons can be placed in headers, in footers, next to headings, or in the open left column of a page.

Color and *screening* can distinguish one part of a document from another or unify a series of documents. (Screening refers to shaded areas that are actually composed of patterns of tiny dots.) Color and screening can set off sections within a document, highlight examples, or emphasize warnings.

DESIGNING THE PAGE

Page design is the process of combining the various components on a page. Each time you plan a design, you need to remain flexible as you make decisions about specific elements. The flexibility and lavishness of your design will be based on the capabilities of your word-processing or typesetting equipment, how the document will be reproduced, and the budget available. (Color printing, for example, is far more expensive than black-and-white printing.)

Using a Grid. As an aid to arranging pages, use a grid to serve as a visual framework to position blocks within the image area. To create a basic reference grid that you can duplicate for many projects, divide an 8½-by-11 page into 10-point units, as shown in part A of Figure 4. You do not need to draw every line, of course. After defining the margins, such as those for the 46-by-70-unit page shown

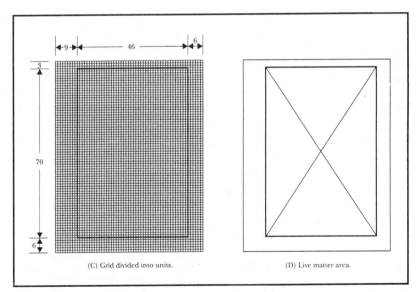

(C) Grid divided into units.　　　　　　　　(D) Live matter area.

Figure 4　Creating a Page-Design Grid

in part A of Figure 4, you can then arrange blocks of material inside the "live matter area" marked with the X in part B of Figure 4. Within the live matter area, you can draw vertical lines to create columns and horizontal lines for blocks of material.

Before you put actual text and visuals on a page, you may wish to create a *thumbnail sketch* with blocks indicating the placement of elements. You can go further by laying out a rough assembly of all the thumbnail pages showing size, shape, form, and general style of a publication. This mock-up, called a *dummy,* allows you to see how a publication will look. As you work with elements on the page, experiment with different designs. Often what seems a useful concept in principle turns out not to work in practice.

Defining Columns. As you design pages, consider early the size and number of columns. Although more variations are possible, Figure 5 shows eight ways of placing text on a page. Pattern A provides maximum text; patterns B and C provide more white space; patterns D and E combine maximum text and readability; and patterns F, G, and H provide ample illustrative space. For typewritten material, such as reports, the maximum block (pattern A) is acceptable if double-spaced. For fairly solid prose set in type, the traditional two-column structure (pattern D) enhances legibility by keeping text columns narrow enough so that readers need not scan back and forth across the width of the entire page for every line.

Avoid starting a new paragraph on the last line of a column. A word at the end of a column is called a *widow.* This term is also used for carried-over letters of hyphenated words. If a widow is carried over to the top of the next column or page, it is called an *orphan.* Avoid both widows and orphans.

Using White Space. White space makes difficult subjects seem easier to comprehend by visually framing information and breaking it into manageable chunks. Even the simple use of white space between paragraphs helps readers see the information in that paragraph as a unit. Use extra white space between sections to signal to the reader that one section is ending and another is beginning—a visual cue indicating the organization of a document. You can also emphasize text—a word, a phrase, or a paragraph—by framing it with white space. You need not have access to sophisticated equipment to make use of white space. You can easily indent and skip lines for paragraphs, lists, and other blocks of material.

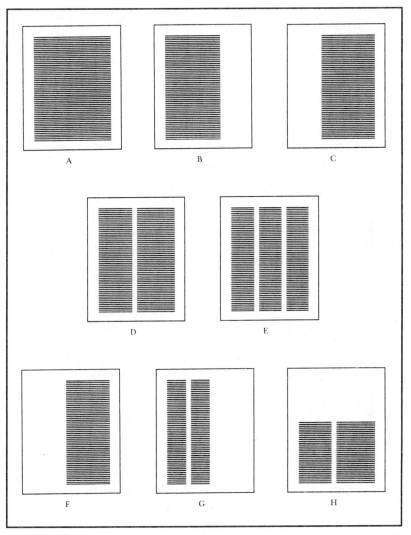

Figure 5 Eight Ways of Using Columns (Courtesy of *Designing with Type* by James Craig; copyright © 1971 by Watson-Guptill Publications)

Using Lists. Lists provide an effective way to use white space; they combine both linguistic and visual elements to highlight words, phrases, and short sentences. Lists are particularly useful for certain types of information:

- steps in sequence
- materials or parts needed
- items to remember
- criteria for evaluation
- concluding points
- recommendations

Follow the advice given in the entry **lists**, such as avoiding both too many lists and too many items in lists.

Using Illustrations.   Readers notice illustrations before text and large illustrations before small ones. Thus, the size of an illustration is the reader's gauge of its importance. Consider the proportion of the illustration to the text. Proportion often means employing the three-fifths rule: page layout is more dramatic and appealing when the major element (photo, drawing, and so on) occupies three-fifths rather than half of the available space.

Illustrations can be gathered in one place (as at the end of a report), but placing them within the text makes them more effective by putting them closer to their accompanying explanations, as well as providing visual relief. (See **illustrations.**)

FURTHER INFORMATION

For more detailed information on design and production, such as packaging, binding, and printing, see the following:

Alred, Gerald J., Walter E. Oliu, and Charles T. Brusaw. *The Professional Writer: A Guide for Advanced Technical Writing.* New York: St. Martin's, 1992.

Bruno, Michael H., ed. *Pocket Pal: A Graphic Arts Production Handbook.* 13th ed. Memphis: International Paper, 1988.

Carter, Rob, Ben Day, and Philip Meggs. *Typographic Design: Form and Communication.* New York: Van Nostrand, 1985.

Romano, Frank J. *The Typencyclopedia: A User's Guide to Better Typography.* New York: Bowker, 1984.

leave/let

As a **verb**, *leave* should never be used in the sense of "allow" or "permit."

> CHANGE *Leave* me do it my way.
>   TO *Let* me do it my way.

As a **noun**, however, *leave* can mean "permission granted."

> EXAMPLE   Employees are granted a *leave* of absence if they have a chronic illness.

lend/loan

Lend or *loan* each may be used as a **verb**, but *lend* is more common.

> EXAMPLES   You can *loan* them the money if you wish.
> You can *lend* them money if you wish.

Unlike *lend, loan* can be a **noun**.

> EXAMPLE   We made arrangements at the bank for a *loan*.

letters (see correspondence)

libel/liable/likely

The term *libel* refers to "anything circulated in writing or pictures that injures someone's good reputation." When someone's reputation is injured in speech, however, the term is *slander*.

> EXAMPLES   When an editorial charged our board of directors with bribing a representative, the board sued the newspaper for *libel*.
> If the mayor supports the bribery charge in his speech tonight, we will accuse him of *slander*.

The term *liable* means "legally subject to" or "responsible for."

> EXAMPLE   Employers are held *liable* for their employees' decisions.

In business writing, *liable* should retain its legal meaning. Where a condition of probability is intended, use *likely.*

> CHANGE   Rita is *liable* to be promoted.
> TO   Rita is *likely* to be promoted.

library research

The key tools for doing library research include the card catalog, periodical indexes, bibliographies, computer-search services, reference books, and, increasingly, information stored on compact disks.

For help in using any of these, as well as in using the library in general, ask a librarian.

THE CARD CATALOG

The card catalog contains a listing of each book a library owns. It is usually found in cabinets near the reference or circulation section, though some larger libraries keep their card catalogs in bound books or on computer terminals. Go to the card catalog to determine whether the library has the book you need and where to find it.

Most books have three types of cards in the catalog—an *author card* and a *title card* (found in the Author/Title Index) and a *subject card* (found in the Subject Index). (See Figures 1, 2, and 3.) Cards are arranged alphabetically: Author cards are filed by the author's last name; title cards are filed by the first important word in the title (excluding *a, an,* and *the*); and subject cards are filed by the first word of the general subject. All three cards include the author, the title, the publisher, the date and place of publication, the number of pages, and the major topics covered in the book. They also indicate whether a book has an index, a bibliography, or any illustrations. At the bottom of a card are subject headings that can lead you to more materials on the same topic.

Each card also includes, in the upper left-hand corner, the *call number,* which indicates where the book is kept in the library. The

Figure 1   Author Card

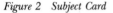

Figure 2   Subject Card

Subject ——————— ACCOUNTING--DATA PROCESSING.

HF
5657
.N5   Newman, Maurice S.
         Financial accounting estimates through
      statistical sampling by computer / Maurice
      S. Newman. New York : Wiley, c 1976.
         xiii, 247 p. : ill. ; 24 cm. (Wiley series
      on systems and controls for financial
      management)
         "A Wiley-Interscience publication."
         Bibliography: p. 225-226.
         Includes index.

WMUW   09 MAR 77   2346105 GZNAnc   76-23400

Title ——————— Financial accounting estimates through
                  statistical sampling by computer

HF
5657
.N5   Newman, Maurice S.
         Financial accounting estimates through
      statistical sampling by computer / Maurice
      S. Newman. New York : Wiley, c1976.
         xiii, 247 p. : ill. ; 24 cm. (Wiley series
      on systems and controls for financial
      management)
         "A Wiley-Interscience publication."
         Bibliography: p. 225-226.
         Includes index.

WMUW   09 MAR 77   2346105 GZNAnc   76-23400

Figure 3   Title Card

call number, written on the book's spine, enables you to find the book on the shelf. Call numbers are actually the book's classification according to the Dewey Decimal System, the Library of Congress System, or the library's own system.

A card catalog also contains *see* cards and *see also* cards. *See* cards indicate that the heading you are looking under is not the one used for your topic and refer you instead to another heading. For example, if you looked up *letter writing,* a *see* card might refer you to *com-*

mercial correspondence. See also cards list additional headings related to the topic. Under *word processing,* for example, a *see also* card might refer you to *computers.*

BIBLIOGRAPHIES AND PERIODICAL INDEXES

Bibliographies and periodical indexes contain lists of books and articles. Bibliographies list books, periodicals, and other research materials published in a particular subject area—for example, in business or engineering. Periodical indexes list journal, magazine, and newspaper articles. (*Periodicals* are publications that are issued at regular intervals—daily, weekly, monthly, and so on.) For a list of some useful bibliographies and periodical indexes, see **reference books**.

Instructions for using bibliographies and periodical indexes are found in the front of each volume (or the first volume of a series). There you will find a key to the **abbreviations** and **symbols** used as well as an explanation of the way that information is arranged in the book. You will also find a list of the specific topics covered and, for periodical indexes, a list of which newspapers, magazines, and journals are included. The following indexes are useful for locating business topics:

Accountant's Index, 1920–
Business Periodicals Index, 1958–
Index to U.S. Government Periodicals, 1851–(bimonthly)
Wall Street Journal Index, 1958–(monthly)

Current issues are often in one area, back issues (which are bound in volumes) in another. Back issues of some journals and most newspapers are generally on microforms, descriptions of which appear at the end of this entry. Libraries generally keep periodicals in a separate room or area. If your library does not have the periodicals you need, you can get them through *interlibrary loan,* a service that permits you to borrow books and buy photocopied periodical articles from other libraries. Consult your librarian for specific details of the system.

COMPUTER-SEARCH SERVICES AND INDEXES

Many academic, industrial, and medical libraries now offer computer-search services. Indexes are electronically stored as data bases in a computer. Librarians can then quickly find, or retrieve, information from the indexes. This computer-search service is an auto-mated method of preparing a bibliography; it provides you with a computer printout of a list of citations, some with **abstracts**, appro-priate to your subject. Data bases are available in medicine, busi-ness, biology, management, engineering, environmental studies, and many other subjects. Ordinarily there is a charge for the service, but the cost is relatively low when the speed and convenience of the search are taken into account.

Computer-search services are usually located in the reference sec-tion of the library. (Searches are almost always conducted by refer-ence librarians skilled in searching computer data bases.) At some large universities, these services are located in satellite libraries. The reference staff can provide information about the range of subjects in the data base, the types and cost of search services, and proce-dures for using the service.

It is generally necessary to set up an appointment with a reference librarian to arrange for the search. Some libraries provide a form to fill out in advance that asks for a brief statement of the research topic and for any pertinent information necessary or helpful for conducting the search.

After completing the search, the librarian generally meets with the researcher to go over the printout. He or she can help you eval-uate the citations for their relevance to your project and can also assist you in finding them. Some libraries provide with the printout a brief guide that indicates where books, periodicals, and micro-form sources on the citation list are located.

REFERENCE WORKS

Additional sources of information include encyclopedias, special-ized dictionaries, handbooks and manuals, statistical sources, and atlases.

Encyclopedias. Encyclopedias—alphabetically arranged collections of articles—are often illustrated and usually published in multivol-ume sets. Some encyclopedias cover a wide range of general subjects, and others specialize in a particular subject. General encyclopedias provide the kind of overview that can be helpful to someone new to a particular subject. The articles in general encyclopedias are useful sources of background information and can be especially helpful in defining the terminology essential for understanding the subject.

Some articles contain bibliographies, which list additional sources. Three major general encyclopedias are the following:

Encyclopedia Americana (30 volumes)
Encyclopaedia Britannica (24 volumes)
New Columbia Encyclopedia (1 volume)

Specialized encyclopedias provide detailed information on a particular field of knowledge. Their treatment of a subject is rather thorough, and so the researcher ought to have some background information on the subject in order to use the encyclopedia's information to full advantage. Specialized encyclopedias contain comprehensive bibliographies. There are specialized encyclopedias on many subjects, two examples of which follow:

Heyel, Carl, ed. *The Encyclopedia of Management*
McGraw-Hill Encyclopedia of Science and Technology (15 volumes plus annual supplements)

Dictionaries. Dictionaries—alphabetical arrangements of words with information about their forms, pronunciations, origins, meanings, and uses—are essential to all writers. For a list of major abridged and unabridged dictionaries, look in the **dictionary** entry of this book. Specialized dictionaries define those terms used in a particular field—for example, computers, architecture, consumer affairs. Their definitions are generally more complete and are more likely to be current. The following specialized dictionaries are typical:

Ammer, Christine, and Dean S. Ammer. *Dictionary of Business and Economics*
Dorland's Illustrated Medical Dictionary
McGraw-Hill Dictionary of Scientific and Technical Terms

Handbooks and manuals. These are compilations of frequently used information in a particular field of knowledge. They are usually one volume in length and generally provide such information as brief definitions of terms or concepts, explanations and details about particular organizations, numerical data in **graphs** and **tables, maps,** and the like. Handbooks and manuals are handy sources of fundamental information on a particular subject, although they are most useful for someone with some knowledge of the topic, particularly in scientific or technical fields. Every field has its own handbook or manual; the following are typical:

Sabin, William A. *The Gregg Reference Manual*
Environmental Regulation Handbook
Merritt, F. S., ed. *Building Construction Handbook*
U.S. Government Manual

Statistical sources. Collections of numerical data, these are the best sources for such information as the height of the Washington Monument; the population of Boise, Idaho; the cost of living in Aspen, Colorado; and the annual number of motorcycle fatalities in the United States. The answers to many statistical questions can be found in almanacs and encyclopedias. The answers to difficult or comprehensive questions, however, are most likely to be found in works devoted exclusively to statistical data, a selection of which follows:

American Statistics Index (1978– with monthly, quarterly, and annual supplements. Lists and abstracts all statistical publications issued by agencies of the U.S. government, including periodicals, reports, special surveys, and pamphlets.)

U.S. Bureau of the Census. *County and City Data Book* (1952–. Issued every five years. Includes a variety of data from cities, counties, metropolitan areas, and the like. Arranged by geographic and political areas, it covers such topics as climate, dwellings, population characteristics, school districts, employment, and city finances.)

U.S. Bureau of the Census. *Statistical Abstract of the United States* (1979– annual. Includes statistics on the U.S. social, political, and economic condition and covers broad topics such as population, education, public land, and vital statistics. Some state and regional data.)

Atlases. Collections of maps, atlases are classified into two categories based on the type of information their maps present—general atlases show physical and political boundaries, and thematic atlases give special information, such as climate, population, natural resources, or agricultural products. The following are several general atlases:

Hammond Medallion World Atlas
National Geographic Atlas of the World
Rand McNally New Cosmopolitan World Atlas
The Times Atlas of the World
U.S. Geological Survey. *The National Atlas of the United States of America*

COMPACT DISK/READ ONLY MEMORY (CD-ROM)

Libraries increasingly make reference materials available that use CD-ROM technology. CD-ROM (compact disk—read-only memory) refers to an optical (rather than magnetic) medium for the storage and retrieval of information. The compact disks used are like the laser disks used in the music industry. The turntable for CD-ROM disks, however, is connected to a microcomputer rather than to an audio receiver and speakers, so that the information can be viewed on the computer screen and printed on demand. (The computer reads the CDs as though they were regular computer floppy disks.) The disks are called "read-only memory" because the computer can read the information from the disks, but the user cannot change information on the disk or write new information to the disk.

The major benefit of this medium is its enormous storage capacity. Each disk can store approximately 275,000 pages. CD-ROM technology also permits full-text subject searches. Every word in a text (except **conjunctions**, **prepositions**, and **articles**) is indexed, thereby simplifying and greatly expanding the user's search capabilities compared with a manual search. Once the information is found, it can be printed on demand for reading ease and reference. The disks can store graphics, voice, and music, as well as text. For example, a "talking" version of *Webster's Ninth New Collegiate Dictionary* is now available, with the voice of a professional announcer reading each of the dictionary's 160,000 entries.

With their capacity to store, index, and permit interaction among text, graphics, music, and voice media, CD-ROMs have virtually unlimited potential for the storage of reference materials, including almanacs, encyclopedias, atlases, general and specialized dictionaries, books of quotations, thesauruses, and numerous economic, demographic, political, legal, and statistical data collections. The U.S. Bureau of the Census alone makes scores of data collections available on CD-ROMs in agriculture, housing, population, transportation, construction, retail and wholesale trade, and many more.

Check with a reference librarian to learn the kinds of CD-ROM databases available and for information about how to access the information using the computer.

MICROFORMS

Some library source materials may require you to use microforms. Reduced photographic images of printed pages, microforms are used by many libraries for storing magazines, newspapers, and other materials. Because they are reduced, microforms must be magnified by machines called microreaders in order to be read. The most common kinds of microforms are microfilm and microfiche.

Microfilm. Rolls of 35-millimeter film, usually with four printed pages per frame, microfilm must be read on manually or electrically operated machines that advance the roll, frame by frame, for viewing.

Microfiche. A flat sheet of film, usually 4 × 6 inches, that can contain as many as 98 pages, microfiche is read on a microreader, where it can be moved horizontally or vertically from frame to frame for viewing.

If you are unsure about where to get microform materials or how to use microreaders, ask a librarian. Microform materials and microreaders are usually located in a special section of the library. Some microreaders are equipped with photocopying devices that for a fee permit you to make paper copies of microforms.

TIPS FOR DOING LIBRARY RESEARCH

Once you find sources with the information you need and actually get your hands on those sources, you must be conscientious about keeping track of them. Besides taking careful notes of any information they contain, you should methodically note certain information about the sources themselves.

When you get the book, magazine, or microform, there are certain shortcuts that can help you decide quickly whether it has information that will be useful to your research. In books it is best to start by looking over the **table of contents** and then by reading the **introductions**, **conclusions**, and **summaries**.

Does the book have an index or a **bibliography**? For a magazine article, it helps first to scan the **heads**, to get an idea of its major topics. Is the magazine an authoritative one, or is it brief and topical in its scope? With microforms, you can quickly flip through the text also looking for major topics. No matter what form your source takes, always consider its date: How current is the information? Timeliness is important in any research; you don't want to use out-of-date information.

Prepare a 3 × 5-inch note card for any source that you include in your research. The card should include the source's call number,

Figure 1   Bibliography Card for a Book

Figure 2   Bibliography Card for a Periodical

author, and publication information (publisher, city, year). Then, when you compile your bibliography, you will have all necessary information on these cards. Figures 1 and 2 are examples of bibliography cards. (See also **note-taking**.)

-like

The **suffix** *-like* is sometimes added to **nouns** to make them into **adjectives**. The resulting **compound word** is hyphenated only if it is unusual or might not immediately be clear.

EXAMPLES childlike, lifelike, dictionary-like, computer-like
Her new assistant works with *machine-like* efficiency.

like/as

To avoid confusion between *like* and *as,* remember that *like* is a **preposition** and *as* is a **conjunction**. Use *like* with a **noun** or **pronoun** that is not followed by a **verb**.

EXAMPLE The new supervisor behaves *like a novice.*

Use *as* before **clauses** (which contain verbs).

EXAMPLES He acted *as though he owned the company.*
He responded *as we expected he would.*

Like may be used in elliptical constructions that omit the verb.

EXAMPLE She took to architecture *like a bird to nest building.*

If the omitted portions of the elliptical construction were restored, however, *as* would be used.

EXAMPLE She took to architecture *as a bird takes to nest building.*

linking verbs

A **verb** that functions primarily to link the **subject** to a **noun** or **modifier** is called a *linking verb.* The most common linking verb is a form of the verb *be.*

EXAMPLE Each department *is* important to the company's overall performance.

However, many other verbs may also function as linking verbs, including *become, remain,* and *seem.*

EXAMPLE He *became* an investment advisor.

Verbs that convey the senses (*look, feel, sound, taste, smell*) often perform only a linking function.

EXAMPLE The bookkeeper *looked* tired.

A few verbs may function either as linking verbs or as transitive or intransitive verbs. When *be* may be substituted, the verb is probably a linking verb.

EXAMPLES   He *grew* angry. (linking verb, equivalent in meaning to *became*)
He *grew* African violets in his office. (transitive verb)
The African violets *grew.* (intransitive verb)

(See also **subjective complements.**)

listening

Listening is a learned skill; it is not automatic or instinctive. Listening requires concentration and mental effort. But it is worth the effort it takes, for good listening facilitates the exchange of ideas, opinions, and information.

The first thing to understand is that there are a number of natural human barriers to effective listening. One of them is that if the speaker says something that is contrary to your own prejudice, you may immediately start to prepare a rebuttal—and stop listening. Another is that your personal feelings about the speaker can get in your way; for example, if you dislike the speaker, your feelings may convince your subconscious mind that he or she will not have anything to say that is worth listening to—and your mind is more likely to stray. Physical barriers can also get in the way of effective listening. If you are hungry or tired, for example, you will certainly find concentrating more difficult. And finally, you may be distracted by noises and sights. The important thing is to be aware of these potential distractions and try to prevent them or, if you cannot, to overcome them.

The following guidelines may help you improve your listening skills:

1. Make a conscious effort to listen carefully, to stay involved, and to react to what is being said. It may help to try to put yourself in the speaker's place.
2. Learn to use the spare time that results from your mind's absorbing information faster than the speaker can present it to listen more effectively and efficiently. For example, you might try to find the speaker's pattern of organization. Identify the introduction, the method being used to develop the topic, the transition (so that you will be alert for the next point), and the conclusion. Or evaluate the evidence the speaker uses to substantiate his or her points. Listen "between the lines" for meaning that may not be in the words. Or review the talk to this point. These

techniques will help you not only probe the meaning of the subject but also remember key points.

3. Don't allow yourself to be distracted by the speaker's personality or mannerisms. Respond thoughtfully to the speaker's words, and avoid making judgments too quickly.
4. Be prepared. Think about the subject of a meeting or workshop ahead of time. This will help you understand and remember the material.
5. Take notes. If you are following a speaker's presentation in order to take notes, your mind will be less likely to wander or be distracted. However, your note taking must enhance your listening and not detract from it. Also, if you have taken notes, you are much more likely to review what you have heard—and reviewing your notes can remedy weaknesses in your listening skills.

The best test of listening well is the ability to respond well. Get into the habit of summarizing and paraphrasing in your own words what has been said. Doing so will both reduce the probability of listening mistakes and increase retention.

lists

Lists can save **readers** time by allowing them to see at a glance specific items, questions, or directions. Lists also help readers by breaking up complex statements that include figures and by allowing key ideas to stand out.

EXAMPLE Before we agree to hold the convention at the Brent Hotel, we should make sure the hotel facilities meet the following criteria:

1. At least eight meeting rooms that can accommodate 25 people each.
2. Ballroom and dining facilities for 250 people.
3. Duplicating facilities that are adequate for the conference committee.
4. Overhead projectors, flip charts, and screens that are sufficient for eight simultaneous sessions.
5. Ground-floor exhibit area that can provide room for thirty 8 × 15-foot booths.

To confirm that the Brent Hotel is our best choice, perhaps we should take a look at its rooms and facilities during our stay in Kansas City.

Notice that all the items in this example have a **parallel structure**. In addition, all the items are balanced—that is, all points are relatively equal in importance and are of the same general length. Consider, however, the following example and its revision:

> CHANGE I believe we should consider several important items at the meeting.
>
> 1. Our 19-- Production Schedule
> 2. The Five-Year Corporate Plan
> 3. We should also develop an agenda for the next meeting that includes a discussion of criteria for relocating the Westdale Division. Perhaps you can give me some tentative ideas at this meeting.
> 4. The draft of our Year-End Financial Report
>
> TO Please bring to the meeting the following items:
>
> 1. Our 19-- Production Schedule
> 2. The Five-Year Corporate Plan
> 3. The draft of our Year-End Financial Report
>
> In addition, you might give me some tentative ideas about criteria for relocating the Westdale Division. Since we must formally discuss this problem soon, we should include such a discussion in the agenda for the committee's next meeting.

In the original version, item 3 is neither parallel in structure nor balanced in importance with the other items. In the revision, item 3 is discussed separately, since it deserves a more developed treatment.

In an attempt to avoid writing **paragraphs**, some writers tend to overuse lists, however. A **memorandum** or **report** that consists almost entirely of lists, for example, can be difficult to understand, for the reader is forced to connect the separate items and mentally to provide **coherence**. Do not expect a reader to deal with unexplained lists of ideas.

To ensure that the reader understands how a list fits with the surrounding sentences, always provide adequate **transitions** before and after any lists. If you do not wish to indicate rank or sequence, which numbered lists suggest, you can use bullets, as shown in the list of tips that follows. In typography a bullet is a small *o* that is filled in with ink.

TIPS FOR USING LISTS

- List only comparable items.
- Use parallel structure throughout.

- Use only words, **phrases**, or short sentences.
- Provide adequate transitions before and after lists.
- Use bullets when rank or sequence is not important.
- Do not overuse lists.

literature

In business contexts, the word *literature* applies to a body of writing pertaining to a specific field, such as finance, insurance, or computers. We commonly speak, for example, of medical literature or campaign literature.

> EXAMPLE Please send me any available *literature* on computerized translations of foreign languages.

literature reviews

A literature review is a summary **report** on the **literature**, or printed material, that is available on a particular subject in a specific period of time. For example, a literature review might describe all material published within the past five years on a special technique for debugging computers, or it might describe all reports written in the past fifteen years on efforts to improve quality control at a particular company. A literature review tells the **reader** what is available on a particular subject and gives him or her an idea of what should be read in full. The review may be self-contained, or it may be part of a larger work.

Industrial research departments often prepare literature reviews, which then serve as starting points for detailed **research**. Managers in business and industry also use literature reviews to keep specialists informed of the latest developments and trends in their fields. Some **journal articles** or theses begin with a brief literature review that brings the reader up to date on current research in the area. The author can then use the review as background for discussion of the subject.

To prepare a literature review, you must begin with **library research** or even a computer search of published material on your **topic**. Since your reader may begin research on the basis of your literature review, be especially careful to cite accurately all bibliographic information. As you review each source, note the scope of the book or article and judge its value to the reader. Save all printouts of computer-assisted searches—you may wish to incorporate the sources in the **bibliography** of the final version of your literature review.

You can arrange your discussion chronologically, beginning with a description of the earliest relevant literature and progressing to the most recent. You can also subdivide the topic, discussing works on various subcategories of the topic.

Begin a literature review by defining the area to be covered and the types of works to be reviewed. For example, a literature review may be limited to articles and reports and not include any books. Remember also to make the review as concise as possible (much like an **abstract** or an **executive summary**). Mention material directly pertinent to your topic, but do not go into any details. (Your readers can go to the original literature if they want detail.) Provide a list of references at the end.

The following literature review (Figure 1) is part of an **introduction** to an annotated **bibliography**. This introduction reviews the literature that is listed later in the bibliography.

As we examined business-writing books written over the last hundred years, we discovered that the turn of the century ushered in a burst of publication. . . . Two developments may be significant in causing this rise in publication. The first is the development of business instruction, when R.M. Bartlett in Philadelphia in 1846 began teaching bookkeeping and other commercial subjects. By 1860 all major cities had at least one such school, and by 1900 business instruction in colleges and universities was not uncommon. Second, the modern typewriter was placed on the market in 1874 by E. Remington and Son. By 1900 the typewriter (both the person and the machine) was commonplace in business. The effect that these two influences—business instruction and the type-writer—had on the genesis of business-writing guides is a potential area for scholarship and study.

   One of the earliest titles on correspondence for the professional in business is the first edition of *Mercantile Correspondence in English and German Languages,* by John Clausen (ca. 1889). This work was designed to train business people in how to read and write letters in German and English. An-

---

Figure 1   Literature Review

other early work is *Hand-Book of Modern Business Correspondence* (1908), by Forrest Crissey. This work was designed to "guide . . . students, stenographers, correspondence clerks, all office men, and managers" in the art of letter writing in business. Calvin Althouse, in an early work simply titled *Business Letters* (1910), asserted that "one of the great needs of the business world today is to find those who can indite a good business letter, cordial in tone, correctly punctuated and expressed in clear, unmistakable English. . . ." One might hear a similar statement today—over seventy years later.

By 1916 a number of books attempted to answer Althouse's call with general treatments of business correspondence (Poole and Buzzell, 1913) and specific treatments of sales letters (Rose, 1915), of direct-mail letters (Ruxton, 1918, and *Sales Promotion by Mail*, 1916), and of house organs (Wilson, 1915).

The publication of textbooks on business writing is directly related to business writing instruction. According to Professor Francis W. Weeks, the first courses in business writing were offered at the University of Illinois (1902) and New York University (1903). Originally published in 1904, *Commercial Correspondence and Postal Information*, by Altmaier, may rank as the first business-writing textbook. It contains not only writing assignments but also cases for study. LaSalle Extension University published *Business English* (1911) by Edwin Herbert Lewis for students from high school through college. Another business writing textbook, by H. W. Hammond and in its fifth edition by 1913, was designed for schools where no teacher of business English was employed, and it served as a supplement to regular business courses.

Edwin Hall Gardner and Robert Ray Aurner's *Effective Business Letters*, originally published in 1915, was based on a business letter writing course at the University of Wisconsin. Nathaniel Waring Barnes's *How to Teach Business Correspondence* (1916) might be considered the earliest work on pedagogy. However, it could also be considered a teacher's manual for his *How to Write Business Letters* (1916). By 1923, two books were exclusively devoted to business writing courses in high schools: *Handbook for Business Letter Writers (1922)* and *Actual Business English* (1923).

Figure 1   Literature Review (continued)

ANNOTATED BIBLIOGRAPHIES

Related to literature reviews are *annotated bibliographies,* which also give readers information about printed material. Rather than discussing the literature in **paragraphs**, however, an annotated **bibliography** lists each item in a standard form (see **documenting sources**) and then briefly describes it. This description (or *annotation*) may include the purpose of the book, its scope, the main topics covered, its historical importance, and anything else the writer thinks the **reader** should know.

The following annotation, among others, followed the historical literature review shown earlier. (The number, 202, appears in the original to help index the over 900 annotations.)

> 202   Davey, Patrick J. *Financial Manuals.* New York: Conference Board, 1971. 77 p.
>
> This work is a report by an independent, nonprofit business-research organization. It is designed "to assist executives who are faced with the task of preparing a new financial manual or updating an existing one." The sections of this report cover the purposes, preparation and maintenance, contents, and physical characteristics of financial manuals. The two indexes include a composite listing of manual subjects (not cross-referenced to the body of this report) and a detailed table of contents of a typical manual. The book gives writing advice primarily by showing models of narrative sections of manuals, focusing on typical content, arrangement, and format.

logic

Logic, or correct reasoning, is essential to convincing your **reader** that your conclusion is valid. Errors in logic can quickly destroy your credibility with your reader. Although a detailed discussion of logic is beyond the scope of this book (see **reference books** for books on logic), the following discussion points out some common errors in logic that you should watch out for in your writing.

LACK OF REASON

When a statement violates the reader's common sense, that statement is not reasonable. If, for example, you stated "New York City is a small town," your reader might immediately question your logic. Common sense would suggest that a city of over eight million people is not a small town. If, however, you stated "Although New York's population is over eight million, it is a city composed of small towns," your reader could probably accept the statement as reasonable—that is, if you then demonstrated the truth of the statement with reasonable examples. Always be sure that your statements are sensible and that they are supported by sound examples.

SWEEPING GENERALIZATIONS

Sweeping generalizations are statements that are too large to be supportable; they generally enlarge an observation about a small group to a generalization about an entire population.

> EXAMPLES   Management is never concerned about employees.
> Computer instructions are always confusing.

These statements are too broad; they ignore any possibility that some managements may be concerned about employees or that some computer instructions are written well. Such generalizations are simply not true; using them will always weaken your credibility. No matter how certain you are of the general applicability of an opinion, exercise great caution when using such all-inclusive expressions as *anyone, everyone, no one, all,* and *in all cases.* Your statement is likely to sound illogical and will not be taken seriously. Certain stereotypical **phrases** are based on sweeping generalizations and should also be avoided: "typical business person," "bureaucratic mentality," and "absent-minded professor."

NON SEQUITUR

A statement that does not logically follow from a previous statement or has little bearing on the previous statement is called a *non sequitur.*

> EXAMPLE   I arrived at work early today, so the weather is calm.

In this example, common sense tells us that arriving early for work does not produce calm weather, or any other kind. Thus, the second part of the sentence does not follow logically from the first. Notice how much more logical the following statement is. It makes sense because each idea is logically linked to the other.

> EXAMPLE   The snow slowed traffic in the city, so although I left for work
> at the usual time, I arrived a bit late.

Of course, most non sequiturs are not so obvious as the first example. They often occur when a writer neglects to express adequately the logical links in a chain of thought.

> EXAMPLE   Last year our laboratory increased its efficiency by 50 percent by using part-time help. I suggest that we hire two full-time laboratory assistants.

Although both the statements are about the same subject—additional laboratory staff—a logical connection is missing. The reader is forced to guess the meaning. Does the writer mean that full-time assistants will be more efficient? Are part-time employees unavailable? Such non sequiturs can cause the reader to misunderstand what he or she is reading or to assume that it is illogical. In your own writing be careful that all points stand logically connected; non sequiturs cause difficulties for reader and writer alike.

POST HOC, ERGO PROPTER HOC

This term means literally "after this, therefore because of this," and it refers to the logical fallacy that because one event happened after another event, the first somehow caused the second.

> EXAMPLE   I didn't bring my umbrella today. No wonder it is now raining.

Many superstitions are based on this error in logic. In on-the-job writing, this error in reasoning usually results from a hasty conclusion that events are related, without the writer examining the logical connection between the two events.

> EXAMPLE   We issued the new police uniforms on September 2. Arrests then increased 40 percent.

In the example, it is not logical to assume that new uniforms would produce such a dramatic increase in arrests. To demonstrate such a claim logically would require an explanation of the special circumstances that produced the result. For example, if the new uniforms resulted in a union settlement with police officers, which in turn caused the officers to end a work slowdown, then the conclusion would be reasonable. Even in that case, however, the new uniforms per se did not increase arrests; rather, a complete chain of events produced the result.

BIASED OR SUPPRESSED EVIDENCE

A **conclusion** reached as a result of self-serving data, questionable sources, or purposely incomplete facts is illogical—and probably dishonest. If you were asked to prepare a **report** on the acceptance of a new policy among employees and you distributed **questionnaires** only to those who thought the policy was effective, the resulting evidence would be biased. If you purposely ignored employees who did not believe the policy was effective, you would also be suppressing evidence. Any writer must be concerned about the fair presentation of evidence—especially in reports that recommend or justify actions.

FACT VERSUS OPINION

Distinguish between fact and opinion. Facts include verifiable data or statements, whereas opinions are personal conclusions that may or may not be based on facts. For example, it is a verifiable fact that distilled water boils at 100°C; that distilled water tastes better than tap water is an opinion. In order to prove a point, some writers mingle facts with opinions, thereby obscuring the differences between them. This is of course unfair to the reader. Be sure always to distinguish your facts from your opinions in your writing so that your reader can clearly understand and judge your conclusions.

EXAMPLES   The new milling machines produce parts that are within 2 percent of specification. (This sentence is stated as a fact and can be verified by measurement.)

The milling machine operators believe the new models are safer than the old ones. (The word *believe* identifies the statement as an opinion—later statistics on the accident rates may or may not verify the opinion as a fact.)

The opinion of experts, or their professional judgment, in their area of expertise is often accepted as valid evidence in court. In writing, too, such testimony can help you convince your reader of the logic of your conclusions. However, be on guard against flawed testimonials. For example, a chemist may well make a statement about the safety of a product for use on humans, but the chemist's opinion would not be as valid as that of a medical researcher who has actually studied the effects of that product on humans. When you quote the opinion of an authority, be sure that his or her expertise is appropriate to your point. Make sure also that the opinion is a current one and that the expert is indeed highly respected.

LOADING

When you include an opinion in a statement and then reach conclusions that are based on that statement, you are *loading the argument.* Consider the following opening for a **memorandum**:

> EXAMPLE   I have several suggestions to improve the *poorly written* policy manual. First, we should change. . . .

By opening with the assumption that the manual is poorly written, the writer has loaded the statement to get readers to accept his arguments and conclusions. Yet, he has said nothing to establish *how* the manual is poorly written. In fact, it may be that only parts of the manual are poorly written. And if so, what are the exact problems? Be careful not to load arguments in your writing, as conclusions reached with loaded statements are weak and ultimately unconvincing.

In your writing you should always take pains to express your ideas logically. Logic not only gives writing **coherence** but also keeps it fair and honest.

long variants

Guard against inflating plain words beyond their normal value by adding extra **prefixes** or **suffixes**, a practice that creates long variants. The following is a list of some normal words followed by their inflated counterparts:

analysis	analyzation
certified	certificated
commercial	commercialistic
connect	interconnect
finish	finalize
orient	orientate
priority	prioritization (or prioritize)
use	utilize (see also **utilize**)
visit	visitation

(See also **gobbledygook** and **word choice**.)

loose/lose

Loose is an **adjective** meaning "not fastened" or "unrestrained."

EXAMPLE He found a *loose* wire.

Lose is a **verb** meaning "be deprived of" or "fail to win."

EXAMPLE I hope we do not *lose* the Acme account.

lowercase and uppercase letters

Lowercase letters are small letters, as distinguished from **capital letters** (known as *uppercase* letters). The terms were coined in the early history of printing when printers kept the small letters in a "case," or tray, below the tray where they kept the capital letters.

The use of all capital letters ("all caps") to emphasize important information should be confined to no more than three or four words at a time. Setting an entire passage in all caps makes it hard to read, because the shapes of capital letters are not as distinctive as are the shapes of lowercase letters or a combination of uppercase and lowercase letters. Uniformity of shape deprives readers of important visual clues about the identities of letters and thus slows them down. Instead, request **boldface** or *italic* for such passages, which makes the words stand out without affecting the unique shapes of the letters. (See also **capital letters** and **layout and design.**)

M

malapropisms

A malapropism is a word that sounds similar to the one intended but that is ludicrously wrong in the context.

> CHANGE The service technician cleaned the printer's *plankton*.
> TO The service technician cleaned the printer's *platen*.

Intentional malapropisms are sometimes used in humorous writing; unintentional malapropisms can embarrass a writer. (See also **antonyms** and **synonyms**.)

male

The term *male* is usually restricted to scientific, legal, or medical contexts (a *male* patient or suspect). Keep in mind that this term sounds cold and impersonal. The terms *boy, man,* and *gentleman* are acceptable substitutes in other contexts; however, be aware that these substitute words also have **connotations** involving age, dignity, and social position. (See also **female**.)

maps

Maps can be used to show specific geographic features (roads, mountains, rivers, and the like) or to show information according to geographic distribution (population, housing, manufacturing centers, and so forth). Bear these points in mind in creating and using maps:

1. Label the map clearly.
2. Assign the map a figure number if you are using enough **illustrations** to justify use of figure numbers. (See Figure 1.)
3. Make sure all boundaries within the map are clearly identified. Eliminate unnecessary boundaries.
4. Eliminate unnecessary information from your map (if population is important, do not include mountains, roads, rivers, and the like).
5. Include a scale of miles or feet to give your **reader** an indication of the map's proportions. (See Figure 1.)

Figure 12. Location of Service Areas of Three Utilities

Source: The U.S. Nuclear Regulatory Commission

Figure 1   Sample Map

6. Indicate which direction is north.
7. Show the features you want emphasized by using shading, dots, cross-hatching, or appropriate symbols when color reproduction cannot be used.
8. If you use only one color, remember that only three shades of a single color will show up satisfactorily.
9. Include a key or legend telling what the different colors, shadings, or symbols represent.
10. Place maps as close as possible to the portion of the text that refers to them.

mass nouns (see **nouns**)

maybe/may be

Maybe (one word) is an **adverb** meaning "perhaps."

EXAMPLE *Maybe* the legal staff can resolve this issue.

May be (two words) is a **verb** phrase.

EXAMPLE It *may be* necessary to ask for an outside specialist.

media/medium

Media is the plural of *medium* and should always be used with a plural verb.

EXAMPLES The *media are* a powerful influence in presidential elections. The most influential *medium is* television.

memorandums

The memorandum is the most frequently used form of communication among members of the same organization. Called memos for short, memorandums are routinely used for internal communications of all kinds—from short notes to small **reports** and **internal proposals**. Among their many uses, memos announce policies, confirm conversations, exchange information, delegate responsibilities, request information, transmit documents, instruct employees, and report results. As this partial list illustrates, memos provide a record of decisions made and virtually all actions taken in an organization. For this reason, clear and effective memos are essential to the success of any organization. The slogan "Put it in writing" reflects the importance of memos and the care with which they should be written. The result of a carelessly prepared memo is a garbled message that could baffle **readers**, cause a loss of time, produce costly errors, or irritate employees with an offensive **tone**.

Memos play a key role in the management of many organizations. Effective managers use memos to keep employees informed about company goals, motivate them to achieve these goals, and keep their morale high in the process. To achieve these ends, managers must be clear and accurate in their memos in order to gain respect and maintain credibility among their subordinates. Consider the unintended secondary messages the following notice conveys:

EXAMPLE It has been decided that the office will be open the day after
Thanksgiving.

The first part of the sentence ("It has been decided") not only sounds impersonal but also communicates an authoritarian management-versus-employee tone: *somebody* decides that *you* work. The passive voice also suggests that the decision maker does not want to say, "I have decided" and thus be identified. One solution, of course, is to remove the first part of the sentence.

EXAMPLE The office will open the day after Thanksgiving.

But even this statement sounds impersonal. A better solution would be to suggest both that the decision is good for the company and that employees should be privy to (if not part of) the decision-making process.

EXAMPLE Because we must meet the December 15 deadline to be eligible
for the government contract, the office will be open the day
after Thanksgiving.

This version is forthright and informative and helps the employees understand the decision.

MEMO PROTOCOL

In many organizations, memos follow both written and unwritten lines of protocol. Protocol is usually reflected in the order of the recipients and those who receive copies. The following description by a public-utility employee illustrates how rank and lines of authority can be revealed in both obvious and subtle ways:

> If I put my immediate supervisor's name AND the vice-president's name on the top (of the memo's heading "to"), it says I really report to both equally. If the supervisor's name is on the top and I send a copy to the vice-president, it means that, though structurally I report to the supervisor, I have direct access to the VP.
> —Carla Butenhoff, "Bad Writing Can Be Good Business," *ABCA Bulletin* 40 (June 1977): 12–13.

Such practices vary, so it is important to learn the etiquette of memos in your organization.

WRITING MEMOS

The writing process described at the beginning of this book will help you compose memos. It is particularly important to **outline** a memo, even if that means simply jotting down the points to be covered and then ranking them in a logical **method of development**. With careful preparation, memos can be both concise and adequately developed. Adequate development is crucial to ensure clarity.

> CHANGE   Be more careful on the loading dock.
>   TO   To prevent accidents, follow these procedures:
>   1. Check . . .
>   2. Load only . . .
>   3. Replace . . .

Although the original version is concise, it is not as clear and specific as the revision. Don't assume your reader will know what you mean. State what you mean explicitly: readers aren't always careful, and some will provide their own interpretation if you are not as specific as possible.

Memos should ordinarily deal with only one subject; if you need to cover two subjects, you may wish to write two memos, since multi-subject memos are difficult to file.

MEMO OPENINGS

Although methods of development may vary in memos, a memo should normally begin with a statement of its main idea. Even if your **opening** will review the background of a problem, begin with the main point.

> EXAMPLE   Because of our inability to serve our present and future clients
>   as efficiently as in the past, I recommend we hire an addi-
>   tional claims representative and a part-time receptionist.
>   (main idea) Last year we did not hire new staff because of
>   the freeze on hiring. . . . (background opening)

As with other writing, if your reader is not familiar with the subject or the background of a problem, provide an introductory background paragraph. A brief background is especially important in memos that serve as records that can provide crucial information months (or even years) later. Generally, longer memos or those dealing with complex subjects benefit most from developed **introduc-**

tions. However, even when you are writing a short memo and the recipient is familiar with the situation, you need to remind your reader of the context. Readers have so much crossing their desks that they need a quick orientation. (Words that provide context are shown below in *italics*.)

EXAMPLES *As we decided after yesterday's meeting,* we need to set new guidelines for. . .
As Jane recommended, I reviewed the office reorganization plan. I like most of the features; however, the location of the reception- ist and word processor. . .

The only exceptions to stating the main point first are (1) when the reader is likely to be highly skeptical and (2) when you are disagree- ing with persons in positions of higher authority. In such cases, a more persuasive tactic is to state the problem first (rather than *your* solution) and then present the specific points that will support your final recommendation. (See also **persuasion**.)

LISTS AND HEADINGS

It is often a good idea to use **lists** to emphasize your points in a memo. If you are trying to convince a skeptical reader, a list of your points—from most to least persuasive—will stand out rather than being lost in a lengthy paragraph. Be careful, however, not to overuse lists. A memo that consists almost entirely of lists is difficult for readers to understand because they are forced to connect the sepa- rate items for themselves and mentally provide coherence. Lists lose their impact when they are overused.

Another useful device, particularly in long memos, is **headings**. Headings have a number of advantages:

1. They divide material into manageable segments.
2. They call attention to main topics.
3. They signal a shift in topic.

Headings also function like the parts of a **formal report** in that readers interested only in one section of a memo can easily identify that section.

WRITING STYLE

Like all **correspondence**, the level of formality in memos depends entirely on your reader and **objective**. For example, is your reader a peer, superior, or subordinate? A memo to an associate who is of equal rank and is a friend is likely to be informal and personal. However, a memo written as an internal proposal to several readers or a memo to someone two or three levels higher in your organization is likely to use the more formal **style** of a report. Consider the following original and revised versions of a subordinate's statement to a superior:

CHANGE   I can't agree with your plan because I think it poses logistical problems. (informal, personal, and forceful)

TO   The logistics of moving the department may pose serious problems. (formal, impersonal, and cautious)

A memo giving instructions to a subordinate will also be relatively formal and impersonal, but more direct—unless you are trying to reassure or praise. Remember, however, if you become too impersonal and formal and use many fancy words, you will create **affectation**. Managers who sound stuffy are assumed to *be* stuffy. They may also be regarded as rigid, lacking a nimble mind capable of moving an organization ahead. When writing to subordinates, also remember that managing does not mean ordering. An officious tone will prevent a memo from being an effective management tool.

FORMAT AND PARTS

Memo format and customs vary greatly from organization to organization. The following are some of the styles used:

preprinted half sheets (8½" × 5½")
message-and-reply forms ("speed messages")
regular 8½" × 11" letter stationery
special 8½" × 11" forms with company name or logo

Although there is no single, standard form, Figure 1 shows a typical memorandum format. When memos exceed one page, use a second-page heading like the one shown in **correspondence**. Some firms also print short-purpose statements on the side or bottom of memos, with space for the writer to make a check mark.

EXAMPLES   ☐ For your information
☐ For your action
☐ For your reply

You can also use this quick-response system for memos sent to numerous readers whose responses you need to tabulate.

PROFESSIONAL PUBLISHING SERVICES
MEMORANDUM

DATE: April 14, 19--

TO: Hazel Smith, Publications Manager

FROM: Herbert Kaufman *HK*

SUBJECT: Schedule for Acme Electronics Brochure

Acme Electronics has asked us to prepare a comprehensive brochure
for their Milwaukee office by August 9, 19--.

We have worked with electronic firms in the past, so this job
should be relatively easy. My guess is that it will take nearly
two months. Ted Harris has requested time and cost estimates.
Fred Moore in accounting will prepare the cost estimates, and I
would like you to prepare a schedule for the estimated time.

Additional Personnel
In preparing the schedule, check the following:

      1.   Production schedule for all staff writers.
      2.   Available free-lance writers.
      3.   Dependable graphic designers.

Ordinarily, we would not need to depend on outside personnel; however,
since our bid for the Wall Street Journal special project is still
under consideration, we could be pressed in June and July. We have
to keep in mind staff vacations that have already been approved.

Time Estimates
Please give me time estimates by April 19. A successful job done on
time will give us a good chance to obtain the contract to do Acme's
publications for their annual stockholders' meeting this fall.

I know your staff can do the job.

lcs
Copies: Ted Harris, Senior Vice-President
            Fred Moore, Accounting Manager

Figure 1   Typical Memo Format

EXAMPLE I can meet at 1 p.m. ☐
2 p.m. ☐
3 p.m. ☐

Regardless of the parts included, perhaps the one requiring the most careful preparation is the subject line, or the title of a memo. Subject lines function much like the titles of reports, aiding in filing and later retrieval. Subject lines are also an important orientation when the reader first sees the memo. Therefore, it is important to make them accurate. That is, the memo should deal only with the single subject announced in the subject line, which also should be complete.

CHANGE Subject: Tuition Reimbursement
TO Subject: Tuition Reimbursement for Time Management Seminar

Remember, too, that subject lines should not substitute for an opening that provides a context for the message.

Capitalize all major words in the title of a subject line. Do not capitalize an **article**, **conjunction**, or **preposition** of fewer than four letters unless it is the first or last word.

The final step is signing or initialing a memo, which lets the reader know that you approve of its contents, especially if you did not type it. Where you sign or initial the memo depends on the practice of your organization: Some writers sign at the end, and others sign their initials next to their typed name. For further secretarial and typing details, we recommend *The Gregg Reference Manual* by William A. Sabin (McGraw).

metaphor

Metaphor is a figure of speech that points out similarities between two things by referring to one of them as being the other. Metaphor states that the thing being described *is* the thing to which it is being compared.

EXAMPLE *The building site was a beehive,* with iron workers still at work on the tenth floor, plumbers installing fixtures on the floors just beneath them, electricians busy on the middle floors, and carpenters putting the finishing touches on the first floor.

The use of metaphor often helps clarify complex theories or objects. For example, the life-sustaining tube connecting space-walking astronauts to their oxygen supply in the spacecraft is called an *umbilical cord.* The person who first drew this **comparison** knew that such a life support tube was new and unfamiliar, so to make its function immediately apparent he used a metaphor that compared it to something with which people were already familiar. A similar purpose was served when the term *window* was used to describe the abstract concept of the point at which a spacecraft reenters the earth's atmosphere. Here the strange and faraway was made near and familiar by the metaphorical use of a term familiar to everyone. Both of these expressions have gained widespread use because they helped clarify new and unfamiliar concepts.

A word of caution: Some writers sometimes mix metaphors, which usually results in an illogical statement.

EXAMPLE   Billingham's proposal *backfired,* and now she is *in hot water.*

This example makes an incongruous statement because a backfiring automobile does not land someone in hot water. (See also **figures of speech**.)

methods of development

One of the most important elements in any writing is its method of development. After you have completed your **research**, but before beginning your **outline**, ask yourself how you can most effectively "unfold" your **topic** for your **reader**. An appropriate method of development will make it easy for your reader to understand your topic and will move the topic smoothly and logically from an **introduction** (or **opening**) to a **conclusion**. There are several common methods of development, each best suited to particular purposes.

If you are writing a set of **instructions**, for example, you know that your readers need the instructions in the order that will enable them to perform some task. Therefore, you should use a **sequential method of development**. If you wished to emphasize the time element of a sequence, however, you could follow a **chronological method of development**.

If writing about a new topic that is in many ways similar to another, more familiar topic, it is sometimes useful to develop the new topic by comparing it to the old one—thereby enabling your readers to make certain broad assumptions about the new topic, based on their understanding of the familiar topic. By doing so, you are using a **comparison method of development**.

When describing a mechanical device, you may divide it into its component parts and explain each part's function as well as how all the parts work together. In this case, you are using a **division and classification method of development**. Or you may use a **spatial method of development** to describe the physical appearance of the device from top to bottom, from inside to outside, from front to back, and so on.

If you are writing a **report** for a government agency explaining an airplane crash, you might begin with the crash and trace backwards to its cause, or you could begin with the cause of the crash (for example, a structural defect) and show the sequence of events that led to the crash. Either way is the **cause-and-effect method of development**. You can also use this approach to develop a report dealing with the solution to a problem, beginning with the problem and moving to the solution, or vice versa.

If you are writing about the software for a new computer system, you might begin with a general statement of the function of the total software package, then explain the functions of the larger routines within the software package, and finally deal with the functions of the various subroutines within the larger routines. You would be using a **general-to-specific method of development**. (In another situation, you might use the **specific-to-general method of development**.)

To explain the functions of the departments in a company, you could present them in a sequence that reflects their importance within the company: the executive department first and the custodial department last, with all other departments (sales, engineering, accounting, and so on) arranged in the relative order of importance they are given in that company. You would be using the **decreasing-order-of-importance method of development**. (In another situation, you might use the **increasing-order-of-importance method of development**.)

Methods of development often overlap, of course. Rarely does a writer rely on only one method of development in a written work. The important thing is to select one primary method of development and then to base your outline on it. For example, in describing the organization of a company, you would actually use elements from three methods of development: you would *divide* the larger

topic (the company) into departments, present the departments *sequentially,* and arrange the departments by their *order of importance* within the company.

For example, assume that you are writing an article about a particular company. You could approach such a topic any number of ways. You could *compare* the company with its major competitor, touching upon such things as each one's historical development, market share, number of employees, revenue produced per employee, gross annual sales, net income, return on investment, research and development expenditures, debt as a percentage of assets, and relative financial condition. Or you could *divide,* or break down the company by departments, and discuss each in turn by decreasing order of importance: the executive department, engineering, sales, production, accounting, data processing, inventory control, advertising, order processing. Or in order to discuss and illustrate the company's operations, you could follow a purchase order through its entire life cycle, from the time an advertisement is placed in a trade journal, to the actual product sale, to the receipt of the order at the factory, to the product being pulled from stock and shipped to the customer, to the invoice being received by the accounting department and the bill being sent to the customer, to the payment being received from the customer . . . and finally to the account being closed.

minutes of meetings

Organizations and committees keep official records of their meetings; such records are known as *minutes.* If you attend many business-related meetings, you may be asked to serve as recording secretary and write and distribute the minutes of a meeting. At each meeting, the minutes of the previous meeting are usually read aloud if printed copies of the minutes were not distributed to the members beforehand; the group then votes to accept the minutes as prepared or to revise or clarify specific items. The bylaws or **policies and procedures** of your organization may specify what must be included in your minutes of meetings. As a general guide, *Robert's Rules of Order* recommends that the minutes of meetings include the following:

1. Name of the group or committee holding the meeting.
2. Place, time, and date of the meeting.

3. Kind of meeting (a regular meeting or a special meeting called to discuss a specific subject or problem).
4. Number of members present and, for committees or boards of ten or fewer members, their names.
5. A statement that the chairperson and the secretary were present, or the names of any substitutes.
6. A statement that the minutes of the previous meeting were approved, revised, or not read.
7. A list of any reports that were read and approved.
8. All the main motions that were made, with statements as to whether they were carried, defeated, or tabled (vote postponed) and the names of those who made and seconded the motions (motions that were withdrawn are not mentioned).
9. A full description of resolutions that were adopted and a simple statement of any that were rejected.
10. A record of all ballots with the number of votes cast for and against.
11. The time that the meeting was adjourned (officially ended) and the place, time, and date of the next meeting.
12. The recording secretary's signature and typed name and, if desired, the signature of the chairperson.

Except for recording motions, which must be transcribed word for word, summarize what occurs and paraphrase discussions.

Since minutes are often used to settle disputes, they must be accurate, complete, and clear. When approved, minutes of meetings are official and can be used as evidence in legal proceedings.

Keep your minutes brief and to the point. Give complete information on each topic, but do not ramble—consider the topic and go on to the next one. Following a set **format** will help you keep the minutes concise. You might, for example, use the heading *TOPIC*, followed by the subheadings *Discussion* and *Action Taken,* for each major point discussed.

Avoid abstractions and generalities; always be specific. If you are referring to a nursing station on the second floor of a hospital, write "the nursing station on the second floor" or "the second-floor nursing station," not just "the second floor."

Be especially specific when referring to people. Avoid using titles (the chief of the Records Department) in favor of names and titles (Ms. Florence Johnson, head of the Records Department). And be consistent in the way you refer to people. Do not call one person *Mr.*

Minutes of the Regular Meeting of the Credentials
Committee

DATE: April 18, 19--

PRESENT: M. Valden (Chairperson), R. Baron,
M. Frank, J. Guern, L. Kingson,
L. Kinslow (Secretary), S. Perry,
B. Roman, J. Sorder, F. Sugihana

Dr. Mary Valden called the meeting to order at
8:40 p.m. The minutes of the previous meeting were
unanimously approved, with the following correction: the name of the secretary of the Department
of Medicine is to be changed from Dr. Juanita
Alvarez to Dr. Barbara Golden.

Old Business

None.

New Business

The request by Dr. Henry Russell for staff
privileges in the Department of Medicine was discussed. Dr. James Guern made a motion that
Dr. Russell be granted staff privileges.
Dr. Martin Frank seconded the motion, which passed
unanimously.
    Similar requests by Dr. Ernest Hiram and
Dr. Helen Redlands were discussed. Dr. Fred
Sugihana made a motion that both physicians be
granted all staff privileges except respiratory-
care privileges because the two doctors had not
had a sufficient number of respiratory cases.
Dr. Steven Perry seconded the motion, which was
passed unanimously.
    Dr. John Sorder and Dr. Barry Roman asked
for a clarification of general duties for active
staff members with respiratory-care privileges.
Dr. Richard Baron stated that he would present a
clarification at the next scheduled staff meeting
on May 15.
    Dr. Baron asked for a volunteer to fill the
existing vacancy for Emergency Room duty.
Dr. Guern volunteered. He and Dr. Baron will
arrange a duty schedule.
    There being no further business, the meeting
was adjourned at 9:15 p.m. The next regular
meeting is scheduled for May 15, at 8:40 p.m.

Respectfully submitted,

Ledie Kinslow   *Mary Valden M.D.*

Leslie Kinslow   Mary Valden, M.D.
Medical Staff Secretary   Chairperson

Figure 1   Sample of a Set of Minutes

Jarrel and another *Janet* Wilson. It may be unintentional, but a lack of consistency in titles or names may reveal a deference to one person at the expense of another. Avoid **adjectives** and **adverbs** that suggest either good or bad qualities, as in "Mr. Sturgess's *capable* assistant read the *extremely comprehensive* report to the subcommittee." Minutes should always be objective and impartial.

If a member of the committee is to follow up on something and report back to the committee at its next meeting, state clearly the person's name and the responsibility he or she has accepted.

When assigned to take the minutes at a meeting, be prepared. Bring more than one pen and plenty of paper. If convenient, you may bring a tape recorder as a backup to your notes. Have ready the minutes of the previous meeting and any other material that you may need. If you do not know shorthand, take notes during the meeting and then expand them with the appropriate details immediately after the meeting. Remember that minutes are primarily a record of specific actions taken. (See also **note taking**.)

Figure 1 is a sample set of minutes.

misplaced modifiers

A **modifier** is misplaced when it modifies, or appears to modify, the wrong word or phrase. It differs from a **dangling modifier** in that a dangling modifier cannot *logically* modify any word in the sentence because its intended referent is missing. The best general rule for avoiding misplaced modifiers is to place modifiers as close as possible to the words they are intended to modify. A misplaced modifier can be a word, a **phrase**, or a **clause**.

MISPLACED WORDS

Adverbs are especially likely to be misplaced because they can appear in several positions within a sentence.

> EXAMPLES   We *almost* lost all of the parts.
> We lost *almost* all of the parts.

The first sentence means that all of the parts were *almost* lost (but they were not), and the second sentence means that a majority of the parts (*almost* all) were in fact lost. Possible confusion in sentences of this type can be avoided by placing the adverb immediately before the word it is intended to modify.

> CHANGE All navigators are *not* talented in mathematics. (The implication is that *no* navigator is talented in mathematics.)
> TO *Not* all navigators are talented in mathematics.

MISPLACED PHRASES

To avoid confusion, place phrases near the words they modify. Note the two meanings possible when the phrase is shifted in the following sentences:

> EXAMPLES The equipment *without the accessories* sold the best. (Different types of equipment were available, some with and some without accessories.)
> The equipment sold the best *without the accessories*. (One *type* of equipment was available, and the accessories were optional.)

MISPLACED CLAUSES

To avoid confusion, clauses should be placed as close as possible to the words they modify.

> CHANGE We sent the brochure to four local firms *that had three-color illustrations*.
> TO We sent the brochure *that had three-color illustrations* to four local firms.

SQUINTING MODIFIERS

A modifier "squints" when it can be interpreted as modifying either of two sentence elements simultaneously, so that the reader is confused about which is intended.

> EXAMPLE We agreed *on the next day* to make the adjustments.

The meaning of the preceding example is unclear; it could have either of the following two senses:

> EXAMPLES We agreed to *make the adjustments on the next day.*
> *On the next day we agreed* to make the adjustments.

A squinting modifier can sometimes be corrected simply by changing its position, but often it is better to recast the sentence:

EXAMPLES We agreed that *on the next day* we would make the adjustments.
(The adjustments were to be made on the next day.)
On the next day we agreed that we would make the adjustments.
(The agreement was made on the next day.)

(See also **dangling modifiers.**)

mixed constructions

A mixed construction occurs when a sentence contains grammatical forms that are improperly combined. These constructions are improper because the grammatical forms are inconsistent with one another. The most common types of mixed constructions result from the following causes:

TENSE

CHANGE The pilot *lowered* the landing gear and *is approaching* the runway. (shift from past to present tense)
TO The pilot *lowered* the landing gear and *approached* the runway.
OR The pilot *has lowered* the landing gear and *is approaching* the runway.

PERSON

CHANGE The *administrator* should take care in choosing *your* equipment. (shift from third to second person)
TO The *administrator* should take care in choosing *the* equipment.

NUMBER

CHANGE My *car,* though not as fast as the others, *operate* on regular gasoline. (singular subject with plural verb form)
TO My *car,* though not as fast as the others, *operates* on regular gasoline.

VOICE

CHANGE *I will check* your report, and then *it will be returned* to you. (shift from active to passive voice)
TO *I will check* your report, and then *I will return* it to you.

(See also **parallel structure** and **agreement.**)

modifiers

Modifiers are words, **phrases**, or **clauses** that expand, limit, or make more precise the meaning of other elements in a sentence. Although we can create sentences without modifiers, we often need the detail and clarification they provide.

EXAMPLES   Production decreased. (without modifiers)
Automobile production decreased *rapidly*. (with modifiers)

Most modifiers function as **adjectives** or **adverbs**. An adjective makes the meaning of a **noun** or **pronoun** more precise by pointing out one of its qualities or by imposing boundaries on it.

EXAMPLES   *ten* automobiles   *this* crane
an *educated* person   *loud* machinery

An adverb modifies an adjective, another adverb, a **verb**, or an entire clause.

EXAMPLES   Under test conditions, the brake pad showed *much* less wear than it did under actual conditions. (modifying the adjective *less*)
The wear was *very* much less than under actual conditions. (modifying another adverb, *much*)
The recording had hit the surface of the disc *hard*. (modifying the verb *hit*)
Surprisingly, the machine failed even after all the tests that it had passed. (modifying a clause)

Adverbs become **intensifiers** when they increase the impact of adjectives (*very* fine, *too* high) or adverbs (*rather* quickly, *very* slowly). As a rule, be cautious in using intensifiers; their overuse can lead to exaggeration and hence to inaccuracies. (See also **dangling modifiers** and **misplaced modifiers**.)

mood

The grammatical term *mood* refers to the **verb** functions—and sometimes form changes—that indicate whether the verb is intended to (1) make a statement or ask a question (indicative mood), (2) give a command (imperative mood), or (3) express a hypothetical possibility (subjunctive mood).

The indicative mood refers to an action or a state that is conceived as fact.

EXAMPLES *Was* the president there?
The president *was* there.

The imperative mood expresses a command, suggestion, request, or entreaty. In the imperative mood, the implied subject "you" is not expressed.

EXAMPLES *Close* the sale today.
Please *keep* this confidential.

The subjunctive mood expresses something that is contrary to fact, that is conditional, hypothetical, or purely imaginative; it can also express a wish, a doubt, or a possibility. The subjunctive mood may change the form of the verb, but the verb *be* is the only one in English that preserves many such distinctions.

EXAMPLES The senior partner insisted that he *be* in charge of the project.
If we *were* to close the sale today, we would meet our monthly quota.
If I *were* you, I would postpone the trip.

Form change for the subjunctive is rare in most verbs other than *be*. Instead, we use **helping verbs** to show the subjunctive function. Be careful, however, not to use unnecessary verbs.

CHANGE If I *would have known* that you were here, I would have come earlier.
TO If I *had known* that you were here, I would have come earlier.
OR *Had I known* that you were here, I would have come earlier.

The advantage of the subjunctive mood is that it enables us to express clearly whether or not we consider a condition contrary to fact. If so, we use the subjunctive; if not, we use the indicative.

EXAMPLES If I *were* president of the firm, I would change several personnel policies. (subjunctive)
Although I *am* president of the firm, I don't feel that I control every aspect of its policies. (indicative)

Be careful not to shift from one to another within a sentence; to do so makes the sentence not only ungrammatical but unbalanced as well.

CHANGE   *Have* the customer sign the contract (imperative); then you *can*
          collect the deposit. (indicative)
     TO   *Have* the customer sign the contract (imperative); then *collect*
          the deposit. (imperative)

Ms./Miss/Mrs.

Ms. is a convenient form of addressing a woman, regardless of her
marital status. Some women indicate a preference for *Miss* or *Mrs.*,
however, and such a preference should be honored. An academic or
professional title (*Doctor, Professor, Captain*) should take preference
over *Ms., Miss,* or *Mrs.* (See also **correspondence**.)

MS/MSS

MS (or ms) is the **abbreviation** for *manuscript.* The plural form is MSS
(or mss). Do not use this abbreviation (or any abbreviation) unless
you are certain that you **reader** is familiar with it.

mutual/in common

When two or more persons (or things) have something in common,
they share it or possess it jointly.

EXAMPLES   What we have *in common* is our desire to make the company
            profitable.
            The fore and aft guidance assemblies have a *common* power
            source.

Mutual may also mean "shared" (as in *mutual* friends), but it usually
implies something given and received reciprocally and is used with
reference to only two persons or parties.

EXAMPLES   Smith mistrusts Jones, and I am afraid the mistrust is *mutual.*
            (Jones also mistrusts Smith.)
            Both business and government consider the problem to be of
            mutual concern.

N

narration

Narration is the presentation of a series of events in a prescribed (usually chronological) sequence. Much narrative writing explains how something happened: an insurance investigator detailing the cause of a fire in a warehouse, a site visit for a proposed new plant, the events and decisions in an important meeting. (A scenario is a form of narrative that raises the question, "What if?" In it, the writer speculates about what could or is likely to happen under certain circumstances.)

Effective narration rests on two key writing techniques: the careful, accurate sequencing of events and a consistent **point of view** on the part of the narrator. Narrative sequence and essential shifts in the sequence are signaled in three ways: chronology (clock and calendar time), transitional words pertaining to time (*before, after, next, first, while, then*), and verb tenses that indicate whether something has happened (past **tense**) or is under way (present tense). The point of view indicates the writer's relation to the information being narrated as reflected in the use of **person**. Narration usually expresses either a first- or third-person point of view. First-person narration indicates that the writer is a participant ("this happened to me"), and third-person narration indicates that the writer is writing about what happened to someone or something else ("this happened to her, to them, or to it").

The narrative shown in Figure 1 describes the financial climate for investors over the course of one year. The chronology is carefully specified throughout the narrative by month or by quarter, as the events require. The narrator uses the first person throughout ("we said"), as is appropriate for a newsletter whose function is to give advice. The chronology of past events ("In September we said . . .") shifts to the present ("Stocks and bonds are behaving more like commodity markets have in the past") as the narrative shifts from past to current market performance.

Once a narrative is under way, it should not be interrupted by lengthy explanations or analyses. Explain only what is necessary for readers to follow the events.

A REVIEW OF 19--

In April, we wrote, "As the reality of the crunch unfolds, the market is apt to react emotionally, with violent selling waves followed by equally dramatic periods of short covering. Investors should take advantage of the current market upswing to liquidate low quality stocks and bonds. Market downdrafts should be used to purchase securities of the highest quality."

In May, we introduced the "Watchlist," a group of companies where both annual and quarterly financial ratios are experiencing some deterioration in their balance sheet and financial ratios.

In June, we introduced the "Buy 90% T-bills plus 10% calls" as a defensive strategy preferable to holding equities. We also recommended:

1. getting fully overwritten
2. buy/writing on high quality securities
3. buying puts aggressively

Chronological development

In July, we said, "This stop/go monetary policy works to increase the inherent volatility and risk in equity and debt markets alike. Therefore, the most appropriate view seems to be that of the informed, negatively biased, but agile contrarian who is willing to don a bullish cap when bearish market forces seem spent." That month we also introduced the "Brignoli Method" of dynamic vs. static method of option over writing.

In September, we said, "While none of us expected the kind of powerful rally we have had in mid-August, . . . it's time to begin looking the other way. While the market still shows few signs of a near-term top, some defensive posturing is in order." We then focused on synthetic puts (sell stock/buy calls deep in the money as a way to protect recent gains) in order to participate in any further upside, and yet limit downside risk.

We would have done better being bullish and abandoning all caution. By being cautious, we participated in a lot of the upside with more limited downside risk, paying some insurance along the way.

Nevertheless, we are uncomfortable riding this kind of roller coaster without seat belts or safety nets. Perhaps the Fed's decision to bail the system out means there is no other stance to take but a bullish one. Yet, it's hard to gauge just how long this reprieve will last.

Current assessment

Stocks and bonds are behaving more like commodity markets have in the past. Typically, commodity prices move between enormous extremes both up and down. What's more, each extreme tends to have little connection to fundamental reality or value. Indeed, psychology tends to be the driving force behind such market moves.

Figure 1   Example of Narration (*Source:* Joseph Bench and Werner Mendel, *Asset Allocation & Strategy Letter,* Shearson/American Express [Winter 1982] 1–3.)

For further information about sequencing narratives, see **sequential** and **chronological methods of development**. Other writing strategies, like **process explanation** and **instructions**, also help sequence information accurately.

nature

Nature, used to mean "kind" or "sort," can—like those words—often be vague. Avoid the word in your writing. Say exactly what you mean.

CHANGE The space program, by its very *nature*, is costly.
TO Because of the need for sophisticated equipment and highly skilled personnel, the space program is costly.

CHANGE The *nature* of the contract caused the problem.
TO The forfeiture clause in the contract caused the problem.

needless to say

Although the **phrase** *needless to say* sometimes occurs in speech and writing, it is redundant because it always precedes a remark that is stated despite the inference that nothing further need be said.

CHANGE *Needless to say*, departmental cutbacks have meant decreased efficiency.
TO Departmental cutbacks have meant decreased efficiency.
OR Understandably, departmental cutbacks have meant decreased efficiency.

neo-

The **prefix** *neo-* is derived from a Greek word meaning "new." It is hyphenated when used with a **proper noun**, and it may be hyphenated when used with a **noun** beginning with the vowel *o*.

EXAMPLES neo-Fascism, neo-Darwinism, neo-orthodoxy
neonatal, neoplasm, neologism

new words

New words (also called neologisms) continually find their way into the language from a variety of sources. Some come from other languages.

EXAMPLES   discotheque (French), skiing (Norwegian), whiskey (Gaelic)

Some come from technology.

EXAMPLES   software, vinyl, nylon

Some come from scientific research.

EXAMPLES   berkelium, transistor

Some come from brand or trade names.

EXAMPLES   Jello, Teflon, Kleenex

Some, called **blend words**, are formed by combining existing words.

EXAMPLE   motor + hotel = motel

Some come from **acronyms**.

EXAMPLES   scuba, radar, laser

Business and technology are responsible for many new words. Some are necessary and unavoidable; however, it is best to avoid creating a new word if an existing word will do. If you do use what you believe to be a new word or expression, be sure to define it the first time you use it; otherwise, your **reader** is certain to be confused. (See also **long variants** and **vogue words**.)

newsletter articles

A newsletter is a company publication or an employee publication that is produced by the employer. Its primary purpose is to keep employees informed about the company and its operations and policies. Many different types of newsletters are found in business and industry—from the gossip sheet to the more sophisticated instruments of company policy that increase the employee's understanding of the company, its purpose, and the business in which it is engaged. If your company publishes a newsletter of the latter type, you may be asked to contribute an article on a subject that you are especially qualified to write about. The editor may offer some general advice but can give you little more help until you submit a draft.

Before beginning to write, consider the traditional *who, what, where, when,* and *why* of journalism (who did it? what was done? where was it done? when was it done? and why was it done?)—and then add *how*, since the *how* of your subject may be of as much interest to your fellow employees as any of the five *w*'s.

Before going any further, determine whether there is an official company policy or position on your subject. If so, adhere to it as you prepare your article. If there is no company policy on your subject, determine as nearly as you can what management's attitude is toward your subject.

Gather several fairly recent issues of your company newsletter, and study the **style** and **tone** of the writing and the approach the company has taken to various kinds of subjects in past issues. Try to emulate these as you work on your own article. Ask yourself the following questions about your subject: What is its significance to the company? What is its significance to employees? The answers to these questions should help you establish the style, tone, and approach for your article. These answers should also heavily influence the **conclusion** you write for your article.

Research for a newsletter article frequently consists of **interviewing**. Interview everyone concerned with your subject. Get all available information and all points of view. (Be sure to give maximum credit to the maximum number of people.)

Writing a newsletter article requires a little more imagination than does writing **reports**. With a newsletter, you do not have a captive audience; therefore, you may want to provide four helpful ingredients to ensure a successful article: (1) an intriguing **title** to catch the **readers'** attention (a **rhetorical question** is often effective); (2) eye-catching **photographs** or **illustrations** that entice them to read your lead **paragraph** to see what the subject is really about; (3) a lead, or first paragraph, that is designed to encourage further reading (this paragraph generally makes the **transition** from the **title** to the down-to-earth treatment of the subject); and (4) a well-developed presentation of your subject to hold the readers' interest all the way to the conclusion.

Your **conclusion** should emphasize the significance of your subject to your company and its employees. Because of its strategic location to achieve **emphasis**, your conclusion should include the thoughts that you want your readers to retain about your subject.

In preparing your newsletter article you will find it helpful to refer to the Checklist of the Writing Process and to follow the steps listed there.

The newsletter article presented in Figure 1 is typical.

TELECOMMUNICATIONS MOVES INTO A NEW DIMENSION

By Sandy Balzo

A seven-story building has been shrunk down into a 3" x 5" rectangle.

Sounds like the work of a supervillain in a comic strip, doesn't it? But this is precisely what telecommunications technology has been able to accomplish over the last few years.

The seven-story building we're talking about is a telephone switching office, filled with equipment to route calls to phones all over the world. The 3" x 5" rectangle is a silicon chip, a chip capable of doing the same work as that of seven floors of equipment.

Telecommunications--telephone communications--has made great strides over the last several years through the use of computer technology. First Wisconsin employees will have a chance to see just how far that technology has taken us when they arrive at the First Wisconsin Center the Tuesday after Memorial Day to find the Center's new Dimension PBX system in place. . . .

The Center has been on Wisconsin Telephone's Centrex system since 1973. Datapoint, a microcomputer system, was added in early 1980. Datapoint eliminated the 13 access codes formerly used for long distance calls, consolidating them into one: 8--area code--seven-digit number. Because of this single code, information on outgoing calls could be recorded and published as summary reports for department heads to use for cost control.

Detailed call information, including the number called and the date, time, and length of call, is also kept; however, this information is not made available unless it is specifically requested by a department head. Even when requested, the information is discussed only with the person who made the calls. This reporting feature also will be part of the Dimension system. . . .

Telecommunications, headed by John Dunlap, is responsible for all voice communications at First Wisconsin. . . . "Dimension offers almost incredible flexibility," says Dunlap. "Over 120 features are available on the system. Granted, many of these features are not applicable to our business right now, but as we change and grow, Dimension will grow with us.

"Right from the beginning, we will be able to utilize a number of features not available in Centrex. For example, automatic callback will allow a caller to be 'rung back' when a busy extension becomes free, so the caller doesn't have to continue trying to get through to a busy department. If the number you are calling is busy, you will dial a code and hang up. When the party you are calling finishes the call and replaces the receiver, your phone will ring. When you pick up your phone, the other line will be rung back, completing the call.

Figure 1   Manuscript of a Newsletter Article

"We'll also be able to forward our calls to another phone just by dialing the appropriate code, or place a conference call with up to six people through an attendant. . . .

"With Centrex," explains Dunlap, "all calls--including interoffice calls--must go through Wisconsin Telephone's central switching office. If I was calling someone on the other side of the floor, for example, the call would originate from my phone, travel out of the Center to the switching office, then back to the Center and finally arrive at the telephone just 100 feet away from me. This wastes time and money. With Dimension, we will have our own switching equipment right here in the Center.

"Another advantage is that we will be able to make any moves or changes in service at a terminal right here in Telecommunications. For example, when someone changes desks now, we have to call Wisconsin Telephone to make the change. With Dimension we will be able to sit down at a terminal and make the change in the time it takes for the employee to walk from one desk to the other. . . .

"All of the equipment we need will fit into one 30' x 30' room," says Dunlap. "Ten years ago, we would have needed the majority of the Clybourn level just to contain the switching equipment."

The Telecommunications department is completing a detailed evaluation of each department to determine the types of equipment and features needed in each area. To facilitate the cut-over to Dimension, a moratorium (or freeze) has been placed on all telephone moves and changes from April 1 through July.

Core groups of employees will receive intensive training on Dimension during March and April. They, in turn, will train the people in their areas.

When Employees go home the evening of Friday, May 27, Centrex will still be in operation. When they return on the Tuesday after Memorial Day, they will find Dimension in place and working.

Communication counselors in each area will be available to help with any question or problems during the shakedown period. Also, detailed instruction cards will be provided with each telephone, along with a new interoffice telephone directory detailing dialing instructions and special features.

"It's important," says Dunlap, "that everyone be thoroughly familiar with the new system. Dimension can do much more for us than Centrex did, but we have to use its features effectively--if we don't, it's just another telephone."

Figure 1   Manuscript of a Newsletter Article (continued) (*Source:* Reprinted with permission from the Spring 1986 issue of *The First Account,* an employee publication of the First National Bank of Milwaukee.)

news releases

Companies and organizations write news releases, or press releases, to announce to the public new products or services, special events (such as plant openings, company anniversaries, or union contracts), management changes, or sponsorship of social-action or cultural programs. The purpose of the news release to both to inform the public about the company and its products and to create a favorable company image. Even the announcement of an unfavorable event, such as a strike, should try to present the company in a good light. Large corporations and institutions usually have their own public relations staffs or use outside agencies. However, a small company without a public relations staff or an agency will often want to give information to the public and will need someone to write news releases. In case you are called upon to write one, the following guidelines may prove useful.

The news release may be clear and concise and should be written with particular attention to the five *w's: who, what, where, when,* and *why.* Write the release so that all critical information is in the first **paragraph**, information of the next level of importance is in the second paragraph, and so on. Editors must make your release fit the space they have available; if they must cut your release, they will delete the last paragraph first, and then the next to last, and so on. Be sure about the accuracy of your facts, and be careful to define any technical terms. Type the release, double-spaced, on company letterhead. Leave the top third of the page blank for editors to mark any necessary heads on the copy. Give the name and phone number of someone who can give further information. Begin with the place and date of the announcement, as is shown in the following sample. If the release is longer than one page, type *More* at the bottom of all pages (except the last). Type *-30-* or *End* at the bottom of the last page. Releases are usually sent to local newspapers, television and radio stations, and other special groups, such as trade publications or professional associations. Send the release to a specific person whenever possible. Otherwise, try to address the news release to a particular editor—for example, to the business editor or the education editor. Figure 1 is a typical news release.

For detailed information in writing news releases, see Doug Newsome and Bob Carrell, *Public Relations Writing: Form and Style* 3rd ed. (Belmont, CA: Wadsworth, 1991).

Bentley Plastic's
3535 Michigan Avenue
Chicago, IL 60653

FOR IMMEDIATE RELEASE

For More Information Call:
Marjorie Kohls
(312) 712-1946

CHICAGO, ILLINOIS, MAY 20, 19-- . . . Mark Williams has
joined Bentley Plastics as vice president-marketing. He
will direct the Illinois and Indiana district sales offices
and coordinate overseas distribution through the company's
Singapore office. Williams will travel extensively to the
Far East while developing marketing channels for Bentley.

Formerly, Williams was director of services with
International Marketing Associates, a consulting group in New
York. While at IMA, he developed a computer-based marketing
center that linked textile firms in the United States,
Finland, and Great Britain. A graduate of the Columbia
University Graduate School of Business, Williams is the
author of Marketing Dynamics, an informal examination of
psychological appeals to the buying public. The book has
been used in marketing classrooms at several universities.

Bentley Plastics, headquartered in Chicago, produces
plastic tubing and coils. The company's main plants are in
Skokie, Illinois, and Gary, Indiana. Since 1978 Bentley
has also been producing tubing for French distribution
through the firm of Jourdan and Sons, Paris.

-30-

Figure 1   News Release

no doubt but

In the **phrase** *no doubt but,* the word *but* is redundant.

CHANGE There is *no doubt but* that he will be promoted.
TO There is *no doubt* that he will be promoted.

nominalizations

We have a natural tendency to want to make our on-the-job writing sound very formal—even "impressive." One practice that contributes to both is the use of *nominalizations,* or a weak **verb** (*make, do, conduct, perform,* and so on) and a **noun** when the verb form of the noun would communicate the same idea more effectively in fewer words.

CHANGE The Legal Department will *conduct an investigation* of the purchase.
TO The Legal Department will *investigate* the purchase.
CHANGE The quality assurance team will *perform an evaluation* of the new software.
TO The quality assurance team will *evaluate* the new software.

You may occasionally find a legitimate use for a nominalization. You might, for example, use a nominalization to slow down the **pace** of your writing. But if you use nominalizations thoughtlessly or carelessly or just to make your writing sound more formal, the result will be **affectation**.

none

None may be considered either a singular or plural **pronoun,** depending on the context.

EXAMPLES *None* of the material *has* been ordered. (always singular with a singular noun—in this case, "material")
None of the clients *has* been called yet. (singular even with reference to a plural noun [*clients*] if the intended emphasis is on the idea of *not one*)
None of the clients *have* been called yet. (plural with a plural noun)

For **emphasis**, substitute *no one* for *none* and use a singular **verb**.

> EXAMPLE   I paid the full retail price for three of your firm's machines, *no one* of which was worth the money.

(See also **agreement**.)

nor/or

Nor always follows *neither* in sentences with continuing negation.

> EXAMPLE   They will *neither* support *nor* approve the plan.

Likewise, *or* follows *either* in sentences.

> EXAMPLE   The firm will accept *either* a short-term *or* a long-term loan.

Two or more singular **subjects** joined by *or* or *nor* usually take a singular **verb**. But when one subject is singular and one is plural, the verb agrees with the subject nearer to it.

> EXAMPLES   *Neither* the manager *nor* the secretary *was* happy with the new filing system. (singular)
> *Neither* the manager *nor* the secretaries *were* happy with the new filing system. (plural)
> *Neither* the secretaries *nor* the manager *was* happy with the new filing system. (singular)

(See also **correlative conjunctions**.)

notable/noticeable

Notable, meaning "worthy of notice," is sometimes confused with *noticeable,* meaning "readily observed."

> EXAMPLES   His accomplishments are *notable.*
> Our advertising campaign is having a *noticeable* effect on sales.

note taking

The purpose of note taking is to summarize and record the information that you extract from your **research** material. The great challenge in taking notes is to condense another's thoughts in your own words without distorting the original thinking. Meeting this challenge involves careful reading on your part, because to compress someone else's ideas accurately, you must first understand them.

When taking notes on abstract ideas, as opposed to factual data, be careful not to sacrifice **clarity** for brevity. You can be brief—if you are accurate—with statistics, but notes expressing concepts can lose their meaning if they are too brief. The critical test of a note is whether after a week has passed, you will still know what the note means and from it be able to recall the significant ideas of the passage. If you are in doubt about whether or not to take a note, take it—it is much easier to discard a note you don't need than to find the source again if it is needed.

As you extract information, be guided by the **objective** of your writing and by what you know about your **readers**. (Who are they? How much do they know about your subject? What are their needs?)

Resist the temptation to copy your source word for word as you take notes. Paraphrase the author's idea or concept in your own words. But don't just change a few words in the original passage; you will be guilty of plagiarism. On occasion, when your source concisely sums up a great deal of information or points to a trend or development important to your subject, you are justified in quoting it verbatim and then incorporating that **quotation** into your paper. As a general rule, you will rarely need to quote anything longer than a **paragraph**. (See also **paraphrasing**.)

If a note is copied word for word from your source, be certain to enclose it in **quotation marks** so that you will know later that it is a direct quotation. In your finished writing, be certain to give the source of your quotation; otherwise, you will be guilty of **plagiarism**. (See also **documenting sources**.)

The mechanics of note taking are simple and, if followed conscientiously, can save you much unnecessary work. The following guidelines may help you take notes more effectively:

1. First, don't try to write down everything. Pick out the most important ideas and concepts to record as notes.
2. Create your own shorthand. Common words can be indicated by symbols. For example, you can use "&" for *and,* " + " for *plus,* "w" for *with,* and so on.
3. Use numbers (5, 10, 20) for numerical terms instead of writing *five, ten,* and *twenty.*
4. Leave out vowels when you can do so and still keep the word recognizable, as in "vwl" for *vowel.*
5. Be sure to record all vital names, dates, and definitions.

6. Mark any notes you need to question. You might put an asterisk beside any note you don't fully understand or think you might need to pursue further.
7. Check your notes for accuracy against the printed material before leaving it.

Consider the information in the following paragraph:

> The arithmetic of searching for oil is stark. For all his scientific methods of detection, the only way the oilman can actually know for sure that there is oil in the ground is to drill a well. The average cost of drilling an oil well is over $300,000, and drilling a single well may cost over $8,000,000! And once the well is drilled, the odds against its containing enough oil to be commercially profitable are 49 to 1. The odds against its containing any oil at all are 8 to 1! Even after a field has been discovered, one out of every four holes drilled in developing the field is a dry hole because of the uncertainty of defining the limits of the producing formation. The oilman can never know what Mark Twain once called "the calm confidence of a Christian with four aces in his hand."

The paragraph says essentially the following:

1. Many scientific methods of detection.
2. Only sure way to know is to drill a well.
3. Average cost of drilling a well over $300,000; actual cost can go over $8,000,000.
4. Odds against profitable well: 49 to 1.
5. Odds against any oil: 8 to 1.
6. If existence of oil is known, 1 of 4 wells still dry because limits of field unknown.

If your objective and readers' needs involved only questions of cost and profit, you might take notes 3 and 4; if they involved only the technical process of oil drilling, you might take 1, 2, and 6. However, if there is any doubt whether you should take a note, *take it.*

So that you will give proper credit when you incorporate your notes into your writing, be sure to include the following with the first note taken from a book: author, title, publisher, place and date of publication, and page number. (On subsequent notes from the same book, you will need to include only the author and page number.) Figures 1 and 2 are examples of a first and a subsequent note taken from the paragraph on oil drilling.

Figure 1 *First Note from a Source*

Figure 2 *Subsequent Note from a Source*

If you do not have time to take careful notes in the library, you may want to check out a book or books to review at home. If you need to take more information from periodical articles (which can not be checked out) than can be conveniently committed to notes, you may want to make a photocopy at the library to take home for fuller evaluation. (See also **library research**.)

nouns

A *noun* names a person, place, thing, concept, action, or quality. The two basic types of nouns are **proper nouns** and **common nouns**.

PROPER NOUNS

Proper nouns name specific persons, places, things, concepts, actions, or qualities. They are usually capitalized.

EXAMPLES Abraham Lincoln, New York, U.S. Army, Nobel Prize, Montana, Independence Day, Amazon River, Butler County, Magna Carta, June, Colby College

COMMON NOUNS

Common nouns name general classes or categories of persons, places, things, concepts, actions, or qualities. Common nouns include all types of nouns except proper nouns. Some nouns (turkey/Turkey) may be both common and proper.

EXAMPLES human, college, knife, bolt, string, faith, copper

Abstract nouns are common nouns that refer to something intangible that cannot be discerned by the five senses.

EXAMPLES love, loyalty, pride, valor, peace, devotion, harmony

Collective nouns are common nouns that indicate a group or collection of persons, places, things, concepts, actions, or qualities. They are plural in meaning but singular in form.

EXAMPLES audience, jury, brigade, staff, committee

Concrete nouns are common nouns used to identify those things that can be discerned by the five senses.

EXAMPLES house, carrot, ice, tar, straw, grease

A count noun is a type of concrete noun that identifies things that can be separated into countable units.

EXAMPLES desks, chisels, envelopes, engines, pencils
There were four *calculators* in the office.

(See also **fewer/less** and **amount/number**.) A mass noun is a type of concrete noun that identifies things that comprise a mass, rather than individual units, and cannot be separated into countable units.

EXAMPLES electricity, water, sand, wood, air, uranium, gold, oil, wheat, cement
The price of *silver* increased this year.

(See also **fewer/less** and **amount/number**.)

NOUN FUNCTION

Nouns may function as subjects of **verbs**, as objects of verbs and **prepositions**, as **complements**, or as **appositives**.

EXAMPLES   The *metal* bent as *pressure* was applied to it. (subjects)
The bricklayer cemented the *blocks* efficiently. (direct object)
The company awarded our *department* a plaque for safety. (indirect object)
The event occurred within the *year.* (object of a preposition)
An equestrian is a *horseman.* (subjective complement)
We elected the sales manager *chairman.* (objective complement)
George Thomas, the *treasurer,* gave his report last. (appositive)

Some words that are usually used as nouns may also be used as **adjectives** and **adverbs**.

EXAMPLES   It is *company* policy. (adjective)
He went *home.* (adverb)

USING NOUNS

Forming the Possessive. Nouns form the possessive most often by adding *'s* to the names of living things and by adding an *of* **phrase** to the names of inanimate objects.

EXAMPLES   The *president's* statement was forceful.
The keys *of the calculator* were sticking.

However, either form may be used.

EXAMPLES   The *table's* mahogany finish was scratched.
Two personal friends *of the chairperson* were on the committee.

Plural nouns ending in *s* need only to add an **apostrophe** to form the **possessive case.**

EXAMPLE   The *architects'* design manual contains many illustrations.

Plural nouns that do not end in *s* require both the apostrophe and the *s.*

EXAMPLE   The installation of the plumbing is finished except in the *men's* room.

With group words and compound nouns, add the *'s* to the last noun.

EXAMPLES   The *chairman of the board's* report was distributed.
My *son-in-law's* address was on the envelope.

To show individual possession with coordinate nouns, use the possessive with both.

EXAMPLES Both the *Senate's* and *House's* galleries were packed for the hearings.

Mary's and *John's* presentations were the most effective.

To show joint possession with coordinate nouns, use the possessive with only the last.

EXAMPLES The *Senate and House's* joint committee worked out a satisfactory compromise.

Mary and John's presentation was the most effective.

Forming the Plural. Most nouns form the plural by adding *s*.

EXAMPLE *Dolphins* are capable of communicating with people.

Those ending in *s, z, x, ch,* and *sh* form the plural by adding *es*.

EXAMPLES How many size *sixes* did we produce last month?

The letter was sent to all the *churches*.

Technology should not inhibit our individuality; it should fulfill our *wishes*.

Those ending in a consonant plus *y* form the *plural* by changing *y* to *ies*.

EXAMPLE The store advertises prompt delivery but places a limit on the number of *deliveries* in one day.

Some nouns ending in *o* add *es* to form the plural, but others add only *s*.

EXAMPLES One tomato plant produced twelve *tomatoes*.

We installed two *dynamos* in the plant.

Some nouns ending in *f* or *fe* add *s* to form the plural; others change the *f* or *fe* to *ves*.

EXAMPLES cliff/cliffs, fife/fifes, knife/knives

Some nouns require an internal change to form the plural.

EXAMPLES woman/women, man/men, mouse/mice, goose/geese

Some nouns do not change in the plural form.

EXAMPLE *Fish* swam lazily in the clear brook while a few wild *deer* mingled with the *sheep* in a nearby meadow.

Compound nouns form the plural in the main word.

EXAMPLES sons-in-law, high schools

Compound nouns written as one word add *s* to the end.

> EXAMPLE Use seven *tablespoonfuls* of freshly ground coffee to make seven cups of coffee.

If in doubt about the plural form of a word, look up the word in a good **dictionary**. Most dictionaries give the plural form if it is made in any way other than by adding *s* or *es*.

nowhere near

The **phrase** *nowhere near* is colloquial and should be avoided in writing.

> CHANGE His ability is *nowhere near* Jim's.
> TO His ability does *not approach* Jim's.
> OR His ability is *not comparable to* Jim's.
> OR His ability is *far inferior* to Jim's.

number

Number is the grammatical property of **nouns**, **pronouns**, and **verbs** that signifies whether one thing (singular) or more than one (plural) is being referred to. Nouns normally form the plural by simply adding *s* or *es* to their singular forms.

> EXAMPLES Many new business *ventures* have failed in the past ten *years*.
> *Partners* in successful *businesses* are not always personal *friends*.

But some nouns require an internal change to form the plural.

> EXAMPLES woman/women, man/men, goose/geese, mouse/mice

All pronouns except *you* change internally to form the plural.

> EXAMPLES I/we
> he, she, it/they

By adding an *s* or *es*, most verbs show the singular of the third **person**, present **tense**, indicative **mood**.

> EXAMPLES he *stands*, she *works*, it *goes*

The verb *be* normally changes form to indicate the plural.

> EXAMPLES I *am* ready to begin work. (singular)
> We *are* ready to begin work. (plural)

(See also **agreement**.)

numbers

GENERAL GUIDELINES

1. Write numbers from zero to ten as words and numbers above ten as figures.
2. Spell out approximate numbers.
3. In most writing, do not spell out ordinal numbers, which express degree or sequence (42nd), unless they are single words (tenth, sixteenth). (See also **numeral adjective**.)
4. When several numbers appear in the same sentence or paragraph, express them alike, regardless of other rules and guidelines.

   EXAMPLE   The company owned 150 trucks, employed 271 people, and rented 7 warehouses.

5. Spell out numbers that begin a sentence, even if they would otherwise be written as figures.

   EXAMPLE   One hundred and fifty people attended the meeting.

   If spelling out such a number seems awkward, rewrite the sentence so that the number does not appear at the beginning.

   CHANGE   Two hundred and seventy-three defective products were returned last month.
   TO   Last month, 273 defective products were returned.

6. Do not follow a word representing a number with a figure in parentheses representing the same number.

   CHANGE   Send five (5) copies of the report.
   TO   Send five copies of the report.

PLURALS

The plural of a written number is formed by adding *s* or *es* or by dropping *y* and adding *ies*, depending on the last letter, just as the plural of any other noun is formed. (See **nouns**.)

   EXAMPLES   sixes, elevens, twenties

The plural of a figure may be written with *s* alone or with *'s*.

   EXAMPLES   5s, 12s or 5's, 12's

DOCUMENT PARTS

In typed manuscript, page numbers are written as figures, but chapter or volume numbers may appear as figures or words.

EXAMPLES   Page 37
Chapter 2 or Chapter Two
Volume 1 or Volume One

Figure and table numbers are expressed as figures.

EXAMPLE   Figure 4 and Table 3

MEASUREMENTS

Units of measurement are expressed in figures.

EXAMPLES   3 miles, 45 cubic feet, 9 meters, 27 cubic centimeters, 4 picas

When numbers appear run together in the same phrase, write one as a figure and the other as a word.

CHANGE   The order was for 12 6-inch pipes.
TO   The order was for twelve 6-inch pipes.

Percentages are normally given as figures, and the word percent is written out, except when the number is in a table.

EXAMPLE   Approximately 85 percent of the area has been sold.

FRACTIONS

Fractions are expressed as figures when written with whole numbers.

EXAMPLES   27½ inches, 4¼ miles

Fractions are spelled out when they are expressed without a whole number.

EXAMPLES   one-fourth, seven-eights

Numbers with decimals are always written as figures.

EXAMPLE   5.21 meters

TIME

Hours and minutes are expressed as figures when a.m. and p.m. follow.

EXAMPLES   11:30 a.m., 7:30 p.m.

When not followed by a.m. or p.m., however, time should be spelled out.

EXAMPLES   four o'clock, eleven o'clock

DATES

The year and day of the month should be written as figures. Dates are usually written in a month-day-year sequence, in which the year may or may not be followed by a comma.

EXAMPLES   The August 26, 19-- issue of *Computer World* announced the new system.
The August 26, 19--, issue of *Computer World* announced the new system.

In the day-month-year sequence, commas are not used.

EXAMPLE   The 26 August 19-- issue of *Computer World* announced the new system.

The slash form of expressing dates (8/24/87) is used in informal writing only.

ADDRESSES

Numbered streets from one to ten should be spelled out except when space is at a premium.

EXAMPLE   East Tenth Street

Building numbers are written as figures. The only exception is the building number *one*.

EXAMPLES   4862 East Monument Street
One East Tenth Street

Highways are written as figures.

EXAMPLES   U.S. 70, Ohio 271, I-94

numeral adjectives

Numeral adjectives identify quantity, degree, or place in a sequence. They always modify count **nouns**. Numeral adjectives are divided into two subclasses: cardinal and ordinal.

A cardinal **adjective** expresses an exact quantity.

EXAMPLES *one* pencil, *two* typewriters, *three* airplanes

An ordinal adjective expresses degree or sequence.

EXAMPLES *first* quarter, *second* edition, *third* degree, *fourth* year

In most writing, an ordinal adjective should be spelled out if it is a single word (*tenth*) and written in figures if it is more than one word (*312th*). Ordinal numbers can also function as **adverbs**.

EXAMPLE John arrived *first.*

(See also **first/firstly**.)

O

objective

What do you want your **readers** to know or be able to do when they have read your finished writing project? When you have answered this question, you have determined the *objective,* or purpose, of your writing project. Too often, however, beginning writers state their objectives in broad terms that are of no practical value to them. Such an objective as "to explain the Model 6000 Accounting System" is too general to be of any real help. But "to explain how to operate a Model 6000 Accounting System" is a specific objective that will help keep the writer on the right track.

The writer's objective is rarely simply to "explain" something, although on occasion it may be. You must ask yourself, "Why do I need to explain it?" In answering this question, you may find, for example, that your objective is also to persuade your reader to change his or her attitude toward the thing you are explaining.

A writer for a company magazine who has been assigned to write an article on the firm's new computer installation, in answer to the question *what,* could state the objective as "to explain the way the computer will increase efficiency and ultimately benefit employees." In answer to the question *why,* the writer might state "to ease the fear of automation that has become evident in employees."

If you answer these two questions exactly and put your answers in writing as your stated objective, not only will your job be made easier but also you will be considerably more confident of ultimately reaching your goal. As a test of whether you have adequately formulated your objective, try to state it in a single sentence. If you find that you cannot, continue to formulate your objective until you *can* state it in a single sentence.

Even a specific objective is of no value, however, unless you keep it in mind as you work. Guard against losing sight of your objective as you become involved with the other steps of the writing process.

objective complements

An objective complement is a **noun** or **adjective** that completes the meaning of a sentence by revealing something about the direct object of a transitive **verb**; it may either describe (adjective) or rename (noun) the direct object.

EXAMPLES   We painted the house *white*. (adjective)
            They call her a *genius*. (noun)

The objective complement is one of the four kinds of **complements** that complete the subject–verb relationship; the others are the direct object, the indirect **object**, and the **subjective complement**.

objects

There are three kinds of objects: direct object, indirect object, and object of a **preposition**. All objects are **nouns** or noun equivalents (**pronoun, gerund, infinitive**, noun **phrase**, noun **clause**) and can be replaced by a pronoun in the objective **case**.

DIRECT OBJECTS

The direct object answers the question "what?" or "whom?" about a **verb** and its **subject**.

EXAMPLES   John built a *business*. (noun)
            I like *jogging*. (gerund)
            I like *to jog*. (infinitive)
            I like *it*. (pronoun)
            I like *what I saw*. (noun clause)
            Sheila designed a new *circuit*. (*Circuit*, the direct object, answers
                the question, "Sheila designed *what?*")
            George telephoned the *chief engineer*. (*Chief engineer*, the direct
                object, answers the question, "George telephone *whom?*")

A verb whose meaning is completed by a direct object is called a transitive verb.

INDIRECT OBJECTS

An indirect object is a **noun** or noun equivalent that occurs with a direct object after certain kinds of transitive verbs, such as *give, wish, cause, tell,* and their **synonyms** or **antonyms**. The indirect object is usually a person or persons and answers the question "to whom or what?" or "for whom or what?" The indirect object always precedes the direct object.

EXAMPLES Wish *me* success.

Their attorney wrote *our firm* a follow-up letter.

Give *the car* a push.

We sent the *general manager* a full report. (*Report* is the direct object. The indirect object, *general manager,* answers the question, "We sent a full report *to whom?*")

The general manager gave the *report* careful consideration. (*Consideration* is the direct object. The indirect object, *report,* answers the question, "The general manager gave careful consideration *to what?*")

The purchasing department bought *Sheila* a new oscilloscope. (*Oscilloscope* is the direct object. The indirect object, *Sheila,* answers the question, "The purchasing department bought a new oscilloscope *for whom?*")

OBJECTS OF PREPOSITIONS

For a discussion of objects of prepositions, see **prepositional phrases**.

observance/observation

An *observance* is the "performance of a duty, custom, or law"; it is sometimes confused with *observation,* which is the "act of noticing or recording something."

EXAMPLES The *observance* of Veterans Day as a paid holiday varies from one organization to another.

The efficiency expert made careful *observations* when she visited our department.

OK/okay

The expression *okay* (also spelled *OK* or *O.K.*) is common in informal writing but should be avoided in more formal **correspondence** and **reports**.

CHANGE Mr. Sturgess gave his *okay* to the project.

TO Mr. Sturgess *approved* the project.

CHANGE The solution is *okay* with me.

TO The solution is *acceptable* to me.

on account of

The **phrase** *on account of* should be avoided as a substitute for *because*.

> CHANGE He felt that he had lost his job *on account of* the company's switch to automated equipment.
> TO He felt that he had lost his job *because* the company switched to automated equipment.

on/onto

On is normally a **preposition** meaning "supported by," "attached to," or "located at."

> EXAMPLE Install the telephone *on* the wall.

Onto implies movement to a position on or movement up and on.

> EXAMPLE The union members surged *onto* the platform after their leader's defiant speech.

on the grounds that/of

The **phrase** *on the grounds that*—or *on the grounds of*—is a wordy substitute for *because*.

> CHANGE *On the grounds of* our friendship, he felt he could ask me to substitute for him at the meeting.
> TO *Because of* our friendship, he felt he could ask me to substitute for him at the meeting.

one

When used as an **indefinite pronoun**, *one* may help you avoid repeating a **noun**.

> EXAMPLE We need a new plan, not an old *one*.

One is often redundant in **phrases** in which it restates the noun, and it may take the proper **emphasis** away from the **adjective**.

> CHANGE The computer program was not a unique *one*.
> TO The computer program was not unique.

One can also be used in place of a noun or **personal pronoun** in a statement such as the following:

> EXAMPLE   *One* cannot ignore *one's* physical condition.

In statements of this kind, to avoid the tedious **repetition** of *one*, it is permissible to use a third-person singular personal pronoun with *one* as the antecedent.

> CHANGE   *One* must do *one's* best to correct the injustices *one* sees.
> TO   *One* must do *his* best to correct the injustices *he* sees.
> OR   *One* must do *her* best to correct the injustices *she* sees.

If you use *one* in this manner, be careful not to shift back and forth between *one* and *you.* Using *one* in this way is formal and impersonal, and so in any but the most formal writing you are better advised to address your **reader** directly and personally as *you.*

> CHANGE   *One* cannot be too careful about planning for leisure time. The cost of *one's* equipment can, for example, force *one* to work more and therefore reduce *one's* leisure time.
> TO   *You* cannot be too careful about planning for leisure time. The cost of *your* equipment can, for example, force *you* to work more and thus reduce *your* leisure time.

(See also **point of view**.)

one of those . . . who

A **dependent clause** beginning with *who* or *that* and preceded by *one of those* takes a plural **verb**.

> EXAMPLES   She is *one of those* executives *who are* concerned about their writing.
> This is *one of those* policies *that make* no sense when you examine them closely.

In the preceding two examples, *who* and *that* are subjects of dependent clauses and refer to plural antecedents (*executives* and *policies*) and thus take plural verbs, *are* and *make.*

Because people so often use singular verbs in such constructions in everyday speech and very informal writing, this rule confuses many writers. The principle behind the rule becomes clearer if *among* is substituted for *one of*. Compare the following examples with the preceding ones:

EXAMPLES She is *among* those executives *who are* concerned about their writing. (You would not write, "She is among those executives who *is* concerned . . .")

This is *among* those policies *that make* no sense when you examine them closely. (You would not write "This is among those policies that *makes* no sense . . .")

Another way to clarify the principle behind the rule is to turn the sentence around. Compare the following examples with the examples given above:

EXAMPLES Of those executives who *are* concerned about their writing, she is one.

Of those policies that *make* no sense when you examine them closely, this is one.

When the sentences are seen turned around in this rather unnatural but perfectly logical way, you would not be likely to use *is* for *are* (in the first sentence) or *makes* for *make* (in the second sentence). It may also be helpful to contrast these sentences with others in which the singular verb is the correct form.

EXAMPLES She is one executive *who is* concerned about her writing. (*Who* refers to a singular antecedent, *executive*, and is therefore singular and takes a singular verb, *is*.)

This is one policy *that makes* no sense when it is examined closely. (*That* refers to a singular antecedent, *policy*, and so requires a singular verb, *makes*.)

There is one exception to the plural-verb rule stated at the beginning of this entry: If the phrase *one of those* is preceded by *the only* (*the only one* . . .), the verb in the following dependent clause should be singular:

EXAMPLES She is *the only one* of those executives *who is* concerned about her writing. (The verb is singular because its subject, *who*, refers to a singular antecedent, *one*. If the sentence were reversed, it would read, "Of those executives, she is the only *one who is* concerned about her writing.")

This is *the only one* of those policies *that makes* no sense when you examine it closely. (If the sentence were reversed, it would read, "Of those policies, this is the only *one that makes* no sense when you examine it closely.")

Finally, it should be repeated that the plural-verb rule given at the beginning of this entry is often ignored in everyday speech and very informal writing. Indeed, in spoken English the singular form of the verb, though technically illogical, is probably far more common than the plural. However, in your work-related writing, in which preciseness is crucial, use a plural verb after *one of those who* or *one of those that.*

only

In writing, the word *only* should be placed immediately before the word or **phrase** it modifies.

> CHANGE We *only* lack financial backing; we have determination.
> TO We lack *only* financial backing; we have determination.

A speaker can place *only* before the **verb** and avoid **ambiguity** by stressing the word being modified; in writing, only the correct placement of the word can ensure **clarity**. Incorrect placement of *only* can change the meaning of a sentence.

> EXAMPLES *Only* he said that he was tired. (He alone said he was tired.)
> He *only* said that he was tired. (He actually was not tired, although he said he was.)
> He said *only* that he was tired. (He said nothing except that he was tired.)
> He said that he was *only* tired. (He was nothing except tired.)

openings

If your **reader** is already familiar with your subject or if what you are writing is short, you may not need to begin your writing project with a full **introduction**. You may simply want to focus the reader's attention with a brief opening.

For many types of on-the-job writing, openings that simply get to the point are quite adequate, as shown in the following examples:

Correspondence

Mr. George T. Whittier
1720 Old Line Road
Thomasbury, WV 26401

Dear Mr. Whittier:

You will be happy to know that we have corrected the error in your bank balance. The new balance shows. . .

Progress Report Letter

William Chang, M.D.
Phelps Building
9003 Shaw Avenue
Parksville, MD 21221

Dear Dr. Chang:

To date, 18 of the 26 specimens you submitted for analysis have been examined. Our analysis indicates. . .

Longer Progress Report

PROGRESS REPORT ON REWIRING
THE SPORTS ARENA

The rewiring program at the Sports Arena is continuing on schedule. Although the costs of certain equipment are higher than our original bid had indicated, we expect to complete the project without exceeding our budget, because the speed with which the project is being completed will save labor costs.

Work Completed
As of August 15, we have. . .

Memorandum

To: Jane T. Meyers, Chief Budget Manager
From: Charles Benson, Assistant to the Personnel Director
Date: June 12, 19--
Subject: Budget Estimates for Fiscal Year 19--

As you requested, I am submitting the personnel budget estimates for fiscal year 19--.

You may also use an intriguing or interesting opening, either by itself or in conjunction with an introduction, to stimulate your reader's interest. Such types of writing as **annual reports, journal articles**, and **newsletter articles** often *require* an interesting opening because you do not have a captive audience for such articles and **reports**.

Such openings have two purposes: to indicate the subject and to catch the interest of the reader. Several types of openings achieve both purposes. The opening should be natural, not forced; an obviously "tacked on" opening will only puzzle your reader, who will be unable to establish any meaningful connection between the opening and the body of your article or report.

STATEMENT OF THE PROBLEM

One way to give the reader the perspective of your report is to present a brief account of the problem that led to the study or project being reported.

> EXAMPLE　Several weeks ago a brewmaster noticed a discoloration in the grain supplied by Acme Farms, Inc. He immediately reported his discovery to his supervisor. After an intensive investigation, we found that Acme...

However, if the reader is familiar with the problem or if the particular problem has been solved for a long period, a problem opening is likely to be boring.

DEFINITION

Although a definition can be useful as an opening, do not define something with which the reader is familiar or provide a definition that is obviously a contrived opening (such as "Webster defines business as ..."). A definition should be used as an opening only if it offers insight into what follows.

> EXAMPLE　*Conglomerate* comes from the Latin verb *conglomerare,* meaning "roll or heap together," and it is used to refer to a corporation composed of many different companies. The remarkable growth of conglomerates over the past decade...

INTERESTING DETAIL

Often an interesting detail of your subject can be used to gain the readers' attention and arouse their interest. This requires, of course, that you be aware of your readers' interests. The following opening, for example, might be especially interesting to members of a personnel department:

> EXAMPLE　The small number of graduates applying for jobs at Acme Corporation is disappointing, particularly after many years of steadily increasing numbers of applicants. There are, I believe, several reasons for this development...

Sometimes an interesting statistic is an effective opening.

> EXAMPLE　From asbestos sheeting to zinc castings, from a chemical analysis of the water in Lake Maracaibo (to determine its suitability for use in steam injection units) to pistol blanks (for use in

testing power charges), the purchasing department attends to the company's material needs. Approximately 15,000 requisitions, each containing from one to fourteen separate items, are processed each year by this department. Every item or service that is bought. . .

ANECDOTE

An anecdote can also be used to catch your reader's attention and interest.

EXAMPLE In his poem "The Calf Path," Sam Walter Foss tells of a wandering, wobbly calf trying to find its way home at night through the lonesome woods. It made a crooked path, which was taken up the next day by a lone dog that passed that way. Then "a bellwether sheep pursued the trail over vale and steep, drawing behind him the flock, too, as all good bellwethers do." At last the path became a country road; then a lane that bent and turned and turned again. The lane became a village street, and at last the main highway of a flourishing city. The poet ends by saying, "A hundred thousand men were led by a calf, three centuries dead."

Many companies today follow a "calf path" because they react to events rather than planning. . . .

BACKGROUND

The background or history of a certain subject may be quite interesting and may even put the subject in perspective for your reader. Consider the following example from a **newsletter article** describing the process of oil drilling:

EXAMPLE From the bamboo poles the Chinese used when the pyramids were young to today's giant rigs drilling in a hundred feet of water, there has been a lot of progress in the search for oil. But whether four thousands years ago or today, in ancient China or a modern city, in twenty fathoms of water or on top of a mountain, the object of drilling is and has always been the same—to manufacture a hole in the ground, inch by inch. The hole may be either for a development well . . .

This type of opening is easily overdone, however; use it only if the background information is of some value to your reader. Never use it just as a way to get started.

QUOTATION

Occasionally, you can use a **quotation** to stimulate interest in your subject. To be effective, however, the quotation must be pertinent— not some loosely related remark selected from a book of quotations simply because it was listed under the subject heading that fits your writing project. Often a good quotation to use is one that predicts a new trend or development.

> EXAMPLE Richard Smith, president of P. R. Smith Corporation, recently said, "I believe that the Photon projector will revolutionize our industry." His statement represents . . .

OBJECTIVE

In reporting on a project or activity of some kind, you may wish to open with a statement of the project or activity's objective. Such an opening gives the reader a basis for judging the actual results.

> EXAMPLE The primary objective of the survey project was to measure consumer response to our new advertising campaign. We began by establishing a sampling procedure based on . . .

SUMMARY

You can provide a summary opening by greatly compressing the results, conclusions, or recommendations of your article or report. Do not start a summary, however, by writing "This report summarizes . . ."

> CHANGE This report summarizes the advantages of having a new product tested by consumers before beginning mass production and distribution of the product. The major advantage is . . ."
>
> TO Having each new product consumer tested before beginning mass production and distribution has several advantages. First, it allows us to . . .

FORECAST

Sometimes you can use a forecast of a new development or trend to arouse the reader's interest.

> EXAMPLE In the very near future, we may be able to call our local library and have a videotape of *Hamlet* replayed on our wall television. This project and others are now being developed at Acme Industries. . . .

SCOPE

At times you may want to present the **scope** of your article or report in your opening. By providing the parameters of your material—the limitations of the subject or the amount of detail to be presented— you enable your readers to determine whether they want or need to read your article or report. Be on guard against letting this kind of opening become a narrated **table of contents** or an **abstract**; if either of those is appropriate, include it—but not as an artificial opening. The scope type of opening is often useful for small writing projects in which an abstract or table of contents would be unnecessary.

> EXAMPLE This pamphlet provides a review of the requirements for obtaining an FAA pilot's license. It is not designed as a textbook to prepare you to take the examination itself; rather, it gives you an idea of the steps you need to take and the costs involved. . . .

oral presentations

Preparing an oral presentation is much like preparing to write; that is, you must determine your purpose, analyze your audience, develop your topic, and prepare an outline.

PURPOSE OF THE PRESENTATION

Summarize your specific message succinctly—in an single sentence if possible: "Tobacco kills!" or "We must reduce costs!" In order to summarize your message in a single sentence, you must know exactly what the purpose of your presentation is. Is it to tell the audience something they didn't know? Is it to update their knowledge? To ask them to take a specific action? To ask them for money?

AUDIENCE ANALYSIS

To communicate effectively with your listeners, you must first know who they are. Are they coworkers? Customers? Fellow members of a professional organization? You should consider their age, their sex, their occupation, their eduction—because who they are largely determines what they are interested in, and you can appeal effectively to an audience only by relating to their desires, needs, and anxieties.

Try to put yourself in your listeners' place. What do they already know about your topic? What do they need to know in order for your presentation to achieve its objective? What is your listeners' attitude toward your subject? Resistance? Apathy? Curiosity? Interest? Must you convince your listeners? Must you motivate them? Your listeners' attitude toward your topic should largely determine your approach. What is your audience's attitude toward *you*? The image you present and the prestige you bring with you will greatly influence their acceptance of you.

ORGANIZATION

Speaking well is mainly thinking logically and then organizing your talk in the same way. Logical reasoning is not only powerful and persuasive but also a necessary ingredient for any speech. Your presentation will lack coherence without it.

Organizing your presentation consists of collecting the necessary data, developing the topic, and **outlining** the presentation.

Collecting the Data. You must be the master of your subject if you expect to be taken seriously. Therefore, it is a good idea to gather more information than you will use in your presentation, just to build your own confidence in your mastery of your subject.

In collecting data, use all the sources of information you can think of, including brainstorming, written material, interviewing others, and your own background (see **research**).

Be sure of your facts. Do not be guilty of unfounded assumptions or unproved assertions.

Developing the Topic. Make certain that your **method of development** is appropriate to both your audience and your objective and is based on your reader's needs.

For work-related presentations, two basic plans can be used to cover most situations:

1. State your facts.
   Argue from them.
   Appeal for action.

or

2. Show that something is wrong.
   Show how to fix it.

Several other methods of development are also good for oral presentations.

The **problem–solution method of development** describes and analyzes the problem, then presents the criteria for evaluating possible solutions, and finally explains the advantages and disadvantages of each solution.

The **comparison-and-contrast method of development** sets your idea side by side with others and lets the audience compare your idea with the others.

The **cause-and-effect method of development** explains why something happened or why you predict something is going to happen.

The **specific-to-general method of development** begins with specific details—such as statistics, expert opinions, and examples—and then uses them to build to a general conclusion.

The **general-to-specific method of development** presents a general statement and then follows it with such supporting details as statistics, expert opinions, and examples.

The **increasing-order-of-importance method of development** develops a topic from the least important to the most important point and thus leaves the audience with the most important points fresh in their minds at the end.

Structuring the Presentation. After selecting the most appropriate method of development, you must prepare an outline that reflects that method. If you used 3-by-5-inch note cards when gathering your data, lay them out on a desk top and group them by topic to organize your outline. When you have grouped and sequenced your note cards correctly, number them. However, don't consider this sequence final. You may find yourself renumbering your notes several times, even after you have typed your outline.

The Opening. Your opening is the most important part of your speech. It should not only catch the interest of your audience but also stimulate curiosity and impress your listeners with the importance of your topic.

For an interesting opening, use your personal experiences and your reading. Remember, however, that your opening must always be tied to your theme. The following are ways you might open a presentation:

- An unusual, startling statement

  EXAMPLE   "'Star Trek's' 'beam-me-up' technology may be the most common mode of transportation in twenty years."

- A rhetorical question

    EXAMPLE   "Will colonizing outer space ever be practical?"

- A dramatic story

    EXAMPLE   Terry Fox's attempt to run across Canada to raise money for cancer research.

- A personal experience
- A quotation from a famous person

    EXAMPLE   "We have nothing to fear but fear itself."
    —Franklin D. Roosevelt

- A historical event

    EXAMPLE   "Do you remember where you were when Neil Armstrong first set foot on the moon?"

- A reference to a current news story
- A reference from literature or the Bible

    EXAMPLE   "We need the kind of frankness in this project that Samuel Pepys displayed in his diary back in the seventeenth century."

You may even use your opening to tell your audience why what you are about to say is important to them.

The Body. Begin the body of your presentation with a statement of your theme. (When delivering your presentation, pause both before and after this statement, to emphasize its importance.) Then relate all the evidence and proof necessary to support your theme statement. The strength of your proof will sell your ideas. Use analogies, stories, testimony, logic, statistics, and examples to support your theme.

Stories can sell your idea. Abraham Lincoln and Jesus Christ used stories to great effect. However, your story must relate directly to your theme, and it must be short. Avoid old stories that the audience has probably heard. Avoid off-color stories at all costs. And don't wait for a response when you have finished your story.

Testimony can provide authority and support for your position from people who have gone on record as agreeing with you. Testimony from an expert is especially helpful for questions of fact, and quotations from a prestigious book or person will help you gain acceptance from the audience. Be sure, however, that the person you are quoting has a right to speak on the subject.

Statistics, properly presented, can be interesting. But they should be presented in a frame of reference to which the reader can relate. "The ship was the length of three football fields" is much better, for example, than just the dry number of feet. You could say that the Astrodome is 210 feet high or that you could put a 20-story building inside it. Do not include endless statistics, however, no matter how interesting they may seem.

Analogies and *similes* can help you communicate by relating the unfamiliar to the familiar. They are comparisons of things that are not really alike but have one thing in common. "Pollution is to the environment what cancer is to the body."

The Closing. Plan your closing just as you planned your opening. Your closing is almost as important as your opening, because what you say in your closing is what your audience is most likely to remember. Therefore, make certain that your closing is tied directly to the purpose of your presentation. Your closing may also be designed to create a specific mood or stimulate a specific action.

If you want your closing to get action, tell your audience what you want them to do! If your objective is not to get your audience to do something, you might close with a summary or a recommendation, or by asking a rhetorical question or for their cooperation.

Whatever the objective of your closing, always try to end on a high note that emphasizes your central theme. And always make your closing as interesting as possible, since it is what is most likely to be remembered.

MAKING THE PRESENTATION

The key to effective delivery is practice. Public speaking isn't natural for anyone, but everyone can learn to do it well with enough practice.

Practice consists of two parts: (1) fixing your outline in your mind and (2) polishing your delivery. Memorize only your opening and your closing, plus perhaps a few important phrases. Read your outline over and over again until you are thoroughly familiar with it. Then try to make your presentation without notes. If you forget a part of the outline, go on as best you can until you have finished the whole talk. Repeat this process as many times as necessary. Rehearse with your outline until you know exactly how you want to move from one idea to another. Become so familiar with your outline that just a skeleton of it will guide you as you make the actual presentation.

To polish your delivery, rehearse on your feet and out loud. Don't be inhibited during rehearsal: force yourself to be dynamic, even though there is no live audience in front of you. Practice your gestures as well as your words and delivery.

Evaluate your voice for projection, inflection, and enthusiasm. Listen to yourself on a tape recorder. Practice a conversational style of presentation. Also listen for "uh," "y'know," and other nervous mannerisms.

In your practice sessions, vary your phraseology, gestures, and vocal inflections. Don't let your talk become canned. Use whatever words and gestures are natural. If you practice, you will have no problem with the gestures and words you want to use—they will come naturally.

If possible, arrange one practice session in the room where the speech is to be delivered so you can get the feel of the room and the equipment.

Last-minute rehearsal is generally not a good idea; in fact, it may actually work against you by making you more tense. It is generally better to try to relax immediately before your presentation.

EQUIPMENT AND ROOM

When you are to make your presentation, arrive well ahead of time to check out the room and equipment. Confirm in advance that the needed equipment is available. Will you need a chalkboard? A screen? A projector? A flipchart? If so, make sure they are available.

Consider the size of the room. Tailor everything to scale. Make sure that your visual aids can be seen from all parts of the room.

Check your slides (is it a rear or forward projector?). Check the location of wall plugs and light switches. Check the room for acoustics; if they are bad, you will know you must speak louder.

VISUAL AIDS

Well-planned visual aids can add interest and emphasis to your presentation. They can clarify and simplify your message because they communicate clearly, quickly, and vividly: we learn much better by seeing than by listening. Visual aids present an idea in a form that the audience can understand more quickly. But use visual aids *only* if they clarify or emphasize a point. Don't try to use them to flesh out a skimpy or weak presentation.

Keep your visual aids simple and uncluttered. Keep the amount of information on each to a minimum (usually one idea to a visual aid). When the visual aid is text, space it so the audience can easily read it.

Slide projectors and *overhead projectors* are easy to use. As you prepare your presentation, decide which slides you will use and where each one will go. Have them made up far enough in advance that you can rehearse with them. A line graph in a slide or overhead is good for showing growth and decline over a specified period, such as the growth of the U.S. population since 1790. Always put a title over a line graph, be sure to label both legs of the graph with horizontal labels, and make sure that the lines are dark enough to be seen from the back of the room. A bar graph in a slide or overhead can be either vertical or horizontal. Be sure to put a title over the bar graph. Label all bars horizontally (putting the label inside the bar helps make identification easy). Use different colors in the contrasting bars. Make sure everything can be read from the back of the room. (See **illustrations**.)

Flip charts are good for small- and medium-sized audiences. They give you good control of what you want the audience to see because you flip over the chart only when you need it. You can even draw illustrations on the flip chart ahead of time with light pencil lines that the audience can't see and then fill in the heavy lines with a felt-tip pen during your presentation (sketching it during the presentation helps hold the audience's attention).

A *chalkboard* is good with small- and medium-sized audiences, as it is easy to use and to control. It gives you complete flexibility to decide what goes on, what comes off, and when. It adds animation to your presentation because you must physically put the information on the board. If your information is too long to put on the board conveniently while you speak, put part of it on the board ahead of time. A disadvantage of using a chalkboard is that you must interrupt your presentation to write on it.

A *poster* can be used for medium- to large-sized audiences of up to 100 people. The poster must be large enough for your audience to see clearly what it contains; a common size is 2 × 3 feet. Prepare the poster ahead of time, and make your lettering large enough to be seen comfortably from the back of the room. Felt-tip markers are good writing instruments for posters. Put the poster on the easel only when you are ready to use it; otherwise, it may distract your audience.

Practice with your visual aids. During the practice sessions, point to the visual aid with both gestures and words. Practice talking to your audience, however, rather than to the visual aid. Be sure you do not block it with your body. Cover your visual aids both before and after discussing them so they won't distract your audience.

When using slides or overheads, give your audience time to absorb the information on the slide or overhead before you comment on it. Don't talk while you are changing overheads or doing something physical. Pause while you do it.

DELIVERY

The speaker's delivery can make the subject interesting or dull to the audience. Never open your presentation with an apology; open forcefully. Don't tell the audience you are a poor speaker; let *them* decide. Don't explain that you didn't have time to prepare; if you didn't, you should not have agreed to speak. If you stumble and apologize, your listeners will begin to question your knowledge of the subject.

Delivery is both audible and visual. Step briskly up to the lectern and take a deep breath. Look directly at your audience and remain silent until you have absolute quiet.

A strong voice, confident manner, and take-charge attitude will impress your audience favorably. If you seem reluctant to take charge, the audience will deny you the authority they would otherwise have granted you as the speaker.

Your first sentence should be forceful and attention getting.

> CHANGE "I would like to speak to you today about the problems we are experiencing with the new payroll management system."
> TO "If we don't meet our current schedule, the new payroll management system will be in jeopardy."

Talk with your audience in a conversational way—don't lecture to them. Make your message personal; don't be afraid of the pronoun *you*. Work at getting expressiveness and enthusiasm into your voice.

To emphasize a point, say it—then pause to let its significance register—and repeat the point. The "pregnant silence" is a great way to get your listeners' attention.

Let your notes guide you. If you lose your place, don't panic—just find it again. Remember that your audience is made up of human beings just like you.

Be sure not to pass out a long handout at the beginning of your presentation. If you do, the audience will read it instead of listening to you.

Nervousness. It is natural to be apprehensive, and that feeling will probably never go away. Stage fright shouldn't worry you. Indeed, perhaps the lack of it should, because it can be a helpful stimulant. But fear is a result of a lack of confidence, and the best defense against butterflies is to be as well prepared as possible. You can expect to be nervous, but if you know what you are going to say and how you are going to say it, you will probably relax as you start to speak.

You can gain strength and confidence simply by standing up and meeting the situation face to face. To avoid stage fright, try to relax both your body and your mind. Relax your body by whatever means works for you: meditation, isometric exercises, deep breathing, progressive relaxation techniques, and the like. Relax your mind by thinking positive thoughts. Avoid attempting to evaluate your ability to speak. Conjure up visual images of what you want to look like and do, and then assume that you will achieve the desired behavior. Give yourself a pep talk: "My subject is important. I am ready. My listeners have come here to hear what I have to say."

When you stand up to speak, take a long, deep breath. It will help calm you. Don't jingle coins in your pocket, fidget with notes or pencils, pull your ear, or run your fingers through your hair. If you can't keep your hands still, put them behind you and keep them there.

Don't mistake the audience's silence for hostility. The audience is on your side. They are eager for your information, not your scalp.

Enthusiasm. You must be convinced that you have something important to tell your listeners and then convey this conviction to them. If you are deeply interested in your subject and enthusiastic about communicating it to your listeners, you will automatically transmit that to your audience. Your presentation is most likely to be on a job-related topic, so you can speak with knowledge and conviction. Reach out and figuratively shake the hands of your listeners.

Eye Contact. It is important to establish rapport with the audience, and eye contact is the best way to do it. Pick out a few people in different parts of the audience and alternately speak directly to each one of them. Maintain eye contact with the good listeners—those who nod and react. In other words, hold a conversation with them. Look at your listeners as you would if you were actually talking to them. And look into the eyes of people—not over their heads. Maintaining eye contact creates an appearance of honesty, dependability, and security. Looking into someone's eyes is equivalent to a handshake; it tells your audience you are someone they can believe and trust.

If you memorize nothing else, memorize your opening and your closing so you can maintain eye contact with your audience during those important parts of your presentation.

Gestures. Use gestures to clarify, amplify, emphasize, demonstrate, and, finally, to draw attention to your visual aids. In other words, make your hands and body support your speaking. If you don't put your hands in your pockets, you will instinctively use them to gesture. But gesture just as naturally as you would in conversation.

Humor and Jokes. A discriminating sense of humor is a valuable asset to any speaker. It is an excellent device for gaining rapport with your audience, and it can offer comic relief when your subject is very serious.

Your humor should always relate directly to your message. Do not use humor from the current edition of a popular magazine or television program, because your audience probably saw it also. Above all, don't be vulgar.

QUESTION-AND-ANSWER SESSION

Try to anticipate what questions you will receive during any question-and-answer session, and be ready with your answers. Be sure you understand a question before attempting to answer it, and then answer it as completely as time allows or the question deserves. Be sure of the accuracy of your answers, and don't be afraid to say "I don't know."

Be polite and objective when responding to a hostile question, but be prepared to go on to the next one if it becomes evident that the questioner simply wants to argue. Do not be defensive, and do not play for laughs at the questioner's expense (you will offend not only him or her but the audience as well).

oral/verbal

Oral refers to what is spoken.

EXAMPLE He made an *oral* commitment to the policy.

Although it is sometimes used synonymously with *oral, verbal* literally means "in words" and can refer to what is spoken or written. To avoid possible confusion, do not use *verbal* if you can use *written* or *oral.*

CHANGE He made a *verbal* agreement to complete the work.
TO He made a *written* agreement to complete the work.
OR He made an *oral* agreement to complete the work.
CHANGE Avoid *verbal* orders.
TO Avoid *oral* orders.

When you must refer to something both written and spoken, you should use both *written* and *oral* to make your meaning clear.

EXAMPLE He demanded either a *written* or an *oral* agreement before he would continue the project.

order letters

One of the most common reasons for writing a letter, especially if you work for a small organization or are self-employed, is to order supplies or equipment. The supplies may be anything from company letterhead to X-ray film. Obviously, an order letter must be specific and complete if you are to receive the exact item you want. But be careful not to clutter the letter with unnecessary details, such as why you need the items or who will use them. Above all, be accurate. Since a misspelled word or misplaced decimal point could cause a staggering error, proofread the letter carefully and double-check all price calculation. If you order several items, it is best to list them.

HOLT TOOL COMPANY
1012 Clarke Street
Phoenix, AZ 85019

(602) 297-3100

                                        September 5, 19--

Downtown Parts Company
109 South State Street
Chicago, IL 60650

Attention: Sales Department

Please send the following items listed in your current parts
catalog:

```
 2   Tempered steel cylinders, 2" diameter and 5"
     long, part number C5789S, @ $25.50 each          $51.00

 4   Aluminium castings with corrosion-resistant
     coating, part number S312A, @ $8.18 each         $32.72

12   Special tempered sheet metal screen, 11/4"
     long with hexagonal heads, @ $1.14 each          $13.68


                                     TOTAL     $97.40
```

The enclosed check for $104.22 covers the price, sales tax,
and parcel post charges.

Please send this material to me by October 1.

                            Sincerely,

                            James Siemer

                            James Siemer
                            Parts Manager

JS:tb
Enclosure: Check

Figure 1   Order Letter

HOLT TOOL COMPANY
1012 Clarke Street
Phoenix, AZ 85019

(602) 297-3100

October 12, 19--

Downtown Parts Company
109 South State Street
Chlcago, IL   60650

Attention: Sales Department

On September 5, I sent you a letter in which I placed an
order for a number of parts listed in your current catalog.
I also sent a check for $104.22.

I have enclosed a copy of that letter, and I request that
you please rush this material to me. If for some reason you
cannot send the material, please cancel my order and return
the check.

Thank you.

Slncerely,

James Siemer

James Siemer
Parts Manager

JS:tb
Enclosure: Copy of order letter

Figure 2   Follow-up Letter

Make sure that the order letter contains any of the following information that is appropriate:

1. The exact name and part number of the item.
2. Any useful description of the item: size, style, color, and so on.
3. The quantity of each item.
4. The price of the item (both unit price and total price).
5. The shipping method: mail, air, express, or whatever.
6. The date of the order and the date by which you need the item (indicate "rush" or other instructions).
7. The place to which the material is to be shipped (including the exact shipping address).
8. The method of payment (including a check or money order, indicating that you will pay c.o.d., or enclosing a purchase order number for the seller to bill your company).

Figure 1 shows a typical order letter.

If you receive no response to an order letter within about ten days after the item was due, you may need to send a follow-up letter. If you do so, be courteous and avoid showing irritation. In your follow-up, identify the order by referring to the original letter by date. It is also wise to include a copy of the letter. Figure 2 is a typical follow-up letter. (See also **correspondence** and **lists**.)

organization

Organization is achieved, first, by developing your **topic** in a way that will enable your **reader** to understand your message and then by **outlining** your material on the basis of that **method of development**.

A logical method of development satisfies the reader's need for a controlling shape and structure for your subject. For example, if you were writing a proposal to your manager, trying to get him or her to fund a project you wanted to undertake, you would probably use an order-of-importance method of developing the topic. You would start with the most important reason that the project should be funded and end with the least important reason. On the other hand, if you were a Federal Aviation Administration agent reporting on an airplane crash, you would probably use a cause-and-effect method, starting with the cause of the crash and leading up to the crash (or starting with the crash and tracing back to the cause).

An appropriate method of development is the writer's tool for keeping things under control and the reader's means of following the writer's development of a theme. Many different methods of development are available to the writer; this book includes those that are likely to be used by business people: **sequential, chronological, increasing-order-of-importance, decreasing-order-of-importance, division-and-classification, comparison, spatial, specific-to-general, general-to-specific,** and **cause-and-effect.** As the writer, you must choose the method of development that best suits your subject, your reader, and your **objective.**

Outlining provides structure to your writing by ensuring that it has a beginning, a middle, and an end. It gives proportion to your writing by making sure that one step flows smoothly to the next without omitting anything important, and it enables you to emphasize your key points by placing them in the positions of greatest importance. Using an outline makes larger and more difficult subjects easier to handle by breaking them into manageable parts. Finally, by forcing you to organize your subject and structure your thinking in the outline stage, creating a good outline allows you to concentrate exclusively on writing when you begin the rough draft.

organizational charts

An organizational chart shows how the various components of an organization are related to one another. It is useful when you want to give your **readers** an overview of an organization or to show them the lines of authority within it. (See Figure 1.)

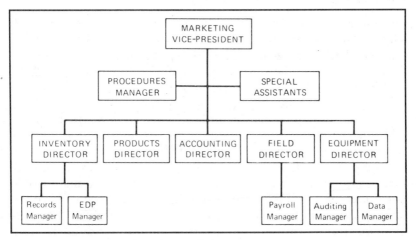

Figure 1   Organizational Chart Showing Positions

```
                    ┌─────────────────────┐
                    │   FIELD DIRECTOR    │
                    │   J. Ann Carlson    │
                    └─────────────────────┘
```

Figure 2   Organizational Box with Name of Person and Position

The title of each organizational component (office, section, division) is placed in a separate box. These boxes are then linked to a central authority. If your readers need the information, include the name of the person occupying the position identified in each box. (See Figure 2.)

As with all **illustrations**, place the organizational chart as close as possible to the text that refers to it.

orient/orientate

Orientate is merely a **long variant** of *orient*, meaning "locate in relation to something else." The shorter form should be used because it is simpler.

> CHANGE   Let me *orientate* your group on our operation.
> TO   Let me *orient* your group on our operation.

outlining

Outlining provides structure to your writing by ensuring that it has a beginning (**introduction**), a middle (main body), and an end (**conclusion**). An outline gives your writing proportion so that one part flows smoothly to the next without omitting anything important. Outlining also enables you to emphasize your key points by placing them in the positions of greatest importance.

Like a road map, an outline indicates a starting point and keeps you moving logically so that you don't get lost before arriving at your conclusion. (Errors in logic are much easier to detect in an outline than in a draft.) Using an outline makes larger and more difficult subjects easier to handle by breaking them into manageable parts; therefore, the less certain you are about your writing ability or about your subject, the fuller your outline should be. The parts of an outline are easily moved about, so you can experiment to see what arrangement of your ideas is the most effective. Perhaps most important, creating a good outline frees you to concentrate on writing when you begin the rough draft (by forcing you to organize your subject and structure your thinking beforehand).

An outline is a tool that helps writers make their writing more logical and coherent. Do not feel that once you have created an outline you must follow it slavishly; as you write the draft, you may still make any changes necessary.

Two types of outlines are generally used: the topic outline and the sentence outline. The topic outline consists of short **phrases** that show the sequential order and relative importance of ideas; in this manner, a topic outline provides order and establishes the relationships of topics to one another. The topic outline alone is generally not sufficient for a large or complex writing job, but it may be used to structure the major and minor divisions of your topic in preparation for creating a sentence outline. (An outline for a small job is not as detailed as one for a larger job, but it is just as important; for example, a topic outline that lists your major and minor points can help greatly even in writing important letters.)

On a large writing project, it is wise to create a topic outline first and then use it as a basis for creating a sentence outline. In a sentence outline, the writer summarizes each idea in a single complete sentence that will become the **topic sentence** for a **paragraph** in the rough draft. The sentence outline begins with a main idea statement that establishes the subject and then follows with a complete sentence for each idea in the major and minor divisions. A sentence outline provides order and establishes the relationship of topics to one another to a considerably greater degree than does a topic outline. A well-developed sentence outline offers a sure test of the validity of your arrangement of your material. If most of your notes can be shaped into controlling topic sentences for paragraphs in your rough draft, you can be relatively sure before you begin its final composition that your paper will be well organized. A good sentence outline, when stripped of its numbering symbols, needs only to be expanded with full details to become a rough draft.

Some outlines begin with a thesis statement, which is a statement of the main idea that you intend to develop in your report. This statement gives you a goal that you can work toward as you create your outline. A thesis statement often suggests a particular **method of development**.

EXAMPLES   The mission director must oversee a rigid chain of events that must occur prior to blast-off. (This thesis statement suggests a **sequential method of development**.)

Increased sales in the Chicago area appear to be a direct result of the new marketing techniques introduced there last year. (This thesis statement suggests a **cause-and-effect method of development**.)

The growth of the computer industry has closely paralleled the growth of conglomerates. (This thesis statement suggests a combination of the **chronological method of development** and the **comparison method of development**.)

Although the following outlining technique is mechanical, it is easy to master and well suited to unraveling the complexities of large and difficult subjects.

The first step is to group naturally related items and write them down on note cards and then to determine whether they are exactly what you need to meet the demands of your **objective**, your **reader**, and your **scope** of coverage. If they are—or when they are—arrange them in the proper order, and label them with roman numerals. For example, the major divisions for this discussion of outlining could be as follows:

> I. Advantages of outlining
> II. Types of outlining
> III. Effective outlining
> IV. Writing the draft from the outline

The second step is to establish your minor points by deciding on the minor divisions within each major head. Arrange them in the proper sequence under their major **heads**, and label them with capital letters. Keep major heads equal in importance and minor heads equal in importance; the purpose of this **parallel structure** is to keep your thinking in order. The major and minor heads for this discussion of outlining could be as follows:

> I. Advantages of outlining
> II. Types of outlining
>   A. The topic outline
>   B. The sentence outline
> III. Effective outlining
>   A. Establish major and minor heads
>   B. Sort note cards by major and minor heads
>   C. Complete the sentence outline
> IV. Writing the draft from the outline

Of course, you will often need more than the two levels of heads illustrated here. If your subject is complicated, you may need four or five levels to keep all of your ideas straight and in proper relationship to one another. In that event, the following numbering scheme is recommended:

    I. First-level head
      A. Second-level head
        1. Third-level head
          a. Fourth-level head
            (1.) Fifth-level head

The third step is to mark each of your note cards with the appropriate roman numeral and capital letter. Sort the note cards by major and minor heads (roman numerals and capital letters). Then arrange the cards within each minor head, and mark each with the appropriate sequential arabic number. Transfer your notes to paper, converting them to complete sentences. You now have a complete rough sentence outline, and the most difficult part of the writing job is over.

The final step is to polish your rough outline. Check to ensure that the **subordination** of minor heads to major heads is logical. Remember that all major heads should be parallel and all minor heads should be parallel.

CHANGE   A. Major and minor heads should be established. (passive voice)
         B. Note cards are sorted by major and minor heads. (passive voice)
         C. Complete the sentence outline. (active voice)
    TO   A. Establish major and minor heads. (active voice)
         B. Sort note cards by major and minor heads. (active voice)
         C. Complete the sentence outline. (active voice)

Make certain that your outline follows your method of development. Check for **unity**. Does your outline stick to the subject, or does it stray into unrelated or only loosely related topics? Stay within your established scope of coverage. Resist the temptation to tell all you know unless it all is pertinent to your objective. It is much easier to correct this problem in the outline stage than in the rough draft. If some information is of importance to only a minority of your readers, consider including that information in an **appendix**; those few readers can then pursue the subject further, and the others will not be interrupted. Check your outline for completeness; scan it to see whether you need more information in any of your divisions, and insert any information that is needed.

You now have a final, polished sentence outline. It isn't sacred, however; change it if you need to as you write the draft; the outline should be your point of departure and return. Return to it to find your place and your direction as you work.

outside of

In the **phrase** *outside of,* the word *of* is redundant.

> CHANGE   Place the rack *outside of* the incubator.
> TO   Place the rack *outside* the incubator.

In addition, do not use *outside of* to mean "aside from" or "except for."

> CHANGE   *Outside of* his frequent absences, Jim has a good work record.
> TO   *Except for* his frequent absences, Jim has a good work record.

over with

In the expression *over with,* the word *with* is redundant; moreover, the word *completed* often better expresses the thought.

> CHANGE   You may use the conference room when the managers' meeting is *over with.*
> TO   You may use the conference room when the managers' meeting is *over.*
> OR   You may use the conference room when the managers' meeting is *completed.*

P

pace

Pace is the speed at which the writer presents ideas to the **reader**. Your goal should be to achieve a pace that fits both your reader and your subject; at times you may need a fast pace, at other times a slow pace. The more knowledgeable the reader is, the faster your pace can be—but be careful not to lose control of it. In the first passage of the following example, facts are piled on top of each other at a rapid pace. In the second passage, the same facts are spread out over two sentences and presented in a more easily assimilated manner, even though the length is no greater; in addition, a different and more desirable **emphasis** is achieved.

> CHANGE The generator is powered by a 90-horsepower engine, is designed to operate under normal conditions of temperature and humidity, produces 110 volts at 60 Hertz, is designed for use under emergency conditions, and may be phased with other units of the same type to produce additional power when needed.
>
> TO The generator, which is powered by a 90-horsepower engine, produces 110 volts at 60 Hertz under normal conditions of temperature and humidity. Designed especially for use under emergency conditions, this generator may be phased with other units of the same type to produce additional power when needed.

Check your draft to determine the pace at which you are presenting your facts and ideas to the reader. If you find that you are jamming your ideas too closely together, you have a problem with pacing. There are at least three solutions to such problems: **subordination**, **sentence construction**, and **transition**.

The best way to solve a pacing problem is to search out minor thoughts and subordinate them to the major points, just as, in the example, "... is designed for use under emergency conditions..." was subordinated to "... this generator may be phased with other units. ..."

Another solution is to consider a different type of **sentence** structure. A complex idea is normally better stated in a simple sentence

481

structure; a series of simple thoughts is better stated in a more complex sentence structure. Notice in the example above that the first passage is one long, complicated sentence, and that the same ideas are expressed in shorter sentences in the revision.

A final solution is to provide words and **phrases** of transition to alter the pace.

> CHANGE   Negotiations had gone on for two days. Neither side wanted a walkout. They agreed to abide by the previous contract.
>
> TO   *Although* negotiations had gone on for only two days, neither side wanted a walkout. *Consequently,* they decided to abide by the previous contract.

(See also **telegraphic style.**)

paragraphs

A paragraph is a group of **sentences** that support and develop a single idea; it may be thought of as an essay in miniature, for its function is to expand the core idea stated in its **topic sentence**. A paragraph may use a particular **method of development** to expand this idea. The following paragraph uses the **general-to-specific method of development**. Its topic sentence is italicized.

> *The cost of training new employees is high.* In addition to the cost of classroom facilities and instructors, an organization must pay employees a salary to sit in the classroom while they are learning. We have determined that for the company to break even on professional employees (such as engineers or systems analysts), they must stay in the job for which they have been trained for at least one year.

The paragraph performs three functions: (1) it develops the unit of thought stated in the topic sentence; (2) it provides a logical break in the material; and (3) it creates a physical break on the page, which in turn provides visual assistance to the **reader**.

TOPIC SENTENCE

A topic sentence states the subject of a paragraph; the rest of the paragraph then supports and develops that statement with carefully related details. The topic sentence may appear anywhere in the paragraph—a fact that permits the writer to achieve **emphasis** and variety—and a topic statement may be more than one sentence if necessary.

The topic sentence is most often the first sentence of the paragraph because it states the subject that the paragraph is to develop. The topic sentence is effective in this position because the reader knows immediately what the paragraph is about, as in the following example:

> *One important objective of automation is the improvement of quality.* Cost alone is no longer the reason that U.S. industry is losing ground to international competitors. Higher-quality products from Japan and West Germany are forcing U.S. firms to look for ways to improve consistency of manufacture, precision of design, and control of quality at all stages of a product's life. Computer-aided design and analysis systems permit better prediction of product performance and assurance that all components of a product will fucntion properly with one another. Robots and other computer-based manufacturing systems can produce components with much greater consistency than can human counterparts. Inspection devices with computer-driven "eyes" and precise coordinate measuring machines can ensure that the product has, indeed, been manufactured to specifications.

On rare occasions, the topic sentence logically falls in the middle of a paragraph, as in the following example:

> It is perhaps natural that psychologists should awaken only slowly to the possibility that behavioral processes may be directly observed, or that they should only gradually put the older statistical and theoretical techniques in their proper perspective. But it is time to insist that science does not progress by carefully designed steps called "experiments," each of which has a well-defined beginning and end. *Science is a continuous and often a disorderly and accidental process.* We shall not do the young psychologist any favor if we agree to reconstruct our practices to fit a pattern demanded by current scientific methodology. What the statistician means by the design of experiments is design which yields the kind of data to which *his* techniques are applicable. He does not mean the behavior of the scientist in his laboratory devising research for his own immediate and possibly inscrutable purposes.
> —B. F. Skinner, "A Case History in Scientific Method," *American Psychologist,* 2 (May 1956): 232.

Although the topic sentence is usually more effective early in the paragraph, when the reader's attention is greatest, a paragraph can lead up to the topic sentence, which is sometimes done to achieve emphasis. When a topic sentence concludes a paragraph, it can also serve as a summary or **conclusion**, based on the details that were designed to lead up to it. The following is an example of a topic sentence in the concluding position:

> The way that most office organizations work has usually developed over a number of years, not through a single comprehensive design, but through a process of continuing evolution. The employees need not understand how their organization works in order to do their part, and few do. Information-handling patterns are largely subconscious and change resistant, since they reflect how people in an organization think of themselves and their organization. Therefore, bringing in equipment and instructing an employee to use it and do things differently from now on is not likely to work—at least not without careful preparation. *The barriers to the effective use of new information techniques, therefore, lie in the way that a company is organized and the ways people customarily work and think about themselves in the organization.*

Because multiple paragraphs are sometimes used to develop different aspects of an idea, not all paragraphs have topic sentences. In this situation, **transition** between paragraphs helps the reader know that the same idea is being developed through several paragraphs.

Topic sentence for all three paragraphs
To conserve valuable memory space, a large portion of the software package remains on disc; only the most frequently used portion resides in internal memory all of the time. The disc-resident software is organized into small modules that are called into memory as needed to perform specific functions.

Transition
The memory-resident portion of the operating system maintains strict control of processing. It consists of routines, subroutines, lists, and tables that are used to perform common program functions, such as processing input/output operations, calling other software routines from disc as needed, and processing errors.

Transition
The disc-resident portion of the operating system contains routines that are used less frequently in system operation, such as the peripheral-related software routines that are useful for correcting errors encountered on the various units, and

the log and display routines that record unusual operating conditions in the system log. The disc-resident portion of the operating system also contains Monitor, the software program that supervises the loading of utility routines and the user's programs.
—*NCR Century Operating Systems Manual* (Dayton: NCR Corporation).

In this example, the reason for breaking the development of the idea expressed in the topic sentence into three paragraphs is to help the reader assimilate the fact that the main idea has two separate parts.

PARAGRAPH LENGTH

Paragraph length should be tailored to aid the reader's understanding of ideas. A series of short, undeveloped paragraphs can indicate poor **organization** of material, in which case you should look for a larger idea to which the ideas in the short paragraphs relate and then make the larger idea the topic sentence for a single paragraph. A series of short paragraphs can also sacrifice **unity** by breaking a single idea into several pieces. A series of long paragraphs, on the other hand, can fail to provide the reader with manageable subdivisions of thought. A good rule of thumb is that a paragraph should be just long enough to deal adequately with the subject of its topic sentence. A new paragraph should begin whenever the subject changes significantly. Occasionally, a one-sentence paragraph is acceptable if it is used as a transition between larger paragraphs or in letters and **memorandums** in which one-sentence **openings** and closings are sometimes appropriate.

A short paragraph sometimes immediately follows a long paragraph to emphasize the thought contained in the short paragraph. Also, short paragraphs increase the pace of your writing, whereas long paragraphs can slow down the pace.

Because it has at times displaced some jobs, automation has become an ugly word in the American vocabulary. But the all-important fact that is so often overlooked is that it invariably creates many more jobs than it eliminates. (The vast number of people employed in the American automobile industry as compared with the number of people that had been employed in the harness- and carriage-making business is a classic example.) Almost always, the jobs that have been eliminated by automation have been menial, unskilled jobs, and those who have been displaced have been forced to increase their skills, which resulted in better and higher paying jobs for them.

In view of these facts, is automation really bad? It has made our country the most wealthy and technologically advanced nation the world has ever known!

WRITING PARAGRAPHS

The paragraph is the basic building block of any writing effort. Careful paragraphing reflects the writer's accurate thinking and logical organization. Clear and orderly paragraphs help the reader follow the writer's thoughts more easily.

Outlining is the best guide to paragraphing. It is easy to group ideas into appropriate paragraphs when you follow a good working outline. Notice how the following outline plots the course of subsequent paragraphs:

Outline

I. Advantages of Chicago as location for new plant
  A. Transport facilities
    1. Rail
    2. Air
    3. Truck
    4. Sea (except in winter)
  B. Labor supply
    1. Engineering and scientific personnel
      a. Many similar companies in the area
      b. Several major universities
    2. Technical and manufacturing personnel
      a. Existing programs in community colleges
      b. Possible special programs designed for us

Resulting Paragraphs

Probably the greatest advantage of Chicago as a location for our new plant is its excellent transport facilities. The city is served by three major railroads. Both domestic and international air cargo service is available at O'Hare International Airport. Chicago is a major hub of the trucking industry, and most of the nation's large freight carriers have terminals there. Finally, except in the winter months when the Great Lakes are frozen, Chicago is a seaport, accessible through the St. Lawrence Seaway.

A second advantage of Chicago is that it offers an abundant labor force. An ample supply of engineering and scientific personnel is assured not only the presence of many companies engaged in activities similar to ours but also by the presence of several major universities in the metropolitan area. Similarly, technicians and manufacturing personnel are in abundant supply. The seven colleges in the Chicago City College system, as well as half a dozen other two-year colleges in the outlying areas, produce graduates with associate degrees in a wide variety of technical specialties appropriate to our needs. Moreover, three of the outlying colleges have expressed an interest in establishing special courses attuned specifically to our requirements.

Consider not only the nature of the material you are developing but also the appearance of your page. An unbroken page looks forbidding.

PARAGRAPH COHERENCE AND UNITY

A good paragraph has unity, **coherence**, and adequate development. Unity is singleness of purpose, based on a topic sentence that states the core idea of the paragraph. When every sentence in the paragraph contributes to developing the core idea, the paragraph has unity. Coherence is holding to one **point of view**, one attitude, one **tense**; it is the joining of sentences into a logical pattern. Coherence is advanced by the careful choice of transitional words so that ideas are tied together as they are developed.

Topic sentence   *Any company which operates internationally today faces a host of difficulties.* Inflation is worldwide. Most countries are struggling
Transition   with other economic problems *as well. In addition,* there are many monetary uncertainties and growing economic nation-
Transition   alism directed against multinational companies. *Yet* there is ample business available in most developed countries if you have the right products, services, and marketing organization. To maintain the growth NCR has achieved overseas, we recently restructured our international operations into four ma-
Transition   jor trading areas. *This* will improve the services and support which the Corporation can provide to its subsidiaries around
Transition   the world. *At the same time* it established firm management con-
Transition   trol, insuring consistent policies around the world. *So* you might say the problems of doing business abroad will be more

> difficult this year but we are better organized to meet those
> problems.
> —*Annual Report* (Dayton: NCR Corporation).

Simple enumeration (*first, second, then, next,* and so on) can also provide effective transition within paragraphs. Notice how the italicized words and **phrases** give coherence to the following paragraph:

> Most adjustable office chairs have nylon hub tubes that hold
> metal spindle rods. To ensure trouble-free operation, lubri-
> cate these spindle rods occasionally. *First,* loosen the set screw
> in the adjustable bell. *Then* lift the chair from the base so that
> the entire spindle rod is accessible. *Next,* apply the lubricant
> to the spindle rod and the nylon washer, using the lubricant
> sparingly to prevent dripping. *When you have finished,* replace
> the chair and tighten the set screw.

Good paragraphs often use details from the preceding paragraph,
thereby preserving and advancing the thought being developed.
Appropriate **conjunctions** and the **repetition** of key words and
phrases can help provide unity and coherence among, as well as
within, paragraphs, as the italicized words do in the following
example:

> *Money market funds* are massive investment pools run by large
> brokerage houses or mutual fund firms, which are not subject
> to the government's interest-rate laws. The *fund managers* buy
> high-interest short-term money market instruments, such as
> U.S. Treasury bills, commercial paper, and bank certificates of
> deposit. Since the securities mature within 30 days to one year,
> the *money market funds* have a dependable flow of cash to pay
> off investors who want to withdraw their money.
>
> From the consumer's point of view, a *money market fund* is not
> much different from a checking account. In most cases, peo-
> ple can write checks against an account, although some *money
> market funds* require that checks be written for a minimum of
> $500.

Sometimes a paragraph is used solely for transition, as in the following example:

> . . . that marred the progress of the company.
>
> There were two other setbacks to the company's fortunes
> that year which contributed to its present shaky condition:
> the loss of many skilled workers through the early retirement

program and the intensification of the devastating rate of inflation.

The early retirement program . . .

parallel structure

Parallel sentence structure requires that sentence elements that are alike in function be alike in construction as well, as in the following example (in which similar actions are stated in similar **phrases**):

EXAMPLES   The stream runs *under the culvert, behind the embankment,* and *into the pond.*

We need a supplementary work force *to handle* peak-hour activity, *to free* full-time employees from routine duties, *to relieve* operators during lunch breaks, and *to replace* vacationing employees.

Parallel structure achieves an economy of words, clarifies meaning, and pleases the **reader** aesthetically. In addition to adding a pleasing symmetry to a sentence, parallel structure expresses the equality of its ideas. This technique assists readers because they are able to anticipate the meaning of a sentence element on the basis of its parallel construction. When they recognize the similarity of word order or construction, readers know that the relationship between the new sentence element and the **subject** is the same as the relationship between the last sentence element and the subject. Because of this they can go from one idea to another more quickly and confidently.

EXAMPLES   The computer instruction contains *fetch, initiate,* and *execute* stages. (parallel words)

The computer instruction contains *a fetch stage, an initiate stage,* and *an execute stage.* (parallel phrases)

The computer instruction contains a fetch stage, it contains an initiate stage, and *it contains an execute stage.* (parallel clauses)

Parallel structure is especially important in creating your **outline**, your **table of contents**, and your **heads** because it enables your reader to know the relative value of each item in your table of contents and each head in the body of your **report** (or other writing project).

In any type of writing, parallel structure channels the reader's attention and helps draw together related ideas or line up dissimilar ideas for comparison and contrast.

EXAMPLE   Her book provoked much comment: *negative from her enemies, positive from her friends.*

The power of many of Lincoln's speeches comes from his use of parallel structure; in them, parallel structure harmonizes the elements within sentences and the relationships among sentences.

EXAMPLE   But in a larger sense, *we cannot dedicate—we cannot consecrate— we cannot hallow*—this ground. The brave men, *living* and *dead*, who struggled here, have consecrated it far above our poor power to *add* or *detract. The world will little note nor long remember what we say here*, but *it can never forget what they did here.*
—Abraham Lincoln, Gettysburg Address

A century later, John F. Kennedy use the same technique with striking effect.

EXAMPLE   We shall *pay any price, bear any burden, meet any hardship, support any friend, oppose any foe* to assure the survival and the success of liberty.
—John F. Kennedy, Inaugural Address

Although parallelism can be accomplished with words, phrases, or **clauses**, it is most frequently accomplished by the use of phrases.

EXAMPLES   I was convinced of their competence *by their conduct, by their reputation,* and *by their survival in a competitive business.* (prepositional phrases)
Filling the gas tank, testing the windshield wipers, and *checking tire pressure* are essential to preparing for a long trip. (gerund phrases)
From childhood the artist had made it a habit *to observe people, to store up the impressions they made upon him,* and *to draw conclusions about human beings from them.* (infinitive phrases)

Correlative conjunctions (*either . . . or, neither . . . nor, not only . . . but also*) should always be followed by parallel structure. Both members of these pairs should be followed immediately by the same grammatical form: two words, two similar phrases, or two similar clauses.

EXAMPLES   Viruses carry either *DNA* or *RNA*, never both. (words)
Clearly, neither *serologic tests* nor *virus isolation studies* alone would have been adequate. (phrases)
Either *we must increase our operational efficiency* or *we must decrease our production goals.* (clauses)

To make a parallel construction clear and effective, it is often best to repeat a **preposition**, an **article**, a **pronoun**, a **subordinating conjunction**, a **helping verb**, or the mark of an **infinitive**.

EXAMPLES   The Babylonians had *a* rudimentary geometry and *a* rudimentary astronomy. (article)

My father and *my* teacher agreed that I was not really trying. (pronoun)

To run and be elected is better than *to* run and be defeated. (mark of the infinitive)

The driver *must* be careful to check the gauge and *must* move quickly when the light comes on. (helping verb)

New teams were being established *in* New York and *in* Hawaii. (preposition)

The history of factories shows both *the* benefits and *the* limits of standardization. (article)

When parallel constructions are closely related in thought and equal in length and construction, they balance one another. Such balance is useful for comparing and contrasting ideas.

EXAMPLE   A qualified staff without a sufficient budget is helpless; a sufficient budget without a qualified staff is useless.

FAULTY PARALLELISM

Faulty parallelism results when joined elements are intended to serve equal grammatical functions but do not have equal grammatical form. Avoid this kind of partial parallelism. Make certain that each element in a series is similar in form and structure to all others in the same series.

CHANGE   Before mowing the lawn, check the following items: the dipstick for the proper oil level, the gas tank for fuel, the spark plug wire attachment, and that no foreign objects are under or near the mower.

TO   Before mowing the lawn, check the following items: the dipstick *for the proper oil level*, the gas tank *for fuel*, the spark plug wire *for attachment*, and the lawn *for foreign objects*.

In work-related writing, **lists** often cause problems with parallel structure. When you use a list that consists of phrases or clauses, each phrase or clause in the list should begin with the same **part of speech**.

CHANGE The following recommendations were made regarding the Cost Containment Committee's position statement:

1. *Stress* that this statement is for all departments.
2. *Start* the statement with "If the company continues to grow, the following steps should be taken."
3. *The statement* should emphasize both department managers and staff.

TO The following recommendations were made regarding the Cost Containment Committee's position statement:

1. *Stress* that this statement is for all departments.
2. *Start* the statement with "If the company continues to grow, the following steps must be taken."
3. *Emphasize* that this statement especially applies to both department managers and staff.

In the first list the items are not grammatically parallel in structure: items 1 and 2 begin with verbs, but item 3 does not. Notice how much more smoothly the corrected version reads, with all items beginning with verbs.

Faulty parallelism sometimes occurs because a writer tries to compare items that are not comparable.

CHANGE The company offers special training to help nonexempt employees move into professional and technical careers like data processing, bookkeeping, customer engineers, and sales trainees. (Notice that occupations—data processing and bookkeeping—are being compared to people—customer engineers and trainees.)

TO The company offers special training to help nonexempt employees move into professional and technical careers like data processing, bookkeeping, *customer services*, and *sales.*

Because faulty parallelism with correlative conjunctions (*either . . . or, neither . . . nor, not only . . . but also*) is one of the most common writing errors, the following examples are worth careful study:

CHANGE You may travel to the new plant either *by train* or *there is a plane.* (different grammatical forms: a prepositional phrase, *by train*; and a clause, *there is a plane*)

TO You may travel to the new plant either *by train* or *by plane.* (parallel grammatical forms: prepositional phrases)

OR You may travel to the new plant by either *train* or *plane.* (parallel grammatical forms: nouns)

CHANGE   We are not only *responsible to our stockholders* but also *to our customers.* (different grammatical forms: an adjective with a modifying prepositional phrase, *responsible to our stockholders;* and a prepositional phrase, *to our customers*)

TO   We are responsible not only *to our stockholders* but also *to our customers.* (parallel grammatical forms: adjectives with modifying prepositional phrases)

CHANGE   We either *will pay the bill* or *we will return the shipment.* (different grammatical forms: a verb with its object, *will pay the bill*, and a clause, *we will return the shipment*)

TO   Either *we will pay the bill* or *we will return the shipment.* (parallel grammatical forms: clauses)

OR   We will either *pay the bill* or *return the shipment.* (parallel grammatical forms: verbs with their objects)

Be careful not to throw your reader off balance. If you make a statement about two subjects and then follow with a further statement about one of them, complete the thought and make a balancing statement about the other subject.

CHANGE   The Commanche Commander and the Cessna Hawk are both small aircraft; *the Commander seats four*.

TO   The Commanche Commander and the Cessna Hawk are both small aircraft; *the Commander seats four* and *the Hawk seats six*.

paraphrasing

When you paraphrase a written passage, you rewrite it to state the essential ideas in your own words. Because you do not quote your source word for word when paraphrasing, it is unnecessary to enclose the paraphrased material in **quotation marks**. However, paraphrased material should be footnoted because the ideas are taken from someone else whether or not the words are identical.

Ordinarily, the majority of the notes you take during the **research** phase of writing your **report** will paraphrase the original material (see also **note taking**.)

Original Material

By definition, the leader is a person who has followers. Thus the quality of a manager is directly related to the quality of the men who work for him, and his own results are essentially those of his workers. Tomorrow's manager will be confronted

with more complex technical and commerical problems than
ever before. He won't be able to do all the work himself even
if he should want to; he will thereby become more dependent
upon good men working for him. If he has built an organization of pipsqueaks, as management development expert Jim
Hayes of Duquesne University put it, "he's nothing more than
chief pipsqueak." On the other hand, if he has pulled together
a team of tigers, he is the head tiger.

—George S. Odiorne, *Management by Objectives—A System of Managerial Leadership*
(New York: Pitman, 1965) 11.

Paraphrased

In the future, managers will be confronted with more complex
technical and commercial tasks than they have been in the
past. Increasingly, those who manage will be dependent on
those who perform these tasks. Since those performing the
work will attain the results, the quality of a manager's leadership will be known by the quality of the people who work for
him.

Note that the paraphrased version includes only the essential information from the original passage. Strive to put the original ideas
into your words without distorting them. (See also **plagiarism** and
quotations.)

parentheses

Parentheses ( ) are used to enclose words, **phrases**, or sentences. The
material within parentheses can add **clarity** to a statement without
altering its meaning. Parentheses de-emphasize (or play down) an
inserted element. Parenthetical information may not be essential to
a sentence, but it may be interesting or helpful to some **readers**.

EXAMPLE   Many American business and industrial leaders (for example,
Andrew Carnegie) have risen from humble origins.

Parenthetical material applies to the word or phrase immediately
preceding it.

EXAMPLE   The development of International Business Machines (IBM) is
a uniquely American success story.

Parentheses may be used to enclose figures or letters that indicate sequence. Enclose the figure or letter with two parentheses rather than using only one parenthesis.

> EXAMPLE   The following sections deal with (1) preparation, (2) research, (3) organization, (4) writing, and (5) revision.

Parenthetical material does not affect the **punctuation** of a sentence. If a parenthesis closes a sentence, the ending punctuation should appear after the parenthesis. Also, a **comma** following a parenthetical word, phrase, or **clause** appears outside the closing parenthesis.

> EXAMPLE   Two of our regional managers, Bob Evans (Houston) and Jane Wright (Denver), do not believe the new marketing approach has had a significant impact on sales.

However, when a complete sentence within parentheses stands independently, the ending punctuation goes inside the final parenthesis.

> EXAMPLE   The new marketing approach appears to be a success; most of our regional managers report sales increases of 15 to 30 percent. (The only important exceptions are the Denver and Houston offices.) Therefore, we plan to continue . . .

Do not follow a spelled-out number with a figure in parentheses representing the same number.

> CHANGE   Send five (5) copies of the report.
> TO   Send five copies of the report.

In some footnote forms, parentheses enclose the publisher, place of publication, and date of publication.

> EXAMPLE   [1]Gerald J. Alred, Walter E. Oliu, and Charles T. Brusaw, *The Professional Writer: A Guide for Advanced Technical Writing* (New York: St. Martin's, 1992), p. 189.

Use **brackets** to set off a parenthetical item that is already within parentheses.

> EXAMPLE   We should be sure to give Emanuel Foose (and his brother Emilio [1812–1882] as well) credit for his part in founding the institute.

Use parentheses with care because they are easily overused. And guard against using parentheses when other marks of punctuation are more appropriate.

participial phrases

A participial phrase consists of a **participle** plus its **object** or **complement**, if any, and modifiers. Like the participle, a participial phrase functions as an **adjective** modifying a **noun** or **pronoun**.

EXAMPLES   The division *having the largest sales increase* wins the trophy.
Finding the problem resolved, he went to the next item.
Having begun, we felt that we had to see the project through.

The relationship between a participial phrase and the rest of the sentence must be clear to the **reader**. For this reason, every sentence containing a participial phrase must have a noun or pronoun that the participial phrase modifies; if it does not, the result is a dangling participial phrase that is misplaced in the sentence and so appears to modify the wrong noun or pronoun. Both of these problems are discussed below.

DANGLING PARTICIPIAL PHRASES

A dangling participial phrase occurs when the noun or pronoun that the participial phrase is meant to modify is not stated but only implied in the sentence. (See also **dangling modifiers**.)

CHANGE   *Being unhappy with the job*, his efficiency suffered. (His *efficiency* was not unhappy with the job; what the participial phrase really modifies—*he*—is not stated but merely implied.)
TO   *Being unhappy with the job*, he grew less efficient. (Now what that participial phrase modifies—*he*—is explicitly stated.)

MISPLACED PARTICIPIAL PHRASES

A participial phrase is misplaced when it is too far from the noun or pronoun it is meant to modify and so appears to modify something else. This is an error that can sometimes make the writer look ridiculous indeed. (See also **modifiers**.)

CHANGE   *Rolling around in the bottom of the vibration test chamber*, I found the missing bearings.
TO   I found the missing bearings *rolling around in the bottom of the vibration test chamber*.
CHANGE   We saw a large warehouse *driving down the highway*.
TO   *Driving down the highway*, we saw a large warehouse.

participles

Participles are **verb** forms that function as **adjectives**.

EXAMPLES The *waiting* driver raced his engine.
Here are the *revised* estimates.
The *completed* report lay on his desk.
Rising costs reduced our profit margin.

Participles belong to a larger class of verb forms called **verbals** or nonfinite verbs. (The other two types of verbals are **gerunds**, which always function as nouns, and **infinitives**, which have several functions.) Because participles are formed from verbs, they share certain characteristics of verbs, even though they are adjectives: (1) they may take **objects** or **complements**; (2) they may be in the present, past, or perfect **tense**; and (3) they may be in the active or passive **voice**. But remember that a participle cannot be used as the verb of a sentence. Inexperienced writers sometimes make this mistake; the result is a **sentence fragment**.

CHANGE The committee chairman was responsible. His vote *being* the decisive one.
TO The committee chairman was responsible, his vote *being* the decisive one.
OR The committee chairman was responsible. His vote *was* the decisive one.

TENSE

The present participle ends in *ing*.

EXAMPLE *Declining* sales forced us to close one branch office.

Do not confuse present participles with gerunds, which are also verbals ending in *ing* but which always function as nouns, as in "*Running* is his favorite sport."
The past participle may end in *ed, t, en, n,* or *d.*

EXAMPLES Repair the *bent* lever.
What are the *estimated* costs?
Here is the *broken* calculator.
What are the metal's *known* properties?
The story, *told* many times before, was still interesting.

The perfect participle is formed with the present participle of the **helping verb** *have* plus the past participle of the main verb.

EXAMPLE *Having gotten* (perfect participle) a large raise, the *smiling* (present participle), *contented* (past participle) employee worked harder than ever.

VOICE

Participles formed from transitive verbs may be in either the active or the passive voice. Some form of the helping verb *be* is used to form the passive voice of the perfect participle.

EXAMPLES *Having finished* the job, we submitted our bill. (active)
The job *having been finished*, we submitted our bill. (passive)

parts of speech

Parts of speech is a term used to describe the class of words to which a particular word belongs, according to its function in the sentence; that is, each function in a sentence (naming, asserting, acting, describing, joining, modifying, exclaiming) is performed by a word belonging to a certain part of speech.

If a word's function is to *name* something, it is a **noun** or **pronoun**. If a word's function is to make an *assertion* about something, it is a **verb**. If its function is to *describe* or *modify* something, the word is an **adjective** or an **adverb**. If its function is to *join* or *link* one element of the sentence to another, it is a **conjunction** or a **preposition**. If its function is to express an exclamation, it is an **interjection**. (See also **functional shift**.)

party

In legal language, *party* refers to an individual, group, or organization.

EXAMPLE The injured *party* brought suit against my client.

The term is inappropriate to general writing; when an individual is being referred to, use *person*.

CHANGE The *party* whose file you requested is here now.
TO The *person* whose file you requested is here now.

Party is, of course, appropriate when it refers to a group.

EXAMPLE Arrangements were made for the members of our *party* to have lunch after the tour.

per

Per is a common business term that means "by means of," "through," or "on account of," and in these senses it is appropriate.

EXAMPLES   *per* annum, *per* capita, *per* diem, *per* head

When used to mean "according to" (*per* your request, *per* your order), the expression is business **jargon** at its worst and should be avoided. Equally annoying is the phrase *as per.*

CHANGE   *Per your request*, I am enclosing the production report.
TO   *As you requested*, I am enclosing the production report.

CHANGE   *As per our discussion*, I will send revised instructions.
TO   *As we agreed*, I will send revised instructions.

per cent/percent/percentage

Percent, which is replacing the two-word *per cent*, is used instead of the symbol (%) except in tables.

EXAMPLE   Only 25 *percent* of the members attended the meeting.

Percentage, which is never used with numbers, indicates a general size.

EXAMPLE   Only a small *percentage* of the managers attended the meeting.

periods

A period (also called a full stop or end stop) usually indicates the end of a declarative sentence. Periods also link (when used as leaders) and indicate omissions (when used as **ellipses**).

Although the primary function of periods is to end declarative sentences, periods also end imperative sentences that are not emphatic enough for an **exclamation mark**.

EXAMPLE   Send me any information you may have on the subject.

Periods may also end questions that are really polite requests and questions to which an affirmative response is assumed.

EXAMPLE   Will you please send me the specifications.

Periods end incomplete sentences when the meaning is clear from the context. These sentences are common in advertising. (See also **sentence faults**.)

> EXAMPLE　Bell and Howell's new Double-Feature Cassette Projector will change your mind about home movies. *Because if you can press a button, now you can show movies. Instantly. Easily.*

IN QUOTATIONS

Do not use a period after a declarative sentence that is quoted in the context of another sentence.

> CHANGE　"There is every chance of success." she stated.
> TO　"There is every chance of success," she stated.

A period is conventionally placed inside **quotation marks**.

> EXAMPLES　He liked to think of himself as a "tycoon."
> He stated clearly, "My vote is yes."

WITH PARENTHESES

A sentence that ends in a **parenthesis** requires a period *after* the parenthesis.

> EXAMPLE　The institute was founded by Harry Denman (1902–1972).

If a whole sentence (beginning with an initial **capital letter**) is in parentheses, the period (or any other end mark) should be placed inside the final parenthesis.

> EXAMPLE　The project director listed the problems facing her staff. (This was the third time she had complained to the board.)

CONVENTIONAL USES OF PERIODS

Use periods after initials in names.

> EXAMPLES　W. T. Grant, J. P. Morgan

Use periods as decimal points with numbers.

> EXAMPLES　109.2, $540.26, 6.9%

Use periods to indicate **abbreviations**.

> EXAMPLES　Ms., Dr., Inc.

When a sentence ends with an abbreviation that ends with a period, do not add another period.

EXAMPLE Please meet me at 8:30 a.m.

Use periods following the **numbers** in numbered **lists**.

EXAMPLE 1.
            2.
            3.

AS ELLIPSES

When you omit words in quoted material, use a series of three spaced periods—called **ellipsis** dots—to indicate the omission (do not use ellipses to indicate a pause). Such an omission must not detract from or alter the essential meaning of the passage.

ORIGINAL "Technical material distributed for promotional use is sometimes charged for, particularly in high-volume distribution to educational institutions, although prices for these publications are not uniformly based on the cost of developing them."

WITH OMISSION "Technical material distributed for promotional use is sometimes charged for . . . although prices for these publications are not uniformly based on the cost of developing them."

When introducing a **quotation** that does not begin with the first word of a sentence (that is, when your quotation starts somewhere in the middle of a sentence of the material from which you are quoting), you do not need ellipsis dots, as the lowercase letter with which you begin the quotation already indicates an omission.

ORIGINAL "Once the client's needs have been evaluated, the sales representative must prepare a proposal designed to meet those specific needs."

WITH OMISSION His letter states that "the sales represenative must prepare a proposal designed to meet those specific needs."

If an ellipsis follows the end of a sentence, retain the period at the end of the sentence and add the three ellipsis dots.

ORIGINAL "During the year, every department participated in the development of a centralized computer system. The basic plan centered on the use of the computer as a cost reduction tool.

> At the beginning of the year, each department received a
> booklet explaining the purpose of the system."
>
> WITH   "During the year, every department participated in the devel-
> OMISSION   opment of a centralized computer system. . . . At the begin-
> ning of the year, each department received a booklet ex-
> plaining the purpose of the system."

AS LEADERS

When spaced periods are used in a **table** to connect one item to
another, they are called *leaders*. The purpose of leaders is to help the
reader align the data. The most common use of leaders is in **tables
of contents**.

New York.. $25,000
Chicago 18,000
Detroit 13,500

The most common use of leaders is in **tables of contents**.

PERIOD FAULTS

The incorrect use of a period is sometimes referred to as a *period
fault*. When a period is inserted prematurely, the result is a **sentence
fragment**.

> CHANGE   After a long day at the office in which we finished the report.
> We left hurriedly for home.
>
> TO   After a long day at the office in which we finished the report,
> we left hurriedly for home.

When a period is left out, the result is a "fused," or run-on, sentence.
Be careful never to leave out necessary periods.

> CHANGE   Bill was late for ten days in a row Ms. Sturgess had to fire him.
> TO   Bill was late for ten days in a row. Ms. Sturgess had to fire him.

(See also **sentence faults**.)

person

Person refers to the form of a **personal pronoun** that indicates
whether the **pronoun** represents the speaker, the person spoken to,
or the person (or thing) spoken about. A pronoun representing the
speaker is in the first person.

> EXAMPLE   *I* could not find the answer in the manual.

If the pronoun represents the person or persons spoken to, the pronoun is in the second person.

EXAMPLE *You* are going to be a good supervisor.

If the pronoun represents the person or persons spoken about, the pronoun is in the third person.

EXAMPLE *They* received the news quietly.

The following table shows first, second, and third person pronouns.

Person	Singular	Plural
first	I, me, my	we, ours, us
second	you, your	you, your
third	he, him, his	they, them, their
	she, her, hers	
	it, its	

Identifying pronouns by person helps the writer avoid illogical shifts from one person to another. A common error is to shift from the third person to the second person.

CHANGE *Managers* should spend the morning hours on work requiring mental effort, for *your* mind is freshest in the morning.
TO *Managers* should spend the morning hours on work requiring mental effort, for *their* minds are freshest in the morning.
OR *You* should spend the morning hours on work requiring mental effort, for *your* mind is freshest in the morning.

(See also **case**, **number**, and **one**.)

personal/personnel

Personal is an **adjective** meaning "of or pertaining to an individual person."

EXAMPLE He left work early because of a *personal* problem.

Personnel is a **noun** meaning a "group of people engaged in a common job."

EXAMPLE All *personnel* should pick up their paychecks on Thursday.

Be careful not to use *personnel* when the word you need is *persons* or *people*.

> CHANGE The remaining two *personnel* will be moved next Thursday.
> TO The remaining two *persons* will be moved next Thursday.

personal pronouns

The personal pronouns are *I, me, my, mine; you, your, yours; he, him, his; she, her, hers; it, its; we, us, our, ours;* and *they, them, their, theirs.*

Don't attempt to avoid using the personal pronoun *I* when it is natural. The use of unnatural devices to avoid using *I* is more likely to call attention to the writer than would use of the pronoun *I.*

> CHANGE *The writer* wishes to point out that the proposed solution has several weaknesses.
> TO *I* wish to point out that the proposed solution has several weaknesses.
> OR The proposed solution has several weaknesses.

Also, avoid substituting the **reflexive pronouns** *myself* for *I* or *me*, or *ourselves* for *we* or *us.*

> CHANGE Joe and *myself* worked all day on it.
> TO Joe and *I* worked all day on it.
> CHANGE He gave it to my assistant and *myself.*
> TO He gave it to my assistant and *me.*
> CHANGE This decision cannot be made by managers like *myself.*
> TO This decision cannot be made by managers like *me.*
> CHANGE Nobody can solve this problem but *ourselves.*
> TO Nobody can solve this problem but *us.*

The use of *we* for general reference ("*We* are living in a time of high inflation") is acceptable. But using the editorial *we* to avoid *I* is pompous and stiff. It may also assume, presumptuously, that "we" all agree.

> CHANGE *We* must state unequivocally that *we* disapprove of such practices.
> TO *I* must state unequivocally that *I* disapprove of such practices.

Especially in business writing, in which it can be important to distinguish individual commitments from corporate commitments, bear in mind that the use of *we* can be legally construed to commit the writer's company as well as the writer personally. If you are speaking for yourself—even in your role as an employee—it is better to use *I.*

One is also acceptable for general reference. Be aware, however, that it is impersonal and somewhat stiff and that overdoing it makes your writing awkward.

> CHANGE *One* must be careful about *one's* work habits lest *one* become sloppy.
>
> TO *People* must be careful about *their* work habits lest *they* become sloppy.

(See also **one** and **point of view**.)

persons/people

When we use *persons*, we are usually referring to individual people thought of separately.

> EXAMPLE We need to find three qualified *persons* to fill the vacant positions.

When we say *people*, we are identifying a large or anonymous group.

> EXAMPLE Many *people* have never even heard of our product.

persuasion

Persuasion in writing attempts to convince the **reader** to adopt the writer's point of view. The range of persuasive writing required on the job varies widely. Business writers may use persuasive techniques when writing **memorandums**, pleading for better working conditions in a shop or office, justifying the expense of a new program, or writing a **proposal** for a multimillion-dollar contract. Persuasive writing is also found in many types of **correspondence**, especially when the **you viewpoint** is used.

In persuasive writing, the way that you present your ideas is as important as the ideas themselves. You must support your appeal with **logic**—a sound presentation of facts, statistics, and examples. You must also acknowledge any real or possible conflicting opinions. Only then can you demonstrate and argue for the merit of your point of view. But remember your audience, and take into account your readers' feelings. Always maintain a positive **tone**. And be careful not to wander from your main point—avoid ambiguity and never make trivial, irrelevant, or false claims. But if a reader may be

```
                              MEMORANDUM

          Date:       December 5, 19--
          To:         Harriet Sullivan, Office Manager
          From:       Christine Thomas, Administrative Assistant  CT
          Subject:    Advantages of Expanding HVS Computing Facilities
```

Because our computing facilities currently operate at maximum
capacity, we are turning away new customers in growing numbers
and will soon have to deny our present customers computer time
for emergencies or overload backups. But by purchasing a new VT-
8000 minicomputer and expanding our staff, we could respond to
new service requests, offer better service to valued customers,
and attract new customers who would not have previously
considered using our service.

Last month we turned away 2I new service requests. At least six
of them were equal to the largest accounts we currently serve.
Furthermore, since our aging mainframe computer cannot handle the
latest software available from VRX Systems, we can neither offer
improved, faster services to our most profitable accounts (such
as First International Savings and Loan) nor attract the new
customers who are eager to take advantage of the most recent
advances in computer technology.

The VT-8000 is a very fast, reasonably priced minicomputer with
massive peripheral memory capacity in the form of removable disk
packs. This machine would triple our current processing capacity
and enable us to use the full range of the VRX software now
available. The following details show how purchasing the VT-8000
System would triple our number of customers and pay for itself
within two years:

          Cost of New Equipment

                VT-8000 minicomputer $12,500
                Two 3033 disks and disk drives   1,800
                One VT80 computer terminal   980
                New VRX software   1,050

                Total cost of equipment $16,330

          Increases in Annual Operating Budget

                Salaries: Computer Operator $17,000
                           Data Entry Technician $14,200

                Total increase/annual operating budget $31,200

          Total Costs

                First year $47,530
                Second year $31,200

                Two-year total cost $78,730
```

*Margin labels:*

Statement
of position

Facts and
statistics
that support
the writer's
position

*Figure 1  Persuasive Memo*
```

Increased Income Generated by Expansion

First-year estimate (45 new customers)	$28,100
Second-year estimate (50 new customers) plus the 45 of the first year	$59,322
Total increase	$87,422

Since the purchase of the VT-8000 system is a one-time investment, <u>a profit of over $8,500 will be generated by the end of the second year</u>. The estimates are based on the $578 average annual value of accounts over the past two years.

Other advantages of the VT-8000 minicomputer are as follows:

- It requires little maintenance and therefore has minimal downtime.
- It is easy to operate and thus requires less highly trained staff.
- It is extremely compact and will easily fit into space already
  available in our computer room.
- Additional peripheral equipment, such as disk drives and remote terminals, can be added at minimal cost if we decide to expand the facility again at a later date.

Acknowledgment of disadvantage

Because this system is reliable, easy to install, and easy to operate, we could have it running in three weeks with little disturbance of our normal office routine. More importantly, buying the VT-8000 will provide a cost-effective solution to the current problem of overburdened computing resources and will clear the way for meeting the demands of a growing base of customers. Because the VT-8000 printer is somewhat noisier than the VT-3400 printer, the computer room may have to be soundproofed.

On the basis of these details, I recommend that we expand HVS services by purchasing the VT-8000 system. An enclosed brochure describes the system in more detail. I will be happy to provide additional information about the system at your request.

mo
Enclosure

Figure 1 Persuasive Memo (continued)

skeptical of your main idea, you may need to build up to it with strong, specific points or arguments that support it. (This *inductive* method is illustrated in **specific-to-general method of development**.)

The memorandum shown in Figure 1 was written to persuade a manager and others to accept a new computer system. Notice that the writer admits that the new printer may be noisier than the old one. In fact, by acknowledging negative details or opposing views, a writer gains credibility. A writer also gains credibility through the readers' impression of him or her as a person. This is why the appearance (**format**) of a **letter of application** and a résumé, for example, is important. (See also **methods of development** and **forms of discourse**.)

phenomenon/phenomena

A *phenomenon* is an observable thing, fact, or occurrence. Its plural form is *phenomena*.

> EXAMPLES   Inflation is a *phenomenon* that continues to stump economists. Rain and snowfall are natural *phenomena* that also affect the economy.

photographs

Photographs are vital to many publications. Pictures are the best way to show the surface appearance of an object or to record an event or the development of a phenomenon over a period of time. Not all representations, however, call for photographs. They cannot depict the internal workings of a mechanism or below-the-surface details of objects or structures. Such details are better represented in drawings or diagrams.

HIGHLIGHTING PHOTOGRAPHIC SUBJECTS

Stand close enough to the object so that it fills your picture frame. To get precise and clear photographs, choose camera angles carefully. A camera will photograph only what it is aimed at; accordingly, select the important details and the camera angles that will record them. To show relative size, place a familiar object—such as a ruler, a book, or a person—near the object being photographed.

USING COLOR

The preparation and printing of color photographs are complex technical tasks performed by graphics and printing experts. If you are planning to use color photographs in your publication, discuss with them the type and quality of photographs required. Generally, they prefer color transparencies (slides) and color negatives (negatives of color prints) for reproduction.

The advantages of using color illustrations are obvious: color is a good way of communicating crucial information. In medical, chemical, geological, and botanical publications, to name but a few, readers often need to know exactly what an object or phenomenon looks like. In these circumstances, color reproduction is the only legitimate option available.

Be aware, however, that color reproduction is significantly more expensive than black and white. Color can also be tricky to reproduce accurately without losing contrast and vividness. For this reason, the original must be sharply focused and rich in contrasts.

TIPS FOR USING PHOTOGRAPHS

Like all illustrative materials, photographs must be handled carefully. When preparing photographs for printing, observe the following guidelines:

1. Mount photographs on white bond paper with rubber cement or another adhesive and allow ample margins.
2. If the photograph is the same size as the paper, type the caption, figure and page numbers, and any other important information on labels and fasten them to the photograph with rubber cement or another adhesive. The labels that identify key features in the photograph are referred to as *callouts*. (Photographs are given figure numbers in sequence with **illustrations** in a publication; see Figure 1.)
3. Position the figure number and caption so that the reader can view them and the photograph from the same orientation.
4. Do not draw crop marks (lines showing where the photo should be trimmed for reproduction) directly across a photograph. Draw them at the very edge of the photograph.
5. Do not write on a photograph, front or back. Tape a tissue-paper overlay over the face of the photograph, and then write very lightly on the overlay with a soft-lead pencil. Never write on the overlay with a ball-point pen.

Figure 1   Example of a Photograph

6. Do not use paper clips or staples directly on photographs.
7. Do not fold or crease photographs.
8. If only a color photograph or slide is available for black-and-white reproduction, have a photographer produce a black-and-white glossy copy or slide for printing. Otherwise, the printed image will not have an accurate tone.

phrases

Below the level of the sentence, there are two ways to combine words into groups: by forming **clauses**, which combine **subjects** and **verbs**, and by forming phrases, which are based on **nouns**, nonfinite verb forms, or verb combinations without subjects. A phrase is the most basic meaningful group of words; it cannot make a full statement as a clause can, however, because a phrase does not contain a subject and verb combination.

EXAMPLE   He encouraged his staff (clause) *by his calm confidence.* (phrase)

A phrase may function as an **adjective**, an **adverb**, a noun, or a verb.

EXAMPLES   The subjects *on the agenda* were all discussed. (adjective)
We discussed the project *with great enthusiasm.* (adverb)
Working hard is her way of life. (noun)
The chief engineer *should have been notified.* (verb)

Even though phrases function as adjectives, adverbs, nouns, or verbs, they are normally named for the kind of word around which they are constructed—**preposition, participle, infinitive, gerund,** verb, or noun.

PREPOSITIONAL PHRASES

A preposition is a word that shows the relationship of its **object** to another word; that is, it combines with its object (a noun or a **pronoun**) to form a modifying phrase. A **prepositional phrase,** then, consists of a preposition plus its object (the noun or pronoun) and its **modifiers**.

EXAMPLE   *After the meeting,* the regional managers adjourned *to the executive dining room.*

PARTICIPIAL PHRASES

A participle is any form of a verb that is used as an adjective. A **participial phrase** consists of a participle plus its object and its modifiers.

EXAMPLE   *Looking very pleased with himself,* the sales manager reported on the success of the policies he had introduced.

INFINITIVE PHRASES

An infinitive is the bare form of a verb (*go, run, talk*) without the restrictions imposed by **person** and **number**; an infinitive is generally preceded by the word *to* (which is usually a preposition but in this use is called the sign, or mark, of the infinitive). An **infinitive phrase** consists of the word *to* plus an infinitive and any objects or modifiers.

EXAMPLE   *To succeed in this field,* you must be willing *to assume responsibility.*

GERUND PHRASES

A gerund phrase, which consists of a gerund plus any objects or modifiers, always functions as a noun.

EXAMPLES *Preparing an annual report* is a difficult task. (subject)
She liked *running the department.* (direct object)

VERB PHRASES

A **verb phrase** consists of a main verb and its **helping verb**.

EXAMPLE Company officials discovered that a computer *was emitting* more data than it *had been asked* for. After investigation, police suggested that an unauthorized program *had been run* through the computer at the coded command of another computer belonging to a different company. The police obtained a warrant to search for electronic impulses in the memory of the suspect machine. The case (involving trade secrets) and its outcome *should make* legal history.

NOUN PHRASES

A noun phrase consists of a noun and its modifiers.

EXAMPLES *Many large companies* use computers.
Have *the two new employees* fill out *these forms.*

plagiarism

To use someone else's exact words without **quotation marks** and appropriate credit, or to use the unique ideas of someone else without acknowledgment, is known as plagiarism. In publishing, plagiarism is illegal; in other circumstances it is, at the least, unethical. (For detailed guidance on quoting correctly, see **quotations**.)

You may quote or **paraphrase** the words and ideas of another if you document your source. (See **documenting sources**.) However, if you intend to publish or reproduce and distribute material in which you have included quotations from published works, you may have to obtain written permission to do so from the **copyright** holder. Although you need not enclose paraphrased material in quotation marks, you must document the source. Paraphrased ideas are taken from someone else whether or not the words are identical. Paraphrasing a passage without citing the source is permissible only when the information paraphrased is common knowledge in a field. (*Common knowledge* refers to historical, scientific, geographical, technical, and other types of information on a topic readily available in handbooks, manuals, atlases, and other references.)

plurals

Nouns, pronouns, and **verbs** may be either singular or plural.

NOUNS

Nouns normally form the plural by simply adding *s* to their singular forms.

EXAMPLES Many new business *ventures* have failed in the past ten *years*.
Partners are not always personal *friends*.

Nouns ending in *s, z, x, ch,* and *sh* form the plural by adding *es*.

EXAMPLES Partners in successful *businesses* are not always friends.
How many size *sixes* did we produce last month?
The letter was sent to all area *churches*.
Technology should not inhibit our individuality; it should fulfill our *wishes*.
The young engineers were known throughout the company as *whizzes*.
The instructor gave three *quizzes* during the course.

Nouns ending in a consonant plus *y* form the plural by changing *y* to *ies*.

EXAMPLE The store advertises prompt delivery but limits the number of *deliveries* it will make in one day.

Some nouns ending in *o* add *es* to form the plural; others add only *s*.

EXAMPLES One tomato plant produced twelve *tomatoes*.
We installed two *dynamos* in the plant.

Some nouns ending in *f* or *fe* add *s* to form the plural; others change the *f* or *fe* to *ves*.

EXAMPLES cliff/cliffs, fife/fifes, knife/knives

Some nouns require an internal change to form the plural.

EXAMPLES woman/women, man/men, mouse/mice, goose/geese

Some nouns do not change in the plural.

EXAMPLE *Fish* swam lazily in the brook while *deer* mingled with *sheep* in a nearby meadow.

Compound nouns form the plural in the main word.

EXAMPLES sons-in-law, high schools

Compound nouns written as one word add *s* to the end.

EXAMPLE Use seven *spoonfuls* of freshly ground coffee to make seven cups of coffee.

PRONOUNS

All pronouns except *you* change to form the plural.

EXAMPLES I/we, he/they, she/they, it/they

A problem sometimes occurs because the masculine pronoun has traditionally been used to refer to both sexes.

EXAMPLE *Each* may stay or go as *he* chooses.

To avoid the sexual bias implied in such usage, use *he or she* or the plural form of the pronoun, *they*.

CHANGE *Each* may stay or go as *he* chooses.
TO *Each* may stay or go as *he or she* chooses.
OR *All* may stay or go as *they* choose.

If you use the plural form of the pronoun, be sure to change the indefinite pronoun *each* to its plural form, *all*.

VERBS

Verbs may also be singular or plural.

EXAMPLES The company *pays* high taxes. (singular)
The companies *pay* high taxes. (plural)

Most verbs show the singular of the third **person**, present **tense**, indicative **mood** by adding an *s* or *es*.

EXAMPLES he *stands*, she *works*, it *goes*

The verb *to be* normally changes its form to indicate the plural.

EXAMPLES I *am* ready to begin work. (singular)
We *are* ready to begin work. (plural)

If in doubt about the plural form of a word, look it up in a **dictionary**. Most dictionaries give the plural if it is formed in any way other than by adding *s* or *es*.

point of view

Point of view indicates the writer's relation to the information presented, as reflected in the use of **person**. The writer usually expresses point of view in first-, second-, or third-person **personal pronouns**. The use of the first person indicates that the narrator is a participant or observer ("This happened to me," "I saw that"). The second and third person indicate that the narrator is writing about other people or something impersonal or is giving directions, instructions, or advice ("This happened to her, them, it"; "Enter the data after pressing the ENTER key once"). The writer may also avoid using personal pronouns, thus adopting an impersonal point of view.

EXAMPLE It is regrettable your shipment of March 12 is not acceptable.

Consider the same sentence written from the personal, first-person point of view.

EXAMPLE I regret that we cannot accept your shipment of March 12.

Although the meaning of both sentences is the same, the sentence with the personal point of view indicates that two people are involved in the communication. Years ago business people preferred the impersonal point of view because they thought it made writing sound more objective and businesslike. Unfortunately, however, the impersonal point of view often prevented clear and direct communication and can cause misunderstanding. Today, good business writers adopt a more personal point of view whenever it is appropriate.

Writers should not avoid *I* by using *one* when they are really talking about themselves. They do not increase objectivity but merely make the statement impersonal.

CHANGE One can only conclude that the new advertising is not effective.
TO *I* can only conclude that the new advertising is not effective.

Writers should never use *the writer* to replace *I* in a mistaken attempt to sound formal or dignified.

CHANGE *The writer* believes that this project will be completed by June 30.
TO *I* believe that this project will be completed by June 30.

However, the personal point of view should not be used when an impersonal point of view would be more appropriate or more effective.

CHANGE   I am inclined to think that each manager should attend the final committee meeting to hear the committee's recommendations.

TO   Each manager should attend the final committee meeting to hear the committee's recommendations.

The preceding examples make clear that when the impersonal point of view is used, the focus shifts from the writer to the person or thing being discussed. For the subject matter to receive more emphasis than either the writer or the reader does, an impersonal point of view should be used.

EXAMPLE   The evidence suggests that the absorption rate is too fast.

In a business letter on company stationery, use of the pronoun *we* may be interpreted as reflecting company policy, whereas *I* clearly reflects personal opinion. Which pronoun to use should be decided according to whether the matter discussed in the letter is a corporate or an individual concern.

EXAMPLES   *I* appreciate your suggestion regarding our need for more community activities.

We appreciate your suggestion regarding our need for more community activities.

The pronoun *we* may commit an organization to what the writer says. If the following statement accurately reflects an organization's opinion, with its implication that the proposal being singled out will be accepted, then it is justified.

EXAMPLE   *We* believe that your proposal was the best submitted.

If, however, the writer can speak only personally instead of for the organization, the statement should be hedged so that the reader understands that it represents the writer's opinion rather than the organization's official position.

EXAMPLE   I *personally* believe that your proposal was the best submitted, but the policy commitee will make the final decision.

Whether the writer adopts a personal or an impersonal point of view should depend on the objective and the reader. For example, in a business letter to an associate, the writer will most likely adopt a personal point of view. But in a report to a large group, the writer will probably choose to emphasize the subject by adopting an impersonal point of view.

In descriptive writing, point of view refers to the physical point or vantage of the writer's presentation. The writer can present a scene from a fixed or moving point of view. Once a vantage has been taken, however, the writer should not shift it without indicating to the reader that the perspective has changed. (See also **"you" viewpoint.**)

policies and procedures

A policy states an organization's posture, or stand, on a subject, whereas a procedure provides **instructions** for carrying out the policy. Policies and procedures, therefore, are often written at the same time. They usually originate at top- or middle-management levels and are always subjected to a careful review process—mainly because they are considered a "bible" for management. Policies and procedures thus require extraordinarily careful thought and planning. Language and **word choices** must be as precise as possible so that policies and procedures are clear and understandable—with no ambiguity.

POLICIES

A statement of policy is often preceded by an explanation of the policy's purpose or rationale, as in the following policy regarding company tuition refunds:

> 1.0 GENERAL
> 1.1 The purpose of the Blaylock Tuition Refund Plan is to encourage the development of employees through college-level academic training consistent with their abilities and interests and consistent with the needs of the company.
> 1.2 Financial assistance is offered through the Tuition Refund Plan to encourage college-level work. The plan supports graduate and undergraduate courses and degree programs when the education is appropriately related to department or division objectives.

Such general statements are then followed by the specific details of the policy—in this case, who is eligible, when the tuition refund is appropriate, and so on.

> 2.0 POLICY
> 2.1.1 The Blaylock Tuition Refund Plan is intended for full-time personnel classified in supervisory, managerial, professional, sales, administrative, technical, and administrative support jobs.
> 2.1.2 An individual must be in the employ of the company at the time of enrollment and the completion of the course in order to receive a refund. Should an individual's employment be terminated because of a reduction in force, fees will be refunded for currently approved courses upon satisfactory completion (the last class meeting having been held and a grade one level above passing having been earned). When courses are not satisfactorily completed, reimbursement may be deferred for those individuals having degree approval if, upon completion of the degree, the individual obtains an accumulative grade average of at least "C" (or "B" for most graduate-degree programs).

Sections of a policy are usually numbered (as in the preceding example) and kept in loose-leaf binders, so they can be easily referred to and updated as the need arises.

PROCEDURES

A statement of procedures provides a step-by-step explanation of how to carry out a policy. It provides instructions not only for employees directly involved in the procedure but also for management, who must ensure that the policy is carried out properly.

As preparation for writing procedures, keep track of who is doing what. An easy and effective way is to draw a line vertically down the page of a note pad, an inch or so to the left of center. Then write the word *actor* at the top of the left column and the word *directions* at the top of the right column. Under *directions* describe each step of the procedure; under *actor* write who is performing the action in each step. Make sure your list describes each step of the procedure fully and in the correct sequence. In effect, this technique serves as an outline. The following is an example of the chart you might prepare to write a degree-approval procedure:

ACTOR	DIRECTIONS
Employee	Determines his or her eligibility for degree program, gains approval of manager, and submits request to Personnel Resources Department.
Personnel Resources	Reviews request and, if reason is not obvious, asks manager to justify, in writing, the benefits of approving the degree program.
Employee	Completes Sections I and II of Form F-6970.
Personnel Resources	Sends form to each of two levels of management above employee for approval.

The following might be the draft created from the preceding chart:

1.0 PROCEDURE

1.1 *Degree Approval*

1.1.1 Individuals who meet school requirements and are interested in receiving tuition refunds should gain the approval of their management and Personnel Resources. Personnel Resources may request a manager to justify, in writing, the benefits of approving a degree request if the reason is not obvious.

1.1.2 After agreement is reached, the employee should complete Sections I and II of Form F-6970. After two levels of management approval have been gained, the form should be forwarded to Personnel Resources. Approval must be given by the "staff" manager before degree approval can be granted. Copies of Form F-6970 will then be returned to the student and the manager.

1.1.3 The employee who has been granted degree approval must complete Sections I and II of Form F-6970 when registering for each course required for the degree, whether or not reimbursement will be granted upon completion of a course or deferred until completion of the degree.

positive writing

Presenting positive information as though it were negative is a trap that specialists fall into quite easily because of the complexity of the

information they must write about. It is a practice that confuses the
reader, however, and one that should be avoided.

> CHANGE If sales do *not* decline, we will *not* change our procedures.
> TO We will change our procedures only if sales decline.

In the first sentence, the reader must reverse two negatives to understand the exception that is being stated; the second sentence presents an exception to a rule in a straightforward manner.

On the other hand, negative facts or conclusions should be stated
negatively; stating a negative fact or conclusion positively can mislead the reader.

> CHANGE New car sales for November have been maintained at 40 per-
> cent of last November's record sales volume.
> TO New car sales for November have dropped to 40 percent of last
> November's record sales volume.

Even if what you are saying is negative, do not use any more negative
words than are necessary or words that are more negative than
necessary.

> CHANGE We are withholding your shipment until we receive your pay-
> ment.
> TO We will forward your shipment as soon as we receive your
> payment.

possessive case

A **noun** or **pronoun** is in the possessive case when it represents a
person or thing owning or possessing something.

> EXAMPLE A recent scientific analysis of *New York City's* atmosphere con-
> cluded that New Yorkers on the street took into *their* lungs
> the equivalent in toxic materials of 39 cigarettes per person
> daily.

Singular nouns show the possessive by adding an **apostrophe** and *s*.

> EXAMPLE company/company's

Nouns that form their **plurals** by adding an *s* show the possessive by
placing an apostrophe after the *s* that forms the plural.

> EXAMPLES a managers' meeting/the technicians' handbook

The following **list** shows the relationships among singular, plural, and possessive nouns that form their plurals by adding *s* or changing *y* to *ies*.

singular	company	employee
singular possessive	company's	employee's
plural	companies	employees
plural possessive	companies'	employees'

Nouns that do not add *s* to form their plurals add an apostrophe and an *s* to show possession in both the plural and the singular forms.

singular	child	man
singular possessive	child's	man's
plural	children	men
plural possessive	children's	men's

Singular nouns that end in *s* form the possessive either by adding only an apostrophe or by adding both an apostrophe and an *s*.

EXAMPLES a *waitress'* uniform/an *actress'* career
a *waitress's* uniform/an actress's career

Singular nouns of one syllable always form the possessive by adding both an apostrophe and an *s*.

EXAMPLE The *boss's* desk was cluttered.

Although exceptions are relatively common, it is a good rule of thumb to use an apostrophe and an *s* with nouns referring to persons and living things and to use an *of* phrase for possessive nouns referring to inanimate objects.

EXAMPLES The *chairperson's* address was well received.
The keys *of the typewriter* were sticking.

If this rule leads to awkwardness or wordiness, however, be flexible.

EXAMPLES The *company's* plants are doing well.
The *plane's* landing gear failed.

Several indefinite pronouns (*any, each, few, most, none,* and *some*) form the possessive only in *of* phrases (*of any, of some*). Others, however, use an apostrophe (*anyone's*).

The established **idiom** calls for the possessive case in many stock phrases.

EXAMPLES a *day's* journey, a *day's* work, a *moment's* notice, at his *wit's* end, the *law's* delay

In a few cases, the idiom even calls for a double possessive using both the *of* and the *'s* forms.

EXAMPLE That colleague *of* George's was at the conference.

When several words make up a single term, add *'s* to the last word only.

EXAMPLES The *chairman of the board's* statement was brief.
The *Department of Energy's* new budget shows increased revenues of $192 million for uranium enrichment.

With coordinate nouns, the last noun takes the possessive form to show joint possession.

EXAMPLE *Michelson and Morely's* famous experiment on the velocity of light was made in 1887.

To show individual possession with coordinate nouns, each noun should take the possessive form.

EXAMPLE The difference between *Thomasson's* and *Silson's* test results were statistically insignificant.

To form the possessive of a **compound word**, add *'s*.

EXAMPLES the *vice-president's* car, the *pipeline's* diameter, the *antibody's* reaction.

When a noun ends in multiple consecutive *s* sounds, form the possessive by adding only an apostrophe.

EXAMPLES Jesus' disciples, Moses' journey

Do not use an apostrophe with possessive pronouns.

EXAMPLES *yours, its, his, ours, whose, theirs*

It's is a contraction of *it is*, not the possessive form of *it*.
    In the names of places and institutions, the apostrophe is often omitted.

EXAMPLES Harpers Ferry, Writers Book Club

The use of possessive pronouns does not normally cause problems except with **gerunds** and indefinite pronouns. Several indefinite pronouns (*all, any, each, few, most, none,* and *some*) require *of* phrases to form the possessive case.

EXAMPLE Both dies were stored in the warehouse, but rust had ruined the surface *of each.*

Others, however, use the apostrophe.

EXAMPLE *Everyone's* contribution is welcome.

Only the possessive form of a pronoun should be used with a gerund.

EXAMPLES The safety officer insisted in *my* wearing a respirator.
Our monitoring was not affected by changing weather conditions.

practicable/practical

Practicable means that something is possible and useful.

EXAMPLE The program is *practical,* but considering the company's recent financial problems, is it *practicable?*

Practical, not *practicable,* is used to describe a person, implying common sense, a commitment to what works, rather than to theory.

predicates

The predicate is that part of a sentence that contains the main **verb** and any other words used to complete the thought of the sentence (the verb's **modifiers** and **complements**). The principal part of the predicate is the verb, just as a **noun** (or noun substitute) is the principal part of the **subject.**

EXAMPLE Bill *piloted the airplane.*

The simple **predicate** is the verb (or **verb phrase**) alone; the complete predicate is the verb and its modifiers and complements.

A compound predicate consists of two or more verbs with the same subject. It is an important device for economical writing.

EXAMPLE The company *tried* but *did not succeed* in that field.

A predicate nominative is a noun construction that follows a **linking verb** and renames the **subject.**

EXAMPLES He is my *lawyer*. (noun)
His excuse was *that he had been sick*. (noun clause)

The predicate nominative is one kind of **subjective complement**; the other is the predicate adjective.

prefixes

A prefix is a letter, or letters, placed in front of a root word that changes its meaning, often causing the new word to mean the opposite of the root word.

Root Word	With Prefix
enter	*re*enter (enter again)
acceptable	*un*acceptable (not acceptable)
operate	*co*operate (operate together)
symmetrical	*a*symmetrical (not symmetrical)
honest	*dis*honest (not honest)
science	*meta*science (beyond science)

When a prefix ends with a vowel and the root word begins with the same vowel, the prefix may be separated from the root word with a **hyphen** (re-enter, co-operate, re-elect); the second vowel may be marked with a dieresis (reënter, coöperate, reëlect), although this practice is rare now; or the word may be written with neither hyphen nor dieresis (reenter, cooperate, reelect). The hyphen and the dieresis are visual aids that help the **reader** recognize that the two vowels are pronounced differently. Since typewriters do not have the dieresis mark, the hyphen is the more practical way to help the reader.

Except between identical vowels, the hyphen rarely appears between a prefix and its root word. At times, however, a hyphen is necessary for clarity of meaning; for example, *reform* means "correct" or "improve," and *re-form* means "change the shape of."

preparation

To write clearly and effectively does not require innate creative talent. It does require a systematic approach, however, which should logically begin with the proper preparation.

Preparation consists of determining the **objective** of your writing project, its **readers,** and the **scope** within which you will cover your subject. Although these fundamentals of the writing process are often overlooked, you must resolve them if you hope to write well. They are the foundations on which all the other steps of the writing process are built.

OBJECTIVE

What *exactly* do you want your readers to know or be able to do when they have finished reading what you have written? When you can answer this question—again, *exactly*—you will have determined the objective of your writing. A good test of whether you have formulated your objective adequately is to state it in a single sentence. This statement may also function as the thesis statement in your **outline**, although such a function should not be a requirement of your stated objective. (For a fuller discussion, see **objective**.)

READERS

Know who your readers are and learn certain key facts about them, such as their educational level, technical knowledge, and needs relative to your subject. Their level of technical knowledge, for example, should determine whether you need to cover the fundamentals of your subject and which terms you must define. (For more detail, see **readers**.)

SCOPE

If you know the objective of your writing project and your readers' needs, you will know the type and amount of detail you will need to include in your writing. This is called *scope*, which may be defined as the depth and breadth to which you cover your subject. If you do not determine your scope of coverage, you will not know how much or what kind of information to include, and therefore you are likely to invest unnecessary work during the **research** phase of your writing project.

One of the most common—and damaging—mistakes that business writers make is to begin writing too soon. The preparation stage of the writing process is analogous to focusing a camera before taking a picture. By determining who your reader is, what your objective is, and what your scope of coverage should be, you are bringing your whole writing effort into focus before beginning to write the draft. As a result, your **topic** will be much more clearly focused for your reader. (See also the Checklist of the Writing Process.)

prepositional phrases

A **preposition** is a word that shows relationship and combines with a **noun** or **pronoun** (its **object**) to form a modifying **phrase**. A prepositional phrase, then, consists of a preposition plus its object and the object's **modifiers**.

> EXAMPLE   *After the meeting*, the district managers adjourned *to the executive dining room.*

Prepositional phrases, because they normally modify nouns or **verbs**, usually function as **adjectives** or **adverbs**.
A prepositional phrase may function as an adverb of motion.

> EXAMPLE   Move the typewriter *onto the desk.*

A prepositional phrase may function as an adverb of manner.

> EXAMPLE   Answer customers' queries *in a courteous fashion.*

A prepositional phrase may function as an adverb of place.

> EXAMPLE   We ate lunch *in the company cafeteria.*

A prepositional phrase may function as an adjective.

> EXAMPLE   The man *with the briefcase* is the new district manager.

When functioning as adjectives, prepositional phrases follow the nouns they modify.

> EXAMPLE   Here are the results *of our study.*

When functioning as adverbs, prepositional phrases may appear in different places.

> EXAMPLES   *By five o'clock* the report will be completed.
> The report will be completed *by five o'clock.*

Be careful when using prepositional phrases, as separating a prepositional phrase from the noun it is modifying can cause **ambiguity**.

> CHANGE   *The man* standing by the drinking fountain *in the gray suit* is our president.
> TO   *The man in the gray suit* who is standing by the drinking fountain is our president.

(See also **misplaced modifiers**.)

prepositions

A preposition is a word that links a **noun** or **pronoun** (its **object**) to another sentence element by expressing such relationships as direction (*to, into, across, toward*), location (*at, in, on, under, over, beside, among, by, between, through*), time (*before, after, during, until, since*), or figurative location (*for, against, with*). Although only about seventy prepositions exist in the English language, they occur frequently. Together, the preposition, its object, and the object's modifiers form a **prepositional phrase**, which acts as a **modifier**.

The object of a preposition, the word or phrase following the preposition, is always in the objective **case**. This situation gives rise to a problem in such constructions as "between you and *me*," a phrase that is frequently and incorrectly written as "between you and *I*." *Me* is the objective form of the pronoun, and *I* is the subjective form.

Many words that function as prepositions also function as **adverbs**. If the word takes an object and functions as a connective, it is a preposition; if it has no object and functions as a modifier, it is an adverb.

EXAMPLES The manager sat *behind* the desk *in* his office. (prepositions)
The customer lagged *behind*; then she came *in* and sat *down*. (adverbs)

AVOIDING ERRORS WITH PREPOSITIONS

Do not use redundant prepositions, such as "off *of*," "in back *of*," and "inside *of*."

CHANGE The client arrived *at about* four o'clock.
TO The client arrived *at* four o'clock. (to be exact)
OR The client arrived *about* four o'clock. (to be approximate)

Do not omit necessary prepositions.

CHANGE He was oblivious and not distracted by the view.
TO He was oblivious *to* and not distracted *by* the view.

Avoid unnecessarily adding the preposition *up* to **verbs**.

CHANGE Call *up* and see if he is in his office.
TO Call and see if he is in his office.

USING A PREPOSITION AT THE END OF A SENTENCE

If a preposition falls naturally at the end of a sentence, leave it there.

> EXAMPLE I don't remember which file I put it *in.*

Be aware, however, that a preposition at the end of a sentence can be an indication that the sentence is awkwardly constructed.

> CHANGE The branch office is where he was *at.*
> TO He was at the branch office.

COMMON USES OF PREPOSITIONS

Certain verbs, adverbs, and **adjectives** are used with certain prepositions. For example, we say "interested *in,*" "aware *of,*" "devoted *to,*" "equated *with,*" "abstain *from,*" "adhere *to,*" "conform *to,*" "capable *of,*" "comply *with,*" "object *to,*" "find fault *with,*" "inconsistent *with,*" "independent *of,*" "infer *from,*" and "interfere *with.*" (See also **idioms**.)

USING PREPOSITIONS IN TITLES

When a preposition appears in a title, it is capitalized if it is the first word in the title or if it has four letters or more. (See also **capital letters**.)

> EXAMPLES *Composition for the Business and Technical World* was reviewed recently by *Time* magazine.
> The book *Managing Like Mad* should be taken seriously in spite of its title.

principal/principle

Principal, meaning an "amount of money on which interest is earned or paid" or a "chief official in a school or court proceeding," is sometimes confused with *principle,* meaning a "basic truth or belief."

> EXAMPLES The bank will pay 6.5 percent per month on the *principal.*
> She is a person of unwavering *principles.*
> He sent a letter to the *principal* of the high school.

Principal is also an adjective, meaning "main" or "primary."

> EXAMPLE My *principal* objection is that it will be too expensive.

process explanation

Many kinds of business writing explain a process, an operation, or a procedure. The explanation involves putting in the appropriate

MEMORANDUM

To: Walter Camburn
From: Leonard Fein
Date: March 25, 19--

Subject: Tuition Refund Procedure

Why it is important to follow the procedure

As you requested in your memo of March 18, I checked with Ron Manuszak Tuition Refund Coordinator, about a tuition refund for the two courses you plan to take this summer at Parkland College. To obtain approval for the courses and to receive the actual refund, you should follow the procedure described below.

You must first gain the approval of your manager, Susan Mueller, of the courses you wish to take. If she approves, you must then meet with Mr. Manuszak in Personnel Resources. He will notify you within one week whether or not Personnel Resources has approved your courses.

Step-by-step process

If they approve, you should then complete Sections I and II of the enclosed Form F-6970 and submit the form to Personnel Resources. They will get Ms. Mueller's signature, and Mr. Manuszak will then send you a memo authorizing you to enroll in the courses.

Once the courses are over, you should send Mr. Manuszak a copy of your grade report as evidence that you have completed them successfully. Mr. Manuszak will then complete Section III of Form F-6970 and send it on to you with your tuition-refund check.

I know that Mr. Manuszak will be happy to answer any specific questions you may have about certain courses. His office is in the Blaylock West Building on River Road and his phone number is extension 8709.

Good luck in your courses.

bb
Enclosure

Figure 1   Explanation of a Process

order the steps that a specific mechanism or system uses to accomplish a certain result. The process itself might range from the legal steps necessary to form a corporation to the steps necessary to fill an order. At the least, you should divide the process into distinct steps and present them in their normal order.

In your opening **paragraph**, tell your **reader** why it is important to become familiar with the process you are explaining. Before you explain the steps necessary to form a corporation, for example, you could cite the tax savings that incorporation would permit. To provide your reader with a framework for the details that will follow, you might present a brief overview of the process. Finally, you might describe how the process works in relation to a larger whole. In explaining the air brake system of a large dump truck, you might note that the braking system is one part of the vehicle's air system, which also controls the throttle and transmission-shifting mechanisms.

An explanation of a process can vary in length, depending on how much detail is necessary. Notice in the memorandum shown in Figure 1 how the method of obtaining a company tuition refund is described as a step-by-step process. The explanation includes each detail necessary for the reader to understand the process. **Illustrations** often help convey your message.

progress and activity reports

A progress report provides information about a project—its current status, whether it is on schedule, whether it is within the budget, and so on. Progress reports are often submitted by a contracting company to a client company. They are issued at regular intervals throughout the life of a project and state what has been done in a specified interval and what has yet to be done before the project can be completed. The progress report is used primarily with projects that involve many steps over a period of weeks, months, or even years. Progress reports help keep projects running smoothly by allowing management to assign workers, adjust schedules, allocate budgets, or schedule supplies and equipment, as necessary.

All reports in a series of progress reports should have the same **format**. Since progress reports are normally sent outside the company, they are often written as letters. (See also **correspondence**.)

The **introduction** to the first progress report should identify the project, any methods and necessary materials, and the date by which the project is to be completed. Subsequent reports should then summarize the progress since the first report.

The body of the progress report should describe the project's present status, including such details as schedules and costs.

The report should end with conclusions and recommendations about changes in the schedule, materials, techniques, and so on. The

conclusion may also include a statement of the work done and an estimate of future progress.

The following example (Figure 1) is the first progress report submitted by an electrical contractor (REMCON) to a client (the Arena Committee).

Within an organization, professional employees often submit reports on the progress and current status of all ongoing projects assigned to them by their managers. The managers combine these *activity reports* (also called *status reports*) into larger activity reports that they, in turn, submit to their managers. Activity reports help keep all levels of management aware of the progress and status of projects within an organization.

An activity report includes information about the status of all current projects, including any problems related to their completion, the action currently being taken to resolve any problems, and the writer's plans for the coming month. A manager's activity report should also indicate the current number of employees.

Because the activity report is issued periodically, often monthly, and contains material familiar to its readers, it normally needs no introduction or conclusion. The format of an activity report may vary from company to company, or even among different parts of the same company. The following sections are typical and would be adequate for most situations:

> *Current Projects*
> This section lists every project assigned to the employee or manager and summarizes its current status.
> *Current Problems*
> This section details any problems confronting the employee or manager and explains the steps being taken to resolve them.
> *Plans for the Next Period*
> This section projects what the writer expects to achieve on each project during the next month or reporting period.
> *Current Staffing Level*
> This section, included by managers and project leaders, lists the number of subordinates assigned to the writer and correlates that number with the staffing level considered necessary for the projects assigned.

The activity report shown in Figure 2, using a **memorandum** form, was submitted by a manager of software development (Wayne Tribinski) who supervises 11 employees. The reader of the report (Kathryn Hunter), Tribinski's supervisor, is the director of engineering.

―――――――――――――――**REMCON ELECTRIC**―――――――――――――――
5099 Seventh Street, St. Paul, Minnesota 55101 (6l2) 555-1212

August 20, 19--

Arena Committee
Minnesota Sports
708 N. Case St.
St. Paul, MN 55101

Subject: Arena Rewiring Progress Report

Introduction
identifies
project and
completion
date

This report, as agreed to in our contract, covers the progress on
the rewiring program at the Sports Arena from May 5 to August 15
of 19--. Although the costs of certain equipment are higher than
our original bid indicated, we expect to complete the project by
December 23, without going over cost; the speed with which the
project is being completed will save labor costs.

Work Completed

On August 15, we finished installing the circuit-breaker panels
and meters of Level I service outlets and of all subfloor
rewiring. Lighting fixture replacement, Level II service
outlets, and the upgrading of stage lighting equipment are in the
preliminary stages (meaning that the wiring has been completed
but installation of the fixtures has not yet begun).

Body details
schedules and
costs

Costs

Equipment used up to this point has cost $10,800, and labor has
cost $31,500 (including some subcontracted plumbing). My
estimate for the rest of the equipment, based on discussions with
your lighting consultant, is $11,500; additional labor costs
should not exceed $25,000.

Work Schedule

I have scheduled the upgrading of stage lighting equipment from
August 16 to October 5, the completion of Level II service
outlets from October 6 to November 12, and the replacement of
lighting fixtures from November 15 to December 17.

Conclusion
indicates
pertinent
changes

Conclusion

Although my original estimate on equipment ($20,000) has been
exceeded by $2,300, my original labor estimate ($60,000) has been
reduced by $3,500; so I will easily stay within the limits of my
original bid. In addition, I see no difficulty in having the
arena finished for the Christmas program on December 23.

Sincerely,

John Remcon

John Remcon
President and Owner

ics

Figure 1 Progress Report

INTEROFFICE MEMORANDUM

Date: June 5, 19--
To: Kathryn Hunter, Director of Engineering
From: Wayne Tribinski, Manager, Software Development W.T.

Subject: Activity Report for May, 19--

Projects

1. The Problem-Tracking System now contains both software and hardware
    problem-tracking capabilities. The system upgrade took place over
    the weekend of May 11 and 12 and was placed online on the 13th.
2. For the <u>Software Training Mailing Campaign</u>, we anticipate producing
    a set of labels for mailing software-training information to
    customers by June 10.

Status of current projects

3. The <u>Search Project</u> is on hold until the PL/I training has been
    completed, probably by the end of June.
4. The project to provide a data base for the <u>Information Management
    System</u> has been expanded in scope to provide a data base for all
    training activities. We are in the process of rescheduling the
    project to take the new scope into account.
5. The <u>Metering Reports</u> project is part of a larger project called
    "Reporting Upgrade." We have completed the Final Project
    Requirements and sent it out for review. The Resource Requirements
    estimate has also been completed, and Phase Three is scheduled for
    completion by June 17.

Problems

    The <u>Information Management System</u> has been delayed. The original
schedule was based on the assumption that a systems analyst who was
familiar with the system would work on this project. Instead, the
project was assigned to a newly hired systems analyst who was
inexperienced and required much more learning time than expected.

Existing problems

    Bill Michaels, whose activity report is attached, is correcting a
problem in the <u>CNG Software</u>. This correction may take a week.
    The <u>Beta Project</u> was delayed for approximately one week because of
two problems: interfacing and link handling. The interfacing problem
was resolved rather easily. The link-handling problem, however, was
more severe, and Debra Mann has gone to the customer's site in France to
resolve it.

Plans for Next Month

Plans for the coming months

    • Complete the Software Training Mailing Campaign.
    • Resume the Search Project.
    • Restart the project to provide a data base on information
      management
      with a schedule that reflects its new scope.
    • Complete the Phase Three project.
    • Write a report to justify the addition of two software engineers
      to my department.
    • Congratulate publicly the recipients of Meritorious Achievement
      Awards: Bill Thomasson and Nancy O'Rourke.

Current Staffing Level

Current staff: 11
Open requisitions: 0

ja
Enclosure

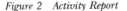

Figure 2   Activity Report

pronoun reference

Avoid vague and uncertain references between a **pronoun** and its antecedents.

> CHANGE Studs and thick treads make snow tires effective. *They* are implanted with an air gun.
>
> TO Studs and thick treads make snow tires effective. *The studs* are implanted with an air gun.

> CHANGE We made the sale and delivered the product. *It* was a big one.
>
> TO We made the sale, which was a big one, and delivered the product.

The **noun** to which a pronoun refers must be clear. Three problems are encountered in regard to pronoun references. One is an ambiguous reference, or one that can be interpreted in more than one way.

> CHANGE Jim worked with Tom on the report, but *he* wrote most of it. (Who wrote most of it, Jim or Tom?)
>
> TO Jim worked with Tom on the report, but *Tom* wrote most of it.

A general (or broad) reference, or one that has no real antecedent, is another problem that often occurs when the word *this* is used by itself.

> CHANGE He deals with personnel problems in his work. *This* helps him in his personal life.
>
> TO He deals with personnel problems in his work. This experience helps him in his personal life.

A hidden reference, or one that has only an implied antecedent, is the third problem.

> CHANGE In spite of the research conducted by our calculator division, we didn't sell *many.*
>
> TO In spite of the research conducted by our calculator division, we didn't sell many calculators.
>
> OR In spite of the fact that we had thoroughly researched the market for calculators, we didn't sell *many.*

For the sake of **coherence**, pronouns should be placed as close as possible to their antecedents. The danger of creating an ambiguous reference increases with distance. Don't force your **reader** to go back too far to find out what a pronoun stands for.

CHANGE The *house* in the meadow at the base of the mountain range was resplendent in *its* coat of new paint.

TO The house, resplendent in *its* coat of new paint, was nestled in a meadow at the base of the mountain range.

Do not repeat an antecedent in **parentheses** following the pronoun. If you feel that you must identify the pronoun's antecedent in this way, you need to rewrite the sentence.

CHANGE The senior partner first met Bob Evans when he (Evans) was a trainee.

TO Bob Evans was a trainee when the senior partner first met him.

When referring to a noun that includes both sexes (student, teacher, clerk, everyone), the pronouns *he* and *his* are traditionally used.

EXAMPLE Each employee is to have *his* annual X-ray taken by Friday.

However, many people feel that this conventional use of the masculine **personal pronoun** implies sexual bias. If there is danger of offending, it is often best to avoid the problem by substituting an **article** or changing the statement from singular to plural. (See also **he/she**.)

EXAMPLES Each employee is to have *the* annual X-ray taken by Friday.

All employees are to have *their* annual X-rays taken by Friday.

pronouns

A pronoun is a word that is used as a substitute for a **noun** (the noun for which a pronoun substitutes is called its *antecedent*). Using pronouns in place of nouns relieves the monotony of repeating the same noun over and over. Pronouns fall into several different categories: personal, demonstrative, relative, interrogative, indefinite, reflexive, intensive, and reciprocal. (See also **pronoun reference**.)

PERSONAL PRONOUNS

Personal pronouns refer to the person or persons speaking (*I, me, my, mine; we, us, our, ours*), the person or persons spoken to (*you, your, yours*), or the person or thing spoken of (*he, him, his; she, her, hers; it, its; they, them, their, theirs*). (See also **person**.)

EXAMPLE *I* wish *you* had told *me* that *she* was coming with *us*.

If *their* figures are correct, *ours* must be in error.

DEMONSTRATIVE PRONOUNS

Demonstrative pronouns (*this, these; that, those*) indicate or point out the thing being referred to.

EXAMPLES *This* is my desk.   *That* will be a difficult job.
These are my coworkers.   *Those* are incorrect figures.

RELATIVE PRONOUNS

The **relative pronouns** are *who* (or *whom*), *which*, and *that*. A relative pronoun performs a dual function: (1) it takes the place of a noun, and (2) it connects, and establishes the relationship between, a **dependent clause** and its main **clause**.

EXAMPLE The personnel manager decided *who* would be hired.

The pronoun *that* is normally used with restrictive clauses and the pronoun *which* with nonrestrictive clauses. (See also **restrictive** and **nonrestrictive elements**.)

EXAMPLES Companies *that adopt the plan* nearly always show profit increases. (restrictive clause)
The annual report, *which was distributed yesterday*, shows that sales increased 20 percent last year. (nonrestrictive clause)

INTERROGATIVE PRONOUNS

Interrogative pronouns (*who* or *whom*, *what*, and *which*) ask questions. They differ from relative pronouns in two ways: They are used only to ask questions, and they may introduce independent interrogative sentences, whereas relative pronouns connect or show relationship and introduce only dependent clauses.

Notice that unlike relative pronouns, interrogative pronouns normally lack expressed antecedents; the antecedent is actually in the expected answer.

EXAMPLES *Who* said that?
What is the trouble?
Which of these is best?

INDEFINITE PRONOUNS

Indefinite pronouns specify a class or group of persons or things rather than a particular person or thing. *All, any, another, anyone, anything, both, each, either, everybody, few, many, most, much, neither, nobody, none, several, some*, and *such* are indefinite pronouns.

EXAMPLE Not *everyone* liked the new procedures; *some* even refused to follow them.

REFLEXIVE PRONOUNS

A **reflexive pronoun**, which always ends with the **suffix** *-self* or *-selves*, indicates that the **subject** of the sentence acts upon itself.

EXAMPLE   The secretary accidentally cut *himself* with the letter opener.

The reflexive and intensive pronouns are *myself, yourself, himself, herself, itself, oneself, ourselves, yourselves,* and *themselves.*
Myself is not a substitute for *I* or *me* as a personal pronoun.

CHANGE   John and *myself* completed the report on time.
TO   John and *I* completed the report on time.

CHANGE   The assignment was given to Wally and *myself.*
TO   The assignment was given to Wally and *me.*

INTENSIVE PRONOUNS

The intensive pronouns are identical in form with the reflexive pronouns, but they perform a different function: to give **emphasis** to their antecedents.

EXAMPLE   I *myself* asked the same question.

RECIPROCAL PRONOUNS

The **reciprocal pronouns** (*one another* and *each other*) indicate the relationship of one item to another. *Each other* is commonly used when referring to two persons or things and *one another* when referring to more than two.

EXAMPLES   They work well with *each other.*
The crew members work well with *one another.*

GRAMMATICAL PROPERTIES OF PRONOUNS

Case. Pronouns have forms to show the subjective, objective, or possessive **case**, as the following chart shows:

	Subjective	*Objective*	*Possessive*
1st person singular	I	me	my, mine
2nd person singular	you	you	your, yours
3rd person singular	he	him	his
	she	her	her, hers
	it	it	its
1st person plural	we	us	our, ours
2nd person plural	you	you	your, yours
3rd person plural	they	them	their, theirs

A pronoun that is used as the subject of a clause or sentence is in the subjective case (*I, we, he, she, it, you, they, who*). The subjective case is also used when the pronoun follows a **linking verb**.

> EXAMPLES   *He* is my boss.
> My boss is *he.*

A pronoun that is used as the **object** of a **verb** or **preposition** is in the objective case (*me, us, him, her, it, you, them, whom*).

> EXAMPLES   Mr. Davis hired Tom and *me.* (object of verb)
> Between *you* and *me,* he's wrong. (object of preposition)

A pronoun that is used to express ownership is in the possessive case (*my, mine, our, ours, his, hers, its, your, yours, their, theirs, whose*).

> EXAMPLE   He took *his* notes with him on the business trip.

Only the possessive form of a pronoun should ever be used with a **gerund**.

> EXAMPLE   The boss objected to *my* arriving late every morning.

Several indefinite pronouns (*any, each, few, most, none,* and *some*) form the possessive only in "of" phrases (*of any, of some*). Others, however, use an **apostrophe** (*anyone's*).

> CHANGE   *Each's* opinion was solicited.
> TO   The opinion *of each* was solicited.

A pronoun **appositive** takes the case of its antecedents.

> EXAMPLES   Two systems analysts, Joe and *I,* were selected to represent the company. (*Joe and I* is in apposition to the subject, *systems analysts,* and must therefore be in the subjective case.)
> The systems analysts selected two members—Joe and *me.* (*Joe and me* is in apposition to *two members,* which is the object of the verb *selected,* and therefore must be in the objective case.)

How to Determine the Case of a Pronoun. To determine the case of a pronoun, try it with a transitive verb, such as *resembled.* If the pronoun can precede the verb, it is in the subjective case; if it must follow the verb, it is in the objective case.

> EXAMPLES   *She* resembled her father. (subjective)
> Her father resembled *her.* (objective)

If compound pronouns cause problems in determining case, try using them singly.

EXAMPLES In his letter, John mentioned *you* and *me*.
In his letter, John mentioned *you*.
In his letter, John mentioned *me*.

They and *we* must discuss the terms of the merger.
They must discuss the terms of the merger.
We must discuss the terms of the merger.

When a pronoun modifies a noun, try it without the noun to determine its case.

EXAMPLES (*We/Us*) pilots fly our own planes.
We fly our own planes. (You would not write "*Us* fly our own planes.")

He addressed his remarks directly to (*we/us*) technicians.
He addressed his remarks directly to *us*. (You would not write "He addressed his remarks directly to *we*.")

To determine the case of a pronoun that follows *as* or *than*, try mentally adding the words that are normally omitted.

EXAMPLES The director does not have as much formal education *as he* [does]. (You would not write "*him* does.")
His friend was taller *than he* [was]. (You would not write "*him* was.")

Gender. A pronoun must agree in **gender** with its antecedent. A problem sometimes occurs because the masculine pronoun has traditionally been used to refer to both sexes.

EXAMPLE *Each* may stay or go as *he* chooses.

To avoid the sexual bias implied in such usage, use *he or she* or the plural form of the pronoun, *they.*

CHANGE *Each* may stay or go as *he* chooses.
TO *Each* may stay or go as *he or she* chooses.
OR *All* may stay or go as *they* choose.

If you use the plural form of the pronoun, be sure to change the indefinite pronoun *each* to its plural form, *all.*

Number. **Number** is a frequent problem only with a few indefinite pronouns (*each, either, neither;* and those ending with *-body,* or *-one,* such as *anybody, anyone, everybody, everyone, nobody, no one, somebody, someone*), which are normally singular and so require singular verbs and are referred to by singular pronouns.

EXAMPLE   As *each arrives* for the meeting and takes *his* seat, please hand *him* a copy of the confidential report. *Everyone is* to return *his* copy before *he* leaves. *No one* should be offended by these precautions when the importance of secrecy has been explained to *him*. I think *everybody* on the committee *understands* that *neither* of our major competitors *is* aware of the new process that we have developed.

Person. Third-person personal pronouns usually have antecedents.

EXAMPLE   John presented the report to the members of the board of directors. *He* (John) first read *it* (the report) to *them* (the directors) and then asked for questions.

First- and second-person personal pronouns do not normally require antecedents.

EXAMPLES   *I* like my job.
You were there at the time.
We all worked hard on the project.

proofreaders' marks

Publishers have established **symbols**, called *proofreaders' marks*, which writers and editors use to communicate with printers in the production of publications. A familiarity with these symbols makes it easy for you to communicate your changes to others. See Figure 1.

proofreading

Proofreading should be done in several stages. Read through the material three times and look for specific things each time, and then read it a final time for content.

During the first time through, ask yourself, "Does it look right?" Then look for:

- accurate and clean typing
- aesthetic page placement of material
- acceptable format
- correct spelling of names and places
- accuracy of numbers

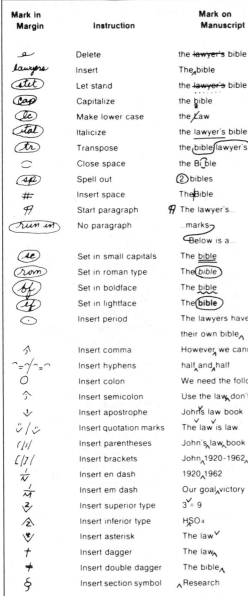

Mark in Margin	Instruction	Mark on Manuscript	Corrected Type
_e_	Delete	the ~~lawyer's~~ bible	the bible
lawyers	Insert	The͜bible	The lawyer's bible
stet	Let stand	the ~~lawyer's~~ bible	the lawyer's bible
cap	Capitalize	the bible	the Bible
_lc_	Make lower case	the Law	the law
ital	Italicize	the lawyer's bible	the *lawyer's* bible
_tr_	Transpose	the bible⁄lawyer's	the lawyer's bible
_⌒_	Close space	the Bi͜ble	the Bible
_sp_	Spell out	②bibles	two bibles
#	Insert space	The͜Bible	The Bible
¶	Start paragraph	¶ The lawyer's...	The lawyer's...
run in	No paragraph	...marks⌐	...marks. Below is a....
		⌐Below is a....	
_sc_	Set in small capitals	The bible	The BIBLE
rom	Set in roman type	The⟨bible⟩	The bible
_bf_	Set in boldface	The bible	The **bible**
_lf_	Set in lightface	The⟨bible⟩	The bible
⊙	Insert period	The lawyers have their own bible͜	The lawyers have their own bible.
⋏	Insert comma	However͜ we cannot....	However, we cannot....
⌒=⸍⁄⌒=⌒	Insert hyphens	half͜and͜half	half-and-half
○	Insert colon	We need the following͜	We need the following:
⋏	Insert semicolon	Use the law͜don't....	Use the law; don't....
⋎	Insert apostrophe	John͜s law book	John's law book
⋎⁄⋎	Insert quotation marks	The law is law.	The "law" is law.
(⁄)⁄	Insert parentheses	John's͜law͜book	John's (law) book
[⁄]⁄	Insert brackets	John͜1920-1962͜went....	John [1920-1962] went....
⁄N	Insert en dash	1920͜1962	1920-1962
⁄M	Insert em dash	Our goal͜victory	Our goal—victory
⋎	Insert superior type	3͜= 9	$3^2 = 9$
⋏	Insert inferior type	H͜SO₄	H_2SO_4
⋎	Insert asterisk	The law⋎	The law*
†	Insert dagger	The law͜	The law†
‡	Insert double dagger	The bible͜	The bible‡
§	Insert section symbol	͜Research	§Research

Figure 1   Proofreaders' Marks

During the second time, ask, "Am I following the rules?" Then check for:

- typographical errors
- capitalization
- punctuation
- spelling
- grammar

During the third time, ask, "Is it complete?" Then look for:

- omissions
- deletions
- doubly typed words

When you read the material for content, make certain that everything is there, is correct, and is in the right place.

To proofread effectively, you must be critical and alert. Much like revising, proofreading requires that you look at your writing objectively. In her article "36 Aids to Successful Proofreading," Ruth H. Turner offered useful tips for proofreading three types of material: short narratives (letters or memorandums), long narratives (manuals or **reports** of ten or more pages), and technical material and statistical tables.*

SHORT NARRATIVES

1. To concentrate on typographical errors, read backwards (from right to left). Of course, since this method will not reveal omissions or duplications, you must read again for content.
2. Arrange with another person to proofread each other's material. However, do not allow this procedure to delay your progress.
3. Concentrate as you slowly read for errors. Speed reading does not help.
4. Pay attention to dates; do not assume they are correct. Check the **spelling** of months and even the correctness of the year.
5. Do not overlook names, addresses, subject or reference lines, signature lines, or even the copies list. Errors can sneak into these items as well as into the body of the letter or memorandum.

---

* Adapted, with permission, from *The Secretary*, Vol. 38, no. 2, p. 12, Feb. 1978 by the National Secretaries Association (International), Kansas City, MO 64108.

6. Examine the end and beginning of lines in the body of the letter or memorandum to make sure that little words like *that* or *and* have not been unnecessarily repeated.
7. If you have duplicated typed material and have ended each line at the same place, check your copy by laying it over the original and holding them both up to a strong light. This procedure will reveal errors without the need for reading.
8. Proofread personalized letters or memorandums that are identical except for names, addresses, or short insertions by carefully examining the personalized portions. Then hold them both up to a light, as described in the previous suggestion.

LONG NARRATIVES

1. Make a style sheet to ensure consistency throughout a manuscript regarding the spelling of specialized terminology or **jargon**, capitalization and **punctuation**, **heads**, **formats** for **outlines** or **tables**, and names and titles. Any items that are unique to your project can be jotted down on this style sheet. Keep this sheet for proofreading later revisions or additional manuals or reports in a series.
2. Proofread in steps. For example, check all the heads and titles first. Be sure that you have consistently followed the style sheet.
3. Scan page numbers. Have you missed or duplicated any?
4. Read the body of the material against the original, sentence by sentence.
5. Make sure any references to other parts of the work are correct. For example, "See page 6 for a similar list." Possibly, in the final typing, the list moved to page 7.
6. Verify the title and page numbers of other reference materials if you have that responsibility. Look up each item if at all possible.
7. When proofreading from a draft that has handwritten inserts, make sure that none have been overlooked in the final draft.

TECHNICAL MATERIAL AND STATISTICAL TABLES

1. If possible, use two people—one reading aloud, the other checking copy—to verify itemized data, codes, budget figures, and so on.
2. If you must do your own proofreading alone, try the following method: When the columns of a table have been typed by tabu-

lating across the page, proofread your copy down the columns, folding the original from top to bottom along the column and laying it next to the corresponding column of the copy.

3. If the draft is typewritten, lay a ruler under each line. This technique will help you keep your place on both the original and the copy. It also helps when the inevitable interruptions occur.

4. Check for both vertical and horizontal alignment of table columns. Proofread across the page, folding the original beneath each line and laying it under the corresponding lines of typed entries so that you can easily read the original against your copy.

5. Count the number of entries in each table column, and compare the total with the number in your copy. If there is a difference, hunt down the culprit.

6. Proofread outlines by breaking the task into components: check headings, then check the mechanics (**numbers**, letters, **indentations**), and finally perform a continuous reading of each item against the original.

A CHECKLIST FOR PROOFREADING

1. Make the **dictionary** your best friend. Is it *privilege, privelege,* or *priviledge; gauge* or *guage; discression* or *discretion; chief* or *cheif?* Never be embarrassed to look up a word, for you might be more embarrassed at an error in the completed work. Watch closely for an omitted *-ed* or final *-s.*

2. Study related words until you understand the differences in their meaning and use: **affect/effect, imply/infer, diagnosis/prognosis, advice/advise, insure/ensure/assure**.

3. Mentally repeat each syllable of long words with many vowels, such as *evacuation, responsibilities, continuously, individual.* It is easy to omit one.

4. Be careful with double letters. They are hard to remember, especially in words like *accommodation* and *occurrence.*

5. Remember that *supersede* is the only word in English ending in *-sede* and that *succeed, proceed,* and *exceed* are the only ones ending in *-ceed.* All others (*cede, recede, precede,* and the like) end in *-cede.*

6. Be careful with silent letters: *rhythm, rendezvous, malign.*

7. Check all punctuation marks after completing all other proofreading. Be careful not to omit a closing **parenthesis** or **quotation mark**.

8. Refer to the dictionary to determine whether to spell **compound words** as separate words, a hyphenated word, or one word. If the dictionary does not list the word as hyphenated or separate words, write it as one word.
9. Be sure that **capital letters** are used consistently. Follow any established style for the type of document or subject matter. If an established style does not exist, adopt one of your own.
10. One last suggestion—proofread tomorrow what you worked on today.

For further information on proofreading, you may wish to consult the following books:

Lasky, Joseph. *Proofreading and Copy-Preparation*
The Chicago Manual of Style. University of Chicago Press
Skillin, M.E., and Gay, R.M., eds. *Words into Type*

proper nouns

A proper noun names a specific person, place, thing, concept, action, or quality and therefore it is always capitalized.

Proper Nouns	*Common Nouns*
John Doe	person
Chicago	city
General Electric	company
Tuesday	day
Declaration of Independence	document

(For the **case** and **number** of proper nouns, see **nouns**.)

proposals

A proposal is a document written to persuade someone to follow a plan or course of action. It may be internal to an organization or be sent outside the organization to a potential client.

An **internal proposal** usually recommends a change or improvement within an organization. The recommendation might be to expand the cafeteria service, to combine multiple manufacturing operations, or to introduce new working procedures. A capital appropriations proposal is a specific type of internal proposal submitted for management approval to spend large sums of money. An internal proposal is normally prepared by an employee or department and then sent to a higher-ranking person in the organization for approval.

A **sales proposal** is a company's offer to provide goods or services to a potential buyer within a certain amount of time and at a specified cost. The purpose of the proposal is to present a product or service in the best possible light and to explain why a buyer should choose it over the competitors. Remember that the survival of some companies depends on their ability to produce effective proposals.

Since proposals offer plans to fill a need, your **readers** will evaluate your plan according to how well your written presentation answers their questions about what you are proposing to do, how you plan to do it, when you plan to do it, and how much it is going to cost.

To answer these questions satisfactorily, make certain that your proposal is written at your reader's level of knowledge. If you have more than one level of reader—and proposals often require more than one level of approval—take into account all your readers. For example, if your immediate reader is an expert on your subject but the next higher level of management (which must also approve the proposal) is not, provide an **executive summary** written in language that is as nontechnical as possible. You might also include a **glossary** of technical terms used in the body of the proposal, or an appendix that explains the information in nontechnical language. On the other hand, if your immediate reader is not an expert but the person at the next level is, write the proposal with the nonexpert in mind and include an appendix that contains the technical details.

Proposals usually consist of an **introduction**, a body, and a **conclusion**. The introduction should summarize the problem you are proposing to solve and your solution. It may also indicate the benefits that your reader will receive from your solution and its total cost. The body should explain in detail (1) how the job will be done, (2) what methods will be used to do it (and if applicable, the materials to be used and any other pertinent information), (3) when work will begin, (4) when the job will be completed, and (5) a cost breakdown for the entire job. The conclusion should emphasize the benefits for the reader and should urge him or her to take action. Your conclusion should have an encouraging, confident, and reasonably assertive **tone**.

proved/proven

Both *proved* and *proven* are acceptable past **participles** of *prove*, although *proved* is currently in wider use.

> EXAMPLES   They had *proved* more obstinate than expected.
> They had *proven* more obstinate than expected.

Proven is more commonly used as an **adjective**.

> EXAMPLE   She was hired because of her *proven* competence as a manager.

pseudo/quasi

As a **prefix**, *pseudo*, meaning "false or counterfeit," is joined to a word without a **hyphen** unless the word begins with a **capital letter**.

> EXAMPLES   *pseudo*science (false science)
> *pseudo*-Americanism (pretended Americanism)

Pseudo is sometimes confused with quasi, meaning "somewhat" or "partial." Unlike *semi, quasi* does not mean half. *Quasi* is usually hyphenated in combinations.

> EXAMPLE   *quasi*-scientific literature

(See also **bi-/semi-**.)

punctuation

Punctuation is a system of **symbols** that help the **reader** understand the structural relationship within (and the intention of) a sentence. Marks of punctuation may link, separate, enclose, indicate omissions, terminate, and classify sentences. Most of the thirteen punctuation marks can perform more than one function. The use of punctuation is determined by grammatical conventions and the writer's intention—in fact, punctuation often performs the same functions in writing that the writer's facial expressions perform in speaking. Misuse of punctuation can cause your reader to misunderstand your meaning. Detailed information on each mark of punctuation is given in its own entry. The following are the thirteen marks of punctuation:

apostrophe	'
brackets	[ ]
colon	:
comma	,
dash	—
exclamation mark	!
hyphen	-
parentheses	( )
period	.
question mark	?
quotation marks	" "
semicolon	;
slash	/

Q

question marks

The question mark (?) has the following uses:
Use a question mark to end a sentence that is a direct question.

EXAMPLE Where did you put the specification?

Use a question mark to end any statement with an interrogative meaning (a statement that is declarative in form but asks a question).

EXAMPLE The report is finished?

Use a question mark to end an interrogative **clause** within a declarative sentence.

EXAMPLE It was not until July (or was it August?) that we submitted the report.

Retain the question mark in a title that is being cited, even though the sentence in which it appears has not ended.

EXAMPLE *Should Engineers Be Writers?* is the title of her book.

When used with **quotations**, the question mark indicates whether the writer who is doing the quoting or the person being quoted is asking the question. When the writer doing the quoting asks the question, the question mark is outside the **quotation marks**.

EXAMPLE Did she say, "I don't think the project should continue"?

If, on the other hand, the quotation itself is a question, the question mark goes inside the quotation marks.

EXAMPLE She asked, "When will we go?"

If the writer doing the quoting and the person being quoted both ask questions, use a single question mark inside the quotation marks.

EXAMPLE Did she ask, "Will you go in my place?"

Question marks may follow a series of separate items within an interrogative sentence.

EXAMPLE   Do you remember the date of the contract? its terms? whether
you signed it?

A question mark should never be used at the end of an indirect
question.

CHANGE   He asked me whether sales had increased this year?
TO   He asked me whether sales had increased this year.

When a directive or command is phrased as a question, a question
mark is usually not used. However, a request (to a customer or a superior, for instance) almost always requires a question mark.

EXAMPLES   Will you be sure that the books are balanced by May.
Will you please let me know if there is any way our Customer
Service Department can assist you?

questionnaires

A questionnaire—a series of questions on a particular topic, sent
out to a number of people—is a sort of interview on paper. It offers
several advantages over the personal interview but has some disadvantages. A questionnaire allows you to sample many more people
than personal interviews can. It enables you to obtain responses
from people in different parts of the country. Even people who live
near you may be easier to reach by mail than in person. Those responding to a questionnaire do not face the constant pressure posed
by someone jotting down their every word—a fact that can produce
more thoughtful answers from questionnaire respondents. And the
questionnaire reduces the possibility that the interviewer might
influence an answer by tone of voice or facial expression. Finally, the
cost of a questionnaire is lower than the cost of numerous personal
interviews.

Questionnaires have drawbacks too. People who have strong opinions on a subject are more likely to respond to a questionnaire than
those who do not. This can slant the results. An interviewer can follow up on an answer with a pertinent question; at best, a questionnaire can be designed to let one question lead logically to another.
Furthermore, mailing a batch of questionnaires and waiting for re-
plies take considerably longer than a personal interview does.

A questionnaire must be properly designed. Your goal should be
to obtain as much information as possible from your recipients with
as little effort on their part as possible. The first rule to follow is to

keep the questionnaire brief. The longer the questionnaire is, the less likely the recipient will be to complete and return it. Next, the questions should be easy to understand. A confusing question will yield confusing results, whereas a carefully worded question will be easy to answer. Ideally, questions should be answerable with a yes or no.

> Would you be willing to work a four-day work week, ten hours a day, with every Friday off?
>
> Yes _____
>
> No _____
>
> No opinion _____

When it is not possible to phrase questions in such a straightforward way, offer an appropriate range of answers. Questions must be neutrally phrased; their wording must not lead respondents to a particular answer.

CHANGE How many hours of overtime would you be willing to work each week?

> 4 hours _____   10 hours _____
>
> 6 hours _____   More than 10 hours _____
>
> 8 hours _____   No overtime _____

TO Would you be willing to work overtime?

> Yes _____
>
> No _____
>
> If yes, how many hours of overtime would you be willing to work each week?
>
> 4 hours _____   10 hours _____
>
> 6 hours _____   12 hours _____
>
> 8 hours _____   More than 12 hours _____

When preparing your questions, remember that you must eventually tabulate the answers; therefore, try to formulate questions whose answers can be readily computed. The easiest questions to tabulate are those for which the recipient does not have to compose an answer. Any questions that require a comment for an answer take time to think about and write and thus lessen your chances of obtaining a response. They are also difficult to interpret. Questionnaires should include a section for additional comments, where recipients may clarify their overall attitude toward the subject. If the information will help interpret the answers, include questions about the recipient's age, education, occupation, and so on. Include your name, your address, the purpose of the questionnaire, and the date by which an answer is needed. (See also **forms design**.)

A questionnaire sent by mail must be accompanied by a letter explaining who you are, the purpose of the questionnaire, how it will be used, and the date by which you would like to receive a reply. If the information provided will be kept confidential or if the recipient's identity will not be disclosed, say so in the letter.

The sample questionnaire in Figure 1 was sent to employees in a large organization who had participated in a six-month program of flexible working hours. Under the program, employees worked a forty-hour, five-day week, with flexible starting and quitting times. Employees could start work between 7 and 9 a.m. and leave between 3:30 and 6:30 p.m., provided that they worked a total of eight hours each day and took a one-half-hour lunch period midway through the day.

Select the recipients for your questionnaire carefully. If you want to survey the opinions of all the employees in a small office, simply send each worker a questionnaire. To survey the members of a professional society, mail questionnaires to everyone on the membership list. But to survey the opinions of large groups in the general population—for example, all word processors working in small firms—is not so easy. Since you cannot include everybody in your survey, you have to choose a representative cross-section.

Each of the following books contains advice on the design and interpretation of sampling techniques:

Arkin, Herbert, and Raymond R. Colton. *Statistical Methods.* 5th ed. New York: Barnes, 1971.
Beardsley, Monroe C. *Thinking Straight: Principles of Reasoning for Readers and Writers.* 4th ed. Englewood Cliffs, NJ: Prentice, 1975.
Weddle, Perry. *Argument: A Guide to Critical Thinking.* New York: McGraw, 1978.

MEMORANDUM

May 18, 19--

To: All Company Employees

From: Nelson Barrett, Director of Personnel _nB_

Subject: Review of Flexible Working Hours Program

      Please complete this questionnaire regarding Luxwear Corporation's trial program of flexible working hours. Your answers will help us to decide whether the program should continue. Return the questionnaire to the Personnel Department by May 28.
      If you want to discuss any item in more detail, call Tania Peters in Personnel at extension 8812.

1. What kind of position do you hold?

    _____   _____
    supervisory   nonsupervisory

2. Indicate your exact starting time under flexitime.

    _____

3. Where do you live?

    Talbot County _____ Greene County _____

    Montgomery County _____ Other, specify _____

4. How do you usually travel to work?

    Drive alone _____   Walk _____

    Car pool _____   Bus _____

    Train _____   Motorcycle _____

    Bicycle _____   Other, specify_____

5. Has flexitime affected your commuting time? If so, please indicate the approximate number of minutes.

    _____   _____   _____
    increase   decrease   no change

6. If you drive, has flexitime affected the amount of time it takes to find a parking space?

    _____   _____   _____
    increase   decrease   no change

Figure 1 Sample Questionnaire

-2-

7. Do you think that flexitime has affected your productivity?

_____ _____ _____
increase   decrease   no change

8. Have you had difficulty getting in touch with colleagues whose work schedules are different from yours?

Yes _____   No _____

9. Have you had trouble scheduling meetings?

Yes _____   No _____

10. Has flexitime affected the way you feel about your job?

_____ _____ _____
feel better feel worse   no change

11. How important is it for you to have flexibility in your working hours?

Very _____   Not very _____

Somewhat _____   Not at all _____

12. If you have children, has flexitime made it easier or more difficult for you to obtain babysitting or day-care services?

_____ _____ _____
easier   more difficult no change

13. Do you recommend that the flexitime program be made permanent?

Yes _____   No _____

14. Do you have suggestions for any changes in the program? If so, please specify.

_____

_____

mo

Figure 1   Sample Questionnaire (continued)

quid pro quo

Quid pro quo, which is Latin for "one thing for another," can suggest mutual cooperation or "tit for tat" in a relationship between two groups or individuals. The term may be appropriate to business and legal contexts if you are sure your **reader** understands its meaning.

EXAMPLE It would be unwise to grant their request without insisting on some *quid pro quo.*

quotation marks

Quotation marks ("") are used to enclose direct **repetition** of spoken or written words. They should not be used to emphasize. There are a variety of guidelines for using quotation marks.

Enclose in quotation marks anything that is quoted word for word (direct quotation) from speech.

EXAMPLE She said clearly, "I want the progress report by three o'clock."

Do not enclose indirect **quotations**—usually introduced by *that*—in quotation marks. Indirect quotations are **paraphrases** of a speaker's words or ideas.

EXAMPLE She said that she wanted the progress report by three o'clock.

Handle quotations from written material the same way: place direct quotations, but not indirect quotations, within quotation marks.

EXAMPLES The report stated, "The potential in Florida for our franchise is as great as in California."
The report indicated that the potential for our franchise is as great in Florida as in California.

If you use quotation marks to indicate that you are quoting, you may not make any changes in the quoted material unless you clearly indicate what you have done. (See **quotations** and **brackets**.)

Quotations longer than four typed lines (at least fifty characters per line) are normally indented (*all* the lines) five spaces from the left margin, single-spaced, and *not* enclosed in quotation marks.

Unless it is indented, a quotation of more than one **paragraph** is given quotation marks at the beginning of each new paragraph, but at the end of only the last paragraph.

Use single quotation marks (on a typewriter use the **apostrophe** key) to enclose a quotation that appears within a quotation.

EXAMPLE John said, "Jane told me that she was going to 'hang tough' until the deadline is past."

Use quotation marks to set off special words or technical terms only to point out that the term is used in context for a unique or special purpose (used, that is, in the sense of *the so-called*).

EXAMPLE Typical of deductive analyses in real life are accident investigations: What chain of events caused an "unsinkable" ship such as the *Titanic* to sink on its maiden voyage?

However, slang, colloquial expressions, and attempts at humor, although infrequent in business writing, seldom rate being set off by quotation marks.

CHANGE Our first six months in the new office amounted to little more than a "shakedown cruise" for what lay ahead.

TO Our first six months in the new office amounted to little more than a shakedown cruise for what lay ahead.

Use quotation marks to enclose titles of reports, short stories, articles, essays, radio and television programs, short musical works, paintings, and other art works.

EXAMPLE Did you see the article, "No-Fault Insurance and Your Motorcycle" in last Sunday's *Journal*?

Titles of books and periodicals are underlined (to be typeset in **italics**).

EXAMPLE Articles in the *Business Education Forum* and *Scientific American* quoted the same passage.

Some titles, by convention, are neither set off by quotation marks nor underlined, although they are capitalized.

EXAMPLES Business Communication (college course title), the Bible, the Constitution, Lincoln's Gettysburg Address, the Montgomery Ward Catalog, the Denver Telephone Directory

Commas and **periods** always go inside closing quotation marks.

EXAMPLE "Reading *World Business Weekly* gives me the insider's view," he writes, adding "it's like having all the top officials sitting in my office for a bull session."

Semicolons and **colons** always go outside the closing quotation marks.

EXAMPLES He said, "I will pay the full amount"; this certainly surprised
          us.
          The following are her favorite "sports": eating and sleeping.

All other **punctuation** follows the logic of the context: if the punctuation is a part of the material quoted, it goes inside the quotation
marks; if the punctuation is not part of the material quoted, it goes
outside the quotation marks.

Quotation marks may be used as ditto marks, instead of repeating
a line of words or numbers directly beneath an identical set. In formal writing, this use is confined to **tables** and **lists**.

EXAMPLE A is at a point equally distant from L and M.
         B   "   "   "   "   "   "   "   S and T.
         C   "   "   "   "   "   "   "   R and Q.

quotations

When you have borrowed words, facts, or ideas of any kind from
someone else's work, acknowledge your debt by giving your source
credit in a footnote. Otherwise, you will be guilty of **plagiarism**. Also
be sure that you have represented the original material honestly and
accurately. (See also **documenting sources**.)

DIRECT QUOTATIONS

Direct word-for-word quotations are enclosed in **quotation marks**.
They are usually, although not always, separated from the rest of the
sentence in which they occur by either a **comma** or a **colon**.

EXAMPLES The noted economist says, "If monopolies could be made to
          behave as if they were perfectly competitive, we would be
          able to enjoy the benefits both of large-scale efficiency and
          of the perfectly working price mechanism."
          The noted economist pointed out: "There are three options
          available when technical conditions make a monopoly the
          natural outcome of competitive market forces: private mo-
          nopoly, public monopoly, or public regulation."

INDIRECT QUOTATIONS

Indirect quotations, which are essentially **paraphrases** and are usually introduced by *that,* are not set off from the rest of the sentence
by **punctuation** marks.

DIRECT   He said in a recent interview, "Regulation cannot supply the dynamic stimulus that in other industries is supplied by competition."

INDIRECT   In a recent interview he said that regulation does not stimulate the industry as well as competition does.

When a quotation is divided, the material that interrupts the quotation is set off, before and after, by commas, and quotation marks are used around each part of the quotation.

EXAMPLE   "Regulation," he said in a recent interview, "cannot supply the dynamic stimulus that in other industries is supplied by competition."

At the end of a quoted passage, commas and **periods** go inside the quotation marks, and colons and **semicolons** go outside the quotation marks.

DELETIONS OR OMISSIONS

Deletions or omissions from quoted material are indicated by three *ellipsis* dots within a sentence and four ellipsis dots at the end of a sentence, the first of the four dots being the period that ends the sentence.

EXAMPLE   "If monopolies could be made to behave . . . we would be able to enjoy the benefits of . . . large-scale efficiency. . . ."

When a quoted passage begins in the middle of a sentence rather than at the beginning, however, ellipsis dots are not necessary; the fact that the first letter of the quoted material is not capitalized tells the **reader** that the quotation begins in midsentence.

CHANGE   He goes on to conclude that ". . . coordination may lessen competition within a region."

TO   He goes on to conclude that "coordination may lessen competition within a region."

Such quotations should be worked into one of your sentences rather than left standing alone. When quoted material is worked into a sentence, be sure that it is related logically, grammatically, and syntactically to the rest of the sentence.

INSERTING MATERIAL INTO QUOTATIONS

When it is necessary to insert a clarifying comment within quoted material, use **brackets**.

EXAMPLE   "The industry is organized as a relatively large, integrated system serving an extensive [geographic] area, with smaller systems existing as islands within the larger system's sphere of influence."

When quoted material contains an obvious error, or might in some other way be questioned, the expression *sic*, enclosed in brackets, follows the questionable material to indicate that the writer has quoted the material exactly as it appeared in the original. (See also **sic**.)

EXAMPLE   In *Basic Astronomy*, Professor Jones noted that the "earth does not revolve around the son [*sic*] at a constant rate."

INCORPORATING QUOTATIONS INTO TEXT

Depending on the length, there are two mechanical methods of incorporating quotations into your text. Quotations of four or fewer lines are incorporated into your text and enclosed in quotation marks. (Many writers use this method regardless of length. When this method is used with multiple **paragraphs**, quotation marks appear at the beginning of each new paragraph, but at the end of only the last paragraph.) Material longer than five lines is now usually inset; that is, it is set off from the body of the text by being indented five spaces from the left margin and by triple-spacing above and below the quotation. The quoted passage is single-spaced and not enclosed in quotation marks.

OVERQUOTING

Do not rely too heavily on the use of quotations in the final version of your **report** or paper. If you do, your work will appear merely derivative. The temptation to overquote during the **note-taking** phase of your **research** can be avoided if you concentrate on summarizing what you read. Quote word for word only when your source concisely sums up a great deal of information or points to a trend or development important to your subject. As a rule of thumb, avoid quoting anything over one paragraph.

R

raise/rise

Both *raise* and *rise* mean "move to a higher position." However, *raise* is a transitive **verb** and always takes an object (*raise* crops), whereas *rise* is an intransitive verb and never takes an object (heat *rises*).

> EXAMPLES If we cannot lower costs, we must *raise* prices.
> If the President signs the bill, the stock market will *rise*.

re

Re (and its variant form *in re*) is business and legal **jargon** meaning "in reference to" or "in the case of." *Re* is sometimes used in **memorandums**.

> EXAMPLE To: Elaine Barr
> From: Edgar Roden
> *Re:*   Revised Office Procedures

Re, however, is now giving way to *subject*.

> EXAMPLE To: Elaine Barr
> From: Edgar Roden
> *Subject:* Revised Office Procedures

readers

The first rule of effective writing is to help the reader; you must accept this commitment if you wish to communicate effectively in writing. If you overlook this consideration in your professional writing, your business or organization will lose time and money and will miss an opportunity to generate goodwill. Whether you are writing a letter, a **report**, or a **memorandum**, you must first determine who the reader is and then decide how to meet that reader's needs.

LETTERS

Letters—whether to customers, clients, or others—are the most personal forms of business writing, since they represent a direct communication between one person and another: you and your reader.

Your task is to communicate some information to this reader. Think of how you might talk to this person, and consider how he or she might respond to what you write. Keep in mind the reader's education, interests, and needs in determining what you will say and how you will say it.

Business letters can and should promote good relations between you and your reader. Businesses and organizations spend millions of dollars to build a relationship with the public, and this relationship can be marred by inconsiderate or insensitive letters. Successful letters are courteous and sincere. Some business writers find it helpful to try to write from the reader's **point of view**. This strategy, often called the **you viewpoint**, does not suggest that you should try to manipulate the reader but, rather, that you should determine how the reader stands to benefit from your letter and then adapt your writing accordingly. For example, if you were asking a customer who had requested a refund to submit a sales slip, the following sentence would *not* build goodwill:

> CHANGE We require that you sign and return the sales slip before we can process a refund.

Notice that the **emphasis** here is on what the writer and the company (*We*) need to *process a refund*; the reader's needs are not mentioned. Consider the following revision:

> TO So you can receive your refund quickly, please sign and return the sales slip.

In this version the reader's benefit—to receive a quick refund—is emphasized, and the tone is more courteous. To ensure that your letters emphasize your reader's benefits and achieve a courteous tone, try asking yourself how you would feel to receive such a letter. For further discussion of courtesy in letters, see **correspondence**, and for advice on specific types of letters, such as **sales letters**, see those entries.

REPORTS

Business reports are normally less personal than business letters are, for they place great **emphasis** on an objective presentation and analysis of information. In writing a business report, consequently, your **tone** must remain somewhat impersonal. Remember that your readers need to grasp your information quickly and that they may base decisions or actions on your interpretation of that information. As you choose facts and data to support your conclusions, consider how much your readers already know about the subject and how they are likely to use the information.

One of the most common mistakes that business writers make is to assume that their readers will be able to understand their writing despite a minimum of details. Often, in a misguided effort to be concise, writers do not provide enough background or supporting detail and fail to clarify logical relationships for their readers. Readers are often busy with other tasks when they read, and so they can all too easily misinterpret information that does not have adequate development or **coherence**. Furthermore, since reports and other documents are filed for future reference, explanations that are clear to the reader today may not be clear in two or three months.

When you write a report for several readers who have similar backgrounds (several financial specialists, for example), try to visualize a single, typical member of that group and write to that reader. You might also make a list of the characteristics (experience, training, and work habits, for example) of that reader. This technique, used widely by professional writers, enables you to decide what should or should not be explained according to that reader's needs. When you are writing for a somewhat more diverse group, it is usually best to aim at those with the least training and experience. The extra information and explanation will not insult those who know more; they can simply read more quickly, perhaps skipping sections with which they are familiar.

When your readership includes people with widely varied backgrounds, however, consider aiming various sections of the document at different sets of readers. Recommendations, **executive summaries**, and **abstracts** can be aimed at busy executives who are interested mainly in the general implications of projects or **proposals**. **Appendixes** containing **tables**, **graphs**, and raw technical data can be aimed at specialists, who wish to examine or use such supporting data. **Glossaries**, of course, must be written for readers who are not familiar with the standard terminology of your **topic**. The body of a report should be aimed at readers with the most serious interest or who need to make decisions based on the entire contents.

MEMORANDUMS AND OTHER KINDS OF WRITING

When writing memorandums, use a combination of the strategies you follow for letters and reports, for memos can vary from personal **correspondence** to single individuals to official reports in memo form for many readers. Whatever the situation, remember that memos serve as permanent records of business operations and thus must be adequately developed and suitably presented.

There are other factors to consider about readers of some less common types of business writing, such as **newsletter articles** and **journal articles**; for discussion of these, refer to the specific entries in this handbook. No matter what your topic or format, never forget that your readers are most important; the most eloquent prose is meaningless unless it reaches its audience.

reason is because

The **phrase** *reason is because* is a colloquial expression to be avoided in writing. *Because,* which in this phrase only repeats the notion of cause, should be replaced by *that.*

> CHANGE Sales have increased more than 20 percent. The *reason is because* our sales force has been more aggressive this year.
>
> TO Sales have increased more than 20 percent. The *reason is that* our sales force has been more aggressive this year.
>
> OR Sales have increased more than 20 percent this year *because* our sales force has been more aggressive.

reciprocal pronouns

The reciprocal pronouns *one another* and *each other* indicate a relationship between two or more persons or things. *Each other* is normally used when referring to two persons or things.

> EXAMPLE The two partners often disagreed with *each other.*

One another is normally used when referring to more than two persons or things.

> EXAMPLE The three vice-presidents talked to *one another* for an hour.

reference books

The following list provides many basic sources for **library research** and general reference:

ABSTRACTS

Accountant's Digest, 1935–. (quarterly)

Accounting and Data Processing Abstracts, 1970–. (eight times per year)

Accounting Articles, 1963–. (monthly)

Dissertation Abstracts International, 1938–. (monthly)

Human Resources Abstracts, 1966–. (quarterly)

Management Literature in Brief, 1968–. (monthly)

Organizational Communication: Abstracts, Analysis and Overview, 1976–. (six times per year)

Personnel and Training Abstracts, 1971–. (eight times per year)

Personnel Management Abstracts, 1955–. (quarterly)

Work Related Abstracts, 1951–. (monthly)

ATLASES

Business Atlas of Western Europe.

National Geographic Atlas of the World.

Oxford Economic Atlas of the World.

Rand McNally Commercial Atlas and Marketing Guide. (updated annually)

Times Atlas of the World: Comprehensive Edition.

United States Geological Survey. *National Atlas of the United States of America.*

BIBLIOGRAPHIES

Alred, Gerald J., Diana C. Reep, and Mohan R. Limaye. *Business and Technical Writing: An Annotated Bibliography of Books, 1880–1980.*

Besterman, Theodore. *A World Bibliography of Bibliographies.*

Bibliographic Index: A Cumulative Bibliography of Bibliographies, 1937–. (three times per year)

Hernes, Helga. *The Multinational Corporation: A Guide to Information Services.*

Sheehy, Eugene P. *Guide to Reference Books.*

Walford, A. J. *Walford's Guide to Reference Material*, 1973–77.

BIOGRAPHIES

Biography Index, 1946–. (quarterly, with cumulations)

Current Biography, 1940–. (monthly, with annual cumulation)

Who's Who in America, 1899–. (every two years)

Who's Who in Banking: The Directory of the Banking Profession.

Who's Who in Finance and Industry, 1936–. (every two years)

Who's Who in Labor.

BOOK GUIDES

Books in Print, 1947–. (annual)

Business Books and Serials in Print, 1977–. (annual)

Cumulative Book Index, 1928–. (monthly, with annual cumulation)

BOOK REVIEWS

Book Review Digest, 1905–. (monthly, with annual cumulation)

Current Book Review Citations, 1976–. (monthly)

The Wall Street Review of Books, 1973–. (quarterly)

COMMERCIAL GUIDES

Encyclopedia of Associations. (annually, with a quarterly supplement, *New Associations and Projects*)

MacRae's Blue Book, five volumes. (annually updated buying directory for industrial material and equipment)

Thomas Register of American Manufacturers, 1905–. (monthly)

DICTIONARIES

For desk dictionaries and unabridged dictionaries, see **dictionaries**. For selected specialized subject dictionaries, see **library research**.

DIRECTORIES

Consumer Protection Directory.

Directory of Business and Financial Services.

Directory of Corporate Affiliations, 1967–. (annual "Who Owns Whom" of industry)

Encyclopedia of Associations. (annual, with a quarterly supplement, *New Associations and Projects*)

Million Dollar Directory.

National Trade and Professional Associations of the United States and Canada, and Labor Unions, 1966–. (annual)

Standard and Poor's Register of Corporations, Directors and Executives, United States and Canada, 1928–. (annual)

Standard Directory of Advertising Agencies, 1907–. (three times per year)

DISSERTATIONS

Dissertation Abstracts International, 1938–. (monthly)

Masters Abstracts, 1962–. (quarterly)

ENCYCLOPEDIAS

Encyclopedia Americana.

Encyclopedia of Accounting Systems.

Graham Irwin. *Encyclopedia of Advertising.*

Heyel, Carl, ed. *Encyclopedia of Management.*

International Encyclopedia of Statistics.

Munn, Glenn G. *Munn's Encyclopedia of Banking and Finance.*

The New Encyclopaedia Britannica.

Sills, David L., ed. *International Encyclopedia of the Social Sciences.*

United States Bureau of Labor Statistics. *Occupational Outlook Handbook,* 1949–. (annual, updated by *Occupational Outlook Quarterly*)

FACTBOOKS AND ALMANACS

The Budget in Brief. (condensed version of annual U.S. budget)

Commodity Year Book, 1939–. (annual)

Demographic Yearbook. (annual U.N. publication on world economics and trade)

Dow-Jones-Irwin Business Almanac, 1977–. (annual)

Facts on File. (weekly)

Johnson, Otto T., et al. *Information Please Almanac, Atlas and Yearbook.*

Standard and Poor's Industry Surveys, 1977–. (quarterly)

Statistical Abstract of the United States, 1879–. (annual)

The Thorndike Encyclopedia of Banking and Financial Tables, 1973. (supplemented annually)

U.S. Industrial Outlook for 200 Industries with Projections for 1984. (annually updated statistics and projections by U.S. Dept. of Commerce)

GOVERNMENT PUBLICATIONS

Index to U.S. Government Periodicals, 1970–. (quarterly)

Monthly Catalog of United States Government Publications, 1895–.

Schmeckebier, Laurence F., and Roy B. Eastin. *Government Publications and Their Use.*

GRAPHICS

American Society for Testing and Materials. *Illustrations for Publication and Projection.*

Arkin, Herbert, and Raymond R. Colton. *Statistical Methods.*

Cardamone, Tom. *Chart and Graph Preparation Skills.*

Carlsen, Rob D., and Donald L. Vest. *Encyclopedia of Business Charts.*

Enrick, Norbert Lloyd. *Handbook of Effective Graphic and Tabular Communication.*

Field, Ron M. *A Guide to Micropublishing.*

Holmes, Nigel. *Designer's Guide to Creating Charts and Diagrams.*

Schmid, Calvin F., and Stanton E. Schmid. *Handbook of Graphic Presentation.*

LANGUAGE USAGE

Bernstein, Theodore M. *The Careful Writer: A Guide to English Usage.*

Copperud, Roy H. *American Usage and Style: The Consensus.*

Morris, William, and Mary Morris. *Harper Dictionary of Contemporary Usage.*

Nicholson, Margaret. *A Dictionary of American English Usage.*

Reader's Digest Association. *Success with Words: A Guide to the American Language.*

LOGIC

Beardsley, Monroe C. *Thinking Straight: Principles of Reasoning for Readers and Writers.*

Brennan, Joseph G. *A Handbook of Logic.*

Copi, Irving M. *Introduction to Logic.*

Weddle, Perry. *Argument: A Guide to Critical Thinking.*

PARLIAMENTARY PROCEDURE

Deschler, Lewis. *Deschler's Rules of Order.*

Robert, Henry M., et al. *Robert's Rules of Order.*

PERIODICAL INDEXES

Accountants Index Supplement, 1921–. (quarterly)

Business Education Index, 1941–. (annual)

Business Periodicals Index, 1958–. (monthly)

Consumer's Index to Product Evaluations and Information Sources, 1973–. (quarterly)

New York Times Index, 1851–. (twice per month)

Readers' Guide to Periodical Literature, 1900–. (biweekly)

SECRETARIAL HANDBOOKS

Doris, Lillian, and Bessemay Miller. *The Complete Secretary's Handbook.*

Hulchension, Lois Irene. *Standard Handbook for Secretaries.*

Janis, Jack Harold, and Margaret H. Thompson. *New Standard Reference for Secretaries and Administrative Assistants.*

Sabin, William A. *The Gregg Reference Manual.*

Tarntor, Sarah Augusta, and Kate M. Monro. *The Secretary's Handbook: A Manual of Correct Usage.*

Webster's Secretarial Handbook.

SPEECH AND GROUP DISCUSSION

Capp, Glen R., and G. Capp, Jr., *Basic Oral Communication.*

Maier, Norman. *Problem-solving Discussions and Conferences: Leadership Methods and Skills.*

Wilcox, Roger P. *Oral Reporting in Business and Industry.*

(See also **oral reports.**)

STYLE GUIDES AND MANUALS

For a list of style guides and manuals, see **documenting sources**.

SUBJECT GUIDES

Corman, Edwin, ed. *Sources of Business Information.*

Brownstone, David M., and Gorton Carruth. *Where to Find Business Information: A Worldwide Guide for Everyone Who Needs the Answers to Business Questions.*

Daniells, Lorna M. *Business Information Sources.*

SYNONYMS

Rodale, J. L. *The Synonym Finder.*

Roget, Peter M. *Roget's International Thesaurus.*

Webster's Collegiate Thesaurus.

reference letters

Almost everyone is called upon at some time to provide a recommendation or reference for a colleague, an acquaintance, or an employee. Reference letters may range from completing an admission form for a prospective student to composing a detailed description of professional accomplishments and personal characteristics for someone seeking employment.

In order to write an effective letter of recommendation, you must be familiar enough with the applicant's abilities or actual performance to offer an evaluation. Then you must *truthfully*, without embellishment, communicate that evaluation to the inquirer. For the reference letter to serve as a valid selection device, you must address specifically the applicant's skills, abilities, knowledge, and personal characteristics in relation to the requested objective. You may also be asked to say what you know about the person's former employment and education or even his or her military discharge and personnel records.

In a reference letter, always respond directly to the inquiry, being careful to address the specific questions asked. For the record, you must identify yourself: name, title or position, employer, and address. You will also have to state how long you have known the applicant and the circumstances of your acquaintance. You should men-

IVY COLLEGE
DEPARTMENT OF BUSINESS
WEST LAFAYETTE, IN 47906

January 14, 19--

Mr. Phillip Lester
Personnel Director
Thompson Enterprises
201 State Street
Springfield, IL   62705

Dear Mr. Lester:

How long writer has known applicant and the circumstances

As her employer and her former professor, I am happy to have the opportunity to recommend Kerry Hawkins. I've known Kerry for the last four years, first as a student in my class and for the last year as a research assistant.

Outstanding characteristics of applicant

Kerry is an excellent student, with above average grades in our program. On the basis of a CPA of 5.6 (A=6), Kerry was offered a research assistantship to work on a grant under my supervision. In every instance, Kerry completed her library search assignment within the time agreed upon. The material provided in the reports Kerry submitted met the requirements for my work and more. These reports were always well written. While working 15 hours a week on this project, Kerry has maintained a class load of 12 hours per semester.

Recommendation and summary of qualifications

I strongly recommend Kerry for her ability to work independently, to organize her time efficiently, and for her ability to write clearly and articulately. Please let me know if I can be of further service.

Sincerely yours,

Michael Paul

Michael Paul
Professor of Business

MP:mt

Figure 1   Reference Letter

tion with as much substantiation as possible, one or two outstanding characteristics of the applicant. Organize the details in your letter in order of importance; put the most important details first. Conclude with a statement of recommendation and a brief summary of the applicant's qualifications.

The Privacy Act of 1974 has had a major impact on reference letters. Under the act, applicants have a legal right to examine the materials in an organization's files that concern them—unless they sign a waiver of their right to do so. Organizations seeking to avoid the privacy issue may offer applicants the option of signing a waiver against reading letters of reference written about them. When you are requested to serve as a reference or asked to supply a letter of reference, you should thus inquire about the confidentiality status of your letter—whether the applicant's file will be open or closed.

Figure 1 is a typical reference letter.

reflexive pronouns

A reflexive pronoun, which always ends with the **suffix** -*self* or -*selves,* indicates that the **subject** of the sentence acts upon itself.

> EXAMPLE The secretary cut *himself* with the letter opener.

The reflexive form of the **pronoun** may also be used as an intensive to give **emphasis** to its antecedent. The reflexive and intensive pronouns are *myself, yourself, himself, herself, itself, oneself, ourselves, yourselves, themselves.*

> EXAMPLE I collected the data *myself.*

Never use a reflexive pronoun as a subject or as a substitute for a subject.

> CHANGE Joe and *myself* worked all day on it.
> TO Joe and *I* worked all day on it.

A common mistake is substituting a reflexive pronoun for *I, me,* or *us.*

> CHANGE John and *myself* completed the report.
> TO John and *I* completed the report.

> CHANGE He gave it to my assistant and *myself.*
> TO He gave it to my assistant and *me.*

CHANGE Nobody can solve the problem but *ourselves*.
TO Nobody can solve the problem but *us*.

refusal letters

When you receive a **complaint letter** or an **inquiry letter** to which you must give a negative reply, you may need to write a refusal letter. For example, a professional organization may have asked you to speak at their regional meeting, but they require your firm to pay your expenses. Because your firm has declined the request, you must write a refusal letter turning down the invitation. The refusal letter is difficult to write because it contains bad news; however, you can tactfully and courteously convey the bad news. In this kind of **correspondence**, that should be your goal.

In your letter you should lead up to the refusal. To state the bad news in your **opening** would certainly affect you **reader** negatively. The ideal refusal letter says no in such a way that you not only avoid antagonizing your reader but keep his or her goodwill. To achieve such an **objective**, you must convince your reader of the justness of your refusal *before refusing*. The following pattern is an effective way to deal with this problem:

1. A buffer beginning.
2. A review of the facts.
3. The bad news, based on the facts.
4. A positive and pleasant closing.

The primary purpose of a buffer beginning is to establish a pleasant and positive **tone**. You want to convince your reader that you are a reasonable person. One way is to indicate some form of agreement with, or approval of, the reader or the project. If your refusal is in response to a complaint letter, do not begin by recalling the reader's disappointment ("We regret your dissatisfaction . . ."). Keep your buffer **paragraph** positive and pleasant. You can express appreciation for your reader's time and effort, if appropriate. Stating such appreciation will soften the disappointment and pave the way for future good relations.

EXAMPLE Thank you for your cooperation, your many hours of extra work answering our questions, and your patience with us as we struggled to make a very difficult decision. We believe

our long involvement with your company certainly indicates our confidence in your products.

Next you should analyze the circumstances of the situation sympa-
thetically. Place yourself in your reader's position and try to see
things from his or her point of view. Establish clearly the reasons you
cannot do what the reader wants—even though you have not yet said
you cannot do it. A good explanation of the reasons should so thoroughly justify your refusal that the reader will accept your refusal
as a logical conclusion.

EXAMPLE   The Winton Check Sorter has all the features that your Abbott
Check Sorter offers and, in fact, offers two additional
features that your sorter does not. The more important of
the two is a backup feature that retains totals in memory,
even if the power fails, so that processing doesn't have to
start again from scratch following a power failure. The second additional feature that the Winton Sorter offers is
stacked pockets, which take less space than do the linear
pockets on your sorter.

Don't belabor the bad news—state your refusal quickly, clearly, and
as positively as possible.

EXAMPLE   After much deliberation, we have decided to purchase Winton
Check Sorters because of the extra features they offer.

Close your letter with a friendly remark, whether to assure the
reader of your high opinion of his product or merely to wish him
success in the future.

EXAMPLE   We have enjoyed our discussions with your company and feel
we have learned a great deal about check processing. Although we did not select your sorter, we were very favorably
impressed with your systems, your people, and your company. Perhaps we will work together in the future on another
project.

Sample refusal letters are presented on pages 000–000. Figure 1
refuses an invitation to speak at a professional organization's regional meeting. Figure 2 refuses a company credit for establishing
an open account. Figure 3 refuses a job offer, and Figure 4 refuses
a claim. (See also **resignation letter or memorandum**.)

Global Insurance Company
301 Decatur Street
Decatur, Illinois 62525

May 2, 19--

George M. Johnson
Good Deal Insurance Company
9001 Cummings Drive
St. Louis, Missouri 63129

Dear Mr. Johnson:

Buffer opening

I am honored to have been invited to address your regional meeting in St. Louis on May 17. To be considered one who might make a meaningful contribution to such a gathering of experts is indeed flattering.

Review of facts, followed by bad news

On checking with those who control the purse strings here at Global Insurance Company, however, I learned that it would be contrary to company policy for Global to pay my expenses for such a trip. Therefore, as much as I would enjoy attending your meeting, I must decline.

Positive and pleasant closing

I have been very favorably impressed over the years with your organization's contribution to the insurance industry, and I am proud to have received your invitation.

Sincerely,

Ralph P. Morgan

Ralph P. Morgan
Adviser/GIC

RPM/mo

Figure 1   Refusal Letter

Titus Packaging, Inc.
2063 Eldorado Dr.
Billings, Montana 59102

April 4, 19--

Ms. Edna Kohls
Graphic Arts Services, Inc.
936 Grand Avenue
Billings, Montana 59102

Dear Ms. Kohls:

Buffer opening

We appreciate your interest in establishing an open account at Titus Packaging, Inc. In the two years since you began operations, your firm has earned an excellent reputation in the business community.

Review of the facts, followed by the bad news

As you know, interest rates have been rising sharply this past year, while sales in general have declined. With the current negative economic climate, and considering the relatively recent establishiment of your company, we believe that an open account would not be appropriate at this time.

Positive and pleasant closing

We will be happy to have you renew your request around the first of next year, when the economic climate is expected to improve and when your company will be even more firmly established. In the meantime, we will be happy to continue our present cash relationship, with a 2-percent discount for payment made in ten days.

Sincerely,

Conrad C. Atkins

Conrad C. Atkins
Manager, Credit Department

CCA/mo

Figure 2   Refusal Letter

```
                                        127 Idlewild Road
                                        Boston, MA 02173
                                        October 17, 19--


          Ms. Juanita Perez
          Director, Personnel Department
          Manchester Iron Works, Inc.
          1258 Halsey Avenue
          Boston, MA 02181

          Dear Ms. Perez:
```

Buffer
opening I was pleased to receive your offer of employment as an Administrative Assistant in the Executive Office. I was very favorably impressed with your company and with the position as you described it.

Review of
the facts, Since interviewing with you, however, I have been offered
followed by another position that is even more in line with my long-
the bad news range goals, and I have accepted that position.

Positive and Thank you for your time and consideration. I enjoyed
pleasant meeting with your staff.
closing

```
          Sincerely yours,

          Jason L. Wytosh

          Jason L. Wytosh
```

Figure 3   Refusal Letter

General Television, Inc.
5521 West 23rd Street
New York, NY 10062

Customer Relations
(212) 574-3894

September 28, 19--

Mr. Fred J. Swesky
7811 Ranchero Drive
Tucson, AZ 85761

Dear Mr. Swesky:

Buffer opening	We have received your letter regarding the replacement of your KL-71 television set and have investigated the situation.
Review of the facts, followed by the bad news	You stated in your letter that you used the set on an uncovered patio. As our local service representative pointed out, this model is not designed to operate in extreme heat conditions. As the instruction manual that accompanied your television set cautioned, such exposure can seriously damage this model. Since your set was used in such extreme heat conditions, we cannot honor the two-year replacement warranty.
Positive and pleasant closing	We trust you will understand our position and we hope to provide for your future television needs.

Sincerely yours,

Susan Siegel

Susan Siegel
Assistant Director

SS/ar

Figure 4   Refusal Letter

relative pronouns

Relative **pronouns** (the most common are *who, whom, which, what,* and *that*) perform a dual function: They substitute for a **noun** and link the **dependent clause** in which they appear to a main **clause**. (Relative pronouns differ in use from relative **adjectives**, which are pronouns in form and have a similar linking function but which *modify* [describe] nouns.) In each of the following examples, two words are italicized: the relative pronoun and the word for which it is substituting:

> EXAMPLES   The specifications were sent to the *manager, who* immediately approved them.
>
> The project was assigned to *Ed Jones, whom* everyone respects for his skill as a designer.
>
> The customer's main *objection, which* can probably be overcome, is to the high cost of installation.
>
> The *memo* from Martha Goldstein *that* you received yesterday sets forth the most important points.

Sometimes a relative pronoun does not stand for another specific noun but does act as a noun in serving as the subject of a clause. In the following example, *what* acts as a subject in the dependent clause while also linking that clause to the main clause:

> EXAMPLE   We invited the committee to come to see *what* was being done about the poor lighting.

The relative pronoun *who* (*whom*) normally refers to a person; *that* and *which* normally refer to a thing; and *that* can refer to either. The pronoun *that* is normally used with restrictive clauses and the pronoun *which* with nonrestrictive clauses. (See also **restrictive and nonrestrictive elements.**)

> EXAMPLES   The annual report, *which was distributed yesterday*, shows that sales increased 20 percent last year.
>
> Companies *that adopt the plan* nearly always show profit increases.

Relative pronouns can often be omitted.

> EXAMPLE   I received the handcrafted ornament (that) I ordered.

Do not omit the word *that*, however, when it is used as a **conjunction** and its omission could cause the **reader** to misread a sentence.

CHANGE   This time delay ensures the operator has time to load the card
           hopper.
   TO   This time delay ensures *that* the operator has time to load the
          card hopper.

(See also **who/whom.**)

repetition

The deliberate use of repetition to build a sustained effort or emphasize a feeling or idea can be quite powerful.

EXAMPLE   Similarly, atoms *come and go* in a molecule, but the molecule
            remains; molecules *come and go* in a cell, but the cell *remains;*
            cells *come and go* in a body, but the body *remains;* persons *come
            and go* in an organization, but the organization *remains.*
            —Kenneth Boulding, *Beyond Economics* (Ann Arbor: U of Michigan P, 1968) 131.

Repeating key words from a previous sentence or **paragraph** can also
be used effectively to achieve **transition.**

EXAMPLE   For many years, *oil* has been a major industrial energy source.
            However, *oil* supplies are limited, and other sources of en-
            ergy must be developed.

Be consistent in the word or phrase you use to refer to something. In
business writing, it is generally better to repeat a word (so there will
be no question in the reader's mind that you mean the same thing)
than to use a synonym in order to avoid repeating it. Your primary
goal in business writing is effective and precise communication
rather than elegance.

CHANGE   Several recent *analyses* support our conclusion. These *studies*
            cast doubts on the feasibility of long-range forecasting. The
            reports, however, are strictly theoretical.
   TO   Several recent theoretical *studies* support our conclusion.
          These *studies* cast doubts on the feasibility of long-range
          forecasting. They are, however, strictly theoretical.

Purposeless repetition, however, makes a sentence awkward and
hides its key ideas.

CHANGE   He *said that* the customer *said that* the order was canceled.
   TO   He *said that* the customer canceled the order.

The harm caused to your writing by careless repetition is not limited to words and **phrases**; the needless repetition of ideas can be equally damaging.

> CHANGE   In this modern world of ours today, the well-informed, knowl-
> edgeable executive will be well ahead of the competition.
> TO   To succeed, the contemporary executive must be well in-
> formed.

(See also **conciseness/wordiness** and **elegant variation**.)

reports

A report is an organized presentation of factual information that answers a request by supplying the results of an investigation, a trip, a test, a research project, and the like. All reports can be divided into two broad categories: formal and informal.

Formal reports present the results of projects that may require months of work and involve large sums of money. These projects may be done either for one's own organization or as a contractual requirement for an outside organization. Formal reports generally follow a stringent **format** and include some or all of the report elements discussed in **formal reports**.

Informal reports normally run from a few paragraphs to a few pages and include only the essential elements of a report: introduction, body, conclusions, and recommendations. Because of their brevity, informal reports are customarily written as a letter (if the report is to be sent to someone outside the organization) or as a **memorandum** (if it is to be sent to someone inside the organization).

The *introduction* serves several functions: it announces the subject of the report, states its purpose, and, when appropriate, gives essential background information. The **introduction** should also summarize any conclusions, findings, or recommendations made in the report. Managers, supervisors, and clients find a concise summary useful because it gives them the essential information at a glance and helps focus their thinking as they read the rest of the report. The *body* of the report should present a clearly organized account of the report's subject—the results of a test carried out, the status of a construction project, and so on. The amount of detail to include depends on the complexity of the subject and on your reader's familiarity with it. In the *conclusion* should summarize your findings and tell the reader what you think their significance may be. In some reports, a final section gives *recommendations*. (Sometimes the **con-**

clusions and recommendations sections are combined.) In this section, you make suggestions for a course of action based on the data you have presented.

Many different types of informal reports are described in separate entries in this handbook: **feasibility reports, investigative reports, progress and activity reports, trip reports**, and **trouble reports**. Many of these can be formal or informal, depending on their length and complexity.

research

Research is the process of investigation, the discovery of facts. As part of the writing process, research must be preceded by preparation (that is, you must first determine your **reader**, objective, and **scope**). During the preparation phase, you establish the extent of the coverage needed for your work, and then during the research stage you can logically determine what information you will need and in how much detail. Without this preparation, the research will not be adequately defined or focused.

Researchers frequently distinguish between primary and secondary information, and depending on the goal of the research, the distinction can be important. *Primary information* refers to the "raw" data compiled from observations, surveys, experiments, **questionnaires**, and the like. This information is frequently gathered or located in notebooks, computer printouts, telephone logs, transcripts of speeches and interviews, tape recordings, and unedited film. *Secondary information* refers to primary information that has been analyzed, assessed, evaluated, compiled, or otherwise organized into accessible form. The forms include books, articles, reports, dissertations, operating and procedure manuals, brochures, and so forth. Use the information most appropriate to your research needs, recognizing that some projects will require both types.

Many projects require information from a variety of sources. The most common ones include written materials, interviews with experts, and firsthand observations. However, before investigating any of them, do not overlook the invaluable resource that *you* may represent. Before going elsewhere, interview yourself to tap into your knowledge and experience. You may find that you already have enough information to get started. This technique, commonly known as *brainstorming*, may also stimulate your thinking about additional places to seek information.

First, write down as many ideas as you can think of about the subject, as well as the objective and scope of your project, and jot them down in random order *as they occur to you.* (This may be done by a group as well as alone.) Put down what you know and, if possible, where you learned of it. For every idea noted, ask what, when, who, where, how and why. List the details these additional questions bring to mind. You can write down these ideas on a chalkboard, pad of paper, or note cards. (Note cards are preferable if you are working alone because they can easily be shuffled and rearranged.) Once your memory runs dry, group the items in the most logical order, based on your objective and your reader's needs.

The end result of this process will be a tentative outline of your project. The outline will have sketchy or missing sections, thus helping to show where additional research is needed, and it will also help integrate the various details of the additional research.

If you must conduct a formal, structured search of published sources, see **library research**. Scan quickly the written material before reading it in order to get an idea of the kind of information it includes. Then if it seems useful, read it carefully, taking notes of any information that falls within the scope of your research. Be sure to note where you found the information so you can find it again if necessary or compile it for a list of works cited. You may think of additional questions about the topic as you read; jot these down and identify them with a question mark. Some of them may eventually be answered in other research sources; those that remain unanswered can guide you to further research. (For detailed guidance on taking notes, see **note taking** and **paraphrasing**.)

If after researching these other sources you still need more information, consider talking to an expert. Not only can someone skilled in a field answer many of your questions, but he or she can also suggest other sources of information. (To make the most of such discussion, see **interviewing for information** and **listening**.)

Finally, you can use your own observations or hands-on experience. In fact, this is the only way to obtain certain kinds of information: the behavior of people and animals, certain natural phenomena, mechanical processes, the operation of tools and equipment, and the like. When planning research that involves observation, choose your sites and times carefully. Also, be sure to obtain permission in advance when necessary. Such observations may be illegal, resented, or contrary to an organization's policy. Keep accurate, complete records, indicating date, time of day, and the like. Save interpretations of your observations for future analysis. Be aware that research involving observations may be time-consuming, complicated, and expensive and that your presence may inadvertently influence what you observe.

If you have to write an operating manual for equipment or a procedure for some task, you must first acquire hands-on experience by operating the equipment or performing the task. Afterwards, you will in effect be interviewing yourself based on your experience. To do so, make a rough outline of your experience using the brainstorming technique described in this entry. After writing the draft, have someone unfamiliar with the equipment operate it or someone unfamiliar with the procedure perform it. When he or she has a problem, rewrite the passage until it is clear and easy to follow.

As with observations, obtain permission to operate the equipment or carry out a procedure. Comply with all safety rules, and make them a part of the manual or procedures you write. (See also **questionnaires.**)

resignation letter or memorandum

Start your letter or memorandum of resignation on a positive note, regardless of the circumstances under which you are leaving. You might, for example, point out how you have benefited from working for the company. You might say something complimentary about how well the company is run. Or you might say something positive about the people with whom you have been associated.

Then explain why you are leaving. Make your explanation objective and factual, and avoid recriminations. Your letter or memorandum will become part of your permanent file with that company, and if it is angry and accusing, it could haunt you in the future: you may need references from the company.

Your letter or memorandum should give enough notice to allow your employer time to find a replacement. It may be no more than two weeks, or it may be enough time to enable you to train your replacement. Some organizations ask for a notice that is equivalent to the number of weeks of vacation you receive.

The sample memorandum of resignation in Figure 1 is from an employee who is leaving to take a job offering greater opportunities. The memorandum of resignation presented in Figure 2 is from an

INTEROFFICE MEMORANDUM

To: W.R. Johnson, Director of Purchasing
From: J.L. Washburn, Purchasing Agent JLW
Date: January 7, 19--
Subject: Resignation from Barnside Appliances,
          effective February 7, 19--

Positive opening

My three years at Barnside Appliances has been an invaluable period of learning and professional development. I arrived as a novice, and I believe that today I am a professional-- primarily as a result of the personal attention and tutoring I have received from my superiors and the fine example set both by my superiors and my peers.

Reason for leaving

I believe the time has come for me to move on, however, to a larger company that can give me an opportunity to continue my professional development. Therefore, I have accepted a position with General Electric, where I am scheduled to begin on February 12. Thus, my last day at Barnside will be February 7. However, if you need more time to hire and train my replacement, I can make arrangements to work longer.

Positive closing

Many thanks for the experiences I have gained, and best wishes for the future.

Figure 1   Sample Resignation Memo (Resignation to Accept a Better Position)

INTEROFFICE MEMORANDUM

To: T.W. Haney, Vice-President, Administration
From: L.R. Rupp, Executive Assistant ʃℛℛ
Date: February 12, 19--
Subject: Resignation from Winterhaven, effective
          March 1, 19--

Positive opening

My ten-year stay with the Winterhaven Company has been a very pleasant experience, and I am sure it has been mutually beneficial.

Reason for leaving

Because the recent realignment of my job leaves no career path open to me, however, I have accepted a position with another company that I feel will give me a better future. I am, therefore, submitting my resignation, to be effective on March 1, 19--.

Positive closing

I have enjoyed working for Winterhaven and wish the company success in the future.

Figure 2   Sample Resignation Memo (Resignation Under Negative Conditions) employee who is leaving under unhappy circumstances. Notice that it opens and closes positively and that the reason for the resignation is stated without apparent anger or bitterness.

respective / respectively

Respective is an **adjective** that means "pertaining to two or more things regarded individually."

> EXAMPLE   The committee members prepared their *respective* reports.

Respectively is the **adverb** form of *respective*, meaning "singly, in the order designated."

> EXAMPLE   The first, second, and third prizes in the sales contest were awarded to Maria Juarez, Gloria Hinds, and Margot Luce, *respectively.*

Respective and *respectively* are often unnecessary because the meaning of individuality is already clear.

> CHANGE   The committee members prepared their *respective* reports.
> TO   Each committee member prepared a report.

restrictive and nonrestrictive elements

Modifying **phrases** and **clauses** may be either restrictive or nonrestrictive. A nonrestrictive phrase or clause provides additional information about what it modifies, but it does not limit, or restrict, the meaning of what it modifies. Therefore, the nonrestrictive phrase or clause can be removed without changing the essential meaning of the sentence. It is, in effect, a parenthetical element, and so it is set off by **commas** to show its loose relationship with the rest of the sentence.

> EXAMPLES   This instrument, *called a backscatter gauge,* fires beta particles at an object and counts the particles that bounce back. (nonrestrictive phrase)
> The annual report, *which was distributed yesterday,* shows that sales increased 20 percent last year. (nonrestrictive clause)

A restrictive phrase or clause limits, or restricts, the meaning of what it modifies. If it were removed, the essential meaning of the sentence would be changed. Because a restrictive phrase or clause is essential to the meaning of the sentence, it is never set off by commas.

EXAMPLES   All employees *wishing to donate blood* may take Thursday afternoon off. (restrictive phrase)

Companies *that adopt the plan* nearly always show profit increases. (restrictive clause)

It is important for writers to distinguish between nonrestrictive and restrictive elements. The same sentence can take on two entirely different meanings depending on whether a modifying element is set off by commas (because nonrestrictive) or not set off (because restrictive). The results of a slip by the writer can be not only misleading but also downright embarrassing.

CHANGE   I think you will be impressed by our systems engineers who are thoroughly experienced in projects like yours.

TO   I think you will be impressed by our systems engineers, who are thoroughly experienced in projects like yours.

The problem with the first sentence is that it suggests that "you may not be so impressed by our other, less experienced, systems engineers."

résumés

A résumé* is an essential element in any **job search** because it is, in effect, a catalog of what you have to offer to prospective employers. Sent out with your **application letter**, it is the basis for their decision to invite you for a job interview. (See **interviewing for a job**.) It tells them who you are, what you know, what you can do, what you have done, and what your job objectives are. It may be the basis for the questions you are asked in the interview, and it can help your prospective employer evaluate the interview, as an organized reminder of what you covered orally. The résumé, then, is an important document that deserves careful planning and execution.

Three steps will help you prepare your résumé:

1. Analyze yourself and your background.
2. Identify those to whom you will submit your résumé (your **readers**).
3. Organize and prepare the résumé.

---

*When typeset, *résumé* is set with accent marks (´) to distinguish it from the verb *resume*.

GATHERING INFORMATION

The starting point in preparing a résumé is a thorough analysis of your experience, education and training, professional and personal skills, and personal traits.

List the major points for each category before actually beginning to organize and write your résumé. (It helps to write each item on a 3- × 5-inch card.) The following questions can serve as an inventory of what you should consider in each category.

Experience. Note all your employment—full-time, part-time, vacation jobs, and free-lance work—and analyze each job on the basis of the following list of questions:

1. What was the job title?
2. What did you do (in reasonable detail)?
3. What experience did you gain that you can apply to another job?
4. Why were you hired for the job?
5. What special skills did you learn on that job?
6. Were you promoted or given a job with more responsibility?
7. Why did you leave it?
8. When did you start and when did you leave the job?
9. Would your former employer give you a reference?
10. What special traits were required of you on the job (initiative, leadership, ability to work with details, ability to work with people, imagination, ability to organize, and so on)?

Education. For the applicant with little work experience, such as a recent graduate, the education category is of primary importance. For the applicant with extensive work experience, education is still quite important, even though it is now secondary to work experience. List the following information about your education:

1. Colleges attended and the inclusive dates.
2. Degrees and the dates they were awarded.
3. Major and minor subjects.
4. Courses taken or skills acquired that might be important to the job you are applying for.
5. Internships, work-study programs, co-op positions.
6. Cumulative grade averages and academic honors.
7. Extracurricular activities.
8. Scholarships and awards.
9. Special training courses (academic or industrial).

ORGANIZING AND WRITING THE RÉSUMÉ

After listing all the items in the preceding three categories, you should analyze them in terms of the job you are seeking, evaluating the items, rejecting some of them, and finally selecting those that you will include in your résumé. Base your decision on the following questions:

1. What exact job are you seeking?
2. Who are the prospective employers?
3. What information is most pertinent to that job and those employers?
4. What details should be included and in what order?
5. How can you present your qualifications most effectively to get an interview?

Résumés should be brief—preferably one or two pages, depending on your level of experience—and should include the following information:

1. Your name, address, and phone number.
2. Your immediate and long-range job objectives.
3. Your professional training.
4. Your professional experience, including the firms where you have worked, and your responsibilities.
5. Your specific skills.
6. Pertinent personal information.

FORMAT OF THE RÉSUMÉ

A number of different formats can be used. The most important thing is to make sure that your résumé is attractive, well organized, easy to read, and free of errors. A common format uses the following **heads**:

Employment Objective
Education
Employment Experience
Special Skills and Activities
References (optional)

Underline or capitalize the heads to make them stand out on the page. Whether you list education or experience first depends on which is stronger in your background. If you are a recent graduate, list education first; if you have substantial job experience, list your most recent experience first, your next most recent experience second, and so on.

The Heading. Center your name in all capital letters (and boldface if you're using a word processor) at the top of the page. Follow it with your address and telephone number, also usually centered.

Employment Objective. State both your immediate and long-range employment objectives. However, if an objective is not appropriate for a particular position (a temporary job, for example), you may exclude it.

Education. List the college or colleges you attended, the dates you attended each one, any degree or degrees received, your major field of study, and any academic honors you earned. First-time applicants frequently give the name of their high school, its location (city, state), and the dates they attended.

Employment Experience. List all your full-time jobs, from the most recent to the earliest that is appropriate. If you have had little full-time work experience, list your part-time and temporary jobs, too. Give the details of your employment, including the job title, dates of employment, and the name and address of your employer. Provide a concise description of your duties only for those jobs whose duties were similar to those of the job you are seeking; otherwise, give only a job title and a brief description. Specify any promotions or pay increases you received. Do not, however, list your present salary. (Salary depends on your experience and your potential value to an employer.) If you have been with one company for a number of years, highlight your accomplishments during that time. List military service as a job. Give the dates you served, your duty specialty, and your rank at discharge. Discuss the duties only if they relate to the job you are applying for.

Some résumés arrange employment experience by function rather than by chronological time. Instead of listing your jobs first, starting with the most recent, you list the functions you've performed ("Management," "Project Development," "Training," "Sales," and the like). The functional arrangement is useful for persons who wish to stress their skills or who have been employed at one job and wish to demonstrate their diversity of experience at that single position. It is also used by those who have gaps in time on their résumé caused by unemployment or illness. Although the functional arrangement can be effective, employment directors know that it may

CAROL ANN WALKER
273 East Sixth Street
Blooomington, Indiana 47401
(913) 321-4567

EMPLOYMENT OBJECTIVE

Financial research assistant, leading to a management position in corporate finance.

EDUCATION

Indiana University (Bloomington)
Bachelor of Business Administration (Expected June 19--)
Major: Finance   Minor: Computer Science
Dean's List: 3.88 grade point average of possible 4.0.
Senior Honor Society, 19--.

EMPLOYMENT EXPERIENCE

FIRST BANK (Bloomington, Indiana)
Research Assistant Intern, Summer and Fall Quarters, 19--.
    Assisted manager of corporate planning and developed computer model for long-range planning.

MARTIN FINANCIAL RESEARCH SERVICES (Bloomington, Indiana)
Editorial Assistant Intern, 19-- to 19--.
    Provided research assistance to staff and developed a design concept for in-house fInancial audits.

SPECIAL SKILLS AND ACTIVITIES

Associate Editor, Business School Alumni Newsletter.
    Wrote two articles on financial planning with computer models; surveyed business periodicals for potential articles; edited submissions.

President, Women's Transit Program.
    Coordinated activities to provide safe nighttime transportation to and from dormitories and campus buildings.

REFERENCES

Available upon request.

Figure 1   Student Résumé

CAROL ANN WALKER
1436 W. Schantz Avenue
Dayton, Ohio 45401
(513) 555-1212

Employment   Senior Research Financial Analyst in corporate offices
Objective   of growth and research-oriented major manufacturing
company.

Employment Experience
(19-- to Present)

January 19-- to Present   KERFHEIMER CORPORATION (Dayton, Ohio)

Senior Financial Analyst (September 19-- to October 19--)
Report to the Senior Vice-President for Corporate Financial
Planning of this $1-billion manufacturer of heavy mining and con-
struction equipment, which is also purchased by various branches
of the federal government and the Department of Defense (DOD).
Work with government procurement officers and engineer's in
developing manufacturing cost estimates for complex and massive
machinery, based on prototypes developed in our research lab.
Develop program funding requirements and determine best available sources, some of which have been in the $100- to $300-million
range. Recipient of the "Financial Planner of the Year" award from
the Association of Financial Planners.

Financial Analyst (January 19-- to September 19--)
Reported to Senior Financial Analyst and assisted in the
development of funding for major DOD contracts for troop carriers,
digging and earth-moving machines, and extension booms. Researched funding options and recommended those with the most
favorable rates and terms. Recommended by Senior Financial
Analyst as the person to replace him on his retirement.

June 19-- to December 19--   FIRST BANK, INC. (Bloomington, IN)

Planning Analyst (September 19-- to December 19--)
Reported to Manager of Corporate Planning and developed
computer models for short- and long-range planning that reduced
by 65 percent the time required to compute costs.

Figure 2   Advanced Résumé: Organized by Job

CAROL ANN WALKER
Page 2

Education

Wharton School, University of Pennsylvania (19-- to Present)
Graduate Seminars Taken
Advanced Corporate Planning and Demographics
Computer Analysis of Corporate Planning
Theory of Corporate Policies
Regulation and Corporate Financial Policy

University of Wisconsin-Milwaukee (June 19--)
Degree: M. B.A.
"Special Executive Curriculum": A special fast-track program for
M.B.A. students who are identified as promising and who are
sponsored by their employer.

Indiana University (June 19--)
Degree: B.B.A. (*magna cum laude*)
Major: Finance
Minor: Computer Science

Special Skills and Activities

Article published in *Midwest Finance Journal*: "Developing Computer
Models for Financial Planning" (Vol. 34, No. 2, 19--), pp. 122–136.

Guest Lecturer at Indiana University (June 29, 19--)

Senior Member, Association for Corporate Financial Planning

Member of Audubon Society, Photographer, and Runner

References and a portfolio of computer financial models on request.

Figure 2   Advanced Résumé: Organized by Job (continued)

CAROL ANN WALKER
1436 W. Schantz Avenue
Dayton, Ohio 45401
(513) 555-1212

Employment objective	Senior Research Financial Analyst in corporate offices of growth- and research-oriented major manufacturing company.

Major Accomplishments

Financial Planning

- Provided research on funding options that enabled company to achieve a 23-percent return on investment.
- Developed long-range funding requirements to respond to government and military contracts that totaled over $1 billion.
- Developed computer model for long- and short-range planning, which saved 65 percent in preparation time.

Capital Acquisition

- Developed strategies enabling employers to acquire over $1 billion at 3 percent below market rate.
- Responsible for securing over $100 million through private and government grants for research.
- Developed computer models for capital acquisition that enabled company to increase its long-term debt during several major building expansions.

Research and Analysis

- Developed sophisticated computer models based on cutting-edge research applied to practical problems of corporate finance.
- Served primarily as a researcher for 11 years at two different types of firms.
- Recipient of the "Financial Planner of the Year" award from the Association of Financial Planners, a group composed of both academics and practitioners.
- Published academic article and am taking doctoral-level seminars at the Wharton School, which are described in the education section that follows.

Figure 3   Advanced Résumé: Organized by Function

CAROL ANN WALKER
Page 2

Education

Wharton School, University of Pennsylvania (19-- to Present)
Graduate Seminars Taken
Advanced Corporate Planning and Demographics
Computer Analysis of Corporate Planning
Theory of Corporate Policies
Regulation and Corporate Financial Policy
University of Wisconsin--Milwaukee (June 19--)
Degree: M.B.A.
"Special Executive Curriculum": A special fast-track program for
M.B.A. students who are identified as promising and who are
sponsored by their employer.
Indiana University (June 19--)
Degree: B.B.A. (*magna cum laude*)
Major: Finance
Minor: Computer Science

Work History

KERFHEIMER CORPORATION (Dayton, Ohio): January 19-- to Present
Senior Financial Analyst (19-- to 19--)
Financial Analyst (19-- to 19--)
FIRST BANK, INC. (Bloomington, IN): June 19-- to December 19--
Planning Analyst (19-- to 19--)
Student Intern (19-- to 19--)

Special Skills and Activities

Article published in Midwest Finance Journal: "Developing Computer
Models for Financial Planning" (Vol. 34, No. 2, 19--), pp. 122–136.
Guest Lecturer at Indiana University (June 29, 19--)
Senior Member, Association for Corporate Financial Planning
Member of Audubon Society, Photographer, and Runner

References and a portfolio of computer financial models on request.

Figure 3   Advanced Résumé: Organized by Function (continued) be used to cover weaknesses, and so you should use it carefully and be prepared to explain any gaps.

Special Skills and Activities. This category usually comes near the end and may replace the Personal Data category. You may include such skills as knowledge of foreign languages, writing and editing abilities, specialized knowledge (such as experience with a computer language or a background in electronics), hobbies, student or community activities, professional or club memberships, and published works. Be selective: do not overload this category, do not duplicate information given in other categories, and do not include any items that do not support your employment objective. Other titles, such as "Abilities" and "Professional Affiliations," may be used for this category.

Personal Data. Federal legislation limits the inquiries an employer can make before hiring an applicant—especially requests for such personal information as age, sex, marital status, race, and religion. Consequently, some job seekers exclude this category because they feel their personal data could have a negative impact on the employer. You may also eliminate this category simply because you need the space for more significant information about your qualifications. However, if you believe the Personal Data category will help you land a particular job, then include your date of birth and your marital status (it's better to give your date of birth than your age, so that your résumé won't become out of date after your next birthday). In any case, you should see yourself through the eyes of your potential employers and provide whatever information would be most useful to them.

References. You can state on your résumé that "references will be furnished upon request" or include references as part of the résumé (only if you need to fill space or if including names is traditional to your profession). Either way, do not list anyone as a reference without first obtaining his or her permission to do so.

Style. As you write your résumé, use action **verbs**, and state your ideas concisely. You can avoid the pronoun *I* since the résumé is only about you.

> CHANGE I was promoted to office manager in June 19--.
> TO Promoted to office manager in June 19--.

The following is a list of typical verbs used in résumés:

administered	managed
analyzed	operated
completed	organized
conducted	oriented
coordinated	prepared
created	programmed
designed	recruited
developed	started
directed	supervised
evaluated	trained
increased	wrote

Be truthful in your résumé. If you give false data and are found out, the consequences could be serious. At the very least, you will have seriously damaged your credibility with your employer.

Make your résumé flawless before mailing it by proofing it and verifying the accuracy of the information. Have someone else review it, too. And do not pinch pennies when you create the résumé. It, and the accompanying application letter, will be the sole means by which you are known to prospective employers until an interview. If you have access to a computer with word-processing software and a laser printer, create the résumé using them. (If you use a dot-matrix printer, make sure it is a high-quality printer.) The word processor also allows you to customize and update the résumé easily for future use. Otherwise, have the résumé professionally typeset and printed. Printing always produces a more professional-looking résumé than does photocopying.

The sample résumés on pages 591–595 are all for the same person. Figure 1 is a student's first résumé, and Figures 2 and 3 show her work experience later in her career (one is organized by job, the other by function). Examine as many résumés as possible, and select the format that best suits you and your goals.

revision

The more natural a work of writing seems to the **reader**, the more effort the writer has probably put into revision. Anyone who has ever had to say of his or her own writing, "Now I wonder what I meant by that," can testify to the importance of revision. The time you invest in review will make the difference between clear writing and unclear writing.

If you have followed the appropriate steps of the writing process, you will have a very rough draft that can hardly be considered finished writing. Revision is the obvious next step.

Allow a couple of days, if possible, to go by without looking at the draft before beginning to revise it. Without a cooling period, you are too close to the draft to be objective in evaluating it. Only when enough time has elapsed so that you can say, "How did I ever write that?" or "I wonder why I said that so awkwardly?" are you ready to start revising.

A different frame of mind is required for revising than for **writing the draft**. Read and evaluate the draft, which should have been written quickly, with cool deliberation and objectivity—from the point of view of a reader or critic. Be anxious to find and correct faults, and be honest. In revising, consider your reader first.

Do not try to do all your revision at once. Read through your rough draft several times, each time searching for and correcting a different set of problems.

Check your draft for completeness. Your writing should give readers exactly what they need, but it should not burden them with unnecessary information or sidetrack them into insignificant or only loosely related subjects. Check your draft against your **outline** to make certain that you did, in fact, follow your plan. If not, now is the time to insert any missing points into your draft. This may mean inserting a line here and there; it may mean writing a **paragraph** or passage on a separate sheet and attaching it to the appropriate page; or it may mean major additions to your rough draft, depending on how carefully you followed your outline.

Take time to examine the facts in your draft for accuracy. Keep in mind that no matter how careful and painstaking you may have been in conducting your **research**, compiling your notes, and creating your outline, you could easily have made errors when transferring your thoughts from the outline to the rough draft. You can quickly and easily check the facts in your draft for accuracy if you took complete notes, and this can be critical if it catches even a single error. Be certain that contradictory facts have not crept into your draft.

Be consistent with names. Make sure, for example, that you have not called the same item a "routine" on one page and a "program" on another.

Your **introduction**, if you use one, should state your **objective** and provide a frame in which your reader can place the detailed in-

formation that follows in the body of your draft. Check your introduction to see that it does, in fact, give the reader such assistance.
If you do not use an introduction, check your **opening** to see that
it is useful and interesting to the reader.

To determine whether you have good **transition**, look for **unity**
and **coherence**. If a paragraph has unity, all its sentences and ideas
are closely tied together and contribute directly to the main idea expressed in the **topic sentence** of the paragraph. Writing that is coherent flows smoothly from one point to another, from one sentence
to another, and from one paragraph to another. Where transition
is missing, provide it; where transition is weak, strengthen it. Also
look for unity in the entire report, and provide any transition that
is needed between paragraphs or sections.

Check your draft for **pace**. If you find that you are jamming your
ideas too closely together, space them out and slow down the pace.

Check your use of **jargon**. If you have any doubt that all your
readers will understand any jargon you may have used, eliminate it.

Check your draft for **conciseness**. Tighten your writing so that it
says exactly what you mean, by pruning unnecessary words, **phrases**,
sentences, and even paragraphs.

Replace **clichés** with fresh **figures of speech** or direct statements.

Watch for words that could carry an undesired **connotation**. Also
delete or replace vague or pretentious words, coined words, and unnecessary **intensifiers**. (See also **word choice**.)

Check your draft for **awkwardness**, determine the reason for any
you may find, and correct it.

Check your draft for possible grammatical errors. Any such errors
should be caught in your check for awkwardness, but a final review
may save you embarrassment.

Finally, check your final draft for typographical errors by **proofreading** it.

rhetorical questions

A rhetorical question is a question to which a specific answer is
neither needed nor expected. The question is often intended to
make the reader think about the subject from a different perspective; the writer then answers the question in the article or essay.

EXAMPLES   Is methanol the answer to the energy shortage?
Does advertising lower consumer prices?

The answer to a rhetorical question may not be a yes or no; in the above examples, it might be a detailed explanation of the pros and cons of the value of methanol as a source of energy or the effect of advertising on consumer prices.

The rhetorical question can be an effective **opening**, and it is often used for a **title**. By its nature, however, it is somewhat informal and should therefore be used judiciously in professional writing. For example, a rhetorical question would not be an appropriate opening for a **report** or **memorandum** addressed to a busy superior in your company. When you do use a rhetorical question, be sure that it is not trivial, obvious, or forced. More than any other writing device, the rhetorical question requires that you know your reader.

run-on sentences

A run-on sentence, sometimes called a fused sentence, is two or more **sentences** without **punctuation** to separate them. The term is also sometimes applied to a pair of **independent clauses** separated by only a **comma**, although this variation is usually called a **comma fault** or comma splice. Run-on sentences can be corrected by (1) making two sentences, (2) joining the two clauses with a **semicolon** (if they are closely related), (3) joining the two clauses with a **comma** and a **coordinating conjunction**, or (4) subordinating one **clause** to the other.

> CHANGE   The new manager instituted several new procedures some were impractical. (run-on sentence)
>
> TO   The new manager instituted several new procedures. Some were impractical. (period)
>
> OR   The new manager instituted several new procedures; some were impractical. (semicolon)
>
> OR   The new manager instituted several new procedures, but some were impractical. (comma plus coordinating conjunction)
>
> OR   The new manager instituted several new procedures, some of which were impractical. (one clause subordinated to the other)

(See also **sentence faults**.)

S

sales letters

A sales letter promotes a product or a service. A sales letter might be a response to an **inquiry letter** or part of a direct-mail campaign. An effective sales letter (1) catches the attention of readers, (2) arouses their interest, (3) convinces them that your product or service will fulfill a need or desire, and then (4) confidently asks them to take the course of action you desire.

Before you can write an effective sales letter, you must determine whom you will send it to. One good source of names is past and present customers. Those who have purchased a product or service from you in the past may well do so again. Another source is people who may be expected to be interested in certain products and services. You can purchase or rent lists of such names, which are drawn from the membership of clubs, fraternal and religious organizations, professional societies, and the like. These lists tend to be expensive, however, and must be selected with care.

Once you determine who is to receive your sales letter, learn as much as you can about the typical **reader**. That reader's sex, age, vocation, geographical location, financial status, and so on, will help determine your approach in your sales letter. You must be aware of your reader's needs and desires because they are what your product or service must satisfy.

With today's personal computers, a mail-merge feature enables you to address potential customers by name rather than as "Dear Homeowner," or whatever other general designation may be appropriate.

Be conscious of your legal ability when you write a sales letter. Make no claims that are not true. And be careful of overstatement. If you say that a product is safe, you are guaranteeing its absolute safety. Therefore, say that the product is safe *provided that normal safety precautions are taken.*

Naturally, you must have a thorough knowledge of the product or service you are offering; in your sales letter, you must convince your reader of its worth.

Like most business letters, a sales letter consists of an **opening**, a body, and a closing.

OPENING

Begin your sales letter by identifying a need or a desire the reader may have—do not begin with a description of the product or service. The reader is much more likely to be interested in what you are selling if you show how it directly benefits him or her. The **you viewpoint** is essential here. (See **correspondence**.) A number of techniques can achieve this objective, as the following examples demonstrate:

Statement of problem
: You have an inventory problem that is costing you money. Our staff of experts would like to help you solve that problem.

Unusual offer
: How would you like to pay 50¢ for a complete restaurant meal? Or buy a $300 topcoat for $80? Or save an incredible 37% on your monthly car payments? How would you like to see movies with your family absolutely free?

Surprising question
: Would you be interested in a "magic" wand that would eliminate the drudgery of lawn care?

Appeal to normal desire
: At this time each year, everyone's thoughts turn to vacation plans and home improvements. If you are considering a major recreational purchase or home improvement this year, you may want to find out about Superloans from Home National Bank.

BODY

The body of your sales letter should supply the details that will convince readers that your product or service will satisfy their needs or desires better than any other can. The body should point out and stress all the benefits your product can offer.

Analyze your product carefully to determine your strongest psychological sales points. (Psychological selling simply means stressing a product's benefits rather than its physical features.) Select the most important psychological selling point about your product or service, and build your sales letter around it. Show how your product or service will make your reader's job easier, increase his or her status, make personal life more pleasant, and so on. In other words, the body of the letter should show how your product or service can satisfy the need or desire identified in your opening. Remember to describe the physical features of your product *in terms of their benefit to your reader.* Help your readers imagine themselves using your product or service—and enjoying the benefits of doing so.

Superloan is a loan that is made against the equity that you have in your home. Remember that equity is money. You wouldn't keep your money stuffed under a mattress or buried in a tin can. Many people do not realize that equity money can be put to work just like any other asset. Because of the rapid increases in the value of real estate in this area, many people who purchased homes several years ago do not really know how much equity they have. In fact, you probably have more than you think. You may even have more than you need.

Superloans can be used to buy the boat or car or airplane you've always wanted. They can also be used for those home improvements that cannot be financed under conventional FHA home improvement loans, such as a private swimming pool.

Of course, a Superloan does not have to be used only for recreational items. You may want to use money that is now in equity to pay for college expenses for your children or grand-children. You may want to open or expand your own business. Or you may need to install a more efficient heating system or put a new roof on your house.

You may need to provide evidence to convince your reader that your product or service is everything you claim it to be. There are many ways to do this. You can offer a money-back guarantee, a free trial use of your product, testimonials, case histories, and the like. The following are three examples:

Free trial use As soon as I receive your okay, I will rush your copy to you. Read and use it for ten full days at no cost or obligation.

Testimonial Senator William Worthington was so impressed by Peter Krump's *Breakthrough Rapid Reading* that he has written a glowing tribute to it. The senator writes that Krump's method is "the least expensive and most efficient way" you can learn rapid reading.

Case history Dozens of case histories are on file and available on request. To cite just one, Cynthia L. was fifty pounds overweight. She suffered constantly from severe arthritis, high blood pressure, and other ailments. Within three weeks of using negative energizer foods with her meals, she lost thirty pounds and her distressing symptoms began to disappear.

Try to minimize the negative effect price can have on your reader. There are a number of techniques that can help you do so. One is to mention the price along with a reminder of the benefits. Another technique is to state the price in terms of a unit rather than a set (50 cents per item instead of $6 per set). Another is to identify the daily, monthly, or even yearly cost based on the estimated life of the product (10 cents a night for a mattress sounds less expensive than $179). Suggest a series of payments rather than the total ($10 a month for the next year instead of $120). Or compare the cost with that of something the reader accepts readily (for the cost of one beer a day, you can have streets that are free from potholes).

CLOSING

If effective, the body of your letter will make your reader want your product or service or at least want more information about it. Your closing should ask the reader to do whatever is necessary to obtain the product or service. Some sales letters ask for the order; others ask only for a show of interest. You might request your reader to provide personal information on an enclosed card, to come to your showroom for a demonstration, to authorize a home sales visit, or to provide personal information.

Your closing should offer incentives that will make your reader want to act. For example, you might send a complimentary item, stress an item's limited availability, offer a special discount for a limited period of time, or suggest a deferred payment plan. Make it as easy as possible for your reader to respond. The following are three examples:

Complimentary item
By initiating and returning the enclosed postpaid card, you will receive at once the special handbook *Seven Steps to Better Managing* without cost—and you will begin to profit from your new subscription to the new *Presidents' Letter.*

Time limit
Just fill out and mail the enclosed invitation card. As soon as I receive it, I'll rush a copy of *How to Live Better and Spend 20% Less* for you to read and use for 10 full days at no cost or obligation. If at the end of 10 days you decide to keep *How to Live Better,* just send $10.95 plus postage and handling, and the book is yours. But act now—the cost will increase to $12.95 on November 30.

Appeal to normal desire
So, if you have equity in your home and would like to talk with someone about the possibility of borrowing against that equity, please complete the postage-paid reply card included with this letter. Just drop it in the mail and a Home National Bank loan officer will call you to explain Superloan possibilities as well as to answer any questions you may have. Let us help to make your dreams come true.

Figure 1 illustrates how the parts of a sales letter work together.

Home National Bank
902 Home Avenue
Portland, Oregon 97207

October 8, 19--

Dear Mr. Jones:

Opening identifies the need or desire the reader may have

      At this time each year, everyone's thoughts turn to vacation plans and home improvements. If you are considering a major recreational purchase or home improvement this year, you may want to find out about Superloans from Home National Bank.

      Superloan is a loan that is made against equity that you have in your home. Remember that equity is money. You wouldn't keep your money stuffed under a mattress or buried in a tin can. Many people do not realize that equity money can be put to work just like any other asset. Because of the rapid increases in the value of real estate in this area, many people who purchased homes several years ago do

Body includes details that will convince the reader you can satisfy the need or desire

not really know how much equity they have. In fact, you probably have more than you think. You may even have more than you need.

      Superloans can be used to buy the boat or car or airplane you've always wanted. They can also be used for those home improvements that cannot be financed under conventional FHA home improvement loans, such as a private swimming pool.

      Of course, a Superloan does not have to be used only for recreational items. You may want to use money that is now in equity to pay for college expenses for your children or grandchildren. You may want to open or expand your own business. Or you may need to install a more efficient heating system or put a new roof on your house.

Closing tells the reader what is necessary to satisfy the need or desire

      So, if you have equity in your home and would like to talk with someone about the possibility of borrowing against that equity, please complete the postage-paid reply card included with this letter. Just drop it in the mail, and a Home National Bank loan officer will call you to explain Superloan possibilities as well as to answer any questions you may have. Let us help make your dreams come true.

Sincerely,

John M. Peters

John M. Peters
President

JMP/ja
Enclosure

Figure 1   *Sales Letter*

sales proposals

The *sales proposal*, one of the major marketing tools in use in business and industry today, is a company's offer to provide specific goods or services to a potential buyer within a specified period of time and for a specified price. The primary purpose of a sales proposal is to demonstrate that the prospective customer's purchase of the seller's products or services would be a wise investment, because doing so will solve a problem, improve operations or offer benefits. Indeed, the sales proposal should sell solutions to problems rather than equipment or services.

Sales proposals vary greatly in size and relative sophistication. Some may be a page or two long and be written by one person; others may be many pages long and be written by several people; still others may take hundreds of pages and be written by a team of professional proposal writers. A short sales proposal might bid for the construction of a single home; a sales proposal of moderate length might bid for the installation of a network of computer systems; and a very long sales proposal might be used to bid for the construction of a multibillion-dollar aircraft carrier.

Your first task in writing a sales proposal is to find out exactly what your potential customer needs. The information in a proposal should be gathered in a survey of the potential customer's business and needs. You must then determine whether your organization can satisfy the customer's needs. Before preparing a sales proposal, you should try to find out who your principal competitors are. Then compare your company's strengths with those of the competing firms, determine your advantages over your competitors, and emphasize them in your proposal. For example, a small software company bidding for an air force contract at a local base would be familiar with its competitors. If the proposal writer believes that his or her company has better-qualified personnel than do its competitors, he or she might include the **résumés** of the key people who would be involved in the project, as a way of emphasizing that advantage.

SOLICITED AND UNSOLICITED PROPOSALS

Sales proposals may be either solicited or unsolicited. The latter are not so unusual as they may sound: companies often operate for years with a problem they have never recognized (unnecessarily high maintenance costs, for example, or poor inventory-control meth-

ods). If you learn of such a company, you might prepare an unsolicited proposal if you were convinced that the potential customer
could realize substantial benefits by adopting your solution to the
problem. You would, of course, need to persuade the customer of
the excellence of your idea and of his or her need for what you are
proposing.

To ensure that you don't waste time and effort, you might precede
an unsolicited proposal with an inquiry to determine any potential
interest. If you receive a positive response, you might then need to
conduct a detailed study of the prospective customer's needs and
requirements in order to determine whether you can be of help and,
if so, exactly how. You would then prepare your proposal on the basis
of your study.

An unsolicited proposal should clearly identify the potential customer's problem, but at the same time it should be careful not to
overstate it. Furthermore, the proposal must convince the customer
that the problem needs to be solved. One way to do this is to emphasize the benefits the customer will realize from the solution being
proposed.

The other type of sales proposal—the solicited sales proposal—is
a response to a request for goods or services. Procuring organizations that would like competing companies to bid for a job commonly issue a *Request for Proposals*. The Request for Proposals (RFP)
is the means used by many companies and government agencies to
find the best method of doing a job and the most qualified company
to do it. A Request for Proposals may be rigid in its specifications
governing how the proposal should be organized and what it should
contain, but it is normally quite flexible about the approaches that
the bidding firms may propose. Normally, the Request for Proposals
simply defines the basic work that the firm needs.

The procuring organization generally publishes its Request for
Proposals in one or more journals, in addition to sending it to certain companies that have good reputations for doing the kind of
work needed. Some companies and government agencies even hold
a conference for the competing firms at which they provide all pertinent information about the job being bid for.

Managers interested in responding to Requests for Proposals regularly scan the appropriate publication. Upon finding a project of
interest, an executive in the sales department of such a company
obtains all available information from the procuring company or

agency. The data is then presented to management for a decision on whether the company is interested in the project. If the decision is positive, the technical staff is assigned to develop an approach to the work described in the Request for Proposals. The technical staff normally considers several alternatives, selecting one that combines feasibility and a price that offers a profit. The staff's concept is presented to higher management for a decision on whether the company wishes to present a proposal to the requesting organization. Assuming that the decision is to proceed, preparation of the proposal is the next step.

When you respond to a Request for Proposals, pay close attention to any specifications in the request governing the preparation of the proposal, and follow them carefully.

WRITING A SIMPLE SALES PROPOSAL

Even a short and uncomplicated sales proposal should be carefully planned. The **introduction** should state the purpose and **scope** of the proposal. It should indicate the dates on which you propose to begin and complete work on the project, any special benefits of your proposed approach, and the total cost of the project. The introduction could also refer to any previous association your company may have had with the potential customer, assuming that the association was positive and mutually beneficial.

The body of a sales proposal should itemize the products and services you are offering. It should include, if applicable, a discussion of the procedures you would use to perform the work and any materials to be used. It should also present a time schedule indicating when each stage of the project would be completed. Finally, the body should include a breakdown of the costs of the project.

The **conclusion** should express your appreciation for the opportunity to submit the proposal and your confidence in your company's ability to do the job. You might add that you look forward to establishing good working relations with the customer and that you would be glad to provide any additional information that might be needed. Your conclusion could also review any advantages your company may have over its competitors. It should specify the time period during which your proposal can still be considered a valid offer. If any supplemental materials, such as blueprints or price sheets, accompany the proposal, include a list of them at the end of the proposal. Figure 1 shows a typical short sales proposal.

PROPOSAL
TO LANDSCAPE THE NEW CORPORATE HEADQUARTERS
OF THE
WATFORD VALVE CORPORATION

Submitted to: Ms. Tricia Olivera, Vice-President
Submitted by: Jerwalted Nursery, Inc.
Date Submitted: February 1, 19--

Introduction states purpose and scope of proposal, indicates when project can be started and completed.

Jerwalted Nursery, Inc., proposes to landscape the new corporate headquarters of the Watford Valve Corporation, on 1600 Swason Avenue, at a total cost of $8,000. The lot to be landscaped is approximately 600 feet wide and 700 feet deep. Landscaping will begin no later than April 30, 19-- and will be completed by May 31.

The following trees and plants will be planted, in the quantities and sizes given and at the prices specified.

Body lists products to be provided, cost per item.

4 maple trees (not less than 7 ft.) @ $40 each—$160
41 birch trees (not less than 7 ft.) @ $65 each—$2,665
2 spruce trees (not less than 7 ft.) @ $105 each—$210
20 juniper plants (not less than 18 in.) @ $15 each—$300
60 hedges (not less than 18 in.) @ $7 each—$420
200 potted plants (various kinds) @ $2 each—$400

Total Cost of Plants = $4,155
Labor = $3,845
Total Cost = $8,000

Conclusion specifies time limit of proposal, expresses confidence, and looks forward to working with prospective customer.

All trees and plants will be guaranteed against defect or disease for a period of 90 days, the warranty period to begin June 1, 19--.

The prices quoted in this proposal will be valid until June 30, 19--.

Thank you for the opportunity to submit this proposal. Jerwalted Nursery, Inc., has been in the landscaping and nursery business in the St. Louis area for thirty years, and our landscaping has won several awards and commendations, including a citation from the National Association of Architects. We are eager to put our skills and knowledge to work for you, and we are confident that you will be pleased with our work. If we can provide any additional information or assistance, please call.

Figure 1   Short Sales Proposal

WRITING A LONG SALES PROPOSAL

Wherever possible in a sales proposal, use eye-catching graphics instead of sentences and paragraphs. **Lists** and **flowcharts** are particularly effective. Customize your proposal whenever possible.

EXAMPLE A PROPOSAL PREPARED EXPRESSLY FOR

Mr. William A. Kurtz
Vice-President
The Cambridge Company
Tucson, Arizona

Also, whenever possible, include testimonial letters from other users, stressing specific benefits. Be sure to include the appropriate advertising literature, a copy of your company's annual report, and the contract.

A large sales proposal should contain the following elements:

- Transmittal letter
- Title page
- Executive summary
- Description of method currently being used
- Description of proposed method
- Comparison of present and proposed methods
- Equipment recommendations
- Cost analysis
- Delivery schedule
- Summary of advantages
- Statement of responsibilities
- Description of vendor
- Advertising literature
- Contract

The **transmittal letter** expresses your appreciation for the opportunity to submit your proposal and for any assistance you may have received in studying the customer's requirements. The letter should acknowledge any previous association with the customer, assuming that it was a positive experience. Then it should summarize the recommendations offered in the proposal and express your confidence that they will satisfy the customer's needs. Figure 2 shows the cover letter for the proposal illustrated in Figures 3 through 11, a proposal that the Waters Corporation of Tampa provide a computer system for the Cookson chain of retail stores. (See pp. 613–624.)

THE WATERS CORPORATION
17 North Waterloo Blvd., Tampa, Florida 33607

September 1, 19--

Mr. John Yeung, General Manager
Cookson's Retail Stores, Inc.
Savannah, Georgia 31499

Dear Mr. Yeung:

Express your appreciation for the opportunity to make the proposal

The Waters Corporation appreciates the opportunity to respond to Cookson's Request for Proposals, dated July 26, 19--. We would like to thank Mr. Becklight, Director of your Management Information Systems Department, for his invaluable contributions to the study of your operations that we conducted before preparing our proposal.

Summarize the proposal's recommendations

Our proposal describes a Waters Interactive Terminal/Retail Processor System designed to meet Cookson's network and processing needs. It will provide all of your required capabilities, from the point-of-sale operational requirements at the store terminals to the host processor. The system uses the proven Retail III modular software, with its point-of-sale applications, and the superior Interactive Terminal with its advanced capabilities and design. This system is easily installed without massive customer reprogramming.

Make a soft sales pitch

The Waters Interactive Terminal/Retail Processor System, which is compatible with much of Cookson's present equipment, not only will answer your present requirements but also will provide the flexibility to add new features and products in the future. The system's unique hardware modularity, efficient microprocessor design, and flexible programming capability will greatly reduce the risk of obsolescence.

Thank you for the opportunity to present this proposal. We are confident that you will select our system, and we look forward to working with you.

Sincerely yours,

Janet A. Curtain

Janet A. Curtain
Account Manager
General Merchandise Systems

JAC/mo

Figure 2   Cover Letter for a Proposal

An **executive summary** follows the transmittal letter. Written to the executive who will ultimately accept or reject the proposal, it should summarize in nontechnical language how you plan to approach the work. Figure 3 shows the executive summary of the Waters Corporation proposal.

If your proposal offers products as well as services, it should include a *general description* of the products, as in Figure 4.

After the executive summary and the general description, explain exactly how you plan to do what you are proposing. Because this section will be read by specialists who can understand and evaluate your plan, you can feel free to use technical language and discuss complicated concepts. Figure 5 shows one part of the detailed solution appearing in the Waters Corporation proposal, which included several other applications in addition to the payroll application. Notice that this discussion, like that found in an unsolicited sales proposal, begins with a statement of the customer's problem, follows with a statement of the solution, and concludes with a statement of the benefits to the customer.

Essential to any sales proposal are a *cost analysis* and a *delivery schedule*. The cost analysis itemizes the estimated cost of all the products and services that you are offering; the delivery schedule commits you to a specific timetable for providing those products and services. Figure 6 (pp. 617–618) shows the cost analysis, and Figure 7 (p. 619) shows the delivery schedule of the Waters Corp. proposal.

Also essential if your recommendations include modifying the customer's physical facilities is a *site preparation description* that details the required modifications. Figure 8 shows the site preparation section of the Waters proposal (see p. 620).

If the products you are proposing require training the customer's personnel, your proposal should specify the *required training* and its cost. Fig. 9 (p. 621) shows the training section of the Waters proposal.

To prevent misunderstandings about what you and your customer's responsibilities will be, you should draw up a *statement of responsibilities*, as shown in Figure 10 (p. 622). It usually appears toward the end of the proposal. Also toward the end of the proposal is a *description of the vendor* (Figure 11, p. 623), which should give a factual description of your company, its background, and its present position in the industry. Following this description, many proposals add what is known as an *institutional sales pitch* (Figure 12, p. 624). Up to this point, the proposal has attempted to sell specific goods and

EXECUTIVE SUMMARY

The Waters 319 Interactive Terminal/615 Retail Processor System
will give your management the tools necessary to manage people
and equipment more profitably with procedures that will yield
more cost-effective business controls for Cookson's.

The equipment and applications proposed for Cookson's will respond
to your current requirements and allow for a logical expansion
in the future.

The features and hardware in the system were determined from
data acquired through the comprehensive survey we conducted
at your stores in February of this year. The total of 71 Interactive
Terminals proposed to service your four stores is based on the
number of terminals currently in use and on the average number
of transactions processed during normal and peak periods. The
planned remodeling of all four stores was also considered, and
the suggested terminal placement has been incorporated into
the working floor plan. The proposed equipment configuration
and software applications have been simulated to determine system
performance based on the volumes and anticipated growth rates
of the Cookson stores.

The information from the survey was also used in the cost justification,
which was checked and verified by your controller, Mr. Deitering.
The cost effectiveness of the Waters Interactive Terminal/Retail
Processor System is apparent. Expected savings, such as the
projected 46-percent reduction in sales audit expenses, are
realistic projections based on Waters's experience with other
installations of this type.

Figure 3   Executive Summary

GENERAL SYSTEM DESCRIPTION

The point-of-sale system that Waters is proposing for Cookson's includes
two primary Waters products. These are the 319 Interactive Terminal
and the 615 Retail Processor.

Waters 319 Interactive Terminal

The primary component in the proposed retail system is the Interactive
Terminal. It contains a full microprocessor, which gives it the flexibility
that Cookson's has been seeking.

The 319 Interactive Terminal gives you freedom in sequencing a transaction.
You are not limited to a preset list of available steps or transactions.
The terminal program can be adapted to provide unique transaction
sets, each designed with a logical sequence of entry and processing
to accomplish required tasks. In addition to sales transactions recorded
on the selling floor, specialized transactions, such as theater tickets
sales and payments, can be designed for your customer service area.

The 319 Interactive Terminal also functions as a credit authorization
device, either by using its own floor limits or by transmitting a
credit inquiry to the 615 Retail Processor for authorization.

Data-collection formats have been simplified so that transaction editing
and formatting are easier. Mr. Sier has already been given the documentation
on these formats and has outlined all data-processing efforts that
will be necessary to adapt the data to your current systems. These
projections have been considered in the cost justification.

Waters 615 Retail Processor

The Waters 615 Retail Processor is a minicomputer system designed
to support the Waters family of retail terminals. The processor will
reside in the computer room in your data center in Buffalo. Operators
already on your staff will be trained to initiate and monitor its
activities.

The 615 will collect data transmitted from the retail terminals, process
credit, check authorization inquiries, maintain files to be accessed
by the retail terminals, accumulate totals, maintain a message-routing
network, and control the printing of various reports. The functions
and level of control performed at the processor depend on the peripherals
and software selected.

Software

The Retail III software used with the system has been thoroughly tested
and is operational in many Waters customer installations.

The software provides the complete processing of the transaction,
from the interaction with the operator on the sales floor through
the data capture on cassette or disk in stores and your data center.

Retail III provides a menu of modular applications for your selection.
Parameters adapt each of them to your hardware environment and operation
requirements. The selection of hardware will be closely related to
the selection of the software applications.

Figure 4　General Description of Products

PAYROLL APPLICATION

Current Procedure

Your current system of reporting time requires each hourly employee to sign a time
sheet; the time sheet is reviewed by the department manager and sent to the Payroll Department on Friday evening. Since the week
ends on Saturday, the employee must show the
scheduled hours for Saturday and not the actual hours; therefore, the department manager
must adjust the reported hours on the time
sheet for employees who do not report on the
scheduled Saturday or who do not work the
number of hours scheduled.

The Payroll Department employs a supervisor
and three full-time clerks. To meet deadlines
caused by an unbalanced work flow, an additional part-time clerk is used for 20 to 30
hours per week. The average wage for this
clerk is $4.25 per hour.

Advantage of Waters's System

The 319 Interactive Terminal can be pro-
grammed for entry of payroll data for each
employee on Monday mornings by department
managers, with the data reflecting actual
hours worked. This system would eliminate the
need for manual batching, controlling, and
keypunching. The Payroll Department estimates
conservatively that this work consumes 40
hours per week.

Hours per week	40
Average wage	× 4.25
Weekly payroll cost	$170.00
Annual savings	$8,840.00

Elimination of the manual tasks of tabulating, batching, and controlling can save .25
units. Improved work flow resulting from
timely data in the system without keypunch

Figure 5   Detailed Solution

processing will allow more efficient use of
clerical hours. This would reduce payroll by
the .50 units currently required to meet
weekly check disbursement.

Eliminate manual tasks	.25
Improve work flow	.75
40-hour unit reduction	1.00
Hours per week	40
Average wage	4.75
Savings per week	$190.00
Annual savings	$9,880.00

TOTAL SAVINGS: $18,720.00

Figure 5   Detailed Solution (continued)

COST ANALYSIS

This section of our proposal provides detailed cost information for the Waters 319
Interactive Terminal and the 615 Waters Retail Processor. It then extends these major
elements by the quantities required at each
of your four locations.

319 Interactive Terminal

	Price	Maint. (1 yr)
Terminal	$2,895	$167
Journal Printer	425	38
Receipt Printer	425	38
Forms Printer	525	38
Software	220	--
TOTALS	$4,490	$281

615 Retail Processor

	Price	Maint. (1 Yr)
Processor	$57,115	$5,787
CRT I/O Writer	2,000	324
Matrix Printer	4,245	568
Software	12,480	---
TOTALS	$75,840	$6,679

The following breakdown itemizes the cost per
store.

Store No. 1

Description	Qty	Price	Maint.
Terminals	16	$68,400	$4,496
Digital Cassette	1	1,300	147
Thermal Printer	1	2,490	332
Software	16	3,520	---
TOTALS		$75,710	$4,975

Figure 6   Cost Analysis

Store No. 2

Description	Qty	Price	Maint.
Terminals	20	$85,400	$5,620
Digital Cassette	1	1,300	147
Thermal Printer	1	2,490	332
Software	20	4,400	---
TOTALS		$93,590	$6,099

Store No. 3

Description	Qty	Price	Maint.
Terminals	17	$72,590	$4,777
Digital Cassette	1	1,300	147
Thermal Printer	1	2,490	332
Software	17	3,740	---
TOTALS		$80,120	$5,256

Store No. 4

Description	Qty	Price	Maint.
Terminals	18	$76,860	$5,058
Digital Cassette	1	1,300	147
Thermal Printer	1	2,490	332
Software	18	3,960	---
TOTALS		$84,610	$5,537

Data Center at Buffalo

Description	Qty	Price	Maint.
Processor	1	$57,115	$5,787
CRT I/O Writer	1	2,000	324
Matrix Printer	1	4,245	568
Software	1	12,480	---
TOTALS		$75,840	$6,679

The following summarizes all costs.

Location	Hardware	Maint.	Software
Store No. 1	$72,190	$4,975	$3,520
Store No. 2	89,190	6,099	4,400
Store No. 3	76,380	5,256	3,740
Store No. 4	80,650	5,537	3,960
Data Center	63,360	6,679	12,480
Subtotals	$381,770	$28,546	$28,100

TOTAL $438,416

Figure 6   Cost Analysis (continued)

DELIVERY SCHEDULE

Waters is normally able to deliver 319 Interactive Terminals and 615 Retail Processors
within 120 days from the date of the contract. This can vary depending on the rate
and size of incoming orders.

All the software recommended in this proposal
is available for immediate delivery. We do
not anticipate any difficulty in meeting your
tentative delivery schedule.

Figure 7   Delivery Schedule

SITE PREPARATION

Waters will work closely with Cookson's to ensure that each site is properly prepared prior to system installation. You will receive a copy of Waters's installation and wiring procedures manual, which lists the physical dimensions, service clearance, and weight of the system components in addition to the power, logic, communication-cable, and environmental requirements. Cookson's is responsible for all building alterations and electrical facility changes, including the purchase and installation of communication cables, connecting blocks, and receptacles.

Wiring

For the purpose of future site considerations, Waters's in-house wiring specifications for the system call for two twisted pair wires and twenty-two shielded gauges. The length of communications wires must not exceed 2,500 feet.

As a guide for the power supply, we suggest that Cookson's consider the following:

1. The branch circuit (limited to 20 amps) should service no equipment other than 319 Interactive Terminals.
2. Each 20-amp branch circuit should support a maximum of three Interactive Terminals.
3. Each branch circuit must have three equal-sized conductors--one hot leg, one neutral, and one insulated isolated ground.
4. Hubbell IG 5362 duplex outlets or the equivalent should be used to supply power to each terminal.
5. Computer-room wiring will have to be upgraded to support the 615 Retail Processor.

Figure 8   Site Preparation Section

TRAINING

To ensure a successful installation, Waters
offers the following training course for your
operators.

Interactive Terminal/Retail Processor Operations

Course number: 8256
Length: three days
Tuition: $500.00 per person

This course provides the student with the skills,
knowledge, and practice required to operate
an Interactive Terminal/Retail Processor System.
On-line, clustered, and stand-alone environments
are covered.

We recommend that students have department store
background and that they have some knowledge
of the system configuration with which they
will be working.

Figure 9   Training Section

RESPONSIBILITIES

On the basis of its years of experience in installing information-processing systems, Waters believes that a successful installation requires a clear understanding of certain responsibilities.

Generally, it is Waters's responsibility to provide its users with needed assistance during the installation so that live processing can begin as soon thereafter as is practical.

Waters's Responsibilities

--Provide operations documentation for each application that you acquire from Waters.

--Provide forms and other supplies as ordered.

--Provide specifications and technical guidance for proper site planning and installation.

--Provide advisory assistance in the conversion from your present system to the new system.

Customer's Responsibilities

--Identify an installation coordinator and system operator.

--Provide supervisors and clerical personnel to perform conversion to the system.

--Establish reasonable time schedules for implementation.

--Ensure that the physical site requirements are met.

--Provide competent personnel to be trained as operators and ensure that other employees are trained as necessary.

--Assume the responsibility for implementing and operating the system.

Figure 10   Statement of Responsibilities

DESCRIPTION OF VENDOR

The Waters Corporation develops, manufac-
tures, markets, installs, and services total
business information-processing systems for
selected markets. These markets are primarily
in the retail, financial, commercial, industrial, health-care, education, and government
sectors.

The Waters total system concept encompasses
one of the broadest hardware and software
product lines in the industry. Waters computers range from small business systems to powerful general-purpose processors. Waters computers are supported by a complete spectrum
of terminals, peripherals, data-communication
networks, and an extensive library of software products. Supplemental services and
products include data centers, field service,
systems engineering, and educational centers.

The Waters Corporation was founded in 1934
and presently has approximately 26,500 employees. The Waters headquarters is located
at 17 North Waterloo Boulevard, Tampa, Florida, with district offices throughout the
United States and Canada.

Figure 11   Description of Vendor

WHY WATERS?

Corporate Commitment to the Retail Industry

Waters's commitment to the retail industry is stronger than ever. We are continually striving to provide leadership in the design and implementation of new retail systems and applications that will ensure our users of a logical growth pattern.

Research and Development

Over the years, Waters has spent increasingly large sums on research and development efforts to ensure the availability of products and systems for the future. In 19--, our research and development expenditure for advanced systems design and technological innovations reached the $70 million level.

Leading Point-of-Sale Vendor

Waters is a leading point-of-sale vendor, having installed over 150,000 units. The knowledge and experience that Waters has gained over the years from these installations ensure well-coordinated and effective systems implementations.

Figure 12   Institutional Sales Pitch

services. The sales pitch, striking a somewhat different chord, is designed to sell the company and its general capability in the field. Less factual than the vendor description, the sales pitch promotes the company and concludes the proposal on an upbeat note.

same

When used as a **pronoun,** *same* is awkward and outmoded.

CHANGE Your order has been received, and we will respond to *same* next week.

TO Your order has been received, and we will respond to *it* next week.

OR We received your order, and we will comply with *it* next week.

scope

If you know your **reader** and the **objective** of your writing project, you will know the type and amount of detail to include in your writing. This is its *scope*, which may be defined as the depth and breadth to which you need to cover your subject. If you do not determine your scope of coverage in the planning stage of your writing project, you will not know how much or what kind of information to include, and as a result, you are likely to invest unnecessary work during the **research** phase of your project.

Your scope should be designed to satisfy the needs of your objective and your reader. By keeping your objective and your reader's profile in mind as you work, you can determine those items that should and should not be included in your writing.

semicolons

The semicolon links **independent clauses** or other sentence elements of equal weight and grammatical rank, especially **phrases** in a series that have **commas** within them. The semicolon indicates a greater pause between clauses than a comma would, but not as great a pause as a **period** would.

When the independent clauses of a **compound sentence** are not joined by a comma and a **conjunction**, they are linked by a semicolon.

EXAMPLE No one applied for the position; the job was too difficult.

Make sure, however, that such **clauses** balance or contrast with each other. The relationship between the two statements should be so clear that further explanation is not necessary.

> EXAMPLE The new marketing approach was very successful; every division reported increased sales.

Do not use a semicolon between a **dependent clause** and its main clause. Remember that elements joined by semicolons must be of equal grammatical rank or weight.

> CHANGE No one applied for the position; even though it was heavily advertised.
>
> TO No one applied for the position, even though it was heavily advertised.

USING A SEMICOLON WITH STRONG CONNECTIVES

In complicated sentences, a semicolon may be used before transitional words or phrases (*that is, for example, namely*) that introduce examples or further explanation.

> EXAMPLE The study group was aware of his position on the issue; that is, federal funds should not be used for the housing project.

A semicolon should also be used before **conjunctive adverbs** (such as *therefore, moreover, consequently, furthermore, indeed, in fact, however*) that connect independent clauses.

> EXAMPLE I won't finish today; moreover, I doubt that I will finish this week.

The semicolon in this example shows that *moreover* belongs to the second clause.

USING A SEMICOLON FOR CLARITY
IN LONG AND COMPLICATED SENTENCES

Use a semicolon between two independent clauses connected by a **coordinating conjunction** (*and, but, for, or, nor, yet*) if the clauses are long and contain other **punctuation**.

> EXAMPLE In most cases these individuals are corporate executives, bankers, Wall Street lawyers; but they do not, as the economic determinists seem to believe, simply push the button of their economic power to affect fields remote from economics.
> —Robert Lubar, "The Prime Movers," *Fortune* Feb. 1960: 98.

A semicolon may also be used if items in a series contain commas within them.

EXAMPLE Among those present were John Howard, president of the Omega Paper Company; Carol Martin, president of Alpha Corporation; and Larry Stanley, president of Stanley Papers.

Do not, however, use semicolons to enclose a parenthetical element that contains commas. Use **parentheses** or **dashes** for this purpose.

CHANGE All affected job classifications; typists, secretaries, clerk-stenographers, and word processors; will be upgraded this month.
TO All affected job classifications (typists, secretaries, clerk-stenographers, and word processors) will be upgraded this month.
OR All affected job classifications—typists, secretaries, clerk-stenographers, and word processors—will be upgraded this month.

Do not use a semicolon as a mark of anticipation or enumeration. Use a **colon** for this purpose.

CHANGE Three decontamination methods are under consideration; a zeolite-resin system, an evaporation and resin system, and a filtration and storage system.
TO Three decontamination methods are under consideration: a zeolite-resin system, an evaporation and resin system, and a filtration and storage system.

The semicolon always appears outside closing **quotation marks**.

EXAMPLE The attorney said, "You must be accurate"; the client said, "I will."

sentence construction

A sentence is the most basic and versatile tool available to the writer. Consider the many different ways the same idea can be expressed to achieve different **emphasis**.

EXAMPLES Every person in the department, from manager to typists, must work overtime this week to ensure that we meet the deadline.

To ensure that we meet the deadline, every person in the department, from manager to typists, must work overtime this week.

From manager to typists, every person in the department must work overtime this week to ensure that we meet the deadline.

To ensure that we meet the deadline, every person in the department must work overtime this week, from manager to typists.

This week, every person in the department, from manager to typists, must work overtime to ensure that we meet the deadline.

When shifting word order for emphasis, however, be aware that word order can make a great difference in the meaning of a sentence.

EXAMPLES   He was *only* the accountant.
He was the *only* accountant.

Except for **expletives**, all words or word groups in a sentence function as a **subject**, a **verb**, a **complement**, a **modifier**, a connective, an **appositive**, or an **absolute**. Subjects, verbs and complements are the main elements of the sentence. Everything else is subordinate to them in one way or another. A sentence that progresses quickly from subject to verb to complement is clear and easy to understand. The problem is to write sentences that contain more information, and in more complicated form, with the same **clarity** and directness.

The basic sentence patterns in English are the following:

EXAMPLES   Sales declined. (subject-verb)
Advertising increased sales. (subject-verb-direct object)
John showed Dr. Barnes the printout. (subject-verb-indirect object-direct object)
Advertising made the sales drive a success. (subject-verb-direct object-objective complement)
The advertising was effective. (subject-linking verb-subjective complement)

Most sentences follow the subject-verb-object pattern. In "The company dismissed Joe," we know the subject and the object by their positions relative to the verb. The knowledge that the usual sentence order is subject-verb-object helps **readers** interpret what they read. The fact that readers tend to expect this order explains why the writer's departures from it can be effective if used sparingly for **emphasis** and variety, but annoying if overdone.

An inverted sentence places the elements in other than normal order.

EXAMPLES   A better job I never had. (direct object-subject-verb)
More optimistic I have never been. (subjective complement-subject-linking verb)

Inverted sentence order may be used in questions and exclamations and also to achieve emphasis.

EXAMPLES   Have you a pencil? (verb-subject-complement)
How heavy your book feels! (complement-subject-verb)
A sorry sight we presented! (complement-subject-verb)

In sentences introduced by expletives (*there, it*), the subject generally follows the verb because the expletive precedes the verb.

EXAMPLES   *There* (expletive) *are* (verb) certain *principles* (subject) of draft-ing that must not be ignored.
It (expletive) *is* (verb) *difficult* (complement) *to work* (subject) in a noisy office.

Beginning sentences with expletives is often wordy.

CHANGE   *There are* certain principles of drafting that must be followed.
TO   Certain principles of drafting must be followed.

CONSTRUCTING CLEAR SENTENCES

It is always best to use uncomplicated sentences to state complex ideas. If readers must cope with a complicated sentence in addition to a complex idea, they are likely to become confused.

CHANGE   When you are purchasing parts, remember that although an increase in the cost of aluminum forces all the vendors to increase their prices, some vendors will have a supply of aluminum purchased at the old price, and they may be willing to sell parts to you at the old price in order to get your business.
TO   Although an increase in the cost of aluminum forces all ven-dors to increase their prices, some vendors will have a sup-ply of aluminum purchased at the old price. When you are purchasing aluminum parts, remember that these vendors

may be willing to sell you the parts at the old price in order
to get your business.

Just as simpler sentences make complex ideas more digestible, a
complex sentence construction makes a series of simple ideas more
palatable.

> CHANGE The computer is a calculating device. It was once known as a
> mechanical brain. It has revolutionized industry.
>
> TO The computer, a calculating device once known as a mechan-
> ical brain, has revolutionized industry.

Do not string together in a series a number of thoughts that should
be written as separate sentences or some of which should be subordinated to others. Sentences carelessly tacked together this way are
monotonous and hard to read because all ideas seem to be of equal
importance.

> CHANGE We started the program three years ago, there were only three
> members on the staff, and each member was responsible for
> a separate state, but it was not an efficient operation.
>
> TO When we started the program three years ago, there were only
> three members on the staff, each having responsibility for
> a separate state; however, that arrangement was not efficient.

It is often easy to improve sentences by eliminating trailing constructions and ineffective **repetition**.

> CHANGE We worked on the report on Friday, but we couldn't finish it
> because some information we needed was not available.
>
> TO Lack of necessary information prevented our completing the
> report on Friday.

CONSTRUCTING PARALLEL SENTENCES

Express coordinate ideas in similar form. The very construction of
the sentence helps the reader grasp the similarity of its components.
(See also **parallel structure**.)

> EXAMPLE Similarly, atoms come and go in a molecule, but the molecule
> remains; molecules come and go in a cell, but the cell re-
> mains; cells come and go in a body, but the body remains;
> persons come and go in an organization, but the organi-
> zation remains.
>
> —Kenneth Boulding, *Beyond Economics* (Ann Arbor: U of Michigan P, 1968) 131.

CONSTRUCTING SENTENCES TO ACHIEVE EMPHASIS

Subordinate your minor ideas to emphasize your more important ideas. (See also **subordination**.)

CHANGE We all had arrived, and we began the meeting early.
TO Since we all had arrived, we began the meeting early.

The most emphatic positions within a sentence are at the beginning and the end. Do not waste them by tacking on **phrases** and **clauses** almost as an afterthought or by burying the main point in the middle of a sentence between less important points. For example, consider the following original and revised versions of a statement written for a company's **annual report** to its stockholders:

CHANGE Sales declined by 3 percent in 1981, but nevertheless the Company had the most profitable year in its history, thanks to cost savings that resulted from design improvements in several of our major products; and we expect 1982 to be even better, since further design improvements are being made.
TO Cost savings from design improvements in several major products not only offset a 3-percent sales decline but made 1981 the most profitable year in the Company's history. Further design improvements now in progress promise to make 1982 even more profitable.

Reversing the normal word order is also used to achieve emphasis.

EXAMPLES I will never agree to that.
That I will never agree to.
Never will I agree to that.

BEGINNING A SENTENCE WITH A COORDINATING CONJUNCTION

There is no rule against beginning a sentence with a **coordinating conjunction**; in fact, coordinating conjunctions can be strong transitional words and at times provide emphasis.

EXAMPLE I realize the project was more difficult than expected and that you have also encountered personnel problems. *But* we must meet our deadline.

Starting sentences with **conjunctions** is acceptable in all but the most formal English. But like any other writing device, this one should be used sparingly lest it become ineffective and even annoying. (See also **sentence variety**, **run-on sentences**, **sentence fragments**, and **sentence faults**.)

sentence faults

A number of problems can create sentence faults.

FAULTY SUBORDINATION

One of the most common sentence faults is faulty **subordination**, which occurs (1) when a grammatically subordinate element, such as a **dependent clause**, actually contains the main idea of the sentence or (2) when a subordinate element is so long or detailed that it dominates or obscures the main idea. Avoiding the first problem (main idea expressed in a subordinate element) depends on the writer's knowing which idea is *meant* to be the main idea. Note that both of the following sentences appear logical; which one really is logical depends on which of two ideas the writer means to emphasize.

> EXAMPLES Although the new filing system saves money, many of the staff are unhappy with it.
> The new filing system saves money, although many of the staff are unhappy with it.

In this example, if the writer's main point is that *the new filing system saves money*, the second sentence is correct. If the main point is that *many of the staff are unhappy*, then the first sentence is correct. It is easier than you may think to slip and put your main idea into a grammatically subordinate element (especially since people commonly do so in conversation, when they can raise their voices and make gestures to stress the main point).

The other major problem with subordination is loading so much detail into a subordinate element that it "crushes" the main point by its sheer size and weight.

> CHANGE Because the noise level on a typical street in New York City on a weekday is as loud as an alarm clock ringing three feet away, New Yorkers often have hearing problems.
> TO Because the noise level in New York City is so high, New Yorkers often have hearing problems.

CLAUSES WITH NO SUBJECTS

Writers sometimes inappropriately assume a subject that is not stated in a clause.

CHANGE   Your application program can request to end the session after
      the next command. (Request *who* or *what* to end the session?
      The reader doesn't know.)
TO   Your application program can request *the host program* to end
      the session after the next command.

CHANGE   This command enables sending the entire message again if an
      incomplete message transfer occurs. (The sentence contains
      no subject for the verb *sending*. The reader doesn't know *who*
      or *what* is doing the sending.)
TO   This command enables *you to send* the entire message again if
      an incomplete message occurs.

(See also **telegraphic style**.)

RAMBLING SENTENCES

Sentences that contain more information than the reader can comfortably absorb in one reading are known as *rambling sentences*. The
obvious remedy for a rambling sentence is to divide it into two or
more sentences. In doing so, however, put the main message of the
rambling sentence into the first of the revised sentences.

CHANGE   The payment to which a subcontractor is entitled should be
      made promptly in order that in the event of a subsequent
      contractual dispute we, as general contractors, may not be
      held in default of our contract by virtue of nonpayment.
TO   Pay subcontractors promptly. Then if a contractual dispute
      should occur, we cannot be held in default of our contract
      because of nonpayment.

MISCELLANEOUS SENTENCE FAULTS

The assertion made by a sentence's **predicate** about its **subject** must
be logical. "Mr. Wilson's *job* is a salesman" is not logical, but "*Mr.
Wilson* is a salesman" is. "Jim's *height* is six feet tall" is not logical, but
"*Jim* is six feet tall" is.

Do not omit a required **verb**.

CHANGE   The floor is swept and the lights out.
TO   The floor is swept and the lights *are* out.

CHANGE   I never have and probably never will write the annual report.
TO   I never have *written* and probably never will write the annual
      report.

Do not omit a subject.

> CHANGE He regarded price fixing as wrong, but until abolished by law,
> he engaged in it, as did everyone else.
>
> TO He regarded price fixing as wrong, but until *it was* abolished
> by law, he engaged in it, as did everyone else.

Avoid **compound sentences** containing **clauses** that have little or no
logical relationship to one another.

> CHANGE My department is responsible for all company publications,
> and the staff includes twenty writers, three artists, and three
> typists.
>
> TO My department is responsible for all publications. The staff
> includes twenty writers, three artists, and three typists.

(See also **run-on sentences** and **sentence fragments**.)

sentence fragments

A sentence fragment is an incomplete grammatical unit that is punctuated as a sentence.

> EXAMPLES He quit his job. (sentence)
> And quit his job. (fragment)

But having a subject and a **predicate** does not automatically make
a **clause** into a sentence. The clause must also make an independent
statement. *I work* is a sentence; *If I work* is a fragment because the
subordinating conjunction *if* makes the statement into a **dependent clause**.

Sentence fragments are often introduced by **relative pronouns**
(*who, which, that*) or **subordinating conjunctions** (such as *although,
because, if, when,* and *while*). This knowledge can tip you off that what
follows is a dependent clause and must be combined with a main
clause.

> CHANGE The new manager instituted several new procedures. *Many of
> which are impractical.* (The last is an adjective clause modify-
> ing *procedures* and linked to it by the relative pronoun *which*.)
>
> TO The new manager instituted several new procedures, many of
> which are impractical.

A sentence must contain a finite verb; **verbals** will not do the job.
The following examples are sentence fragments because their ver-

bals (*providing, to work, waiting*) cannot perform the function of a finite verb.

EXAMPLES *Providing* all employees with hospitalization insurance.
To work a forty-hour week.
The customer *waiting* to see you.

Fragments usually reflect incomplete and sometimes confused thinking. The most common type of fragment occurs because of the careless addition of an afterthought.

CHANGE These are my coworkers. *A fine group of people.*
TO These are my coworkers, a fine group of people.

The following examples are common types of sentence fragments:

CHANGE Some of our customers prefer to pay at the time of purchase. *While others find installment payments preferable.* (adverbial clause)
TO Some of our customers prefer to pay at the time of purchase, while others find installment payments preferable.

CHANGE The board approved the project. *After much discussion.* (prepositional phrase)
TO The board approved the project after much discussion.

CHANGE We reorganized the department. *Distributing the work load more evenly.* (participial phrase)
TO We reorganized the department, distributing the work load more evenly.

CHANGE The staff decided to take a break. *It being midafternoon.* (absolute phrase)
TO The staff decided to take a break, it being midafternoon.

CHANGE The field tests showed the prototype to be extremely rugged. *The most durable we've tested this year.* (appositive phrase)
TO The field tests showed the prototype to be extremely rugged, the most durable we've tested this year.

CHANGE We have one major goal this month. *To increase the strength of the alloy without reducing its flexibility.* (infinitive phrase)
TO We have one major goal this month: to increase the strength of the alloy without reducing its flexibility.

Such fragments should either be a part of the preceding sentence or converted into their own sentences. Explanatory **phrases** beginning with *such as, for example*, and similar terms often lead writers to create sentence fragments.

> CHANGE The staff wants additional benefits. For example, the use of company automobiles. (fragment)
>
> TO The staff wants additional benefits, such as the use of company automobiles. (one sentence)
>
> OR The staff wants additional benefits. For example, one possible benefit is the use of company automobiles. (two sentences)

A hopelessly snarled fragment simply has to be rewritten. This rewriting is best done by pulling out the main points of the fragment, listing them in the proper sentence, and then rewriting the sentence. (See also **garbled sentences**.)

> CHANGE Removing the protection cap and the piston secured in the housing by means of the spring placed between the piston and the housing.
>
> MAIN 1. Remove the protection cap.
> POINTS 2. The piston is held in the housing by a spring.
> 3. The spring is connected to the piston at one end and the housing at the other.
> 4. To remove the piston, disconnect the spring.
>
> TO Removing the protection cap enables you to remove the piston by disconnecting a spring that connects to the piston at one end and the housing at the other.

(See also **sentence construction**, **sentence faults**, **subjects of sentences**, and **run-on sentences**.)

sentence types

Sentences may be classified according to *structure* (simple, compound, complex, compound-complex); *intention* (declarative, interrogative, imperative, exclamatory); and *stylistic use* (loose, periodic, minor).

BY STRUCTURE

A **simple sentence** consists of one **independent clause**. At its most basic, the simple sentence contains only a **subject** and a **predicate**.

> EXAMPLES Profits (subject) rose (predicate).
> The strike (subject) finally ended (predicate).

Either the subject or the predicate, or both, may be compounded without changing the structure of the simple sentence. A simple sentence need not necessarily be short. Although **modifiers** may extend the length of the simple sentence, they do not alter its basic structure.

EXAMPLES *Tom, Janet, and Harry* worked on the sales brochure. (compound subject)

Tom *designed the layout and supplied the art.* (compound predicate)

A **compound sentence** consists of two or more independent clauses connected by a **comma** and a **coordinating conjunction**, by a **semicolon**, or by a semicolon and a **conjunctive adverb**.

EXAMPLES We expect sales to increase next year, but we cannot guarantee that they will. (comma and coordinating conjunction)

There is little similarity between the chemical composition of sea water and that of river water; the various elements are present in entirely different proportions. (semicolon)

It was 500 miles to the site; therefore, we made arrangements to fly. (semicolon and conjunctive adverb)

The **complex sentence** provides a means of subordinating one thought to another. A complex sentence contains one independent clause and at least one **dependent clause** that expresses a subordinate idea.

EXAMPLE When you have finished the report (dependent clause), bring it to my office (independent clause).

A **compound-complex sentence** consists of two or more independent clauses plus at least one dependent clause.

EXAMPLE Productivity is central to controlling inflation (independent clause), for when productivity rises (dependent clause), employers can raise wages without raising prices (independent clause).

BY INTENTION

By intention, a sentence may be declarative, interrogative, imperative, or exclamatory. A declarative sentence conveys information or makes a factual statement.

EXAMPLE James Evans is president of Acme Corporation.

An interrogative sentence asks a direct question.

EXAMPLE   Who is Acme's vice-president?

An imperative sentence issues a command.

EXAMPLE   Get the contract.

An exclamatory sentence is an emphatic expression of feeling, fact, or opinion. It is a declarative sentence that is stated with great feeling.

EXAMPLE   We got the contract!

BY STYLISTIC USE

A *loose* sentence is one that makes its major point at the beginning and then adds subordinate **phrases** and **clauses** that develop the major point. It is the pattern in which we express ourselves most naturally and easily. A loose sentence could be ended at one or more points before it actually does.

EXAMPLE   One of the foundations engaged me (.) to edit the manuscripts of a socioeconomic research report (.) designed for the thoughtful citizen (.) as well as for the specialist.

Compound sentences are generally classed as loose, since the sentence could end after the first independent clause.

EXAMPLE   The union agreed to accept an arbitrated settlement, but management refused.

Complex sentences are loose if their subordinate clauses follow their main clause.

EXAMPLE   The health care delivery system today is largely a private endeavor (.) despite the fact that about 40 cents of each supporting dollar comes from the public purse.

A *periodic* sentence delays its main idea until the end by presenting subordinate ideas or modifiers first, thus holding the reader's interest until the end. If skillfully handled, a periodic sentence lends force, or **emphasis**, to the main point by arousing the reader's anticipation and then presenting the main point as a climax.

EXAMPLE   During the last decade or so, the attitude of the American citizen toward automation has undergone a profound change.

Do not use periodic sentences too frequently, however, for overuse results in a **style** that is irritating to the **reader**.

A *minor* sentence is an incomplete sentence. It makes sense in its context because the missing element is clearly implied by the preceding sentence.

> EXAMPLE In view of these facts, is automation really useful? *Or economical?* There is no question that it has made our country one of the most wealthy and technologically advanced nations the world has ever known.

In short, minor sentences are elliptical expressions that are equivalent to complete sentences because the missing words are clearly understood without being stated.

> EXAMPLES Why not?   At last!
> How much?   This way, please.
> Ten dollars.   So much for that idea.

Minor sentences are common in advertising copy and fictional dialogue; they are not normally appropriate to business writing.

> CHANGE You can use the one-minute long-distance rate any time after eleven at night all the way until eight in the morning. *Any night of the week.*
> TO You can use the one-minute long-distance rate any time after eleven at night all the way until eight in the morning, any night of the week.

(See also **sentence construction**, **sentence variety**, and **sentence faults**.)

sentence variety

Sentences may be long or short; loose or periodic; **simple, compound, complex**, or **compound-complex**; declarative, interrogative, exclamatory, or imperative—even elliptical. There is never a legitimate excuse for letting your sentences become tiresomely alike. However, sentence variety is best achieved during **revision**; do not let it concern you when you are **writing the draft**.

SENTENCE LENGTH

Varying sentence length makes writing more interesting to the **reader** because a long series of sentences of the same length is monotonous. For example, avoid stringing together a number of short **independent clauses**. Either connect them with subordinating **con-**

nectives, thereby making some dependent, or make some **clauses** into separate sentences.

> CHANGE   The company was founded ten years ago, *and* it now employs fifty people, *and* it has branch offices in two other states.
> TO   The company, *which* was founded ten years ago, now employs fifty people and has branch offices in two other states.
> OR   The company was founded ten years ago. It now employs fifty people and has branch offices in two other states.

Short sentences can often be effectively combined by converting **verbs** into **adjectives**.

> CHANGE   Three files *have been misplaced*. Please find those files.
> TO   Please find the three *misplaced* files.

Although too many short sentences make your writing sound choppy and immature, a short sentence can be effective at the end of a passage of long ones.

> EXAMPLE   In the last two decades, many changes have occurred in American life, the extent, durability, and significance of which no one has yet measured. *No one can.*

In general terms, short sentences are good for emphatic, memorable statements. Long sentences are good for detailed explanations and support. There is nothing inherently wrong with a long sentence, or even with a complicated one, as long as its meaning is clear and direct. Sentence length becomes an element of **style** when varied for **emphasis** or contrast; a conspicuously short or long sentence can be used to good effect.

WORD ORDER

When a series of sentences all begin in exactly the same way, the result is likely to be monotonous. You can make your sentences more interesting by occasionally starting with a modifying word, **phrase**, or clause. This could be a single adjective, **adverb**, **participle**, or **infinitive**; a **prepositional phrase**, a **participial phrase**, or an **infinitive phrase**; or even a subordinate clause. (See also **emphasis** and **subordination**.)

> EXAMPLES   *Exhausted*, the project director slumped into a chair. (adjective)
> *Recently*, sales have been good. (adverb)
> *Smiling*, he extended his hand. (participle)
> *To advance*, one must work hard. (infinitive)

In the morning, we will finish the report. (prepositional phrase)
Reading the report, she found several errors. (participial phrase)
To reach the top job, she presented constructive alternatives when
current policies failed to produce results. (infinitive phrase)
Because we now know the result of the survey, we may proceed with
certainty. (adverb clause)

But overdoing this technique can be monotonous, so use it in moderation.

Inverted sentence order can be an effective way to achieve variety.

EXAMPLES Then occurred the event that gained us the contract.
Never have sales been so good.

Too many inverted sentences, however, can lead to the kind of criticism that was aimed at *Time* magazine's writing style many years ago: "Backwards ran the sentences until reeled the mind." Use inverted sentence order sparingly.

Be careful to avoid the unnecessary separation of **subject** and verb, **preposition** and **object**, and parts of a **verb phrase**.

CHANGE The marketing manager worked closely with, despite personality differences, the advertising chief. (preposition and object separated)
TO Despite personality differences, the marketing manager worked closely with the advertising chief.

This advice, however, does not mean that a subject and verb should never be separated by a modifying phrase or clause.

EXAMPLE John Stoddard, who founded the firm in 1943, is still an active partner.

Vary the position of **modifiers** in your sentences to achieve variety as well as precision. The following examples illustrate four different ways that the same sentence could be written by varying the position of its modifiers:

EXAMPLES Carefully, with the printed side forward, place the deck of punched cards in the hopper of the card reader.
With the printed side forward, carefully place the deck of punched cards in the hopper of the card reader.
With the printed side forward, place the deck of punched cards carefully in the hopper of the card reader.
With the printed side forward, place the deck of punched cards in the hopper of the card reader carefully.

LOOSE/PERIODIC/INSERTION SENTENCES

A loose sentence makes its major point at the beginning and then adds subordinate phrases and clauses that develop or modify the point. A periodic sentence delays its main idea until the end by pre-senting modifiers or subordinate ideas first, thus holding the read-er's interest until the end.

> EXAMPLES The attitude of the American citizen toward automation has undergone a profound change during the last decade or so. (loose)
>
> During the last decade or so, the attitude of the American citi-zen toward automation has undergone a profound change. (periodic)

Experiment in your own writing, especially during revision, with shifts from loose sentences to periodic sentences. Avoid the sing-song monotony of a long series of loose sentences, particularly a series containing coordinate clauses joined by **conjunctions**. Sub-ordinating some thoughts to others makes your sentences more interesting.

> CHANGE The auditorium was filled to capacity, *and* the chairman of the board came onto the stage. The meeting started at eight o'clock, *and* the president made his report of the company's operations during the past year. The audience of stockhold-ers was obviously unhappy, *but* the members of the board of directors all were reelected.
>
> TO By eight o'clock, *when* the chairman of the board came onto the stage and the meeting began, the auditorium was filled to capacity. *Although* the audience of stockholders was obvi-ously unhappy with the president's report of the company's operations during the past year, the members of the board of directors all were reelected.

For variety, you may also alter the normal sentence order with an inserted phrase or clause.

> EXAMPLE Our sales projection, drawn up six months ago, appears quite accurate.

The technique of inserting such a phrase or clause is good for **emphasis**, for providing detail, for breaking monotony, and for regulating **pace**. (See also **sentence construction**, and **sentence faults**.)

sequential method of development

The sequential, or step-by-step, method of development is especially effective for explaining a process or describing a mechanism in operation. It would also be the logical method for writing **instructions** and procedures. (See also **policies and procedures**.)

INTEROFFICE MEMORANDUM

TO: All Employees
FROM: Steven J. Scott, Personnel Manager *SJS*
SUBJECT: Flex-time
DATE: September 15, 19--

Over the past month, the Personnel Office has received numerous calls about the approval process for using the new "flex-time" working schedule. So that you know how to take advantage of this system, please keep this notice in your records.

First, you must determine if you are eligible to use a flex-time schedule. The flex-time system is designed for those employees whose jobs do not require them to answer telephones or to be available to the public <u>between the hours of 8 and 5</u>. In addition, an employee must receive written permission from his or her department manager.

After you have established your elligibility, you must submit a copy of Form FT, signed by your manager, to the Personnel Office. This form will then be sent to your division manager for his or her signature and returned to the Personnel Office.

The Personnel Office will notify you when approval is cleared; you may then begin your new schedule on the first Monday thereafter. Three weeks following this notification, your manager must advise the Personnel Office in writing that your flex-time schedule has not interfered with the smooth functioning of your department.

You may obtain copies of Form FT from Margaret Dienstein in Room 129. If you have any questions, see your department manager--do not contact the Personnel Office directly.

SJS/mo

Figure 1   Sequential Method of Development

The main advantage of the sequential method of development is that it is easy to follow because the steps correspond to the elements of the process or operation being described.

The disadvantages of the sequential method are that it can become monotonous and does not lend itself very well to achieving **emphasis**.

Practically all **methods of development** have elements of sequence within them. The **chronological method of development**, for example, is also sequential: to describe a trip chronologically, from beginning to end, is also to describe it sequentially.

The notice presented in Figure 1 to employees of a company uses the sequential method of development.

service

When used as a **verb**, *service* means "keep up or maintain" as well as "repair."

> EXAMPLE   Our company will *service* your equipment.

To mean providing a more general benefit, use *serves*.

> CHANGE   Our company *services* the northwest area of the state.
> TO   Our company *serves* the northwest area of the state.

set/sit

Sit is an intransitive verb; it does not, therefore, require an **object**. Its past tense is *sat*.

> EXAMPLES   I *sit* by a window in the office.
> We *sat* around the conference table.

Set is usually a transitive verb, meaning "put or place," "establish," or "harden." Its past tense is *set*.

> EXAMPLES   Please *set* the trophy on the shelf.
> The jeweler *set* the stone beautifully.
> Can we *set* a date for the tests?
> The high temperature *sets* the epoxy quickly.

Set is occasionally intransitive.

> EXAMPLES   The sun *sets* a little earlier each day.
> The glue *sets* in 45 minutes.

shall/will

It was at one time fairly common to use *shall* for first-person constructions and *will* for second- and third-person constructions.

EXAMPLES I *shall* go.
You *will* go.
He *will* go.

This distinction is unnecessary, however, because no one could be confused by *I will go* to express an action in the near future. *Shall* is sometimes used in all **persons**, nonetheless, to emphasize determination.

EXAMPLE Employees *shall* submit a written reason for a leave of absence.

sic

Latin for "thus," *sic* is used in **quotations** to indicate that the writer has quoted the material exactly as it appeared in the original source. It is most often used when the original material contains an obvious error or might in some other way be questioned. *Sic* is placed within **brackets**.

EXAMPLE In *Basic Astronomy*, Professor Jones noted that the "earth does not revolve around the son [*sic*] at a constant rate."

simile

A simile is a direct **comparison** of two essentially unlike things, making the comparison with the word *like* or *as*. Similes state that A is *like* B.

EXAMPLE His feelings about his business rival are so bitter that in recent conversations with his staff he has returned to the subject compulsively, *like a person scratching an itch.*

Like **metaphors**, similes can help illuminate difficult or obscure ideas.

EXAMPLE The odds against having your plant or business destroyed by fire are at least as great *as the odds against hitting the jackpot on a Las Vegas slot machine.* Because of the long odds, top management may consider sophisticated fire protection and alarm systems more costly than the risk merits and refuse to approve the expenditure. The plant fire protection chief is free to recommend whatever system he likes, but unless the system is required by fire codes or ordered by the insurance company, chances are it will never win top management's approval.

And yet, plants are destroyed by fire, *just as gamblers sometimes hit the jackpot on a one-armed bandit.* Losing big if fire strikes the plant, or winning big on a slot machine both depend on the chance alignment of three events or factors. . . .

—Jay R. Asher and Daniel T. Williams, Jr., "How Not to Lose the Fire Protection Gamble," *Occupational Hazards* Sept. 1974: 130.

simple sentences

A simple sentence has one **clause**. At its most basic, the simple sentence contains only a **subject** and a **predicate**.

> EXAMPLES Profits rose.
> The strike ended.

Both the subject and the predicate may be compounded without changing the basic structure of the simple sentence.

> EXAMPLES *Tom, Janet, and Harry* worked on the sales brochure. (compound subject)
> Tom *designed the layout and supplied the paragraphs.* (compound predicate)

Although **modifiers** may lengthen a simple sentence, they do not alter its basic structure.

> EXAMPLE The *recently introduced* procedure works *very well.*

Inverting the subject and predicate does not alter the basic structure of the simple sentence.

> EXAMPLE A better job I never had.

A simple sentence may contain noun phrases and **prepositional phrases** in either the subject or the predicate.

> EXAMPLES The man *in the blue suit* is my boss. (prepositional phrase in the subject)
> I wrote the report *in a day.* (prepositional phrase in the predicate)

A simple sentence may include modifying **phrases** in addition to the **independent clause**. This fact causes most of the confusion about simple sentences. The following sentence, for example, is a simple sentence because the introductory phrase is an adjective phrase and not a **dependent clause**:

EXAMPLE   *Hard at work in my office,* I did not realize how late it was.

It is better to use simple sentences to state complex ideas. If readers must cope with a complicated **sentence** in addition to a complex idea, they are likely to become confused.

CHANGE   Throughout the year our company, like other companies, was confronted with a combination of management challenges—such as more intense competition in several markets, increased operating costs, and start-up costs for a number of new products—which put heavy pressure on earnings.

TO   Throughout the year our company, like other companies, was confronted with a combination of management challenges. Typical of these challenges are the intense competition in several markets, increased operating costs, and start-up costs for a number of new products. These challenges put heavy pressures on earnings.

Although simple sentences make complex ideas more digestible, a series of simple ideas should be written in a more complex sentence.

CHANGE   The computer is a calculating device. It was once known as a mechanical brain. It has revolutionized industry.

TO   The computer, a calculating device once known as a mechanical brain, has revolutionized industry.

-size / -sized

As **modifiers**, the **suffixes** *-size* and *-sized* are more common to advertising copy than to general writing.

EXAMPLES   a *king-sized* bed, an *economy-sized* carton

However, they are usually redundant unless they are part of the name of a product and should generally not be used.

CHANGE   It was a *small-size* desk.
TO   It was a *small* desk.

slashes

Although not always considered a mark of **punctuation**, the slash performs punctuating duties by separating and showing omission. The slash is called a variety of names, including slant line, virgule, bar, shilling sign.

The slash is often used to separate parts of addresses in continuous writing.

> EXAMPLE   The return address on the envelope was Ms. Rose Howard/62
> W. Pacific Court/Dalton/Ontario/Canada.

The slash can indicate alternative items.

> EXAMPLE   David's telephone number is 549–2278/2335

The slash often indicates omitted words and letters.

> EXAMPLES   miles/hour for "miles per hour"
> c/o for "in care of"
> w/o for "without"

In fractions the slash separates the numerator from the denominator.

> EXAMPLES   2/3 (2 of 3 parts); 3/4 (3 of 4 parts); 27/32 (27 of 32 parts)

The slash is sometimes used to indicate **brackets** on a typewriter that has no bracket key.

> EXAMPLE   Professor Smith wrote that the earth "does not revolve around
> the son /sic/ at a constant rate."

In informal writing, the slash is also used to separate day from month and month from year in **dates**.

> EXAMPLE   12/29/87

(See also **he/she** and **and/or**.)

so/such

So is often vague and should be avoided if another word would be more exact.

> CHANGE   She writes faster, *so* she finished before I did.
> TO   *Because* she writes faster, she finished before I did.

Another problem occurs with the **phrase** *so that*, which should never be replaced with *so* or *such that*.

CHANGE The report should be written *such that* it can be copied.
TO The report should be written *so that* it can be copied.

Such, an **adjective** meaning "of this or that kind," should never be used as a **pronoun**.

CHANGE Our company does not need computers and we do not anticipate using *such*.
TO Our company does not need computers and we do not anticipate using *any*.

some

When *some* functions as an **indefinite pronoun** for plural count **nouns**, or as an **indefinite adjective** modifying plural count nouns, use a plural **verb**.

EXAMPLES *Some* people *are* kinder than others.
Some of us *are* prepared to leave.

Some is singular, however, when used with mass nouns.

EXAMPLES *Some* sand *has* trickled through the crack.
Some oil *was* spilled on the highway.
Some stationery *is* missing from the supply cabinet.
Most of the water evaporated, but *some* remains.

some/somewhat

Some, an **adjective** meaning "an undetermined quantity" or "certain unspecified persons," should not replace the **adverb** *somewhat*, which means "to some extent."

CHANGE His writing has improved *some*.
TO His writing has improved *somewhat*.
OR His writing is *somewhat* improved.

some time/sometime/sometimes

Some time refers to a duration of time.

EXAMPLE We waited for *some time* before calling the customer.

Sometime refers to an unknown or unspecified time.

EXAMPLE We will visit with you *sometime*.

Sometimes refers to occasional occurrences at unspecified times.

> EXAMPLE He *sometimes* visits the branch offices.

spatial method of development

In a spatial sequence, you describe an object or a process according to the physical arrangement of its features. Depending on the subject, you may describe the features from top to bottom, side to side, east to west (or west to east), inside to outside, and so on. Descriptions of this kind rely mainly on dimension (height, width, length), direction (up, down, north, south), shape (rectangular, square, semicircular), and proportion (one-half, two-thirds). Features are described in relation to one another.

> EXAMPLE One end is raised six to eight inches higher than the other end to permit the rain to run off.

Features are also described in relation to their surroundings.

> EXAMPLE The lot is located on the east bank of the Kingman River.

The spatial method of development is commonly used in **descriptions** of laboratory equipment, **proposals** for landscape work, construction-site **progress and activity reports**, and, in combination with a step-by-step sequence, in many types of **instructions**.

The instructions given in Figure 1, which explain how a two-person security team should conduct a methodical room search, use spatial sequencing (see p. 651).

specie/species

Specie means "coined money" or "in coin."

> EXAMPLE Paper currency was virtually worthless, and creditors began to demand payment in *specie*.

Species means a category of animals, plants, or things having some of the same characteristics or qualities. *Species* is the correct **spelling** for both singular and plural.

> EXAMPLES The wolf is a member of the canine *species*.
> Many animal *species* are represented in the Arctic.

Conducting a Methodical Room Search

First, look around the room to decide how the room should be divided
for the search and to what height the first searching sweep should
extend. The first sweep should include all items resting on the floor
up to the selected height.

As nearly as possible, divide the room into two equal parts.
Base the division on the number and type of objects in the room, not
on the size of the room. Divide the room with an imaginary line that
extends from one object to another--for example, the window on the
north wall to the floor lamp next to the south wall.

Next, select a search height for the first sweep. Base this
height on the average of the majority of objects resting on the floor.
In a typical room, this height is established by such objects as table
and desk tops, chair backs, and so on. As a rule, the first sweep
will be made hip high and below.

After dividing the room and establishing the first search height,
go to one end of the agreed upon room division. This point will be
the starting point for the first and all subsequent search sweeps.
Beginning back to back, work your way around the room along the walls
toward the other team member at the other end of the imaginary dividing
line. Check all items resting on the floor adjacent to the walls;
be sure to check the floor under the rugs. When you meet your partner at
the other end of the room, return to the starting point and search
all items in the middle of the room up to the first search height.
Include all items mounted in or on the walls in the first sweep, such
as air conditioning ducts, baseboards, heaters, built-in storage units,
and so on. During this and all subsequent searches, use an electronic
or a medical stethoscope.

Then determine the search height for the second search sweep.
This height is usually set at the chin or at the top of the head of
the searchers. Return to the starting point and repeat the searching
technique up to the second search height. This sweep typically covers
objects hanging on walls, built-in storage units, tall standing items on
the floor, and the like.

Next, establish the third search height. This area usually includes
everything in the room from the top of the searcher's head to the
ceiling. In this sweep, features like hanging light fixtures and
mounted air conditioning units are examined.

Finally, if the room has a false or suspended ceiling, perform
a fourth sweep. Check flush or ceiling light fixtures, air conditioning
or ventilation ducts, speaker systems, structural frames, and so forth.

Figure 1   Spatial Sequencing

> ### The Facts about Seat Belts
>
> Statistic Recently the Highway Safety Foundation studied the use of seat belts in 4,500 accidents involving nearly 13,000 people. Nearly all these accidents occurred on routes which had a speed limit of at least 40 mph. Only 20 percent of all the vehicle occupants were wearing any kind of seat belt.
>
> Statistic The shoulder-type belts were even more unpopular than the lap belts, and only 4 percent of the occupants who had shoulder belts were wearing them.
>
> Statistic In this study, as in other studies, it was found that vehicle passengers not using seat belts were more than 4 times as likely to be killed as those using them. The driver in some cases escaped a more serious injury by being thrown against the steering wheel.
>
> General conclusion A conservative estimate is that 40 percent of the front-seat passenger car deaths could be prevented if everyone used the seat belts, which the law requires the manufacturer to put into each automobile. If you are in an accident, your chances of survival are far greater if you are using your seat belt.
>
> —*The Safe Driving Handbook* (New York: Grosset, 1970) 84–85.

Figure 1   Specific-to-General Method of Development

specific-to-general method of development

The specific-to-general **method of development** begins with a specific statement and builds to a general conclusion. It is somewhat like the **increasing-order-of-importance method of development** in that it carefully builds its case, often with examples and **analogies** in addition to facts or statistics, and does not actually make its point until the end. For example, if your subject were highway safety, you might begin with a specific highway accident; then, you might go on to generalize about how details of the accident were common enough to many similar accidents that recommendations could be made to reduce the probability of such accidents. Figure 1 is an example of the specific-to-general method of development.

(See also **general-to-specific method of development**.)

spelling

Learning to spell requires a systematic effort. The following system will help you learn to spell correctly:

1. Keep your **dictionary** handy, and use it regularly. If you are unsure about the spelling of a word, don't rely on memory or guesswork—consult the dictionary. When you look up a word, focus on both its spelling and its meaning.
2. After you have looked in the dictionary for the spelling of the word, write the word from memory several times. Then check the accuracy of your spelling. If you have misspelled the word, repeat this step. If you do not follow through by writing the word from memory, you lose the chance of retaining it for future use. Practice is essential.
3. Keep a list of the words you commonly misspell, and work regularly at whittling it down. Do not load the list with exotic words; many of us would stumble over *asphyxiation* or *pterodactyl*. Concentrate instead on words like *calendar, maintenance,* and *unnecessary*. These and other frequently used words should remain on your list until you have learned to spell them.
4. Check all your writing for misspellings by **proofreading**.

spin-off

In business usage, *spin-off* usually refers to the common stock received by stockholders of the parent corporation from the creation of a new corporation; however, it also refers to the new corporation. In technical usage, *spin-off* refers to benefits that come about in one area (for example, housing materials) as the result of achievements in another area (for example, space technology research). Because the term is **jargon**, do not use it unless you are certain that all your **readers** understand it.

> EXAMPLE The Teflon coating on cookware is a *spin-off* from the space
> program.

strata

Strata is the plural form of *stratum*, meaning a "layer of material."

> EXAMPLES The land's *strata are* exposed by erosion.
> Each *stratum is* clearly visible in the cliff.

style

A **dictionary** definition of style is "the way in which something is said or done, as distinguished from its substance." Writers' styles are determined by the way they think and transfer their thoughts to paper—the way they use words, sentences, images, **figures of speech**, and so on.

A writer's style is the way his or her language functions in particular situations. For example, a letter to a friend would be relaxed, even chatty in **tone**, whereas a job **application letter** would be more restrained and deliberate. Obviously, the style appropriate to the one letter would not be appropriate to the other. In both letters, the audience and situation determine the manner or style the writer adopts.

Standard English can be divided into two broad categories of style—formal and informal—according to how it functions in certain situations. Understanding the distinction between formal and informal writing styles helps writers use the appropriate style in the appropriate place. We must recognize, however, that no clear-cut line divides the two categories and that some writing may call for a combination of the two.

A formal writing style can perhaps best be defined by pointing to certain material that is clearly formal, such as scholarly and academic articles in professional journals, lectures read at meetings of professional societies, and legal documents.

Material written in a formal style is usually the work of a specialist writing to other specialists, or writing that embodies laws or regulations. As a result, the vocabulary is specialized and precise. The writer's tone is impersonal and objective because the subject matter looms larger in the writing than does the author's personality. (See **point of view**.) Unlike an informal writing style, a formal writing style does not use **contractions**, slang, or dialect. (See **English, varieties of**.) Sentences may be elaborate because complex ideas are generally being examined.

Formal writing need not be dull and lifeless, however. By using such techniques as the active **voice** whenever possible, **sentence variety**, and **subordination**, a writer can make formal writing lively and even interesting, especially if the subject matter is inherently interesting to the **reader**.

EXAMPLE Business graphics has emerged as a significant applications area for computer graphics systems. Many business managers today have discovered the availability and potential benefits of computer graphics. Their appeal lies in their ability to generate graphs quickly that summarize the relations inherent in a set of data, and to make changes and revisions to the graphs quickly and easily. The ultimate purpose of the resulting graphs is the rapid apprehension (and possible retention) of these relationships.

However, computers do not automatically create good graphs. They merely provide the tool for doing so quickly and easily. The design of good graphs must be based on a systematic method that plays upon the interaction between the relations or information that we wish to communicate and our perception of these relations.

—William A. Simcox, "A Design Method for Graphic Communication," *ABCA Bulletin* 47 (Mar. 1984): 3.

Whether you should use a formal style in a particular instance depends on your reader and **objective**. When writers attempt to force a formal style when it should not be used, they are likely to fall into **affectation, awkwardness**, and **gobbledygook**.

An informal writing style is a relaxed and colloquial way of writing standard English. It is the style found in most private letters and in some **correspondence, memorandums**, nonfiction books of general interest, and mass-circulation magazines. There is less distance between the writer and reader because the tone is more personal than in a formal writing style. Contractions and elliptical constructions are commonplace. Consider the following passage, written in an informal style, from a nonfiction book:

EXAMPLE All you need is a talent for spotting the idiocies now built into the system. But you'll have to give up being an administrator who loves to run others and become a manager who carries water for his people so they can get on with the job. And you'll have to keep a suspicious eye on the phonies who cater to your uncertainties or feed your trembling ego on press releases, office perquisites, and optimistic financial reports. You'll have to give substance to such tired rituals as the office party. And you'll certainly have to recognize, once you get a hunk of your company's stock, that you aren't the last man who might enjoy the benefits of shareholding. These elegant simplicities require a sense of justice that won't be easy to hang on to.

—Robert Townsend, *Up the Organization* (New York: Knopf, 1970) 11.

As this example illustrates, the vocabulary of an informal writing style is made up of generally familiar rather than unfamiliar words and expressions, although slang and dialect are usually avoided. An informal style approximates the cadence and structure of spoken English, while conforming to the grammatical conventions of written English.

656 **subjective complements**

When we consciously attempt to create a "style," we usually defeat our purpose. One writer may attempt to impress the reader with a flashy writing style, which can lead to affectation. Another may attempt to impress the reader with his or her education and produce a style that is dull and lifeless. Business writing need be neither affected nor dull. It can, and should, be simple, clear, direct, and even interesting—the key is to master the basic writing skills and always to keep your reader in mind. What will be both informative and interesting to your reader? When this question is uppermost in your mind as you apply the steps of the writing process, you will achieve an interesting and informative writing style. (See the Checklist of the Writing Process at the beginning of the book.)

The following guidelines will help you produce a brisk, interesting style. Concentrate on them as you revise your rough draft.

1. Use the active voice—not exclusively but as much as possible without becoming awkward or illogical.
2. Use **parallel structure** whenever a sentence presents two or more thoughts that are of equal importance.
3. Avoid the monotony of a sing-song style by using a variety of sentence structures. (See **sentence variety**.)
4. Avoid stating positive thoughts in negative terms (write *40 percent responded* instead of *60 percent failed to respond*). (See also **positive writing**.)
5. Concentrate on achieving the proper balance between **emphasis** and subordination.

Beyond an individual's personal style, there are various kinds of writing that have distinct stylistic traits, such as **business writing style**.

subjective complements

A subjective complement is a **noun** or **adjective** in the **predicate** of a sentence; it completes the meaning of a **linking verb** by describing or renaming the subject of the **verb**.

> EXAMPLES The project director seems *confident*. (adjective)
> Acme Corp. is *our major competitor*. (noun phrase)
> His excuse was *that he had been sick*. (noun clause)
> She is a *lawyer*. (noun)

The subjective complement is also known as a **predicate nominative** (noun) or a **predicate adjective** (adjective).

subjects of sentences

The subject of a sentence is a word or group of words about which the sentence or **clause** makes a statement. It indicates the topic of the sentence, telling what the **predicate** is about. It may appear anywhere in a sentence but most often appears at the beginning.

EXAMPLES *To increase sales* is our goal.
The wiring is defective.
We often work late.
That he will be fired is now doubtful.

The simple subject is a **substantive**; the complete subject is the simple subject and its **modifiers**. In the following sentence, the simple subject is *procedures;* the complete subject is *the procedures that you instituted.*

EXAMPLE The procedures that you instituted have increased efficiency.

Grammatically, a subject must agree with its **verb** in **number**.

EXAMPLES The *departments have* much in common.
The *department has* several advantages.

The subject is the actor in active-**voice** sentences.

EXAMPLE *Steve* wrote the report.

A compound subject has two or more elements as the subject of one verb.

EXAMPLE *The president* and *the treasurer* agreed to withhold the information.

Alternative subjects are joined by *or* and *nor.*

EXAMPLE Either *cash* or a *check* is acceptable.

Be careful not to shift subjects in a sentence, as doing so may confuse your **reader**.

CHANGE *Radio amateurs* stay on duty during emergencies, and *sending messages* to and from disaster areas is their particular job.
TO *Radio amateurs*, who stay on duty during emergencies, are responsible for sending messages to and from disaster areas.
OR *Radio amateurs* stay on duty during emergencies, sending messages to and from disaster areas.

subordinating conjunctions

Subordinating conjunctions connect sentence elements of varying importance, normally **independent clauses** and **dependent clauses**; they usually introduce the dependent clause. The most frequently used subordinating conjunctions are *so, although, after, because, if, where, than, since, as, unless, before, though, when,* and *whereas.* They are distinguished from **coordinating conjunctions**, which connect elements of equal importance.

> EXAMPLES He finished his report, *and* he left the office. (coordinating conjunction)
> He left the office *after* he finished his report. (subordinating conjunction)

A clause introduced with a subordinating conjunction is a dependent clause.

> EXAMPLE *Because we were late,* the client was angry.

The word *because* is a subordinating conjunction. Do not use the coordinating conjunction *and* as a substitute for it.

> CHANGE We were late, *and* the client was angry.
> TO The client was angry *because* we were late.

When the subordinating conjunction begins the sentence, a comma should follow the dependent clause in which it appears.

> EXAMPLE *Because* we were late, the client was angry.

When a dependent clause beginning with a subordinating conjunction comes at the end of the sentence, do not separate the independent clause and the dependent clause with a comma.

> EXAMPLE The client was angry *because* we were late.

Be aware that words may serve multiple functions. *When, where, how,* and *why* serve as both interrogative **adverbs** and subordinating conjunctions.

> EXAMPLES *When* will we go? (interrogative adverb)
> We will go *when* he arrives. (subordinating conjunction)

Since, until, before, and *after* are used as both subordinating conjunctions and **prepositions**.

EXAMPLES *Since* we all had arrived, we decided to begin the meeting early. (subordinating conjunction)
I have worked on this project *since* May. (preposition)

subordination

Subordination is a technique used by writers to show, in the structure of a sentence, the appropriate relationship between ideas of unequal importance by subordinating the less important ideas to the important ideas. The skillful use of subordination is a mark of mature writing.

CHANGE Beta Corp. now employs 500 people. It was founded just three years ago.

TO Beta Corp., *which now employs 500 people*, was founded just three years ago.

OR Beta Corp., *which was founded just three years ago*, now employs 500 people.

Effective subordination can be used to achieve **sentence variety**, **conciseness**, and **emphasis**. For example, consider the following sentence: "The city manager's report was carefully illustrated, and it covered five typed pages." See how it might be rewritten, using subordination, in any of the following ways:

EXAMPLES The city manager's report, *which covered five typed pages*, was carefully illustrated. (adjectival clause)
The city manager's report, *covering five typed pages*, was carefully illustrated. (participial phrase)
The city manager's *five-page* report was carefully illustrated. (single modifier)
The carefully illustrated report of the city manager covered five typed pages. (participial phrase)
The city manager's report, *five typed pages*, was carefully illustrated. (appositive phrase)

We sometimes use a **coordinating conjunction** to concede that an opposite or balancing fact is true; however, a subordinating connective can often make the point more smoothly.

CHANGE Their bank has a lower interest rate on loans, *but* ours provides a fuller range of essential services.

TO *Although* their bank has a lower interest rate on loans, ours provides a fuller range of essential services.

The relationship between a conditional statement and a statement of consequences will be clearer if the condition is expressed as a subordinate clause.

> CHANGE　The bill was incorrect, *and* the customer was angry.
> TO　The customer was angry *because* the bill was incorrect.

Subordinating connectives (such as *because, if, while, when, though*) and **relative pronouns** (*who, whom, which, that*) achieve subordination effectively when the main clause states a major point and the **dependent clause** establishes a relationship of time, place, or logic with the main clause.

> EXAMPLE　Jane got the job *because* she was the most qualified applicant.

Relative pronouns (*who, whom, which, that*) can be used effectively to combine related ideas that would be stated less smoothly as independent clauses or sentences.

> CHANGE　Roger Smith is president of Interstate Insurance. He spoke at the national insurance forum last month.
> TO　Roger Smith, *who* is president of Interstate Insurance, spoke at the national insurance forum last month.

Avoid overlapping subordinate constructions, with each depending on the last. Often the relationship between a relative pronoun and its antecedent will not be clear in such a construction.

> CHANGE　Shock, *which* often accompanies severe injuries, severe infections, hemorrhages, burns, heat exhaustion, heart attacks, food or chemical poisoning, and some strokes, is a failure of the circulation, *which* is marked by a fall in blood pressure *that* initially affects the skin (*which* explains pallor) and later the vital organs of kidneys and brain; there is a marked fall in blood pressure.
> TO　Shock often accompanies severe injuries, severe infections, hemorrhages, burns, heat exhaustion, heart attacks, food or chemical poisoning, and some strokes. It is a failure of the circulation, initially to the skin (this explains pallor) and later to the vital organs of kidneys and brain; there is a marked fall in blood pressure.

substantives

A substantive is a word, or a group of words, that functions in its sentence as a subject. It may be a noun, a **pronoun**, or a **verbal (ger-**

und or **infinitive**), or it may be a **phrase** or even a **clause** that is used as a noun.

EXAMPLES The *report* is due today. (noun)
We must finish the project on schedule. (pronoun)
Several college graduates applied for the job. (noun phrase)
Drilling is expensive. (gerund)
To succeed will require hard work. (infinitive)
What I think is unimportant. (noun clause)

suffixes

A suffix is a letter or letters added to the end of a word to change its meaning in some way. Suffixes can change the **part of speech** of a word.

EXAMPLES The market survey was *useful*. (adjective)
Its *usefulness* should be obvious to all. (noun)

The report was issued at just the right *time*. (noun)
The report was very *timely*. (adjective)

sweeping generalizations

When the scope of an opinion is unlimited, the opinion is called a *sweeping generalization*. Such statements, though at times tempting to make, should be qualified during **revision**. Consider the following:

EXAMPLES Anyone who succeeds in business today is dishonest.
Engineers are poor writers.

These statements ignore any possibility that someone may have succeeded in business without being dishonest or that there might be an engineer who writes superbly. Moreover, one person's definition of "success" or "dishonesty" or "poor writing" may be different from another's. No matter how certain you are of the general applicability of an opinion, use such all-inclusive terms as *anyone, everyone, no one, all, always, never,* and *in all cases* with caution. Otherwise, your opinions are likely to be judged irresponsible. (See also **logic**.)

syllabication

When a word is too long to fit on a line, the proper place to divide it is often a troublesome question. The most general rule is to divide words between syllables. The following guidelines may be useful:

1. One-syllable words should not be divided.
2. Words with less than six letters should normally not be divided.
3. Fewer than three letters should not be left at the end of a line or carried over to begin a new line.
4. Words with **suffixes** or **prefixes** should be divided at, rather than within, the suffix or prefix.

> CHANGE su-permarket
> TO super-market

5. A hyphenated word should not be divided at the **hyphen** if the hyphen is essential to the meaning of the word. For example, *re-form* (to change the shape of something) and *reform* (to improve something) have different meanings. Thus it could be confusing to divide *re-form* at the hyphen.
6. **Abbreviations** and **contractions** should never be divided.
7. Proper names and company titles should not be divided.
8. The last word of a **paragraph** should not be divided.
9. The last word on a page of a typewritten manuscript should not be divided.

Secretarial handbooks with **spellings** and word divisions and **dictionaries** that indicate syllable breaks can be helpful—for example, *Webster's Instant Word Guide* (Springfield, MA: Merriam, 1980).

symbols

From highway signs to mathematical equations, people communicate in written symbols. When a symbol seems appropriate in your writing, either be certain that your **reader** understands its meaning or place an explanation in **parentheses** following the symbol the first time it appears. However, never use a symbol when your reader would more readily understand the full term. (See also **abbreviations** and **proofreader's marks**.)

synonyms

A synonym is a word that means nearly the same thing as another word does.

> EXAMPLES purchase, acquire, buy
> seller, vendor, supplier

The **dictionary** definitions of synonyms are usually identical; the **connotations** of such words, however, may differ. (A *seller* may be the same thing as a *supplier*, but the term *supplier* does not suggest a commercial transaction as strongly as *seller* does.)

Do not try to impress your **reader** by finding fancy or obscure synonyms in a **thesaurus**; the result is likely to be **affectation**. (See also **connotation/denotation** and **antonyms**.)

syntax

Syntax refers to the way that words, **phrases**, and **clauses** are combined to form sentences. In English, the most common structure is the **subject-verb-object** pattern. (For more information about the word order of sentences, see **sentence construction**, **sentence faults**, **sentence fragments**, **sentence types**, and **sentence variety**.)

T

table of contents

A table of contents is a list of **heads** in a **report** or chapters in a book. It lists them in their order of appearance and cites their page numbers. Appearing at the front of a work, a table of contents permits **readers** to preview what is in the work and assess the work's value to them. It also aids readers who may want to read only certain sections.

The length of your report should determine whether it needs a table of contents. If it does, use the major **heads** and subheads of your **outline** to create your table of contents, as in the following sample:

Table of Contents

To punctuate a table of contents, see "leaders" in **periods**, and for guidance on the placement of the table of contents in a report, see **formal reports**.

tables

A table is useful for showing large numbers of specific, related facts or statistics in a small space. A table can present **data** more concisely than text can, and it is more accurate than graphic presentations are because it provides numerous facts that a **graph** cannot convey. A table facilitates **comparisons** among data because of the arrangement of the data into rows and columns. Overall trends about the information, however, are more easily seen in charts and graphs.

GUIDELINES FOR CREATING TABLES

Tables typically include the following elements, as shown in Figure 1.

Table Number. If you are using several tables, assign each a number, and then center the number and title above the table. The numbers are usually arabic, and they should be assigned sequentially to the tables throughout the text. Tables should be referred to in the text by table number rather than by direction ("Table 4" rather than "the above table"). If there are more than five tables in your **report** or paper, give them a separate heading ("List of Tables"), and list them by title and page number, together with any figure numbers, on a separate page immediately after the **table of contents**. The first text reference to the table should *precede* the table. If a document contains several chapters or sections, tables can be numbered by chapter or section (Table 1-1, 1-2, . . . 3-1, 3-2).

Title. The title, which is placed just above the table, should describe concisely what the table represents.

Boxhead. The boxhead carries the column headings. These should be kept concise but descriptive. Units of measurement, where necessary, should be specified either as part of the heading or enclosed in **parentheses** beneath the heading. Avoid vertical lettering if possible.

Stub. The left-hand vertical column of a table is the stub. It lists the items about which information is given in the body of the table.

Body. The body comprises the data below the boxhead and to the right of the stub. Within the body, columns should be arranged so that the terms to be compared appear in adjacent rows and columns. Leaders are sometimes used between figures to aid the eye in following data from column to column. Where no information exists for a specific item, leave an empty space to acknowledge the gap.

Table number → Table 1   Recreational fresh-water angling by water-body type and geographical region*

Caption
Column captions
Body

Boxhead
Stub

Geographical Regions	Reservoirs	Man-Made Ponds	Natural Lakes & Ponds	Rivers & Streams	Farm Ponds
New England	130	40	570	410	410
Middle Atlantic	710	290	780	1200	630
East North Central	1200	760	3100	1600	1300
West North Central	810	550	1200	970	980
South Atlantic	1100	760	640	1500	1600
East South Central	890	630	190	670	1200
West South Central	1700	610	430	880	1300
Mountain	820	50	280	600	230
Pacific	950	200	820	1400	470
Totals	8300	3900	8000	9200	7800

Rule

Footnote — *In thousands of anglers. Anglers who fished in more than one water body or region are represented in more than one category.

Source line — Source: U.S. Department of the Interior

Figure 1   Table of Data

Rules. These are the lines that separate the table into its various parts. Horizontal lines are placed below the title, below the body of the table, and between the column headings and the body of the table. They should not be closed at the sides. The columns within the table may be separated by vertical lines if they aid clarity.

Footnotes. Footnotes are used for explanations of individual items in the table. Symbols (*, #) or lowercase letters, rather than numbers, are ordinarily used to key table footnotes, because numbers might be mistaken for the data in a numerical table.

Source Line. The source line, which identifies where the data were obtained, appears below any footnotes (when a source line is appropriate).

Continued Lines. When a table must be divided so that it can be continued on another page, repeat the boxhead and give the table number at the head of each new page with a "continued" label ("Table 3, continued").

INFORMAL TABLES

To list relatively few items that would be easier for the reader to grasp in tabular form, use an informal table; be sure you introduce it properly.

Dear Customer:

To order replacement parts, use the part numbers and prices on the following list:

Part No.	Part	Price ($)
2-912	Diverter Valve	12.50
2-776	Gasket Kit	0.95
3-212	Adaptor	0.90
7-211	Hose Assembly	3.50

Although informal tables do not need titles or table numbers to identify them, they do require column headings that accurately describe the information listed.

telegraphic style

Telegraphic style condenses writing by omitting **articles, pronouns, conjunctions**, and transitional expressions. Although **conciseness** is important in writing, writers sometimes make their sentences too brief by omitting these words. Telegraphic style forces the reader to mentally supply the missing words. Compare the following two **memorandums**, and notice how much easier the revised version reads (the added words are *italicized*).

CHANGE   Per 1/21 memo, 12 copies of instruction sheet and question-naire enclosed. Report can be complete as soon as above materials received. March filling quickly so let's set date. Please advise.

TO   *As I promised in my* 1/21 memo, enclosed *are* 12 copies of *the* instruction sheet and *the* questionnaire. *We can* complete *the* report as soon as *we* receive *the questionnaires. Our* March *calendar is* filling quickly so *we should* set *a* meeting date *soon.* Please *give me a possible date when you return the questionnaire.*

Telegraphic style can also produce **ambiguity**, as the following example demonstrates:

CHANGE   The director wants the report written by the New York office.

Does this sentence mean that the director wants a report that the New York office *wrote in the past,* or does he or she want the New York office *to write a report in the future?*

TO   The director wants the report *that was* written by the New York office.

OR   The director wants the report *to be* written by the New York office.

Some writers excuse telegraphic style with the claim that their readers will "understand." Maybe so, but they will probably have to work hard to do so—and may therefore even misunderstand. Though telegraphic writing can save space, it never really saves time. As a writer, remember that although you may save yourself work by writing telegraphically, your readers will have to work that much harder to read—or decipher—your writing. (See also **transitions**.)

tenant/tenet

A *tenant* is one who holds or temporarily occupies a property owned by another person.

EXAMPLE   The *tenants* were upset by the increased rent.

A *tenet* is an opinion or belief held by a person or an organization.

EXAMPLE The idea that competition will produce adequate goods and
services for a society is a central *tenet* of capitalism

tense

Tense is the grammatical term for **verb** forms that indicate time distinctions. There are six tenses in English: past, past perfect, present,
present perfect, future, and future perfect. Each of these has a corresponding progressive form.

Tense	Basic	Progressive
Past	I began	I was beginning
Past Perfect	I had begun	I had been beginning
Present	I begin	I am beginning
Present Perfect	I have begun	I have been beginning
Future	I will begin	I will be beginning
Future Perfect	I will have begun	I will have been beginning

Perfect tenses allow you to express a prior action or condition that
continues in a present, past, or future time.

EXAMPLES I *have begun* to write the annual report, and I will work on it
for the rest of the month. (present perfect)
I *had begun* to read the manual when the lights went out. (past
perfect)
I *will have begun* this project by the time funds are allocated.
(future perfect)

Note from the table that the progressive forms are created by combining the **helping verb** *be*, in the appropriate tenses, with the
present **participle** (*-ing*) form of the main verb.

PAST TENSE

The simple past tense indicates that an action took place in its en-
tirety in the past. The past tense is usually formed by adding *-d* or
-ed to the root form of the verb.

EXAMPLE We *closed* the office early yesterday.

PAST PERFECT TENSE

The past perfect tense indicates that one past event preceded another. It is formed by combining the helping verb *had* with the past
participle form of the main verb.

EXAMPLE He *had finished* by the time I arrived.

PRESENT TENSE

The simple present tense represents action occurring in the present, without any indication of time duration.

EXAMPLE I *see* the client.

A general truth is always expressed in the present tense.

EXAMPLE He learned that the saying "time *heals* all wounds" is true.

The present tense can be used to present actions or conditions that have no time restrictions.

EXAMPLE A neat desk *increases* efficiency.

The present tense can be used to indicate habitual action.

EXAMPLE I *pass* the paint shop on the way to my department every day.

The present tense can be used as the "historical present" to make things that occurred in the past more vivid.

EXAMPLE He *asks* for more information on production statistics and *receives* a detailed report on every product manufactured by the company. Then he *asks*, "Is each department manned at full strength?" In his office, surrounded by his staff, he *goes* over the figures and *plans* for the coming year.

PRESENT PERFECT TENSE

The present perfect tense describes something from the recent past that has a bearing on the present—a period of time before the present but after the simple past. The present perfect tense is formed by combining a form of the helping verb *have* with the past principle form of the main verb.

EXAMPLES He *has retired*, but he visits the office frequently.
We *have finished* the draft and are ready to begin revising it.

FUTURE TENSE

The simple future tense indicates a time that will occur after the present. It uses the helping verb *will* (or *shall*) plus the main verb.

EXAMPLE I *will finish* the job tomorrow.

Do not use the future tense needlessly.

CHANGE This system *will be* explained on page 3.
    TO This system *is* explained on page 3.

CHANGE When you press this button, the card *will be* moved under the
        read station.
    TO When you press this button, the card *is* moved under the read
        station.

FUTURE PERFECT TENSE

The future perfect tense indicates action that will have been completed at a future time. It is formed by linking the helping verbs *will have* to the past participle form of the main verb.

EXAMPLE As of tomorrow, I *will have worked* here two years.

TENSE AGREEMENT OF VERBS

The verb of a subordinate **clause** should usually agree in tense with the verb of the main clause. (See also **agreement**.)

EXAMPLES When Ms. Jones *dictates* a letter, she *wants* it typed immediately.
          When Ms. Jones *dictated* a letter, she *wanted* it typed immediately.

Shift in Tense. Be consistent. The only legitimate shift in tense records a real change in time. When you choose a tense in telling a story or discussing an idea, stay with that tense. Illogical shifts in tense will only confuse your **reader**.

CHANGE Before Tom *called* the irate client, he *made* sure he *undstands* the
        problem.
    TO Before Tom *called* the irate client, he *made* sure he *understood* the
        problem.

that

Avoid the unnecessary repetition of *that*.

CHANGE I think *that* when this project is finished *that* you should write
        the results.
    TO I think *that* you should write the results when the project is finished.
    OR Write the results when the project is finished.

CHANGE You will note *that* as you assume greater responsibility and as your years of service with the company increase, *that* your benefits will increase accordingly.

TO You will note *that* as you assume greater responsibility and as your years of service with the company increase, your benefits will increase accordingly.

OR You will note *that* your benefits will increase as you assume greater responsibility and as your years of service with the company increase.

However, do not delete *that* from a sentence in which it is necessary for the **reader's** understanding.

CHANGE Quarreling means trying to show the other person is in the wrong.

TO Quarreling means trying to show *that* the other person is in the wrong.

CHANGE Some department managers fail to recognize sufficiently the people in their departments constitute a source of new ideas.

TO Some department managers fail to recognize sufficiently *that* the people in their departments constitute a source of new ideas.

(See also **conciseness/wordiness**.)

that/which/who

Who refers to persons, whereas *that* and *which* refer to animals and things.

EXAMPLES John Brown, *who* is retiring tomorrow, has worked for the company for twenty years.
Please return the files *that* you borrowed.
Our Atlanta store, *which* opened last year, is very profitable.

That is often overused. (See **that**.) However, do not eliminate it if to do so would cause **ambiguity** or problems with **pace**.

CHANGE We ask you return the contract to us by the fifteenth.

TO We ask *that* you return the contract to us by the fifteenth.

Which, rather than *that*, should be used with nonrestrictive **clauses** (clauses that do not change the meaning of the basic sentence).

EXAMPLES   After John left the restaurant, *which* is one of the best in New
York, he came directly to my office. (nonrestrictive)
A company *that* diversifies often succeeds. (restrictive)

(See also **who/whom**, **relative pronoun**, and **restrictive and nonrestrictive elements**.)

there/their/they're

There, their, and *they're* are often confused because they sound alike.
There is an **expletive** or an **adverb**.

EXAMPLES   *There* were more than 1,500 people at the conference. (expletive)
More than 1,500 people were *there*. (adverb)

Their is the **possessive** form of *they*.

EXAMPLE   Our employees are expected to keep *their* desks neat.

They're is a **contraction** of *they are*.

EXAMPLE   If *they're* right, we should change the design.

thesaurus

A thesaurus is a book of words with their **synonyms** and **antonyms**,
arranged by categories. Thoughtfully used, it can help you with **word
choice** during the **revision** phase of the writing process. However,
this variety of words may tempt you to choose inappropriate or
obscure synonyms just because they are available. Use a thesaurus
to clarify your meaning rather than to impress your **reader**. Never
use a word unless you are sure of its meanings; **connotations** of the
word that might be unknown to you could mislead your reader. (See
"synonyms" in **reference books** for the names of thesauruses and
also see **affectation** and **defining terms**.)

thus/thusly

Thus is an **adverb** meaning "in this manner" or "therefore." The *-ly*
in *thusly* is superfluous and should be omitted.

CHANGE　The committee's work is done. *Thusly* we should have the report by the end of the week.
TO　The committee's work is done. *Thus* we should have the report
by the end of the week.

'til/until

'Til is a nonstandard **spelling** of *until*, meaning "up to the time of."
Use *until*.

CHANGE　We worked *'til* eight o'clock.
TO　We worked *until* eight o'clock.

titles

The title of a document should indicate its topic and announce its
scope and **objective**. Often the title is the only basis on which readers can decide whether they should read something. Titles are also
increasingly used by information specialists as a source of key terms
by which documents can be indexed for automated information
storage and retrieval systems. Imprecise titles thus defeat human and
automated information retrieval.

To create accurate titles, keep the following guidelines in mind:

1. Be specific. Do not use general or vague terms when specific
ones will pinpoint the topic and its scope. Although the title
"Electric Fields and Living Organisms" announces the topic of
a report, it leaves the reader with important unanswered questions: What is the relationship between electric fields and living
organisms? What kind of organisms does it refer to? What is the
intensity of the electric field? What stage in the organism's life
cycle does it discuss? The addition of details identifies not only
the topic but its scope and objective as well: *Effects of 60-Hz Electric
Fields on Embryo and Chick Development, Growth, and Behavior.*
2. Be concise, but don't make your title short just for the sake of
being short. As the examples above indicate, making a title accurate may mean adding a few terms. Conciseness, instead, means
eliminating words that do not contribute to accuracy. Avoid titles
that begin "Notes on . . .," "Studies on . . .," "A Report on . . .," or
"Observations on. . . ." These notions are self-evident to the
reader. On the other hand, certain works, like **annual reports** or

feasibility studies should be identified as such in the title because this information helps define the purpose and scope.

3. Do not indicate dates in the title of a periodic or progress report, but put them in a subtitle:

> The Effects of Acid Rain on Red Spruce
> in the White Mountains
> Quarterly Report
> January–March 19—

4. Avoid using **abbreviations, acronyms and initialisms**, chemical formulas, and the like *unless* the work is addressed exclusively to specialists in the field.

5. Do not put titles in sentence form.

> CHANGE   How Residential Passive Solar Heating Could Affect Seven
>   Electric Utilities
>   TO   Potential Effects of Residential Passive Solar Heating on Seven
>   Utilities

6. For multivolume publications, repeat the title on each volume. The distinction among the volumes is made by the volume number (Volume 1, 2, 3, and so on), and sometimes each volume will have a different subtitle. For example, Volume 1 could be an **executive summary**; Volume 2 could be the main report; and any subsequent volumes could be lengthy **appendixes**.

(For guidelines on how to capitalize titles and when to use italics and quotation marks, see **capital letters**, **italics**, and **quotation marks**.)

to/too/two

To, *too*, and *two* are confused only because they sound alike. *To* is used as a **preposition** or to mark an **infinitive**.

> EXAMPLES   Send the report *to* the district manager. (preposition)
>   I wish *to* go. (mark of the infinitive)

Too is an **adverb** meaning "excessively" or "also."

> EXAMPLES   The price was *too* high. ("excessively")
>   I, *too*, thought it was high. ("also")

Two is a number.

> EXAMPLE   Only *two* buildings have been built this fiscal year.

tone

In writing, tone is the writer's attitude toward the subject and his or her **readers**. The tone may be casual or serious, enthusiastic or skeptical, friendly or hostile. In business writing, the tone in **correspondence**, **memorandums**, and **formal reports** may range widely—depending on the **objective**, situation, and context. For example, in a memo read only by an associate who is also a friend, your tone might be casual and friendly.

> EXAMPLE   I think your proposal to Smith and Sons is great. If we get the contract, I owe you a lunch! I've marked a couple of places where we could cover ourselves on the schedule. See what you think.

In a memo to a superior, however, your tone might be quite different.

> EXAMPLE   I think your proposal to Smith and Sons is excellent. I have marked a couple of places for your consideration where we could ensure that we are not committing ourselves to a schedule we might not be able to keep. If I can help in any other way, please let me know.

In a memo that serves as a **report** to numerous readers, the tone would again be different.

> EXAMPLE   The Smith and Sons proposal appears complete and thorough, based on our department's evaluation. Several small revisions, however, would ensure that Acme is not committing itself to an unrealistic schedule. These are marked on the copy of the report being circulated.

Your tone will be set by many factors in your writing. As illustrated above, a formal writing **style** will normally have a different tone than will an informal writing style. (See also **business writing style**.) **Word choice**, the **introduction** or **opening**, and even your **title** all contribute to the overall tone. For instance, a title such as "Some Observations on the Diminishing Oil Reserves in Wyoming" clearly sets a tone quite different from that of "What Happens When We've Pumped Wyoming Dry?" The first title would most likely be appropriate for a report; the second title would be more appropriate for a **newsletter article**. The important thing is to make sure that your tone is the one best suited to your objective, by always keeping your reader in mind.

In business correspondence, tone is particularly important because the letter represents a direct communication between two people. Moreover, good business letters establish a rapport between your organization and the public, and a positive and considerate tone is essential. (See **you viewpoint**.)

topics

On the job, the topic of a writing project is usually determined by need. In a college writing course, on the other hand, you may have to select your own topic. If you do, keep the following points in mind:

1. Select a topic that interests you.
2. Select a topic that you can **research** adequately with the facilities available to you.
3. Limit your topic so that its **scope** is small enough to handle within the time you are given. A topic like "Air Pollution," for example, would be too broad. On the other hand, keep the topic broad enough so that you will have enough to write about.
4. Select a topic for which you can make adequate **preparation** to ensure a good final **report**.

topic sentences

A topic sentence states the controlling idea of a **paragraph**; the rest of the paragraph supports and develops that statement with carefully related details. The topic sentence may appear anywhere in the paragraph—which permits the writer variety in **style**—and a topic statement may also be more than one sentence if necessary.

The topic sentence is often the first sentence because it states the subject.

EXAMPLE *The arithmetic of searching for oil is stark.* For all his scientific methods of detection, the only way the oil driller can actually know for sure that there is oil in the ground is to drill a well. The average cost of drilling an oil well is over $300,000, and drilling a single well may cost over $8,000,000! And once the well is drilled, the odds against its containing any oil at all are 8 to 1! Even after a field has been discovered, one out of every four holes drilled in developing the field is a dry hole because of the uncertainty of defining the limits of the producing formation. The oil driller can never know what Mark Twain once called "the calm confidence of a Christian with four aces in his hand."

On rare occasions, the topic sentence logically falls in the middle of a paragraph.

EXAMPLE   It is perhaps natural that psychologists should awaken only slowly to the possibility that behavioral processes may be directly observed, or that they should only gradually put the older statistical and theoretical techniques in their proper perspective. But it is time to insist that science does not progress by carefully designed steps called "experiments," each of which has a well-defined beginning and end. *Science is a continuous and often a disorderly and accidental process.* We shall not do the young psychologist any favor if we agree to reconstruct our practices to fit the pattern demanded by current scientific methodology. What the statistician means by the design of experiments is design which yields the kind of data to which *his* techniques are applicable. He does not mean the behavior of the scientist in his laboratory devising research for his own immediate and possibly inscrutable purposes.

—B. F. Skinner, "A Case History in Scientific Method," *American Psychologist* 2 (May 1956): 232.

Although the topic sentence is usually most effective early in the paragraph, a paragraph can lead up to the topic sentence; this is sometimes done to achieve **emphasis**. When a topic sentence concludes a paragraph, it can also serve as a summary or **conclusion**, based on the details that were designed to lead up to it.

EXAMPLE   Energy does far more than simply make our daily lives more comfortable and convenient. Suppose you wanted to stop— and reverse—the economic progress of this nation. What would be the surest and quickest way to do it? Find a way to cut off the nation's oil resources! Industrial plants would shut down; public utilities would stand idle; all forms of transportation would halt. The economy would plummet into the abyss of national economic ruin. *Our economy, in short, is energy-based.*

—*The Baker World* (Los Angeles: Baker Oil Tools).

Occasionally, the controlling idea of a paragraph—what would normally be its topic sentence—is not explicitly stated but only implied.

Nevertheless, if the paragraph has **unity**, a sentence stating the controlling idea *could* be written, and all the sentences in the paragraph would be found to be related directly to it. However, people writing in business and industry are well advised to make their topic sentences *explicit*.

toward/towards

Both *toward* and *towards* are acceptable varient spellings of the **preposition** meaning "in the direction of." *Toward* is more common in the United States, and *towards* is more common in Great Britain.

> EXAMPLES We walked *toward* the Golden Gate Bridge.
> They were headed *towards* London Bridge.

transition

Transition is the means of achieving a smooth flow of ideas from sentence to sentence, **paragraph** to paragraph, and subject to subject. Transition is a two-way indicator of what has been said and what will be said; that is, it provides a means of linking ideas to clarify the relationship between them. You can achieve transition with a word, a **phrase**, or even a paragraph. Without the guideposts of transition, **readers** can lose their way. Transition can be quite obvious.

> EXAMPLE *Having considered* the economic feasibility of this alloy as a transformer core, *we turn now* to the problem of inadequate supply.

Or it can be more subtle.

> EXAMPLE Even if this alloy is economically feasible as a transformer core, there still remains the problem of inadequate supply.

Either way, you now have your reader's attention fastened on the problem of inadequate supply, exactly what you set out to do.

Certain words and phrases are inherently transitional. Consider the following terms and their functions:

Result: *therefore, as a result, consequently, thus, hence*
Example: *for example, for instance, specifically, as an illustration*
Comparison: *similarly, likewise*
Contrast: *but, yet, still, however, nevertheless, on the other hand*
Addition: *moreover, furthermore, also, too, besides, in addition*

Time: *now, later, meanwhile, since then, after that, before that time*
Sequence: *first, second, third, then, next, finally*

Within a paragraph, such transitional expressions clarify and smooth the movement from idea to idea. Conversely, the lack of transitional devices can make the going bumpy for the reader. Consider first the following passage, which lacks adequate transition:

> EXAMPLE People had always hoped to fly. Until 1903 it was only a dream. It was thought by some that human beings were not meant to fly. The Wright brothers launched the world's first heavier-than-air flying machine. The airplane has become a part of our everyday life.

Now read the same passage with words and phrases of transition added (in **italics**), and notice how much more smoothly the thoughts flow:

> EXAMPLE People had always hoped to fly, *but* until 1903 it was only a dream. *Before*, it was thought by some that human beings were not meant to fly. *In 1903* the Wright brothers launched the world's first heavier-than-air flying machine. *Now* the airplane has become a part of our everyday life.

And finally, read the same passage with stronger transition provided:

> EXAMPLE People had always hoped to fly, but until 1903 it was only a dream. *Before that time*, it was thought by some that human beings were not meant to fly. *However*, in 1903 the Wright brothers launched the world's first heavier-than-air flying machine. *Since then* the airplane has become a part of our everyday life.

If your **organization** and **outline** are good, your transitional needs will be less difficult to satisfy (although they must nonetheless *be* satisfied). Just as the outline is a road map for the writer, transition is a road map for the reader.

TRANSITION BETWEEN SENTENCES

In addition to using transitional words and phrases such as those shown above, the writer may achieve effective transition between sentences by repeating key words or ideas from preceding sentences, by using **pronouns** that refer to antecedents in previous sentences, and by using **parallel structure**—that is, by repeating the pattern of a phrase or **clause**. Consider the following short paragraph, in which all these means are employed. (A few examples are indicated by italics; however, to mark them all would be confusing.)

EXAMPLE Representative of many American university towns is Millville. *This midwestern town*, formerly a *sleepy farming community*, is today the home of a large and bustling *academic community*. Attracting students from all over the Midwest, *this university* has grown very rapidly in the last ten years. *This same decade* has seen a physical expansion of *the campus*. The state, recognizing *this expansion*, has provided additional funds for the acquisition of land adjacent to the university. The *university* has become *Millville's* major industry, generating most of *the town's* income—and, of course, many of *its* problems, too.

Another device for achieving transition is enumeration:

EXAMPLE The recommendation rests upon *three conditions. First*, the department staff must be expanded to a sufficient size to handle the increased work load. *Second*, sufficient time must be provided for the training of the new members of the staff. *Third*, a sufficient number of qualified applicants must be available within the alloted time.

TRANSITION BETWEEN PARAGRAPHS

All the means discussed above for achieving transition between sentences—and especially the repetition of key words or ideas—may also be effective for transition between paragraphs. For paragraphs, however, longer transitional elements are often required. One technique is to use an opening sentence that summarizes the preceding paragraph and then to move ahead to the business of the new paragraph.

EXAMPLE Each year, forest fires in our region cause untold destruction. For example, wood ashes washed into streams after a fire often kill large numbers of fish. In addition, the destruction of the vegetation along stream banks causes water temperatures to rise, making the stream unfit for several varieties of coldwater fish. Forest fires, moreover, hurt the tourist and recreation business, for vacationers are not likely to visit flame-blackened areas.

The loss of valuable forest, of wildlife, of tourist and recreation business, and many other indirect losses caused by such fires, damage not only the quality of life but also the economy of our region....

Ask a question at the end of one paragraph and answer it at the beginning of the next.

EXAMPLE   Automation has become an ugly word in the American vocabulary because it has at times displaced some jobs. But the all-important fact that is often overlooked is that it invariably creates many more jobs than it eliminates. (The vast number of people employed in the great American automobile industry as compared with the number of people that had been employed in the harness-and-carriage-making business is a classic example.) Almost always, the jobs that have been eliminated by automation have been menial, unskilled jobs, and those who have been displaced have been forced to increase their skills, which resulted in better and higher-paying jobs for them. *In view of these facts, is automation really bad?*

    Certainly automation has made our country the most wealthy and technologically advanced nation the world has ever known. . . .

A purely transitional paragraph may be inserted to aid readability.

EXAMPLE   . . . that marred the progress of the company.

    There were two other setbacks to the company's fortunes that year that also marked the turning of the tide: the loss of many skilled workers through the Early Retirement Program and the intensification of the devastating rate of inflation.

    The Early Retirement Program . . .

CHECKING FOR TRANSITION DURING REVISION

Check for **unity** and **coherence** to determine whether the transition is effective. If a paragraph has unity and coherence, the sentences and ideas will be tied together and contribute directly to the subject of the paragraph. Look for places where transition is missing, and add it. Look for places where it is weak, and strengthen it.

transmittal letters

The transmittal letter, also known as a cover letter, identifies the item being sent, the person to whom it is being sent, and the reason for sending it. A transmittal letter provides a permanent record of the transmittal for both the writer and the **reader**.

Keep your remarks brief in a transmittal letter. Open with a **paragraph** explaining what is being sent and why. In an optional second paragraph, you might include a summary of any information you're sending. A letter accompanying a **proposal**, for example, might point out any sections in the proposal that may be of particular

WATERFORD PAPER PRODUCTS
P.O. BOX 413
WATERFORD, WI 53474

(414) 738-2191

November 12, 19--

Ms. Nancy Melcher
2021 State Street
Racine, WI 53307

Dear Ms. Melcher:

Thank you for your interest in Waterford Paper Products. The enclosed
brochure describes our product line and our current prices.

If I can be of future help, please call me at extension 2349.

Sincerely,

Lawrence Smith

Lawrence Smith
Customer Relations

LS/ik
Enclosure

Figure 1   Transmittal Letter

interest to the reader. The letter could then go on to present evidence that the writer's firm is the best one to do the job. This paragraph could also mention the conditions under which the material was prepared, such as limitations of time or budget. The closing

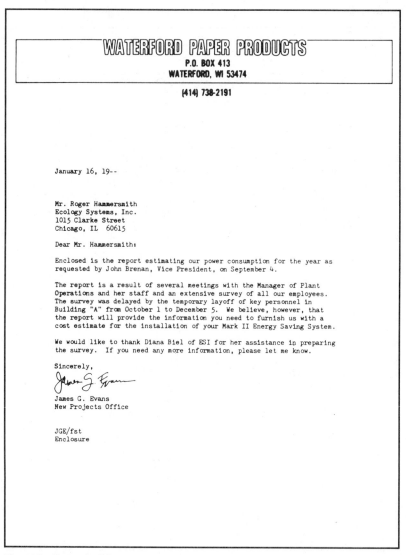

Figure 2   Transmittal Letter

paragraph should contain acknowledgments, offer additional assistance, or express the hope that the material will fulfill its purpose.

Figure 1 is brief and to the point. Figure 2 is a bit more detailed,
for it touches on the manner in which the information was gathered.

trip reports

Many companies require or encourage reports of the business trips their employees take. A trip report both provides a permanent record of a business trip and its accomplishments and enables many employees to benefit from the information that one employee has gained.

MEMORANDUM

To: Manuel Cruz, Manager, Customer Relations
From: Isoroku Somoto, Field Service Engineer
Date: May 31, 19--
Subject: Trip to Inspect New Power Unit Installations, May 26-30

The purpose of this trip was to inspect the installation of Taylor Auxilliary Power Units in five hospitals and to train the maintenance staffs at those hospitals to operate the units during a commerical power failure. I visited the New Orleans General Hospital on the 26th, Our Lady of Mercy Hospital in San Antonio on the 27th, Dallas Presbyterian Hospital on the 28th, St. Elizabeth Hospital in Oklahoma City on the 29th, and the Jefferson Davis Memorial Hospital in Atlanta on the 30th.

At each site, I found that the installation of the equipment had been done properly. I made arrangements, in each hospital, with the administrative office and then placed the hospital on auxilliary power for one hour as a trial run. In every location, the transfer from commercial power to auxilliary power was made without problems.

After inspecting the equipment and its installation, I held a brief training session with the maintenance staff. The training consisted of instruction in starting the unit's engine, in operating the generator's controls to produce 220 volts of electricity at 60 Hertz, and in activating the operating unit in the event of a commercial power failure.

In all five hospitals, both the administrative and maintenance staffs appeared to have a favorable opinion of the Taylor Power Equipment Company, its product, and its field personnel. Our sales staff and installers seem to be doing a good job.

IS/bb

Figure 1   Trip Report

A trip report should normally be in the **format** of a **memorandum**, addressed to your immediate superior. On the subject line give the destination and dates of the trip. The body of the **report** will explain why you made the trip, who you visited, and what you accomplished. The report should devote a brief section to each major event and may include a **head** for each section (you needn't give equal space to each event, but instead, elaborate on the more important events). Follow the body of the report with any appropriate **conclusions** and recommendations.

The trip report shown in Figure 1 is typical.

trite language

Trite language is made up of words, **phrases**, or ideas that have been used so often that they are stale.

> CHANGE *It may interest you to know* that all the folks in the branch office are *hale and hearty*. I should finish my report *quick as a wink*, and we should *clean up* on it.
>
> TO Everyone here at the branch office is well. I should finish my project within a week, and I'm sure it will prove profitable for us.

Trite language shows that the writer is thoughtless in his or her **word choice** or is not thinking carefully about the **topic** but is relying instead on what others have thought and said. (See also **affectation**.)

trouble reports

The trouble report is used to report an accident, an equipment failure, an unplanned work stoppage, and so on. The **report** enables the management of an organization to determine the cause of the problem and to make any changes necessary to prevent its recurrence. The trouble report normally follows a simple **format** (and is often a **memorandum**), since it is an internal document and is not large enough in either size or **scope** to require the format of a **formal report**.

In the subject line of the memorandum, state the precise problem you are reporting. Then begin your description of the problem in the body of your report. What happened? Where did it occur? When did it occur? Was anybody hurt? Was there any property damage?

MEMORANDUM

To: James K. Arburg, Safety Officer
From: Lawrence T. Baker, Foreman of Section A-40 LTB
Date: November 30, 19--

Subject: Personal-Injury Accident in Section A-40
            October 10, 19--

On October 10, 19--, at 10:15 p.m., Jim Hollander, operating
punch press #16, accidentally brushed the knee switch of his
punch press with his right knee as he swung a metal sheet over
the punching surface. The switch activated the punching unit,
which severed Hollander's left thumb between the first and second
joints as his hand passed through the punch station. While an
ambulance was being summoned, Margaret Wilson, R.N., administered
first aid at the plant dispensary. There were no witnesses to
the accident.
        The ambulance arrived from Mercy Hospital at 10:45 p.m., and
Hollander was admitted to the emergency room at the hospital at
11:00 p.m. He was treated and kept overnight for observation,
then released the next morning.
        Hollander returned to work one week later, on October 17.
He has been given temporary duties in the tool room until his
injury heals.

Conclusions About the Cause of the Accident

The Maxwell punch press on which Hollander was working has two
switches, a hand switch and a knee switch, and both must be
pressed to activate the punch mechanism. The hand switch must be
pressed first, and then the knee switch, to trip the punch
mechanism. The purpose of the knee switch is to leave the
operator's hands free to hold the panel being punched. The hand
switch, in contrast, is a safety feature. Because the knee
switch cannot activate the press until the hand switch has been
pressed, the operator cannot trip the punching mechanism by
touching the knee switch accidentally.
        Inspection of the punch press that Hollander was operating
at the time of the accident made it clear that Hollander had
taped the hand switch of his machine in the ON position,
effectively eliminating its safety function. He could then pick
up a panel, swing it onto the machine's punching surface, press
the knee switch, stack the newly punched panel, and grab the next
unpunched panel, all in one continuous motion--eliminating the
need to let go of the panel, after placing it on the punching
surface, in order to press the hand switch.
        To prevent a recurrence of this accident, I have conducted a
brief safety session with all punch press operators, at which I
described Hollander's experience and cautioned them against
tampering with the safety features of their machines.

mo

Figure 1   Trouble Report

Was there a work stoppage? Since insurance claims, worker's compensation awards, and, in some instances, lawsuits may hinge on the information contained in a trouble report, be sure to include precise times, dates, locations, treatment of injuries, names of any witnesses, and any other crucial information. Give a detailed analysis of what caused the problem. Be thorough and accurate in your analysis, and support any judgments or conclusions with facts. Be careful about your **tone**; avoid any condemnation or blame. If you speculate about the cause of the problem, make it clear to your **reader** that you are speculating. In your **conclusion**, state what has been done, what is being done, or what will be done to correct the conditions that led to the problem. This may include training in safety practices, better or improved equipment, protective clothing (for example, shoes or goggles), and so on.

The report given in Figure 1, about an accident involving personal injury, was written by the foreman of a group of punch press operators for the plant's safety officer, at the safety officer's request. Since there were no witnesses, the foreman obtained the information for the report by talking to the plant nurse, hospital personnel, and the victim—and by inspecting the equipment used by the victim at the time of the accident.

try and

The **phrase** *try and* is colloquial for *try to*. Unless you are writing a casual personal letter, it is better to use *try to.*

> CHANGE   Please *try and* finish the report on time.
> TO   Please *try to* finish the report on time.

U

unity

Unity is singleness of purpose and treatment, the cohesive element that holds a piece of writing together; it means that everything in an article or paper is essentially about one thing or idea.

To achieve unity, the writer must select one **topic** and then treat it with singleness of purpose—without digressing into unrelated paths. The prime contributors to unity are a good outline and effective **transition**. After you have completed your outline, check it to see that each part relates to your subject. Be certain that your transitional terms make clear the relationship of each part to what preceded it.

Transition dovetails sentences and **paragraphs** like the joints of a well-made drawer. Notice, for example, how neatly the sentences in the following paragraph are made to fit together by the italicized words and **phrases** of transition:

EXAMPLE Any company that operates internationally today faces a host of difficulties. Inflation is worldwide. Most countries are struggling with other economic problems *as well. In addition,* many monetary uncertainties and growing economic nationalism are working against multinational companies. *Yet* ample business is available in most developed countries if you have the right products, services, and marketing organization. To maintain the growth Data Corporation has achieved overseas, we recently restructured our international operations into four major trading areas. *This* reorganization will improve the services and support that the corporation can provide to its subsidiaries around the world. *At the same time,* the reorganization establishes firm management control, ensuring consistent policies around the world. *So* you might say the problems of doing business abroad will be more difficult this year, but we are better organized to meet those problems.

The logical sequence provided by a good outline is essential to achieving unity. An outline enables the writer to lay out the most direct route from **introduction** to **conclusion** without digressing into side issues that are not related, or that are only loosely related, to the subject. Without establishing and following such a direct route, a writer cannot achieve unity.

up

Adding the word *up* to **verbs** often creates a redundant **phrase**.

CHANGE We have opened *up* ten new markets this year.
TO We have opened ten new markets this year.

CHANGE He wrote *up* the report.
TO He wrote the report.

(See also **conciseness**.)

usage

Usage is a term used to describe the choices we make among the various words and constructions available in our language. The line between standard English and nonstandard English, or between formal and informal English, is determined by these choices. Your guideline in any situation requiring such choices should be appropriateness: is the word or expression you use appropriate to your **reader** and subject? When it is, you are practicing good usage.

This book has been designed to help you sort out the appropriate from the inappropriate: just look up the item in question in the index. A good **dictionary** is also an invaluable aid in your selection of the right word.

utilize

Utilize should not be used as a **long variant** of *use,* which is the general word for "employ for some purpose." When you are tempted to use this term, try to substitute *use.* It will almost always prove a clearer and less pretentious word.

CHANGE You can *utilize* the fourth elevator to reach the fiftieth floor.
TO You can *use* the fourth elevator to reach the fiftieth floor.

V

vague words

A vague word is one that is imprecise in the context in which it is used. Some words encompass such a broad range of meanings that there is no focus for their definition. Words such as *real, nice, important, good, bad, contact, thing,* and *fine* are often called "omnibus words" because they can mean everything to everybody. In speech we sometimes use words that are less than precise, but our vocal inflections and the context of our conversation make their meanings clear. Since writing cannot rely on vocal inflections, avoid using vague words. Be concrete and specific. (See also **abstract words/concrete words.**)

> CHANGE It was a *meaningful* meeting, and we got *a lot* done.
> TO The meeting resolved three questions: pay scales, fringe benefits, and work loads.

verb phrases

A verb phrase is a group of words that functions as a single **verb**. It consists of a main verb preceded by one or more **helping verbs**.

> EXAMPLE He *is* (helping verb) *working* (main verb) hard this summer.

The main verb is always the last verb in a verb phrase.

> EXAMPLES You *will file* your tax return on time if you begin early.
> You *will have filed* your tax return on time if you begin early.
> You *are* not *filing* your tax return too early if you begin now.

Questions often begin with a verb phrase.

> EXAMPLE *Will* he *audit* their account soon?

Words can appear between the helping verb and the main verb of a verb phrase.

> EXAMPLE He *is* always *working*.

The **adverb** *not* may be appended to a helping verb in a verb phrase.

EXAMPLES   He *cannot work* today.
He *did not work* today.

verbals

Verbals, which are derived from **verbs**, function as **nouns, adjectives**, and **adverbs**. There are three types of verbals: gerunds, infinitives, and participles.

When the *-ing* form of a verb is used as a noun, it is called a **gerund**.

EXAMPLE   *Seeing* is *believing.*

An **infinitive** is the root form of a verb, usually preceded by *to* (*to analyze, to build*). Infinitives can be used as nouns, adjectives, or adverbs.

EXAMPLES   He likes *to jog.* (noun)
That is the main problem *to be solved.* (adjective)
The valve acts *to control* the flow of liquid. (adverb)

When a verb is used as an adjective, it is called a **participle**; present participles commonly end in *-ing,* past participles in *-ed, -en, -d,* or *-t.*

EXAMPLES   A *burning* candle consumes stale tobacco smoke.
The *published* report contains up-to-date information.

verbs

A verb is a word, or a group of words, that describes an action (The antelope *bolted* at the sight of the hunters), states the way in which something or someone is affected by an action (He *was saddened* by the death of his friend), or affirms a state of existence (He *is* a wealthy man now).

TYPES OF VERBS

Verbs may be either transitive verbs or intransitive verbs.

Transitive Verbs. A transitive verb is a verb that requires a direct object to complete its meaning.

EXAMPLES   They *laid* the foundation on October 24. (*foundation* is the direct object of the transitive verb *laid*)
George Anderson *wrote* the treasurer a letter. (*letter* is the direct object of the transitive verb *wrote*)

Intransitive Verbs. An intransitive verb is a verb that does not require an object to complete its meaning. It is able to make a full assertion about the **subject** without assistance (although it may have modifiers).

EXAMPLES The water *boiled.*   The engine *ran.*
              The water *boiled* rapidly.   The engine *ran* smoothly.

Although intransitive verbs do not have an **object**, certain intransitive verbs may take a **complement**. These verbs are called **linking verbs** because they link the complement to the subject. When the complement is a **noun** (or **pronoun**), it refers to the same person or thing as the noun (or pronoun) that is the subject.

EXAMPLES The conference table *is* an antique.
              Mary *remains* the director.

When the complement is an **adjective**, it *modifies* the subject.

EXAMPLES The study *was* thorough.
              The report *seems* complete.

Such intransitive verbs as *be, become, seem,* and *appear* are almost always linking verbs. A number of others, such as *look, sound, taste, smell,* and *feel,* may function as either linking verbs or simple intransitive verbs. If you are unsure about whether one of these verbs is a linking verb, try substituting *seem;* if the sentence still makes sense, the verb is probably a linking verb.

EXAMPLES Their antennae *feel* delicately. (simple intransitive verb)
              Their antennae *feel* delicate. (linking verb—You could substitute *seem.*)

Some verbs, such as *lie* and *sit,* are inherently intransitive.

EXAMPLE The patient should *lie* on his back during treatment. (*On his back* is an **adverb** phrase modifying the verb *lie.*)

FORMS OF VERBS

By form, verbs may be described as being either finite or nonfinite.
Finite Verbs. A finite verb is the main verb of a **clause** or sentence. It makes an assertion about its subject and can serve as the only verb in its clause or sentence. Finite verbs may be either transitive or intransitive (including linking) verbs. They are subject to changes in

form to reflect **person** (I *see*, he *sees*), **tense** (I *go*, I *went*), and **number** (he *writes*, they *write*).

EXAMPLE The telephone *rang*, and the secretary *answered* it.

A **helping verb** (sometimes called an *auxiliary verb*) is used in a **verb phrase** to help indicate **mood**, tense, and **voice**.

EXAMPLES The work *had* begun.
I *am* going.
I *was* going.
I *will* go.
I *should have* gone.
I *must* go.

The most commonly used helping verbs are the various forms of *have* (*has*, *had*), *be* (*is*, *are*, *was*, and so on), *do*, (*does*, *did*), and *can*, *could*, *may*, *might*, *must*, *shall*, *should* and *will*, *would*. **Phrases** that function as helping verbs are often made up of combinations with the sign of the infinitive, *to*: for example, *am going to* and *is about to* (compare *will*), *has to* (compare *must*), and *ought to* (compare *should*).

The helping verb always precedes the main verb, although other words may intervene.

EXAMPLE Machines *will* never completely *replace* people.

Nonfinite Verbs. Nonfinite verbs are **verbals**, which, although they are derived from verbs, actually function as nouns, adjectives, or **adverbs**.

When the *-ing* form of a verb is used as a noun, it is called a **gerund**.

EXAMPLE *Seeing* is *believing*.

An **infinitive**, which is the root form of a verb (usually preceded by *to*), can be used as a noun, an adverb, or an adjective.

EXAMPLES He hates *to complain*. (noun, direct object of *hates*)
The valve closes *to stop* the flow. (adverb, modifies *closes*)
This is the proposal *to select*. (adjective, modifies *proposal*)

A **participle** is a verb form used as an adjective.

EXAMPLES His *closing* statement was very *convincing*.
The *rejected* proposal was ours.

PROPERTIES OF VERBS

Person is the grammatical term for the form of a **personal pronoun** that indicates whether the pronoun refers to the speaker, the person spoken to, or the person (or thing) spoken about. Verbs change their forms to agree in person with their subjects.

EXAMPLES I *see* (first person) a yellow tint, but he *sees* (third person) a yellow-green hue.

I *am* (first person) convinced, and you *are* (*second person*) convinced; but unfortunately he *is* (third person) not convinced.

Voice refers to the two forms of a verb that indicate whether the subject of the verb acts or receives the action. If the subject of the verb acts, the verb is in the active voice; if it receives the action, the verb is in the passive voice.

EXAMPLES The aerosol bomb *propels* the liquid as a mist. (active)

The liquid *is propelled* as a mist by the aerosol bomb. (passive)

In your writing, the active voice provides force and momentum, whereas the passive voice lacks these qualities. The reason is not difficult to find. In the active voice, the verb plays the key role in identifying what the subject is doing. The passive voice, on the other hand, consists of a form of the verb *to be* and a past participle of another verb. In the passive voice, the **emphasis** is on what is being done to the subject. (See also **nominalizations**.)

EXAMPLES Things are seen by the normal human eye in three dimensions: length, width, and depth. (*Things* takes precedence over the eye's function.)

The normal human eye sees things in three dimensions: length, width, and depth. (Here the eye's function—which is what the sentence is about—receives the emphasis.)

Number refers to the two forms of a verb that indicate whether the subject of a verb is singular or plural.

EXAMPLES The machine *was* in good operating condition. (singular)

The machines *were* in good operating condition. (plural)

Tense refers to verb forms that indicate time distinctions. There are six tenses: present, past, future, present perfect, past perfect, and future perfect. All verb tenses are derived from the three principal parts of the verb: the infinitive (without *to*, which normally precedes it); the past form; and the past participle. Following are the six tenses of *write* (infinitive), whose other two principal parts are *wrote* (past form) and *written* (past participle):

EXAMPLES I *write* (present, based on infinitive)
I *wrote* (past, based on past form)
I *will write* (future, based on infinitive)
I *have written* (present perfect, based on past participle)
I *had written* (past perfect, based on past participle)
I *will have written* (future perfect, based on past participle)

Note that *write* is an irregular verb; that is, its past and past participle forms are produced by internal changes: *write, wrote, written.* Regular verbs, on the other hand, form the past and past participle by the addition of the suffixes *-ed, -d,* or *-t: talk, talked; believe, believed; spend, spent.* The tenses of regular verbs, like those of irregular verbs, are derived from the three principal parts.

EXAMPLES I *believe* (present, based on infinitive)
I *believed* (past, based on past form)
I *will believe* (future, based on infinitive)
I *have believed* (present perfect, based on past participle)
I *had believed* (past perfect, based on past participle)
I *will have believed* (future perfect, based on past participle)

Each of the six tenses also has a progressive form. The progressive form is created by adding the appropriate tense of *be* to the present participle (*-ing*) form of the verb.

EXAMPLES I *am writing.* (present progressive)
I *was writing.* (past progressive)
I *will be writing.* (future progressive)
I *have been writing.* (present perfect progressive)
I *had been writing.* (past perfect progressive)
I *will have been writing.* (future perfect progressive)

(See also **tense.**)

CONJUGATION OF VERBS

The conjugation of a verb arranges all forms of the verb so that the differences caused by the changing of the tense, number, person, and voice are readily apparent. The following is a conjugation of the verb *drive*:

Tense	Number	Person	Active Voice	Passive Voice
Present	Singular	1st	I drive	I am driven
		2nd	You drive	You are driven
		3rd	He drives	He is driven
	Plural	1st	We drive	We are driven
		2nd	You drive	You are driven
		3rd	They drive	They are driven
Progressive Present	Singular	1st	I am driving	I am being driven
		2nd	You are driving	You are being driven
		3rd	He is driving	He is being driven
	Plural	1st	We are driving	We are being driven
		2nd	You are driving	You are being driven
		3rd	They are driving	They are being driven
Past	Singular	1st	I drove	I was driven
		2nd	You drove	You were driven
		3rd	He drove	He was driven
	Plural	1st	We drove	We were driven
		2nd	You drove	You were driven
		3rd	They drove	They were driven
Progressive Past	Singular	1st	I was driving	I was being driven
		2nd	You were driving	You were being driven
		3rd	He was driving	He was being driven
	Plural	1st	We were driving	We were being driven
		2nd	You were driving	You were being driven
		3rd	They were driving	They were being driven
Future	Singular	1st	I will drive	I will be driven
		2nd	You will drive	You will be driven
		3rd	He will drive	He will be driven
	Plural	1st	We will drive	We will be driven
		2nd	You will drive	You will be driven
		3rd	They will drive	They will be driven
Progressive Future	Singular	1st	I will be driving	I will have been driven
		2nd	You will be driving	You will have been driven
		3rd	He will be driving	He will have been driven
	Plural	1st	We will be driving	We will have been driven
		2nd	You will be driving	You will have been driven
		3rd	They will be driving	They will have been driven

(continued)

Tense	Number		Person	Active Voice	Passive Voice
Present Perfect	Singular		1st	I have driven	I have been driven
			2nd	You have driven	You have been driven
			3rd	He has driven	He has been driven
	Plural		1st	We have driven	We have been driven
			2nd	You have driven	You have been driven
			3rd	They have driven	They have been driven
Past Perfect	Singular		1st	I had driven	I had been driven
			2nd	You had driven	You had been driven
			3rd	He had driven	He had been driven
	Plural		1st	We had driven	We had been driven
			2nd	You had driven	You had been driven
			3rd	They had driven	They had been driven
Future Perfect	Singular		1st	I will have driven	I will have been driven
			2nd	You will have driven	You will have been driven
			3rd	He will have driven	He will have been driven
	Plural		1st	We will have driven	We will have been driven
			2nd	You will have driven	You will have been driven
			3rd	They will have driven	They will have been driven

very

The temptation to overuse **intensifiers** like *very* is great. Evaluate your use of them carefully. When you do use them, clarify their meaning.

> EXAMPLE Bicycle manufacturers had a *very* good year: sales across the country were up 43 percent over the previous year.

In many sentences, however, the word can simply be deleted.

> CHANGE The board was *very* angry about the newspaper report.
> TO The board was angry about the newspaper report.

via

Via is Latin for "by way of."

> EXAMPLE The equipment is being shipped to Los Angeles *via* Chicago.

The term should be used only in routing instructions.

> CHANGE His project was funded *via* the recent legislation.
> TO His project was funded *through* the recent legislation.
> OR His project was funded *as the result of* the recent legislation.

vogue words

Vogue words are words that suddenly become popular and, because of an intense period of overuse, lose their freshness and preciseness. They may become popular through their association with science, technology, or even sports. We include them in our vocabulary because they seem to give force and vitality to our language. Ordinarily, this language sounds pretentious in our day-to-day writing.

EXAMPLES *super, interface* (as a verb), *bottom line, input, mode, state of the art, impact* (as a verb), *cutting edge, parameter, communication, feedback,* and many words ending in *-wise.*

Obviously, some of these terms are appropriate in the right context. It is when they are used outside that context that imprecision becomes a problem.

EXAMPLE An *interface* was provided between the two computers. (appropriate)
CHANGE We must *interface* with the Purchasing Department. (inappropriate)
TO We must *cooperate* with the Purchasing Department.

This book discusses some vogue terms individually; use the index to find the word in question. For those not included, check a current **dictionary**. (See also **gobbledygook** and **trite language**.)

voice

In grammar, voice indicates the relation of the subject to the action of the verb. When the **verb** is in the active voice, the **subject** acts; when it is in the passive voice, the subject is acted upon.

EXAMPLES David Cohen *wrote* the advertising copy. (active)
The advertising copy *was written* by David Cohen. (passive)

Both of the sentences say the same thing, but each has a different **emphasis**: In the first sentence emphasis is on the subject, *David Cohen,* whereas in the second sentence the focus is on the object, *the advertising copy.* Notice how much stronger and more forceful the active sentence is.

One of the rules of good writing is always to use the active voice unless there is good reason to use the passive. Because they are wordy and indirect, passive sentences are hard for the **reader** to understand. Notice how much clearer the following passive sentence becomes when it is rewritten in the active voice:

> CHANGE Things *are seen* by the normal human eye in three dimensions: length, width, and depth.
>
> TO The human eye *sees* things in three dimensions: length, width, and depth.

Passive-voice sentences are wordy because they always use a **helping verb** in addition to the main verb, and an extra preposition if they identify the doer of the action specified by the main verb.

> ACTIVE Employees *resent* changes in policy.
>
> PASSIVE Changes in policy *are resented by* employees.

The active-voice version takes one verb (*resent*) and one preposition (*in*); the passive-voice version takes two verbs (*are resented*) and two prepositions (*in* and *by*). The passive-voice version is also indirect because it puts the doer of the action behind the verb instead of in front of it.

One difficulty with passive sentences is that they can bury the subject, or performer of the action, in **expletives** and prepositional phrases.

> CHANGE It *was reported* by Engineering that the new relay is defective.
>
> TO Engineering *reported* that the new relay is defective.

Sometimes writers using the passive voice fail to name the performer—information that might be missed.

> CHANGE The problem *was discovered* yesterday.
>
> TO The Engineering Department *discovered* the problem yesterday.

Very often the passive voice can be just plain confusing, especially when used in **instructions**.

> CHANGE Plates B and C should be marked for revision. (Are they already marked?)
>
> TO You *should mark* plates B and C for revision.
>
> OR *Mark* plates B and C for revision.

Another problem that sometimes occurs with the passive voice is **dangling modifiers**.

CHANGE Hurrying to complete the work, the wires *were connected* improperly. (Who was hurrying, the wires?)

TO Hurrying to complete the work, the technician improperly *connected* the wires. (Here, *hurrying to complete the work* properly modifies *technician.*)

There are, however, certain instances when the passive voice is effective or even necessary. Indeed, for reasons of tact and diplomacy, you might need to use the passive voice to *avoid* identifying the doer of the action.

CHANGE Your sales force didn't meet the quota last month. (active)

TO The quota wasn't met last month. (passive)

When the performer of the action is either unknown or unimportant, use the passive voice.

EXAMPLES The copper mine *was discovered* in 1929.
Fifty-six barrels *were processed* in two hours.

When the performer of the action is less important than the receiver of that action, the passive voice is sometimes more appropriate.

EXAMPLE Ann Bryant *was presented* with an award by the president.

When you are explaining an operation in which the reader is not actively involved (but not when you are giving the reader **instructions**) or when you are explaining a process or a procedure, the passive voice may be more appropriate.

EXAMPLE Area strip mining *is used* in regions of flat to gently rolling terrain, like that found in the Midwest and West. Depending on applicable reclamation laws, the topsoil may *be removed* from the area to be mined, *stored,* and later *reapplied* as surface material during reclamation of the mined land. After the removal of the topsoil, a trench *is cut* through the overburden to expose the upper surface of the coal to be mined. The length of the cut generally corresponds to the length of the property or of the deposit. The overburden from the first cut *is placed* on the unmined land adjacent to the cut. After the first cut *has been completed,* the coal *is removed,* and a second cut *is made* parallel to the first.

Anyone could be the doer of the action in this example; it really doesn't matter who does it. Therefore, it would be pointless for the writer to put this passage in the active voice. Do not, however, simply assume that any such explanation should be in the passive voice. Ask yourself, "Would it be of any advantage to the reader to know the doer of the action?" If you can answer no, then use the passive voice. But if your honest answer is yes, then use the active voice. The following example uses the active voice to explain an operation:

> EXAMPLE   In the operation of an internal combustion engine, an explosion in the combustion chamber *forces* the pistons down in the cylinders. The movement of the pistons in the cylinders *turns* the crankshaft. The crankshaft, in turn, *operates* the differential. The differential *turns* the rear axles, which *turn* the wheels and *move* the automobile.

Whether you use the passive or the active voice, however, be careful not to *shift* voices in a sentence.

> CHANGE   Ms. McDonald *corrected* the malfunction as soon as it *was identified* by the technician.
>
> TO   Ms. McDonald *corrected* the malfunction as soon as the technician *identified* it.

W

wait for/wait on

Wait on should be restricted in writing to the activities of waitresses and waiters—otherwise, use *wait for*. (See also **idioms**.)

> EXAMPLES Be sure to *wait for* Ms. Sturgess to finish reading the report before asking her to make a decision.
> Joe's feet ached from *waiting on* tables at the diner.

when and if

When and if (or *if and when*) is a colloquial expression that should not be used in writing.

> CHANGE *When and if* your new position is approved, I will see that you receive adequate staff help.
> TO *If* your new position is approved, I will see that you receive adequate staff help.
> OR *When* your new position is approved, I will see that you receive adequate staff help.

where . . . at

In **phrases** using the *where . . . at* construction, *at* is unnecessary and should be omitted.

> CHANGE *Where* is his office *at*?
> TO *Where* is his office?

where/that

Do not substitute *where* for *that* to anticipate an idea or fact to follow.

> CHANGE I read in the *Wall Street Journal where* the semiconductor industry is expected to expand over the next decade.
> TO I read in the *Wall Street Journal that* the semiconductor industry is expected to expand over the next decade.

whether or not

When *whether or not* is used to indicate a choice between alternatives, omit *or not*; it is redundant, since *whether* itself communicates the notion of a choice.

> CHANGE The project director asked *whether or not* the request for proposals had been issued.
> TO The project director asked *whether* the request for proposals had been issued.

(See also **as to whether**.)

while

While, meaning "during an interval of time," is sometimes substituted for connectives like *and, but, although,* and *whereas*. Used as a connective in this way, *while* often causes **ambiguity**.

> CHANGE John Evans is sales manager, *while* Joan Thomas is in charge of research.
> TO John Evans is sales manager, *and* Joan Thomas is in charge of research.

Do not use *while* to mean *although* or *whereas*.

> CHANGE *While* the office manager was angry with his assistant, he didn't fire him.
> TO *Although* the office manager was angry with his assistant, he didn't fire him.

Restrict *while* to its meaning of "during the time that."

> EXAMPLE I'll have to catch up on my reading *while* I am on vacation.

who/whom

Writers often have difficulty with the choice of *who* or *whom*. *Who* is the subjective **case** form, *whom* is the objective case form, and *whose* is the possessive case form. When in doubt about which form to use, try substituting a **personal pronoun** to see which one fits. If *he* or *they* fits, use *who.*

> EXAMPLES *Who* is the congressman from the tenth district?
> *He* is the congressman from the tenth district.

If *him* or *them* fits, use *whom.*

EXAMPLES   It depended on *them.*
It depended on *whom?*

It is becoming common to use *who* for the objective case when it begins a sentence, although some still object to such an ungrammatical construction. The best advice is to know your **reader**.

The choice between *who* and *whom* is especially complex in sentences with interjected **clauses**.

CHANGE   These are the men *whom* you thought were the architects.
TO   These are the men *who* you thought were the architects.

The parenthetical clause *you thought* tends to attract the form *whom,* a form that appears logical as the object of the verb form *thought.* In fact, *who* is the correct form, since it is the subject of the verb form *were.* Note that the interjected clause *you thought* can be omitted without disturbing the construction of the clause.

EXAMPLE   These are the men *who* were the architects.

whose / of which

Whose should normally be used with persons; *of which* should normally be used with inanimate objects.

EXAMPLES   The man *whose* car had been towed away was angry.
The mantle clock, the parts *of which* work perfectly, is over one hundred years old.

If these uses cause a sentence to sound awkward, however, *whose* may be used with inanimate objects.

EXAMPLE   There are added fields, for example, *whose* totals should never be zero.

who's / whose

Who's is a **contraction** of *who is.*

EXAMPLE   *Who's* scheduled to attend the productivity seminar next month?

Whose is the possessive for *who* or *of which.*

EXAMPLE   *Whose* department will be affected by the budget cuts?

Who's and *whose* are not interchangeable.

-wise

Although the **suffix** *-wise* often seems to provide a tempting short-cut, it leads more often to inept than to economical expression. It is better to rephrase the sentence.

CHANGE Our department rates high efficiencywise.
TO Our department has a high efficiency rating.

The *-wise* suffix is appropriate, however, to **instructions** that indicate certain space or directional requirements.

EXAMPLES Fold the paper *lengthwise*.
Turn the adjustment screw half a turn *clockwise*.

word choice

As Mark Twain once said, "The difference between the right word and almost the right word is the difference between 'lightning' and 'lightning bug.'" The most important goal in choosing the right word in business writing is the preciseness implied by Twain's comment. **Vague words** and **abstract words** defeat preciseness because they do not convey the writer's meaning directly and clearly. Vague words are imprecise because they can mean many different things.

CHANGE It was a *meaningful* meeting.
TO The meeting helped both sides understand each other's position.

In the first sentence, *meaningful* ironically conveys no meaning at all. See how the revised sentence says specifically what made the meeting meaningful. Although abstract words may at times be appropriate to your **topic**, their unnecessary use creates dry and lifeless writing.

ABSTRACT work, fast, food
CONCRETE sawing, 110 m.p.h., steak

Being aware of the **connotation** and denotation of words will help you anticipate the **reader's** reaction to the words you choose. Connotation is the suggested or implied meaning of a word beyond its dictionary definition. Denotation is the literal, or primary, dictionary meaning of a word.

Understanding **antonyms** and **synonyms** will increase your ability to choose the proper word. Antonyms are words with nearly the opposite meaning (*fresh/stale*), and synonyms are words with nearly the same meaning (*notorious/infamous*).

Malapropisms and **trite language** are likely to irritate your readers, by either confusing or boring them. Malapropisms are words that sound like the intended word but have different, sometimes even humorous, meanings.

> CHANGE   The repairperson cleaned the typewriter's *plankton.*
> TO   The repairperson cleaned the typewriter's *platen.*

Trite language consists of stale and worn phrases, frequently **clichés.**

> CHANGE   We will finish the project *quick as a flash.*
> TO   We will finish the project *quickly.*

Avoid using **jargon** unless you are certain that all of your readers understand the terms. Avoid choosing words with the objective of impressing your reader, which is called **affectation**; also avoid using **long variants**, which are elongated forms of words used only to impress (*utilize* for *use, telephonic communication* for *telephone call, analyzation* for *analysis*). Using a **euphemism** (an inoffensive substitute for a word that is distasteful or offensive) may help you avoid embarrassment, but the overuse of euphemisms becomes affectation. Using more words than necessary (*in the neighborhood of* for *about, for the reason that* for *because, in the event that* for *if*) is certain to interfere with **clarity**.

Understanding the use of **clipped forms of words, compound words, blend words, idioms,** and **foreign words in English** will help you find the appropriate word for a specific use. Clipped forms of words are created by dropping the beginning or ending of a word (*phone* for *telephone, ad* for *advertisement*). Compound words are made from two or more words that are either hyphenated or written as one word (*mother-in-law, nevertheless*). Blend words are created by using two words to produce a third word (*smoke* + *fog* = *smog*).

A key to choosing the correct and precise word is to keep current in your reading and to be aware of new words in your profession and in the language. Be aware also, in your quest for the right word, that there is no substitute for a good **dictionary**.

word processing

Word processing enables you to input rough drafts into a computer, edit your text on a video screen, print out a well-formatted paper copy of your final draft, and store that version electronically for future use or revision.

ENTERING AND EDITING TEXT

As you type text, a cursor (a solid or flashing spot of light) marks your position on the screen. When the cursor and text reach the end of a line, you need not press "carriage return" to position the cursor on the line below; the software does so automatically in a process called *automatic wordwrap*. You use the *carriage return* (or *enter*) key to add one or more lines of space between paragraphs, between text and a topic heading, between the end of a letter and its complimentary close, and elsewhere.

The software also allows you to enter text *regardless* of where a page ends. Some programs display a dotted line across the screen to indicate the end of one page and the beginning of the next, but you can continue entering text at that point without interruption. Page breaks become important only when you end your document and add page numbers and headers or footers. (These features are discussed later in this entry, under "Format.")

The *screen* on which text is entered usually permits 24 lines of vertical text with 64 characters on each line. (A space counts as a character.) Thus, you cannot see an entire page on screen unless your word-processing program has a *page preview mode* (see below). The screen also displays a *status line* that appears at either the top or bottom of the screen information about the line, page, and column where the cursor is located. It also indicates whether you are using a special typeface (bold, italic, underline), all capital letters, and whether the text is being entered in insert or overwrite mode. *Insert mode* means that text being entered in the middle of other text moves the old text to the right and to subsequent lines to accommodate the new text. *Overwrite mode* means the new text "types over" the old text as it is being entered.

After the first draft has been entered, you can make any changes, insertions, and deletions without retyping the entire document. As you add new text between or within sentences, the *automatic wordwrap* feature adjusts all subsequent lines to the end of the paragraph.

If the insertion is a paragraph or longer, all subsequent paragraphs shift automatically to the end of the section, chapter, or document, as appropriate.

As an aid during revision, you can use the *search and replace* feature to locate and replace a letter, number, word, or phrase with another throughout your document. You can instruct the computer to do so automatically or to stop at each instance during the search to allow you to verify the change. The second option is preferable; otherwise you could miss those places where a term needs a capital letter or an **apostrophe** to indicate possession.

You can use the *macro* feature to simplify entering repetitious information. This feature allows you to store a long phrase, an address, standard paragraphs in a form letter or contract, or other material and insert it where you wish with one or two keystrokes.

Block operations allow you to move, delete, reposition, or file blocks of text for later use. A "block" can range in size from a single letter to an entire document.

After text has been entered and organized to your satisfaction, you can use your system's spell-checker and **thesaurus** to fine-tune it. Online *spell-checkers* help with on-screen proofing by stopping at each misspelled word, repeated word (*the the*), words with numbers instead of letters (*wi11* with two ones rather that two letter *l*'s), and common errors in capitalization made during typing (*THere*). When the spell-checker finds a word or **acronym** not found in its dictionary, it stops, awaiting your response, and may offer one or more suggested spellings at that point.

Although a spell-checker is an invaluable tool, it is not infallible. It cannot tell whether you meant *their* or *there* in a given context, since both words are spelled correctly, and so will pass over each. Nor can a spell-checker help you with numbers (except when they're incorrectly used as letters). You still must print a paper copy of your document and proof it carefully.

You can also fine-tune your language by using an online **thesaurus** that searches for and displays **synonyms** for specific terms you select. Using a special dictionary, it displays a list of synonyms for the word you've selected, sometimes displaying one or more **antonyms** for it as well. However, a thesaurus cannot make the fine discriminations in meaning that the human mind can. Like a spell-checker, the thesaurus matches terms literally and cannot take the context into account.

FORMAT

You can apply a variety of word-processing features to enhance the layout and other elements affecting the **format** of your text. Equipped with the proper software and printer, you can also vary the style and size of type used for text, **headings**, captions, and footnotes. (See also **layout and design**.)

Margins. The page margins are usually preset for one inch on all sides of a printed page and are visible only when a page is printed or in preview mode; the margins do not appear on the work screen. Margin settings can be changed for the whole page or for blocks of text within a page.

Columns. Most word processors allow you to arrange the text on the page in two or more columns, a feature that can be used to create newspaper-style columns of text. This feature can also be used to create membership lists, financial statements, rosters, and similar materials without having to use tab stops to separate each row into the appropriate columns.

Margin Alignment. Page columns can be printed with the text aligned (or "justified") on the right margin as well as the left. Be aware, however, that text justified along the right margin will contain extra white space between some words. (See "Line, Word, and Letter Spacing" below.)

Widow and Orphan Control. This feature automatically protects against the awkward appearance of stand-alone words or lines at the top or bottom of a page. A *widow* refers to a word or several words, generally preceding a new paragraph, that appear as the first line on a page. An *orphan* refers to the first line of a paragraph appearing alone at the bottom of a page. These can occur when the word processor divides the text of a document into pages for printing. When you activate this feature, the software recognizes and prints widows on the previous page and orphans on the next page.

Centering. As the name implies, this feature allows you to center a word, line, or block of text on the page. Centering is especially useful for creating **titles**, letterhead stationery, and captions for tables and figures.

Line, Word, and Letter Spacing. The word processor single-spaces all text unless you instruct it otherwise. However, text can be separated by as many spaces as you choose in full or fractional increments (2, 2.5, 3.33, and so on). This feature, most useful for creating drafts on which you or others will comment, also permits you to vary line spacing from one block of text to another within a document.

You can also change the spacing between words and letters if you have a printer that supports these options. These features are most useful for fine-tuning the look of a block of right-justified text containing too much white space.

Headers and Footers. Word processors allow you to enter the header or footer at the beginning of a document and automatically position it on every page when the document is printed. Headers and footers do not appear on the work screen, although they can be seen in preview mode (see below).

Footnotes. Footnotes may be placed at the foot of a page or at the end of a chapter or document. The software positions and numbers them automatically according to your instructions. Most word processors will update the numbering automatically from the point where a note has been added or deleted. Once a note is linked by the footnote number in text, it will move to the foot of the same page automatically if the text to which it is "tagged" moves.

Page Numbers. The positioning of page numbers, like headers and footers, is done automatically after you specify where you want the numbering to begin and where on the page you want the numbers to appear. By convention, the first page of a letter, chapter, or report is unnumbered. You can instruct the word processor to begin numbering the second page, and it will number all following pages in sequence automatically. The word processor will also number the front matter pages of a **formal report** sequentially with small roman numerals. Once you establish the numbering style (*page 3, -3-, #3,* and so on), the word processor will repeat it throughout. Page numbers can be centered at the top or bottom of the page or located in the upper or lower right or left corner.

The software will even distinguish between even and odd pages, positioning the page number at the top or bottom left corner for even pages and at the top or bottom right corner for odd pages. The software can also create a **table of contents** after you identify the elements—usually your chapter titles and other headings—to be included in it. Using the same principle, you can create a *subject index.* You can either move through the text marking the appropriate words and phrases that will appear as headings and subheadings, or you can create a separate listing of words and phrases and have the software search through the text for them, listing the page number of each occurrence next to it in a separate subject index at the end of your document. (See also **indexing**.)

Type Style Options. You can vary the style and size of type used for text and headings and highlight important words and phrases by the text font you select. A *font* is a complete set of letters, numbers, and other type characters of distinctive and uniform design. They are divided into families of several sizes (for text, headings, and footnotes), weights (**boldface** or roman), and other features (*italic* or underscore) that share the same design and that distinguish them from other fonts. These features, used in conjunction with the guidelines in **layout and design**, can help you to create distinctive documents and **correspondence**.

Preview Mode. Your work screen shows only 24 lines of text from top to bottom. To see more text, you must scroll up or down, but even when you reach the point at which a page begins or ends, you cannot see headers, footers, or page numbers as they will appear on the printed page. Nor can you see the font you specified—you see only the generic style displayed on the work screen. Some word processors, however, permit you to view a reduced version of the full 8½-by-11-inch page before you print it. Called *preview mode,* this feature lets you see each page and all the format characteristics you created for it—columns, line and letter spacing, justification, pagination, headers, footers, footnotes, and the overall "look" of everything together. It also displays all the fonts your printer can create. If anything looks amiss, you can correct it before you print it. However, you must leave preview mode and return to the regular work screen to correct or revise material.

Style Sheets. After you have created the format features for a document, you can save them for future use as a *style sheet*—a set of user-defined text-format codes stored as a separate file with a unique name. They include such features as paragraph indention and spacing; line and page breaks; and line, word, and letter spacing, in addition to type font style and size. They are useful for creating recurrent uniform documents, such as monthly reports, form letters, **proposals**, and newsletters. Once created, a style sheet can be applied to as many documents as you wish.

PRINTING

After you have entered, revised, formatted, and previewed the text, you can print one or more copies of the entire document or specific pages. You can print on 8½-by-11-inch or 8½-by-14-inch plain or letterhead paper. Many printers also print pages in landscape (side-

```
This is an example of dot matrix printing in draft mode.

This is an example of dot matrix near-letter quality printing.

This is an example of letter quality printing.

This is an example of laser printing with **bold**, *italic*, and **enlarged** typefaces.
```

Figure 1   Varying Typeface Quality for Different Printers

ways) orientation for tables and graphics that will not fit on a page in portrait (conventional) orientation. Most printers also have paper-feeding mechanisms for printing nonstandard forms and even address labels.

Microcomputers use *dot matrix, letter quality,* and *laser* printers, each of which produces typefaces of varying quality, as shown in Figure 1. *Dot matrix* printers print characters composed of tiny dots that give them a "fuzzy," indistinct look. They can produce better quality print for memos and informal reports in double-strike or overstrike mode. *Letter quality* printers are slower than dot matrix printers and use a plastic daisy wheel or thimble and ribbon to print a clear, dark typeface similar in quality to that of an office typewriter. *Laser* printers work on the same principle as photocopy machines by using a jet-spraying device to deposit carbon images directly on paper. Laser printers can produce a great variety of typefaces at a quality comparable to professionally printed material.

Most word processors enable you to merge information from different files and then print them as one document. Using the merge feature, you can combine several sections of a letter, report, or proposal done at different times, each stored as a separate file, and print them as a single document. This feature permits firms to send "personalized" form letters to thousands of potential customers. Such form letters merge standard language with individual names and addresses on a target mailing list.

OUTLINING

Word-processing software makes **outlining** easier by providing the shell for you to fill in, rearrange, and update, regardless of the length and complexity of your outline. This feature also makes it easier for you to experiment with the organization and scope of information in the outline. Rearranging sections of the outline on screen is far less cumbersome than cutting and taping the paper version. Most word processors allow you to select from more than one style of outline shell or to specify your own style, such as the decimal numbering system (1, 1.1, 1.1.2, and so on).

WORD PROCESSING AND THE WRITING PROCESS

Word processing can help you record your ideas quickly, enhance your writing and revising skills, and create well-designed documents. Remember, however, that good writing is still the result of careful planning, constant practice, and thoughtful revision. In some cases, word-processing technology can initially intrude on the writing process and impose certain limitations that many beginners overlook. The ease of making minor, sentence-level changes and the limitation of a 24-line viewing screen, for example, may focus your attention too narrowly on surface problems of the text so that you lose sight of larger problems of scope and organization. The fluid and rapid movement of the text on the screen, together with last-minute editing changes, may allow undetected errors to creep into the text. Also, as you master word processing and become familiar with its revision capabilities, you may begin to "overwrite" your documents: Inserting phrases and rewriting sentences becomes so easy that you may find yourself generating more but saying less. The following tips will help you avoid these initial pitfalls and develop writing strategies that take full advantage of the benefits offered by word-processing technology.

TIPS ON USING THE WORD PROCESSOR
TO IMPROVE WRITING SKILLS

1. Do not write first drafts on the computer *without any planning or outlining*. Plan your document carefully by identifying your objective, readers, and scope and by completing your research and preparing an outline *before* you begin **writing a draft** on the computer.
2. Use the word processor's outline feature to brainstorm and organize an initial outline for your topic.
3. When you're ready to begin writing, you can overcome writer's block by practicing freewriting on the computer within the structure of your outline. Freewriting means typing your thoughts as quickly as possible for five to ten minutes without stopping

to correct mistakes or to complete sentences—correct these when you revise.

4. Use the search command to find and delete wordy phrases such as *that is, there are, the fact that,* the overuse of the verb *be,* and unnecessary **helping verbs** such as *will.*

5. Use a spell-checker and other specialized programs to identify and correct typographical errors, misspellings, and **grammar** and **diction** problems. Maintain a file of your most frequently misspelled or misused words and use the search command to check them in your documents.

6. Avoid excessive editing and rewriting on the screen. Print out a double-spaced copy of your draft periodically for major revisions and reorganizations.

7. Always **proofread** your final copy on paper because the fluidity of the viewing screen makes it difficult to catch all the errors in your manuscript. Print out an extra copy of your document for your colleagues to comment on before making final revisions.

8. When writing a single document for a variety of readers, use the search command to locate technical terms and other data that may need further explanation for secondary readers or for inclusion in a **glossary**.

9. Use the computer for effective page **layout and design** by emphasizing major **headings** and subheadings with bold print, by using the copy command to create and duplicate parallel headings throughout your text, and by inserting blank lines and tab-key spaces in your text to create extra white space around examples and **illustrations**.

10. Frequently "save" or store your text on disk during long writing sessions, if your computer does not have an automatic storage backup feature. Routinely create an extra or "backup" copy of your documents on floppy disks for safekeeping.

11. Keep the standard version of certain documents, such as your **résumé** and **application letters**, on file so you can revise them to meet the specific needs of each new job opportunity.

writing a draft

You are well prepared to write a rough draft when you have established your **objective, readers'** needs, and **scope**, and when you have done adequate **research** and **outlining**. Writing a rough draft is simply transcribing and expanding the notes from your outline into **paragraphs**, without worrying about **grammar**, refinements of language, or such mechanical aspects of writing as **spelling**. Refinement will come with **revision**.

To write a rough draft quickly, concentrate on converting your outline into sentences and paragraphs (see also **sentence construction**). Write as though you were explaining your subject to someone across the desk from you. Don't worry about a good opening. Just start. There is no need in a rough draft to be concerned about an **introduction** or **transitions** unless they come easily—concentrate on *ideas*. Don't try to polish or revise. Writing and revising are different activities. Keep writing quickly to achieve **unity** and proportion.

Even with good preparation, however, writing a draft remains a chore and an obstacle for many writers. Experienced writers use the following tactics to get started and keep moving. Discover which ones are the most helpful to you.

- Set up your writing area with the equipment and materials (paper, dictionary, source books, and so forth) you will need to keep going once you get started.
- Use whatever writing tools—separately or in combination—are most comfortable for you: pencil, felt-tip pen, typewriter, word processor, or whatever.
- Remind yourself that you are beginning a version of your writing project that no one else will read.
- Remember the writing projects you've finished in the past—you have completed something before, and you will this time.
- Start with the section that seems easiest to you—your reader will not know or care that you first wrote a section in the middle.
- Give yourself a time limit (10 or 15 minutes, for example) in which you will keep your pen or fingers on the keyboard moving, regardless of how good or bad your writing seems to you. The point is to *keep moving*.
- Don't let anything stop you when you are rolling along easily—if you stop and come back, you may not regain the momentum.
- But stop writing before you're completely exhausted; when you begin again, you may be able to regain your momentum.
- When you finish a section, give yourself a small reward—a short walk, a cup of coffee, a chat with a friend, an easy task, and so on.

- Reread what you've written when you resume writing. Often seeing what you've written will trigger the frame of mind that was productive.
- Switch the writing tools you were using when you stopped: go from ball-point pen to typewriter, for example.
- If all else fails, use a tape recorder to dictate a rough draft. (See the entry on **dictation**.)

The most effective way to start and keep going, however, is to use a good outline as a springboard and map for your writing. Your outline notes can become the **topic sentences** for paragraphs in your draft, as shown below. For example, notice that items III.A. and III.B. in the following topic outline become the topic sentences of the succeeding two paragraphs. And notice, too, that the subordinate items in the outline become sentences in the two paragraphs.

Outline

III. Advantages of Chicago as Location for New Plant
   A. *Outstanding Transport Facilities*
      1. Rail
      2. Air
      3. Truck
      4. Sea (except in winter)
   B. *Ample Labor Supply*
      1. Engineering and scientific personnel
         a. Many similar companies in the area
         b. Several major universities
      2. Technical and manufacturing personnel
         a. Existing programs in community colleges
         b. Possible special programs designed for us

Resulting Paragraphs

Probably the greatest advantage of Chicago as a location for our new plant is its excellent transport facilities. The city is served by three major railroads. Both domestic and international air cargo service is available at O'Hare International Airport. Chicago is a major hub of the trucking industry, and most of the nation's large freight carriers have terminals there. Finally, except in the winter months when the Great Lakes are frozen, Chicago is a seaport, accessible through the St. Lawrence Seaway.

> *A second advantage of Chicago is that it offers a large labor force.*
> An ample supply of engineering and scientific personnel is
> assured not only by the presence of many companies engaged
> in activities similar to ours but also by the presence of several
> major universities in the metropolitan area. Similarly, tech-
> nicians and manufacturing personnel are in abundant supply.
> The seven colleges in the Chicago City College system, as well
> as half a dozen other two-year colleges in the outlying areas,
> produce graduates with associate degrees in a wide variety of
> technical specialties appropriate to our needs. Moreover,
> three of the outlying colleges have expressed an interest in es-
> tablishing courses attuned specifically to our requirements.

Remember that as you write, your function as a writer is to communicate certain information to your readers. Do not try to impress
them with a fancy writing **style**. Write in a plain and direct style that
is comfortable and natural for both you and your reader—the first
rule of good writing is to *help the reader*.

As you write your rough draft, keep in mind your reader's level
of knowledge of the subject. Doing so will not only help you write
directly to your reader, it will also tell you which terms you must
define. (See also **defining terms**.)

When you are trying to write quickly and come to something difficult to explain, try to relate the new concept to something with
which the reader is already familiar. Although **figures of speech** are
not used extensively in technical writing, they can be very useful in
explaining a complex process. In the rough draft, a figure of speech
might be just the tool you need to keep moving when you encounter
a complex concept that must be explained or described.

Above all, don't wait for inspiration to write your rough draft—
you need to treat writing a draft in business writing as you would
any on-the-job task. Use the tips in this entry to help you complete
the task. (See also the Checklist of the Writing Process at the
beginning of this book.)

X

Xmas

X is similar to the symbol for the Greek letter chi. Because it looks like a cross, it is often used as a symbol for Christ—thus, the abbreviation *Xmas*. The expression *Xmas* is often used in advertising; however, even in advertising *Xmas* is best avoided, since to some people, the term detracts from the religious significance of the holiday.

Y

you viewpoint

The *you viewpoint* (or "you attitude") is a writing technique that places the readers' interests foremost in your writing. It is based on the principle that your readers are more concerned about their own needs than they are about yours. The you viewpoint often, but not always, means using the words *you* and *your* rather than *we, our, I,* and *mine.* Consider the following sentence that focuses on the writer's, rather than the reader's, needs:

> EXAMPLE   *We must receive* your receipt with the merchandise before *we can process* your refund.

Even though the sentence uses *your* twice, the words in italics suggest that the **point of view** centers on the writer's need to process the refund. You can make the request more polite, as in the following example:

> EXAMPLE   Please enclose the sales receipt with the merchandise, so that we can process your refund promptly.

Although the **tone** is more polite and friendly (which is important in most **correspondence**), this version still emphasizes the writer's need to get the receipt "so that *we* can process your refund promptly."

But what is the reader's interest? The reader is not interested in helping the business process its paperwork. He or she simply wants the refund—and by emphasizing that need, the writer encourages the reader to act quickly. Consider the following revision written with the you viewpoint.

> EXAMPLE   So you can receive your refund promptly, please enclose the sales receipt with the merchandise.

In this example, the reader's benefit is stressed as the reason the reader should enclose the receipt. The writer using this sentence, therefore, is more likely to accomplish his or her **objective**: to get the reader to act. Consider another example:

CHANGE   So that we can complete our file records, please send your
Form 1040-A by March 10.

TO   So that your file is complete, please send your Form 1040-A
by March 10.

As the revision illustrates, the you viewpoint can suggest that the recipient's interests are at stake, even though the recipient has little incentive to send the form.

Obviously, using the you viewpoint means more than using *you* and *your*; it means seeing a situation from the reader's viewpoint and writing accordingly. (See also **persuasion**.)

Z

zeugma

A zeugma is a construction in which an adjective or verb is forced to apply to two words, even though it is grammatically or logically correct only for one of them. Poets, and occasionally public speakers, use zeugma deliberately for rhythmic effect; but it is imprecise and should therefore be avoided in business writing.

> CHANGE The walls of the office *are* green, the rug, blue.
>   TO The walls of the office *are* green; the rug *is* blue.

In this case *are* (a plural **verb**) is used for both subjects, *walls* (a plural **noun**) and *rug* (a singular noun), which is grammatically and logically incorrect.

Index

Index terms followed by page numbers refer to the titles of hand-book entries. Terms without page numbers refer either to synonyms for entries or to topics discussed within an entry.